1992

The Reform of the United Nations

The Reform of the United Nations

A Volume In The Series
Annual Review of United Nations Affairs

Joachim W. Müller

Volume I

REPORT

Oceana Publications, Inc.
New York*London*Rome

Library of Congress Cataloging-in-Publications Data

Müller, Joachim W.
        The reform of the United Nations
        Contents: v. 1. Report
1. United Nations - - Finance.   I. Title.
JX1977.8.F5M85   1992   341.23- -dc20   91-50824
ISBN 0-379-20671-4 (Series)
        0-379-20672-2 (Vol. I)

PUBLISHER'S NOTE

Annual Review of United Nations Affairs is now edited by professional specialists who are part of the staff of the United Nations itself. They are:

> Kumiko Matsuura
> Programme Planning Officer,
> United Nations Industrial Development
> Organizations (UNIDO)

> Dr. Joachim W. Müller
> Programme Planning and Budget Officer,
> United Nations Office at Vienna (UNOV)

> Dr. Karl P. Sauvant
> Acting Assistant Director,
> United Nations Centre on Transnational Corporations,
> United Nations

We recently issued 1988 in two volumes, developing a totally new format and new focus which brings subscribers in depth coverage of the work of the United Nations.

In an effort quickly to bring the service completly up-to-date, 1989 has been prepared and will be released early in 1992. 1990 will be published sometime in late Spring; and 1991 sometime in late Fall. This will bring the service up-to-date. We are grateful for the patience of our subscribers.

Additionally, we have in the past from time to time published special volumes in ARUNA, such as the periodic *Chronology and Fact Book of the UN.* We here made available a most significant special UN volume *The Reform of the United Nations,* prepared by one of our ARUNA editors, Joachim W. Müller, a participant in the reform process.

The two-volume set will come to subscribers to ARUNA automatically. It is the publisher's conviction that this title is intrinsic to the character and quality of the material now being published as part of the Annual Review. The work is separately offered to purchasers not subscribers to ARUNA.

Dr. Joachim W. Müller is currently Programme Planning Budget Officer, United Nations Office at Vienna (UNOV). He has previously been with the Programme Planning and Budget Division, United Nations, New York, the German Society for Technical Co-operation (GTZ) and Bank of America. Current address: Vienna International Centre, UNOV, E-1485, P.O. Box 600 A-1400 Vienna, Austria.

FOREWORD

Dramatic changes in today's world have created new opportunities and challenges for international collaboration. The United Nations entered this new era after surviving a crisis which had threatened its very existence. The response to the crisis was a reform effort which was remarkable on a number of counts: some viewed it as an attempt to save, others as an attempt to break, the organization; every facet of its activities was affected; and the public interest was unprecedented. The reform process was concluded at the end of 1990. Is the United Nations better equipped today to meet the global challenges?

The Reform of the United Nations is an important publication which provides the information needed to examine this question. Dr. Müller gives a detailed account of the reform process rather than a prescription of what should be done. This is not necessarily a bad thing. A number of proposals on how to reform the United Nations have recently been made, but little has been done to understand the actual process of 'reform making'. This publication fills the gap by making a detailed presentation of past experience, on the basis of which the limitations and potential of 'reform making' in the United Nations become clear. To this end, the publication provides a wealth of information taken from primary sources. The positions and justifications put forward by the main actors - the representatives of Member States and the United Nations Secretariat - are recorded, together with the reform proposals which were developed, rejected, modified, approved and implemented. This is a unique historical record of an important reform process.

My own view, as one who was not only associated with it but has long been involved in successive attempts at reforming the United Nations, including the 1969 Jackson Report, is that the results fell considerably short of the aspirations. This is not surprising to anyone familiar with the enormous difficulties of bringing about rational change and consistent management policies in an organization as complex as the United Nations. Comparison with the private sector is much in vogue these days. What is not usually appreciated among those urging such emulation is that the enterprise in this case has the equivalent of a Board of 166 Directors, each with a particular set of interests and priorities. It is in this context that the practical implications of reforms when they come to be implemented often turn out to be much less appealing and hence more complicated than was anticipated when they were approved in theory.

This study demonstrates some of these difficulties. It also provides the foundation for developing a vision of what should be done in the future. Clearly, reform of the United Nations is still far from complete, but it must inevitably be a continuous process. This publication will help us to learn from the past in order to master the challenges ahead.

Margaret Joan Anstee
Director-General of the United Nations Office at Vienna
Previously the Secretary-General's Special Co-ordinator for the
Implementation of Reforms Arising From the Group of 18 Report

PREFACE

The United Nations has undergone a remarkable change. A few years ago, the end of multilateralism was announced and the United Nations was pushed to the brink of financial insolvency. Today, the United Nations has been established as a key player in international affairs. The involvement of the United Nations in Namibia, Central America, Afghanistan, the Iran-Iraq war, Western Sahara, Cambodia or Kuwait are recent cases which highlight its new-found importance. This renaissance was accompanied by two major developments, one external and one internal to the United Nations. Externally, the end of the Cold War and the lessening of ideological competition resulted in a dramatic improvement of the climate in which the United Nations was operating. Internally, the organization undertook a major reform effort. This publication is a comprehensive report and documentation of the initiation, approval and implementation of reform in the United Nations. It provides an understanding of the process of decision-making and policy formulation that will shape the United Nations for decades to come.

The initiative for reform came at a time when the world body was severely threatened by political and financial crises. In particular, the major contributing countries were dissatisfied with specific programme activities, the utilization of resources, decision-making on budgetary matters and the apportionment of costs. Most of all, the USA as the major contributor wanted a larger say in the budgetary process. As well as demanding reforms, it opted to withhold part of the financial contribution it was required to pay towards the expenses of the organization. Although withholding of assessed contributions had been practised by a number of countries in the past, the sudden increase in the amount outstanding as a result of the US decision made it appear likely that the United Nations would become insolvent. The majority of member states, the developing countries, in particular, were suspicious of the motivation behind a reform which was accompanied by action to create financial instability. In fact, they viewed the reform initiatives as an attempt to challenge the democratic character of the organization by increasing the influence of the developed, at the expense of the developing, countries, and threatening what is known as the sovereign equality of member states.

Faced with the organization's imminent financial collapse, the diverging views were brought together in an attempt to reform the United Nations. The reform movement was thus born out of a crisis and was to be implemented under the most difficult political and financial conditions. While the crisis posed a grave threat to the organization it also harboured potential rewards. It created a climate in which a major redirection of the organization appeared possible, to the benefit of all member states. The need for change would soon become even more apparent. It so happened that the transformation of relations between East and West coincided with the reform initiative and there was an obvious need to redirect the United Nations to enable it to seize the new opportunities and face the challenges resulting from global developments.

The threat of bankruptcy and improvements in international relations were of major importance for the reform process. These issues were also the main reasons for the considerable public interest which the reform process attracted. Suddenly, the United Nations was back in the headlines. The reform process was closely followed by a wide audience and recommendations for change were regularly put forward by outside observers. This renewed interest was certainly a welcome development, but it also highlighted the limited understanding of the United Nations in general and the process of reform in particular. Clearly, detailed information is needed to make the process more transparent. That is what this publication seeks to achieve. While no solutions are offered, information is provided which will allow the reader to make his own judgement. The publication thus restricts analysis and focuses on a description of the initiation, approval, implementation and conclusion of the reform process, relying mainly on primary sources. Moreover, the documentation is complete in that it covers the reform effort from start to finish. It is a unique publication, providing an insight into the complete process of 'reform making' by drawing together all relevant primary information. Only by understanding the limitations and potential of this process will it be possible to recommend serious proposals for change in the future.

The reform of the United Nations was carried out over a period of five years. It was launched in 1985 with the establishment of the Group of 18, composed of high-level experts, mandated to review the efficiency of the administrative and financial functioning of the United Nations. Based on the recommendations of the group, a programme of reform was approved by the General Assembly and implemented in the political, economic and social fields as well as in the administrative area. Among the measures taken were the introduction of new planning and budget procedures, reductions in personnel, the restructuring of the secretariat, the streamlining of the intergovernmental machinery, an improvement in the management of public information activities, a reorganization of conference services and changes in monitoring, evaluation and inspection. The process concluded with the review of an analytical report on the implementation of the reforms by the General Assembly in December 1990.

The publication tells an exciting story. It highlights the positions of the major interest groups: the critical attitude of the USA, the 'rediscovery' of the United Nations by the USSR, the emergence of Japan as a major financial backer of the organization, the broker function of the Western European countries in the negotiating process and the strong support of the developing countries for the United Nations. It gives a detailed account of the discussions in intergovernmental bodies and the response of the secretariat. The main reports containing the proposed reforms, their assessment and justification are also presented. Finally, it records the relevant resolutions and decisions, including those which were approved as well as those which were rejected.

The general view is that the reform effort has achieved quite disparate results in the various areas it initially targeted. In fact, it was judged as having largely failed in the economic and social fields. As a result, a new reform initiative was launched by the General Assembly in 1991 building on the discussions documented in this publication. The new initiative to reform the United Nations in the economic and social fields will be the subject of a future publication.*

The Reform of the United Nations is divided into two volumes. Volume I (Report) gives a detailed account of the reform process. After an introduction to the United Nations, there is a short review of previous reform efforts, followed by a description of the build-up to the financial crisis and the start of the new reform effort with the establishment of the Group of 18. There is a detailed account of the discussions at the General Assembly and ECOSOC. Wherever appropriate, draft resolutions submitted during the negotiations, but not approved, are presented in order to document the process of negotiations. The resolutions and decisions which were adopted are shown in volume II as outlined below. Volume I ends with the final review of the reform process by the General Assembly and some concluding comments. The Volume also includes four indices: a subject and name index, an index of draft decisions and resolutions, an index of adopted decisions and resolutions and a document index.

Volume II (Resolutions, Decisions and Documents) brings together 11 of the main resolutions and decisions and 41 documents associated with the reform process. The resolutions and decisions are those approved by the

---

*Joachim W. Müller, *The Reform of the United Nations in the Economic and Social Fields* (Dobbs Ferry, New York: OCEANA, forthcoming).

General Assembly and the Economic and Social Council. The documents include those submitted by the Administrative Committee on Co-ordination (ACC), the Advisory Committee on Administrative and Budgetary Questions (ACABQ), the Committee for Programme and Co-ordination (CPC), the Fifth (Administrative and Budgetary) Committee of the General Assembly, the Group of 18, the International Civil Service Commission (ICSC), the Secretary-General and the Special Commission of the Economic and Social Council on the In-depth Study of the United Nations Intergovernmental Structure and Functions in the Economic and Social Fields. This documentation provides the background and reference material for understanding the process of reform as described in Volume I.

Finally, I would like to express my appreciation to those who have helped in making this publication possible. Special thanks go to Ms. Julieta Ocampo for her assistance. Most of all, I am grateful to my wife Kumiko for her advice and patience. Needless to say, I alone bear responsibility for all the shortcomings, and the views expressed do not necessarily reflect those of the institutions with which the author is affiliated.

Vienna, 1991   Joachim Müller

TABLE OF CONTENTS FOR VOLUME I

Page

TABLE OF CONTENTS FOR VOLUME II

PART II
DOCUMENTS

LIST OF ABBREVIATIONS

ACABQ	Advisory Committee for Administrative and Budgetary Questions
ACC	Administrative Co-ordinating Committee
CCAQ	Co-ordinating Committee for Administrative Questions
CCISUA	Co-ordinating Committee for Independent Staff Unions and Associations of the United Nations System
CCSQ	Co-ordinating Committee for Substantive Questions
CPC	Committee for Programme and Co-ordination
CSDHA	Centre for Social Development and Humanitarian Affairs
CSTD	Centre for Science and Technology for Development
CTC	Centre on Transnational Corporations
DAM	Department of Administrative and Management
DIEC	Director-General's Office for International Co-operation and Economic Affairs
DIESA	Department of International Economic and Social Affairs
DPI	Department of Public Information
DTCD	Department of Technical Co-operation for Development
ECA	Economic Commission for Africa
ECDC	Economic Co-operation among Developing Countries
ECE	Economic Commission for Europe
ECLAC	Economic Commission for Latin America and the Caribbean
ECOSOC	Economic and Social Council
EEC	European Economic Community
ESCAP	Economic and Social Commission for Asia and the Pacific
ESCWA	Economic and Social Commission for Western Asia
FAO	Food and Agricultural Organization
G77	Group of Seventy-Seven
GATT	General Agreement on Tariffs and Trade
GSTP	Global System of Trade Preferences
HABITAT	United Nations Centre for Human Settlement
IAEA	International Atomic Energy Agency
IBRD	International Bank for Reconstruction and Development (World Bank)
ICAO	International Civil Aviation Organization
ICJ	International Court of Justice
IDA	International Development Association
IDDA	Industrial Development Decade for Africa
IDS	International Development Strategy
IFAD	International Fund for Agricultural Development
IFC	International Finance Corporation
ILO	International Labour Organization
IMCO	Intergovernmental Maritime Consultative Organization
IMF	International Monetary Fund
IMO	International Maritime Organization
INSTRAW	International Research and Training Institute for Advancement of Women
ITC	International Trade Centre
ITU	International Telecommunication Union
JAB	United Nations Joint Appeals Board
JIU	Joint Inspection Unit

LDCs	Least Developed Countries
MULPOC	Multinational Programming and Operational Centre
NAM	Non-Aligned Movement
NGO	Non-Governmental Organization
NIEO	New International Economic Order
OECD	Organization for Economic Co-operation and Development
OGS	Office of General Service
OHRM	Office of Human Resource Management
OPPBF	Office of Programme Planning, Budget and Finance
SWAPO	South West African People's Organization
TCDC	Technical Co-operation among Developing Countries
TNC	Transnational Corporation
UK	United Kingdom of Great Britain and Northern Ireland
UN	United Nations
UNCHS	United Nations Centre for Human Settlements (Habitat)
UNCSDHA	United Nations Centre for Social Development and Humanitarian Affairs
UNCSTD	United Nations for Science and Technology for Development
UNCTAD	United Nations Conference on Trade and Development
UNCTC	United Nations Centre on Transnational Corporations
UNDP	United Nations Development Programme
UNDRO	Office of the United Nations Director Relief Co-ordinator
UNEP	United Nations Environment Programme
UNESCO	United Nations Educational, Scientific and Cultural Organization
UNFDAC	United Nations Fund for Drug Abuse Control
UNFICYP	United Nations Peace-keeping Force in Cyprus
UNFPA	United Nations Fund for Population Activities
UNGOMAP	United Nations Good Offices Mission for Afghanistan and Pakistan
UNHCR	Office of the United Nations High Commissioner for Refugees
UNICEF	United Nations Children's Emergency Fund
UNIDO	United Nations Industrial Development Organization
UNIFIL	United Nations Interim Force in Lebanon
UNITAR	United Nations Institute for Training and Research
UNJSPB	United Nations Joint Staff Pension Board
UNMOGIP	United Nations Military Observation Group in India and Pakistan
UN-PAAERD	United Nations Programme of Action for African Economic Recovery and Development
UNRISD	United Nations Research Institute for Social Development
UNRWA	United Nations Relief and Works Agency for Palestine Refugees in the Near East
UNTAG	United Nations Transition Group in Namibia
UNIIMOG	United Nations Iran-Iraq Military Observer Group
UNU	United Nations University
UPU	Universal Postal Union
USA	United States of America
USSR	Union of Soviet Socialist Republics
WFP	World Food Programme
WHO	World Health Organization
WIPO	World Intellectual Property Organization
WMO	World Meteorological Organization

CHAPTER 1
THE UNITED NATIONS UNDER REFORM
AND THE GROUP OF 18

1.1 Introduction

Since its creation in 1946, the United Nations (UN) has been the subject of periodic reviews. These have resulted in a continuous process of reforming the organization. In fact, the word 'reform' has acquired a particular meaning at the UN. First, it is seen as a response to new challenges or emerging concerns of members states. There are, however, also other interpretations. Reform efforts have been viewed as attempts to undermine the interests and concerns of member states which consequently react to preserve the status quo. Others see reform as a process through which economies can be achieved by curtailing or cutting activities, often without concern for substance. Still others view reform as a conspiracy: conspiracy on the part of the secretariat to enhance its position or on the part of member states to promote their interests at the expense of others. Quite often, such attempts have resulted in a stalemate and the exchange of accusations, including laments over the absence of vision or the lack of political will.

These views can also be found in the latest efforts to reform the UN. Touching all aspects of the organization, the reform process was carried out over a five-year period. It was launched in December 1985 by the decision of the General Assembly (GA) to establish the Group of 18 to review the efficiency of the administrative and financial functioning of the UN. It was concluded in December 1990 when the GA considered and approved the final assessment of the implementation of the reform. This is therefore an appropriate time to look back on a critical period for the UN. This will help to understand both the potential and the limitations of the organization and provide the foundation for deciding how to proceed in the continuous process of reform. The questions which should be asked are numerous. What were the interests of the major players in the reform process, namely the various groups of members states and the UN secretariat? What was the impact of the reform on the different fields of UN activities, such as the areas of peace and security as opposed to economic and social issues? How did the reform change the intergovernmental structure of the UN as compared to the organization and operation of the secretariat? Did this impact improve or weaken the UN? Did it support the interests of a particular group? Is the renaissance of the UN the result of a successful reform or the lessening of the Cold War? Is the UN now better equipped to fulfil the new demands emanating from the breathtaking changes in the international climate? These are only a few of the questions which merit serious attention in order to understand what has happened.

This report will provide the information needed to form a judgement. It is a detailed documentation which relies on primary sources and focuses on two basic and interrelated perspectives. Firstly, details are provided on the mechanics of reform-making in the UN, identifying and describing the participants, the decision-making procedures, the actual process of implementation and the assessment of results. Secondly, the mechanics of reform-making are viewed in the wider context in which the effort was carried out. This includes the growing dissatisfaction of UN member states prior to the reform effort, the build-up of the financial crisis, the end of the Cold War characterised by a lessening of the ideological competition and the rediscovery of the role of the UN in the areas of peace and security.

The following section gives a short introduction to the UN system. These issues are emphasized to facilitate the understanding of the reform process. Subsequently, details are provided on the previous reform initiatives started in the 1950s, the build-up to the financial crisis during the early 1980s, and the establishment of the Group of 18 in 1985, its work and final report. The following chapters describe events on an annual basis, beginning with the year 1986 (chapter 2) during which the main reform resolution 41/213 is approved. This resolution mandates the implementation of specific changes in the administrative and budgetary area, as well as the launching of further reviews. With the start of 1987 (chapter 3) these reviews are initiated. A first progress report is presented which highlights organizational changes in the political and administrative fields. During the year 1988 (chapter 4) the review of the economic and social area is concluded. A second progress report on the overall reform effort is discussed. Major decisions are taken with regard to the implementation of staff reductions and on budgetary matters. The year 1989 (chapter 5) sees a consolidation of the reform process and the submission of a final progress report. The first major test for the newly established procedures is recalled, namely the approval of the UN programme budget for 1990-1991. The year 1990 (chapter 6) marks the end, with the discussion of an analytical report and the approval of a concluding resolution on the reform process. This is followed by some final comments.

1.2   The United Nations[1]

The UN is part of the UN system, also known as the UN family.   An illustration of this rather complex set-up is shown in the following illustration.

The United Nations System[2]

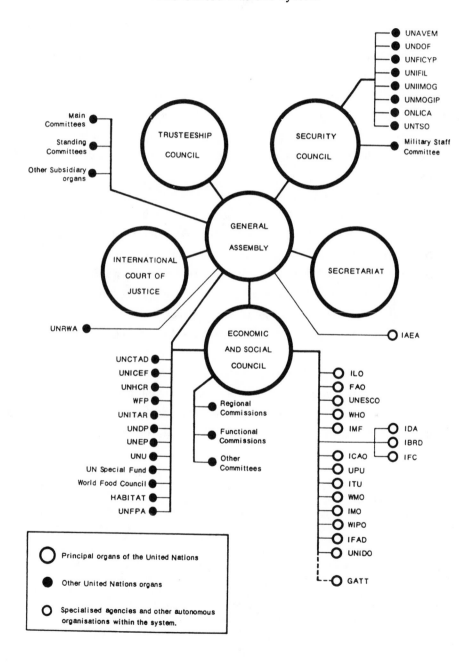

As illustrated, the UN system includes 14 specialized agencies* and the Bretton Woods institutions**. The UN itself is at the centre and concerned with the maintenance of international peace and security and the promotion of development and international co-operation as well as the co-ordination of the overall UN system. Other organizations are working in areas such as health, education, international trade or postal administration. The creation of some of them, such as ITU which was founded in 1865, predates the establishment of the UN in 1946. Each organization has a legislative body composed of representatives of member states and a secretariat which implements the programme of the organization. The secretariats of the UN system employ over 60,000 staff members in more than 150 countries. The whole system spends some $6 billion a year, one third funded through mandatory assessments on member states and two thirds from voluntary contributions.*** The secretariats of the specialized agencies are financially and administratively independent of the UN.

The UN itself has 166 member states and constitutes approximately half of the UN system in terms of staff and budget. The UN has six principal organs, namely the GA, the Security Council, the Economic and Social Council (ECOSOC), the Trusteeship Council, the International Court of Justice (ICJ) and the secretariat, headed by the Secretary-General. In addition, a number of specific organs, such as programmes or bodies, were established by the GA or the Secretary-General to carry out certain tasks. They relate to the UN through the principal organs - as is the case for the specialized agencies and the World Bank institutions.

The GA is the main deliberative organ of the UN. Composed of representatives of all member states, it meets in regular session from September to December each year. The negotiations conducted during the sessions result in the approval of resolutions. They may be divided into two categories. Firstly,

---

*Food and Agriculture Organization (FAO), General Agreement on Tariffs and Trade (GATT), International Atomic Energy Agency (IAEA), International Civil Aviation Organization (ICAO), International Fund for Agricultural Development (IFAD), International Labour Organization (ILO), International Maritime Organization (IMO), International Telecommunication Union (ITU), United Nations Education, Scientific and Cultural Organization (UNESCO), United Nations Industrial Development Organization (UNIDO), Universal Postal Union (UPU), World Health Organization (WHO), World Intellectual Property Organization (WIPO), World Meteorological Organization (WMO).
**International Monetary Fund (IMF), International Bank for Reconstruction and Development (IBRD) or World Bank with the affiliated organizations International Development Association (IDA) and International Finance Corporation (IFC).
***Exclusive of the capital funding of the financial institutions IBRD, IDA, IFAD, IFC and IMF.

those which are directed towards member states in order to guide their conduct. Secondly, those which address the Secretary-General and provide the mandates and instructions for the activities carried out by the secretariat. Resolutions are approved on the basis of drafts which are submitted by member states or a group of member states for discussion. Quite often, by the time the final draft of a resolution is agreed upon, the process of negotiations has included the submission of competing drafts, the revision of drafts and the withdrawal of drafts. Decisions are made by a majority of the members present and voting, except for 'important questions' which require a two-thirds majority. Important questions include issues such as recommendations with respect to the maintenance of peace and security, the election of non-permanent members to the Security Council or budgetary questions. In accordance with article 18.1 of the UN Charter, each member of the GA has one vote. Often, resolutions which find general approval are adopted by consensus which does not require the taking of a vote.

The GA allocates most of the questions to its seven main committees.* In addition, under the GA's rules of procedure, two standing committees have been established. The Committee on Contributions advises the Assembly on all questions relating to the apportionment of the expenses of the UN. The Advisory Committee on Administrative and Budgetary Questions (ACABQ), examines the reports on the budget and the accounts of the UN and the administrative budgets of the specialized agencies and advises the GA on other financial and administrative issues. Created in 1946, the ACABQ is made up of 16 experts who serve in their personal capacity. They are chosen by the GA, normally by consensus. Experts are selected from each of the groups of states. The composition, however, gives particular weight to the major contributors, and experts from the USA, USSR and Japan are always included. ACABQ has its own small secretariat.[3]

---

*First Committee (disarmament and related international security matters); Special Political Committee; Second Committee (economic and financial matters); Third Committee (social, humanitarian and cultural matters); Fourth Committee (decolonization matters); Fifth Committee (administrative and budgetary matters); Sixth Committee (legal matters).

Finally, the GA establishes subsidiary, *ad hoc* and other bodies.* Two of these bodies, the International Civil Service Commission (ICSC) and the Joint Inspection Unit (JIU) are funded jointly by organizations within the UN system.

The ICSC aims to develop a single, unified international civil service through establishing common standards, methods and arrangements for the organizations participating in the UN common system.** This is to allow for easy interchange of personnel and to limit competition in recruitment. The four World Bank organizations maintain their own system of remuneration, pensions and personnel policies which is more attractive to staff members than that of the UN common system. The Commission is responsible for making recommendations to the GA for the regulation and co-ordination of conditions of service, including issues of pay, allowances, benefits and the classification of duty stations. In this function, the Commission is an advisor to the legislative organ and restricts its activity to providing technical advice. For certain issues, ICSC also has decision-making functions and acts on behalf of the governing bodies. The ICSC comprises 15 independent experts appointed in their individual capacity by the GA and a small secretariat. The ICSC meets for three weeks, twice a year, when representatives of executives heads and of staff have the opportunity to address the Commission.

The JIU's mandate is to examine, in an independent manner, the management of the organizations.*** The Unit consists of 11 inspectors appointed by the GA supported by a small secretariat. The inspectors serve in their personal capacity and have special experience in administrative and financial matters. They can make on-the-spot enquiries and have broad powers of investigation in matters relating to the efficient and proper use of funds. They do not, however, have any decision-making power and are limited to proposing reforms or making recommendations aimed at improving management and achieving greater co-ordination between organizations.

---

*They include among others, the Board of Auditors, Investment Committee, International Law Commission, United Nations Joint Staff Pension Fund, United Nations Administrative Tribunal, Committee on the Peaceful Uses of Outer Space, Special Committee against Apartheid, Special Committee on Peacekeeping Operations, United Nations Council for Namibia, Committee on Conferences, United Nations Disarmament Commission, Conference on Disarmament (CD), Committee on Information, International Civil Service Commission (ICSC) and the Joint Inspection Unit (JIU).

**Participating organizations in ICSC are: UN, ILO, FAO, UNESCO, ICAO, WHO, UPU, ITU, WMO, IMO, WIPO, IFAD, UNIDO, IAEA and GATT.

***Following organizations participate in JIU: UN, ILO, FAO, UNESCO, ICAO, WHO, UPU, ITU, WMO, IMO, WIPO, UNIDO and IAEA.

Furthermore, the GA has established committees to monitor the implementation of treaties and to report to states parties and to the GA. Such treaty bodies include the Committee on the Elimination of Racial Discrimination (CERD), the Human Rights Committee, and the Committee Against Torture. Finally, some UN affiliated organs report directly to the GA through their intergovernmental body, board of trustees or head of secretariat.*

The Security Council has primary responsibility for the maintenance of international peace and security and reports to the GA. Its functions include the investigations of disputes, threats to peace or acts of aggression and recommending appropriate action. It can call on members to apply economic sanctions, and undertake military action, such as peace-keeping missions. The Council has five permanent members (China, France, the USSR, the UK, the USA) and 10 members each elected by the GA for a two-year term. Decisions require nine votes, including those of all five permanent members, which therefore have the right of veto. The Security Council is assisted by a Military Staff Committee composed of the chiefs of staff of the permanent members of the Security Council. Finally, the Security Council supervises a number of peace-keeping organizations.**

ECOSOC is the principal organ for co-ordinating the economic and social work of the UN system. The intergovernmental bodies of a number of the UN specific organs report to ECOSOC.*** In addition, the specialized agencies are to co-ordinate their work through the machinery of ECOSOC. For example, they submit annual reports to the Council. Finally, two joint specific organs report to ECOSOC: the International Trade Centre (ITC), jointly financed by the UN/UNCTAD and GATT and the World Food Programme (WFP), a specific organ of the UN and FAO. ECOSOC meets twice yearly and has a number of subsidiary bodies including six functional commissions****,

*This include the UN Disaster Relief Organizations (UNDRO), UN Relief and Worlds Agency for Palestine Refugees in the Near East (UNRWA), UN Institute for Training and Research (UNITAR).

**These include the United Nations Truce Supervision Organization (UNTSO), United Nations Disengagement Observer Force (UNDOF), United Nations Interim Force in Lebanon (UNIFIL), United Nations Military Observation Group in India and Pakistan (UNMOGIP), and United Nations Force in Cyprus (UNICYP).

***The UN High Commissioner for Refugees (UNHCR), UN Conference on Trade and Development (UNCTAD), World Food Council (WFC), UN Environment Fund (UNEP), International Narcotics Control Board (INCB), UN Children's Fund (UNICEF), UN Development Programme (UNDP), UN Population Fund (UNFPA), UN Fund for Drug Abuse Control (UNFDAC).

****Statistical Commission, Population Commission, Commission on Social Development, Commission on Human Rights, Commission on the Status of Women, Commission on Narcotic Drugs.

five regional commissions*, six standing committees** and a number of standing expert bodies***. CPC, one of the six standing committees, was established in 1962 as the main subsidiary body for planning, programming and co-ordination. In particular, the Committee reviews the secretariat's proposed medium-term plan, programme priorities, the translation of legislation into programmes and programme evaluation. Recommendations on the work programme are made to the GA and ECOSOC with the view to avoiding overlap and duplication of activities. Decisions are taken on the basis of consensus. Since 1970, the Committee has included 21 government representatives, nominated by ECOSOC and elected by the GA, namely five African, five West European and others, four Asian, four Latin American and three East European members.

The Trusteeship Council supervises the administration of territories placed under the trusteeship system to promote their progressive development towards self-government or independence. Ten of the initial eleven trust territories have attained independence, so that the Council has few remaining responsibilities. The Trusteeship Council reports to the Security Council.

The International Court of Justice (ICJ) is the principal judicial organ of the UN and is located in The Hague (The Netherlands). It decides cases and provides advisory opinions on questions submitted to the court by member states or organs of the UN and the specialized agencies. The Court consists of 15 judges elected by GA and the Security Council.

The secretariat services the legislative bodies of the UN and administers the activities and policies decided by them. It is headed by the Secretary-General who is appointed by the GA on the recommendation of the Security Council. The Secretary-General in turn appoints the members of his staff. In the case of the most senior level, this is often done in consultation with member states. As well as being chief administrative officer of the secretariat, the Secretary-General is responsible for alerting the Security Council to threats to international peace and security and to using his good offices to help resolve

---

*Economic Commission for Africa (ECA) in Addis Ababa, Economic and Social Commission for Asia and the Pacific (ESCAP) in Bangkok, Economic Commission for Europe (ECE) in Geneva, Economic Commission for Latin America (ECLAC) in Santiago, Economic Commission for Western Asia (ESCWA) in Baghdad.

**Committee for Programme and Co-ordination (CPC), Committee on Natural Resources, Committee on Transnational Corporations, Committee on Human Settlements, Commission on Non-Governmental Organizations, Commission on Negotiations with Intergovernmental Agencies.

***Bodies on subjects such as development planning, crime prevention and control, the transport of dangerous goods, and tax treaties between developed and developing countries.

international conflicts. The secretariat employs more than 16,000 international civil servants from over 140 countries. The staff is responsible to the organization and is not to seek or receive instructions from any government or outside authority. The secretariat's responsibilities include administering the peace-keeping operations, surveying world economic and social trends and problems, organizing international conferences, preparing studies on subjects such as disarmament and the development of human rights, translating documents, providing interpretation services at meetings and disseminating information to the world's public.*

The secretariat is organized into departments, centres and offices which serve one or more intergovernmental bodies or provide services to the organization as a whole.** These entities posses varying degrees of autonomy in the areas of financial control, accounting, recruitment and the provision of administrative services. In addition, there exist varying degrees of independence from the assessed budget of the UN due to funding through voluntary contribution. In fact, one can distinguish between those entities which are more closely affiliated with the UN*** and those which are more autonomous****.

For the biennium 1990-1991, the UN has approximately 10,000 posts, 3,800 for professional staff and 6,200 for general service staff. In addition, approximately 2,500 posts are funded by voluntary contributions. In accordance with article 101.3 of the UN Charter, 'the paramount consideration in the employment of the staff and in the determination of the conditions of service shall be the necessity of securing the highest standards of efficiency,

---

*For a detailed description of the annual activities of the United Nations see: Kumiko Matsuura, Karl P. Sauvant, Joachim W. Müller, *The Annual Review of United Nations Affairs* (Dobbs Ferry, New York: OCEANA, 1991-continuing).

**Those providing services to the organization as a whole are: Department of Public Information (DPI); Department of Administration and Management (DAM), including Office of Programme Planning, Budget and Fiance (OPPBF), Office of Human Resource Management (OHRM) and Office of General Services (OGS); United Nations Office at Vienna (UNOV) and the United Nations Office at Geneva (UNOG).

***Closely affiliated are, for example: the Executive Office of the Secretary-General, Offices of the Secretary-General; Department of Political and Security Council Affairs, Department of Specialized Political Questions, Regional Co-operation, Decolonization and Trusteeship; Department of Political and Security Council Affairs, Department for Disarmament Affairs, Director General's Office for International Co-operation and Economic Affairs (DG's Office); Department of International Economic and Social Affairs (DIESA), Department of Technical Co-operation for Development (DTCD), Centre for Science and Technology for Development (CSTD); UN Centre on Transnational Corporations (UNCTC); the Secretariat of Regional Commissions; CSDHA, Human Rights, UNHCR, UNCTAD, WFC, UNDRO, UNEP, HABITAT and the entities providing services to the organizations as a whole.

****More autonomous are, for example: UNDP, UNICEF, UNITAR, UNRWA, UNU, INCB.

competence and integrity.' In the same article, it has been laid down that 'due regard shall be given to the importance of recruiting the staff on as wide a geographical basis as possible'. The composition of staff in the professional category from various countries follows approximately the distribution of assessments to the regular budget. As such, the largest contingent are US nationals. General service staff are recruited locally at the place of employment, without regard to geographical distribution. Staff are initially recruited on fixed-term appointments and are generally offered permanent contracts after a certain period. Some staff members are seconded from their national civil service for a number of years to work at the UN. These staff members, in general, remain on fixed-term contracts. Until recently, nearly all staff members from socialist countries were seconded to the UN.

The pay of professional and higher category staff includes two components. Firstly, the salary is determined by reference to the civil service system of a comparator country, which has so far been the USA. Secondly, a flexible post adjustment component is added so as to ensure that the purchasing power of staff members stationed throughout the world is equal. The system, therefore, takes into account changes in the local cost of living and exchange rates. The staff in the general service category are in general recruited locally and their compensation is determined in accordance with best prevailing local conditions. The levels of posts are determined in accordance with a job classification scheme, which is generally applied throughout the UN common system. All organizations, with the exception of UPU, which are member of the UN common system, participate in the UN Joint Pension Fund. The pension fund is governed by a board, composed of representatives of legislative bodies, executive heads and staff. It submits its recommendations for decision to the GA. The fund is financed two-thirds by the organizations and one-third by the staff. There is no common system of health insurance, but various schemes are established at the local level under a cost-sharing arrangement between organizations and staff. The organizations of the common system provide similar benefits to all professional staff, including home leave on a biennial basis, annual leave of 30 days and the payment of education grants for children of internationally recruited staff members. Other allowances include the payment of a rental subsidy at certain duty stations during the first years of employment, essentially most important for junior level professional staff. For duty stations with very difficult living conditions, additional financial incentives and entitlements exist, such as more frequent home leave. The interests of UN staff members are represented by staff organizations at the various duty stations. They are brought together in the Co-ordinating Committee for Independent Staff Unions and Associations (CCISUA). The various UN organizations and those of the specialized agencies are organized in the Federation of International Civil Servants' Associations (FICSA). Both organizations attend the meetings of ICSC. Appeals by staff members are dealt with by the United Nations Administrative Tribunal (UNAT), which is responsible for litigations concerning the UN as well as the UN Joint Staff Pension Fund. The operations of the UN are assessed by internal and external auditors. A Board of Auditors is appointed by and reports to the General Assembly. The board selects national auditing bodies, which in turn appoint the external authors. The co-ordination between external auditors of the UN organizations is entrusted to the Panel of External Auditors.

The UN programme budget is divided into two major parts: the regular budget, financed from assessed contribution, and the budget funded from voluntary contributions. The programme budget covers the period of a biennium, starting with the beginning of a calender year. Prior to the reform, described in the following chapters, the Secretary-General initiated the preparation of the programme budget proposal 18 months prior to its implementation. The proposal is based on the six-year medium-term plan previously approved by the GA. In the May preceding the budget period, the proposals are reviewed by CPC and ACABQ. CPC focuses its review on the programmatic presentation, including issues such as the setting of priorities and mandates for specific activities. ACABQ reviews the administrative and financial aspects of the programme budget and scrutinizes the proposal for possible economies. Both committees are expected to reach a decision by consensus. The proposed programme budget, along with the recommendations of ACABQ and CPC, are subsequently submitted to the fall session of the General Assembly and taken up by the Fifth Committee. The committee, which is composed of government representatives, reviews the Secretary-General's proposals, considers the recommendations of CPC and ACABQ, amends the proposal where applicable and passes the programme budget on to the plenary after voting on each budget section as well as on the programme budget as a whole. The GA finally approves the biennial programme budget towards the end of the session in December, just before the start of the first year of implementation. In accordance with article 18.2 of the UN Charter, budgetary questions are included in 'Decisions of the General Assembly on important questions', which require a two-thirds majority. Subsequent changes necessitated by inflation and exchange rate movements are introduced to the approved budget once towards the end of the first year of its implementation and again towards the end of the second year. In addition to these rather technical adjustments, the approved programme budget can be modified in accordance with two procedures. Firstly, the secretariat can request the GA's approval for revised budget estimates. Those may be put forward to reflect the implementation of major changes in the approved programme budget, e.g. a Secretary-General's proposal to merge two departments or to implement a comprehensive office automation plan. Secondly, the programme budget can be modified as a result of programme budget implication statements. Such statements are approved in connection with new GA resolution, mandating the implementation of new activities which cannot be absorbed into the previously approved programme of work. In fact, the GA cannot take any decision on a draft resolution which has programme budget implications before being presented with an implication statement by the secretariat. Budget increases which result from revised estimates or programme budget implication statements are also known as add-ons. The initial programme budget for 1990-1991 includes estimated regular budget expenditure of approximately $1,975 million, partly offset by income of $367 million, leaving net requirements of $1,608 million and shows expected voluntary contributions of approximately $2,500 million.

Approximately half of the UN regular budget is spent in the USA. Other major centres of expenditure are located in Switzerland, Austria, Ethiopia, Thailand, Chile and Iraq. The assessments for individual countries are decided by the GA every three years on the recommendation of the 18-member Committee for Contributions. The primary criterion applied when deciding on the scale of assessments is the ability of each member country to pay in terms of national income, but also taking into account the size of population and per capita income. The level of contributions also determines the desirable range of professional posts in the secretariat for each country. In the first scale in 1946, the USA assessment was 49.89 per cent. A first revision let to a reduction of the US contribution to 39.89 per cent and the establishment of a minimum assessment of 0.04 per cent for all states. With the admission of new countries, such as Japan, Italy, Austria, Spain and the two Germanies, as well as a large number of developing counties, the scale was further revised. The maximum contribution, i.e. the US contribution, was reduced to 30 per cent in 1957 and 25 per cent in 1974. The minimum contribution was reduced to 0.02

---

*For a detailed breakdown of the 1990-1991 programme budget see annex, table 1.

per cent in 1974 and to 0.01 per cent in 1978.* If its contribution were calculated based only on the criteria currently applied, without a maximum or minimum ceiling, the US would have to pay substantially more and some developing countries would pay even less than the minimum contribution. Currently, it is possible that member states which contribute 1.88 per cent could form the two-thirds majority required to approve the budget in 1991. In fact, member states which account for almost 80 per cent of the assessed budget either cast a negative vote or abstained from voting for the approval of the 1986-1987 programme budget.

The work of the 19 organizations in the UN system is brought together at the secretariat level through the Administrative Committee on Co-ordination (ACC). The ACC is composed of the Secretary-General and the executive heads of specialized agencies and World Bank institutions. The ACC meets three times a year and supervises the implementation of agreements between the participating organizations and co-ordinates their activities. Prior to the ACC session, the organizational committee of ACC meets to determine its future work. The discussions at ACC centre mostly on the general political environment and the identification of common targets. Decisions are binding on all member organizations and are reached by consensus. The ACC is assisted by, or delegates decision-making to, subsidiary machinery. This includes the Consultative Committee on Administrative Questions (CCAQ), the Consultative Committee on Substantive Questions (CCSQ) including programme and development activities, and a number of sub-committees, such as the Advisory Committee on the Co-ordination of Information Systems (ACCIS) or committees on statistics and nutrition. A secretariat unit in the UN serves as the focal point in the UN system for matters relating to interagency affairs. It provides support for ACC, CCSQ and the sub-committees. CCAQ, however, has its own inter-organizational secretariat which is jointly funded by all participants.** CCAQ is also divided in two different branches: CCAQ (PER) deals with personnel and administrative questions, especially with issues concerning salaries, allowances, entitlements or job classification, and CCAQ (FB) is concerned with financial and budgetary matters, in particular with the development of common approaches to budgetary and financial operations. It

---

*The scale of assessments for 1991 is as follows: USA 25.00%, Japan 11.38 %, USSR 9.99%, Germany 9.36%, France 6.25%, UK 4.86%, Italy 3.99% and Canada 3.09%. Eight countries contribute between 2.00-1.00%, 11 countries 0.99-0.50%, 52 countries 0.49-0.02% and 80 countries the minimum of 0.01%. For detailed scale of assessments see annex, table 2.
**UN, UNDP, ILO, FAO, UNESCO, ICAO, WHO, UPU, ITU, WMO, IMO, WIPO, IFAD.

carries out its work through consultations between the senior administrators of the participating organizations.

Essentially, the secretariat implements the decision of the governing bodies. The actual method of implementation depends, however, on the interaction between both groups. This reflects not only their legitimate differences of interests, but also longstanding 'unwritten rules', and relations between delegations and senior secretariat staff. Whereas the main actors at the secretariat level are the Secretary-General and his senior officials, it is the national delegations of members states who work at the governing level. Delegations are composed of staff from foreign ministries and representatives of organizations responsible for the subject matter in question in the home country, such as ministries of finance. One might distinguish between those permanently placed at UN duty stations and those who come from member states to attend a specific meeting of a governing body. The latter are often highly specialized experts, such as scientists or senior staff, ministers or even the country's head of state. The former are members of permanent national delegations, who are posted to the location for a number of years. All member states have such permanent delegations in New York, and most of them also in Geneva and Vienna. Members of regional commissions also maintain permanent delegations in Addis Ababa, Santiago, Baghdad and Bangkok. In some places, the functions of the permanent delegation to the United Nations are often taken care of by the embassy to the UN host country. Delegations often act in accordance with strict and binding instructions received from their national capital; in other cases they are more flexible and take decisions in accordance with general guidelines. Continuous consultations between delegations and their capitals during negotiations are part of the process of reaching a balanced decision at the intergovernmental level. In general, delegations based in New York are higher ranking than those in other UN duty stations. This implies that, prior to taking a decision, a delegation based in Geneva might have to receive clearance from its delegation in New York. Decision-making by governing bodies is a rather complex system of group dynamics as well as national interests and influence. In order to facilitate the exchanging of views, a number of groups of countries have been formed. The best known and largest is certainly the Group of 77 (G77) which represents the interests of some 130 developing countries in the economic and social fields.[*]

---

[*]A detailed account of the work of the Group of 77 is provided in: Karl P. Sauvant, Joachim W. Müller, *The Collected Documents of the Group of 77* (Dobbs Ferry, New York: OCEANA, vol. 1-15, continuing).

A representative of the G77 often speaks on behalf of the group during meetings of intergovernmental bodies or submits on behalf of the group draft resolutions for decision. The G77 in turn is organized into regional groupings, including the African, the Latin American and the Asian groups. In order to organize their political interests, the developing countries have established the Non-aligned Movement (NAM) with some 100 members. A similar composition of member states, including mainly Western countries, can be found in the Western European and Others group, the Geneva group (G10) operating in the European-based UN organizations and Group B at UNCTAD. Furthermore, there is the European Community group of 12 member states, the Nordic group of five member states and, until recently, the group of socialist countries.

Decisions by governing bodies are often taken on the basis of documentation prepared by the secretariat which also assists in the conduct of the negotiations. In fact, the secretariat plays a crucial part in this process: since the secretariat is well informed on the technical issues involved, the governing body often accepts its expertise and seldom rejects or modifies it. In fact, the organizational complexity and the multitude of issues, make it difficult, in particular for individual developing countries sometimes with a staff of less than five in a permanent delegation, to cover adequately, with the required specialization and preparation, all meetings. As a result of their larger staff, delegations from the main countries are in a better position to keep a more visible profile *vis-à-vis* other delegations and the secretariat and make their views known in the negotiations.

There does not exist a co-ordinating body at the legislative level which is similar to the ACC at the secretariat level. Although the GA is the legislative body of the system, it does not provide for an organized exchange of views between the governing bodies of the UN system. Due to the diversity of the composition of national delegations, the complexity of the UN legislative level and its lack of co-ordination, one can often find differences in the positions of delegations from the same country expressed at different forums of the UN system or even at the UN itself.

1.3 Previous Reform Efforts

As noted above, efforts to reform the UN have been a continuous process. There have been a multitude of initiatives from various quarters inside the UN secretariat, the governing bodies or from outside the organization. Reform proposals have, for example, emanated internally from the Secretary-General, the JIU, the ICSC, the Department of Administration and Management, the Joint Appeals Board and the Administrative Tribunal.[4] The GA has covered reform issues under the agenda item "Question of the Composition of the Relevant Organs of the United Nations" since 1977 and "Question of Equitable Representation on and Increase in the Membership of the Security Council" since 1979. The most influential, however, have included the setting up of committees of experts or government representatives, appointed by the Secretary-General or the GA. The secretariat services such committees by providing, for example, the necessary documentation. The reports of the committees are submitted to the GA for further consideration. The Assembly might in turn adopt some of the proposed recommendations in the form of a GA resolution instructing the secretariat to implement the decision.

The first major effort at reform was carried out in the 1950s. It covered a review of the salary and allowances system as well as the initial expansion of the secretariat. With regard to the latter, changes were introduced which led to the decentralization of the secretariat from Headquarters to the regional commissions. Issues of salary and allowances were entrusted to expert groups for review.[5] The Committee of Experts on Salary, Allowances and Leave System was established in 1949, composed of three experts who made a comprehensive review of the salary and allowances system, including a comparative study of the arrangements in other international organizations. The committee reported through the Secretary-General to the GA and its recommendations led to the reduction of grade levels and the regrouping of posts into four categories instead of the previous nineteen grades and one-category system based on the US federal administration model. A Salary Review Committee of nine member states was established in 1955 to examine salary issues and the desirability of the common system in view of the considerable deviations. The committee supported the common system but with some flexibility. It made recommendations on salaries, allowances, recruitment and the co-ordination of conditions of service within the common system.

By the late 1950s, major disenchantment with peace-keeping operations, the geographical distribution of senior level posts and the implementation of technical co-operation activities triggered a review of the activities of the UN. This disenchantment also resulted in the organization's first financial crisis. The crisis started when the Security Council could not agree on the funding of the peace-keeping operation in the Congo (ONUC) and Middle East (UNEF). As a result of this deadlock, the GA allocated the expenses by the same formula as was used to assess the regular UN budget. France and the socialist countries refused to pay on the grounds that UNEF and ONUC were unconstitutional, since the power to decide on the funding belonged solely to the Security Council where France and the USSR had a veto right. They argued that UNEF and ONUC were not proper expenses of the organization and should be charged directly to those countries responsible for the conflict. The refusal to pay brought on a financial crisis as a deliberate effort to prevent the power of deciding on peace-keeping operations shifting from the Security Council to the GA.[6]

Committee of Experts on the Review of the Activities and Organization of the Secretariat: the Committee of 8 (1961)

The committee of eight experts* was appointed by the Secretary-General as requested by GA resolution 1446 (XIV) "to work together with the Secretary-General in reviewing the activities and organization of the secretariat of the UN with a view to effecting or proposing further measures designed to ensure maximum economy and efficiency in the secretariat." The group was requested to pay special attention to examining the categories of posts subject to geographical distribution and the criteria for determining the range of posts for each member state. The report was characterized by the divergence in views between the expert from the USSR and the other experts. The expert disagreed strongly with the others on the issue of the geographical distribution of posts. He argued that the senior staff in particular was composed, of an overwhelming majority of nationals of countries belonging to Western military alliances. This imbalanced composition of the secretariat, he argued, distorted the implementation of Security Council decision, as was the case with the resolution concerning the Republic of the Congo. The expert also rejected the financial system governing operational activities, where socialist countries were virtually excluded from participating in operations in developing countries even though they bore the expenses incurred. In fact, he argued that the funding of operational activities through the regular budget was not authorized by the UN charter. He further argued that there existed serious defects in the secretariat's organizational structure, with an unduly large number of senior posts, a cumbersome and ill-defined structure, an unjustifiably large staff and an excessive division of functions. He proposed to radically reorganize the secretariat in such a way that the UN should not be headed by a single person,

---

*France, Colombia, USSR, United Arab Republic, UK, Ghana, India, USA.

the Secretary-General, but by three persons representing three main groups of States - the socialist states, the neutral states and the members of Western military blocs. The proposals of the expert from the USSR were strongly opposed by the other experts. As a result of this deadlock, very little could be agreed on. Some limited adjustments in the allocation of top-level responsibilities were made in order to achieve a more equitable and balanced geographical distribution. In the area of economic and social activities, attention was drawn to the question of decentralization and the particular need to strengthen the regional economic commission for Africa. Other issues concerned the call for limiting budget increases, proposals to reduce the staffing of the Department of Trusteeship and Information from Non-Self-Governing Territories, proposals to develop a UN library service, and emphasis was placed on better scheduling and servicing of meetings. With regard to budget stabilization, concern was expressed about the steady increase.

Working Group of Fifteen on the Examination of the Administrative and Budgetary Procedures of the United Nations (1961)

In response to the financial crisis emanating from the refusal of some member states to contribute to peace-keeping operations, a working group composed of representatives from 15 member states was established to review the methods for covering the cost of peace-keeping operations and the relationship between such methods and the existing administrative and budgetary procedures of the organization. The working group was not able to present a set of recommendations to the GA for approval because of the divergence of opinion among its members.[7] Instead, the GA decided to submit the issues to the International Court of Justice and requested an advisory opinion on whether the expenditures of UNEF and ONUC constituted expenses to be born by the member states as apportioned by the GA. The International Court decided in the affirmative by a vote of 9 to 5 and declared the non-payment illegal. A confrontation seemed likely since the refusal to pay was still maintained. Instead, the problems were shelved, mostly due to the conciliating efforts of the members states from the Non-Aligned Movement.

During a special session of the GA in 1963, it was decided to assess contributions for peace-keeping separately from those for the regular budget. The scale of assessments approved for peace-keeping shifted the financial burden onto those willing and able to pay additional contribution. Furthermore, a Special Account was established - financed by voluntary contributions - as a working capital fund to cover short-term imbalances between income and expenditure. Finally, and most importantly, countries which supplied troops agreed informally to bear the costs of their participation in peace-keeping operations themselves. In 1962 the UN issued long-term bonds to cover parts of the costs of UNEF and ONUC. The annual payments needed for servicing the loans were included in the regular budget. Most of the countries which refused to participate in the financing of UNEF and ONUC did not make contributions to the regular budget to cover these annual payments.

Special Committee on Peace-Keeping Operations (1964)

The financial difficulties created by peace-keeping operations, however, were not resolved, and a deficit of approximately $100 million was reached. As a result, the GA decided in 1964 to establish a committee of 34 member states to undertake a comprehensive review of peace-keeping operations. The committee was charged to work out a compromise solution for the financing of future peace-keeping operations, but was not able to do so. The USSR and France insisted that the Security Council should decide on peace-keeping operations. The USA referred to the decision of the International Court of Justice. Some informal rules were established. New peace-keeping forces would be established only by the Security Council. When voluntary financing was not agreed upon, contributions to peace-keeping would be assessed. This would be done separately from the regular budget of the UN, but on the basis of a formula reflecting a similar scale of assessment. The formula reduced the contributions from developing countries and increased those, for countries which held a permanent seat in the Security Council. In 1967, the committee was requested to study matters relating to facilities, services and personnel for peace-keeping operations. This work continued until 1983 and was resumed in 1988.

Ad Hoc Committee of Experts to Examine the Finances of the United Nations and the Specialized Agencies: the Committee of 15 (1965)

The financial crisis was not only created by peace-keeping operations. Member states also started to withhold their assessed contributions for other activities which they considered objectionable. On the initiative of the French delegation, an attempt was made to find a package deal solution to the financial problems. A committee made up of representatives from fifteen member states was set-up to analyze the finances of the UN. In particular, the committee was to analyze actual expenditure by type of activities, including the amounts committed for the different peace-keeping operations since their inception, the resources utilized to meet them and, where applicable, the debts contracted by the UN. In addition, the committee was to examine according to GA resolution 2049 (XX) the entire range of the budgetary problems of the UN and the specialized agencies, "notably their administrative and budgetary procedures, the means of comparing and, if possible, standardizing their budgets and the financial aspects of their expansion, with a view to avoiding needless expenditure, particularly expenditure resulting from duplications". The purpose of the review was "on the one hand, to secure better utilization of the funds available through rationalization and more thorough co-ordination of the activities of the organizations and, on the other, to ensure that any expansion of those activities takes into account both the needs they are intended to meet and the costs member states will have to bear as a result".

The committee presented two reports. The first report[8] dealt with the finances and the financial situation of the UN. It noted the concern of some member states that the expenditures of the UN had more than doubled between 1956 and 1965. The reasons were identified as: the increase in the number of organs and conferences, the marked increase in the size of the UN secretariat, the rising expenditure for secretariat salaries, the higher cost of living in the countries in which the main agencies of the UN were located, expansion of membership, the need for increasing developmental activities in view of the ever-widening gap between industrialized and developing countries with respect to their rates of economic growth. It was felt desirable, however, that any savings resulting from more effective utilization of resources and improved co-ordination should be used as additional resources for the benefit of developing countries. The concern of the socialist countries was to be met by separating those expenditures to which they objected and transferring them to the income section of the budget. This applied to the expenditure of the UN Commission for the Unification and Rehabilitation of Korea (UNCURK) and the interest payment on the 1962 bond issue for the Congo peace-keeping mission. The socialist countries, as well as some Western countries, were to be pleased by removing all technical cooperation activities from regular budget. The experts from the developing countries in the Committee of 15 supported this proposal on the understanding that equivalent voluntary contribution would be made to UNDP. Finally, all member states would commit themselves to paying their assessment in full, starting with 1973. These proposals were not accepted. The committee members from China, USSR and Poland wanted the expenditure for UNCURK and the bond issue completely removed from the budget. In addition, they did not accept a commitment for the future. Those developing countries which were not represented in the committee did not accept the removal of the expenditure for technical co-operation from the regular budget when the proposal was put forward to the Fifth Committee. Apparently, they did not trust the implicit commitment to increase the voluntary contributions to UNDP.

In its second report[9] the committee presented 52 recommendations concerning long-term planning, programme formulation, budget preparation and evaluation as well as issues concerning conferences servicing, documentation and standardization. Central to the recommendations on programme planning and budgeting was the idea of presenting a plan based on an analysis of alternative means and costs of accomplishing specific objectives within a definite time-frame. It was suggested that the plan should cover a six-year period; with a biennial programme budget for the first two years, a plan for the second two, and a tentative plan for the last two years. A partial implementation of these recommendations was approved by the GA in 1967, when it established new budgetary procedures involving the submission of the proposed annual budget together with planning estimate for the succeeding one-year budgetary period on the basis of long-term plans developed by programme-formulating bodies, including ECOSOC and its subsidiary bodies. Subsequent efforts eventually led to the approval of a biennial programme budget cycle and a six year medium-term plan in 1972, starting with a first biennial programme budget for 1974-1975 and a medium term plan for 1974-1977.

Committee on Reorganization of the Secretariat: the Committee of 7 (1968)

The Secretary-General decided in 1986 to appoint a committee of seven members with a wide geographical distribution to review the organization of the secretariat of the UN, including the offices in Geneva, the secretariats of UNCTAD, UNIDO and the regional economic commissions, with a view to ensuring the most efficient functioning of the secretariat and the optimum use of available resources. The committee was requested to examine, in particular, the top echelon of the secretariat, to review management procedures and propose detailed studies. Whereas the main concern was to ensure maximum efficiency in the functioning of the secretariat, the committee's recommendations aimed at reducing staffing levels and achieving a substantial reduction in costs. The report covered a multitude of issues: the grading of senior officials; the reduction of the amount of documentation and number of conferences to avoid further increases in work load; the reorganization of the executive office of the Secretary-General; the promotion of increased decentralization in the economic and social fields; the financial management of UNDP and other activities financed from voluntary contributions; the pooling and cutting of expenditures for public information; the establishment of a budget review committee under the chairmanship of the Secretary-General; the need for a systematic study of the utilization of manpower in the secretariat; the creation of a management service to carry out, for example, organizational studies and review administrative procedures and manpower utilization; improved recruitment procedures; the rotation of senior officials; staff mobility; training; promotion; and retirement. The expert from the USSR particularly criticized the recent expansion of the staff and demanded a reduction by 8 or 10 per cent. He proposed the abolition of permanent appointments and their replacement by fixed-term contracts. The implementation of some of the recommendations was within the authority of the Secretary-General, whereas others needed the approval of the GA. Although a large number of these recommendations were implemented, they did not lead to a reduction in the total UN budget as initially assumed by the Committee.

Jackson Report (1969)

A UN formerly dominated by relations between the larger, established countries had by the 1960s shifted its emphasis to the political, economic and social concern of the new countries. These countries had recently achieved independence from their colonial past under the guidance of the UN and were now looking to the UN for help to match their political independence with economic progress. In 1965, the UN Development Programme (UNDP) was established to implement technical co-operation activities in developing countries and it was expected that such activities, funded from voluntary contribution of member states, would grow considerably over the next few years. Despite the creation of UNDP, the implementation of technical co-operation programmes by the UN system remained fragmented, hampered by a plethora of independent agencies, semi-independent organizations, units and funds.

Sir Robert Jackson and a team of experts was commissioned by the Governing Council of UNDP to undertake a study of the capacity of the system to handle the resources made available through the organization. The 'Jackson report', also known as the 'capacity study', was issued in 1969. The report outlined a number of recommendations which aimed to strengthen the role of UNDP, ECOSOC and inter-agency co-ordination. In particular, UNDP was seen as a central co-ordinating organization, since it already controlled the largest share of technical co-operation funds in the UN system. The report was the subject of a rather lengthy review by the Governing Council. Comments were also received from the Inter-Agency Consultative Board (IACB). The final debate took place subsequently in ECOSOC and the GA. The study was welcomed by most of the member states, but strongly opposed by the specialized agencies, which did not want to accept any limitations of their independence.[10]

It was proposed that UNDP would become the centre of UN system development work, which was expected to double in the coming five years. Most of the voluntary funds were to be channelled through UNDP to the specialized agencies. This concentration of resources was expected to reenforce co-ordination and restrain inter-agency rivalry. This has not happened. Firstly, the initial assumption that resources for development activity would increase did not materialize. Secondly, the relative importance of UNDP resources *vis-à-vis* those of the specialized agencies has even declined. It was also proposed that ECOSOC would become a 'one-world parliament' - a policy centre for development in the system. ECOSOC's mandate was in fact to supervise and co-ordinate the activities of the specialized agencies. This, however, it could not do, since the agencies were not formally accountable to either ECOSOC or the Secretary-General. Other proposals aiming at inter-agency co-ordination were similarly not taken up, such as a system-wide computerized information system for development activities, the creation of a combined UN Development Service and the harmonization of development policy through the ACC Development Resources Panel under the UNDP Administrator.[11]

Other recommendations were implemented more successfully. In accordance with the Jackson report, UNDP developed a system of country programming, based on indicative planning figures. Governments had to project development programmes over a period of five to ten years to qualify for UNDP grants. Furthermore, the UNDP resident representatives in the developing countries were appointed co-ordinator of the activities of other agencies in the field. UNDP's headquarters was reorganized and the old Technical Assistance and Special Fund programmes were merged.

Quite clearly, the reform of UNDP appears to have been more successful than the implementation of recommendations aiming at inter-agency co-ordination, which would have required the cooperation of the specialized agencies. The success of this reform was limited by what Jackson pointed out as a lack of co-ordination within the governments of member states. Delegations from the same states to different specialized agencies often support contradictory policies by following the lead of the various executive heads.

Special Committee for the Review of the United Nations Salary System (1970)

In 1970, concern over increases in the salaries of professional staff prompted the GA to establish a "Special Committee for the Review of the United Nations Salary System". The committee consisted of experts from eleven member states and was to carry out a review of the long-term principles and criteria which governed the level of salaries. It was noted by the committee that the pension provisions were too generous, the operation of the post adjustment system unsatisfactory and the large number of higher graded personnel not justified. It confirmed the Noblemaire principle as the formula for establishing professional salaries, but noted that the existing compensation was too high compared to national standards. Based on the committee's recommendation, a margin was introduced by which UN salaries could deviate from those of the comparator system, the US government salary system. It also proposed the establishment of the International Civil Service Commission (ICSC), created in 1975, to regulate and co-ordinate conditions of service within the UN common system.

Ad Hoc Committee on the Restructuring of the Economic and Social Sectors of the United Nations System: the Group of 25 (1974)

Whereas the Jackson Report was initiated to adapt the UN system to the needs of implementing technical co-operation for development more effectively, the following major reform originated from quite different causes. In fact, the limited success of development activities to support economic progress in developing countries prompted demands for fundamental structural changes in the world economic system. Such negotiations were pursued in UNCTAD, basically between the developing countries, organized in the Group of 77, and the developed countries. The developed countries, however, were not prepared to surrender important economic advantages to their weaker negotiating partners. This disappointing outcome led the latter to switch negotiations from UNCTAD to the GA and the specialized agencies during the mid-1970s. Following the demands of the developing countries, in 1974 the sixth special session of the GA adopted the Declaration and Programme of Action for the

Establishment of a New International Economic Order (NIEO), covering issues such as trade, commodities, industrialization, technical co-operation and transfer of technology. The new emphasis was also subsequently reflected in related documents, such as the Charter of Economic Rights and Duties of States and the Lima Declaration. As already experienced in UNCTAD, the developed countries were rather reluctant to accept the new emphasis and expressed many reservations which fell short of open opposition.

In order to support its implementation, the developing countries pressed for making the UN system more receptive to the NIEO and for increased control over the UN machinery. The sixth special session of the GA in 1974 decided to establish a high level group of experts to be appointed by the Secretary-General. This group of experts, known as the 'Group of 25', was to make recommendation on structural changes and presented their report to the seventh special session of the GA in 1975. The group recommended that the post of a Director-General should be established to co-ordinate all activities within the UN system in the field of economic and social affairs; a new consultative procedure should be established to achieve consensus on controversial issues; UNCTAD should be replaced by an international trade organization; ECOSOC should be revitalized; the role of the specialized agencies should be redefined; and pre-investment funds should be consolidated.[12]

During the seventh special session, the developing countries objected to some recommendations made in the report. Although no specific recommendations were approved, the special session established an *Ad Hoc* Committee on the Restructuring of the Economic and Social Sectors of the United Nations System. The committee was to discuss and propose structural adjustments to the UN system in accordance with the requirements for implementing NIEO and the Charter of Economic Rights and Duties of States. One meeting was held in 1975 and three in 1976. Positions papers were submitted to the committee by the Group of 77, the USA and the members of the European Community.

In general, the developing countries preferred a strengthening of those UN bodies, such as the GA and UNCTAD, which they considered favourable to their own views. In particular, the GA was to be empowered to provide direction to the World Bank and GATT. The Group of 77 supported the creation of the office of the Director-General for economic development and the concentration of development activities in the regional commissions. The group opposed, however, the consolidation of development funds, since it was expected that this would lead to a decrease in such funds.

The USA advanced only a few recommendation for reform since it was more interested in preserving the status quo. It expressed opposition to strengthening the GA and limiting the autonomy of the World Bank, GATT and IMF as well as to the establishment the office of Director-General. Emphasis was placed on managerial reforms and on issues of planning, programming, budgeting, evaluation and co-ordination. Furthermore, the USA favoured a reduction of the subsidiary machinery of ECOSOC and a consolidation of funds as recommended by the Group of 25.

The European and socialist countries adopted a position similar to that of the USA, although some differences could be noted. The Nordic countries were more supportive of the demands of the Group of 77 and the socialist countries supported the group in their demands for a NIEO.

In December 1977, the GA finally approved resolution 32/197 on the reform after strenuous negotiations. The resolution was supported unanimously and reflected a compromise. In addition, the record of implementation was somewhat mixed. The compromise was evident in the call for the strengthening of the GA, which made no reference to the World Bank, IMF or GATT. Nevertheless, in accordance with the main thrust of the resolution, these organizations have become more involved in inter-agency co-operation through the ACC. Moreover, the resolution established the office of the Director-General for International Economic Co-operation (DIEC) to ensure co-ordination and provide leadership within the UN system, as strongly supported by the Group of 77. The new office, however, was not given sufficient resources and authority to fulfil its new mandate effectively.

Other changes which were implemented fully or with at least partial success, included the holding of a single pledging conferences and the reorganization and streamlining of the ACC machinery, in particular to make it responsible for inter-agency co-ordination in the area of development activities. Furthermore, a secretariat to ACC and ECOSOC was created, known as the Office of Secretariat Services for Economic and Social Matters (OSSECS). The Department for Technical Co-operation and Development (DTCD) was set up to bring together staff dealing with development activities with a corresponding restriction of the mandate for the Department for International Economic Co-operation (DIESA) to inter-disciplinary research, programme planning and co-ordination. The regional commissions were strengthened through decentralization, for example, by granting authority to the commissions as executing agencies for technical co-operation activities. The streamlining of the work of the GA resulted in the rationalization of methods, especially for the Second Committee which is entrusted with economic and social issues. A network of country co-ordinator was established, replacing the UNDP resident representative, to oversee the activities of the UN system in developing countries. Finally, the UNDP country programme was used as a frame of reference for the UN system development activities.

Other important reforms, as mandated by resolution 32/197, were not realized. Those included the rationalization of the ECOSOC subsidiary machinery and work programme, the strengthening of UNCTAD's role in international economic negotiations and the creation of a single governing body for the control of operational activities. The former was resisted by developing and the latter by developed countries.

Committee on the Charter of the United Nations and the Strengthening of the Role of the Organization (1975)

In 1975, the GA established the Special Committee on the United Nations Charter and Strengthening of the Role of the Organization. The Committee meets every year to consider proposals to strengthen the role of the UN in the maintenance of international peace and security. This relates to issues such as the peaceful settlement of disputes between states and the rationalization of existing UN procedures. So far, however, only a few modest changes have been approved and implemented.

Negotiating Committee on the Financial Emergency of the United Nations (1975)

The reform efforts did not lead to the resolution of the financial difficulties of the UN. Problems persisted and a new attempt was made to find a comprehensive solution with the establishment of the Negotiating Committee on the Financial Emergency of the United Nations in 1975. The committee reported in 1976, however, that no common approach could be found. The socialist and Western countries became concerned at the rapid growth in the UN budget and were not willing to commit themselves in advance to paying their assessments. In fact, these countries now viewed restraint or a cut in expenditure as a requirement for financial viability. The developing countries held a different view - they looked to a strong and growing UN to support their demands for a New International Economic Order. The Committee is still in existence today, but has not met since 1976. The deficits continued to grow, although at a modest pace. A temporary solution had to be found in 1981 when the Working Capital Fund (WCF) was increased from $50 million to $100 million.

Committee of Governmental Experts to Evaluate the Present Structure of the Secretariat in the Administrative, Finance and Personnel Areas: the Committee of 17 (1980)

In 1980 the Secretary-General Kurt Waldheim approached the GA indicating that a committee of experts should be established to evaluate the administrative structure of the secretariat. He viewed this as a similar initiative to the one launched by Secretary-General U Thant in 1968, when the Committee on the Reorganization of the Secretariat had been established. After twelve years, it was thought opportune to undertake a review of the administrative machinery, analyzing its short-comings, its strengths and possible improvements. The GA took up the initiative and requested the Secretary-General to appoint 17 experts with due regard to equitable geographical distribution through consultations with regional groups. This committee was to deal with issues similar to those covered by the Group of 18 some years later. After a year, the committee requested more time to complete its analysis due to the complexity of the issues involved. In the meantime, a new Secretary-General, Javier Pérez de Cuéllar, took office in 1991 and immediately initiated a number of administrative changes. The final report submitted by the committee of 17 in 1982, identified a number of issues, but made no recommendations for reform. The committee noted the changes implemented by the new Secretary-General, in particular, the establishment of the Programme Planning and Budgeting Board (PPBB), an internal senior level board to review and approve programme budget issues, and the Central Monitoring Unit to monitor programme performance. Clearly impressed by the new initiatives, the committee did not see any need to intervene within the area of responsibility of the new chief administrative officer, the Secretary-General. Little notice was taken of this reform effort, possibly since it was not conducted in an atmosphere of crisis as would be the case in a few years time.

High-level Advisory Group on Administrative Reform (1983)[13]

As an internal mechanism, the Secretary-General established an advisory group of high-level officials whose task was to identify issues and areas where administrative changes were necessary and possible. The group was chaired by the USG for Administration and Management and consisted of eight members.

It met regularly during 1983, either alone or with invited representatives from various parts of the secretariat. The committee's final report was submitted in February 1984. It identified priority areas where improvements in the organization and functioning of the secretariat were necessary and suggested possible courses of action for the Secretary-General to increase the operational effectiveness and efficiency of the organization. Upon receipt of the group's report, the Secretary-General directed. the USG for Administration and Management to develop a programme of management improvement. This resulted in a number of proposals being presented to the Secretary-General in June 1984 and the implementation of measures such as the modernization of the communications system; changes in UN peace-keeping operations; the establishment of a staff incentive programme; and new procedures to control travel on official business and the disposal of excess UN property.

1.4   Build-up to the Financial Crisis

The new effort to reform the UN was preceded by the growing dissatisfaction of member states with the organization. The criticism focused initially, however, on two specialized agencies, namely UNESCO and FAO. The USA decided in 1985, followed by the UK in 1986, to withdraw from UNESCO. This was the final conclusion of a period of criticism which had focused on the programme and management of the organization. In particular, the proposals for a New World Information and Communication Order were seen as an attempt to control the free press and license journalists. Support for the Palestine Liberation Organization (PLO) and the South West African People's Organization (SWAPO) was seen as unacceptable politicization. Criticism of the management focused on budget growth, personnel management, inadequate financial control and, in particular, on the leadership of the Director-General, M.A. M'Bow. The withdrawal resulted in a 30 per cent reduction of UNESCO's budget. The USA's decision was taken under the Reagan Administration and influenced by the Heritage Foundation, a Washington-based conservative think-tank. A new Director-General, Mr. Federico Mayor, was elected by the General Conference in 1987, and he immediately initiated a number of changes in order to regain the support of the countries which had left the organization. This has evidently not been sufficient, since the USA and the UK have not rejoined UNESCO so far. A second UN organization which was singled out for censure by the USA and other countries was FAO. Criticism again focused on issues of politization, mismanagement and the leadership of the Director-General, Edouard Saouma. The USA, the UK, Australia and Canada suspended payment of their contributions and demanded budgetary budget reform. The re-election of the Director-General for a third term in 1987 was not received favourably by the critics.

The most serious threat of all, however, was targeting the UN itself. The anti-UN attitude of some countries was amplified by a declining faith in multilateralism and support of terrorist organizations."[14] Perhaps the most irritating incident for the USA at the UN was the passing of GA resolution 3379 (XXX) in 1975 which compared zionism to racism. Another concrete example was the North-South dialogue conducted at UNCTAD. The problems included "assistance to the Palestinian people, economic cooperation among developing countries, efforts to redistribute world shipping and 'compulsory' transfer of technology. In the management category, lack of transparency and accountability in the budget process, excessive amounts of documentation, often technically deficient and biased (management and ideology), wasteful and duplicative programs, questionable financial management."[15] The Reagan Administration intensified its critical attitude and its ambassador to the UN, Jeane Kirkpatrick, complained about UN attempts to regulate international business, such as proposals for a code of conduct for transnational corporations, a marketing code for infant formula and codes for pesticides and toxic chemicals.[16] In 1982, the Reagan Administration refused to sign the Law of the Sea Convention, a convention which had been supported by the previous US Administration. The USA now found itself quite often on the defensive, complaining of being outvoted and singled out when blame was assigned. Following an initiative of Senator Robert W. Kasten in 1983, a law was passed in the USA which mandated the annual compilation of records on the voting results, distinguishing between countries voting for or against US positions.[17] While the same concerns were shared by a number of Western governments, the reaction of the USA was certainly the harshest.

A first attempt by US legislators to press for change in the UN can be found in section 503 (a) of the Foreign Relations Authorization Act for 1978, which required President Carter to submit a report on the UN system with recommendations on restructuring and reform.[18] Congressional hearings were held in 1979 on a reform of the UN and its finances. The issues raised included concern over the increase in the UN budget and the politicization of financial matters. Interest was also expressed in the possibility of introducing weighted voting in UN decision-making in accordance with the size of the financial commitment. The hearings marked the first Congressional attempt to intervene in UN affairs. Previously, this had been left to the State Department and the White House. The USA was not the only country pressing for financial restraint. The USSR and the USA became "at least partial accomplices" and showed "solidarity in demanding fiscal austerity" from the Secretary-General in 1983.[19]

The second congressional attempt to influence the management of the UN had more serious implications. It marked a shift of attitude arising out of a more widespread disagreement with the UN. A symbol of this disagreement was the Kassebaum Amendment to the Foreign Relations Authorization Act of 1985 for the fiscal years 1986 and 1987. According to Kilgore, it emanated from a coalition of political forces with quite different intentions. "First are the isolationists - an ever present force within Congress - who are suspicious of most international organizations and who sometimes go so far as to advocate US withdrawal from the United Nations and the removal of its headquarters from US soil. ... Secondly, there are those who see the United Nations as useful body only insofar as it can be used as an instrument of US foreign policy. ... It is identified with the work of the Heritage Foundation and overall is concerned to reassert US authority over UN activities. ... Thirdly, there is a core of sincere reformists who on the whole support the UN system, though not in all its aspects, and whose intent ... was to promote genuine reform within the organization in order to improve the credibility in the United States."[20] It was the latter group, including Senator Nancy Kassebaum, who sponsored the amendment. Their intention was not destructive, but in order to be successful they had to rely on a coalition that was more hostile to the UN system than they were themselves. The amendment stipulated that the US should pay 20 per cent of the assessed annual budget of the UN or any of the specialized agencies which did not adopt weighted voting procedures on matters of budgetary consequences, e.g. votes in proportion to the contribution of each member state; that the amount required to enable the US to fulfil its full obligations to the UN in 1985 and 1987 should be included in the Department of State authorization legislation; and that 'the authorization for funds in excess of 20 per cent will remain available to permit payment of a further assessed contribution should the intended reforms be achieved in the UN fiscal year for which the funds are provided'. The intention was to promote meaningful reform in budget procedures at the UN and its specialized agencies and not to reduce the US assessed contribution. The Amendment was passed by the Senate by a vote of 71 in favour and 13 against. The Reagan Administration indicated that it share the concern about UN budget reform.

The growing disillusion with the organization had taken a toll even on those who were friendly to the UN, as can be seen by Senator Kassebaum's introduction to the amendment, which he justified by criticizing the construction of a UN conference centre in Ethiopia: "the cost of the first phase of this building will be $73.5 million, of which the United States' share will be 25 per cent and it will cost us $18.5 million to pay for that conference centre in Ethiopia so that they can stand on the twenty-ninth floor and watch the rest of the country starve to death."[21] Once approved, the Amendment became law with no expiration date and no need for renewal. A conscious act by the legislative bodies would be needed in order to amend or repeal the law.

Weighted voting existed in the 'financial' organizations, namely the World Bank and IMF, of which the socialist countries were not members. Introducing such a system into the UN budgetary procedure would require an amendment of the charter by a vote of two-thirds of the member states, including the five permanent members of the Security Council. The requirements of the Kassebaum Amendment could only be satisfied if most of the small or poor countries gave up the influence they possessed over the budgetary procedure. Major powers, such as the USSR or China, would have substantially fewer votes than the USA. Quite clearly, such changes were too far-reaching. This was also realized by the sponsors of the Kassebaum legislation. To ensure payment of the full contribution to the UN, the hurdles were lowered in autumn 1985. A reconsideration of the Kassebaum legislation was considered justified once the UN had met a number of less demanding conditions, such as a freeze in UN salaries and the introduction of changes in the programme budget approval process.

The Kassebaum legislation became the spearhead of a drive to restrict payment of the US contribution to the UN. In 1985, the USA paid only $124 million of its assessed contribution of $198 million. The new shortfall of $74 million brought the USA's cumulative deficit to $86 million. But the worst was still to come. Along with the strengthening of the anti-UN mood in the USA, other legislation, such as the Sundquist Amendment, was approved by the US Congress which stipulated further withholdings. In addition, one other effort which was not aimed at the UN in particular had major implications for the organization. Approved by the US Congress in December 1985, the Gramm-Rudman-Holding law (Budget Deficit Reducing Act) mandated an across-the-board reduction in government spending with the aim to balance the federal budget by 1991. The law was not aimed at the UN in particular, but rather imposed progressive cuts in federal spending over the coming five years.

Congress and the Reagan Administration would be responsible for meeting the target set by the law in the subsequent annual budgets. At that stage, in late 1985, the cumulative effect of the various pieces of legislation on actual payments to the UN in the coming years was not clear. The Kassebaum Amendment reduced the US assessment of $210 million for 1986 by $42 million. The Gramm-Rudman-Holding law could result in a further cut of $70 million. In addition to those already mentioned, there were other legislative initiatives which aimed to cut US contributions even further. In fact, there was a possibility that the USA would only paying $60 million of its $210 million assessment.

Financial problems at the UN were not a new thing.* According to the financial regulations, assessed contributions are payable in January of each year. Members states, however, have increasingly opted to pay later in the year, to delay payment even further or to withhold contributions for reasons of principles. As a result, the UN was faced with a permanent cash flow crisis and the deficit created by unpaid contribution had grown from $71 million at the end of 1974 to $504 million by the end of 1985.[22] Out of this $504 million, $242 million was the result of arrears and withholdings from the regular budget, $262 million for withholdings from UNIFIL, UNEF and UNDOF peace-keeping operations outlined above. The major debtor nations for peace-keeping operations were the USSR ($164 million), the Ukrainian SSR ($18 million), the German Democratic Republic ($16 million) and Poland ($12 million). Despite this serious and growing deficit, peace-keeping activities remained in operation since the troop-contributing member states agreed to temporarily absorb the deficit. Reimbursement for the cost of the troops was expected to be made at a later stage once the financial situation had improved.

The regular budget withholdings and arrears of $242 million - as compared to an annual budget of approximately $800 million - was mainly attributed to the USA ($86 million), USSR ($41 million), South Africa ($24 million) and Brazil ($16 million). Just one year before, the total outstanding contribution had been only $166 million, out of which only $12 million was attributed to the USA. The new arrears of $74 million brought the accumulated US deficit up to $86 million and increased the total deficit considerably. The total UN arrears for 1985 of $242 million were composed of withholdings on grounds of principle and the deficit resulting from delays in payment. Contributions were withheld by 18 states on grounds of principle, related to interest payments on

---

*For details on the financial situation see annex, table 3 and 4.

the 1962 bond issue, opposition to the inclusion of technical assistance in the regular budget and support for the PLO and SWAPO. For those countries, which included the USSR ($41 million), South Africa ($24 million), USA ($7 million), Ukrainian SSR ($6 million), France ($4 million) and China ($4 million), the amounts totalled $93 million. The balance of the arrears of $149 million was the result of delays in payments which were expected to be made eventually. In fact, the member states with no arrears at all were a minority. Out of 159 member states, only 69 had no contributions outstanding at the end of 1985. In accordance with article 19 of the charter, a state could loose its right to vote if the amount of its arrears equalled or exceeded the amount of its contribution for the preceding two years. This had only ever happened in the case of South Africa.[23]

The shortfall in payments for the regular budget resulted in an immediate shortage in respect of the day-to-day cash needs, essentially the UN payroll and payments to vendors. Unlike national governments, the UN was not allowed to borrow funds in the commercial market. To meet its obligations, it could use the Working Capital Fund (WCF) to cover short-term imbalances in expenses and income. The WCF was set up in 1945 with $40 million, financed by assessed contribution. In 1982, the GA approved an increase to $100 million which represented 13.2 per cent of the appropriation for that year. For 1985, this figure amounted to 12.2 per cent. In addition, the GA had established a UN Special Account in 1965, funded by voluntary contribution, for the purpose of clearing up past financial difficulties and covering short-term deficits. At the end of 1985, the account held $77 million, the major donors being Japan ($13 million), UK ($10 million), China ($5 million), France and Canada ($4 million each). As a further measure to deal with the cash crisis, the GA approved the suspension of the financial regulations which governed the refund of savings to member states. According to the regulations, the UN had to return to member states as a credit against their assessed contributions in the next biennium their share of the balance of the appropriations not required. The effect of the suspension of the regulations increased temporarily the monies available to the UN, but the refunds were expected to be made once the financial situation had improved. In 1985, the monies thus realized amounted to $30 million. The total amount of $207 million from these various sources, still fell short of the regular budget deficit, which amounted to $242 million. To fill such a gap, the Secretary-General had been authorized by the GA in 1958 to borrow cash from accounts and special funds in its custody for purposes which normally related to the WCF. This temporary use of trust fund accounts funded by voluntary contributions or   peace-keeping funds was granted on the condition that normal current rates of interests would be paid. Despite all these measures, it appeared possible that the UN might not be able to meet its day-to-day cash obligations during 1986 if the expected increase in withholdings from the USA materialized.

The imminent crisis prompted further reform initiatives. In order to meet the immediate cash needs, the Secretary-General put forward a number of proposals and ideas.[24] These included the increase of the WCF to not less than $150 million, the borrowing of funds from member states, the issuance of long-term bonds or the assessment of contributions on a biennial rather than an annual basis. None of the proposals, however, were taken-up. The countries which had fulfilled their obligations were not willing to cover the additional bill for those not willing to pay. Another proposal which was widely discussed related to the reduction of the US assessment to the UN. In October 1985, two distinguished UN officials, Prince Sadruddin Aga Khan of Pakistan and Maurice Strong of Canada, proposed a revision of the scale of assessment with a maximum contribution of 10 instead of 25 per cent, with no increase for the poorer nations and corresponding increases for the middle size countries.[25] This had also been recommended by the Swedish Prime Minister, Olaf Palme, on the assumption that there would be corresponding increases for the middle-size powers.[26] The Secretary-General supported a reduction in the maximum assessment from 25 per cent to 15 per cent. One might assume that this would have been welcomed by the main contributor. The reaction of the USA to such proposals, however, "was generally one of hostility and embarrassment".[27] In fact, there was strong evidence that the USA did not want to pay less, but rather to use the financial leverage to induce change. In addition, this option was unlikely to find the support among the majority of members states who did not wish to legitimize unilateral reductions by the USA. Such option could only be considered, if at all, once the USA had fulfilled its current commit-ments. The members states of the European Community clearly stated that "the financial crisis ... is not to be resolved by compensatory contributions from other members states".[28]

A more comprehensive reform initiative was put forward by Maurice Bertrand, a member of the Joint Inspection Unit (JIU), on the occasion of the fortieth anniversary of the UN.[29] He admitted that his critical judgement was meant to surprise or even to shock. So it did. He first argued that the current UN system was built on three fallacious notions: first, that the maintenance of peace could be achieved through an institution, second, that the development of poor countries could be achieved through a sectoral approach, and third, that negotiations among 159 states were possible without a prior definition of agreed negotiation structures. He argued that the current structure could not be modified but needed to be transformed system-wide. After the League of Nations (first-generation) and the current organization (second-generation), there was a need to build a new, third-generation, UN. After highlighting shortcomings of the current system - the lack of co-ordination, the extraordinary complexity of inter-governmental and secretariat structures, the inordinately ambitious content of the programmes, the extreme fragmentation of the activities, the mediocre quality of programme outputs, the lack of staff qualifications, the lack of realism - he outlined his vision of reform. He saw little room for improving the structures of the 'political' UN, in particular the Security Council, and limited himself to encouraging the member states to make the most of the current structure in this field. Transformation, he argued, should focus on the structures in support of development. An 'economic' UN should be built up side by side with the 'political' UN. Towards this end, three major reforms were envisaged. First, there should be a genuine world forum to deal with economic problems to replace current dual system of ECOSOC and UNCTAD. The new forum should have a restricted membership of 23 members and function as an 'economic security council'. Second, the secretariats of the UN and the specialized agencies should be reorganized under the authority of one or more semi-independent commissions made up of independent persons of distinction. This structure of council-commission was similar to the European Community model. Third, regional or subregional development agencies or enterprises should be established in place of the current sectoral approach of independent specialized agencies working without co-ordination. The proposals for change would result in a substantial reduction of the activities of the specialized agencies. Bertrand's report was a rather personal account. In fact, the JIU distanced itself from his initiative, since the scope of the report went beyond what had jointly been approved by the inspectors and its release was in violation of JIU working procedures.[30] For these reasons, the ACC found it inappropriate to comment on the report and characterized it as a personal vision of the UN system.[31] Despite the critical comments, the report received widespread attention and served as an important input into the work of the Group of 18.

In its report on the work of the organization to the GA, the **Secretary-General**[32] noted:

"It is ironic that, as we enter a phase in history in which the practical necessity of co-operative internationalism is so patent, there should, in some quarters at least, be a retreat from it. Questioning of international organizations striving to create greater order in the world polity and economy is widespread, and the United Nations is the subject of especially heavy criticism ...

There is no question that the difficulties of making the United Nations work to their [member states'] satisfaction has an important bearing on the attitude of some Governments towards the Organization. Certainly the new complexity of the expanded membership and new voting patterns, as well as instances where division and conflict have been highlighted at the expense of broad areas of agreement and common interest, have had an impact. ...

I am bound, however, to express my deep concern at the practice of certain Member States of selectively withholding their duly assessed contribution. This can only have a most detrimental effect on the future viability of our Organization."

1.5   The Group of 18

The 40th session of the GA held at the end of 1985 brought together approximately 100 national presidents to commemorate the 40th anniversary of the UN. The celebrations were conducted under the long shadow of the financial crisis. Clearly, the major donors, in particular the USA, wanted to put an end to 'business-as-usual'. Major changes were expected to be required to regain their support for the organization. It was not only the developed countries which had become disenchanted; the developing countries, always know as staunch supporters, had also adopted an ambivalent attitude towards the UN.[33] The UN had been credited with bringing about the decolonization process and for providing a forum in which major powers could be held accountable for their international conduct. At the same time, a more critical attitude had emerged which focused on the inability of the Security Council to ensure peace in the Middle East, to abolish apartheid by imposing comprehensive sanctions and to bring independence to Namibia. The failure of the 'global negotiations' remained a deep disappointment for the developing world. Hence, there was widespread perception of the need for change. The motives of the various groups involved in supporting a new reform effort, however, were quite different, as has been noted.

The idea for such a new reform effort was first introduced by Mr. Abe, Foreign Minister of **Japan**[34], during the general debate at the beginning of the 40th session of the GA.

"In carrying out its activities over the past 40 years the secretariat of the United Nations and its specialized agencies have steadily expanded and it may well be that some of their activities are outdated, not urgently needed or even redundant. I am concerned that the United Nations system may be losing the unwavering support of peoples around the world. It is thus imperative that the Organization itself make a determined effort towards effective administrative and financial reform so that it can function more efficiently. Only in this way will Member States - developing countries beset with difficulties in economic management as well as major contributing countries experiencing severe financial strain and striving to regain fiscal health - be able to gain the understanding of their peoples and continue their support of the United Nations for many years to come. ...

In an effort toward comprehensive administrative and financial reform, I should like to propose the establishment of a "group of eminent persons for a more efficient United Nations," so that the world body and its specialized agencies would function efficiently into the twenty-first century. Comprised of a small number of individuals from developed and developing countries, the group would contribute to a thorough review of the administrative and financial operations of the organizations within the United Nations system. At the same time, it would provide an opportunity for undertaking an objective study of the management of those organizations with a view to guaranteeing their efficiency, so that they would be of greater use to the people of both developed and developing countries in meeting their genuine needs now and in the future. I hope that a concrete proposal on this question will be considered at this session of the General Assembly, and I call upon all Member States to act today to assure that this irreplaceable Organization will operate more efficiently."

Following this initiative, Australia, Comoros, Finland, Japan, New Zealand, Norway and Sweden put forward the draft resolution entitled **Improvement of the Administrative Efficiency and Financial Soundness of the United Nations (A/40/L.42)** under the agenda item relating to the commemoration of the 40th anniversary of the UN. The draft resolution reads as follows:

"The General Assembly,

Reaffirming the purposes and principles of the Charter of the United Nations,

Reaffirming that the Organization is based on the principle of the sovereign equality of all its Members,

Mindful of the vital role of the United Nations in the maintenance of international peace and security and in the promotion of international co-operation,

Convinced that the improvement of the administrative efficiency and the enhancement of the financial soundness of the United Nations could help fully to implement the purposes and principles of the Charter,

Considering the overwhelming support for the United Nations, expressed by Heads of State or Government or their special envoys and by the representatives of Member States during the commemoration of the fortieth anniversary of the United Nations,

Noting that a number of participants stressed the need to promote confidence in the United Nations and enhance the political will of Member States to render more positive support to the Organization,

Reaffirming the necessity of securing the highest standards of efficiency competence and integrity in the employment of the Secretariat staff and the importance of recruiting the staff based on the principles of equitable geographical distribution,

Noting with appreciation the efforts being made by the Secretary-General, as the chief Administrative Officer of the Organization, to improve the efficiency and effectiveness of the Secretariat,

Bearing in mind the work of the relevant subsidiary organs of the General Assembly,

Taking fully into account the views expressed during the discussion of other relevant items on the agenda of the fortieth session of the General Assembly,

1.   *Decides* to establish a High-level Group of Knowledgeable Persons, with a term of one year, entrusted with the following tasks:

(a) To conduct a thorough review of the administrative, budgetary and financial matters of the United Nations, in full accordance with the principles and provisions of the Charter of the United Nations, with a view to identifying measures for ensuring the administrative efficiency and the financial soundness of the United Nations;

(b) To submit to the General Assembly, through the Secretary-General, before the opening of its forty-first session, a report containing the observations and recommendations of the Group;

2.   *Requests* the President of the General Assembly and the Secretary-General, in consultation with Governments of Member States, to appoint immediately the Chairman and the Vice-Chairman and, from among the candidates recommended by their Governments, no more than 14 other members of the Group, with due regard to broad geographical representation and bearing in mind that the Chairman and the Vice-Chairman should have experience in high-level policy-making in their Governments, a demonstrated interest in United Nations affairs and the ability to stimulate and maintain the interest of the international community in the work of the Group, and that the other members of the Group should be knowledgeable in the Organization's affairs;

3.   *Requests* the Secretary-General to provide the Group with the necessary staff and services on the understanding that the staff members will be appointed to him in consultation with the Chairman of the Group;

4.   *Also requests* the Secretary-General to provide full assistance to the Group, in particular by submitting his views, providing information necessary to conduct the review and organizing meetings with relevant review bodies and members of the Secretariat;

5.   *Invites* the relevant subsidiary organs of the General Assembly to submit, through their chairmen, upon the request of the Group, information and comments on matters pertaining to their work;

6.   *Requests* the Secretary-General to submit his comments on the report of the Group of the General Assembly at its forty-first session;

7.   *Decides* to include in the provisional agenda of its forty-first session the item entitled "Improvement of the administrative efficiency and financial soundness of the United Nations: report of the High-level Group of Knowledgeable Persons."

Negotiations on the draft resolution led to its revision and the support of additional sponsors, including Australia, Austria, Bangladesh, Barbados, Canada, Finland, Jamaica, Japan, New Zealand, Norway, Samoa and Sweden. On 18 December 1985, the Plenary Assembly adopted by consensus the draft A/40/L.42/Rev. 1 as resolution entitled **Review of the Efficiency of the Administrative and Financial Functioning of the United Nations**

(40/237). By resolution 40/237, the GA decided to establish a Group of High-level Intergovernmental Experts - known as the Group of 18 - with a term of one year to carry out the following task: (a) to conduct a review of the administrative and financial matters of the UN, with a view to identifying measures for further improving the efficiency of its functioning, (b) to submit to the GA, 41st session, a report containing the observations and recommendations of the group. The group had two major goals: first, to identify permanent economies which could be made in the UN secretariat, most likely along the lines of the economy measures already introduced; second, to develop a new decision-making mechanism for approving the programme budget which would satisfy the demands of a minority, the major contributors, and still be acceptable to the majority of members states. The group had no mandate to review the scale of assessments, although the issue would be discussed by the group.

In a communication dated 7 February 1986, the President of the GA informed the Secretary-General that he had appointed the following individuals as members of the Group of 18[35]:

Mr. Mark Allen (UK)

Mr. Maurice Bertrand (France)

Mr. Bi Jilong (China)

Mr. Lucio García del Solar (Argentina)

Mr. Ignac Golob (Yugoslavia)

Mr. Natarajan Krishnan (India)

Mr. Kishore Mahbubani (Singapore)

Mr. Hugo B. Margain (Mexico)

Mr. Elleck Mashingaidze (Zimbabwe)

Mr. Fakhreddin Mohamed (Sudan)

Mr. Ndam Njoya (Cameroon)

Mr. Vasiliy Stepanovich Safronchuk (USSR)

Mr. Shizuo Saito (Japan)

Mr. Edward O. Sanu (Nigeria)

Mr. David Silveira da Mota (Brazil)

Mr. José S. Sorzano (USA)

Mr. Tom Vraalsen (Norway)

Mr. Layachi Yaker (Algeria)

'See volume II, 1.1.

The Group of 18 was intergovernmental in nature, so as to ensure that its work and recommendations reflected the views of a wide cross-section of members states; the group represented all five regions, as well as the countries holding the current and forthcoming chairmanship of the Non-Aligned Movement and the chairmanship of the Group of 77, the five permanent members of the Security Council, and most of the major contributors to the UN budget. The group included political leaders, former cabinet ministers, senior officials and permanent representatives.

In late 1985, having been apprised of the likelihood of a significant shortfall in the assessed contribution of the USA, the Secretary-General had taken action and approved a set of economy measures which he considered to be under his own authority. They included a severe recruitment freeze, the deferment of cost-of-living salary increases for staff in the general service category, the deferment of promotions for six months; the deferment of a number of maintenance and alteration projects and the reduction in travel costs, temporary assistance and overtime by 20 per cent. Total savings as against the 1986 approved budget were estimated to amount to $30 million. In addition, the Secretary-General proposed a second package of economy measures for which he requested the approval of member states. In order to obtain their approval and to emphasize the seriousness of the situation, he requested the 40th GA to reconvene from 28 April to 9 May 1986 to consider the following modifications to the approved programme budget for 1986: changes in the calendar of meetings and conferences; reductions in the provision of verbatim and summary records; and the deferral of certain programme activities, major construction projects for ECA in Africa and ESCAP in Asia, of publications and the purchase of furniture and equipment. The second package was expected to save an additional $30 million bringing the total savings for 1986 to $60 million or approximately 8 per cent of the approved budget.

Not surprisingly, the US withholdings came under strong attack by developing countries during the reconvened 40th session. They accused the USA of blackmailing the UN in order to change the very foundation on which it was based, i.e. the principle of the sovereign equality of all member states. This principle was seen to being threatened by demands for weighted voting in decision-making. The developing countries were opposed to the economy measures and, instead, demanded full payment of its assessed contribution by the USA. African countries, in particular, objected strongly to the deferral of the construction projects, one of which was located in Africa and constituted the largest single saving measure proposed.

The USA supported the Secretary-General's proposal. In defending its withholdings, the USA argued that it had only joined other countries which had used this practice in the past. Moreover, the withholding reflected dissatisfaction at how little influence the main contributor had on the way the funds were spent. The USSR and the European countries criticized the withholdings, the USSR, in particular, demanding that the USA should bear the 'financial and political responsibilities' for the financial crisis. These countries, however, did support the economy measures and stressed the need for financial restraint. In fact, it was felt that there was even scope for further savings.

An attempt by the developing countries to discuss the individual proposals separately was not rejected by the Western countries in order to avoid the restoration of the proposed cuts. The resulting deadlock in the negotiations over the proposed economy measures was finally overcome. The imminent danger of financial collapse persuaded the developing countries to swallow the 'pill'. In a strong appeal to the GA, the Secretary-General declared that if his pill was refused "next time I will have to come as a surgeon with a knife".[36]

The economy measures were finally approved by resolution 40/472, as temporary measures only for 1986. Clearly they could not resolve the crisis, and would merely provide short-term cash-flow relief. As such, the economy measures could only buy time and delay the expected insolvency. During this time, the UN would have the opportunity to initiate reforms which might persuade member states to resume payment of their assessed contributions.

This prospect prompted a search for solutions both inside and outside the UN. New reform efforts were proposed in the hope of regaining, in particular, the support of the USA. The first was a private initiative by two high-ranking UN officials - Prince Sadruddin Aga Khan and Maurice Strong - who had already put forward proposals in October 1985 for a reform of the scale of assessments. They commissioned a study on the UN financial emergency as a privately sponsored supplement to the Group of 18 report. The study was carried out by George Davidson, a former USG for Administration, and reviewed by a panel of fourteen members, known as the friends and supporters of the UN. The idea was to introduce new options to which a more political body such as the Group of 18 could possibly not agree. As previously proposed by Prince Sadruddin Aga Khan and Maurice Strong, the Davidson study included a proposal to change the scale of assessments by reducing the maximum contribution from 25 per cent to 15 or 10 per cent. The corresponding deficit, which should be rather small due to the expected reduction in the total UN budget, should be covered by increased contributions from middle-sized states. The recommendations to reduce the maximum contribution was also put forward by the Secretary-General, who proposed a decrease to 20 or 15 per cent, coupled with an equal share for all Security Council members and increases for middle-ranking member states.[37] The Davidson report, however, went further. Detailed recommendations were put forward, such as a general reduction in the salaries of UN staff by 3 per cent, and a reduction in the annual leave entitlement. It pointed to over-staffing at the top level of the UN, the excessive number of meetings and the need to rationalize secretariat structures. The expansion of UN activities was criticized as having often included marginal and incremental tasks which did not lend themselves to meaningful international action. Special attention was given to the interrelationship between the programme funded under the regular budget and extrabudgetary activities. Whereas the former was estimated at $700 million annually, the latter amounted to $1,250 million. Davidson argued that activities should be shifted from the regular budget to extrabudgetary funding, in accordance with the preference of the funding organizations. This would particularly strengthen the operational programmes such as UNDP, UNFPA and UNEP.[38] The Davidson study was made available to the members of the Group of 18.

A second major privately-sponsored effort was initiated by the UN Association of the USA (UNA-USA) in early 1986. Financed by a grant from the Ford Foundation, the association carried out a two-year research project on the UN management and decision-making. The objective was to offer constructive criticism regarding the management, governance and role of the UN. The project consisted of two parts. At its centre was a high-level, 23-member international panel.[*] The panel was supported by project staff who produced several research papers during 1986 and 1987.[**] These papers provided the background for the deliberations of the panel which released a preliminary report in early December 1986 and a final report in the summer of 1987.[39] In its final conclusions, the UN malaise was attributed to two major

---

[*]Elliot L. Richardson (chairman), Andres Aguilar Mawdsley, Otto Borch, Andrew F. Brimmer, Enrique V. Iglesias, Senator Nancy L. Kassebaum, Prince Sadruddin Aga Khan, Jean J. Kirkpatrick, T.T.B. Koh, K.B. Lall, Jacques Leprette, Robert S. McNamara, Frederic V. Malek, Olusegun Obasanjo, Philip A. Odeen, Sadako Ogata, Paul H. O'Neill, Olara A. Otunnu, Mohamed Sahnoun, Salim A. Salim, Helmut Schmidt, Brian Urquhart, Cyrus R. Vance.
[**]Peter Fromuth (staff director), Prince Sadruddin Aga Khan, Maurice Bertrand, Frederick K. Lister, Edward C. Luck and Ruth Raymond as authors of research papers.

problems: the ambiguity of its specific world role and its failure to change that role as the world had changed. To correct the situation, it was proposed that the UN should take the following three steps: firstly, it should identify common interests among its members, secondly, it should convert these common interests into common views, and thirdly, it should strive to convert the common views into cooperative action. In accordance with these three steps, the UN should engage in a 'global watch', the identification of emerging issues of urgent global significance; 'consensus-building', including agreement on issues such as focusing only on those countries directly affected or ensuring speed of consultation and minimal procedural delays; and 'consensus conversion', the stimulation of collective action by proposing specific mechanisms for co-operation. The current structure was not considered able to engage in these activities, especially in the economic and social area, due to: overlap between the GA, ECOSOC and UNCTAD; low level of representation; lack of intellectual authority; the weakness of co-ordination and joint planning in the UN system and the absence of a system for identifying emerging global issues. With regard to the latter, it was proposed to establish in affiliation with ECOSOC a small ministerial board of not more than 25 governments to conduct global watch consultations. Such a board would cover all issues not within the jurisdiction of the Security Council. The Board should report to the GA as well as to ECOSOC and be supported by a new 'Bureau of Global Watch' to be located in DIESA. In order to achieve a more integrated UN system, it was proposed to establish a single commission, composed of the Directors-General of all the main agencies in the economic and social fields, mandated to develop integrated responses to global issues through joint programming, and the development of a consolidated UN system budget. In order to reduce overlap and duplication in the implementation of technical co-operation, a single Development Assistance Board should be established in place of the separate executive boards of UNDP, UNFPA, WFP and UNICEF. Further recommendations included the elimination of the Second and Third Committees of the GA, the expansion of ECOSOC to plenary size, the merger of the Special Political Committee with the Fourth Committee and the merger of DIESA and DIEC into a single department headed by a Director-General. In the area of peace and security, it was proposed to strengthen cooperation with regional bodies, to establish multilateral inspection teams for monitoring arms reductions and to establish an *ad hoc* compliance review group under the Security Council to examine questions relating to multilateral agreements arising from the reports of the proposed multilateral inspection teams. Finally, it was proposed that the position of the Secretary-General should be strengthened. To this end, election to this office should be for a single term not to exceed seven years.

The report by Maurice Bertrand, the proposals put forward by Prince Sadruddin Aga Khan and Maurice Strong as well as the activities of UNA-USA provided the Group of 18 with a host of materials to work on.

The Group of 18 met for the first time on 25 February 1986 and held a total of 67 closed meetings, the last on 15 August 1986. Mr. Tom Vraalsen (Norway) was elected Chairman of the group, supported by four Vice-Chairmen. The final report entitled **Report of the Group of High-level Intergovernmental Experts to Review the Efficiency of the Administrative and Financial Functioning of the United Nations (A/41/49)** was issued in August 1986. It included 71 recommendations for reform and was submitted to the 41st session of the GA for consideration.

Some insight into the work of the group was provided by one of its members, Mr. Maurice Bertrand. As noted, he had previously been a member of the UN Joint Inspection Unit and had produced several reports on problems of the organization and functioning of the UN system. In fact, one of his reports submitted at the occasion of the 40th anniversary of the UN, has been discussed above. Mr. Bertrand was quite hesitant to accept the invitation to become a member of the Group of 18, since he believed that the UN was "totally incapable of reforming itself."[40] All the group members were ambassadors and, according to Mr. Bertrand, "were more familiar with political problems than with the mysteries of budgetary and financial problems, or the substance of the economic, social and humanitarian programs which they should have been able to discuss. They were even less familiar with the organizational chart of the agencies or with the details of the vast machinery of the intergovernmental committees or committees of experts which were to be made 'more efficient'".[41] He described the working atmosphere of the group as cordial. It was difficult, however, to define a method of work. A number of Mr. Bertrand's observations are recalled below[42]:

"We had elected a very large 'Bureau', consisting of a Chairman and four Vice-Chairmen, but we had no rapporteur and no mechanism had been established to enable the United Nations to help us, either by seriously studying various problems or by preparing draft chapters of the report."

See volume II, 2.1.

"We requested a vast amount of documentation that few of us had the time or even the desire to read, and we spent a great deal of time in trying to understand just what our task was."

"Our discussions were greatly influenced by the financial crisis, which we were not called upon to resolve in the immediate future and which many of my colleagues from countries belonging to the Group of 77 regarded as a form of blackmail practised on the United Nations by the United States."

"Each of us felt that we had been burdened with responsibilities which should have been assumed either by the Secretary-General or by the member states and that we had not been given the resources to deal seriously with either the administrative problems or the political problems".

All members were requested to put forward suggestions for improving the functioning of the UN. This yielded a highly disparate list of over 150 ideas including general comments such as "more efficient organization of conferences and meetings", "raise the fees for garage use", "increase in the sale and scope of distribution of United Nations stamps" and "freeze all recruitment for 3 to 5 years".

According to Bertrand, it was this disparate list of ideas which became the basis of the final report, and not an agreement on the general political orientation of any reform or restructuring. In the absence of such an agreement, no decision could be reached on any problem of importance which had a connection with the political and financial crisis. There was a failure to agree on issues ranging from the "principles for establishing a new scale of contributions, to the possible 'debudgetization' of some of the activities financed from the budget, to the restructuring of various programmes, to the definition of priorities between programmes, to the possible elimination of some intergovernmental committees or committees of experts whose usefulness was not obvious, and, last and most important, to the procedure for approving the programme budget, which was the heart of the problem."

One of the most spectacular recommendation related to the reduction in staff. The US expert proposed a reduction of one third. The expert from the USSR, the UK and Japan finally agreed with him on a reduction of one fourth. Bertrand expressed his surprise that the experts from developing countries were inclined to accept such a drastic reduction. They appeared to be content with the formulation in the recommendation which noted that such a reduction should be possible without causing any negative impact on the current level of programme activities of the UN. Only after a strong appeal by the Secretary-General was the reduction limited to fifteen per cent, to be realized over three years. On the recommendation of the Soviet expert, the higher figure of 25 per cent was only applied to the top-echelon posts. The other recommendations were mostly a restatement of recommendations made many time before: a reduction in the number of conferences, better co-ordination, reduced travel costs, competitive recruitment of young professionals and plans for career development. Some recommendations were new, such as the suggestion that at least 50 per cent of the nationals of any country recruited as international civil servants should hold permanent appointments. This provision of the report was not approved by consensus but opposed by the expert from the USSR. According to Bertrand it was designed primarily to hinder socialist countries, which follow a practice of not permitting their nationals to accept permanent appointments. Finally, the recommendations called for drastic reductions in staff benefits, such as the elimination of the education grant for post-secondary studies and the reduction of staff members' annual leave.

The group called for further studies for those difficult areas where no agreement could be reached, such as recommendations 8 (structure of the intergovernmental machinery in the economic and social sphere), 16 (the political departments), 25 (economic departments and programs), 26 (Department of Technical Co-operation for Development), 27 (regional economic commission) and 37 (Department of Public Information).

With regard to the procedure for approving the programme budget, the hope of reaching agreement was entertained until the last minute. A number of issues were considered, each essentially aiming to preserve the principle of sovereign equality of states in the budgeting process as well as giving major contributors sufficient relative weight. Bertrand argued that the fact that the dialogue had been undertaken under the threat of the USA to withhold its contribution essentially made it impossible to work out a compromise solution. The group finally submitted three different options to the GA for further discussion. The first option envisaged three major changes. First, the possibility of increasing the approved budget through add-ons would be controlled. Such add-ons would be funded and limited by a contingency fund of no more than 2 per cent of the approved budget. Second, the Secretary-General would provide a proposed budget outline two years prior to the implementation of the budget. The outline would define the major programme content and the resource ceiling for the subsequent detailed programme budget exercise. Third, the role of CPC in the budget process would be strengthened. CPC would not only focus on programmatic issues but also be involved in financial decisions which had previously been left exclusively to ACABQ.

Furthermore, CPC would review the budget outline and recommend to the GA its approval by consensus. This did not imply weighted voting, but it gave the right to veto to each member of CPC quite early in the budget process when the major parameters were fixed. Since the major contributors had always been represented in this committee, no consensus could be reached without their approval. Consensus would also be required in CPC when reviewing the detailed programme budget. Subsequent approval of outline and programme budget by the GA, however, could still be given by majority decision. This procedure allowed for a rather strict control in accordance with three innovations: the outline would provide a ceiling; the consensus requirements in CPC gave a veto right; and the contingency fund constituted a cap on subsequent add-ons. The second option was less demanding. The recommendations concerning the budget outline, contingency fund and strengthening of CPC were similar to those of the first option. However, the second option did not formally require decision making at CPC by consensus and the budget outline was seen as an indicative figure rather than a fixed ceiling. The third option went the farthest. Consensus would be required in CPC and the Fifth Committee. The financial limits of the budget would be set prior to determining the programme content and would derive from what member states could and were prepared to make available.

Although Bertrand approved of the work of the group, he noted that he "did not much feel like signing such a report. Many of its recommendations struck me as either useless and too general or else inadequate, while some were dangerous for the future of the United Nations. Above all, it had not been possible to give the problem as much careful thought as such a group should have done."[43]

What is most striking in the Group of 18 report is that most of the recommendations were concerned with the secretariat and implied a critical assessment. In fact, it was stated in the final report that the quality of work should be improved, that personnel were not sufficiently qualified and that working methods were not efficient. Staff had been the target of criticism since the beginning of the crisis and the development of discontent of member states with the UN. As noted above, cost-of-living adjustments for general service staff and promotions had been deferred by a decision made in early 1986. For professional staff, salary scales had not been increased since 1975. Cost-of-living adjustments for this group had already been frozen in December 1984. Having stopped any increase in the pay of professional staff, the GA decided in 1985 to limit the range by which UN salaries could exceed the comparator salaries, based on the US federal civil service rates. The range was fixed between 110 and 120, with a desirable mid-point of 115. In other words, UN pay for professional staff could exceed that of US civil service staff based in Washington by 15 per cent. By this decision, the GA overturned an ICSC decision of 1984 on the basis of which the margin would be determined in a pragmatic manner. As a result, UN pay was frozen and did not even increase to offset inflation for nearly six years. This was done in parallel to a cut in pension benefits. Measures during the first half of the 1980s included an increase in the period of employment required to qualify for retirement benefits, an increase in the percentage deducted from salaries for pension fund contributions and a reduction of pensionable remuneration. Finally, the Group of 18 called for a drastic reduction of those benefits which might be considered in Western Europe as social achievements, namely the period of vacation and the education grant. Why was there such a concentrated effort to reduce staff enumeration and benefits? Obviously it could not be attributed to the stated intention to improve the quality of work by attracting more competent staff. Based on his work in the Group of 18, Mr. Bertrand might have had an explanation when he noted that, whereas there was no agreement on the general political orientation, "the only area in which there was any chance of obtaining a consensus was the criticism of the Secretariat."[44]

Notes

1. *United Nations Handbook 1990* (Wellington, New Zealand: Ministry of External Relations and Trade, 1990); *Basic Facts About the United Nations* (New York: United Nations, Department of Public Information, 1990); Jacques Tassin, *Administrative Coordination in the United Nations Family*, in Chris De Cooker (ed.), *International Administration: Law and Management Practices in International Organizations* (Dordrecht, the Netherlands: Martinus Nijhoff Publishers, 1990).
2. *United Nations Handbook 1990*, p. 5.
3. Paul Taylor, 'Reforming the UN System: Value for Money', *The World Today*, XLIV (1988), No. 7, p. 124.
4. John de Gara, *Administrative and Financial Reform of the United Nations: A Documentary Essay* (Academic Council on the UN System, 1989), Appendix I.
5. Yves Beigbeder, *Management Problems in United Nations Organizations. Reform or Decline?* (London: Frances Pinter, 1987), pp. 45-47.
6. Thomas M. Franck, *Nation Against Nation* (Oxford: Oxford University Press, 1985), pp. 82-83.
7. A/4971, p. 6.
8. A/6289, p. 6.
9. A/6343.
10. P. Collins, 'Administrative Reforms in International Development Organizations', *Public Administration and Development*, VII (1987), Special Issue, pp. 125-142.

11. Douglas Williams, *The Specialized Agencies and the United Nations - The System in Crisis* (New York: St. Martin's Press, 1987), pp. 47-49.
12. David Nicol, John Renninger, 'The Restructuring of the United Nations Economic and Social System: Background and Analysis', *Third World Quarterly*, IV (1982), No. 1, pp. 74-92.
13. A/C.5/39/83.
14. Yves Beigbeder, *Administrative and Structural Reform in the Organizations of the United Nations Family*, in: De Cooker (ed.), *op.cit.*, II. 4/7.
15. *Ibid.*
16. Ruth Pearson, 'U.N. Cries "Uncle"', *Bulletin of the Atomic Scientists*, XLIV (October 1988), p. 36.
17. Christian Tomuschat, 'Die Krise der Vereinten Nationen', *Europa-Archiv*, XLII (1987), No. 4, pp. 100-101.
18. Arthur Kilgore, 'Cut Down in the Crossfire?', *International Relations*, XXXIII (November 1986), p. 599.
19. Pearson, *op.cit.*, p. 39.
20. Kilgore, *op.cit.*, pp. 594-595.
21. *Congressional Record*, S7793, 7 June 1985.
22. A/C.5/40/16; ST/ADM/SER.B/283.
23. ST/ADM/SER.B/276; ST/ADM/SER.B/283.
24. A/C.5/40/16.
25. Prince Sadruddin Aga Khan, Maurice F. Strong, 'Proposals to Reform the UN, 'Limping' in its 40th Year', *The New York Times*, 8 October 1985; Prince Sadruddin Aga Khan, Maurice F. Strong, 'United Nations: Reform Might Help its Work', *International Herald Tribune*, 9 October 1985.
26. Louis Wiznitzer, 'Sweden's Combative Prime Minister Stands Firm on Austerity', *The Christian Science Monitor*, January-February 1983.
27. Taylor, *op.cit.*, p. 123,
28. Michael J. Berlin, 'Lowering the Boom', *The Interdependent*, March-April 1986.
29. Maurice Bertrand, *Some Reflections on Reform of the United Nations*, JIU/REP/ 85/9, Joint Inspection Unit, United Nations, Geneva, 1985.
30. UN Press Release WS/1304.
31. A/41/639.
32. *Official Records of the General Assembly, Fortieth Session, Supplement No. 1* (A/40/1), pp. 5-6.
33. James Jonah, 'The United Nations has its Problems', *International Affairs/ Mezhdunarodnaya Zhizn*, XXXIV (November 1988), p. 102.
34. A/40/PV.7, pp. 24-26.
35. A/40/1085/Add.1.
36. 'The Knife Next Time', *The Economist*, 17-23 May 1986, p. 41.
37. Elaine Sciolino, 'UN Chief Suggests U.S. Contribution to be Cut', *The New York Times*, 29 April 1986.
38. Gene M. Lyons, 'Reforming the United Nations', *International Social Science Journal*, XLI (May 1989), pp. 252-253.
39. Final and preliminary panel reports as well as research papers can be found in Peter J. Fromuth (ed.), *A Successor Vision - The United Nations of Tomorrow* (Lanham: United Nations Association of the United States of America and University Press of America, 1988).
40. Maurice Bertrand, *The Third Generation World Organization* (New York: UNITAR, and Dordrecht, the Netherlands: Martinus Nijhoff Publishers, 1989), p. 107.
41. *Ibid.*, p. 109.
42. *Ibid.*, pp. 109-112.
43. *Ibid.*, p. 114.
44. *Ibid.*, p. 112.

2.1 Financial Situation

The deficit under the regular budget at the end of 1985 had amounted to $242 million, out of which the USA owed $86 million.* The future looked even worse. There was the possibility that the USA would pay as little as $60 million in 1986. The actual amount, however, would not be known until the end of the year, when the USA traditionally paid its assessment. In addition, when preparing the budget for 1987 the Reagan Administration requested an amount which was $140 million short of what was required to meet the obligations to the UN and the specialized agencies. The shortfall included the withholdings mandated by the Kassebaum amendment. The resources requested did not include any funds which could be made available for disbursement once the UN had met the USA's demands. As Kilgore put it "the Administration had eaten the carrot that was intended to reward reforming agencies".[1] When the budget was considered in Congress, an additional cut of $47 million on the allocation for international organizations was approved in order to meet budget targets. Further cuts of $130 million were introduced under the Senate outlay ceiling. The final budget allocation was so small that the potential US contribution in 1987 could again be as low as $60 million - the minimum amount expected for 1986. There was, however, a glimmer of hope. In July 1986, the US Supreme Court ruled that the Gramm-Rudman-Holding Act was unconstitutional in so far as it obliged the Comptroller General to institute automatic across-the-board cuts should the Administration or Congress fail to meet the targets specified in the legislation. This left the Administration and the Congress some flexibility, allowing them to exempt contributions to international organizations from across-the-board cuts, although the overall budget ceiling established by the legislation had to be respected. Any exemption would, of course, need the political will for its approval. There was already some feeling that the magnitude of potential cuts was getting out of control, in particularly in view of the fact that the UN had initiated a reform process with the submission of the report of the Group of 18 to the GA. Furthermore, Secretary-General Javier Pérez de Cuéllar, whose

---

*For details on the financial situation see annex, table 3 and 4.

continuation in office the USA supported, announced that he would not stay for a second five-year term starting in 1987 should the UN go bankrupt. During summer of 1986, the Reagan Administration tried again some control over the problems created by the impending financial crisis in the United Nations. It assigned authority over UN issues to a higher level within State Department, from the Assistant Secretary of State responsible for International Organizations to the office of the Secretary of State. In September, the White House and the State Department attempted to get some of the Congressional cuts rolled back. The effort did not, however, go as far as reversing the entire package of cuts, but merely to removed the Senate outlay ceiling.[2] In fact, the critical attitude of the Reagan Administration had not changed. In September 1986, the USA announced that it would stop contributing to the UN Family Planning Agency (UNFPA) and divert its previous contribution to other volunteer family planning programmes. UNFPA was accused of supporting forced sterilization and abortions in China, charges which were denied by both the Agency and China.

The economy measures approved in 1986, including the reduction of maintenance levels of premises and equipment, produced just enough savings to keep the organization afloat. There were also some bright spots in the financial picture. China decided to pay off its past withholdings with regard to the 1962 bond issue and other budget items, while still maintaining its continuous disagreement with those expenditures. In addition, Brazil, Argentina, Czechoslovakia, Poland and Yugoslavia substantially reduced their arrears. In response to an appeal by the Secretary-General for early payment of assessed contributions, 48 member states had paid their assessed contribution in full by 30 June 1986 as compared to 33 member states one year earlier. In response to a further appeal, the USSR made a voluntary contribution of $10 million to augment the Special Account, bringing up the total amount to $94 million.[3]

2.2 The 41st Session of the General Assembly

After twelve to eighteen months of angry exchanges and bad feelings about the withholding of assessments, the 41st session of the GA set out to discuss the report of the Group of 18 (A/41/49)*. In his report on the work of the organization, the **Secretary-General**[4] commented on the problems ahead:

---

*See volume II, 2.1.

"Regrettably, in marked contrast to sentiments expressed during the fortieth anniversary, 1986 has witnessed the United Nations subjected to a severe crisis challenging its solvency and viability. Precisely at the time when renewed efforts have been called for to strengthen the Organization, its work has been shadowed by financial difficulties resulting primarily from the failure of Member States to meet obligations flowing from the Charter. It is essential to lift this cloud so that the United Nations can, both now and in the longer term, be that strong constructive force in world affairs that is vitally needed in our increasingly interdependent world. The strengthening and revitalization of the present structure of multilateral institutions is critical to the resolution of problems confronting the international community relating to peace, security and development. To ignore this necessity is to imperil the future prospects of a better world."

There was a feeling of pessimism about the prospects of reaching agreement on the proposed economy measures or on any of the three proposed options for a new programme budget procedure. Most of the G77 and NAM members supported option two, which did not require consensus in decision-making and modified current procedure least. The USA and the socialist countries favoured option three, which included the most radical changes, although it was not clear how the final procedure under option three would look. Finally, option one - somehow a compromise between two and three - including consensus voting in CPC, was mainly supported by Western countries. With regard to the economy measures, the African group was particularly opposed to the cuts although a minority of the G77 appeared to have accepted budgetary reductions.

The report of the Group of 18 was taken up under agenda item 38 (Review of the Efficiency of the Administrative and Financial Functioning of the United Nations: Report of the Group of High-level Intergovernmental Experts to Review the Efficiency of the Administrative and Financial Functioning of the United Nations). The financial crisis, which had provided the impetus, was technically or legally a separate matter from the reform initiative. Both issues were separate items on the GA agenda. The Group of 18 did not have a mandate to deal with the immediate financial crisis, as the Group itself pointed out in paragraph 8 of its report. In reality, however, there was an important relationship between the two subjects. In addition to the report of the Group of 18, the GA also had before it the Secretary-General's note on the report of the Group of 18 (A/41/663) and the ACC's comments on the report of the

Group of 18 (A/41/763).* The GA decided that agenda item 38 would be considered in plenary meetings of the Assembly, and that the Fifth Committee would, within the scope of its responsibilities, undertake a factual examination of the report and submit its findings to the plenary. In view of the importance of the subject and the keen interest by member states, the discussion of the report of the Group of 18 was taken up early in the session in order to give adequate time for its consideration. The plenary sessions on the report were preceded by the annual general debate, during which high-level national representatives - heads of state, prime ministers and foreign ministers - gave a summary introduction of their country's position on the world situation and on particular items to be subsequently considered during the GA session. Since the issue of reform and the report of the Group of 18 were among the main topics, frequent reference was made to these items during the general debate. Those comments made are recalled below, followed by a report on the plenary meetings of the GA on the report of the Group of 18.

2.2.1 The Issue of the Reform of the United Nations during the General Debate

Before the general debate was opened, Mr. Humayun Rasheed Choudhury, **President of the General Assembly**, emphasized the importance of the reform issue during the first meeting of the 41st session of the GA:

"This session of the General Assembly has the crucial role to play in restoring confidence in the United Nations and its ability to deal promptly and effectively with the various international issues and problems ... there is a general feeling that the United Nations today needs revitalizing in a number of aspects in order to bring it into line with the priorities of a changing world.

Undoubtedly there is scope to cut bureaucratic waste, to reorient expenditure to priority areas and generally to streamline the administration to make this world body more functional and cost-effective.

No attempt at revitalizing the United Nations can succeed without strengthening the role of the Security Council and the General Assembly as well as the Office of the Secretary-General. ...

I would urge this General Assembly to make a conscious effort to break with the past. Let us attempt to re-examine the way we conduct our business."

---

*See volume II, 2.2, 2.3.

Following this statement, the general debate was opened. The comments on the reform issue and the report of the Group of 18 are recalled below[*].

Ronald Reagan, **President of the United States of America**[6]

"This Organization itself faces a critical hour - that is usually stated as a fiscal crisis. But we can turn this "crisis" into an opportunity. The important reforms proposed by the Group of Experts can be a first step towards restoring this Organization's status and effectiveness. The issue, ultimately, is not one of cash but of credibility. If all the Members of this universal Organization decide to seize the moment and turn the rhetoric of reform into reality, the future of the United Nations will be secure. And members have my word for it: My country, which has always given the United Nations generous support, will continue to play a leading role in the effort to achieve its noble purposes."

Mr. Siddiky, **Bangladesh**[7]

"Whatever doubt that one may have about the efficacy of the United Nations it has far less to do with its role *per se* in international relations, than to do with the attitude of those in doubt. It is not so much a crisis of confidence in the United Nations; rather it is a crisis of political will."

Mr. Wagner Tizon, **Peru**[8]

"any reform to improve the efficiency of the United Nations and to make more democratic the taking of decisions can only be welcomed by the international community. But if the Organization's distressing financial problems led us into situations that were incompatible with making the system more democratic, we should have no hesitation in choosing a more democratic and independent, but at the same time more austere, system given no State decision-making power over the Organization's fate on the basis of its economic contribution."

Mrs. Gro Harlem Brundland, **Prime Minister of Norway**[9]

"The financial crisis is the manifestation of a fundamental crisis of credibility which has been festering for some time. There has been a widespread and deepening loss of confidence in the United Nations on the part of many Member States and their publics that believe that the Organization is not sufficiently effective in meeting its original objectives or in serving the interests of its Members.

Even the strongest champions of the United Nations - countries like Norway and many others - must now concede that these concerns have some validity.

---

[*]For the general debate, the name of the speaker is provided. In addition, the title is given for a speaker who is a head of state or a prime minister. For other debates, the speaker is only identified as a representative of a country.

The political and economic issues on the agenda of the United Nations persist. Its budget is burdened by unnecessary duplication and overlapping of functions, and the budgetary process lacks the discipline required to evoke the full support of all Member States.

The task of renewing the effectiveness of the United Nations is basically political in nature. It requires that Member States manifest the political will to place the financing of the Organization on a viable basis and provide the Secretary-General with the mandate and the support he needs to carry out the major organization, staffing and budget changes which will reduce costs, improve effectiveness and restore confidence."

Mr. Dhanabalan, **Singapore**[10]

"It will not be easy to rebuild this Organization. The small States, which make up the vast majority of the membership, have never lost faith. They know that global adherence to the principles of the United Nations Charter is crucial for their survival. ...

Yet a United Nations composed only of small States would be a pointless Organization. The threats to small States will always come from the medium-sized States and the big Powers. We need their continued adherence to the principles of the United Nations Charter. And we need their continued commitment to the Organization.

... we have constantly passed resolutions, routinely, recklessly and often selectively condemning a great Power. This has not brought us any closer to our goal of convincing any great Power to behave otherwise. All our resolutions should be carefully crafted, tempered by wisdom and judgement, to persuade great Powers that it is in their interest to take cognizance of the needs of small States. The reckless attacks of previous years have led to the inevitable result that both the Soviet Union and the United States decided, no matter what their other disagreements may be, to ignore and sometimes to undermine the United Nations. It is not surprising that the largest financial withholdings have been made by the Soviet Union and the United States. The art of political moderation must be relearned by all of us. ...

Fortunately for us, the Group of High-Level Intergovernmental Experts ... has come up with a reasonable report recommending some reforms. Staff should be reduced by 15 per cent and the overstaffed higher levels by 25 per cent. Fewer consultants should be hired. Official travel should be curtailed. The political departments should be consolidated. The forty-first session of the General Assembly should quickly endorse those recommendations.

There is, unfortunately, one unresolved issue in the report of the Group of High-Level Intergovernmental Experts, and this concerns the critical question of budgetary management. ... As they make up the vast majority of the membership, the small States can easily vote in any budgetary procedure they like - as they have tended to do, against the wishes of the larger States, in regard to budgetary matters. This reckless use of our votes has unfortunately led us to the present crisis and will only ensure the continuation of the crisis. If we try to do the same with the budgetary procedure, we shall only aggravate the problems of the United Nations, and solve none. ...

Consensus is what we should aim for in financial matters. ...

Consensus, in our definition, consensus does not mean that any Member State, large or small, has the power of veto. It means a spirit of give and take, a spirit of understanding each other's interests."

Mr. Shevardnadze, **Union of Soviet Socialist Republics**[11]

"Recent events have once again focused attention on an odd phenomenon: the country that once offered the site the United Nations Headquarters today all-too-often shows intense hostility towards the Organization. It slams the door and refuses to fulfil its obligations, as has been the case with the United Nations Educational, Scientific and Cultural Organization (UNESCO), or tries to assert the principle that whoever has the most money is right. It puts spokes in the wheels of the collective machinery with the notion that by so doing that machinery can be made to function according to its will. The United States has adopted the practice of lecturing, punishing and arbitrarily threatening the Organization as a whole and those of its members it dislikes for some reason. Lately, the States Members of the United Nations have begun to ask with increasing frequency whether the United Nations can function normally in a country whose Government shows such undisguised disrespect for them and for the Organization itself. Perhaps that question should be heeded."

Sir Geoffrey Howe, **United Kingdom**[12]

"We support the creation of a new mechanism to consider the programme and budget, structured so as to ensure effective decision-making and to contribute to greater rationalization and efficiency within the system. ... Greater budgetary discipline, improved co-ordination, and rigorous adherence to priorities can only strengthen the Organization and ensure its future stability and vigour."

Mr. Kuranari, **Japan**[13]

"concern has been expressed that the United Nations might suffer functional paralysis should it fail to promptly achieve the reforms necessary to rectify the very serious administrative and financial situation, caused in part by organizational over-expansion. ...

None of the similar efforts to reform the United Nations in the past has produced as comprehensive and constructive a report as the one submitted by this Group [of 18].

The Group's report contains many constructive recommendations for making the United Nations a more efficient organization, and I wholeheartedly support them. I very much hope that ... they will be implemented as soon as possible with the support of all Member States. The United Nations should then be able to regain the trust of all the peoples of the world, gain the ability to respond promptly and effectively to any situation that may arise, and in this way serve as a model for all the bodies within the United Nations system."

Mr. Taleb Ibrahimi, **Algeria**[14]

"The United Nations must be maintained, preserved and protected. International relations without the United Nations not only are inconceivable, but would be dangerous. The United Nations is the order of dialogue and co-operation itself. Finally, the United Nations is the most promising augury for the world of tomorrow. If it is challenged or weakened, that long-desired better world will be compromised.

It is our shared goal to ensure that the United Nations becomes more efficient, effective and influential in the conduct of world affairs. If this means the rationalization of structures, better use of available institutions, the elimination of unnecessary expenditure and the abolition of overlapping of functions and duplication, no one will object.

On the other hand, if all it means is challenge multilateralism and the central role therein of the United Nations, there will be reason to question the implications of such a fatal cycle. None of use will benefit if that happens; we shall all be the losers."

Mr. Ellemann-Jensen, **Denmark**[15]

"As I see it, we must pursue two objectives simultaneously: first, we must make a determined effort towards administrative and financial reform; second, and probably more important, we must seek a more realistic common understanding of what can be expected from the United Nations."

Mr. Pires de Miranda, **Portugal**[16]

"Austerity is now called for. The figures show - in such a way that no doubts can be entertained about this point - that expectations have to be reduced to the level of existing resources. The financial crisis certainly reflects a crisis that could be called a "growing up crisis" but which reflects a reality we can only call political. ...

The United Nations will overcome the present crisis. However, it will have to fight atavism, to abandon theoretical needs that are frequently translated into requests which sometimes make the Secretariat look like a research department. We must be realistic: where there is no room for agreement, we must work to create the conditions necessary to obtain it, without trying to disguise, with bureaucratic initiatives, difficulties that are known to all."

Mr. Wu Xuequian, **China**[17]

"The financial crisis confronting the United Nations at the present time has caused widespread concern. We are of the view that the United Nations should undergo rational structural reforms, but such reforms must be aimed at strengthening, not weakening, the role of the Organization and must observe, not violate, the principle of the sovereign equality of all Member States, as provided for in the Charter."

Mr. Chirac, **France**[18]

"It is my feeling, however, that the general realization of past disarray and inadequacies has, for the first time, led to a commitment to real reform, as evidenced by the conclusions of the Group of 18.

No one disputes the existing shortcomings in co-operation between Members of the United Nations, but this necessary clear-sightedness should not lead us to take a pessimistic view."

Mr. Oscar Arias Sanchez, **President of the Republic of Costa Rica**[19]

"We are concerned about the distaste shown by certain powerful nations for the whole question of the political equality of all States. It appears to be reflected, at least in part, in the financial crisis affecting the United Nations. It seems that small and weaker nations are being denied the right to a dialogue of equals, a dialogue free from constraints or conditions."

Mr. Clark, **Canada**[20]

"Our acceptance or rejection of the report of the Group of 18 will be the litmus test of our commitment to renew the capacity of the United Nations to fulfil its mandate.

Our budgets here are swollen by the accumulation of outdated and misguided programmes. A thorough review would free resources for meeting needs that have long been relatively neglected. These include large ares of development, in particular the promotion of women and the promotion of human rights in general. ...

The adoption of the report of the Group of 18 and the settlement of arrears and withholdings would address half the problem. The other half is more basic. There simply is no escaping the fact that world-wide support for this institution depends on its performance. There may be some who think that if the United Nations were flush with funds all would be well. But the stark reality is that the United Nations must be reformed politically as well as financially.

We are in danger of becoming a caricature of the hopes expressed in 1945. This was to be a forum in which difficult decisions were to be taken: it has become a means to avoid them. When there is crisis, we have endless debate. When there is a need for hard compromise, we draft resolutions which defy agreement. ...

The place to start is with administrative and financial reforms. Obviously, putting our house in order in order will not put the world in order, but it will protect and strengthen the only organization that can. Canada is a strong find of the United Nations, but Canadians who are making sacrifices at home do not want to subsidize inefficiency here."

Mr. van den Broek, **Netherlands**[21]

"The financial crisis in itself reflects political dissent among the Members of the United Nations. No doubt the present crisis, if left unresolved, would soon become an institutional one, jeopardizing the viability and integrity of the whole Organization. Apart from the urgent task of balancing the budget, the financial crisis requires long-term structural solutions. ...

We agree ... on the need for re-examination of the structure, staff and procedures aimed at bringing about a tighter, less costly Secretariat. We support his efforts and expect continued leadership in pursuance of more efficiency and streamlining of the Secretariat.

But streamlining and personal cuts are not enough. Furthermore, such measures cannot be properly carried out in isolation; they should be accompanied by a reform of the intergovernmental machinery and its functioning. Over the years we have, as the Group of 18 correctly notes, built an overly complex structure which suffers from a lack of cohesion and makes co-ordination extremely difficult, if not impossible. ...

On the subject of working methods, we feel that an overloading of agenda items should be avoided. In general, it does not seem wise to duplicate in the United Nations work done in specialized forums."

Mr. Tindemans, **Belgium**[22]

"one must cut bureaucratic waste, redirect expenditure to priority areas and streamline the administration. I might add that one should rationalize and lighten the intergovernmental mechanism, which is the responsibility of Member States and for which the United Nations Secretariat is but a support. ...

We should also be able to agree on a method of planning and budgeting procedures which would ensure a positive consensus on the budget and on the programmes of the United Nations. That would help to avoid a situation in which Member States contributing the largest share of the budget find themselves obliged to abstain or vote against the budget."

Mr. Orzechowski, **Poland**[23]

"We are in favour of reducing the operating costs of the United Nations, but the extent of that reduction has to be determined by the need to maintain the ability of the United Nations to fulfil its statutory functions under the Charter."

Mr. Andersson, **Sweden**[24]

"How is it that some Member States express their support for the activities of the United Nations while, at the same time, in violation of existing obligations, refuse to pay for them fully and loyally? How is it that so many Member States are in arrears with their assessed contributions?

The amounts in question are modest. They cannot reasonably be a great financial burden to any country. The reason for this is rather short-term political considerations and a lack of solidarity with the United Nations. ...

We must now find solutions that ensure a sound financial basis for the United Nations. At the same time, it must be possible for the United Nations to adapt to changed circumstances and conditions through reforms. The Member States must be able to feel fully confident that the United Nations is using its resources in an effective way. ...

The present scale of assessment makes the United Nations too vulnerable and dependent on individual large contributors. When a major contributor, drastically and in violation of existing obligations, cuts its contributions - in the way that is now about to take place - the basis for the work of the entire Organization is undermined. If assessments were distributed more evenly among all Members, we would be able to reduce this vulnerability in the future."

Mr. Dizdarevic, **Yugoslavia**[25]

"The United Nations is the best expression of one of the greatest achievements in the development of international relations: equitable participation of all countries in the solution of questions that concern the destiny of the whole world. We must safeguard and promote this achievement. We, therefore, do not accept the attempts to determine the rights of the United Nations Members according to their might and wealth."

Mr Mwangale, **Kenya**[26]

"Although the crisis is described as financial, it must be quite obvious to all of us by now that the United Nations is facing one of its worst political crises yet, a crisis of which the financial difficulties being encountered are mere symptoms. It is therefore incumbent upon all Member States to demonstrate their faith and commitment to our Organization in deeds rather than in words. Kenya, for its part, welcomes the report of the Group of High-level Intergovernmental Experts entrusted by the General Assembly at its fortieth session with studying ways and means of enhancing the effectiveness of the financial and administrative capabilities of the United Nations. In the group's recommendations, we find a number of positive elements which deserve serious consideration by this Assembly."

Mr. Al-Sabah, **Kuwait**[27]

"Kuwait views with great concern the crisis which the United Nations is facing. We believe that in order to deal with it fairly and prudently we must all refrain from exploiting the Organization for political purposes - as are certain countries with their own ideas of what the effective role of the United Nations should be. Instead, efforts should be focused on the definitive fulfilment by all countries of their political and financial obligations in accordance with the Charter. ...

We must try with all the vigour at our command to transform that crisis into momentum for administrative reform, rationalization of expenditure and the creation of an exemplary world structure within which constant efforts are made for the well-being of all humanity. ...

In this regard, we wish to place on record our appreciation of the efforts of the Group of High-Level Intergovernmental Experts in reviewing the efficiency of the administrative and financial performance of the United Nations."

Mr. Malmieraca Peoli, **Cuba**[28]

"we are now witnessing new attempts by the United States Government to undermine the principles of the United Nations through immoral pressure which constitutes blatant violations of the Charter. It is true that the Organization requires administrative and managerial adjustments, but it is sheer fiction to call a political phenomenon, which has its roots in the design of one Government to subject the action of States in United Nations forums to its own will, a "financial crisis". The Kassebaum amendment and other legal schemes of the United Nations must not hang over our heads like so many swords and Damocles. The mere formulation of such schemes by United States legislative bodies is not enough, for those very bodies have established international commitments and obligations under the Charter of the United Nations.

The problem we are facing is political and therefore it requires political solutions."

Mr. Hameed, **Sri Lanka**[29]

"It is clear that what we are confronting is a fundamental crisis of political proportions far beyond a financial shortfall. At the root is antagonism towards multilateralism and a tendency to lapse into myopic unilateralism, which appears as an attractive and convenient path to those with economic or political might, or both.

Wisely, long-term and medium-term remedies were sought, attacking the cause rather than the symptoms. During the current session this crisis is likely to affect the consideration of all issues on the agenda. Let us be realistic. If we reform the United Nations structurally, administratively and financially to present a model of rectitude, wise management and good husbandry, we will still need to deal with this tendency that seeks to drift away from multi-lateralism and global co-operation."

Mr. Fall, **Senegal**[30]

"When the causes of the malaise are analyzed, stress is often placed on the crisis of confidence of the third-world countries with regard to the effective-ness of the United Nations. ... However, this crisis of confidence is really more like a lovers' quarrel than a rejection. It reflects the profound and sincere commitment of the countries of Africa, Latin America and Asia to the United Nations. The most serious threat comes from the larger States, which, unable to continue to control the decision-making process in the Organization, are trying to remove particularly important questions from its consideration, adopting a position of systematic obstruction in its agencies or trying to deprive it of any real meaning by systematically denigrating its procedures and continually violating its rules and principles."

Mr. Kusumaatmadja, **Indonesia**[31]

"Indonesia recognizes that there is indeed room for improvements and greater economy in the workings of our Organization. We therefore welcome the report of the High-Level Group of 18 and stand ready to consider its valuable recommendations in a most positive spirit. At the same time, however, Indonesia believes that the crisis, which is essentially of a political nature, has reached a point where efficiency and rationalization measures alone will not suffice to provide a comprehensive and durable solution. This effort must be accompanied by a renewed commitment of explicit support to the United Nations by all Member States in accordance with their treaty obligations."

Mr. Totu, **Romania**[32]

"The financial difficulties confronting the Organization at present can and must be resolved through the improvement and simplification of the Organization's activities, without negatively affecting its democratic priorities and structures, based on the participation of all Member States in conditions of equality, and on the powers of the General Assembly as the most representative United Nations body."

Mr. O'Flynn, **New Zealand**[33]

"It is long-standing political indifference or, in some cases, hostility, which is the cause of the United Nations financial crisis. The selective withholding of contributions - a practice in which one major contributor has recently joined another - cannot be condoned. Nor can the action of those who allow dues to fall into arrears. But we have all contributed to the current crisis. We have pretended to believe that political problems could be solved simply by calling for more financial resources, more studies, more staff. Well, we were wrong. Entirely new measures are necessary, at once more dramatic and more constructive. ...

We in New Zealand welcome the report of the High Level Group. We strongly endorse its consensus findings. We commend them to the membership. We must go on to develop quickly an agreed approach to the reform of the programme and budget process. We must begin to run this important Organization like any self-respecting business - in the interests, that is, of its shareholders, the Member States. In the process, all of us are going to have to accept some curtailment of our favourite programme. We accept that. Compromise from all will be required.

Reform of our finances, management and administration is the first requirement, for it is the prerequisite to efficiency."

Mr. Akinyemi, **Nigeria**[34]

"Yet this cherished Organization is currently undergoing the gravest crisis in its history. Some call it a crisis of multilateralism. Others define it as a financial crisis. Fundamentally, it is a political crisis inflicted on the United Nations by its membership. Disagreements about the management and control of the Organization's budget and the determination of its programmes are mere symptoms of a deeper difference in perceptions of the role and capability of the United Nations. ...

In any process of reform, difficult choices have to be made. New priorities will have to be set. Cost-saving measures must be instituted. Indeed, readjustments in assessed contributions may even become necessary. However, such measures should not be dictated or imposed by any Member State or group of States. Instead, they should derive from negotiated agreement among all Member States. To do this successfully, we will all have to be tolerant and to appreciate each other's legitimate interests and concerns. Let us move away from apportioning blame and accept that the United Nations can only function on the basis of a consensus that adequately respects the concerns of each and all. ...

Surely, a United Nations that grinds to a halt as the result of financial constraints cannot even engage in reform.. One thing we all agree upon is that the United Nations is worth preserving. If it were not, we would not all be present here. A testament to the continued validity of the United Nations lies in the fact that the very countries that have been most vocal in calling attention to its shortcomings continue to exploit the forum it offers to address the world community on major issues of concern to them. Clearly, it is better to talk at the United Nations than to fight on the battlefield.

In addition, it is the view of the Nigerian delegation that the necessary reforms should be carried out in full accordance with the provisions of the United Nations Charter. The principle of sovereign equality of all Member States should not be derogated directly or indirectly, and essential programmes and activities of high priority should continue to attract the lion's share of available resources. In other words, we must ensure that we do not end up cutting the bone while we trim the fat."

Mr. Mahathir bin Mohamad, **Prime Minister of Malaysia**[35]

"The reality is that a few wealthy and powerful nations have always, in spite of charges of "automatic majorities" and "extreme" and "useless" resolutions, had the edge in shaping the United Nations. If the Organization falls short of expectations, the responsibility rests heavily on the shoulders of those same powerful nations, which perhaps expect the United Nations to be a creature in their own image, serving only certain perceived ends, for certain perceived interests.

To be sure, the responsibility also lies with the smaller developing nations. ... There is a need for us to temper the majority we enjoy by what is relevant, practical and realistic. Most important, we should not allow ourselves to be proxies, basing our decisions on ideological attachments or bloc interests, without regard for the principles involved. ...

Certainly, over the years some "fat" has accumulated which needs to be trimmed. Its efficacy must be reviewed periodically in order to enhance its role, but the motive for improving the United Nations must always be premised on the precepts enshrined in the Charter. ...

While we commend the efforts of the Group of 18 to reduce the staff levels in the Secretariat and to rationalize the Organization's administrative and budgetary procedures, we cannot agree with any rationale that obligatory contributions by any Member country can be withheld in order to force the acceptance of conditions unilaterally decided by a country's own national legislature. ...

Amy hint or suggestion that a Member country, however big or small, could unilaterally impose conditions would only bring about difficult precedents inconsistent with the spirit and the Charter upon which the United Nations was founded. Rules and procedures built around such a basic concept of the equality of States must not be tempered with, for that is one of the fundamental pillars upon which the United Nations was established."

Mr. Abdel Meguid, **Egypt**[36]

"Recently the relevance of the United Nations has been called into question. For our part, we believe that this question is baseless and absolutely irrelevant. ...

Any effort aimed at increasing the effectiveness of the Organization must stem first and foremost from the necessary political will. ... In that regard, we welcome the important role played by the Group of 18.

... an end must be put to the practice of bringing financial pressure to bear on the Organization, and to the attempt to channel reforms towards predetermined goals that express only short-term interests."

Mr. Consalvi, **Venezuela**[37]

"The criticisms that are sometimes levelled at [the United Nations] often lose sight of the deep meaning of the existence of an organization in which it is still possible to convene the overwhelming majority of States in order to urge them to face their problems by means of dialogue and civilized debate. ...

Venezuela is committed to the strengthening of the United Nations and will decisively challenge any attempts to make it inoperative or set it aside as one more symbol of lost illusions."

Mr. Mahabir, **Trinidad and Tobago**[38]

"the Assembly is taking place under the threatening shadow of a financial crisis which is endangering the viability of the United Nations. This crisis is but one aspect of a much deeper malaise which could ultimately unravel the very fabric of international political and economic relationships and co-operation so painstakingly woven over the past four decades.

Evidence of this malaise is manifested by the increasing efforts to subordinate the sovereignty of the weak to the might of the strong; by the growing trend towards unilateralism with the concomitant undermining of multilateral institutions."

Mr. del Valle, **Chile**[39]

"The United Nations today is but a pale reflection of the Organization that emerged from the ashes of the Second World War, as an example of the international community's enlightened interest in giving concrete expression to mankind's hope for lasting peace. Today that institution, which gave rise to so many hopes, is experiencing not only a financial crisis but also one of confidence and destiny. ...

In addition to this crisis, there is another, one which is far more serious. It arises from our peoples' loss of confidence in the system and in its ability to achieve the objectives for which it was created. Although it was created to be an instrument for assuring peace, the United Nations has instead become a forum of sterile confrontation. The Organization has thereby lost its ability to be a protagonist in international life and its ability to impose prudence in the conduct of States and to generate efficient initiatives for solving problems. ...

The successive efforts made to bring about change have not been sufficient to generate effective and necessary dialogue capable of pulling the Organization out of its state of immobility. Immobility cannot be concealed by an excessive increase in the number of meetings or by the proliferation of documents which the meetings produce. Through inertia and lack of courage to check a senseless process that seems to be leading nowhere, it has foundered into a voracious calendar that only consumes time, money and hopes.

The impossibility of facing up to this reality, which is becoming more and more complex and dynamic, has led the United Nations to a position so far removed from reality that the world it reflects today is a fictitious one."

Mr. Barré, **Somalia**[40]

"The consensus which emerged from the celebration of the fortieth anniversary of the United Nations was that the world Organization, with all its faults, still represented mankind's best hope for peace and progress. That consensus, I believe, envisaged two lines of action: it called for the reform of those shortcomings typical of any 40-year-old bureaucracy, and it called for the strengthening of the central role of the United Nations in the system of collective security established by the Charter.

The first line of action has been set in motion as a result of the efforts of the Group of high-level intergovernmental experts set up to review the administrative and financial functioning of the world body. My Government welcomes the recommendations of the Group as a valuable starting point for the process of reform, and we believe that they should receive careful consideration."

Mr. de Luz, **Cape Verde**[41]

"The financial difficulties are above all, as we know, a reflection of political positions which work to deny the United Nations its role as an institutional framework for dialogue on the major international issues of the present day, on the basis of the sovereign equality of States. Thus, if the financial crisis were to be resolved, this wold undoubtedly help to resolve the institutional crisis that now besets the United Nations. The institutional crisis, in its turn, cannot be resolved without the political will of all countries. Our common destiny requires us to make national sacrifices in this way.

There is no doubt that a great deal could be done towards streamlining the work of the United Nations in order to improve its administrative and financial effectiveness."

Mr. Barrow, **Belize**[42]

"Whatever proposals emerge for the strengthening of the United Nations system must take account of the fundamental need of small States to be involved actively in the international community, not with a limited spectator status but as equal participants in the real work of the international system. Hence membership of the Security Council, for example, can no longer be the preserve of the large and the powerful but must reflect the evolutionary nature of international reality. States large and small should be accommodated on a manageable rotation basis so as to allow all nations the benefit of constructive participation, regardless of wealth or military power.

Reform, of course, is not a one-way street. If the third world countries which make up the bulk of the United Nations membership are to persuade the great Powers to be responsive to the need for a more egalitarian framework for the Security Council they must also be prepared to exercise the power of their majority in the General Assembly with restraint and responsibility.

In particular, those of us who belong to the non-aligned group of nations should use our force of numbers to act in an unbiased fashion as regards the super-Powers and their respective world views and alliances. Too often it appears that our positions are anything but non-aligned. We need to put our own house in order and get back to a situation in which we apply the principles of our movement uniformly and without selectivity. The General Assembly ought not to be a forum for sterile agenda and one-aided resolutions, rammed home by what increasingly appears to be an unbalanced use of our majority."

Colonel Denis Sassou-Nguesso, **President of the People's Republic of the Congo**[43]

"The Organization must certainly be kept in being. Consequently we are deeply concerned by the crisis of multilateralism. We believe that crisis in which the Organization now finds itself, and which is the subject of an in-depth analysis by the Secretary-General in his annual report, as well as by the Group of 18 intergovernmental experts, can not be regarded merely as a financial crisis. It touches upon the very philosophy of international relations in our time, and the degree of credibility given to the multilateral system, which has been patiently built up over 40 years. We therefore say yes to reform, if its purpose is to strengthen this valuable instrument."

Mr. Mandungu Bula Nyati, **Zaire**[44]

"my delegation would like to reaffirm its steadfast devotion to the principle of the sovereign equality of Member States enshrined in the United Nations Charter. We ardently hope that those recommendations [of the Group of 18] may lead to the strengthening of the role of the United Nations and the purposes and principles of its Charter, which must not be infringed."

Mr. Masri, **Jordan**[45]

"While we continue to believe in the vital need for the existence of the United Nations, we feel, unfortunately, that there is a campaign being waged against this Organization. Although I do not want to go into the details of this campaign, I feel it is essentially unjust and prejudiced."

Mr. Mladenov, **Bulgaria**[46]

"We are ... concerned at the attempts of certain Member States to impose on the Organization methods of work and aims that are incompatible with its Charter and to create difficulties that would impede the normal and undis-turbed activities of Member States. Today we are all responsible for keeping alive and consolidating trust in the United Nations, which like a living organism develops and breathes in a changing political climate."

Mr. Hayden, **Australia**[47]

"The Australian Government has some understanding of the impatience expressed about the United Nations and its operations. We would argue that there is room for more efficient administration of the Organization, less wasteful duplication of function and operation and a more rational decision-making process for its budget. In view of its high mission and the poverty and exploitation against which it is struggling, it is quite wrong that the United Nations should be in any way an example of conspicuous consumption. In view of the high expectations of it in every part of the world, it would be a shame if the United Nations were to degenerate into a broadcasting agency for pointless, meaningless and ultimately useless declarations. ...

Our Government feels very strongly that the Organization is in danger so long as it refuses or postpones reform, but it believes equally strongly that there is no substitute for the United Nations in a multilateral system of co-operative management of global problems and the maintenance of world peace."

Mr. Manuel Pinto Da Costa, **President of the Democratic Republic of Sao Tome and Principe**[48]

"A careful reading of the report submitted by the high-level Group of Experts is an unquestionable confirmation of our assertion. Beyond interests and intentions whose motivations we question, beyond hard-to-conceal measures which seek to subvert the fundamental principles of the Charter, beyond proposals whose efficacy we question as a viable alternative to the present situation, is the unquestionable fact that adjustments, reforms in methods and institutions, elimination of some practices and procedures are all required.

To maintain the *status quo* or limit the range and efficacy of the numerous recommendations included in the report, in the name of questionable interests, would be, in our modest opinion, to fall short of our collective responsibility; it would be to put at risk our determination to reform the United Nations into an operative instrument for resolving the problems of our time."

Mr. Mugabe, **Zimbabwe**[49]

"I wish to commend for its good work the Group of High Level Intergovernmental Experts. ... The Group's observations, analyses and recommendations ... are a realistic attempt to find solutions to the problem besetting our Organization, and I sincerely trust that the Assembly will see them in that serious light."

Mr. Poos, **Luxembourg**[50]

"It would seem that this financial crisis is political in nature and must be treated as such. It reveals profound disagreement between Member States as to the role that should be played by the Organization and even by some of its specialized agencies.

I must say in this context that it seems to me to be crucial that all States Members meet the international commitments to which they have solemnly subscribed. On the other hand, it cannot be denied that after 40 years of existence we must review all the United Nations programmes in order to redirect them towards spheres in which their effectiveness in not called into question and they can tackle matters or real priority, some of which are tragic in nature.

In this spirit, my country will join in any effort aimed at restructuring the Secretariat and rationalizing the use and cost of its human resources. Since the situation is till alarming, despite the economy measures adopted at the Secretary-General's initiative, this matter remains extremely urgent. Only in this way can we create an atmosphere favourable to the restoration of confidence in the future of the United Nations."

Mr. Al-Dali, **Democratic Yemen**[51]

"We are aware of the importance of the proposed administrative reforms aimed at improving the Organization's performance. However, we believe that the real crisis facing the United Nations stems from the weakness or total lack of political will on the part of some Member States who put their own selfish interests above those of the international community, who circumvent United Nations resolutions and obstruct their implementation in their drive to settle international problems outside the United Nations."

Mr. Blamo, **Liberia**[52]

"In addition to the fundamental problems confronting it, the United Nations is faced with the current financial crisis, which threatens its very foundations and survival. ... It is my Government's considered view that much could be achieved by streamlining the vast United Nations bureaucracy. However, to cut programmes arbitrarily would, in my delegation's view, seriously hamper international economic and technical co-operation."

Mr. Bassolé, **Burkina Faso**[53]

"The United Nations and its different agencies are subjected to underhand attacks for having dared to lend an attentive ear to our legitimate claims. More and more, there are blatant attempts at weakening and restricting the role of the United Nations system, thus threatening to undermine the principles of sovereign equality and of democratic procedures on which it rests.

We were aware that within this institution an underground battle was going on between the old and the new order. ...

Today, there is much talk about the crisis of the United Nations, and of the lack of confidence it causes among States and peoples. But surely this loss of confidence is the joint result of the disappointed hopes of those who have overestimated the real capacities of the United Nations, and the failed attempts of those who wanted to continue to ben the United Nations to their wishes. It may be an Utopian illusion to want to accelerate the march of history, but it is suicidal to try to reverse it.

A real danger is threatening the United Nations today. The financial crisis it is going through is due to its failure to avoid the childhood ailment of all government administrations: over-expansion. We recognize that through the years the United Nations has become an enormous machine for swallowing up resources which have gone mainly to pay for an administration whose efficiency has often been questioned. No one could seriously oppose reforms to improve the productivity of this Organization, to increase its effectiveness and to streamline its structures to make them more efficient. But in no case could Burkina Faso be a party to any action directed not to those aims but to depriving the Organization of its content and substance by diverting it from its basic purpose."

Mr. Abdullah, **United Arab Emirates**[54]

"on objective review of the events of this year does not justify optimism, since certain parties have been trying to weaken the United Nations and diminish its role, a development which poses a threat to the existing international order. There is no doubt that the present financial crisis is but one aspect of the international political crisis. Although we believe it is necessary to introduce the necessary administrative and financial reform, this should not be used as a pretext for undermining the effectiveness of the United Nations."

Mr. Tudor, **Barbados**[55]

"The report of the Group of High-level Inter-Governmental Experts ... has generated a level of attention and concern unprecedented in recent times. And with good reason. Because what is at stake is the very existence of this Organization and the way in which it functions. So amid all of the deliberation, consultation and negotiation, two things seemed to be accepted by all of us: first, that it is important for all of us to settle this matter quickly and quietly;

secondly, that whatever happens, the United Nations will never be the same again.

My delegation believes that the report represents an excellent foundation on which to develop a series of reforms with a view to cutting the fat, tightening the belt, firming the muscle and generally improving the health of the Organization. Beyond that, a package of reform, based on that foundation, might even lead to an improved process of decision-making that would satisfy the interests of all Member States, complying with the concept of universality and generally uphold the principles embodied in the Charter."

Mr. Van Lierop, **Vanuatu**[56]

"A great deal has been written, and even more has been said, on the subject of the imperfections of the United Nations. Critics point to our lengthy debates, repetitive speeches, strident resolutions, and our frequent waste and inefficiency. The criticisms are not completely without merit. There is considerable room for improvement.

However, one must ask why the United Nations' most vociferous critics do not begin with a candid self-examination. What measures have they taken to correct similar, if not worse, shortcomings in the various national and local governmental bodies of their own respective jurisdictions? Are we to believe that the United Nations is unique in its frequent waste and inefficiency? Is this the only place where there are too many lengthy speeches and too many divisive resolutions? Or course not."

Ms. Chiepe, **Botswana**[57]

"My delegation would like to appeal to those who have done so not to withhold their contributions at a time when the United Nations needs more, not less financial resources. The great importance we attach to the survival of the Organization impels us to caution against the erroneous thinking popular in certain quarters that the Organization has too much money to spend or waste, the corollary to that fallacy being that, if you deny it more money, then the problem will disappear. The fact is that the United Nations needs more money, not less, to finance the many humanitarian projects all of us expect it to carry out."

Mr. Gurinovich, **Byelorussian Soviet Socialist Republic**[58]

"The range of issues facing the United Nations is wide indeed. If they are to be resolved successfully, it is necessary to make collective efforts to increase the efficiency of the United Nations and to enhance its prestige.

However, a trend to the opposite on the part of certain Western States has emerged recently, that is, to undermine the Organization, to impede its activities, to bring tough pressure to bear on some Member States and to apply arbitrary discriminatory measures against others. We are witnessing a situation whereby the United Nations is being subjected to political-financial blackmail. In any society blackmail is considered to be an abominable phenomenon. It is doubly abominable when used against this universal Organization which is the symbol of mankind's hope for a better world."

Mr. Al-Mahdi, **Sudan**[59]

"The United Nations membership has grown steadily over the past 40 years. Its bodies and committees have indeed multiplied. This expansion has had a negative impact on the effective utilization of its resources and its ability to co-ordinate its numerous and sometimes overlapping activities. It has become necessary ow to study the administrative and financial shortcomings of the Organization with a view to drawing up a comprehensive plan to improve its administrative and financial performance along the lines of the recommenda-tions of the Group of Intergovernmental Experts.

In the light of the experience of four decades, the Charter of the United Nations should be revised to incorporate new provisions, such as economic rights, protection of the environment and outer space, and particularly to enhance the effectiveness of the means of maintaining peace and security. In this context, we believe that permanent membership of the Security Council should be expanded to give a seat to every recognized regional group and that the General Assembly should be empowered to override, by a certain majority, a veto in the Security Council, in order to ensure that no one permanent member may be able to paralyse the international will as expressed by a large majority of Member States."

Mr.Mboumoua, **Cameroon**[60]

"despite the financial aspects of the present crisis, it is really a reflection of the political will of certain Member States which already enjoy considerable influence and privilege in the Organization to get almost exclusive and sometimes abusive control of its decision-making machinery, thus endangering the ethical basis and even the future of multilateralism."

Sir Satcam Boolell, **Mauritius**[61]

"We should not accept any proposal which would attempt, indirectly or otherwise, to change the Charter objectives or weaken the role of the legislative organs. This Organization is the only world body whose membership represents practically the whole of mankind, based on the principle of sovereign equality. It is the only world body where weaker nations have a chance to voice their feelings and where they can find the moral checks and balances against encroachment on their hard-won independence and sovereign existence."

Mr. Lopez Contreras, **Honduras**[62]

"The concern that led to the report of the Group of 18 doubtless reflects an awareness of the international community regarding wastage and an erosion of the credibility of our Organization. It will be a working tool to enhance the effectiveness of this Organization, provided it does not promote the progressive paralysis of the United Nations, provided it does not a sidetrack it from its essential task, and provided "savings" do not kill all its activities and the United Nations does not depart from its responsibility and its fundamental objectives."

Mr. Chagula, **United Republic of Tanzania**[63]

"My delegation notes that, contrary to the impression now being created, there was no consensus or evident agreement in the Group of 18 on matters related to the vital subject of planning, programming and budgeting in the United Nations. ... I should like to state that Tanzania will very strongly oppose any proposals to establish mechanisms, no matter what they are called, that will infringe the principle of the sovereign equality of Member States under the United Nations Charter, alter the power and prerogatives of the main organs of the United Nations and impair the prerogatives of the Secretary-General as chief administrative officer of the Organization."

Mr. Wolde, **Ethiopia**[64]

"The Ethiopian delegation is convinced that the crisis is not financial; we believe it is essentially political. ... Indeed, it is a political crisis caused by lingering sentiments and outmoded receptions inimical to the democratization of international relations, to the recognition of, and respect for, the sovereign equality of nations and to a constructive accommodation of inevitable changes in international relations. These obviously arise from apprehensions in some circles that the multilateral approach to problems and acceptance of changing situations will rob them of their positions of power and unfair privileges. These circles promote and rationalize their perceptions under the convenient guise of protecting the United Nations from "irresponsible diktat of a mechanical majority.

Such an attitude, I submit, represents a threat to the sovereignty and the national interests of the developing countries. Furthermore, it represents an erosion of faith in the cardinal principles enunciated in the Charter and a negation of the inexorable historical tide of change which, in the last forty years has altered not only the system of international relations, but also the United Nations itself."

Mr. Peters, **Saint Vinceant and the Grenadines**[65]

"We, the small nations of the world, whose contributions are very modest but to which the existence of the United Nations is most important, would want to see a vibrant United Nations. Perhaps the United Nations has been too ambitious, expanding too many programmes in too many areas too quickly. This has always meant the expansion of administrative costs, and in the long run we get away from serving the basic principles of the Charter.

We should hope that in the restructuring that is being undertaken the opportunities for the meaningful participation of those of us that are relatively new Members of this Organization will not be eroded."

2.2.2 Plenary Meetings on the Report of the Group of 18

Following the general debate, the report of the Group of 18 was considered in plenary meetings of the Assembly. At the beginning following introduction was given by Mr. Vraalsen (Norway), **Chairman of the Group of 18**[66]

"The matter before us is of direct concern to each and every Member State. It is not an East-West issue. It is not an issue between opposing forces from the North and from the South, between developing and developed countries, between regional groups or between the major contributors to the United Nations system and the rest of the membership. It is a matter of common interest and common concern. Either we succeed together or we fail together.
...

During the past months I have sensed that among some delegations there continues to be a lingering feeling of doubt and uneasiness about the reform process, in particular regarding the efforts to develop improved machinery and procedure for planning and programme budgeting. I really hope that during the forthcoming debate we can put those concerns firmly to rest. ...

The present planning and budget procedure is inadequate. It does not give Member States - and here I mean all of us, all Member States - the possibility to exercise the necessary intergovernmental leadership, particularly in setting priorities within the resources likely to be available. Reforms in that area would serve the interest of us all. ...

I wish to convey to all representatives the following with a strong sense of urgency: that we must during this session of the General Assembly develop a practical procedure that can facilitate and encourage broad agreement on the budget; that the report of the Group of 18 provides a good basis for shaping such a procedure; and that we must start working on this questions now. ...

Let us be very clear about this: whatever measures of reform we undertake, the financial viability of the United Nations can be fully restored and secured only if all Member States pay their assessed contributions in full and on time. Anything short of that is a violation of their obligations under the Charter. Anything short of that makes orderly management of the Organization virtually impossible. Withholdings at the level which we are experiencing at present, if allowed to continue, will threaten the very existence of the Organization."

The statements of national delegations are recalled below.

The representative of **Brazil**[67]

"In general, my Government is prepared to accept most of the recommendations proposed, with any technical adjustments that may prove necessary.

On the other hand, there are clearly different levels of accuracy, appropriateness and validity in the proposed recommendations. Some, such as recommendations 20 and 30, are extremely vague or only restate previous recommendations. Others are either excessively specific or excessively rigid - recommendation 3 (e) is an example. Still others are poorly elaborated or based on insufficient information or inadequate premises, such as recommendation 25 (2), in regard to which I have serious reservations. Despite these shortcomings, however, the general lay-out of the report and the bases underlying its work are sound and consistent. ...

I do not wish to enter into details at this stage, but two examples ... merit immediate attention: first, the need to ensure the participation of Member States at an early stage of the budgetary process, with due respect for the responsibilities of the Secretary-General; and secondly, the introduction of the concept of a budgetary envelope that would encase, with some adjustments to the current definition of add-ons, the totality of resources available for a biennium.

This latter concept still requires some refinement, specifically in relation to the procedure for the determination of the envelope and the related contingency fund, but the basic agreement is already there. My delegation does not deem it appropriate, however, that we should limit ourselves to the three choices presented by the Group of 18 when considering this item. We would prefer a broader discussion, that would not necessarily impose the selection of one of three choices, which the Group of 18 itself could not make. ...

I should like ... to indicate two areas dealt with by the Group which we feel should be examined very closely in order to dispel some concerns, which I am sure are shared by other delegations.

The first relates to the recommendations directed to the United Nations Development Programme (UNDP) and other, similar organizations subsidiary to the Economic and Social Council and the General Assembly. Owing to the specific characteristics of those organizations, some recommendations directed primarily at the United Nations proper but applicable to them as well should be agreed upon only after careful consultations have been carried out with all directly interested parties. ...

The second area that we feel should be closely examined is that of personnel. The Group of 18, appropriately, devoted a great deal of attention to this issue and has formulated 22 recommendations in the relevant chapter of its report. In addition, one further recommendation - number 15, is in the chapter devoted to the structure of the Secretariat, but nevertheless has a direct bearing upon personnel.

The Group of 18 concurred as to the need to ensure that more equitable and selective methods of recruitment be applied to improve the standards of efficiency, competence, independence and integrity of the Secretariat. The Group also agreed that reduction of the number of staff members would be desirable and could be attained without hampering the current level of programme activities of the United Nations. These two sets of recommendations, although distinct, have the same objective, namely, more efficiency, agility and responsiveness in the Secretariat.

My delegation fully shares these objectives and believes that the recommendations, with the necessary adjustments, should be accepted and implemented. There is, however, a pervasive objective sought by some, which is sometimes clearly spelt out, sometimes disguised behind other goals. I refer to the idea of indiscriminate reduction of expenditures. We are concerned at the level of the United Nations budget, and my own country's assessed contribution is not paid without some sacrifice. But we cannot accept the idea that this concern should be the determinant factor in undertaking alterations or restructuring. ... For that reason, we have severe reservations with regard to the present formulation of recommendation 61."

The representative of the **Union of Soviet Socialist Republics**[68]

"In our view, on the whole the results of the activities of the Group can be assessed positively. ... The recommendations concerning limiting the number and length of meetings of United Nations bodies and reducing the volume of the documentation, and so on, seem useful. Nor can there be any doubts regarding the recommendation on a study of the structure of the Secretariat in order to simplify and streamline it and improve co-ordination among various subdivisions, in particular in the social and economic sphere. The recommendation on reducing the number of United Nations personnel by 15 per cent and the number of higher-level employees by 25 per cent is also of great significance. ...

It should also be noted that the report of the Group of 18 contains a number of recommendations on which agreement was not reached, which in our view is totally unacceptable. For example, one recommendation which was not agreed upon in the Group, but was included in the report, states that not less than 50 per cent of the nationals of any State working in the Secretariat should have permanent contracts. This can only be described as a cynical recommendation aimed at strengthening the over-representation in the Secretariat of one group of States and even further aggravating the under-representation of another group. We are profoundly convinced that such an approach runs counter to the objectives and purposes of the United Nations. It is understandable that we firmly reject this kind of recommendation. There are other recommendations on personnel issues which impede the implementation of the principle of just geographical distribution in staffing the Secretariat. In the view of the Soviet delegation, recommendations on personnel matters should be referred to the International Civil Service Commission for further study."

The representative of **Japan**[69]

"My delegation ... believes that we, the Member States, should consider the recommendations as a single entity and endorse them in their entirety. ...

I should like briefly to highlight those of the wide-ranging recommendations that my delegation regards as the most important. The first regards the so-called principle of scrap-and-build in the planning and setting up of programmes. In the course of the 41-year history of the United Nations, the priorities of Member States have undergone certain changes. New activities have been added, but those activities that have achieved their objectives and those that have lost their relevance have not been properly eliminated. As a result, the ever lengthening agenda of the United Nations has led to a constant expansion of the intergovernmental machinery without sufficient attention being paid to the elimination of redundant or obsolete activities. When work programmes are fragmented among too many United Nations subsidiary bodies, it becomes extremely difficult for delegations to participate in them in a meaningful way. Co-ordination among those bodies also suffers. It is important to ensure that new bodies are created only as existing ones that have lost their relevance are discontinued. My delegation therefore fully supports the Group's recommendations that the number, frequency and duration of meetings of intergovernmental bodies and machinery should be rationalized. Although we had hoped that the Group could have been more specific in its recommendations for structural reforms of the intergovernmental machinery, my delegation agrees with the need for a comprehensive review of the entire structure of the United Nations. ...

The second point relates to staff. Concomitant with the considerable growth of the intergovernmental machinery, there has been a dramatic expansion of the structure and size of the Secretariat over the years. We fully agree with the analysis of the Group of 18 that the structure of the Secretariat is top-heavy, too complex and too fragmented. Even with the present organizational structure, the size of the Secretariat could be reduced by eliminating duplication, simplifying the hierarchical structure and improving personnel policies. A leaner and more efficient Secretariat would be able to respond more readily to the needs and expectations of the international community. My delegation therefore believes that streamlining the organizational structure of the Secretariat and increasing its administrative and financial accountability are urgent tasks. ...

The third question is that of personnel management. The quality of the Organization is a function of the quality and dedication of its staff. Similarly, the efficiency of the Organization depends in large part on the efficiency of its staff. As stipulated in the United Nations Charter, it is essential to maintain the highest standards of efficiency, competence and integrity in managing the Secretariat staff. In order fully to mobilize the entire staff to achieve the goals of the United Nations, it is important also to guarantee that personnel management is based on a clear, coherent and transparent set of staff rules and regulations. My delegation heartily welcomes the contribution made by the Group of 18 towards achieving these objectives.

The fourth point is that of budget procedure. Ensuring that the United Nations is placed on a stable financial footing is perhaps the most important objective of the reforms. To this end, it is essential that a general agreement be reached among Member States regarding the desirable level of the programme budget and that priorities be set to determine the appropriate allocation of resources among various programmes.

It is a startling fact that since 1979 Member States that account for 70 to 80 per cent of assessed contributions have either voted against or abstained on the regular budget of the United Nations. If this trend continues and the Member States contributing the bulk of budgetary resources continue to be dissatisfied with matters relating to the regular programme budget, the financial operations and the overall capacity of the United Nations will be gravely affected. My delegation therefore welcomes the serious efforts the Group of 18 has made to rectify the deficiencies of the present planning and budget mechanism. The Group agreed on many important points regarding new budgetary procedures, including the active participation of Member States at each stage and the need for member Governments to give guidance on the level of resources needed to cover all expenditures during a biennium. As for the remaining issues that must be addressed during the current session of the General Assembly, my delegation is ready to support alternative A, which is more specific on the mandate to indicate the level of total resources for the biennium and on the decision-making procedure of the new committee. ...

Finally, on monitoring and follow-up, on many occasions in the past recommendations on the administrative and financial efficiency of the United Nations have been made, but they have never been effectively implemented. This was due mainly to the lack of mechanisms to ensure and monitor implementation. My delegation is pleased, therefore, that the Group of 18 has proposed target dates and follow-up procedures to ensure full implementation of its recommendations. Once the General Assembly decides to adopt those recommendations at this session we shall have to see to it that the General Assembly itself monitors progress and ensures their implementation as speedily and as effectively as possible."

The representative of **Canada**[70]

"My delegation firmly believes that, taken together, the 71 recommendations on which a consensus was achieved could significantly improve the operation of the United Nations. It is out of that conviction that we urge this General Assembly to endorse the consensus recommendations as a prelude to speedy implementation, which would significantly strengthen the financial recommendations already implemented by the Secretary-General.

As my delegation believes that improvement of the programme planning and budgetary procedure is vital, we were concerned that here there was no overall consensus; but we are not dispirited. ... There was a consensus on the need for improvements in the intergovernmental machinery of the budgetary process, on the need for Member States to become involved at the earliest possible stage in the budgetary process, on the importance of co-ordination between programme planning and programme budgeting and on the need for the General Assembly to establish at an early date a level of resources available for the United Nations regular budget. My delegation believes that this high degree of agreement gives us a basis for moving forward. ...

Adoption of the reform measures discussed in the report of the Group is only part of what will be required to restore the viability of our Organization. The financial crisis, brought about by the arrears and the withholding by Member States of their contributions, must not be ignored. Canada expects that as part of the reform process those countries that have long criticized the United Nations - sometimes using non-payment of assessment as a pressure tactic - will then act so as to eliminate the problems caused by arrears and withholdings."

The representative of **Australia**[71]

"my delegation has some reservations about several of the points made by the Secretary-General in his preliminary observations on the Group of High-level experts' report. We acknowledge the legitimate concerns of the staff associations, but we think these must be addressed in the broader context of the overall viability of the Organization. They cannot be allowed to stand in the way of reforms agreed upon by the membership of the United Nations.

The specific recommendations contained in Part A of Chapter II of the Group's report have the full support of the Australian delegation. We have long argued for such reforms, particularly with regard to the number and length of meetings and conferences. We also need to find new procedures and methods of work which will enable us better to utilize the time available. Too much time is currently used in the repetition of national positions in debates and not enough time is spent on constructive dialogue and negotiation. ...

Part B of chapter II calls for an in-depth study to identify measures to rationalize and simplify the intergovernmental structure. We understand the thinking behind this recommendation, but would have preferred to see a more concrete formulation. There is clear evidence of functional overlap and duplication, which steps should be taken to eliminate.

We particularly welcome the recommendations in part A of chapter III, based on the recognition that the Secretariat is overstaffed, particularly at senior levels. As I have already indicated, we look to the Secretary-General to implement recommendation 15, within the three-year period identified by the Group of Experts. In our view the opportunity should not be lost to reduce inefficiency while redeploying competent staff in accordance with recommendations 16 to 24. It would not, in our view, be adequate for the Secretariat to seek to implement recommendation 15 simply by means of attrition.

The recommendations contained in part D of chapter III deserve careful consideration and follow-up. It seems to my delegation that the lack of precision in a number of these recommendations could give rise to problems of implementation. The Secretariat should be in no doubt of our resolve to reduce administrative overheads by streamlining the Organization.

Chapter IV contains 26 recommendations, many of which are in the form of exhortations to implement existing rules and regulations. There are, however, a number of proposals which deserve particular attention. Recommendation 54 calls, for example, for limits on the length of service of senior officers of the Secretariat. This is consistent with the Australian Government's proposal that, as a general principle, heads of all United Nations bodies should be limited to two terms in office. If implemented, this principle would serve to break down rigidity, inject new ideas and make organizations more responsive to current needs.

We also endorse recommendation 61, which calls for a reduction in the total entitlements of staff members. Like the Organization as a whole, staff members must accept that times have changed. As the Australian Foreign Minister said in his general debate statement, it would be wrong for the United Nations in any way to be seen as setting an example of conspicuous consumption. ...

We are concerned at the apparent level of mistrust which has arisen in relation to consideration of chapter VI. We very much hope it will be possible to resolve any differences in this area between groups in a positive and constructive manner.

Whatever budget decision-making mechanism is finally adopted, it should, in our view, contain the following five essential elements.

First, Member States must be able to determine resource allocations in accordance with more clearly defined priorities.

Secondly, Member States must be consulted fully prior to the preparation of the biennial programme budget and medium-term plan.

Thirdly, an upper limit on the level of the budget must be agreed by Member States before the Secretariat submits its expenditure proposals. This limit should be determined on the basis of the actual resources available to the Organization.

Fourthly, any additional expenditure which becomes necessary after the preparation of the programme budget should be accommodated within the approved budget ceiling.

Fifthly, to the greatest extent possible, decisions should be taken by consensus. Only in exceptional circumstances should voting become necessary. It should be a matter of principle that the budgets of the Organization should in future enjoy the widest possible support."

The representative of **Singapore**[*72]

"I propose that the General Assembly adopt this report, imperfect as it is, because it embodies, in my view, a clear and reasonable call to action.

In endorsing the report, the United Nations General Assembly would also be sending an important message to the United Nations Secretariat. We know that over the years the Secretariat has grown out of control. The Member States have never collectively protested against this growth. In fact many Member States have individually contributed to the problem. It is obvious to any management analyst that no chief executive officer can function with over 80 deputies, which I believe is the situation our Secretary-General faces. Yet, in spite of this large number of Assistant Secretaries-General and Under-Secretaries-General, there is always pressure upon him to appoint more. ...

The biggest weakness of the report of the Group of 18, however, is its lack of agreement on the recommendations in its chapter VI on the planning and budgetary procedure, which is probably the most critical chapter. Ironically, in the introduction to the chapter, especially in paragraphs 65 to 68, all members of the Group have agreed on the deficiencies of the present planning and budgetary procedures. They have also agreed on the need to rectify these deficiencies. Given this agreement, the lack of consensus on the recommendation in paragraph 69 is all the more tragic.

I suspect that most representatives must be as puzzled as I was when I first read proposals (a) and (b) of that paragraph. The differences seem so minute that it is strange that no agreement was possible. More tragically, even though the differences appear so minute, a heavy cloud of suspicion already surrounds those proposals. I am not discussing proposal (c), because I understand it is not being seriously considered.

Let me state clearly, for the record, what proposals (a) and (b) do not call for. First, neither calls for weighted voting in any form. Neither proposal would transform the United Nations into the United Nations Industrial Development Organization. Secondly, neither would take the final decision-making power on the budget away from the General Assembly, which, as Article 17 of the Charter states, "shall consider and approve the budget of the Organization".

As a small State, Singapore is fundamentally opposed to any weighted voting in the United Nations, because it would undermine the fundamental principle

---

[*]The representative of Singapore was Mr. Kishore Mahbubani, who was a member of the Group of 18.

of sovereign equality. I was sorry, therefore, to learn that some members believe that some form of weighted voting is hidden in Chapter VI, although I have to acknowledge that recommendation H of proposal (a) has a misleading reference to the decision-making record of the Committee for Programme and Co-ordination (CPC).

Is it possible to explain proposals (a) and (b) in simple terms? I shall try. The proposals revolve round two United Nations Committees, the Advisory Committee on Administrative and Budgetary Questions (ACABQ) and the Committee for Programme and Co-ordination, both of which have been in existence for some time. I believe that committees, like human beings, develop and take on a life and character of their own. Hence the ACABQ, especially under the outstanding chairmanship of Ambassador Conrad Mselle, is universally acknowledged to have done a good job, while the CPC is generally said to have failed in both its planning and its co-ordination functions.

Not surprisingly, therefore, both proposals (a) and (b) recommend that the CPC be strengthened through the election of expert members. Both proposals (a) and (b) also agree that the improved CPC should look more carefully at the programme budget each year. Even more significantly, both proposals agree on the need to define the level of resources for the budget. They also agree that a limited financial envelope should cover additional expenditures, although proposal (a) is more specific in calling for a contingency fund of only 2 per cent of the estimated budget, which, incidentally, should have been adequate to meet the additional expenditures incurred in previous years. Both proposals also stress that any new additional expenditures outside the financial envelope would have to be obtained through redeployment of resources from low-priority to high-priority areas. Having participated in the Group of 18 discussions, I wish to assure you, Mr. President, that agreement on those points was not easily arrived at. If we cannot agree on anything else, let us at least agree on those critical points.

What, then, is the heart of the dispute between proposals (a) and (b)? It revolves round the roles of the ACABQ and the CPC. Significantly, both proposals acknowledge that there would be inevitable problems in having two committees looking at the same budget simultaneously. To understand what problems that might create, try to think of a human body with two heads, each giving simultaneous instructions to the one pair of hands and one pair of legs on what to do. Unless the two heads co-operate, the hands and legs will become entangled and the body will trip over.

In the same way, if the CPC and the ACABQ are given responsibilities over the United Nations budget without careful definition of their respective roles, the budget will have two heads, possibly pulling in different directions. Why, then, can we not agree on one head instead of two? In an ideal world, that would be the best solution. In the real world, we have to live with untidy solutions. Hence I fear that the United Nations will have to live with those two Committees. Consequently, their roles and functions will need to be carefully defined."

The representative of **Finland**[73]

"In our view, the proposed staff cuts lack the detailed criteria which are absolutely necessary for this measure to be effective. In addition, the programmatic priority setting as a basis for the cuts will not be decided, according to the recommendations, by the Member States but by the Secretary-General. On the personnel recommendations as a whole, I concur with the observations set forth in the Secretary-General's note.

My delegation regrets that the Group of 18 did not reach agreement on the revision of the scale of assessments. We believe that there is broad support for the idea that the present scale does not adequately correspond to the Organization's needs.

Finland also regrets that it was not possible for the Group to reach agreement on planning and budget procedures. Consensus should be our aim also in programming and budgeting decisions, and it must be found on the basis of agreement on our operational requirements. The content of our programme of work is, in United Nations reality, the only reasonable point of departure in determining the scope of resources needed. That aim would be greatly facilitated by strengthening the intergovernmental mechanisms. We welcome all the proposals of the Group of 18 to that effect. An effective intergovernmental preparatory mechanism is a prerequisite for better planning and implementation of United Nations programmes. It is necessary, in particular, in order to provide an instrument for establishing the priorities for the United Nations programme of work. That would contribute to our better judgement on the need for and use of resources."

The representative of **Algeria**[74]

"The study undertaken by the Group of Experts ... clearly shows that the proliferation of United Nations activities in response to the needs of a world in evolution poses management problems relating to co-ordination and the demarcation of mandates. The result has been the administrative top-heaviness and excesses the Group of 18 has diagnosed in its report.

Constraints of all types prevented the Group from carrying out a deeper analysis of all these problems. It is therefore essential that the Assembly entrust that task to an intergovernmental committee, which in the view of my delegation could be the Committee for Programme and Co-ordination (CPC), whose terms of reference and experience appear to make it the most appropriate body to carry out that task.

In doing so, the Committee should be guided by a desire to strike a balance between the need to merge or eliminate certain bodies and the need to strengthen others.

We believe that the same approach should prevail in the study of the number and frequency of the meetings and conferences which obviously constitute a basic part of the Organization's activities.

The Group of Experts has proposed detailed recommendations on the restructuring of the Secretariat. ... While noting the cogency of many of the recommendations, we believe it is appropriate to call for the advice of the Secretary-General, in his capacity as the highest officer of the Organization, to enable us to take the necessary decisions with due regard for his authority and the need to preserve the Secretariat's dynamism and skills.

It goes without saying that in this restructuring exercise the continuity of the Organization's activities must be borne in mind. The Secretary-General must therefore be allowed full scope to exercise his prerogatives in this respect. ...

The Group of Expert's diagnosis ... emphasizes that Member States are not fully involved in the preparation of the budget. The remedy lies not in restructuring the budget machinery but rather in adopting a new method so that Member States can participate and that the level and content of the programme budget would be negotiated throughout the budgetary process.

Consequently we could consider accepting alternative (b), contained in chapter VI of the report of the experts, who, according to what we know of the Group's work, sought to strike a compromise that, although based on a different original position was designed to take account of the efforts to improve the budget machinery contained in alternative (a).

Certain elements of alternative (b) suggest a procedural solution for a problem identified as one of methods of work, but the acceptance of other elements of that same proposal would demand sacrifices of us, which we are nevertheless ready to make if that would ensure the financial stability of the Organization's programmes.

The procedure we have in mind for examining the programming and financial aspects of the Organization's activities ... could be as follows: first, the negotiation of the general plan for the future programme budget, which the Secretary-General would submit to the Fifth Committee, through the CPC and the Advisory Committee on Administrative and Budgetary Questions (ACABQ), in a non-budgetary year; and, secondly, the drawing up of the draft programme budget on the basis of guidelines which the Assembly would in the main have already negotiated in the CPC, the ACABQ and the Fifth Committee.

In order to ensure the broadest possible agreement among Member States on the budget's content, the CPC's functions in planning and co-ordination of programmes must be strengthened to include examination of the order of priority of programmes and to make the medium-term plan the principal directive of general policy in establishing the programme budget. The responsibility for establishing priorities among activities should remain the prerogative of the CPC and the intergovernmental bodies concerned, and presupposes agreement on the specific and objective criteria that should prevail.

The question of additional expenditure could be solved by including the more foreseeable expenditures in the body of the budget and by establishing a fund to finance the impact of inflation and currency fluctuations.

This new procedure presupposes the full implementation of the rules and regulations governing the planning of programmes and the application of all the provisions of the terms of reference of the CPC and the ACABQ, the carrying out of the process of improving the functioning of the CPC and its conditions of work, the broadening of the membership of the ACABQ, the strengthening of the co-ordination between the two budgetary structures through the holding of joint meetings and the allocation of the time necessary for negotiations on the content and level of the budget in those two Committees and in the Fifth Committee, whose functions as a committee dealing with programme and budget matters should never be in any way altered or restricted."

The representative of **Jamaica**[75]

"The report has usefully highlighted the problem of co-ordination. This, along with proper planning, execution, monitoring and evaluation and inspection will ensure that the United Nations system does not squander the limited resources made available to it. Many of the problems have been identified in earlier reports, so they are not entirely unknown.

In this regard, we consider that the function of evaluation, like audit, should be carried out by an independent internal unit in the Secretariat, as well as by the external system - like the Joint Inspection Unit and the Board of External Auditors. This would ensure timely identification of activities that are "obsolete, of marginal usefulness or ineffective".

Most of the money for development activities now comes from voluntary funds. While these are sincerely appreciated, we cannot help but note that by the increasing shift to voluntary funding the principle of collective responsibility enshrined in the Charter is being undermined, since these funds can easily be withheld and impair the impartial treatment of all participants in the multilateral process.

It is for this reason that my delegation cautions against the funding of developmental activities totally from voluntary contributions. If developmental activities are to be "rationalized", how can funding be assured where funding is voluntary - as is the case, for example, with the United Nations Development Programme (UNDP) - when the activities now in the regular budget are funded from assessed contributions?

We have also noted recommendation 8 (3) (d) calling for the management and control, at the intergovernmental level, of United Nations operational activities for development. While my delegation has no fundamental objection to this proposal, we need to make sure that it does not result in an unwieldy body that would have little time to give to individual programmes. The experience of the Economic and Social Council in seeking to carry out its mandate should be borne in mind.

We agree that the established procedures for selection of the criteria for setting the relative priorities should be strictly applied by the intergovernmental machinery and the Secretariat, and that the medium-term plan should be made to serve as "the principal policy directive" for the programme budget. The oversight and legislative bodies - the Committee for Programme and Co-ordination (CPC) and the Economic and Social Council - should ensure fulfilment of their mandates. We note that a start has been made in addressing these issues. ...

The Group of High-level Intergovernmental Experts has recommended that a comprehensive study of the intergovernmental machinery and its function be carried out, and its findings presented to the General Assembly no later than at its forty-third session. At the same time, the Group has recommended a substantial reduction in the number of staff members at all levels. While we think that this is a laudable goal, we would prefer to have these reductions considered in relation to the study, in order to ensure that there is no negative impact on the programme activities determined by the General Assembly and other legislative bodies. The suggested percentages seem to have been taken out of the air. We note that the Secretary-General has emphasized the relationship between possible changes in the intergovernmental machinery and modifications in the size, composition and work of the Secretariat staff.

My delegation strongly supports the maintenance of a highly motivated, efficient and competent international civil service. Proposed changes in the conditions of service should be examined by the International Civil Service Commission to ensure system-wide application. We believe that only with predictable personnel policies will the United Nations be able to attract and retain the calibre of staff needed to implement its programmes. ...

The recommendations concerning the number of staff on fixed-term contracts do not appear to have taken into account those Member States that have fewer than 10 nationals - sometimes two or three - employed in the Secretariat. We also believe that permanent appointments should be related to job performance, and not to the staff member's country of origin.

My delegation has studied carefully the different proposals submitted by the Group on the planning and budget mechanism. ... At this time ... I will note that my delegation believes that the functions of CPC and of the Advisory Committee on Administrative and Budgetary Questions should be retained in their present form. It would, however, be useful for CPC to have available to it information on the level of resources required for implementing the programme budget. ...

We agree ... that the procedures and methods of work of the General Assembly, the Economic and Social Council and their subsidiary bodies should be streamlined, and that the Committee on Conferences should be strengthened. It seems to us, however, that the level of resources allocated to conference services must be an integral part of the budget process, since conferences and meetings are mandated by legislative bodies. Similarly, the creation of a new body by the General Assembly cannot be arbitrarily linked to the discontinuing of an existing one, without regard to the functions mandated. We assume that the recommendation was intended to emphasize the need for periodic review by the General Assembly of the functions and work programmes of its subsidiary bodies.

There are other recommendations about which my delegation has some serious reservations. These include recommendation 24, in which it is suggested that UNDP take over the functions performed by the Office of the United Nations Disaster Relief Co-ordinator - an obvious incompatibility - and recommendation 25 (2) on the integration of the Centre for Science and

Technology for Development into the Department of International Economic and Social Affairs and the Department of Technical Co-operation for Development."

The representative of **Rwanda**[76]

"First, there must be full respect for the Charter, one of the cardinal principles of which is the sovereign equality of States. That principle cannot be brought into disrepute or violated in any way.

Secondly, we must safeguard the prerogatives of intergovernmental bodies, particularly as regards programming future activities, co-ordination and monitoring. In this respect the prerogatives of the General Assembly, the Economic and Social Council and the Secretary-General as regards programming and drawing up priorities must be respected.

Thirdly, the reforms envisaged should not place the Secretary-General, who is the chief administrative officer responsible for the managing and carrying out of programmes, in a rigid institutional framework within which his freedom of action and right to take initiative would be impeded. We re-elected him only four days ago. ...

Fourthly, the mechanisms for drawing up programmes and setting the order of priorities for programmes and sub-programmes are perhaps not operating to the full satisfaction of all Member States. We must have the courage to acknowledge that, if it is the case. But we must also have the courage to improve their effectiveness if, after careful consideration, we realize that the rules and regulations governing their operation are outdated. If, on the other hand, this examination shows that the present rules and regulations are satisfactory, we must look for the reasons why they have not been respected and apply the appropriate remedy.

My delegation does not believe that it was a good idea to propose the creation of alternative mechanisms before this thorough, objective consideration of the rules under which the existing mechanisms operated had taken place. It could only agree to this approach if it were assured that the needs that justified the establishment of the existing mechanisms no longer existed or that the new substitute mechanisms would be more effective.

Fifthly, the right to establish priorities in programmes cannot be the prerogative of certain countries, but must be the right of all Member States of the Organization and of the deliberative bodies, particularly the General Assembly and the Economic and Social Council.

Sixthly, the idea of large and small contributors, which is being increasingly introduced, could distort the facts of the problem and divert our discussion, which we want to be sincere, objective and constructive. My delegation is convinced that, in order to collect the contributions due to the Organization, all the contributing Member States must make an effort which is perhaps quantitatively disproportionate, if one takes into account the figures, but qualitatively comparable. The disproportion in the amounts paid to the Organization should not be the basis for unequal treatment among Member States or confer any prerogative for speaking on behalf of so-called small contributors."

The representative of **Bangladesh**[77]

"First, since no single suggestion mentioned in section C of chapter VI of the report can attract universal acceptance, the points of agreement must lie somewhere in between. Secondly, existing planning and budget mechanisms, comprising the Committee for Programme and Co-ordination and the Advisory Committee on Administrative and Budgetary Questions, continue to enjoy a degree of acceptance owing to their proved utility. We should therefore aim at rationalizing those mechanisms further, particularly specifying their respective roles *vis-à-vis* each other. Thirdly, to change the mode of decision-making in the budgetary process so as to give virtual power of veto to one Member State or a group of Member States would be tantamount to amending the Charter, which would be unacceptable. A practical procedure might therefore be devised to facilitate broad agreement while fully preserving the principle of the sovereign equality of States as enshrined in the Charter. Fourthly, the Fifth Committee, in accordance with its existing mandate, should continue to have a say in budgetary matters.

Deliberations on the budgetary process will remain incomplete if we limit ourselves to a discussion on allocation and disbursement, leaving the funding aspect untouched. Consideration of the scale of assessment therefore assumes importance. The scale of assessment is an important index of the financial commitment of Member States to the United Nations. There appears to be an intrinsic linkage between the need for consensus on the budgetary process and the need for agreement on the scale of assessment. We had expected that the Group would give its views on this important aspect as well.

As for the specific recommendations in the report, particularly those dealing with personnel, the structure of the Secretariat and the functioning of the intergovernmental machinery, we believe that these can be implemented without undue delay, in the interest of securing a leaner, healthier and more effective United Nations. Those recommendations are the product of a long deliberative process spread over the course of years on which there is scarcely any scope for further disagreement by Member States. We should like in this connection to emphasize that this process of streamlining the United Nations system need not end with the implementation of these recommendations. Should we find during this process of implementation that we need to go further, the Assembly must not hesitate to take the necessary action."

The representative of **Egypt**[78]

"The decision-making procedure of the General Assembly stems from the nature of the United Nations itself and gives expression to the historical reality and democratic character of this Organization. We must not lose sight of the fact that the adoption of resolutions by consensus, though attractive, is a double-edged weapon that could completely paralyse the General Assembly, or at the very least confine its activities to a very limited number of areas; and it could lead to obstruction of the Organization's pioneering role in many other fields concerning which consensus may be reached gradually.

Egypt believes that all Member States of the Organization are responsible for and keenly interested in the management of its finances in such a way as to achieve optimum rationalization and efficiency. Egypt believes that it is necessary to give all Member States the opportunity to play their part and that no committee dealing with that matter should have its membership confined to a limited number of States, whether representation in such committees is at the level of experts or of States."

The representative of **Romania**[79]

"We could never accept measures which would limit and then reduce essential political and economic activities or affect the democratic principles which underlie the functioning of the United Nations, first and foremost of which is the equal sovereignty of States, whether small, medium-sized or large. We should emphasize especially the importance that should be attached to the General Assembly as the major political body of the United Nations, where all States, regardless of their size, can voice their views and act in accordance with their own rights and interests. In this connection we believe that no measures or decisions should be taken that might limit the prerogatives or competence of the General Assembly, the conditions for its functioning, or its ability to consider any issue pertaining to international peace and security and international relations in general. It is not by weakening the role of the General Assembly that we shall increase the administrative and financial efficiency of the United Nations. On the contrary, we can do that only by permanently strengthening its position as the most representative body of the United Nations. ..."

It is quite clear that major savings could be made by improving the structures and functioning of the Secretariat and by substantially reducing the excessive and constantly increasing administrative costs of the Organization, above all staff costs. Accordingly we should take firm and consistent action to improve the intergovernmental machinery of the United Nations and simplify the Secretariat, eliminate useless structures and overlapping, improve working methods and reduce bureaucracy, substantially increase productivity and make full use of working hours. Only thus can we succeed in improving the efficiency of the administrative functioning of the Organization and significantly reduce administrative costs as a whole, and staff costs in particular. The staffing of the Secretariat must be both rational and equitable, so that all Member States are properly represented. ...

Another category of recommendations would appear, at least in their current wording, to be totally unacceptable, since they are in flagrant contradiction with previous decisions of the General Assembly and even with the Charter. ...

I should like to make myself perfectly clear. We are not against permanent contracts, even though the quality of work would not necessarily depend directly on the type of commitment. However, we are concerned about the exaggerated proportion of permanent contracts in the total number of Secretariat staff contracts. The actual relationship between permanent contracts and fixed-term contracts, in our view, is disproportionate and is in favour of the former.

This situation has a negative impact on the equitable representation of States Members, as well as on the efficiency and work productivity of the Secretariat. Consequently, we are of the view that this ratio should be corrected substantially in the near future so as to enable all States Members to be represented in an equitable manner.

The acceptance of permanent contracts comes within the exclusive purview of each State Member. No one can dictate to a State Member a policy to be adopted in this regard or how many of its nationals should have permanent or fixed-term contracts. Consequently, the recommendations in the report of the Group of experts, which seem to impose some rules and regulations in this regard, are completely unacceptable to the Rumanian delegation. ...

It is a legitimate requirement that all States Members can have the opportunity to take part on an equal footing in all stages of the process of preparing and approving the budget. By the same token, we should prevent any situation arising whereby a State Member might be able to attach conditions to the amount of its contribution to the budget. Through this increased involvement of States Members, we do not at all mean stricter monitoring of programmes by States which make larger contributions. It might seem superfluous to emphasize that the programming of the Organization's activities should be quite consistent with the financial resources available to it. I would add, nevertheless, that these resources should not in any way be viewed as constantly increasing amounts. On the contrary, what we should do, without delay, is to undertake a reduction in budget expenditures, an aim which States Members and the General Assembly have always tried to achieve. ...

Special attention, we feel, should be paid to the idea that we should establish consensus in the process of preparing and approving the United Nations budget. To be sure, it is always preferable - and for Romania this is the preferred method - that consensus be constantly encouraged and used in order to adopt the largest possible number of resolutions and decisions in the General Assembly.

Romania has always striven to have its own proposals adopted by general agreement. Nevertheless, the Rumanian delegation is of the view that we should be very careful so that the laudable intention of adopting budgetary decisions by consensus does not result in deadlock. In fact, the introduction of a second right of veto - above and beyond that already officially enshrined in the Charter - would be more than the Organization could bear."

The representative of **Saudi Arabia**[80]

"This Organization is at present being subjected to challenges, not only to its sovereignty but also to its very viability. The current financial and institutional difficulties should not let us forget the experience of the League of Nations in the 1930s, when policies based on short-term political interests glorified nationalism, unilateralism, the erosion of the rule of law, and the cult of power politics destroyed the League of Nations and led directly to global conflagration. ...

If this world body falls short of expectations, the responsibility must be heavily shared by the big contributors, who, perhaps, expect the United Nations to be modelled on their own image. Therefore we simply cannot agree with any rationale that obligatory contributions by any Member State can be withheld. ... Moreover, the decision-making process of the United Nations should give full recognition to the principle of the sovereign equality of all States. The balance of influence in favour of the wealthy and the powerful is already manifest in some major organs: the Security Council and the Economic and Social Council, to mention only two. ...

The present scale of assessments makes the United Nations too vulnerable since it is dependent upon the few big contributors. When any of them cuts its contributions, the basis for the work of the entire Organization is affected. If assessments were distributed more evenly among Members which are able to pay, we should be able to reduce this vulnerability in the future. ...

As far as the Group's proposals to streamline the Secretariat are concerned, we support the proposal that the number of staff members be reduced by 15 per cent and the number at the higher levels by 25 per cent. ... The rotation of senior posts, every one of them, should also be a basic principle of administrative streamlining. Moreover, the total entitlements, salaries and other conditions of service of staff members should be considered in the light of levels of worth and standards that would encourage the recruitment of highly qualified and capable international staff. It is quality that should be stressed rather than quantity. ...

Streamlining and personnel cuts should, however, be accompanied by a reform of the intergovernmental machinery and its functioning as well. Over the years we have - as the Group of 18 notes - built an overly complex institutional structure which lacks cohesion in certain areas and which makes co-ordination difficult. A long-term solution to the present crisis must be found in a more coherent and effective programme. Member States should therefore give guidance for the rationalization of this Organization and should set the relevant priorities. ...

While we support budget cuts to meet reductions in assessed contributions, the objective of the entire exercise should not be the maximum budget reduction, regardless of consequences, but rather the achievement of a coherent and effective programme of activity for the Secretariat and the Organization as a whole. Reforms should be carried out in full accordance with the provisions of the United Nations Charter. The principle of the sovereign equality of all Member States should not be tampered with, and essential programmes and activities of high priority pertaining to live and burning issues, such as those concerning Palestine, South Africa, Afghanistan and others, should continue to attract their proper share of available resources."

The representative of **Argentina**[81]

"Chapter VI, concerning methods of analyzing the Organization's planning and budget procedure, remains an outstanding issue. That is not surprising, because politically it is one of the most delicate subjects the Group of Experts had to deal with. ...

We agree with a number of representatives who have already spoken that we must not confine ourselves to choosing one of the alternative formulas put forward by the Group of Experts. The solution might be to combine some elements of alternatives (a) and (b). ... Ideas such as the earlier participation of Governments in the budget process and earlier notification to the Secretary-General of the amount of available resources might be a practical basis for agreement at the current session.

As regards the specific planning and budget machinery, if a single body is not established to deal with both those problems together, and we are instead to continue with the present division of labour between the Committee for Programme and Co-ordination and the Advisory Committee on Administrative and Budgetary Questions, we believe that any solution we adopt must make perfectly clear the sphere of competence of each body, to avoid any overlapping, which might create undesirable conflicts. ...

As regards what method should be followed in the decision-making process, we believe that here, as elsewhere, it is necessary to exhaust all efforts to achieve a consensus and ensure the broadest possible basis for understanding. However, we cannot rule out the decision-making procedures provided for in the Charter. Anything of essential importance to the work of the United Nations, such as the budget, must be adopted within certain time-limits, if the Organization is not to be paralysed."

The representative of **Trinidad and Tobago**[82]

"There are many facets to the situation: there is a financial crisis, there is a political crisis, there is a challenge to multilateralism and there is in a most fundamental sense a crisis of confidence. ...

In the 40 years of its existence changing international circumstances and challenges have led to a significant expansion in the scope and volume of the work of the Organization, as demonstrated by the agenda of the United Nations, the programmes and activities undertaken, the number of conferences and meetings and the growth of the United Nations Secretariat itself. Even if that growth was gradual, there is no evidence that it was planned and orchestrated; rather, the Organization has undertaken numerous *ad hoc* measures to cope with immediate requirements at various times. ...

If we consider those recommendations related to the Secretariat and to personnel, many questions come to mind. There are specific recommendations related to a substantial reduction in the number of staff members, and there are general recommendations relating to the streamlining of departments and offices. But what is not clear is whether the streamlining exercise is to be pursued independently of, or in order to achieve, the 15 or 25 per cent recommended reduction.

Furthermore, the specific reductions suggested do not appear to have been arrived at in a scientific manner but, rather, appear to have leapt out as convenient targets. The same is true of the recommendation regarding the reduction in the use of outside consultants. It seems that before making a decision on those recommendations it will be necessary for us to examine possible ways in which they may be implemented and the various implications of those possibilities.

For example, we should have some basic framework and guidelines for effecting reductions in staff while maintaining the principles of geographic distribution, the highest standards of staff competence and the situation of women in the Secretariat. It is simply not enough to claim that this can be achieved by attrition, without specifying how all relevant conditions, including the continuing need to recruit new staff members and avoid any negative effects on the implementation of programmes, could be satisfied.

The recommendation regarding the reduction of the total entitlements of staff members is dangerously open-ended. It is likely to engender great unease among staff and unions. In an Organization in which 80 per cent of expenses can be attributed to staff costs, it is obvious that the staff will have to bear a part of the necessary financial paring, but this must not be done without due regard for the effects of staff morale and efficiency - the efficiency not only of those who have been affected, but even more of those who are not sure whether they will be. It is therefore necessary to ensure improvements in personnel management and career-development policies as part of the overall framework of reforms. It is imperative that in arriving at decisions which relate directly to staff there be full consultation with staff representatives in accordance with accepted industrial relations principles and practices. ...

It is also important that the planning and budget procedure which is finally adopted by us conform to the established rules and practices of decision-making within the Organization.

The founding nations conferred upon certain members of the Security Council the power of veto. The General Assembly was left unfettered, assuring each nation of sovereign equality. We must not permit the introduction of any such disabilities in this area of decision making."

The representative of **Côte d'Ivoire**[83]

"the search for greater efficiency at any price must not serve as a convenient pretext for implicit questioning of what constitutes the common denominator of the Organization, gives it its originality and constitutes its essence - that is, the principle of the absolute equality of all States Members and of respect for their sovereignty, whatever the level of their contribution to the Organization's budget. To tamper even indirectly with that principle under the cover of apparently neutral technical reforms would be to deprive the Organization of its ethic, its soul and its *raison d'être*. That would be, in the final analysis, gradually to condemn it, through disaffection and disillusionment to inertia. It would be to destroy a great hope, for which the peoples would never forgive us. ...

Furthermore, the United Nations, given its responsibilities, is an essentially political organization, therefore its administration and financial functioning cannot always accommodate methods and evaluation criteria in use in other financial or economic organizations. Its efforts, no doubt slow but patient, gradual, persevering and praiseworthy, in favour of peace, international co-operation, development and a better understanding among peoples, which is its mission and its final objective, could not be measured solely in terms of financial ratios or economic cost-effectiveness. ...

Taking into account the foregoing, it goes without saying that a voting system which called into question the principles I have mentioned or any violation of the prerogatives of legislative bodies, which would be tantamount to a *de facto* revision of the Charter, would not have the support of my delegation.

The first part of the report emphasizes the agreement among the experts in Chapters I to V and therefore makes clear-cut recommendations. In this connection and as regards the report's recommendations on the structure of the Secretariat and on the staff, my delegation agrees with the views of the experts who ask that there be a secretariat structure which might be more rational, streamlined and less top-heavy and the establishment of a staff policy which would be more consistent and orderly. The recommendations formulated by the experts with that end in view, favouring a reduction of certain posts, on management, staff, as well as those on recruitment procedures and on the proportion of permanent and fixed-term staff present no difficulty to my delegation. ...

There can be no doubt that the sensitive question of the budget and planning machinery is the nexus of the entire report of the Group of High-level Experts. ...

What we need is a negotiated political solution. The truth is that we cannot lay down a practical procedure which might facilitate and encourage overall agreement on the budget as long as there continue to be political differences which set State Members against each other on questions of substance. That is where the problem lies.   No intergovernmental machinery, however intelligent it might be, will fill the chronic budgetary deficit of the United Nations if the profound divisions continue among members of the Organization on the programme budget."

The representative of **Tunisia**[84]

"My delegation is open to any solution that would improve the administrative and financial functioning of the Organization as stipulated in the mandate of the Group of Experts.   However, we cannot endorse any form of rigid machinery that might impede the functioning of the Organization, rather than facilitate it. It now seems to be agreed and accepted that many delegations are opposed to any budgetary process that would exclude States whose contributions are at a fairly low level. My delegation is in favour of a budgetary process that would first and foremost take into account the desire of Member States to take part, from the outset, in the preparation of the budget and in the choice of priorities. These objectives can be achieved and we already have proposals in this connection."

The representative of **Nigeria**[85]

"On the whole, our attitude to the recommendations on which there was consensus agreement in the Group is quite positive. I feel able to state that Nigeria can support these recommendations in principle, although we shall need to know how the Secretary-General proposes to implement them. ...

We are concerned by the apparent lack of in-depth analysis of the issues considered by the Group and the apparent undue emphasis on expenditure reduction, which seems to us to suggest that the Group was more concerned with reducing the budget than with identifying lasting and meaningful measures for real improvement of the Organization. We note that the review called for in recommendation 8 of the report is restricted to intergovernmental bodies in the economic and social fields only and does not cover intergovernmental bodies dealing with political and other activities. ... We will support such reviews only if the objective is to strengthen and enhance the role and, indeed, the responsibility of the United Nations in promoting the economic and social development of its Members. We will not be able to support any review of this sector that aims at reducing the scope and role of the United Nations at a time when multilateral co-operation for development is being eroded.

We welcome recommendations to reduce the number of conferences, rationalize the work agenda of intergovernmental organs and their subsidiaries, and streamline and merge departments. These measures, in combination with other measures substantially to reduce documentation and publications, will, if properly implemented, be healthy for our Organization. However, "rationalization", "consolidation", "streamlining" and other such terms, should not become code words for deprogramming. ...

All recommendations touching on the acquired rights, salary and other entitlements of United Nations staff should properly, we believe, be referred to the International Civil Service Commission, because of the obvious legal and contractual issues involved, which only the Commission is competent to handle. The Assembly's decision should be taken only after the Commission has submitted its views. ...

We are all aware of the fact that there has been disagreement over the content and level of the budget for a number of years, owing largely to political disagreement among Member States on the scope of the United Nations programme, which many Member States find beneficial. However, a new, added dimension to the problem is the emerging notion that Member States that account for the major part of the budget should have a greater vote in decisions relating to budgetary matters.

Although we all remain eloquently silent on this dimension of the problem, no one can ignore the fact that it has a major bearing on the failure within the Group of 18 to agree on the procedure for programme planning and the budget process. An acceptable solution must preserve the authority of the General Assembly and indeed the prerogatives of the Secretary-General in the formulation of budget proposals."

The representative of **Jordan**[86]

"Thirdly, many of the recommendations call for consolidation of departments, reduction of the staff of certain departments, the streamlining of the activities of some and the abolition of others. This is particularly relevant to chapter III, sections B, C, and D. We find much merit in many of these recommendations, especially in view of the growth in the activities undertaken by the Organization, the changing needs of its Member States and the ability of the United Nations to respond to these needs. There are, however, specific cases, such as recommendation 22, dealing with special economic assistance programmes, that have to be further examined. ...

We attach great importance to personnel questions because we are dealing with the human element and we are talking about the largest component in the budget. Our judgement is guided by a number of criteria: maintenance and upgrading of the quality, integrity, and competence of the staff; more equitable geographical distribution; non-application of pressure by Member States; competitive working conditions to attract and maintain the best; reduction of staff and redeployment allowing for a turnover of new and young blood. In this respect my delegation is ready to endorse recommendation 15 and we look forward to the submission by the Secretary-General of a co-ordinated and sequential plan. ...

Sixthly, a lack of co-ordination has been the cause of many deficiencies and much waste. This is true at Headquarters and it is also true in the field. Attempts have been made in the past and are suggested in the report to redress such situations. In the wake of attempts towards a restructuring of the United Nations system, the creation of the post of Director-General for Development and International Economic Co-operation, with its limitations, and the designation of Resident Co-ordinators in the field, one is sorry to conclude that co-ordination has not improved. The contrary seems to be true. One major reason for such a deteriorating situation is the position taken by Member States themselves. We, the Governments, or our representatives in the different legislative bodies of the United Nations system allow and even encourage the proliferation of departments and field offices, or call for an organ or organization to undertake activities that are already covered by an existing one. ...

The budgetary process is of paramount importance. There seems to be a convergence of views on a number of points, including: the participation of Member States in the decision-making process; adherence to rules and procedures set by the General Assembly on priorities; improvement of intergovernmental machinery; and the importance of co-ordinated programme planning and programme budgeting. This convergence of views should be carried further to make it possible for practical procedures to be adopted and for broad agreement to be reached on the content and level of the budget."

The representative of **Sri Lanka**[87]

"The specific recommendations in chapter II, section A of the report deals with a number of suggestions relating to changes in the intergovernmental machinery of the United Nations, some of which can be implemented without much delay if the Assembly approves. Sri Lanka can certainly support most of them. But, we must keep in mind that any changes should not act to the detriment of important political and economic objectives and programmes being pursued through this intergovernmental machinery. We can certainly rationalize the functioning of many United Nations bodies, like the Economic and Social Council (ECOSOC) and the Main Committees, but we must not cripple them either by overloading them or by paring down their resources to the extent of reducing them to the point of ineffectiveness.

While the Secretariat of the United Nations certainly needs reorganization, our eventual decisions in respect of chapters III and IV of the report must not trim the fat to the extent of damaging essential muscle and sinew. The quality, commitment and competence of the staff must be maintained at a high level if the Secretariat is to live up to the high expectations all of us have of it. Salaries, terms and conditions must be kept at a level attractive enough to bring in, develop and retain the best international talent available. The nurturing, with due consideration for geographical balance, of a professional cadre with a high sense of loyalty, motivation and dedication as impartial international civil servants will be a major contribution to the efficient running of the United Nations. ...

We observe that Member States have very little opportunity to put in a word about the size of the budget or the apportionment of resources to the programmes of the United Nations. Hence the need to make practical arrangements to draw up a budget which is both financially sound and reflective of liabilities is vital. All Members should have a hand in its formulation. The question of seeking the widest possible level of support, if not unanimity, both on the level and content of the budget and on the methodology for deciding and implementing priorities in many respects constitutes the crux of the problem. ...

Although not part of the report, my delegation sees some merit in a review of the provisions of Article 19 of the Charter with the view to perhaps reducing the grace period for arrears. A stricter adherence to Article 17 and prompt payment of assessed contributions will assist in the short term."

The representative of **Colombia**[88]

"My delegation supports, in general, the proposals presented by the Group of 18, but we are not prepared to support each and every one of the recommendations in detail. Some of the recommendations are worded too vaguely, and in fact some recommendations contradict others. In addition, there are some proposals for which proper justification is not given, and if they were adopted they might just give rise to new problems. Therefore, the Assembly should refrain from taking a hasty decision that would only postpone dealing with problems, or even create or worsen problems."

The representative of **Pakistan**[89]

"We consider it vital for the future of this Organization that any changes in the machinery and procedures for evolving a broader agreement on budgetary matters should be entirely consistent with the Charter. The powers of the General Assembly in this field must be fully respected. It is equally important to maintain the necessary balance between the Secretary-General's prerogative to propose and the intergovernmental responsibility to review the budget of the Organization. ...

In the administrative sector there is a clear need to minimize administrative costs so that maximum resources can be allocated to substantive activities. Unfortunately, the High-level Group has not made any concrete recommendations in this area. We would have welcomed clearer guidelines for improving efficiency and reducing costs, such as a possible benchmark or target figure for administrative costs as a proportion of the total budget.

With regard to personnel, my delegation agrees entirely with the view expressed by the Secretary-General that the United Nations must continue to attract the most qualified staff in order to fulfil its functions effectively. Merit should be the paramount consideration in recruitment and retention of staff. Any reduction to be carried out should take into account the need for humane and fair treatment. Furthermore, any formula for staff reductions should allow for flexibility as to precise numbers or percentages. In this field, more than any other, the prerogatives of the Secretary-General as the chief administrative officer under the Charter should be fully respected.

In the common services area we see considerable scope for improvements and cost reductions without affecting the quality of services provided to Member States. In this regard, among other measures, a review of standard costs which were established a long time ago could yield positive results.

There are many important areas which reflect on the efficiency of the Secretariat and the intergovernmental machinery which have escaped the attention of the High-level Group. One of the most important questions in this regard relates to the scale of assessment which, based on our recent experience, must be taken up in any comprehensive exercise aimed at making the United Nations more effective and financially viable."

The representative of **China**[90]

"Equality of all States irrespective of size is the most basic principle of the Charter and the very foundation on which the Organization is established. The effectiveness of the Organization will be lasting and just only when it is based on universal equality among all Member States. In essence, the advantage of the United Nations lies precisely in the fact that all Member States, rich or poor, big or small, enjoy equal rights. We should not only affirm but, above all, endeavour to uphold this principle. Only when the weak are free from the bullying of the strong, the small have the respect of the big, can the United Nations play a fuller role. Should the principle of equal rights be trampled on and replaced by such ideas as "buying rights with money", or "more money, more rights", or "no more rights, no more money", thereby turning the United Nations into a commercial entity where issues are judged not on merits but on the criterion of money, the great edifice built here by the founding fathers would be shaken to its very foundation. We should understand that the United Nations, entrusted with a noble historical mission, has from its very inception never been based on money. ...

The present crisis confronting the United Nations is the result of the syndrome of financial shortage and political inaction. While neither of the two should be overlooked, the latter is of a more fundamental character. Any prescription that may enable the Organization to weather the current crisis will have to be found in the self-criticism of Member States and sought in the necessary reforms. ...

There are indeed areas of great waste in the United Nations. The proliferation of documents and meetings has not only overstrained our financial capacities but has also seriously undermined our efforts to improve efficiency. The reform of intergovernmental bodies has become imperative. The Secretariat is bloated. The overlapping and overstaffing of departments and offices must be corrected. ...

The Chinese delegation cannot concur in certain recommendations in the report. For instance, proposal (a) in chapter VI suggests that decisions on budgetary matters be made by consensus, which may well result in abuse and invite a quasi-veto. We are in favour of efforts to seek consensus but can never agree to nullify the existing democratic procedures provided by the Charter on account of such consensus. Again in the report, recommendations 55 and 57 reflect different propositions with regard to the ratio between fixed-term and permanent contracts of staff members employed in the United Nations. We hold that the question of the length of employment of a staff member is a matter which has been affirmed by General Assembly resolutions in the past and should not be changed."

The representative of the **German Democratic Republic**[91]

"It is ... completely inconceivable and unacceptable that, using the pretext of shortcomings as regards its efficiency in the administrative and financial fields, the material and financial basis for the entire activities of the Organization should be jeopardized by the unilateral measures of one Member State. Under such a pretext, it is intended that the Organization should not only abandon consideration of its main tasks but should also be politically blackmailed.

... recommendations as those on the rationalization of conferences and documentation, on the avoidance of duplication of work and overlapping of agendas, on the simplification of structures or on the reduction of staff could be adopted by the General Assembly immediately after consideration of the modalities of their implementation by the Fifth Committee and ensuring their adequate control by relevant intergovernmental bodies. Such measures would favourably influence cost-effectiveness and make budgetary reductions possible. ...

The German Democratic Republic welcomes ... the recommendation that an intergovernmental body, to be designated by the General Assembly, should study how a higher degree of effectiveness of the organs in the economic and social fields can be achieved by modified structuring and organization. It should also be the task of that body, in the view of my delegation, to study the usefulness and feasibility of the recommendation on merging the management of operational activities and funds with the United Nations Development Programme (UNDP), and on improving the co-ordination of the co-operation of organs and organizations within the United Nations system in the economic and social fields. ...

Like other delegations, my delegation holds the view that the responsibility of the General Assembly for the size of the budget, for the stipulation of priorities and for financing certain activities must be strengthened. It should be clearly stated that the actual available resources and the priorities jointly set by the Member States must be taken into account to a greater extent than before.

Therefore, it is important, above all, that the process of planning and budgeting be unified and that the Member States have the opportunity to examine the proposals more thoroughly prior to their adoption. ...

A few recommendations, however, do not promote the attainment of the declared objective of enhancing the effectiveness of the United Nations. Indeed, they are diametrically opposed to that aim, contradict the Charter and fundamental decisions of the General Assembly and are designed exclusively to promote one-sided political interests. I refer to some points contained in the recommendations regarding personnel, especially the issue of the ratio between permanent staff members and staff members on fixed-term appointments. ...

We agree with the demand that the standards for the selection of competent candidates for the respective posts have to be constantly reviewed and raised. It remains to be seen, however, whether the procedure of competitive examinations, which, owing to its enormous cost is questioned by other countries besides mine, will lead to an improvement. At least the general extension of that procedure to P-3 posts seems to be inadmissible and in contradiction with the resolutions of the General Assembly. As regards the second component, namely, "recruiting the staff on as wide a geographical basis as possible", although this has been repeatedly described by the General Assembly as a necessity for equitable geographical representation, it has by no means been substantially taken into account. ...

It is not for lack of qualified candidates that the under-representation has not been overcome, but the fact that a large number of existing posts are occupied by staff with permanent contracts. Consequently, for a staff member of the Secretariat, after he has been appointed on a permanent basis, his efficiency and qualifications matter only with regard to his promotion or upgrading, not with regard to his employment as such. Frankly, this outdated type of personnel policy is not only in contrast to the principle of performance which determines employment in government administration, science, industry and agriculture in my own country but also completely contrary to the performance standards applied in science and industry in, for instance, the United States.

The endorsement of permanent contracts as a desirable principle for the United Nations Secretariat cannot be supported by my delegation. The ratio of no more than 50 per cent of nationals appointed on a fixed-term basis, as proposed in recommendations 55 and 57, is totally unacceptable. Such an approach constitutes discriminatory interference in the freedom of choice of a candidate of the conditions under which he wants to serve in the world Organization.

We are not opposed to repeated or even long-term renewals of fixed-term contracts, since an experienced and competent staff is indispensable. We recommend, however, consideration of whether it would not better serve the enhancement of effectiveness if the performance and qualifications of a staff member were examined in relation to the required standards for his post as a pre-condition of renewal of the contract each time the fixed-term contract expired.

Furthermore, the German Democratic Republic would have appreciated it if the Group of 18 had developed new ideas on ensuring application of the principle of equitable geographical representation in the international Secretariat of the United Nations and had reaffirmed, at least for under-represented countries, the procedure of replacement as it applied previously. The recruitment freeze further increased the existing disproportions. This trend of development absolutely must be stopped. In view of the complexity of the questions dealt with in chapter IV of the report, my delegation is ready to support the proposal already put forward several times in this debate to refer the entire complex of problems to the International Civil Service Commission (ICSC) for further consideration."

The representative of **Mexico**[92]

"The delegation of Mexico is prepared to accept most of the recommendations of the Group, as they appear in the report. However, we agree with those delegations which have said that some of the recommendations require further consideration and require certain alterations and refinements if they are to be implemented effectively, and if they are really to be directed to improving the efficiency of the administrative and financial functioning of the Organization. Here, without now going into details, we would refer the Assembly to recommendations 3 (e); 8 (3) (d); 15, 22 and 24. ...

Regarding Chapter VI, on Planning and budget procedure, we noted that the 18 experts could not reach agreement, in spite of the fact that the views expressed coincided on many points. Here, my delegation would like to express its preference for what is called the alternative (b). ...

Rather than clinging to any of the opinions which have been set forth in the report it might be best to work on the basis of commonly agreed aims, which should include strengthening the efficiency of the Organization, in strict accordance with the purposes and provisions of the Charter, establishing budgetary machinery that would allow Member States to participate more actively in the preparation of the medium-term plan and the programme budget, in order to carry out the necessary intergovernmental orientation, from the very beginning of the budgetary process; improving the functioning of the Committee on Programme and Co-ordination (CPC), while ensuring that its terms of reference are applied strictly in keeping with the rules governing programme planning and the programming aspects of the budget; establishing a clear division of responsibilities between CPC and the Advisory Committee on Administrative and Budgetary Questions (ACABQ), and establish a system whereby Member States could agree at the outset on an indicative total for the funds needed for the budgetary biennium, together with a specification of the so-called "add-ons", or additional expenses. ...

It has been said that the process of reform in the procedures for planning and budgeting has caused a lingering feeling of doubt and concern. If that is true, it is because it cannot be accepted that the process of reform should be used to disguise a desire for a weighted voting system in the decision-making process, either openly or in a covert manner, or to employ budgetary pressure to coerce the Organization. There certainly cannot be agreement, if that is indeed the intention. If it is not the intention, then there is no reason why this process should be a painful one."

The representative of the United Kingdom, speaking on behalf of the 12 member States of the **European Community**[93]

"Every country, both large and small, should not only have its voice heard, but be assured that it is heard. But we should also face up to political realities. As the Secretary-General pointed out last December, even though the budget then adopted by the Fifth Committee provided for a real growth of only 0.1 per cent, Member States which accounted for almost 80 per cent of the assessed budget either cast a negative vote or abstained in the vote. ... It is plainly unsatisfactory when the budget, which reflects the Organization's work, is a matter for serious contention. The Twelve believe that a solution must be found to the problem of promoting agreement on key budgetary issues.

The recommendations of the Group of 18 comprise administrative and financial reforms of the kind which any organization must implement if it is to achieve efficiency and effectiveness. After 40 years of growth and activity it is appropriate for the United Nations to have a spring-cleaning. The recommendations will help us to do that. They provide an essential basis for the changes which the Organization will need to implement if it is to secure its long-term well-being. ...

The bulk of the experts' recommendations - in Chapters I to V of the report - seem to us to be valuable, constructive, necessary and at times self-evident. That is why we can accept them broadly as they stand. ...

The Twelve have given careful consideration to those issues, which in our view go to the heart of the political and financial problems that beset the Organization. We believe that changes should be made in the system, changes which will produce broader consensus on financial issues and help overcome the reluctance of some members to meet their financial obligations. In particular, we support the creation of an improved mechanism to consider the programme budget, structured so as to ensure effective decision-making and to contribute to greater rationalization and efficiency within the system. We are firm in our support for the Charter and for a strong and effective

Organization. Greater budgetary discipline, improved co-ordination and rigorous adherence to priorities can only strengthen the Organization and ensure its future stability and vigour."

The representative of **India**[94]

"We must stress, however, that in the name of reform no action must be taken that would dilute the principle of sovereign equality and the democratic functioning of the Organization. ...

A number of recommendations relate not only to the United Nations but also to its subsidiary organizations, the specialized agencies, the International Monetary Fund and the World Bank. We concur with the view that co-ordination between those organizations needs to be strengthened so that common approaches and strategies are developed to deal with pressing economic and social problems. However, our delegation wishes to reiterate that in the entire system the position of primacy held by the United Nations at the apex of the hierarchy must be maintained. Those recommendations of the Group, along with their implementation, must be viewed in such a perspective.

The Group has noted that there has been a significant growth in the intergovernmental machinery resulting from the expansion of an agenda which has become not only more diversified but also more complex. A reflection of this growth is the increase in the number of conferences and meetings and the concomitant growth in the volume of documentation. The volume of documentation has increased beyond the limits which allow delegations to use it productively. The rapid growth of the agenda has not made it possible always to permit the required attention to be paid to co-ordination. My delegation concurs with these findings. However, we wish to state that the growth in the size of the agenda over the last 40 years is a reflection of the increasing importance of the United Nations and the expanding number of areas in which Member States have decided to take action in a multilateral framework. The growth in the size of the agenda is not necessarily a bad thing in itself, though we also believe that attention needs to be paid to improving the manner in which these agenda items are dealt with in the various forums of the United Nations. Such improvements could facilitate the concentration of effort by Member States on reaching agreements on ways and means of solving the problems facing them.

Though we agree that the volume of documentation is excessive, our delegation believes that another aspect, that of the quality of documentation, also needs to be seriously addressed. There is no doubt that high quality, action-oriented documentation can play a catalytic role in negotiations.

Another related aspect of documentation is the need to strengthen the independence of thinking and approach of the Secretariat officials who prepare the reports. ...

The Group has concluded that the Secretariat is top-heavy and overmanned, and has consequently recommended that the total number of posts funded from the regular budget should be reduced by 15 per cent over three years and the number of regular budget posts at the Under-Secretary-General and Assistant-Secretary-General levels should be reduced by 25 per cent within a period of three years or less. We welcome those recommendations. ...

My delegation has noted the Group's conclusion that the salaries and allowances of staff have reached an excessively high level and that these should be reduced. Decisions in this area would affect not only the United Nations but the entire common system, which is based and maintained on common personnel standards and conditions of employment. It is therefore important to reaffirm at this stage the central role played by the International Civil Service Commission in the development and maintenance of the entire common system."

The representative of **Uganda**[95]

"Some of the political viewpoints have given rise to at least two broad notions which have been put forth by critics of the United Nations. The first is that the United Nations is under the control of an oppressive majority of countries from the third world, which use their numerical clout in a way which gives them total and absolute control of the Organization, and which totally frustrate the aspirations and desires of the minority which provide the financial back-up of the Organization. The budget has been cited as a case in point where small States wield greater power than corresponds with their financial contribution and where there is need for fundamental change.

The second notion or assumption has been that the smaller countries, in particular those of Africa, are against reforms aimed at improving the working of the United Nations and that their attitude is motivated by nothing more than a desire to safeguard and perpetuate their in-built privileges and advantages.

Allow me to point out the fallacies in those notions. On the question of the alleged oppressive majority, we know that the powers of the organs of the United Nations, particularly those of the General Assembly and of the Security Council, are set out in detail in the United Nations Charter. We know that the permanent members of the Security Council have reserved powers which are of critical and overriding importance in the running of this Organization and over which the General Assembly has no control whatsoever, despite the so-called oppressive majority.

Here I have in mind the power of veto, the appointment of the Secretary-General and the levels of staffing within the organs of the United Nations. So far as this last point is concerned, representatives may wish to examine document A/C.5/41/L.2, which is a report of the Secretary-General on personnel questions and which sets out the composition of the Secretariat. Even a cursory study of the report shows the extent to which "the oppressed minority" exercises influence in the Secretariat as compared to members belonging to the "oppressive majority group". I should point out that, according to that report, some members of the latter group have no representation whatsoever within the Secretariat and that others have one or two members only.

On questions of finance, it is also worthy of note that the small countries have no say in respect of that part of the United Nations budget that is financed through voluntary contributions, controlling such important organs as the United Nations Development Programme and the World Health Organization, all of vital importance to the developing countries. It should also be remembered that developing countries vote with the developed countries on many issues that come up before the United Nations.

As regards the allegation that smaller countries are not in favour of proposals for the improvement of the running of the Organization, nothing could be further from the truth. ...

My delegation ... fully supports all moves to streamline the Organization in order to render it more effective in achieving the objectives for which it was established and in the light of present-day conditions. ...

Some have suggested that since many of the recommendations were adopted unanimously by the Group, whose composition represents all regions, the report should, as a result, be endorsed as a package. My delegation does not subscribe to the notion of a package. We believe that we should examine the recommendations on their merit and modify or adopt them according to how acceptable we find them. ...

Regarding the proposal that the number of regular budget posts at the levels of Under-Secretary-General and Assistant Secretary-General should be reduced by 25 per cent within a period of three years or less, we are of the opinion that the optimum number of these posts, as well as other posts, will be determined only after the reorganization of the departments as recommended by the experts. After such an exercise it may well be that the appropriate number of Under-Secretaries-General and Assistant Secretaries-General will be even lower than 75 per cent of the present levels of these posts.

So far as the planning and budget procedures are concerned, the report itself indicates that existing regulations prescribed by the General Assembly in relation to these matters have not been complied with fully in the past...That being the case, it appears to us that rather than create new organs in this field - for example, the committee for programme, budget and co-ordination, which is proposed under option (a) - measures should be taken to ensure that present regulations, particularly those relating to consultation with Member States at an early stage of the budget, should be complied with. Those existing regulations have not been proved to be inadequate, since they have never been put into effect, and therefore they should be implemented before they can be assessed objectively.

What concerns my delegation is that the body which some have proposed to supplant the Committee for Programme and Co-ordination (CPC), and which it is suggested "should take part in the planning and budget procedure from the very beginning and throughout the process," might well usurp the powers of the Member States on the issues relating to the budget, contrary to the existing General Assembly resolutions. This is particularly so as regards the preamble to option (a) as set out at page 29 of the report. If this happened, the sovereign rights of Member States would be prejudiced and this is a move which my delegation would find unacceptable. We are also concerned that any proposals in this field should not detract from the prerogative of the Secretary-General in the formulation and the presentation of the budget."

The representative of **Yugoslavia**[96]

"Over the 40 years of its existence, the United Nations has witnessed a sustained growth of its agenda, followed by a parallel growth of intergovernmental machinery and of the number, frequency and duration of conferences and meetings, which sometimes may have surpassed the real needs. The volume of documentation has also increased to the extent that it surpasses the limit of what can be studied and used constructively. The United Nations Secretariat has undergone a parallel growth as well, so that the number of posts funded from the regular budget of the United Nations has increased from 1,546 in 1946 to over 11,000 in 1986. Today's structure of the Secretariat is too complex, fragmented and top-heavy and is divided into too many departments, offices and divisions. ...

The reason that its growth has sometimes been disproportionate to our expectations lies in the absence of the political will of some countries to seek substantial solutions to international problems through this Organization. Here I have in mind the procrastination over the crises in, for example, southern Africa, the Middle East and other regions, as well as over the economic and social problems that many countries are facing today. Because of this, there has been a tendency to resort to setting up new intergovernmental bodies, increasing the volume of documentation, and so on. This situation contributed to the growth of the bureaucracy of our Organization. ...

There is room, as well as a need, for a general improvement of the work and efficiency of the United Nations. The proposals and recommendations open up a process which by its scope and importance surpasses the limits of the administrative and financial functioning of the world Organization. Therefore, they should be viewed and implemented exclusively in the context of the need to strengthen the role of the United Nations in international relations. ...

The planning and budgetary procedure is undoubtedly an important component of the efforts to enhance the efficiency of the administrative and financial functioning of the United Nations. However, it is our impression that those issues have given rise to a certain mistrust, which is not unfounded. The process of establishing the programme budget should not be artificially divided, still less merged with a ring of restrictive intentions. ...

The procedure for achieving agreement on the content of the programme and the size of the budget is of particular importance. The adoption of the programme budget should be the result of the broadest agreement. It is therefore necessary to strive for consensus in the process of decision-making, in the interests of all. However, that should not hamstring the proceedings and make possible the vetoing of decisions of vital importance for substantial activities of the United Nations, and thus virtually block its work. It is quite understandable that the usual procedure in accordance with the General Assembly's rules of procedure and with the Charter should be applied in cases when all possibilities of achieving consensus have been exhausted. ...

The changes under consideration are not, and must not be, aimed at creating a new type of organization or a new correlation of forces within the United Nations; rather, they should seek to strengthen the existing Organization by promoting democracy of its structure, diversification of its activities and equality of its members."

The representative of **New Zealand**[97]

"My delegation made it clear at the resumed fortieth session in April that we saw blemishes in the Organization and its staffing and management. That assessment may be seen as an understatement if one reads the report of the high-level review group. It is a most courageous and innovative piece of work. There is no questioning of the existence of a crisis. There is a tough and yet fair assessment of the inadequacies, distortions and excesses of the system. There is no evasion of the issues raised. There are relevant and in most cases, extremely sound recommendations for reform or review. We can support that part - 95 per cent of the report - on which consensus was reached. ...

We have to acknowledge that consensus produced the High-level Group's report. There was virtually full agreement on Chapters II to V among members of the Group. Among the valuable recommendations in those chapters I would recall ... that concerning the commitment to improved co-ordination of United Nations activities, and particularly recommendation 11, regarding the role of the United Nations Development Programme (UNDP) in technical assistance delivery. This concerns all small countries, including some in the South Pacific, which deal with United Nations agencies. How does a one-man or two-man planning office handle a multiplicity of apparently competing agencies from within the United Nations family? Better co-ordination and a clear assignment of leadership are called for. They do not at the moment exist. ...

We can see merit in ensuring that the cluster of recommendations in the report dealing with co-ordination are implemented without too much delay and that the UNDP's primacy in delivering technical assistance is reaffirmed. ...

We consider that a consolidated body for programme and budget consideration is required. That body should be in a position to make recommendations to the General Assembly on the medium-term plan and the programme budget, on the priorities among programmes and on the redeployment of funds from areas of low to those of higher priority. We note that both options (a) and (b) in chapter VI agree on the need to define the level of resources for the budget and to provide a limited envelope of funds to cover contingencies. We support that principle and consider the level of 2 per cent in option (a) looks about right, although we are not inflexible on that figure. Our concern is that we should work within the budget levels previously decided by the General Assembly and that, apart from the contingency envelope, proposals for additional expenditure should be accommodated - as options (a) and (b) both provide - by a reordering of priorities. They should otherwise be deferred.

In considering these recommendations my delegation reaffirms the importance we attach to the membership as a whole having full opportunity to determine the direction and programmes of the Organization. There appears to be concern on the part of some that reform of the budget programming process will undermine the role of the Assembly. We do not believe that to be the case. We must ensure that it does not happen."

The representative of the **United Republic of Tanzania**[98]

"The central mandate in General Assembly resolution 40/237 was that, in conducting a thorough examination of the United Nations administration, recommendations would be made to improve the administrative and financial efficiency of the Organization. My delegation sincerely sympathizes with the Group of 18 because of the difficult mandate entrusted to it and the time constraints under which the report had to be prepared. But even when all this is taken into account fully, it is difficult to see a link between many of the recommendations in the report and the administrative and financial efficiency referred to in resolution 40/237 of the General Assembly. Anyone who knows something about our Organization may, with justification, ask why the statements and recommendations in the report of the Group of 18 do not differentiate clearly problems related to policy, management, structure or procedures. Had this distinction been made, it would have been possible to minimize the confusion, ambiguity, and vagueness inherent in several of the recommendations and thereby avoid making inaccurate statements. ...

It is very disturbing to hear statements about accepting the report as a package, as if such a package exists, or about proposals to impose recommendations which would then be subject to different interpretations. It should therefore not surprise anyone if delegations become very uneasy about time-saving devices such as forcing a quick decision on the report by limiting discussion in the plenary Assembly or in the Fifth Committee. ...

Recommendation 1 on the Committee on Conferences causes considerable difficulties to my delegation. This recommendation mixes and confuses the roles of the Secretariat, inter-governmental and other bodies and organs like the Economic and Social Council, the Advisory Committee on Administrative and Budgetary Questions (ACABQ) and the Fifth Committee in conference matters. My delegation supports fully the general objective sought by the General Assembly for many years to reduce meetings, conferences and documentation. Indeed, too many meetings and too much documentation are more detrimental to smaller delegations like Tanzania. But I believe that the goal of reducing documentation and meetings should be achieved by following agreed procedures. The General Assembly has adopted a number of recommendations affecting the role of the Committee on Conferences. Therefore, my delegation sees no justification in giving that Committee the additional sweeping powers in Recommendation 1, particularly in paragraphs

(d) and (e) of that recommendation. The Tanzania delegation does not accept the implication that the Committee, on its own, should reorder the programme of meetings approved by intergovernmental bodies like the Economic and Social Council, nor do we accept the notion that the General Assembly should single out and put a ceiling on conference resources without looking at these resources in the context of the overall programme of work and budget of the Organization.

Recommendations 2 to 7 cover areas where, in some cases, changes are already taking place such as biennial meetings and conferences. Accordingly, although my delegation does not accept every one of these recommendations, they do not cause us as much trouble as Recommendation 1. We note, however, that Recommendation 3 (e) is unrealistic and impractical; Recommendation 3 (f) is difficult to implement and Recommendation 4 is a restrictive interpretation of General Assembly resolution 40/243. My delegation will not accept Recommendation 5 if it is aimed at abolishing projects already approved by the General Assembly.

Recommendations 8 to 13 on co-ordination, and on a comparative study of the intergovernmental machinery and its functioning, have to be examined and implemented in conjunction with those on the structure of the Secretariat. My delegation trusts that if the study called for in Recommendation 8 is carried out, the outcome will not be a reduction in the capacity and scope of work of the United Nations in the economic and social fields. Each intergovernmental entity in the United Nations has been established for a specific purpose and therefore before it is decided to abolish, merge or restructure such an entity, it should first be ascertained whether the mandate entrusted to such a body is still valid. My delegation also believes that the study should cover political and other intergovernmental structures. My delegation does not accept Recommendation 8, subparagraphs (3) (b) and (3) (d), as criteria for the study for they are unrealistic and difficult to implement. Recommendations 9 to 13 on co-ordination cover matters relating to the United Nations system and it might be useful if the General Assembly would request the Secretary-General, as Chairman of the Administrative Committee on Co-ordination (ACC), to give his views about the implementation of these recommendations. Recommendation 13 is unnecessary and can be dispensed with altogether. In the first place, the subject of harmonizing budgets in the United Nations system is a continuing activity under the aegis of the ACC; this work has gone on for many years. The ACABQ also deals with this question in the context of its report on administrative and budgetary co-ordination between the United Nations and the specialized agencies and the International Atomic Energy Agency (IAEA). The inclusion of United Nations affiliates in Recommendation 13 shows lack of full appreciation of the purposes of the format of a programme budget document. For example, the purposes served by a United Nations Development Programme (UNDP) budget document may not allow that document to be prepared in a form similar to a document submitted to the Executive Committee of the Programme of the High Commissioner for Refugees (UNHCR), and so forth.

With respect to Recommendations 14 to 40 on the structure of the Secretariat, I should like to make some general comments. In the first place, I should point out that the structure of the Secretariat reflects the history of the Organization, the structure of the programme of work entrusted to the administration and decisions of intergovernmental bodies. It is therefore essential that this be taken into account in the implementation of many of the recommendations of the Group of 18. I strongly believe, therefore, that proposals to abolish, restructure, merge or consolidate departments, centres and offices should be submitted to the General Assembly before they are implemented, especially since Member States would like to know how the Group's recommendations would affect the activities the Secretariat has been carrying out. Member States are also interested in ensuring that the Group's recommendations do not in any way adversely affect the scope and capacity of the United Nations to carry out approved work programmes. My delegation would like to emphasize that recommendations which touch on the role of some autonomous bodies, such as United Nations Development Programme, the United Nations Children's Fund, the Office of the United Nations High Commissioner for Refugees, the World Food Programme and others, must be implemented with extreme care. We should not cause disruption of the work of these organizations under the guise of reform. Full consultations with the executive heads and the governing bodies of these programmes should be undertaken not only in connection with recommendations concerning the structure of the Secretariat but also in connection with the study called for in recommendation 8.

Let me now offer a few specific comments. I see no reason why recommendations 14, 16, 25 and 27, and others such as recommendations 17, 18 and so on, have been submitted separately. My delegation notes that few instances of duplication have been cited and that the basis on which proposals have been made for rationalizing, merging or abolishing an office or department is not indicated. The proposals to reduce staff - in recommendation 15 - are arbitrary, since the percentages given do not result from any in-depth examination of the programme of work of the United Nations. The phrase "limiting the programmes and services" in recommendation 19 should be replaced by "reducing the programmes and services". Recommendation 20 is so vague as to be meaningless. Concerning recommendation 24, my delegation believes that the United Nations should retain the function of disaster relief co-ordination since the United Nations Development Programme is not the proper office for this function. Recommendation 25 (4) is impractical. Recommendation 33 is too vague to be useful. Recommendation 35 is unnecessary, since reductions have already been made, and it is not clear to which biennium the 30 per cent refers. Finally, I believe, as regards recommendation 36, that each case must be dealt with on its own merits, and I believe that the General Assembly should ignore recommendations 39 and 40 and let the Secretary-General decide those matters as he sees fit.

For the time being I have little to say about chapter IV, on measures regarding personnel, except to support the Secretary-General's view that the financial crisis should not be resolved at the expense of the entitlements of the staff of the United Nations. In pursuing measures for reform, it is imperative to bear in mind that an Organization like the United Nations cannot discharge fully whatever mandate is entrusted to it unless the staff serving it are qualified, dedicated and adequately remunerated. In this connection, my delegation believes that the roles of the International Civil Service Commission and the Pension Board should be fully respected. Therefore I believe that some proposals in chapter IV, such as recommendation 61, may have to be referred to the International Civil Service Commission.

As regards chapter V, my delegation was amused but not surprised at the prominence given to the Joint Inspection Unit by the Group of 18. My delegation does not accept the implication in this chapter that evaluation in the United Nations system and the Joint Inspection Unit are somewhat synonymous. They are not. Mechanisms and procedures for evaluation, monitoring and inspection are already in place. The statute of the Joint Inspection Unit provides, in article 5, paragraph 2, that inspectors "shall provide an independent view through inspection and evaluation aimed at improving management and methods". In article 5, paragraph 4, of the statute, the Unit is requested to assist intergovernmental bodies in carrying out external evaluation of programmes and activities. In view of this, my delegation does not support recommendation 63, which seeks to entrust the Joint Inspection Unit with more powers of external evaluation in contravention of article 5 of the Joint

Inspection Unit statute. Recommendations 64 and 66 are already covered by the statute of the Joint Inspection Unit. Recommendation 65 might interfere with the Joint Inspection Unit's independence. Enlarging the scope of audits as proposed in recommendation 67, might entail large expenditures with questionable results. We do not accept the involvement of the Joint Inspection Unit in co-ordinating and monitoring some recommendations of the Group as suggested in recommendation 70. It is doubtful whether such a role is proper for a unit whose inspectors operate more individually than collectively.

I now come to chapter VI, which deals with the planning, programming and budgeting procedure. ...

In view of the controversy over planning and budgeting in the United Nations and the extensive discussions in the Group of 18, may I be allowed a moment of reflection. I honestly do not believe the controversy is over the size of the budget; otherwise how does one explain the evident paradox of a declining United Nations budget and the mounting level of denunciation directed at the United Nations and its Member States? It is very disappointing to hear sweeping statements and declarations such as that some Member States are being taxed without being represented, that the majority is despotic and tyrannical over the minority, that a whole group of Member States has no influence over the affairs of the Organization, and that budget and planning procedures are not working. ... May I say that these statements are not accurate and that thorough research will disprove them. For example, present planning procedures do allow Member States the opportunity to consider in depth the work programme of the Organization. It may be that Member States do not avail themselves of the opportunity the planning procedures allow them, but that is a different matter altogether. It is not a question of organizational structure either. Look at the United Nations Industrial Development Organization (UNIDO). Some members of the Group of 18 thought the UNIDO model would save the United Nations, but that model, new as it is, did not prevent some influential Member States from voting against the first budget of UNIDO.

... may I say that not everything in the options, as presented in chapter VI of the report of the Group of 18, is acceptable to my delegation. Although option (a) is a premature infant of the objectives under option (c), with proper care, through the reform process, the goal of option (c) could be fully attained. Among other proposals, the two options are seeking the establishment of a single programme and budget committee by replacing the Committee for Programme and Co-ordination (CPC) and the Advisory Committee on

Administrative and Budgetary Questions (ACABQ) either gradually (option (a)) or immediately (option (c)). These options are based on the mistaken premise that the programme of work and the related priorities of the Organization can be formulated, set and approved in one committee. Some may argue that similar structures exist in several but not in all of the specialized agencies. On this latter point, may I point out that since no two specialized agencies have identical constitutions, programme structures or intergovernmental machinery, then no two specialized agencies have the same planning and budgetary process. Therefore, to transfer a mechanism from one organization to another may raise fundamental constitutional problems which cannot be ignored. Option (b) is equally unacceptable to my delegation since it merely confuses option (a). It has, however, one redeeming feature in the attempt to retain both the ACABQ and the CPC.

In conclusion, may I say the following: let us not continue to make a fundamental error made by outsiders who are not quite familiar with how the programmes and priorities of the Organization are formulated, set and approved. We should not assume, as some seem to do, that the crisis we are facing on the question of the planning and budgeting process can be solved by mere structural tinkering, and that the ACABQ and the CPC, or a combination of the two, or giving the CPC budgetary functions, will somehow bring satisfaction and harmony."

The representative of **Nepal**[99]

"To come back to the report itself: We endorse the "Specific Recommendations", numbered 1 to 7, concerning the intergovernmental machinery, but hope that an exception will be made for the least developed countries with reference to recommendation 4, in much the same way that an exception has been made with respect to reimbursement of the travel costs of representatives of least developed Member countries attending the General Assembly, as specified in recommendation 6.

My delegation understands that it was not possible for the Group of High-level Experts to address in depth issues relating to intergovernmental machinery and its functioning. While therefore endorsing recommendation 8, on the need for a careful and comprehensive study on that subject, we believe that a new body, if created, should be more representative in its nature and number. My delegation shares the urgency felt by the Group in regard to bringing about greater co-ordination of the policies and activities of the specialized agencies of the United Nations, as reflected in recommendations 9 to 13 - in particular recommendation 10, that the heads of the specialized agencies should hold an annual one-week session, under the chairmanship of the Secretary-General, to discuss major questions in the economic and social fields and improve the co-ordination of their programmes.

With respect to the report's recommendations regarding the structure of the Secretariat, we are in agreement with its basic premise that the Secretariat has become, by and large, "too top-heavy and too complex" (A/41/49, para. 30). However, as far as reductions and changes suggested in the strength and structures of the Secretariat are concerned, we are of the view that it would be best to entrust the matter to the wise judgement of the Secretary-General for implementation in an orderly and sequential manner. ...

My delegation is in total agreement with the Secretary-General's legitimate concern that the Secretariat be staffed by personnel with "the highest standards of efficiency, competence and integrity". We also believe that "Working conditions, including salaries and entitlements" (A/41/663, para. 9) must be such as to attract and retain them. We sometimes wonder, however, whether such a concern is not over-emphasized.

While still on matters concerning the Secretariat, permit me to point out that my delegation has also taken favourable note of the many recommendations regarding administrative and other fields as they relate to the Secretariat. In particular, we wish to record our endorsement of the proposal to ban the practice of hiring retired staff members as consultants.

Where measures concerning personnel are concerned, my delegation is in full agreement that no political or other pressures should be brought to bear in selection of the staff. We also support the proposal of the Secretary-General that nationals of developing countries be duly represented at senior levels, in accordance with relevant General Assembly resolutions. We wish to suggest that to that end consideration be given also to each developing country's level of representation and that special consideration be given to least developed countries and to women in that respect.

My delegation supports all the recommendations on monitoring, evaluation and inspection contained in the report. Regarding the chapter on planning and budget procedure, we support those elements on which there was agreement in the Group. ...

While we believe that the specifics of the report's recommendations on planning and budget procedure will be dealt with in the Fifth Committee, we cannot help but express some uneasiness over the suggestion to introduce the consensus principle for decisions on programme and budgetary matters by the Committee concerned. In our view, whenever there are differences of view in the Committee the matter should be referred to the General Assembly for guidance instead of delaying the decision by searching for consensus.

... the package does perhaps represent the last chance to effect long-overdue changes. That can be done, we believe, by adopting the recommendations as a whole. In doing so, we would give a visible and magnificent demonstration of our collective willingness to make our Organization a truly responsive and responsible institution, thereby ensuring its vitality and enhancing its credibility."

The representative of **Burma**[100]

"the United Nations understandably needs to expand its machinery to cope with the increasing demands on its resources. As the Group of Experts has rightly pointed out in the report, this faces the intergovernmental machinery with a situation in which there is much duplication of work. To remedy this, co-operation is necessary within the intergovernmental machinery itself, particularly from its Members. Conferences and meetings are essential for the effective functioning of the intergovernmental machinery, but the present situation seems to be that there is obviously ample opportunity for curtailment in this area. ...

Needless to say, planning and programming of expenditures are essential prerequisites for the United Nations to carry out its activities and programmes. The General Assembly, through the recommendations of the Fifth Committee, is a determining authority on matters of budgetary importance, but the present procedures and mechanisms are not conducive to the effective participation of members in the programming and budgeting process. ... We would like to stress that in attempting to resolve this issue, it is essential to maintain the principle of equitable representation in accordance with the Charter."

The representative of **Kuwait**[101]

"It is no secret that there are persistent attempts to include the United Nations in the list of the bones of contention between the international blocs, and thus its programmes, its budget and the contributions of some Member States have, regrettably, become hostage to domestic political considerations and to the emotional positions adopted by certain lobbying groups in those countries. We remain fully confident that a carefully thought out international consensus will eventually prevent the exploitation of our Organization by certain countries with the aim of tightening unilateral control and imposing non-consensus views.

It is hardly appropriate for Western societies, which pride themselves on their democratic institutions and systems, that their political circles and representative establishments should call for the reallocation of votes in the world Organization in proportion to each Member State's contribution. Such calls demonstrate nothing but a contradiction of the essence of the genuine democratic philosophy. ...

We had hoped that the report would be more specific and that it would incorporate some important procedural details. It also lacks a recommendation on finding a radical solution to the problem of the scale of assessments, a solution providing a proper pattern, based on the principles of justice and equality among Member States. ...

We also wish to express our opposition to the concept of a unified body for the budget and programmes, for in it we foresee an opening for some countries to influence the selection of programmes and the rejection of others that do not suit their narrow domestic interests or desires. We believe that merging the Committee for Programme and Co-ordination with the Advisory Committee would undermine the latter's vital role."

The representative of **Zaire**[102]

"To attempt to resolve the financial difficulties of the United Nations at the expense of the rights of the staff members would clearly be a very short-sighted policy and would result in failure of the reform, since it would call into question the common system by which the whole professional category of Secretariat personnel is governed. In this connection, the International Civil Service Commission should continue to play its central role regarding the regulation and co-ordination of terms and conditions of service under the common United Nations system. ...

Secondly, paragraph 18 of the report, dealing with duplication, which clearly takes place in the agendas and programmes of the intergovernmental machinery and its functioning, deserves exhaustive study which should lead to a co-ordination of the activities engaged in by the Secretariat, and by the whole United Nations system. Activities in the economic and social sectors should be reviewed as a whole, redefined and rationally reallocated among the bodies, whose authority should no longer be disputed. ...

Thirdly, my delegation would like to express its support for recommendation 10 of the Group of Experts to the effect that the executive heads of the International Labour Organization, the United Nations Educational, Scientific and Cultural Organization, the Food and Agriculture Organization of the United Nations, the World Health Organization, the United Nations Industrial Development Organization, the United Nations Conference on Trade and Development, the International Atomic Energy Agency, the General Agreement on Tariffs and Trade, the International Bank for Reconstruction and Development and the International Monetary Fund should be invited to hold an annual one-week session under the chairmanship of the Secretary-General, assisted by the Director-General for Development and International Economic Co-operation and the Under-Secretary-General for International Economic and Social Affairs, to discuss major policy questions in the economic and social fields. The report of these co-ordinating sessions should come before each session of the General Assembly for its consideration.

Fourthly, in taking up that section of the report which deals with the Secretariat structure, the Group of Experts formulated recommendations 14 and 15 which, in my opinion, hinge upon the conclusions reached by the study to be carried out by the intergovernmental body whose task it will be to go into matters of intergovernmental structure, in accordance with recommendation 8.

Consequently, it would seem, at first blush, rather awkward to envisage any kind of reduction in staff, either by 15, 20 or even 5 per cent, as long as a global study redefining the organic authorities and competence of the various departments of the Secretariat has not been submitted, and as long as the targets and programmes for these various departments have not been redefined, in the light of available personnel and a rational utilization of human resources. ...

Fifthly, my delegation considered very closely recommendation 20, which deals with the Department for Disarmament Affairs. It believes that at the present time this Department is functioning with limited staff but that, nevertheless, it has evidenced its effectiveness in that the publications put out by this Department make it possible for Member States to better follow the disarmament negotiations."

The representative of **Bolivia**[103]

"It is inadmissible that the report should be discussed as a whole and that all the recommendations should be adopted as a package. While some of the recommendations are good, others are unacceptable to my delegation, and we shall examine them one by one in the Fifth Committee, as I have said.

As for the structure of the report, I shall refer to its main chapters. The first concerns the state of the intergovernmental machinery and its functioning. My delegation has no trouble with regard to recommendations 1 to 5, in section A, but we find it impossible to accept recommendations 6 and 7, because they jeopardize the participation of small States lacking the financial resources to make full use of the organs of the United Nations except through existing machinery.

My delegation cannot accept any of the recommendations in sections **B and** C, that is, recommendations 8 to 13. While we recognize the need to emphasize co-ordination within the system, we cannot agree that, under the pretext of better co-ordination, the spheres of competence of organs and agencies of the United Nations which are already working selflessly should be diminished, although we would concede that there is room for improvement in their performance.

Here again my delegation wishes to point out that the Bolivian Government supports the United Nations Development Programme (UNDP). We believe that this is the most important body for carrying out the development functions of the Organization. We do not think it is a good idea to mix development functions with emergency relief functions, which have always been a major field of United Nations work. ...

The United Nations has tried several times to make reforms and readjustments. Experience shows that reforms designed to bring about improvements very often destroyed working structures and that previous activities ceased, very much to the detriment of the countries that benefited from the work of the existing bodies that disappeared. I am thinking particularly of the reforms that took place 10 years ago in the social sectors of the United Nations. On the basis of the principles of unified development, the entire social programme of the United Nations was merged with the economic programme. Ten years later social development has practically disappeared. The reports have declined in quality. ...

An important aspect of this report is that it points out the need to strengthen the functions of the Director-General for Development and International Economic Co-operation and the officers serving under him. In the field of development, a few years ago, in view of the optimism we felt concerning the ability of the United Nations to carry out development functions, the Member States succeeded in establishing a second high-level post - a kind of development tsar - at the United Nations. The results have not lived up to the expectations of many delegations. I believe that neither the will nor the performance of the officials concerned is to blame, but that, with the present international situation and the duplication of effort in many fields, the Director-General for development has not been able to meet our expectations. If reform is to take place now, we should give some thought to the possibility of restoring those functions to the Department of International Economic and Social Affairs, which is now without the functions it should have. ...

The report also clearly states the need for a 25 per cent cut in senior posts and a 15 per cent overall cut in staff. In principle it is important to make this reduction, and my delegation does not object to these proposed cuts in the senior level posts, but we need some justification for them. It is not just a question of making percentage cuts in order to reduce budgetary costs without discussing the justification for these posts, because when the posts were originally established they had to be justified. ...

My delegation has some problems with the chapter on personnel measures ... my delegation believes it can detect in the report of the Group of 18 some degree of prejudice against the international official. Otherwise it is hard to understand why they should wish to cut what they describe as "privileges" but which are in fact an important part of staff incentives such as for example the education grant. While my delegation can see the need for changes and adjustments in staff policies, we believe the Secretary-General should be the one to propose such changes, but in any case there should be no cuts in the system of incentives, because that is detrimental to the staff and to their morale. Being an international civil servant is not necessarily an agreeable task. It means that the official has to leave his own country for long periods, and remain at a distance from his family, and from his cultural background. As far as the educational grant is concerned, very often the children of the international official, in whom he places his hopes, are the reason why he feels obliged to accept a post as an international civil servant. Consequently we do not believe that we should consider it legitimate to make the international official pay for the financial crisis of the Organization. The financial crisis is not the responsibility of the international official any more than it is that of the Secretary-General. ...

It is important to refer here to certain particular aspects of personnel questions. Sometimes the Secretary-General is unable to withstand pressure from certain States, particularly the larger States, the permanent members of the Security Council. We should be very clear on this point, because it is incomprehensible to my delegation that certain of the Under-Secretary-General posts should have become the property of particular countries. The report of the Group of 18 beats about the bush in making this point, but we should bring it into the open. It is unacceptable that for 40 years we should have had an Under-Secretary-General for Political and General Assembly Affairs from the same Member State, or that the same country should have held the post of Under-Secretary-General for Political and Security Council Affairs. The permanent members of the Security Council hold that position only in the

Security Council, they are not permanent members of the Secretariat. At that level we must adopt a rule providing for a compulsory rotation of countries each time that an Under-Secretary-General has come to the end of his career. In this way we could give a more democratic and ecumenical character to the posts in question. ...

We firmly believe that the information centres should represent the universal character and scope of the United Nations. Rather than acquiescing in those centres becoming a kind of appendage to the policy of the host country we should close them down. We would do better to save money instead of maintaining arrangements which are counterproductive and do nothing to improve the image of the United Nations. For example, since there has been an American official at the information centre in Washington the image of the United Nations held by the United States authorities has never been worse. A further point is that the information centre in Washington was supposed to serve as a link between the Organization of American States (OAS) and the United Nations, but in the past five years neither the United Nations nor the OAS has received any service from that information centre. ...

My delegation has no problems on chapter V, dealing with monitoring, evaluation and inspection.

Lastly, ... Chapter VI must undergo a most careful analysis by all Member States to ensure that the changes proposed will not affect the future of the Organization and will not mean any loss of authority on the part of States, or of their equal footing as established in the Charter."

The representative of **Venezuela**[104]

"Even now, however, I can say that we agree generally with those recommendations designed to make better use of the services of the Secretariat, to reduce the number and duration of conferences and meetings - without jeopardizing the substantive work of the Organization, to apply the principle that organs of the United Nations should meet at their respective headquarters, to reduce the volume of documentation, to embark upon the comparative study of intergovernmental machinery and its functioning, and to improve the mach·nery for co-ordination between bodies through prior consultation and due analysis of the views of all of them, as well as those recommendations pertaining to the simplification of the organic structure of the Secretariat. ...

As I have said, however, we do have reservations about some of the measures pertaining to personnel recommended by the Group of Experts, particularly that having to do with a major reduction in the number of staff - recommendation 15 - and specifically the reduction by 15 per cent over a three-year period of the total number of posts financed out of the regular budget and an immediate reduction by 30 per cent of outside-consultant services. These are not based on objective reasoning or considerations but seem, rather, to be a response to the current financial crisis of the Organization, the study of which, as the introduction to the report of the Group of 18 rightly points out, is not part of the Group's mandate.

We have reservations also about recommendation 61, concerning the total benefits, salary and other conditions of service to which staff are entitled."

The representative of **Indonesia**[105]

"On the question of the intergovernmental machinery and its functioning, my delegation fully concurs with the analysis contained in chapter II of the report, and in general has no difficulty in accepting its pertinent recommendations. In particular, we strongly support the recommendation that the Committee on Conferences be strengthened and be given broader responsibilities. In fact, we should like to see its mandate expanded to cover also the Economic and Social Council and its subsidiary bodies. To this end we would suggest that the status of the Committee be enhanced by its becoming concurrently a subsidiary body of both the General Assembly and the Economic and Social Council as is the case with the Committee for Programme and Co-ordination (CPC). Moreover, the Committee should be given a greater supervisory role with regard to the organization of meetings of autonomous bodies such as the United Nations Conference on Trade and Development (UNCTAD) and the regional commissions. ...

With respect to chapter III, "Structure of the Secretariat", my delegation sees merit in the recommendation to reduce substantially the number of staff members at all levels, especially in the higher echelons, within a given time frame. On the other hand, we also concur with the Secretary-General's pertinent observation that there is an inevitable relationship between changes in the intergovernmental machinery and modifications in the size, structure and operations of the Secretariat. ...

We would, however, like to be assured that any measures taken to reduce the number of staff members will in no way hinder the effort to correct the current imbalances in geographical distribution. It also goes without saying that such a reduction should not be at the expense of a productive and capable Secretariat. The Group of 18 also recommends a review of a number of Secretariat units with a view to their streamlining and possible merging. In this connection, it is important to recall that in many cases Secretariat units were created by intergovernmental bodies and global conferences with specific purposes and considerations in mind.

... like many other delegations, we find it difficult to endorse Recommendation 61 on the reduction of staff entitlements. We tend to agree with the Secretary-General that to achieve efficiency at the cost of the conditions of service of the staff could be counter-productive. On the other hand, it should also be clearly understood that the staff must continue to meet the highest standards of efficiency, competence and integrity.

We have also studied chapter V, "Monitoring, evaluation and inspection", and we are ready to endorse the five important recommendations contained therein.

Chapter VI, "Planning and budget procedure", is at the same time a very important and a very difficult one. The chapter is closely linked with the root causes of the current financial crisis, and the way in which the matter is to be handled will certainly have an important bearing on the effort to promote confidence in the United Nations. ... a large measure of convergence appears to have been reached on a number of principal aspects to which we fully subscribe; for example, the need for improved intergovernmental machinery dealing with the questions relating to programme budgeting; the desirability of an earlier formal involvement and participation of Member States in the programme budgeting process; and the importance of co-ordinated programme planning and programme budgeting. ...

However, we should be rather circumspect on the question of pre-determining the level of resources. Without the benefit of a thorough technical examination, the line between a genuine effort to increase efficiency and effectiveness, and an attempt to reduce arbitrarily the role of the United Nations, is indeed thin."

The representative of **Austria**[106]

"the Austrian delegation advocates acceptance of the report as a package.

We should not underestimate the signal such a common enterprise would give to public opinion. It would demonstrate our common interest in the increased efficiency of our Organization and testify to the viability of the United Nations, a United Nations able to take bold steps to master its crisis. In fact, it would constitute the first step towards overcoming the crisis.

As far as the question of the planning and budgetary decision-making processes is concerned, Austria has consistently favoured the creation of a committee for programme and budget. This seemed to be a logical consequence of the adoption of the system of programming and planning, specifically after the adoption of the first programme budget in 1974. But suddenly this question has taken on a political dimension. The creation of such a committee seems to some Member States to represent a pragmatic and reasonable method for ensuring that the views of the main contributors, which pay more than 80 per cent of the United Nations budget regarding the amount and content of the budget are duly taken into account. Other Member States tend to regard the creation of such a single committee as a threat to the principle of the universality of this Organization, and particularly as an attempt to modify the provisions of Articles 17 and 18 of the Charter. ...

At this stage we do not want to go into details. Although we would favour a solution along the lines described in (a), my delegation, in a spirit of compromise, is open to working on a formula acceptable to all Member States. We firmly believe that the re-establishment of a broad consensus on budgetary and financial matters must be the ultimate priority for us all."

The representative of **Czechoslovakia**[107]

"we most firmly oppose any efforts to exert pressure on the United Nations, undertaken through various types of manoeuvres and overt and covert encroachments on the result of its activities, making use for these purposes of the most varied pretexts, such as the well-known phrase "the end justifies the means". Here we should also add those pre-programmed actions aimed at provoking the financial crisis of the United Nations, forcing it to work in accordance with some people's specific notions and selfish interests. ...

We support those recommendations which are aimed at enhancing the productivity of the existing structure of the United Nations Secretariat and the more effective co-ordination of the work of its individual elements, as well as the recommendations which propose concrete reductions in the number of members of the Secretariat, including those in higher-level posts.

At the same time we cannot endorse those recommendations in the report which not only were not agreed upon within the Group but also would have consequences which would entail discrimination against a particular group of countries as a result of their implementation - I am referring here to the recommendation that 50 per cent of the nationals of any State working in the Secretariat should have permanent contracts. Those recommendations would undoubtedly further aggravate the under-representation of certain countries and would bring about serious violations of the proclaimed principle of an equitable geographical distribution of posts. We therefore support the proposals which have already been heard here that recommendations on personnel issues should be referred for further study to the International Civil Service Commission."

The representative of **Cuba**[108]

"It is generally accepted that we are confronting the greatest political crisis that has faced the Organization since its foundation. The financial pressures brought to bear upon the Organization are only intended to obtain political reforms that will increase privileges and the control of a few over the immense majority of the Members of the Organization. ...

The Group did not have a mandate to examine the effectiveness of the United Nations in the achievement of the purposes and principles for which the Organization was established, since it is an undeniable axiom that the effectiveness of the Organization depends upon the political will of its Members and their willingness to abide by the terms of the Charter and the resolutions adopted in the course of the Organization's existence. ...

However, we believe it is vitally important that we do not confuse the idea of achieving greater efficiency with that of achieving economies. We should be trying to be more efficient and thus to achieve economies. Efficiency, in our opinion, means obtaining better results with the available resources, obtaining the present results with fewer resources or, in the best of cases, obtaining better results while using fewer human and financial resources. If the present endeavour means that the programmes of the Organization are to be adversely affected, we are setting out on a very uncertain and probably mistaken path. Therefore, first and foremost, and constantly, we must ask ourselves what we are seeking through the present exercise. ...

For example, my delegation is firmly opposed to any formulation that might be interpreted as violating the principles of the Charter, therefore we could not accept the idea of introducing the consensus method into the decision-making process in the administrative and budgetary field if that would mean the establishment of an individual or collective veto in regard to that very important aspect of the Organization's work.

Furthermore, we do not believe it wise to merge the functions of programming and budgeting, since greater complications would be created than already exist. We believe that we should strengthen the present functions of the Committee for Programme and Co-ordination and the Advisory Committee on Administrative and Budgetary Questions, so that these two bodies would be able to fulfil their functions. The work of the Committee for Programme and Co-ordination could be improved on the basis of the existing regulations, and that would meet the concern of certain Member States. ... I should like to say that the second alternative given in chapter VI could serve as a very useful basis on which to reach a generally acceptable agreement."

The representative of **Congo**[109]

"it must be accepted that there was no agreement among the experts regarding the decision-making machinery in the financial and budgetary fields, the subject of chapter VI in the report of the Group of Experts.

In our view this disagreement results from certain demands made by some States designed to challenge the prerogatives of the Fifth Committee and of the General Assembly, as well as their essential bodies, the Committee for Programme and Co-ordination (CPC) and the Advisory Committee on Administrative and Budgetary Questions (ACABQ), which up to now have guaranteed the role and the responsibility of Member States in the formulation and implementation of General Assembly decisions. Therefore it could be concluded that there would be serious risks to the authority and the prerogatives both of the General Assembly and the Secretary-General in having the policies of the Organization determined by an uncontrollable structure in which only the opinion or influence of States or groups of States called "major contributors", are taken into account. In the final analysis this is precisely what we are talking about. If we believe that the development of the activities of the Organization which have caused the present excessive expenditure can only be justified by the growing influence of the small States on the decision-making machinery and on control, then, as some imagine, we could set up a kind of administrative and financial veto which would complement the other right of veto used in the Security Council. On the other hand, if one deems essential the overriding concept of sovereign equality of Member States and of their role in determining the interests of the international community as a whole, then it should follow that the United Nations must first and foremost be concerned not with curtailing the responsibility of small States but rather with the strict application of the most democratic procedures provided for by the relevant provisions of the General Assembly. It is non-compliance with these provisions which has led to those abuses which we all regret and to the relative inefficiency of the system."

The representative of **Sudan**[110]

"it is imperative that we weigh the options contained in chapter VI and ask ourselves why the planning and budgetary procedure should be changed. If the goal is general agreement among the Member States on the size of the budget, the priorities to be established and the way the programme budget is to be used in Member States in order to ensure the optimum utilization of the financial and human resources at the disposal of the Organization, my delegation could endorse the recommendations without reservations. If, on the other hand, the objective is to change the method of decision-making and of the adoption of the programmes and the allocation of parts of the budget, then we shall certainly reach a stalemate which will only heighten the controversies among the Members of the United Nations and completely destroy any kind of planning.

If, therefore, we must make one of the two choices contained in Chapter VI, we would prefer alternative (b). ...

The Assembly is considering the report in an atmosphere of suspicion and apprehensions, some of which are real enough, while others are imaginary. We believe that the Assembly cannot adopt an objective decision on the report immediately without alleviating at least some of the suspicions and fears aroused."

The representative of **Peru**[111]

"First of all, we believe that it was a mistake not to take up the challenge of the major contributor in threatening to reduce its contribution, the result being that we are continuing to subordinate the independence of the Organization to the financing of an administrative forest that we do not need. We trust that the future work of the machinery of reform will allow us to achieve the goal of an Organization that is increasingly independent and democratic, and in which none can wield a financial weapon to influence its decisions or claim privileges.

Once again, we stress that we need an independent and worthy Organization more than a wealthy and large Organization. I repeat: if having more money means our Organization being more dependent, it is better to have less money. If being large means being more vulnerable and weak, it is better to be smaller.

Secondly, we would also have like the report to have set in motion the dismantling of the hereditary fiefdoms in the Organization so that, in keeping with resolution 35/210 of the General Assembly, no high-level post should any longer be the exclusive domain of any Member State or group of States. Only thus shall we give effect to the principle of the legal equality of States which for that reason was expressly included in the Group's terms of reference.

Thirdly, we must achieve a coherent and reasonable interrelationship of the United Nations system in the field of economic and social co-operation, in accordance with the terms of Chapter IX of the Charter, which empowers the Organization to make the necessary recommendations for the co-ordination of the policies and activities of the specialized agencies.

Suffice it to recall that the Protocol signed by the Organization and the International Monetary Fund (IMF) on 15 April 1948 clearly provides that the Fund give consideration to inclusion on its agenda of items proposed by the United Nations. The Protocol further sets forth that its members commit themselves to carry out the decisions of the Security Council.

The pertinent recommendations of the report should not, therefore, be restricted to the subsidiary organs of the United Nations; they should include the whole range of specialized agencies if we really wish to give cohesion and political direction to our efforts. Consequently, the exercise of co-ordination with the executive heads of those agencies as advocated in the report - which far from being a technical is fundamentally a political exercise - should be carried out with the assistance not only of the Secretary-General and the Director-General for Development and International Economic Co-operation, but also of the Presidents of the General Assembly and of the Economic and Social Council, and for that matter even the President of the Security Council."

The representative of **Kenya**[112]

"Ironically, even though the Group's study was prompted by a political preoccupation of certain Member States, namely, the voting mechanism on financial matters, the terms of reference of the Group carefully, and in our view properly, excluded the question of the decision-making process within the Organization and instead focused on its administrative and financial function-ing.

... as a political Organization based on the sovereign equality of all its Members, large and small, the United Nations decision-making process is governed by the Charter, which stipulates that each Member shall have but one vote. Decisions by the Organization are, therefore, by simple majority. However, in recognition of the fact that certain matters are important enough to require a much stronger indication of support than a simple majority, the rules of procedure of the Organization already provide for a two-thirds majority in respect of certain specified matters, including in this instance voting on the budget of the Organization. A notable exception, as Members well know, is the Security Council, wherein permanent members enjoy the right of veto.

In the circumstances, a debate on the decision-making process, in the context of consideration of this item, would not only be beyond the mandate of the Group of Experts, but would also be contrary to the Charter and would to that extent be strenuously opposed. We remain convinced that it is neither desirable nor necessary to interfere with the decision-making process or to introduce diversionary ideas such as that of a pre-determined level and content of the budget of the Organization in order to consider measures necessary to assure the efficient administrative and financial functioning of the Organization. My delegation is convinced that effective ways and means of ensuring involvement by the Member States in the budget process can and should be worked out within the existing intergovernmental machinery, without flouting the Charter. It is in that light that we understand and welcome the remarks in paragraph 9 of the Secretary-General's note (A/41/663)."

The representative of **Poland**[113]

"Secondly, as far as the review of intergovernmental machinery and its functioning is concerned, this is a matter - as the report rightly indicates - falling within the competence of Governments. We consider that a number of subsidiary bodies can be merged or disposed of. But special care should be taken in reviewing the United Nations activities concerning peace and international security.

We should also bear in mind that in the economic and social fields a number of bodies, especially regional economic commissions, play an important role as platforms for dialogue and co-operation, as is the case with the Economic Commission for Europe. Any measures aiming at improving the financial efficiency of the United Nations should not undermine the scope and level of international co-operation achieved so far.

Thirdly, we consider chapter VI to be the most fundamental part of the report. Its content will have a long-standing impact on the functioning of the Organization. The Polish delegation supports the necessity of ensuring that the resources available to the Organization are used most effectively, and thus, in the spirit of good co-operation, is ready for further discussion in order to achieve a decision based on the principle of consensus.

Fourthly, we agree with the proposal that some subsidiary bodies, such as, for example, the Committee on Conferences, should be given broader responsibilities in order to strengthen the efficiency of the Organization. However, we are of the opinion that no subsidiary body should have broader responsibilities than the General Assembly itself. Such a body cannot be transformed into the policy-making body.

Fifthly, Poland has always attached great importance to the problem of personnel. ... It is with deep regret and concern, therefore, that we note that the Group of High-level Intergovernmental Experts has demonstrated a lack of sensibility to the interests, needs and policies of, especially, smaller States.

We consider that it is the sovereign right of every State to decide on the type of each appointment. Parts of recommendations 55 and 57 concerning the ratio of permanent to fixed-term contracts run counter to the principle of equitable geographical distribution."

The representative of the **Ukrainian Soviet Socialist Republic**[114]

"The actions of the United States administration openly aimed at undermining the United Nations cannot be masked by rhetoric, regardless of the high level on which this rhetoric may be uttered.

This time, the major weapon in the arsenal of subversive means used against the United Nations is financial pressure. This is the means now selected by the United States. Everyone is well aware of the dedication of the United States to the ideals of private enterprise. However - and this also should be particularly stressed - the idea of transforming the General Assembly into something like a meeting of bank stockholders, in which the decisive voice is held by the richest of them, a man whose views and behaviour are not open to discussion and are decisive, runs counter to the very principles of the universal international Organization and to the fundamental provisions of its Charter.

... in recent times Member States have expressed their concern regarding a lack of efficiency in the use of conference resources. What deserves serious consideration in this respect are the recommendations of the Group of 18 regarding a restructuring of the intergovernmental machinery, the need to eliminate obvious duplication in conference agendas, the programmes of the work of various bodies, cut-backs in the number of meetings and reduction of the volume of documentation. A specific role in this restructuring must be played by the Committee on Conferences. ...

I think that on the whole there is no basis for casting any doubt on the present level of skills and the dedication of the majority of the United Nations Secretariat staff members. What is of the greatest importance here is a carefully thought out, comprehensive, balanced selection of personnel based on broad geographical representation. The delegation of the Ukrainian SSR believes that the entire section of the Group's recommendations on personnel matters should be studied and considered in the most serious way possible before the General Assembly takes a final decision on it. The most appropriate and competent body for such work is the International Civil Service Commission. Such careful consideration is necessary because this section contains a number of recommendations which were not agreed upon and which, in our view, are totally unacceptable. First and foremost here, I am referring to recommendations 55 and 57."

The representative of **Sweden**[115]

"A few recommendations contain elements that are perhaps not fully in harmony with traditional Swedish policy in international organizations. Some of the Secretary-General's observations on staff entitlements and related issues seem particularly pertinent to my delegation. I do not wish to go into details, but one such recommendation is recommendation 61. ...

I regret that the High-Level Group has not addressed the sharing of the expenses of the Organization. The Swedish Government believes that a revision of the present method of assessing contributions is an essential reform that should be included in a comprehensive solution of the problems facing the United Nations. ...

It remains the conviction of my Government that a more even apportionment of assessments would reflect, better than at present, the fact that the United Nations is the instrument of all nations. The Organization would be less dependent on contributions from any single Member State. This, in turn, would be likely to improve the balance and coherence in the functioning of the world body, thereby enhancing its efficiency and effectiveness.

It is the clear impression of the Swedish Government that the idea of a different and more even distribution of assessments is receiving favourable responses in principle from a number of countries. The main reason that neither the High-Level Group nor the Committee on Contributions have been able to address this issue seems to be, in my judgement, a basic reluctance on the part of delegations and individual experts to recommend that their Governments assume, together with others, a somewhat greater financial responsibility. Another reason could be the formal objection that the apportionment so far is based broadly on capacity to pay. A different scale based on evenness as one major criterion would perhaps depart from the traditional interpretation of the concept of capacity to pay. Therefore, what would be required is a new interpretation, whereas the concept itself, in my opinion, need not necessarily be revised."

The representative of **Bulgaria**[116]

"We support the recommendations aimed at reducing the number of conferences and meetings and shortening their duration. We view as acceptable the recommendation to merge the United Nations departments and offices dealing with questions of a similar or related character. We also support the recommendations to reduce the number of staff members at all levels, particularly in the higher echelons, which in our view should be done in accordance with the principle of equitable geographical distribution. The recommendation that the staff unions or associations finance all their activities from their own funds also seems fairly reasonable to us.

Other positive recommendations are those proposing the reduction of expenses for outside consultants and official travel. ...

The Group of High-level Intergovernmental Experts rightly points out that a major weakness of the current budgeting and programming process is the lack of a clear linkage between priority setting and resource requirements either in the medium-term plan or in the programme budget.

It seems to us that a sound approach for providing such linkage would be to merge the budgeting and programme planning process, as suggested in recommendation 68, option C, and to entrust those two functions to a single intergovernmental body. Similarly, recommendation 68 B also proposes the establishment of such a body and specifically suggests that this body be renamed the Committee for Programme Budget and Co-ordination, which should take part in the planning and budget procedure throughout the process. ...

In our view, decision-making in the new body should retain the principle of consensus, and it should discharge its obligations in close co-operation with the Secretary-General and the Advisory Committee on Administrative and Budgetary Questions.

As can be seen from the report, there have been certain disagreements among the Group's members concerning some questions of personnel. ...

Recommendation 57, in particular, infringes upon the sovereign right of Member States to determine themselves the mode of employment of their nationals in the United Nations Secretariat. Furthermore, many Member States have been of the view over the years that renewable fixed-term appointments offer certain advantages in terms of efficiency by bringing new talent and experience, as well as fresh ideas and energy, to the Secretariat.

We would also recall that widespread resort to permanent contracts has contributed to the present lack of equitable geographical distribution of posts in the Secretariat. In our view, it would therefore be premature to consider these recommendations now, before they have been carefully studied by other relevant bodies such as the International Civil Service Commission."

The representative of **Philippines**[117]

"First, with regard to recommendation 6, concerning the reimbursement of travel costs, we feel that travel costs for all representatives of Member States should be borne by the Governments concerned. My Government is currently operating under financial strain, but if we must we shall bear the additional burden.

It is in that spirit that we urge this body to consider the financial implications of the proposal contained in recommendation 10, which suggests the holding of an annual one-week session of the executive heads of the United Nations agencies to discuss major policy questions in the economic and social fields and to improve the co-ordination of their programmes. Since such a session will surely result in additional expenses, it is suggested that it be held at such a time and in such a venue as would limit or reduce unavoidable expenses.

With regard to recommendation 13, my delegation notes with interest the determined effort to harmonize the format of the programme budgets of the organizations of the United Nations system and wishes to stress its desire to see this accomplished. That would not only expedite budget preparation but facilitate budget analysis as well.

My delegation notes from recommendation 35 that the United Nations is spending over $8 million for outside consultants. We consider this amount excessive, and my delegation believes that we can reduce it even further than the proposed 30 per cent cut. We believe the United Nations could make more constructive use of the expertise of the members of its own staff and thereby minimize to a great extent the use of outside consultants. The Secretariat is supposed to be composed of highly qualified personnel specialized in different fields and disciplines. My delegation sees little justification for hiring so many consultants unless the required expertise is not available within the existing staff of the Organization.

The Philippine delegation strongly endorses recommendation 38, proposing the reduction of the present level of official travel by 20 per cent. This could be cut further without prejudicing the efficiency of the Organization. We recall the proposal of my delegation at the thirty-seventh session on the reduction of travel of the staff and we hope to see it carried out.

Recommendation 38 concerns fact-finding missions, inspection of offices, and the number of staff personnel attending conferences. Sometimes, inspection of premises of United Nations regional headquarters is duplicated by officials of different offices and oftentimes the inspectors have similar comments and recommendations. It is not the intention of my delegation to hamper the work of the United Nations, especially in relation to fact-finding missions, but, whenever possible, duplication should be avoided.

For meetings and conferences, particularly those held outside Headquarters, the Department of Conference Services should, as a rule, maintain a minimal Secretariat staff.

My delegation reaffirms its support for the principle of equitable geographical distribution in the recruitment of Secretariat staff. It believes, however, that the second part of recommendation 55 ... violates that principle.

My delegation does not believe that the principle of equitable geographical distribution can be ensured by requiring that "at least 50 per cent of the nationals of any Member State working in the Secretariat should be employed on a permanent basis", as proposed in recommendation 57. In fact, that will create unnecessary inflexibility which will adversely affect the efficiency of the Organization. It contemplates the appointment of personnel on the basis of the need to fill up permanent and fixed-term quotas rather than performance or the needs of the Organization for specific expertise. A qualified and deserving national of any country should not be deprived of the opportunity to receive a permanent appointment simply because that appointment would be in excess of the quota allotted to his country. ...

As for the planning and budget mechanism, we register our support for the third proposal, which is to merge consideration of the financial and administrative aspects of the budget and review of the content of the programmes within a single intergovernmental expert body. We believe that by doing this we could minimize costs to a great extent, since we should be able to save on time as well as resources. Furthermore, the budgeting and programme planning processes are so closely related that they require the highest degree of co-ordination and harmony, which could better be achieved if the Committee for Programme and Co-ordination and the Advisory Committee on Administrative and Budgetary Questions were merged into one intergovernmental expert body."

The representative of the **United States of America**[118]

"Like other Member States, the United States entered the search for reform with major objectives in mind. Most clearly, our domestic law called for voting rights on budgetary matters proportionate to Member States' contributions to correct the current gross imbalance between those that dominate the decision-making process in determining budget levels and programme priorities and those that bear the heaviest financial responsibility for the Organization. We wanted a means to instil control and discipline into the General Assembly's practice of approving unending add-ons to the budget, which denigrates the role of the Secretary-General and makes a mockery of the overall programme planning and budgeting process. We wanted major staff reductions to eliminate waste and ensure a reordering of priorities within the Organization. These, we believe, are required to achieve efficiency and effectiveness. We wanted a major streamlining and simplification of the Secretariat structure in order to overcome duplication and fragmentation of effort. ...

The agreed recommendations of the Group of 18 could eliminate a great deal of the waste, mismanagement and irresponsibility which now drain so much of the United Nations limited resources and erode donor confidence in the institution. Of critical importance to us among the agreed recommendations is the call for staff reductions. We believe still greater reductions would have better assured the necessary reordering of programme priorities, but we can accept the reductions recommended by the Group of 18 as a good start.

Unfortunately, the Group of 18 was not able to reach agreement on the recommendations in chapter VI on the programme and budget decision-making process. The recommendations in this chapter are at the heart of the reform effort: indeed, it is these recommendations that are required to assure the fulfilment and long-term effectiveness of the recommendations upon which the Group of 18 was able to reach agreement. If we are to find a solution to the key question of the programme budget procedures, we must first understand clearly the different viewpoints and the reasons why they exist.

For a number of years the Member States which contribute the bulk of the Organization's budget have, as the Secretary-General has pointed out, opposed or abstained in the voting approving the biennial budgets. There is a belief among those Member States that the majority has not adequately considered their views when deciding how much the Organization should spend and on what it should be spent. On the other hand there is concern among a number of Member States that a new decision-making process which requires agreement by all Member States could bring the operation of the United Nations to a standstill. In plain terms, there is a lack of understanding and a lack of confidence among different groups of Member States concerning the motives of other groups. It is my view that the United Nations cannot continue to function in this fashion: rather we must seek a solution in which the interests of all - I repeat all - Member States can be protected.

It is my delegation's strong belief that the solution lies in establishing a process that will include agreement on the level and content of the Organization's programme budget at the very beginning of the cycle and an ability on the part of Member States to make sure that agreement has been taken into account in the budget. We recall that both of the committees currently involved in the programme budget process - the Committee for Programme and Co-ordination and the Advisory Committee on Administrative and Budgetary Questions - have traditionally taken their decisions by consensus, and we believe that consensus decision-making is the only appropriate approach to the key decisions to be entrusted to the new mechanism.

The United States supports, at an absolute minimum, the establishment of a programme and budget decision-making mechanism which would operate on the basis of consensus in establishing both an agreed budget level and clear-cut priorities for the Organization within that level. The United States is prepared, in the spirit of compromise, to accept the Chairman's version of chapter VI, since it does establish such a programme and budget committee based on consensus. There should, however, be no misunderstanding on this point by the membership. Chairman Vraalsen's proposal represents a major compromise for the United States, as it does for other Member States. We are reassured to see that support for the Chairman's version of chapter VI reaches well beyond the usual North-South division on such issues."

The representative of **Iraq**[119]

"Chapter II deals with the intergovernmental machinery and its functioning. Here I must share with the representatives in this Hall my own personal scepticism when it comes to intergovernmental machinery. Ever since I can remember - and that is a very long time stretching through three decades - we have been trying to restructure and review the restructuring of the intergovernmental machinery in this house, especially in the economic and social fields, and almost invariably, at every turn, the net result has been to add yet another complexity and another layer of unco-ordinated activity. ...

The report of the Group of 18 is studded with the following terms - and many of its recommendations do not go beyond them: to study, to study in depth, to review, to streamline, to restructure, to rationalize, to co-ordinate. The representative of Singapore, one of the members of the Group of 18, said himself, that quite often, or most of the time, these are substitutes for inaction and for a lack of precision as to what needs to be done. ...

Why has the Group of 18 not commented on what should be done about the meetings of the Board of the United Nations Conference on Trade and Development (UNCTAD), with the Conference itself meeting every three years, as compared with the Second Committee and the Economic and Social Council and the concomitant recommendations on them? We know why they did not do it. It was because they knew there would be no consensus, and even if there were a consensus, they would be unable to persuade representatives in this Hall to accept it. But to ask for yet another in-depth study - by whom, by us who have created this monster, if I want to call it that - is, as I have said, not very appealing. ...

The one additional comment I want to make on the structure of the Secretariat is on Recommendation 24 concerning the Office of the United Nations Disaster Relief Co-ordinator (UNDRO). ... I think the recommendation that this function should be given to the United Nations Development Programme (UNDP) could be improved upon. I would advocate that UNDRO should simply be abolished and that the post of Co-ordinator should be transferred to the office of the Secretary-General. ...

With regard to chapter IV ... The recommendations do not get anywhere near what is really ailing the Secretariat. ...

In recommendation 54 the Group of 18 could only agree that no Under-Secretary-General or Assistant Secretary-General should serve more than 10 years, but it skirted what we have talking about for 20 years: that, especially at the top, immediately under the Secretary-General, the reform should be begun by rotating those posts. There is no clear-cut recommendation on that or even an indication that it was discussed. There is no indication why it was rejected or why it was not recommended. ...

Mr. President ... why should the man on your left always be an American? Why should the man who is always seated on the left of the president of the Security Council be a citizen of the Soviet Union? Why should a Frenchman have been head of the Departments dealing with economic and social affairs at the United Nations for the last 35 years? ... We would not be taking anything from the permanent members; we would not be saying that no national of any of the five permanent members should be an Assistant Secretary-General or an Under-Secretary-General. But can we discuss it, even privately, and see whether we can agree on this? Perhaps a deal could be made so that the Secretary-General could begin to take action. Many of the problems, both reported and unreported, ensue from the fact, not that any P-3 or P-4 post is frozen, but that the important posts at the top are frozen. There is no rotation there, and these bailiwicks keep building up, with overlapping, perhaps with a lack of co-ordination and even with a lack of supervision from the top. ...

With regard to recruitment, we beat about the bush; we talk about examinations, and we talk about Member States putting pressure on the Secretary-General. Let us face it, in eight out of 10 cases - and that might be a conservative estimate - we find jobs for people; we do not recruit the best people for the job. We are all guilty of that, every delegation is guilty. The

Secretary-General is under pressure, and we should face this. ... There must be identification of the qualifications needed for a job, no matter what it is, before we start seeing to whom we should give the job. ... I think that in this area the Group of 18 has been unusually timid, more timid than in some other areas. ...

Recommendations 63 to 67 are all about one unit, the Joint Inspection Unit. ... I understand that the Unit costs some $4 million. I should like to ask this question and all of us should try to answer it: is the Joint Inspection Unit worth $4 million on the basis of the results that it has achieved? ... Whatever good reports were implemented, with resultant savings or streamlining or better administrative methods, I would say - and I would challenge anyone to disprove this - that this could have been done by other means, such as through top-notch consultants, for a fraction of the cost of the Joint Inspection Unit. ... We all know that the Group of 18 could not say that the Joint Inspection Unit should be abolished, because it would have been strung up on the nearest tree to Headquarters. There are too many with vested interests - not only those that have inspectors on the Joint Inspection Unit but those that want to be on it or support those that are on it. We have not discussed whether the solution is to give more power to the Joint Inspection Unit, to streamline its methods or to ask Member States - a pious hope - to upgrade the qualifications required of their candidates for that Unit. ... It is not going to be the best qualified man from country A that gets the job. We know that, and no amount of recommendations is going to change that. ...

We cannot say that, as Senator Kassebaum put it initially, we will withhold our contribution unless there is weighted voting, and then change our position and say that nobody wants weighted voting; the Group of 18 is against it; what we want is consensus. What is consensus? Ultimately, it means abolishing all voting, weighted or unweighted. If every Member of the Assembly or of any group has to vote positively for everything, consensus means something much worse than weighted voting; it means transferring the veto of the five permanent members of the Security Council to others - going back to the League of Nations, where every member of the Council of the League of Nations had a veto. ...

If the largest contributor, or the next largest contributor, or one of the two or three below that says it will not pay unless we do certain things, and we all discuss reforms under that kind of duress, we shall be setting the worst kind of precedent. I can think of horrible results that would perhaps strike at the heart of the Organization. We cannot accept that. ...

On the three options in chapter VI, (a), (b) and (c), I am glad that not much support has surfaced for recommendation (c), because that would indeed be catastrophic. ...

We talk about the Advisory Committee on Administrative and Budgetary Questions (ACABQ) and the Committee for Programme and Co-ordination (CPC), and the gist of all three options is that they would deprive the Secretary-General of the limited authority he now has to prepare programme and budget estimates. ...

We would agree that perhaps there should be consultations, indications and some kind of consensus on the overall ceiling of what the United Nations should do in the economic and social sphere, before the Secretary-General presents the medium-term plan, certainly, and perhaps even the programme budgets for the biennium. But the Secretary-General is the number one political animal in this house and he is not going to propose fantastically unacceptable levels of expenditure. ...

Ideally, in the economic and social area that would be the best way to do it, but we must first separate what is really the heart of the purposes of the United Nations, namely, the political area. I saw in the report of the Group of 18 an estimate that some 10 per cent is spent in the political area. This part of the budget has two characteristics. First, it is not subject to sudden changes unless there is a big crisis, and if there are such changes the Member States, because of the enormous political pressure, have no problem in voting the funds. So we are not talking about the part of the budget which is to service the political activities. If the Security Council decides to do something, even from the regular budget, the practice has been that Member States go along with it.

It is in the economic and social areas that the real difficulties arise. Here I must admit one thing. I am absolutely convinced that in the area of establishing priorities Member States would never agree. There would always be one or two countries or a group of countries, or certain vested interests in the Secretariat that - sometimes contrary to the wishes of the Secretary-General - would want to perpetuate one or other part of the budget. We are never going to get priorities; priorities must come and can only come from the man who knows most about it and from the principal body working full time on it, and that is the Secretariat.

I would have preferred the Group of 18, whichever combination of proposals in chapter VI is accepted, to separate the two things. I think we need to remedy the situation with regard to the general availability of funds by some kind of general agreement, but priorities must first come from the Secretary-General. We may take those priorities and throw them in the East River, as we have done so often, but if we were to leave it arbitrarily to any group of intergovernmental organs I do not think we should advance the cause of programme budgeting in the United Nations. ...

Let us take as a basis the economic and social activities of the United Nations, which constitute the bulk and by far the largest amount of the expenditure, which are the ones that keep on increasing and which call for control. In that I would decide or indicate to the Secretary-General what is the level of money available for the United Nations, and then ask him to present, within the limits of that level, what he thinks should be abolished, despite all the recommendations and the decisions of the intergovernmental bodies, including this Assembly. I would encourage, I would push, I would pester the Secretary-General to tell us which parts of the Secretariat, which parts of the expenditures are no longer really valid, which ones should be instituted, which ones should be downgraded, which ones should be put into category B and if additional funds are available in the next round, should be given priority. ...

Member States will never be able to tell the Secretary-General from the outset what the priorities should be. I think not only that the first step in deciding priorities should be left to the Secretary-General, but that we should insist that he should perform that task, and after that we will examine his proposal and see what we can do. ...

The four specific recommendations - a 15 per cent reduction in posts, 25 per cent in assistant secretaries-general and under-secretaries-general, 20 per cent in outside consultants, 20 per cent in official travel - these come to my mind as being perhaps the only ones - with one or two others - that are actually specific. We support them. But why 15 per cent? Why 20 per cent? Why not 20 per cent? Why not 12 per cent? We are not told why, and we are not told where to cut. Still, they are arbitrary. Yes. But the Secretary-General has indicated, at least indirectly in his report, that he can live with them, and he will do it.

We would have preferred the Group of 18, at least in regard to the under-secretaries-general and the assistant secretaries-general, to indicate to the Secretary-General which ones should be cut. In our own view, since we established all these posts, which ones are no longer valid? Where should the Secretary-General go for cutting? Should he cut the post of Mr. Buffum or Mr. Smirnov? Or should he go somewhere else? There is no indication there.

... we are sorry that there is nothing ... in the report of the Group of 18 about the scale of assessments. There is nothing in the Charter about the scale of assessments. What is in the Charter is that the Assembly is to apportion the budget of the Organization. We have invented the "capacity to pay". We have lived with it. But now, as this distinguished American said last summer, the capacity to pay may be turned into the capacity to destroy. And that is that. That is bad for those who intentionally or unintentionally would destroy the United Nations. The capacity to pay should not be raised to the level of the capacity to destroy through budgetary manoeuvring."

The representative of **Guyana**[120]

"There is a need to ensure participation by Member States at an earlier stage of the budget process than is at present the case. It is necessary to keep in mind that the current financial crisis was precipitated by withholdings by Member States resulting from disagreement on the content and level of the budget of the Organization due to political disagreement on parts of the substantive activities included in the programme budget. It is therefore necessary to devise a mechanism and practical procedures that would facilitate and encourage broad agreement on the budget, notwithstanding political differences on substantive issues that may persist among Member States. ...

We agree that one aim of the reform should be to improve the functioning of the CPC in the submission of recommendations on the medium-term plan and the programme budget. If there must be reform, then let it be; but there must be no compromise of or encroachment on the authority of the General Assembly and the Fifth Committee to decide on the content and level of the budget of the Organization, and all procedures must be in full compliance with the principles and provisions of the Charter."

The representative of **Nicaragua**[121]

"Generally speaking, we have no substantive difficulty with the recommendations contained in part A of chapter II; those recommendations relate to the need to rationalize the number and duration of meetings and conferences, documentation and so forth. As for part C, concerning co-ordination, we would have wished to see more clear and precise recommendations. ...

In view of the fact that the report we are considering proposes changes that will have a decisive impact on the future of the Organization, we believe that the active participation of all the Member States, on the basis of the principle of sovereign equality, must be guaranteed. We find it paradoxical that States that have always waved high the banner of domestic democracy should now seek to impose the concept of limited democracy and limited sovereignty on

smaller States, merely because the latter make smaller contributions to the Organization's budget. To yield to such pressures would imply accepting the imposition of such concepts and violating the principles of the Charter. In such an event, my delegation considers that the correct decision would be to take at their word those who have threatened to reduce the level of their contributions.
...

With regard to the decision-making process, we must express our opposition to any attempt to undermine the democratic decision-making system that has prevailed in this Organization and that is based on the principle of the sovereign equality of all the Member States - a principle at the very root of the grandeur and strength of this Organization."

The representative of the **Libyan Arab Jamahiriya**[122]

"It might be argued that there is over-staffing in the administrative structure. I certainly agree that the organizational structure should be streamlined and its efficiency increased, especially the top echelon, as indicated in the Group's report, since those senior posts have become bargaining chips in certain dealings with certain countries. Thus the Secretary-General has been made powerless to act in the face of the special pressures brought to bear upon him, either directly by some countries or in other cases, on a regional basis. Furthermore, there will have to be reforms with regard to over-staffing and the great privileges that the staff enjoy.

In that connection there is a subject which I must address, namely, the absence of a genuine or equitable representation of States in the Secretariat at either the senior or the lower levels. In fact, many countries are either under-represented or not represented at all. However, the solution of this problem should not divert us from examining the political aspects of the problem.

Some have tried to convince us that the problem is the financial crisis and that pressure should be brought to bear on the United Nations. Attempts have been made to convert the General Assembly into another Security Council, where the veto could be exercised because one Power has greater political clout or contributes a larger share of the budget. If such attempts were allowed to succeed it would be the beginning of the end of the United Nations, which, as I have said, continues to be the symbol of hope for nations large and small.

The agenda of the United Nations General Assembly has undoubtedly been growing over the past 40 years. Not all the problems on that agenda have been solved. Some problems are examined under various agenda items in the

General Assembly. The merging of such items may simplify procedures and achieve big financial savings, but it will not solve the problems...

Why is that campaign waged against the United Nations, and the General Assembly in particular, after the Security Council has turned itself into a sort of General Assembly through the frustration of its resolutions by the use of the right of veto? The purpose of the campaign is to achieve the same thing in the General Assembly through the introduction of another right of veto into its procedures. The time has come to amend or even abrogate the right of veto in the Security Council, not to introduce another veto into the General Assembly."

The representative of **Uruguay**[123]

"we agree with certain comments made by a number of delegations concerning the vagueness of certain recommendations and the excessive rigidity of others, as is the case with recommendation 3 (e), or the rather simplistic or too generalized nature of the solutions proposed, as in recommendation 15.

... measures, which are designed to achieve greater administrative and financial efficiency, will in many cases lead to a welcome reduction in expenditure, but that reduction in itself cannot be a basic aim of the proposed reforms. Like other delegations, we particularly wish to warn against any tendency to seek an indiscriminate reduction of expenditure. The critical financial situation, resulting essentially from the non-payment of assessed contributions by some Member States, must not obscure our clear perception of the mission and purposes of the Organization, for which it must have the resources it needs, rationally and efficiently administered but not arbitrarily limited.

... with regard to chapter VI, concerning the question of planning and budget procedure, ... my delegation leans towards option (b) in the report of the Group of 18."

The representative of the **Lao People's Democratic Republic**[124]

"My Government sees the need for the proposed restructuring of the intergovernmental machinery because the administrative clumsiness and paralysing bureaucracy make it impossible for our Organization to carry out efficiently and effectively the noble task entrusted to it by the Charter. This is especially true because the international situation develops and changes quickly and also because the initial economic and social needs of Member States, most of which have not been completely satisfied, have been supplemented by new ones, by more urgent and complex problems, and the satisfaction of those needs is of overriding importance. ...

My delegation was surprised to learn that at the present time there are many departments and offices dealing with political, economic and social matters, that there is an excessive number of committees, sub-committees, commissions, sub-commissions and working groups within the United Nations. The effort to regroup or to merge these bodies or entities, where necessary, and to co-ordinate their activities is clearly desirable. Quality should, unquestionably, take priority over quantity. It goes without saying that a reform of this type would involve a considerable reduction in administrative expenditure. But in no circumstances should this operation be carried out to the detriment of the recognized interests of the States Members of the United Nations, especially those in which the level of economic and social development is very low, among which countries my own is to be found.

I now come to the problem of restructuring the Secretariat. My Government endorses in principle the recommendation by the Group of High-level Intergovernmental Experts for a reduction of the number of staff members at all levels but particularly in the higher echelons. The spirit and letter of recommendation 15 seem acceptable to us on the whole. Concerning the measures relating to staff, my Government feels that a large number of recommendations by the Group of 18 deserve serious consideration by the Assembly. It would be very desirable for the Secretary-General to ensure that the principle that no post should be considered the exclusive preserve of any Member State, or group of States, a principle reaffirmed by the General Assembly in resolution 35/210 of 17 December 1980, be applied faithfully in accordance with the principle of equitable geographical distribution. My delegation is in full agreement with recommendation 47 because thus far there has been a tendency to neglect the legitimate interests of the developing countries with regard to equitable representation of their nationals at senior levels."

The representative of **Senegal**[125]

"First, it has been recommended that the number and duration of United Nations conferences and meetings be reduced. On principle we agree. None the less we must not lose sight of the fact that these meetings and conferences often provide an excellent framework for negotiations and agreement on issues of common interest, above all those that involve international peace and security or the economic and social development of the international community. In making reductions, we must not lose sight of these points. Secondly, a substantial reduction of Secretariat staff at all levels is proposed. Indiscriminate increases in Secretariat staff must be avoided, because the quality of work would suffer. With savings in mind and in view of the need to absorb the present budgetary deficit, it is tempting to support this. It could be a palliative, but not a remedy. That is why my delegation believes that this recommendation warrants much more thorough study, especially since the implementation of the measure with undue speed could seriously affect the implementation of certain programmes. Staff reductions, therefore, must not be made too hastily."

The representative of **Burundi**[126]

"For the most part, the recommendations contained in the first five chapters of the report are acceptable, with certain alterations. ...

The General Assembly must be fully informed about the motivations that dictated certain recommendations. Even a superficial analysis shows that the over-all steps taken by the Group seem to have given priority to the suppression of certain bodies, to programme cuts, to a reduction in staff and to revenue-generating activities. My delegation doubts that this is the right course implied by General Assembly resolution 40/237. ...

Some proposals seem to us to challenge, without sufficient justification, decisions laboriously negotiated and adopted by the General Assembly. Other recommendations deal with the conditions of employment of Secretariat personnel, without taking their views into account.

Although we agree on the need to lighten the machinery of the Secretariat and to bring the number of staff down to a reasonable level, we must bear in mind, when we reshuffle offices and services, the reasons for which they were created. In any case, we cannot support the policy of throwing the baby out with the bath water.

With regard to measures affecting personnel, my delegation will support those measures that are compatible with resolutions 39/245 and 40/258, which seek a balanced and equitable geographical distribution of staff throughout the Secretariat. We hope that, by means of the reforms being undertaken, representation of the developing countries at the executive level will finally be improved, in order to reflect the universal character of the Organization.

The main difficulty lies in the proposals contained in chapter VI of the report of the Group of 18, relating to planning and budget procedure. ...

The bitterness of the present debate derives from the fact that the conclusions of the Group of 18 seem rather weighted in favour of the major contributor States, to the detriment of the sacrosanct principle of the sovereign equality of Member States.

We believe that solutions (a) and (c) examined in the report do not deserve further consideration by the General Assembly. A merger of planning and budgetary functions is not to be recommended and cannot solve the problem being addressed.

If our goal is to seek rationalization in order to establish a wider basis for agreement on the budget, what is required is not so much the creation of new structures than the strengthening of existing ones. ...

Changes should be carried out cautiously, but my delegation could not go along with any attempt to modify the relationships of authority within the United Nations or to alter the democratic decision-making process in the subsidiary bodies of the General Assembly which are responsible for planning and budget - that is, the Advisory Committee on Administrative and Budgetary Questions (ACABQ) and the Committee for Programme and Co-ordination (CPC)."

The representative of **Ghana**[127]

"In the view of the Ghana delegation, since add-ons have become such a controversial issue, despite the statistics which show their marginal impact on the budget, it should be possible for the General Assembly to take measures at the level of ACABQ to address those problems. In the meantime, in order to reduce any possible impact of add-ons, we suggest the following measures. First, the initial budget should include all foreseeable elements of expenditure. Secondly, decisions requiring supplementary funding should be taken into account in the formulation of the next programme budget, unless any of those decisions are considered priority items which cannot be postponed. Thirdly, we should institute a practice of not returning to Member States savings on currency and inflation until the financial period is over. Fourthly, we should set up a contingency fund. Its level should be established when the General Assembly adopts appropriations for a particular financial period. ...

Since it is necessary to involve Member States fully in the budgetary process from the very beginning to the end, the following suggestions may also be worthy of consideration. The budgetary instructions issued to various programme managers by the Secretary-General should be based on guidelines prepared by him during the off-budget period and approved by the Fifth Committee, after a review by CPC and ACABQ in accordance with their respective mandates. It goes without saying that during the budget year the normal consideration of the budget through CPC, ACABQ and the Fifth Committee will follow. ...

The other recommendations by the Group of 18 need not pose any serious difficulties, given a spirit of positive negotiations. On the question of personnel reduction, we agree that there is room for improvement. In the general reduction, while maintaining the principle of equitable geographical distribution care should be taken not to damage the morale of the staff through arbitrary decisions. In this respect, outside bodies like the International Civil Service Commission could be requested to assist with the exercise. ...

With regard to the structure of the Secretariat, my delegation finds the proposals to be generally satisfactory. The exercise of restructuring, however, should be conducted on rational principles and should not be based on individuals, otherwise the already delicate balance of geographical distribution could be disturbed.

Let me take the opportunity at this stage to comment on certain misconceptions about the underlying causes of the crisis that the United Nations is now facing. It is said that there is lack of agreement among the various Member States on how to finance and utilize the Organization, and for what purposes. There is the perception that this lack of agreement has been the consequence of exasperation on the part of the major contributors at what they considered fiscal irresponsibility of the developing countries and the erosion of their own influence on the world body. This is not correct. The problem is the large-scale withholding of assessed payments intended to coerce the Organization into following a line acceptable to those who feel they have the power to do so. Some of the statements in the present debate clearly attest to this; yet even without the reforms called for, their influence, which they complain is not commensurate with their financial contributions to the United Nations, has been all-pervasive. A case in point was the introduction during the thirty-seventh session of the policy of zero growth without any meaningful consultations with the developing countries, yet the policy has halted development projects beneficial to the developing countries.

There is yet another misconception which must be clarified. The United Nations is criticized for taking as much as 75 per cent of the regular budget as salaries for its staff. That criticism conceals the essential nature of the staff to the world body and the countries from which they hail but it is they who form the resources and assets of the Organization and it is upon them that the task of translating mandates by Member States into activities depends. Such use of the budget cannot therefore be considered wasteful."

The representative of **Viet Nam**[128]

"While welcoming most of the recommendations of the Group of Experts, my delegation feels that some points within some of the recommendations, leave something to be desired, for technical reasons and because of possible political implications. ...

It is necessary to define precisely the appropriate procedures, rules and methods for the functioning of the General Assembly and the Main Committees and, if necessary, to simplify them with a view to greater effectiveness. However, we must show caution when we take decisions on the number and duration of meetings and conferences, as well as on the number of resolutions that can be adopted. The best way to do this would be to establish jointly an order of priority for all questions, especially questions of international security and disarmament, economic and social questions and development questions. ...

With regard to the structure of the Secretariat, we approve the principle of a significant reduction in personnel which would nevertheless guarantee the requirement of greater effectiveness in the work of the Secretariat while keeping the activities of the Organization at their present level. Moreover, such reduction should not prejudice the principle of equitable representation at all levels of the Secretariat."

The representative of **Somalia**[129]

"My delegation wishes to give particular support to the recommendations contained in chapter II, which addresses the need to streamline and co-ordinate the intergovernmental machinery. These recommendations touch upon the heart of the matter: what do we, the Member States, expect from the United Nations? What are our priorities? ... Avoiding duplication, merging overlapping activities, developing criteria to phase out redundant programmes - to do all this is more than desirable; it is essential for the continued functioning of the United Nations. ...

Indeed, the Secretariat is top-heavy, too complex, too fragmented, and it could be leaner. In that, it mirrors the intergovernmental machinery. My delegation strongly supports the proposals made to simplify the structure of the Secretariat, and it agrees that reductions are needed in the number of staff. However, such cuts should not be made across the board, since this would damage the Secretariat's effectiveness in crucial areas while still leaving too much slack in redundant parts of the Organization. The planning for staff reductions should be closely linked to the process whereby priorities are set for the Secretariat, and this, in turn, depends on our ability to redefine the intergovernmental structure. Particularly at the top, any reductions in the number of Under-Secretaries-General and Assistant Secretaries-General will depend on the type of leadership needed in a leaner United Nations, and thus on the new areas of emphasis developed in the review of intergovernmental priorities. Therefore my delegation would like to see these reductions introduced as the outcome of any streamlining in the intergovernmental framework, not as a prelude to such reforms. ...

While its many proposals are timely and useful, the Group of Experts has stopped short of pressing for the key reforms that must be introduced to strengthen the personnel function: the completion of a comprehensive and accessible data base, the strengthening of the job classification system, the rationalization of the management structure and the development of a comprehensive planning system.

Moreover, many specific recommendations require further analysis, in order to ensure that their literal implementation does not jeopardize the intentions that inspired them. Let me give just one example. We fully share the Group's view that more appointments should be made at the junior levels. This, in turn, requires a thorough redesigning of jobs in order to create more functions at the lower levels. But there are limits to this, and these are set by the objective staffing needs of the Organization. Do we need a staff with considerable national and international experience, who can submit work of substance and authority, or do we want to create a training-ground for future international civil servants? The proposal to hire some 200 young people every year, while reducing the overall number of staff, might imply that mid-level and senior staff doing crucial work have to be terminated in order to make room for relatively inexperienced aspirants to a career. ...

As to the proposals on monitoring, evaluation and inspection in chapter V, I can indeed voice support for the recommendations made by the Group. The question arises, nevertheless, why the monitoring function of bodies other than the Joint Inspection Unit has not been addressed. If the Group believes that the ICSC should play a more important role in monitoring the implementation of personnel standards, as set out in recommendation 53, should the recommendations in this chapter not be expanded to address the ICSC as well? ...

The Charter does not distinguish between rich and poor, large and small. Indeed, if the place of each country in this Organization were limited from the outset by its ability to contribute financially, many of us would not be here. The contribution that some of us make can be measured by other criteria, however. There are qualitative elements, the coherence of our views, the intellectual reach of our proposals, the moral vision of our leadership, which cannot be ranked on the basis of per capita income. The budgetary process is not just a technical matter: it is a process whereby we set priorities and allocate resources. ... For example, rather than accepting cuts across the board, even in a period of austerity, we should focus on those programmes that must remain inviolate in order not to undo what has been built in the past. In particular, I should like, *inter alia*, to mention our efforts in the area of technical co-operation, our programmes for refugees, our activities to combat *apartheid*, and our support for the rights of the Palestinian people.

Achieving a consensus is desirable, but must not become a paralysing constraint. On the other hand, sufficient consideration should be given to the interests and concerns of the major contributors, and decisions on the budget should not lead to polarization or confrontation."

The representative of **Barbados**[130]

"The recommendations dealing with the entitlements of staff members ... should be carefully considered. Much thought should be given to their likely effects on the common system. Recommendation 43 (1) contains a proposal that recruitment by competitive examinations should be extended to the P-3 level. This proposal had previously been made to the Fifth Committee and was opposed by a number of delegations, including mine. We can see no reason to change our position on this proposal, which, if implemented, might well result in serious disadvantage to candidates from a wide range of Member States. Recommendation 43 (2) is even less appealing."

The representative of **Cameroon**[131]

"Some of our number, which pay the largest contributions to the United Nations budget, are seeking more complete control over the budgetary process; in this they are armed also with various new mechanisms by which they hope to block any decisions inconsistent with their perspectives. Whether or not they are justified in seeking control would ordinarily be a side issue, which could be determined by an appropriate examination of their complaints and alleged frustrations. As now presented, it has become fundamental. It is our sincere hope that the complaints and frustrations of the so-called minor contributors will receive the same hearing and treatment. ...

In the restructuring recommended for the Department of Political Affairs, Trusteeship and Decolonization, the priority given to the Namibian situation must not be lowered, directly or indirectly. ...

The study requested by that chapter must further promote the decentralization mandated by resolution 32/197 of 20 December 1977, in order to reinforce the activities of regional commissions, especially at the sub-regional level. Furthermore, it is imperative that the Department of Technical Co-operation for Development be strengthened and the Office of the Director-General streamlined. The Department of Administration and Management will need similar streamlining in order to enhance further efficiency and effectiveness. Further streamlining will also be necessary at United Nations offices in Geneva, Vienna and so on, for purposes of cost-effectiveness. That is a very important, and sometimes overlooked, issue.

I turn now to chapter IV, relating to measures regarding personnel, and would briefly make the following comments.

First, the recommendation to cut posts at the top level by 25 per cent and those at the lower level by 15 per cent requires further study by the Fifth Committee. We believe it is necessary to have a clear picture of the scope of the financial implications and their consequences on the capacity of the Secretariat to carry out the workload of mandates given to the Secretary-General by Member States.

Secondly, some of the recommendations which touch upon the common system would benefit from further expert studies by the International Civil Service Commission as well as commentary by the Administrative Committee on Co-ordination (ACC).

Thirdly, in accordance with the relevant resolutions of the General Assembly it must be ensured that the personnel, through their representatives, have a say on the various reforms proposed under this chapter.

Fourthly, with regard to recommendation 57, we note that it touches upon the prerogatives of Member States and, consequently, we would request that it be carefully reviewed in order to avoid encroachments on those prerogatives. We need not commence an activity which would turn out to be an exercise in futility. ...

Sections A and B of Chapter VI, in particular paragraphs 58 to 68, are based on a series of false premises and debatable issues. There are many sweeping and contradictory assertions which are not based on facts. Three alternatives are presented. Alternatives A and C seek the same objective, despite different formulations and the use of codes. That objective is to establish a single programme and budget committee to replace the Committee for Programme and Co-ordination and the Advisory Committee on Administrative and Budgetary Questions, so for the purposes of discussion we must treat recommendations A and C as having the same objectives.

That committee will, as we analyze it, predetermine the level and content of the United Nations budget before the Secretary-General prepares it; allocate resources in accordance with the priorities it has determined; or take decisions by consensus.

The creation of such a committee and its system would imply that the Fifth Committee would have little or no authority, and, by extension, it is understood that neither the General Assembly itself nor the other principal legislative organs be in a position to exercise fully their prerogatives under the Charter. It would complicate, furthermore, the prerogatives of the Secretary-General as chief administrator in the formulation and presentation of the budget.

To establish such a committee, alternatives A and C suggest either the suppression of the Committee for Programme and Co-ordination and the Advisory Committee on Administrative and Budgetary Questions or the transformation of the former. It is in that context that alternative A proposes the "reinforcement" of the Committee for Programme and Co-ordination by changing the name, mandate, composition and decision-making process of that committee and by establishing a permanent secretariat for the so-called new organ. On that question we want to make the following comments.

First, the creation of a programme budget committee would be unjustifiable and indeed undesirable. It has been proposed several times in the past and rejected on each occasion for the reasons I have just stated. Secondly, the setting up of the proposed programme budget committee would, *ipso facto*, face complications in terms of the establishment of a mandate in a way that would avoid revision of the Charter. If it must not revise the Charter - which we are all agreed it must not - then we would face the issue of the role of a new body with a mandate that duplicated and provided no greater efficiency than existing ones. That would offer an inappropriate structural answer to problems relating to policy and management. Thirdly, the system has been tried in the United Nations Industrial Development Organization (UNIDO) and, even given the limited sphere of that organization's activities, it has not quite worked there yet. Experience is much too short for conclusions to be drawn of the application of such a system over a more complicated organization such as the United Nations. Fourthly, what is worse, the implications of the current proposals as they stand would result in unacceptable amendments to the United Nations Charter and instruments deriving from it.

Alternative B is really an alternative to recommendations A and C and is simply an amendment to recommendation A, submitted by some experts in the Group in order to achieve a consensus - not to reflect their positions - which unfortunately was not achieved. It does postulate interesting ideas which could be further refined to form an excellent basis for compromise."

The representative of **Solomon Islands**[132]

"there is one particular recommendation that concerns my delegation: it is recommendation 6, in chapter II. ...

The provision for reimbursing travel costs for our representatives to these sessions is important to us. Without it we would not have been able to participate as we have done up to the present. The recommendation to limit reimbursement of these costs to the least developed countries would cut us off completely from this useful assistance, as we are not listed as a least developed country.

While I do not wish to resort to calling this recommendation unfair, I am obliged to point out that the present formulation does not seem to take into account the basic need for this form of assistance. To my delegation the important purpose of this provision is to enable delegations to have the necessary personnel from their capitals to assist in covering and participating in the various Committees of this Assembly. Hence the criteria for qualifying for this assistance should not be based entirely on a Member State's listing as a least developed country. This assistance should be given to those Member States that need it most."

The representative of **Syrian Arab Republic**[133]

"It is true that the changing international conditions and the emerging challenges have led to a gradual expansion of the functions of the Organization, its size, the size of its agenda and the emergence of new functions in addition to the persistence of old functions which led to the establishment of new bodies and committees at various levels. However, this expansion and growth, we believe, must be viewed as a healthy phenomenon which expresses the vitality of the Organization and its responsiveness to the growing needs of the international community under extremely complicated international conditions. It is only natural, as a result, that there must be a greater number of meetings and conferences held under the auspices of the United Nations to deal with political, social and economic problems and developments resulting from the current imbalance in the present system of international relations.

The convening of such conferences and meetings is inevitable in order to redress this imbalance and impose respect for law in the interests of security, peace and co-operation in the world. Hence, we feel that any reduction in the number of these meetings and conferences or any curtailment of their duration is inconsistent with the reality of our contemporary international life.

This statement also applies to the recommendations regarding the reduction or cancellation of documents or certain committees or the merging of some committees. We believe that such actions, regardless of the arguments adduced to justify them, will no doubt lead to a curtailment of the activities of the United Nations and its effective role and to its transformation into an international organization unable to respond to the developing and continuously growing needs of the international community.

Our real aim must not be to achieve financial savings but to enhance the role of the United Nations through reorganizing its basic structure in order to enable it to play its role effectively as envisioned by the Charter. We should all recall that in any process of reform the current financial crisis is fundamentally the result of the lack of political will on the part of some Member States. Unless such political will is demonstrated, reform measures will be to no avail in enhancing the effectiveness of the Organization; rather, their effects will be completely limited to the financial and administrative areas. I do not believe that this is our common objective or rather the objective of the overwhelming majority of the States Members of this Organization.

It is clear that the aim of bringing financial pressures to bear on the United Nations is to restructure its basic organs in such a way as to restore to a small group of strong and influential Member States, the positions which they enjoyed in the past and through which they controlled international affairs in a manner compatible with their interests. Hence, we will oppose any reform measures aimed at achieving such a goal. ...

What concerns and interests us most in this report is the content of chapter VI described by many previous speakers as constituting the central question in this context. ... In brief, my delegation supports option (b) which preserves the existing procedures that have proved their effectiveness. My delegation cannot but express its opposition to any attempt to introduce the principle of consensus into the General Assembly regarding administrative, financial or other matters since such a principle is an extension of the right of veto. This would impede the adoption of resolutions in the interests of the international community and of the future of our Organization."

In accordance with the procedure previously approved, the debate was suspended in plenary, while the Fifth Committee undertook, within the scope of its responsibilities, a factual examination of the report of the Group of 18. Its findings were subsequently submitted to the Plenary Assembly for final consideration.

2.2.3 Consideration of the Report of the Group of 18 by the Fifth Committee

The Fifth Committee met informally from 16 to 23 October 1986 to consider the report of the Group of 18 chapter by chapter. In addition, the Fifth Committee was also required to study and take decisions on items that affected the organization's staff and their condition of service. This included a discussion of the report of the ICSC (A/41/30) on the UN pension system. Since these items also affected the interests of the specialized agencies which were members of the common system, the ACC also submitted their comments on the staff issue to the Fifth Committee (A/C.5/41/28). For the discussion of chapter VI (planning and budget procedure), a distinction was made between measures on which agreement was imminent and those which were still pending. The committee was required to express an opinion only on the latter. During the informal meetings, a number of questions were posed by delegations to which answers were subsequently provided, at formal meetings, by the Chairman of the Group of 18, the Chairman of the ACABQ, the Chairman of ICSC and the representatives of the Secretary-General. The Fifth Committee also decided to invite a representatives of the staff of the UN secretariat and of the Federation of International Civil Servants' Associations (FICSA) to present their views to the Committee. Further informal consultations were held from 24 October to 5 November to elaborate a draft of the committee's submission to the plenary, which was approved on 5 November 1986.

Statements made during the formal meetings are recalled below. They provide further interpretation and explanation of the report of the Group of 18, not by member states, but by the Chairman of the Group of 18, ACABQ, ICSC and representatives of the secretariat and staff. These statements were followed by the approval of the Fifth Committee report on the Group of 18 report. First of all, however, a statement made by the **Secretary-General**[134] on the issues affecting the staff is recalled:

"the climate of uncertainty surrounding the Organization and the impression of a gradual erosion of the conditions of service - and even of what were considered by many to be acquired rights - was not conducive to the efforts required within the Secretariat to meet the challenge of the current situation. ... He felt it was fair and appropriate, therefore, to ask the Fifth Committee, once again, for such understanding and support, especially with regard to the equitable treatment of the staff and the maintenance of standards which could ensure an environment that would allow the Secretariat to focus its energies on the immense task before it, rather than dissipating them in fears about deteriorating conditions of services."

In response to the questions raised during the informal consultations on the report of the Group of 18, following relies were provided to the Fifth Committee.

Mr. Akwei, **Chairman of the ICSC**[135]

"that the Commission had not been consulted by the Group of High-level Intergovernmental Experts on those matters which were within the Commission's mandate. It had, therefore, followed with great interest the comments made by delegations, noting those proposing that some items should be referred to it, especially those affecting other organizations of the common system as well as the United Nations, and the expressions of caution in that regard. ...

The restructuring and reform of the Secretariat were administrative matters which were within the province of the Secretary-General. However, they involved some fundamental principles which concerned the Commission. It was not explained in the report of the Group of Experts on what basis the percentage reductions of staff had been selected and whether those reductions resulted from a prior analysis of restructuring requirements, as should have been the case, or from a purely budgetary requirement. In the absence of such analysis, it was not established that a particular percentage reduction would produce greater efficiency in the administrative functioning of the Organization. Given the importance of good management-staff relations and the inevitable effect of reductions on staff morale, the Commission hoped that any reductions deemed necessary for efficiency would be effected after a convincing analysis and close consultations with the staff. ... It was also necessary that any reductions should be made after a proper performance appraisal and review of comparative job performance. The Commission had made several recommendations to guide organizations in that regard. No doubt the Secretary-General was also aware of the difficulty of recommending termination of inefficient staff in different office units with dissimilar levels of inefficiency. ...

In regard to recommendations 43 and 57, in particular he noted that matters bearing on the geographical distribution of staff must be decided ultimately by the General Assembly in view of their political nature as well as their effect on the administrative functioning of the Secretariat. In view of differences in the nature, membership and objectives of the various organizations, the Commission had not yet adopted a common approach to the question, which was still under study.

Many delegations had commented on competitive examinations, in particular the level up to which they should be conducted. That had been a matter of considerable controversy in the Fifth Committee and even in the Joint Inspection Unit. In 1985, the Commission had recommended competitive examinations "for recruitment, especially for the junior levels", and also for promotion from the General Service to the Professional level. It could therefore support recommendation 43.

The ratio of fixed-term to permanent appointments had also been a matter of concern and much study in the Commission. The Commission had given its view on the question in 1979, when it had stated that a core career staff was needed in the international civil service, the core varying in size from one organization to another depending on each organization's specific needs, and that the determination of the proportion of permanent and fixed-term staff should be made on an organization-by-organization basis. The proposals in recommendation 57, therefore, would best be decided on by the General Assembly. If any organization wished to refer them to the Commission for study and recommendation, it could always do so.

The period during which the performance of staff should be evaluated before a permanent contract was granted had changed in the United Nations in recent years. Earlier, many Professional staff had been recruited on a two-year probationary contract, usually leading to a permanent contract. Subsequently, the United Nations, in addition to many other organizations, had introduced a system whereby staff were employed on a series of fixed-term appointments, normally of two years' duration, before being considered for probationary contracts leading to permanent appointments. After reviewing the practice throughout the common system, the Commission had recommended, and the General Assembly had decided, in resolution 37/126 in 1982, that staff members on fixed-term appointments upon completion of five years of continuous good service should be given every reasonable consideration for a career appointment. In recommendation 45, the Group of High-level Intergovernmental Experts recommended a three-year eligibility period without making a case for it. Some clarification at least was needed. One aspect of shortening the period not mentioned was the question of United Nations implementation of General Assembly resolution 38/232, recommending that organizations should normally dispense with the requirement for a probationary appointment as a prerequisite for a career appointment following a period of five years' satisfactory service on fixed-term contracts. As far as he knew, that common system recommendation had not yet been followed up by the United Nations at Headquarters or other duty stations. The Group's radical proposal would need to be considered by the Commission. ...

Turning to recommendations 48, 49 and 50, he said that the Commission's current report (A/41/30) and its recommendations on career development in its previous annual reports were very clear. The implementation of those recommendations in regard to human resources development and the needs of the United Nations were a matter for the Secretary-General. The Commission had addressed the question of improving the performance evaluation system for rating staff comparatively and had recommended a format for the common system, but no organization was using it. If, as he assumed, the restructuring and reduction of staff was to be carried out on the basis of merit as stated, the Commission's recommendation deserved serious attention.

Regarding recommendation 53, he said it was not clear why the Group considered it necessary to modify the mandate of the Commission so that it could monitor implementation of personnel standards by the United Nations. A question had also been asked whether any inter-agency body was responsible for monitoring the compliance of organizations with decisions affecting the common system. That role was already assigned to the Commission under its statute ... What was required was for the Committee to consider what action to take regarding delay or non-progress in implementation. ...

Regarding recommendation 61, which dealt with total entitlements (salaries and conditions of service) of staff, he said that the assertion that total entitlements had reached a level that gave reason for serious concern had unfortunately not been substantiated. Since the basis for comparison was the conditions of service of the comparator civil service, they should be reviewed not just selectively but on the basis of total compensation comparison of the overall value of both United Nations and United States entitlements. That would conform more closely to the true meaning of the Noblemaire principle, which had never implied selection of individual entitlements for comparison but rather a general comparison of the conditions of service on both sides with due consideration for differences between the two services. If it was found that the value of United Nations entitlements was too high, only then could measures be introduced to reduce individual entitlements. At present there was no yardstick for measurement because no margin had yet been established for the total compensation comparison; the current methodology used by ICSC was incomplete because it was based on non-expatriate entitlements only.

Until the Assembly authorized a total compensation comparison methodology that embraced both non-expatriate and expatriate entitlements, no meaningful judgement could be made about the level of total entitlements. The two elements cited in recommendation 61, namely education grant and annual leave, were an expatriate entitlement and a partly expatriate entitlement respectively, and hence they could not be judged for the time being in a comprehensive comparison but only on an individual and incomplete basis. ...

A specific question had been asked about which national civil services had a benefit equivalent to that of the United Nations education grant, which reimbursed the cost of post-secondary studies up to the end of the fourth year or the award of a first university degree, whichever was earlier. The information in the Commission's possession on that question was not very specific in many cases and needed to be updated. For example, where an age limit for reimbursement was provided, it was not specified whether it included university education. Most countries provided scholarships and grants for university studies for children of qualifying nationals, under varying conditions, which were not available to non-nationals such as United Nations expatriates. Some even provided free university education. The United States and many other Governments provided more generous assistance for studies up to the secondary level than the United Nations, in many cases total reimbursement. The United States total reimbursement varied according to duty station and could, for example, go up to $20,000 per annum. If the proposal regarding the elimination of the education grant for post-secondary education was intended to bring the United Nations benefit into line with United States practice, the same logic should presumably apply to the education grant up to the secondary level, which would mean more expenditure for the United Nations. The Group had been silent on that point. Further, in respect of post-secondary education, the United States, for example, provided reimbursement for post-secondary education-related travel for children of nationals returning to the United States for university education. ...

Questions had also been raised about the amount of annual leave enjoyed by public servants in other countries and the estimated saving from a reduction in annual leave from six to four weeks in the United Nations Secretariat. It would, of course, be misleading to cost a reduction of six weeks leave to four as a pure saving of two weeks per staff member, both General Service and Professional, since it would not necessarily result in increased productivity or efficiency. No doubt the United Nations should be able to provide estimates. The information possessed by the Commission on annual leave entitlements in many Member States did not include paid official holidays, which were considerable in some countries, and needed to be updated. All United Nations salary review committees which had reviewed the leave system had recommended the same leave for General Service and Professional staff. If a new system was introduced whereby the leave entitlements of General Service staff were to be patterned on prevailing conditions at the duty station the amount could vary from well below six weeks to well above. In Rome, for example, the norm was 42.5 working days, or eight and a half weeks. In Vienna, the norm was 40.9 working days, or eight weeks. The policy of the United Nations system had been to have a standard amount that did not vary by duty station.

All those rather complex issues affected not only the United Nations but the rest of the organizations of the common system. Presumably, the Committee would not wish to introduce one system for the United Nations that would result in different leave and education entitlements for staff of different organizations at the same duty station, thus changing the concept of equal compensation for work of equal value. Further, in recommendation 61, the Group called for prompt implementation of its proposals regarding the education grant and the four weeks annual leave. Taken in conjunction with recommendation 42, that was a very disturbing approach.

In recommendation 42, the Group emphasized its belief that a coherent common system was highly desirable, but it then proceeded to recommend the "applicability of these new rules and regulations to other organizations in the United Nations system". That recommendation raised two concerns which affected the very foundation of the common system. First, the Group seemed to be saying in effect that what was good for the United Nations was good for all other organizations. That was not necessarily so, for it was only by harmonizing and co-ordinating the different practices of the various organizations in the common system that the Commission could evolve a general pattern suitable for the whole system. Secondly, the application of any of the Group's recommendations to the common system could proceed only after consultation with the other organizations. Adopting those recommendations might well, therefore, strike a blow at the very foundations of the common system. The "prompt implementation" proposed in recommendation 61 also concerned the common system. To proceed in that unilateral manner would damage the cohesion of the system. Indeed, the very fact that such recommendations were being entertained by the General Assembly was likely to raise fears in the other organizations that the United Nations might be seeking to "dictate", as it were, to the common system."

Mr. Akwei, **Chairman of ICSC**[136] continued

"With regard to the Noblemaire principle, the conditions of service must be such as to attract candidates of the highest calibre and must be comparable to the most favourable conditions of service offered by a national civil service. Each year, the commission reported on the margin between the net remuneration of the United Nations and that of the United States federal civil service, the current comparator. That comparison was obviously incomplete, since it did not take into account the full range of entitlements which made up the compensation package. Consequently, since 1976, the Commission had been seeking the Assembly's approval to undertake a comparison of total compensation. All elements having a bearing on the conditions of service would thus be taken into account, which was the ideal. It could therefore be said that the Noblemaire principle was not being fully applied.

... if only salary was taken into account, as was currently the case, the comparison with the United States federal civil service was still valid, since the margin was around 15 per cent; however, no comparison was made on the basis of total compensation, for the good reason that the General Assembly had not yet approved such a procedure. ICSC had made some informal comparisons on that basis which showed that for some duty stations the margin was reversed, with the compensation of United States civil servants exceeding that of United Nations staff by as much as 30 per cent in some cases."

Mr. Ruedas, **USG for Administration and Management**[137]

"The Secretary-General did not agree with the judgement that the qualifications of staff, particularly in the higher categories, were inadequate. While the Secretary-General did not feel that the quality of work in the Secretariat had worsened, he did, however, recognize that there was room for improvement in the structural and other arrangements required to manage the vast array of activities of the Secretariat and was giving particular attention to the possibilities for streamlining, consolidation and better co-ordination. ...

Turning to recommendation 1, and the request for information concerning the relationship between the Committee on Conferences and various legislative organs, and whether that Committee should be the final determining body, he said that it might be helpful to clarify the existing situation with respect to how the draft calendar of conferences was drawn up and the existing relationship between the Committee on Conferences and other organs.

In drawing up the draft calendar for the approval of the Committee on Conferences, the Secretariat was guided by three principal elements, namely, specifications of the legislative mandates of individual organs, practical considerations, such as reporting obligations and the need to avoid clashes in the timetable, and legislation governing the pattern of conferences and the drawing up of the draft calendar, the most recent one being resolution 40/243. The Secretariat assumed that the Assembly would retain final authority to approve the calendar of conferences. On that basis it would be possible for the Committee on Conferences, while taking into account the factors he had just mentioned, to investigate the technical aspects of submitting a draft calendar of conferences with a view to making better use of conference facilities and established resources as recommended by the Group of Experts. The legal relationships between the Assembly and the Committee on Conferences or other United Nations organs and between the Committee and those other organs would therefore not change. The Committee would simply be assuming a stronger co-ordinating role but the draft calendar would continue to be prepared by the Secretary-General.

The Committee was also mandated to act on behalf of the Assembly in dealing with requests for departures from the approved calendar when the Assembly was not in session and it also advised the Assembly on other matters connected to the optimum apportionment of conference resources. That advisory and consultative role would not be expected to change. He interpreted paragraph (c) of recommendation 1 as a request to the Committee on Conferences to monitor the manner in which the Secretary-General ensured the harmonization of working procedures of conference services rather than to ensure such harmonization to itself.

Referring to recommendation 2, and to the request that the Secretariat provide information on the relationship between conferences and meetings on the one hand, and programmes on the other, including percentages of resources allocated to each, he said that out of a net budgetary appropriation of approximately $1,388 million for 1986-1987, some $316 million (23 per cent of the net budget) were direct conference-servicing activities such as language services, reproduction of documentation and related services. It did not include such services as sound engineering, security, electricity or the cost of services provided by substantive departments to the meetings. About 15 per cent of the output of those departments enumerated in the 1986-1987 budget related to substantive servicing of the preparation of reports to meetings and conferences. If the number, duration and frequency of meetings and conferences were reduced, there would be a substantial reduction of directly related expenditure.

As to whether that reduction could be accomplished without negative programme impact, he said that three major areas warranted careful study. The first concerned the mandates of existing intergovernmental bodies - currently there were over 150 standing and semi-permanent bodies on the calendar of conferences. The second concerned the process whereby a subject was reviewed and discussed in more than one intergovernmental body and the third concerned the frequency of meetings. In that connection he pointed out that the Second Committee had established a biennial cycle for bodies reporting to it.

Responding to the question relating to recommendation 3 (e) how the Secretariat would scrap a subsidiary body before establishing a new one, he said that the creation or discontinuance of subsidiary organs was a prerogative of the General Assembly. Generally, new subsidiary bodies were created when new activities were envisaged. Normally that should mean that the mandate of the new body would differ substantially from those of existing bodies, although that was not always the case.

Numerous questions had been raised in connection with recommendation 5 concerning construction. Whenever there was a need for construction, the Secretary-General submitted to the Advisory Committee a statement of requirements in the manner recommended by the Joint Inspection Unit and the Advisory Committee. If the Advisory Committee's review was positive, a description of the project and an estimate for an architectural and engineering study was submitted through that Committee to the General Assembly. Following the architectural and engineering study, the Secretary-General provided an estimate for the total cost of the project. The General Assembly reviewed that and approved, in principle, a total project cost. At that time the Assembly usually appropriated a first instalment to cover the cost during an initial one- or two-year period, the resources thus appropriated being placed in a construction account and the balance being carried forward at the end of each year.

With respect to the Economic and Social Commission for Asia and the Pacific, the approved project cost was $44,177,700; the final design phase had been completed and 41 submissions had been received from construction contractors. Following the resumed fortieth session of the General Assembly, the project had been held in abeyance. If the project was resumed in 1987 the main construction contract, committing the United Nations to the project cost in full would be awarded in July 1987. To date $22,698,000 had been appropriated, of which $2,268,000 had been committed. In accordance with the proposal contained in document A/40/1102, $9 million of the appropriation had been deferred to 1987.

Concerning the Economic Commission for Africa, detailed evaluations of the entries for the design competition were under way. If the project was resumed in 1987, a detailed architectural design would be drawn up after a firm was selected and the construction contract could be awarded in 1988. Of an approved total cost of $73.5 million, $3,120,000 had been appropriated, of which $520,000 had been committed to date.

Concerning recommendation 6, which related to the reimbursement of travel costs of representatives of Member States attending the General Assembly, he said that if such reimbursements were limited to the 37 least developed countries, the average annual cost would be $425,500 per annum or $851,000 each biennium. Currently the biennial appropriation for that purpose came to $3,787,300 although in the past two years the actual cost had been $2,066,300 as only 134 Member States had exercised their entitlements. ...

A great many questions had been asked in connection with chapter III. In general terms, the Secretary-General would interpret recommendation 15 as requiring him to undertake a reduction of 15 per cent over three years in the number of regular budget posts, and a reduction of 25 per cent, also over the next three years in the number of posts at the USG and ASG level, and a number of reviews, covering political departments and offices (recommendation 16), departments and programmes in the economic and social area (recommendations 25 and 26), public information (recommendation 37), administration and management (recommendations 30-32), and conference services (recommendation 34). Only after those reviews were completed would the Secretary-General be able to submit clear proposals for change in those areas. The process of reviewing and reducing posts could, however, begin as soon as the Assembly approved the report of the Group of Experts. Reductions could take place but until such time as the Assembly approved any structural changes in the Secretariat, the Secretary-General would need authority to implement reductions with flexibility, within the total level of posts for the Secretariat as a whole. The Secretary-General would also intend to recruit staff at the P-1, P-2 and P-3 levels in the course of 1987 and would not wish to be held to an exact figure or to those three levels alone.

The Secretariat was in the process of preparing the programme budget proposals for the biennium 1988-1989 for submission to the Committee for Programme and Co-ordination and the Advisory Committee. Thus the budget was being finalized prior to any decisions which might be taken on the recommendations of the Group of Experts. Given those circumstances and the financial situation of the Organization, the Secretary-General would approach implementation of recommendation 15, if approved, in the following manner: post reductions would be done on a pragmatic basis designed to cause the least possible disruption to programmes and to the lives and rights of the people involved. A final determination of the reductions in 1988 and 1989 could be made only after the full impact of retrenchments in 1987 had been assessed. Reductions would be achieved as far as possible through the attrition mechanism. However, that might not be compatible with minimizing disruptions to programmes. If that were to be the case, additional financial costs might be required to achieve the targeted post reductions; mechanisms such as redeployment of staff between programmes and duty stations might also need to be applied. The Secretary-General would need to proceed with flexibility under the provisions of the Charter and the Staff and Financial Regulations and Rules. Some flexibility would be needed to defer or modify approved programmes or to terminate approved activities considered to be of low priority.

Referring to a request for a comparison between the 9 political and 11 economic and social departments, centres and offices that currently existed and the situation in 1980, he replied that only one new department - the Department for Disarmament Affairs replacing the Centre for Disarmament - had been created since 1980. In addition the Office for Field Operations and External Support Activities had been established in 1982. The major organizational changes had occurred in the 1970s. ...

Recommendation 15 referred not to the number of staff members but to the number of posts; 15 per cent of the current 11,423 posts was 1,713 posts. The average rate of recruitment at levels P-1 to P-3 for the years 1982, 1983 and 1984 had been 176 posts per annum. Attrition over the past six years had been quite uniform, averaging 3 per cent in the Professional category and 3.1 per cent in the General Service category. If the retirement factor was added in, the figures were just over 4 per cent in each case. Between 1983 and 1985 overall vacancy rates for established posts in the regular budget had been on the order of 7.3 to 7.4 per cent. In 1986, because of measures taken by the Secretary-General including a recruitment freeze, the average rate up to the end of August had been 9.4 per cent.

A 15 per cent reduction in the number of posts would result, at current costs, in direct savings of approximately $141 million per biennium; the indirect savings had not been calculated. A 25 per cent reduction in the higher echelons would result in savings of approximately $3.3 million per biennium on salaries and common staff costs. As to the Joint Staff Pension Fund, if a 15 per cent reduction were achieved by attrition, the number of active participants would decline by 1 per cent a year over three years, and the actuarial imbalance would be up to 0.17 per cent of pensionable remuneration, so that the Fund would need additional contributions of up to $3 million a year.

A preliminary review of existing vacancies and projected attrition indicated that it might be possible, at least initially, to maintain recruitment at P-1 to P-3 levels at a rate comparable to the rates occurring in the period 1982-1984, but that would depend in part on the overall reduction of posts and its effects on the reduced career progression of junior and middle-level staff. It might not be possible to maintain the same level of appointments after the first year.

In connection with recommendation 17, there were 247 locally recruited and 271 internationally recruited Field Service established posts in UNTSO, UNMOGIP and the Supply Depot in Pisa in the 1986-1987 biennium; that percentage had remained unchanged over the past five years.

The responsibility for the dissemination of news and for political analysis within the Secretariat, referred to in recommendation 18, was shared by various departments: the Executive Office of the Secretary-General prepared for him on a weekly basis an extensive compendium of international press and wire service coverage, on a wide range of matters including situations that might threaten the maintenance of international peace and security; the Political Reports Unit of the Office for Field Operational and External Support Activities prepared briefing material regarding developments in the United Nations in the political field for the United Nations information centres; the Department of Public Information sent press cables to the information centres regarding meetings of the General Assembly and the Security Council; the News Service of the Department of Political and Security Council Affairs based its information on news agencies and the daily press and issued daily news bulletins, a daily press review and selected wire service printouts for the use of senior officials and staff in the political departments of the Organization; and the Department of Political Affairs, Trusteeship and Decolonization prepared analyses on developments relevant to its mandate.

Expenditure related to Namibia, referred to in recommendation 19, had totalled $15.6 million in 1984-1985, not including conference-servicing costs; expenditure on Namibia in 1985 had included $3,046,000 for the Council for Namibia, $1,055,000 for the Department of Political Affairs, Trusteeship and Decolonization, $3,056,800 for the Office of the Commissioner for Namibia,

$880,800 for the Department of Public Information and $102,400 for the Office of the Special Representative of the Secretary-General for Namibia.

Regarding recommendation 21, although the number of Non-Self-Governing Territories had decreased from 33 to 18 in the past 10 years, the mandates and activities of the Council for Namibia, for which the Department of Political Affairs, Trusteeship and Decolonization provided substantive servicing, had gradually expanded over the same period, and the number of meetings, missions, conferences and seminars had increased considerably. The Department had also been assigned responsibility for co-operation between the United Nations and the Organization of the Islamic Conference; servicing of the *Ad Hoc* Committee of the International Conference on Kampuchea; and, especially since 1983, fact-finding and good offices on certain political issues.

The questions that had been raised regarding recommendation 24 had to be viewed in the light of other recommendations, including recommendation 23. It was clear that a careful review was needed. The possibility of UNDP taking over responsibility for disaster relief would depend on the outcome of the study proposed in the recommendation.

The Secretary-General did not agree with the assessment in paragraph 39 regarding the lack of responsiveness of the offices concerned with research, analysis and operational activities. As to the extent of duplication between the Department of International Economic and Social Affairs and UNCTAD, the activities of those bodies corresponded to the tasks entrusted to them by their respective governing bodies. It should be one of the central purposes of the review of intergovernmental machinery, especially in the economic and social sectors, to undertake a careful analysis of the mandates and activities of those two bodies.

On the question of the cost and advantages of further enhancing the authority of the Director-General for Development and International Economic Co-operation, the latter's role and responsibilities as set forth in General Assembly resolution 32/197 and subsequent resolutions, most recently Economic and Social Council resolution 1986/74, were clear, and the Secretary-General believed that no further legislative authority was required. Significant progress had been made in promoting system-wide co-operation in many areas, for example operational activities in general, global programmes and country-level operations. The effective exercise of the Director-General's responsibility for system-wide co-ordination required the support of Member States. Economic and Social Council resolution 1986/74 was a significant step in that direction; thus, no additional costs were envisaged.

In connection with recommendation 27, it should be noted that many of the regional projects funded by UNDP were in fact executed by regional commissions; in selecting an executing agency, UNDP applied criteria approved by its Governing Council based mainly on the spheres of competence of the technical agencies of the United Nations system.

The budget of ECE, referred to in recommendation 28, did not include any provision for conference services or common services because the United Nations Office at Geneva had an integrated common services support structure which was at the disposal of each of the substantive organizational units located in Geneva, including ECE. That arrangement provided for greater administrative cohesion and achieved economies of scale. In the 1984-1985 programme budget, a very approximate estimate of costs for conference and common services of $35 million had been made, about two thirds of which had been for conference and library services, but because of its lack of precision, that method had been abandoned when preparing the 1986-1987 programme budget. However, it would be possible, for information purposes, to apportion the conference-servicing budget of the United Nations Office at Geneva among the different users, including ECE.

The Secretary-General interpreted the recommendations of the Group, if approved by the General Assembly, to require him to review and report on a number of issues, including administration and management. The objective of recommendation 30 was a search for greater effectiveness and efficiency, with a view also to a possible reduction in the proportion of administrative costs.

In connection with recommendation 32, the difficulties encountered in the past in respect of co-ordination and planning, programming and budgeting had not been insuperable and had been dealt with at the Programme Planning and Budgeting Board (PPBB). The heads of the Office of Financial Services and the Office of Programme Planning and Co-ordination, and also of the respective departments to which they belonged, were members of the PPBB, which was thus constituted so as to permit the coherent resolution of any difficulties of co-ordination in those areas. Future action on merging the budgeting and programme planning functions, if approved by the General Assembly, must be dealt with in the light of the intergovernmental review in those areas.

The definition of support activities for liaison functions in recommendation 33 was not entirely clear.

In connection with recommendation 34, the cost per page was determined by dividing total costs of internal printing by the total number of pages printed.

In 1985 a total of 825 million page impressions had been produced internally in all official languages at an average cost of less than 1 cent per page impression. That output represented 44 million individual documents which had been distributed at an average cost of 8.6 cents per document. Three quarters of all printing costs were for internal printing. External printing was resorted to mainly when the technical requirements of a job exceeded internal capacity, and the average cost was approximately $21 per typeset page. Occasionally work was performed externally when internal capacity was overloaded, sometimes at a lower cost per page impression, but lead times were usually much longer.

The absolute prohibition against the hiring of retired staff members advocated in recommendation 35 might not be in the interest of Member States, since retired staff members often provided specific expertise on temporary assistance in a more effective and less costly manner than could otherwise be obtained, notably in the language services.

In connection with recommendation 36, two permanent members of the Security Council occupied a total of 972 square feet in the Secretariat building, free of charge. The Group of 77 occupied a total of 2,160 square feet in the Secretariat building, at a cost of $10,886 per annum, plus $1,696 for rental of furniture. Five specialized agencies occupied space in the UNDC I and UNDC II buildings. FAO, IAEA, IMF and WHO paid $24 per square foot (an amount representing the average rental rate paid by the Organization for occupancy in those two buildings). Annual rental income to the Organization amounted to $243,744. UNESCO was not charged rent for the space it occupied in United Nations buildings by virtue of reciprocal arrangements regarding United Nations space at UNESCO headquarters.

Regarding recommendation 38, the total level of expenditure in 1984-1985 for official travel of staff had been $28.8 million, compared to the budgetary provision of $27.5 million for the biennium 1986-1987. Economy measures in 1986 had reduced that amount by $4.5 million.

In connection with recommendation 39, while it was theoretically possible for the Internal Audit Division to report directly to the Secretary-General, the advisability of that move would have to be seen in relation to other factors, such as whether the already heavy schedule of the Secretary-General should be burdened by further direct supervisory responsibilities."

Mr. Ruedas, **USG for Administration and Management**[138], continued "he was aware that he had not answered in due detail all the questions that had been asked, in particular those referring to chapter III on the structure of the

Secretariat. The main reason for that, as he had stated in general terms in describing how the Secretary-General would approach the implementation of recommendation 15 if approved, was that a clear and convincing basis for action would be needed in the form of the studies that the Group itself recommended that the Secretary-General should undertake. For example, he had not answered the question about the Management Advisory Service, although his view was that the function in that difficult field would have to continue somehow, especially in view of the studies that had been called for. He could not say, as matters now stood, whether the Service should exist as a separate unit and whether it should be part of the Department of Administration and Management. The decision would have to follow the general study of the Department currently in progress. ...

In answer to the question whether the Secretariat had been consulted by the Group when recommendation 5 was drafted, he replied that the Secretariat had not been consulted on that recommendation or on any other. The recommendations were the work of the Group of High-level Intergovernmental Experts alone. ...

Travel was essential to the Organization, with its seven main duty stations and smaller offices throughout the world. The Secretary-General had always sought to limit travel costs as far as possible. The measures already taken had reduced expenditure on travel by some $4.5 million in 1986, and would produce a total saving of $23 million for the biennium 1986-1987. While that did not represent a reduction of 20 per cent, as proposed in recommendation 38, it was significant. If the number of meetings was reduced it would clearly be possible to reduce expenditure on travel still further. ...

Turning to the question of how the representation of Member States could be adjusted so that all had a "fair share of the cake", the United Nations Charter stressed the importance of efficiency, competence, and integrity, with due regard to geographical distribution, in the recruitment of staff. The fact that some States were underrepresented did not mean that the two considerations were contradictory, but was, rather, a legacy of the way in which the Organization had been constituted in an earlier period. Overrepresentation was partly due to geographical location, in that a majority of the General Service staff were nationals of the host country in question, which tended to affect geographical distribution when movement to the Professional category occurred."

Mr. Ruedas, **USG for Administration and Management**[139] continued

"with respect to the timing of any action taken to implement recommendation 15, that the Secretary-General would be able to take some initial steps in 1987 provided that he was allowed adequate flexibility. Proposals for the biennium 1988-1989 would be formulated only after the completion of detailed studies, as recommended by the Group of Experts itself. The exact nature of the Secretary-General's plans for implementation of the recommendation would depend upon the specific conditions in each case, so that, for example, if there was a need to restructure the Secretariat, General Assembly approval would be required. There was no reason to suppose that the Secretary-General's authority was being encroached upon in that, as a matter of course, he took those decisions that fell within his competence and requested General Assembly approval of any others. In practice, any plans for implementation in 1987 would have to go before the Assembly at the current session. The Secretary-General would, in any event, comment further on the recommendations, as necessary, as the debate proceeded.

As the Secretary-General had informed the staff, any reduction would be achieved, as far as possible, by attrition. In fact, the vacancy rate for 1986 was 9.4 per cent anyway. The question of an expanded mandate for the Committee on Conferences was not within the competence of the Secretariat, but rather of that Committee and the Group of Experts."

Mr. Ruedas, **USG for Administration and Management**[140] continued

"With regard to chapter IV, he pointed out that, since the United Nations played the leading role in the United Nations system, even those recommendations which were applicable directly to the United Nations alone would have an impact on the other organizations. Consequently, it was the opinion not only of the Secretary-General but also of the executive heads of the specialized agencies that all the recommendations contained in chapter IV should first be transmitted for review to the one body which the Assembly had established for the regulation and co-ordination of conditions of service, namely the International Civil Service Commission, whose role was accepted by all and which performed its tasks on the basis of the decisions of the governing bodies and also with the participation of those who were governed.

The Secretary-General concurred with the views expressed in paragraphs 45 to 49 of the report. As far as the recommendations proper were concerned, he considered that recommendation 41 set objectives which could be supported by all, but which at the same time implied criticism of the management of the Secretariat which was not substantiated by any factual evidence. As far as recruitment was concerned, both the Office of Personnel Services and the advisory appointment bodies were always guided by the provisions of the Charter, but in a political organization, political pressure was perhaps inevitable and it was legitimate for Member States to present candidates for appointment or to seek to ensure that they were adequately represented in the Secretariat. The Secretary-General had always resisted pressure aimed at securing the appointment of individuals who were not the best qualified.

The Secretary-General intended to review all the delegations of authority he had made in personnel matters, but the view that all other senior officials should "refrain from influencing the selection of staff" (recommendation 41) disregarded the necessity of co-operation between heads of departments which would employ the candidates recruited and the officials in charge of personnel services, who were responsible for maintaining the standards and guidelines established by the General Assembly. ...

The Secretary-General noted that recommendation 54 took account of the current situation in the Secretariat. Because of the nature of the posts in question, their occupants were older and therefore did not stay very long. Having said that, the Secretary-General was the firm opinion that he should have complete authority in regard to the length of service of his senior staff.

With regard to recommendation 55, the provisions of paragraph 3 of resolution 35/210 were strictly observed: no post was considered the exclusive preserve of any State or group of States. The main factors considered in the selection of staff were those set forth in the Charter and the targets set forth by the General Assembly in respect of equitable geographical representation. It might, nevertheless, be necessary to replace one staff member by another who was a national of the same State or group of States. Resolution 35/210 did not prohibit that in the case of Member States whose nationals served primarily on fixed-term contracts. ...

The Secretary-General was in agreement with recommendation 56. Replying to the question whether it would be practical to implement recommendation 57, Mr. Ruedas recalled that the General Assembly, in its resolution 37/126, had recommended that organizations of the common system "should establish their needs for permanent and fixed-term staff on a continuing basis in conjunction with the human resources planning process, taking into account the criteria considered by the Commission" for that purpose. There had been no determination of any proportion in the United Nations; instead a pragmatic exercise had taken place with the result that, as of 30 June 1986, 63.9 per cent of staff had permanent appointments and 36.1 per cent had fixed-term appointments. It should be noted that a number of States from all regions preferred to release their nationals for service with the Secretariat only on secondment. There were currently approximately 400 staff members on secondment. The Secretary-General did not consider that the type of appointment in any way affected the principle of equitable geographical distribution. ...

With regard to recommendation 59, the Secretariat had provided the Group with a document giving the overall activities relating to staff-management relations and an estimate of their direct and indirect costs, which amounted to $1 million per year. The bulk of that estimate related to the cost of time spent by staff members on those activities, which were related not only to Staff Union matters but also to the work of joint bodies established in accordance with the Staff Regulations adopted by the General Assembly. To insist that staff unions or associations should finance all their activities from their own funds would be a step backwards in staff-management relations; moreover, as the Secretary-General was of the view that staff representational activities did not derogate from his managerial prerogatives. ...

The Secretary-General had already expressed his views on recommendation 61. ... Specifically, he did not believe that the level of the total entitlements of staff should be reduced. The remuneration of Professional staff had been frozen for the past two years. If the Assembly believed that he matter needed further study, it should put the issues, and the reasons for its concern, to ICSC for review and advice. ...

While the Group of 18 had emphasized the need for external evaluation, it had not emphasized the importance of self-evaluation. In response to concerns expressed by other intergovernmental bodies, evaluation units had been established in various parts of the Secretariat since the late 1970s. Since then, internal evaluation had gathered momentum, as reflected in the number of evaluations at programme level, and their follow-up, undertaken by the Secretariat for review by the Committee for Programme and Co-ordination (CPC) and other intergovernmental bodies concerned. At the same time, evaluation methodologies had been refined under the guidance of CPC. ...

Concerning chapter VI of the report, he recalled that two delegations and the Chairman of the Fifth Committee had asked what the Group of Experts had meant when it had asked what the Group of Experts had meant when it had said that the Organization's budget was high. For purpose of comparison, hey had asked what the 1946 budget, calculated in current dollars and taking inflation into account, had been and what percentage had been devoted in 1946, by comparison with the present budget, to staff costs. In 1946, the Organization's annual budget had been approximately $20 million. The programme budget for the biennium 1986-1987 was almost $700 million. At 1986 rates, the 1946 budget would be approximately $100 million. In 1946, 5 per cent of expenditures had been devoted to salaries and common staff costs. In 1986, those items represented approximately 75 per cent of the budget. ...

One delegation had asked for a brief summary of the programme planning and programme budget processes in other organizations of the system ... the manner in which agencies performed those functions varied greatly, demonstrating that organizational mechanisms should be tailored to the needs of the specific organization. It should therefore be said, as the Advisory Committee had pointed out, that the structure of an organization was a function of its programmes, rather than the reverse; while the Advisory Committee had not weighed the advantages and disadvantages of each method, it had concluded that the harmonization of programming and budgeting arrangement was not necessarily a desirable or even a feasible goal.

One delegation had asked whether it was true, as stated in the report of the Group of 18, that the medium-term plan was not taken seriously into consideration when the programme budget was being prepared, whether the plan was in fact presented almost as a final document which Member States could not modify and whether the Committee for Programme and Co-ordination played only a minor role in its examination. The formulation of the medium-term plan and the programme budget was governed by two sets of regulations adopted by the General Assembly, namely the Financial Regulations and the Regulations governing programme planning annexed to resolution 37/234 ... The structure of the budget was derived from that of the plan. As required by programme planning regulation 3.2, the objectives and strategies of the plan were derived from the policy orientations and goals seat by intergovernmental organs and reflected Member States' priorities as set out in legislation adopted by functional and regional intergovernmental bodies and by the General Assembly. The plan was presented in draft form to sectoral, functional and regional organs prior to its presentation in final form, through CPC, to the Economic and Social Council and the General Assembly as required by programme planning regulations 3.4 and 3.13. As a result Member States did have an input into its formulation, a process which took the better part of two years.

The Committee for Programme and Co-ordination was actively involved in the review of both the medium-term plan and the proposed programme budget.

It advised the Assembly on the programmes which should be accepted, curtailed, reformulated or rejected in accordance with regulation 3.14. In conformity with regulations 3.16 and 3.17, it made proposals to the Assembly on priorities for both the medium-term plan and the programme budget. It was responsible, under regulation 4.2, for checking that programme proposals in the proposed programme budget were in conformity with the strategy laid down in the medium-term plan.

Two delegations had asked about involving Member States earlier in the budget process. He wished to point out that participation by Member States began with the consideration and adoption of the medium-term plan. Member States were represented in a number of governing bodies, commissions, councils and related intergovernmental machinery whose deliberations had a direct bearing on the shape and size of the Organization's budget. Member States could, of course, become involved earlier in the budget process, perhaps in the year preceding the issuance of the budget instructions, by giving their views on the desirable extent of budgetary growth and the assignment of relative priorities. Such an arrangement would not in any way increase the burden on the Secretariat.

One delegation had asked how, specifically, the Secretariat expected Member States to oversee the planning and budget process as mentioned in paragraph 68 of the Group's report, which said it was important to ensure that Member States took part throughout the process. Their involvement would be threefold: overseeing the preparation of the proposed programme budget; indicating the resources likely to be available; and establishing priorities.

Clearly the consultation process described above (intergovernmental bodies, CPC, ACABQ) gave Member States plenty of opportunity to oversee the compilation of the proposed programme budget. If one added that the plans and programmes presented in the budget derived from resolutions and decisions adopted by Member States, it was undeniable that States determined the programmatic content of the Organizations's plans and budgets.

On the question of the funds available, it was clear that Member States had the option of itation process described above (intergovernmental bodies, CPC, ACABQ) gave Member States plenty of opportunity to oversee the compilation of the proposed programme budget. If one added that the plans and programmes presented in the budget derived from resolutions and decisions adopted by Member States, it was undeniable that States determined the programmatic content of the Organizations's plans and budgets.

On the question of the funds available, it was clear that Member States had the option of CPC, for its part, would continue to review priorities at the programme element level.

It had been asked whether the Fifth Committee could, instead of adopting a decision on the financial implications of each individual resolution, adopt a decision in the context of the programme budget as a whole, keeping in mind programme priorities as defined in the medium-term plan. It was true that a consolidated statement was being prepared in the case of conference-servicing costs, and that was a method that could be used as a model in other areas, such as public information. However, the advantages of doing so were not immediately clear. Several years earlier, the Secretariat had considered presenting to the Assembly at each session a "mini-budget", in which the financial implications of all decisions or resolutions would be presented as a whole at the end of the session. It had been felt at the time, however, that would delay the Assembly's work considerably, since no decision could be taken until the review of the "mini-budget" had been completed. That was because, under the Assembly's rules of procedure, no resolution with financial implications could be put to a vote without a report from the Fifth Committee. The process would therefore considerably lengthen the negotiations that took place in the case of each draft resolution. The "mini-budget" procedure did offer the advantage of improving the information given to the Assembly. However, at the past two sessions much more detailed information on the programme implications of draft resolutions had meant that the Assembly had received considerably more detailed information. Obviously, there was no reason not to look into the procedure's advantages and disadvantages further."

Mr. Vraalsen, **Chairman of the Group of 18**[141]

"At the outset the Group had decided that its meetings were to be closed and that there would be no records, so as to encourage a direct exchange of views. He had no mandate or authority to speak on behalf of the Group, or to refer to the informal discussions which had taken place behind closed doors.

...

Several representatives had said that the report departed from the established priority goals of the Organization, particularly in recommendation 19, concerning Namibia. Nothing could be further from the truth; it was stated explicitly in the report that the aim of the recommendations on the Secretariat structure for Namibia was to enhance the Organization's capacity to deal with that important matter without in any way limiting the programmes and services in that area. The situation in which issues relating to Namibia were dealt with by several departments and units of the Secretariat was not the optimal way of dealing with the issue.

The fears expressed by several representatives that some of the recommendations on personnel might be discriminatory were completely unfounded. The Group had stressed that the Secretary-General, in selecting and managing the staff, should be guided by Articles 100 and 101 of the Charter, and that in any question regarding personnel policy, the responsibility and prerogatives of the Secretary-General as chief administrative officer of the United Nations must be acknowledged and his authority under the Charter must in no way be prejudiced. The Group had endeavoured to rectify some of the existing imbalances, as should be clear from recommendations 46, 47 and 51.

Many comments had seemed to question the judgement of members of the Group. He had already noted that the Group was truly representative, and expert, in nature, and had been able to reach consensus on nearly all the recommendations.

Some delegations had asked what was meant by ensuring the highest level of membership on the Committee on Conferences (recommendation 1). That expression was frequently used in the United Nations and implied that the current level of representation was inadequate and that Member States should ensure that they were represented by senior officials with considerable knowledge and experience of the United Nations. No particular level was suggested, since it was a matter for each Member State to decide.

Several delegations had asked how it would be possible to effect a significant reduction in the number of conferences and meetings without affecting the substantive work of the Organization (recommendation 2). It had been quite clear to the members of the Group, who had considerable experience of all parts of the system, including the Secretariat, that the number of meetings could be significantly reduced. They believed that it was not necessary for various intergovernmental bodies to meet as often as they did, or for different bodies to take up the same subjects. Many conferences and meetings did not utilize the time allocated to them. At the request of the Group, the Secretariat had provided information showing that in some bodies 60 to 70 per cent of the time allotted remained unused; the funds wasted would be much better used for other purposes. Such bodies, and the time unused, included the *Ad Hoc* Committee on the Indian Ocean (65 per cent), the Special Committee on Enhancing the Effectiveness of the Principle of Non-Use of Force in International Relations (50 per cent), the *Ad Hoc* Committee on the World Disarmament Conference (70 per cent), the Commission on the

Status of Women (44 per cent), the Industrial Development Board (54 per cent) and the Committee on the Peaceful Uses of Outer Space (56 per cent). The Group had included specific provisions in recommendation 2, intended to ensure that useful activities and bodies were not adversely affected.

It would be for the General Assembly to decide how to implement recommendation 3 (f). The Group felt that it was important to draw the General Assembly's attention to the problem, as had been done before, since too many resolutions were being proposed and adopted by the General Assembly each year. When the General Assembly could not agree on a certain line of action, it was an easy way out to ask the Secretariat to study the matter, seek views and report back. Such studies involved considerable effort and expenditure which should be spent on other activities to benefit Member States.

Decisions on construction (recommendation 5) were not for the Secretary-General to take, but for the General Assembly. In a situation where limited funds were available, the General Assembly would have to decide on priorities, and construction work should not be one of them.

It had been asked what body would undertake the study proposed in recommendation 8 and whether the least developed countries would be properly represented; it was for the General Assembly to decide whether to entrust the task to an existing body or establish a new body and then decide on its size and composition; the Group had completed its work and therefore would not be available to undertake the study.

A number of delegations had asked what scientific or other basis had been used in suggesting a reduction of 15 per cent in the number of regular budget posts (recommendation 15). The recommendation was based on information provided to the Group about the number of staff members and posts, tasks, and the necessity of the work performed; the Group had also discussed the matter with the Secretary-General. The Group was fully aware of the need to avoid any adverse effects on the efficiency of the Organization's activities and had therefore recommended that the Secretary-General should submit to the General Assembly a plan for the implementation of the proposal, taking into account that requirement.

The review suggested in recommendation 16 should clearly be carried out by the Secretary-General, since all matters pertaining to the Secretariat were his responsibility under the Charter. The same applied to the reviews suggested in recommendations 25 and 37.

The suggestion made in recommendation 22 was definitely not aimed at weakening the obligation of Member States to contribute to special economic assistance programmes, which in any case were largely funded from voluntary contributions. The activities carried out under such programmes were very similar to those undertaken by UNDP, and UNDP had the knowledge and infrastructure to deal with such assistance. The process suggested had already been started, and a decision on the subject had been taken by the Economic and Social Council at its summer session in 1986. The Group wished to ensure that the resources of the United Nations were used as effectively as possible, without affecting the programmes or reducing their effectiveness.

Recommendation 24 referred to the Office of the United Nations Disaster Relief Co-ordinator (UNDRO) because that office was affiliated with the United Nations and its posts were funded from the regular budget. The Group wished to ensure the best possible use of funds, and had merely requested UNDP to consider the feasibility of taking over the functions of UNDRO.

The review suggested in recommendation 25 would be undertaken by the Secretary-General; the purpose was to make the best possible use of available resources and avoid duplication. The Group had suggested that the General Agreement on Tariffs and Trade should be invited to participate in the review because it dealt with the same and related questions as the other bodies referred to.

Regarding recommendation 29, it had been asked why the functions of the Office of Secretariat Services for Economic and Social Matters could not be merged with the Office of the Under-Secretary-General for Political and General Assembly Affairs. That possibility had been considered at length, but the Group had finally decided on recommendation 29.

There was no scientific basis for the suggested 20 per cent reduction in official travel (recommendation 38); clearly, however, there were too many missions, involving too many staff members, especially from the Department of Public Information. The Group felt that the reduction could be made without prejudice to the quality of the services of public information coverage.

Commenting on chapter IV of the report, he said, with regard to recommendation 41, that the Secretary-General would retain ultimate responsibility for all staff matters. There was no doubt that political pressure had influenced the selection of staff. In recommendation 45, the Group of Experts had concluded, taking account of the rights of staff members, that a period of three years was sufficient to determine suitability for a permanent appointment. In pursuance of recommendation 46, the Secretary-General could give preference to female candidates in recruitment.

Recruitment on a post-by-post basis, mentioned in recommendation 48, limited flexibility. Employment on the basis of occupational groups would make it easier to transfer staff members in response to changing needs, ensuring optimum use of their qualifications and experience.

In formulating recommendation 61, the Group of Experts had considered the question of total entitlements, and had concluded that total remuneration had reached a level which gave rise to concern. In particular, consideration should be given to the elimination of the education grant for post-secondary studies and the establishment of a four-week annual leave system. Should the recommendation be adopted by the General Assembly, the question should be thoroughly reviewed by ICSC before a final decision was taken.

Turning to chapter V, he said that the Group had concluded that the Joint Inspection Unit should place more emphasis on evaluation, and that it should be renamed accordingly. Although the Group of Experts could not guarantee that adoption of the recommendations in chapter V would mean that Member States would pay increased attention to JIU reports, it would be a step in the right direction.

With regard to chapter VI, the development of procedures to facilitate agreement on budgetary matters was of the greatest significance to the future of the Organization. While differences existed over how current deficiencies could be corrected, the chapter offered a firm basis for agreement, and it was his hope that a consensus would emerge at the current session."

Mr. Vraalsen, **Chairman of the Group of 18**[142], continued

"the statement made in the introduction, to the effect that the qualifications of staff, particularly in the higher categories, were inadequate, reflected the consensus within the Group and should be looked at together with recommendation 41, which referred to the political and other pressures that had influenced the selection of staff. ...

With regard to recommendation 2, subparagraph (c), about which certain representatives, particularly the representative of Sri Lanka, had spoken with emotion, he cited the example of the *Ad Hoc* Committee on the Indian Ocean, which, having shortened its session to two weeks, had been able to carry out its work within that time. Without disputing the need for consultations, the Group of Experts saw that as proof of its contention that by providing a more realistic assessment of their needs, United Nations bodies could avoid wastage of conference-service resources, which accounted for a considerable portion of the Organization's budget. ...

With regard to recommendation 5, it was clear that budgetary matters were the responsibility of the General Assembly; for its part, the Group of Experts felt that at a time of crisis, priorities should be set and that construction of conference facilities was not a priority task in that context.

With regard to recommendation 15, he repeated that there was no scientific way to determine the extent of the staff cuts to be made. The Group of Experts had based itself on a number of factors which had been the subject of detailed discussions with the Secretary-General. Conscious of the need to avoid any negative effects on the implementation of programmes, the Group of Experts had recommended that the Secretary-General should submit to the General Assembly a plan for the implementation of staff cuts. The representative of Cameroon had implied that since the recommendation did not have a scientific basis in should not be taken literally. The Group of Experts was quite categorical on that point: a reduction must be made in the overall number of staff and in the number of posts at the senior levels and the percentages quoted represented a reasonable estimate of the cuts needed. Doubts had been expressed regarding the possibility of implementing those cuts smoothly. The Group was convinced that the Secretary-General, who had just been re-elected, would take all aspects of the problem, particularly the interests of the staff, duly into account when implementing the recommendation. Finally, it should be pointed out that the recommendation came from the Group of Experts alone and hand not been drafted with the Secretary-General.

Recommendation 16 had been formulated advisedly, on the basis of the information provided by the Secretariat regarding the structure and functioning of the departments dealing with political questions. The recommendation was designed to help the Organization to better carry out its mandate in that area.

...

Recommendation 59 should not be seen as an attempt to curtail the activities of the Staff Union. The Secretary-General had said that he was very pleased with the collaboration that had been established with the Union and the Group of Experts had taken note of the fact. It should, however, be recalled that the Group had recommended that a comprehensive review of the intergovernmental machinery of the United Nations and of its report structure should be undertaken and had made specific proposals in that connection, including in respect of personnel. ...

With regard to recommendation 61, the Group of Experts had felt that the education grant in respect of post-secondary education should be discontinued and that the amount of annual leave should be reduced. It realized that those were sensitive issues and it hoped that its recommendations, if accepted, would be considered by the competent bodies. That did not in any way mean that the proposed measures could be ignored for members of the Group had been unanimous on those two points. ...

The Group had considered the question of the scale of assessments, but since it had been unable to reach any conclusion it had decided not to mention the discussions in its report."

Ms. Frangipani-Campino, **representative of the staff**[*143]

"The staff was prepared and willing to contribute to the reforms needed to extricate the Organization from its present difficulties and to restore its strength and vitality. They supported enthusiastically a comprehensive and rational approach to the problems generated or exacerbated by the present crisis. Their goal was not only to safeguard the legitimate career expectations and interest of the staff, but also to ensure the integrity and prestige of the Organization. Arbitrary reforms adopted in an atmosphere of panic would not solve any problems. The reforms envisaged must strengthen, not weaken, the basic structures of the Organization. While noting with appreciation the efforts being made to seek long-term financial stability for the Organization through financial and budgetary reforms, the staff were concerned at several aspects of the report of the Group of Experts.

First, with regard to the proposals for reductions in staff, increases or decreases in the size of the Secretariat were of little importance in themselves; what was crucial was how and why they were carried out. If the object was not just to make short-term savings but also to improve the efficiency of the overall functioning of the Organization, then it was important that reductions be made systematically, taking due account of their impact on programme performance. That required a certain amount of lead time and provision for consulting those directly affected. Any effort to maximize productivity and effectiveness must be based on a clear definition of programme priorities and objectives and of the human skills and experience necessary to implement those programmes, and no streamlining was justified unless it improved delivery. No across-the-board approach could possibly be consonant with those objectives.

---

*Speaking on behalf of the Co-ordinating Committee for Independent Staff Union and Associations of the United Nations System, which represented over 13,000 staff throughout the world.

Secondly, reductions in personnel must be carried out in full respect for the Staff Rules and Regulations and in full recognition of the need to maintain gender and geographical balance. Proper structural distribution was equally important. Since 1974-1975, the number of Under-Secretaries-General and Assistant Secretaries-General had increased by over 50 per cent. By contrast, the number of P-1/P-2 posts had increased by only 9 per cent. Any reduction in staff must take that pattern of growth into account, lest the distorted structure be maintained.

Effective management of resources would require keeping recruitment to a minimum, for to allow skilled staff to leave while contemplating the recruitment of new staff was neither intelligent nor cost-effective. Furthermore, an appropriate redeployment plan should be devised and those areas of the Secretariat which would be responsible for it should be reinforced.

With regard to chapter IV of the Group's report, on measures regarding personnel, she welcomed the general recommendations aimed at modernizing personnel management. She wished to offer specific comments on the recommendations applicable to the Staff Rules and Regulations, which she would take up one by one.

Recommendation 43: the staff supported the principle of competitive examinations but believed that the format of those examinations should continue to be improved and to reflect the differences in experience of internal candidates. Candidates for the P-4 and P-5 levels should also be tested by objective methods for qualifications which included managerial and drafting abilities.

Recommendation 44: the proportion of posts at the junior Professional level was obviously far too low. The filling of vacancies at the higher levels by external candidates tended to frustrate the career development of in-house staff and failed to make maximum use of skills and experience acquired in United Nations service.

Recommendation 45: while implementation of the recommendation would give staff greater security of tenure, a standardized mechanism still needed to be developed to eliminate the discretionary nature of the present system for granting permanent appointments.

Recommendations 46 and 47: the Secretariat should indeed take additional measures to implement the resolutions of the General Assembly on increasing the proportion of posts in the Professional category filled by women, especially at the higher levels, especially if women were not to be disproportionately affected by austerity measures. The staff also supported the measures recommended to ensure that nationals of developing countries were represented at the senior levels. The two recommendations were perfectly compatible with the requirements of competence and integrity.

Recommendation 48: the staff endorsed the concept of greater horizontal and vertical mobility and believed that an occupational group approach might facilitate career development and mobility, provided that it was applied in a rational manner consonant with available resources.

Recommendation 49: career development plans should, wherever possible, encourage a meaningful system of rotation among the various duty stations for staff in the Professional category.

Recommendation 50: The staff were opposed to the content of that recommendation, which would undermine the authority of the Secretary-General as the chief administrative officer of the Organization. Moreover, it was difficult to see how the General Assembly could in such a fashion fruitfully monitor the performance of staff members. It was to be hoped, nevertheless, that the planned review of the performance evaluation system would result in proposals to remedy the defects of the existing system.

Recommendation 51: The staff recognized the necessity of improving the performance evaluation reporting system, but it could not agree that the defects of the existing system stemmed from the functions and composition of the appointment and promotion bodies, or from the latter's failure to exercise fairness or objectivity. The appointment and promotion of staff were governed by clear criteria, which might be improved upon by more explicit reference to career development along occupational lines, but at the present juncture, a restructuring of the bodies concerned purely on the basis of occupational groups seemed ill-advised. Such a restructuring might also be very costly.

Recommendation 52: The staff supported the recommendation and considered that, especially in the present circumstances, the mandatory age of retirement should be strictly applied.

Recommendation 53: ICSC should continue to regulate and co-ordinate conditions of service for the entire United Nations system, and not just for the United Nations. To ask the Commission to assume monitoring functions would undermine and limit the exercise of the legitimate authority of the Secretary-General and the proposed modification would therefore be counter-productive.

Recommendation 54: Under-Secretaries-General and Assistant Secretaries-General should normally be subject to the same performance criteria and periodic evaluation as other categories of staff.

Recommendation 55 and 57: The staff were dedicated to the principle of an independent international civil service in which permanent contract status clearly had a role. That position was not in any way run incompatible with the principle of geographical distribution.

Recommendation 56: The notion that vacancies should be filled only if the work-load of the organizational unit required was entirely reasonable.

Recommendation 58: The staff believed that training and retraining programmes were extremely important and that they needed to be strengthened, particularly with regard to instruction in modern management techniques.

Recommendation 59: The staff union was not a union in the usual sense, dealing with the Administration as an adversary. Its purpose was to work with the Administration towards the same goals, although not always from the same perspective. It had been established to make proposals to the Secretary-General on matters relating to staff welfare, it had assisted the Secretary-General in correcting the shortcomings of the system and it had proposed new ideas for improving the Organization. A staff association that merely rubber-stamped the Administration's decision would serve no purpose.

The figure given by the Under-Secretary-General for Administration and Management referred to the costs of management/staff consultations and not the costs of the activities of staff representatives. The administrative support provided to staff representatives was far outweighed by the benefits resulting from those activities.

The Secretary-General, the staff and the Administration all agreed that staff representative bodies had not infringed the managerial prerogatives of the Secretary-General. The existing arrangement was the backbone of the entire system of staff/management relations in the international civil service, and it was vital to the smooth functioning of the Organization.

Recommendation 60: Any measures taken to improve the administration of justice must include the establishment of an appeals system independent from the Administration. In addition, opinions issued in first instance should constitute decisions, not merely recommendations, appealable to the Administrative Tribunal by either party.

Recommendation 61: The staff noted that the Secretary-General firmly rejected the recommendation to reduce staff entitlements. The staff strongly supported that position and the stand taken by the Chairman of ICSC. The recommendation would do nothing to improve efficiency of the international civil service and would seriously damage the concept of a truly international, and hence, by definition, expatriate, civil service.

In conclusion, she wished to reaffirm a number of principles, namely that no post should be considered the exclusive preserve of any Member State, that States should refrain from exerting political pressure on the Administration in the selection of senior staff, and that technical competence and professional experience should be the criteria for membership on bodies responsible for determining the Organization's programme and budget. Member States should work with the Secretary-General to ensure respect for those principles. The medium- and long-term reforms envisaged would require two things: first, that the Organization be provided with the financial resources it needed to function in the mean time; and, second, that Member States which paid lip-service to support for the Organization should give tangible proof of that support by honouring their financial obligations. In the difficult times ahead the thousands of staff members who were proud to serve the Organization would be its greatest asset, and they were confident that the intention of Member States was not to demoralize them further by denigrating their contribution to the work of the Organization."

Ms. Dam, **Chairwoman of the Federation of International Civil Servants' Associations (FICSA)** [144]

"Recommendation 59 stated that "Staff unions or associations should finance all their activities from their own funds". Both in the private sector and in national service, including the comparator civil service, staff representatives were allowed to devote time to their representative functions. In the United Nations system, the cost of staff activities was covered in full by funds of the staff associations and unions. FISCA had a permanent secretariat in Geneva and a small office in New York. The salaries of the secretariat were paid in full from the Federation's budget, which amounted to $300,000 a year.

FICSA could not accept the statement in recommendation 61 that "the total entitlements ... of staff members have reached a level which gives reason for serious concern", that the annual-leave entitlement was excessive and that the education grant for post-secondary studies should be abolished. Any change in entitlements must be studied by ICSC, which had never been consulted by the Group of 18 in connection with the recommendation. There would be serious repercussions if the General Assembly approved recommendation 61 as part of a "package". It was extremely doubtful that the governing bodies of

---

[*]The association represents 30,000 staff members of the common system, staff serving in United Nations offices in Vienna and Santiago, as well as the staff of United Nations-affiliated bodies and nearly all the specialized agencies.

other organizations in the common system would follow suit. The common system would thus be broken up.

The staff had always advocated a total-compensation approach to the comparison of United Nations remuneration with that of the comparator civil service. It was only through such an approach that a true picture of the situation could be drawn. The Fifth Committee should therefore request ICSC to pursue the total compensation comparison, including expatriate benefits. Staff entitlements could not be dealt with piecemeal.

There was evidence that the current level of entitlements was such that the organizations were experiencing difficulties in recruiting staff. Nationals of some of the major contributor countries could receive higher remuneration when working abroad for their own Governments, or when working in the private sector, than they would in the United Nations system, as was indicated in the latest report of ICSC (A/41/30, para. 202). Reducing staff entitlements in response to the current liquidity crisis, which had been precipitate by the failure of Member States to meet their obligations, was likely to affect the long-term ability of the United Nations to pursue its goals.

Since its establishment in 1946, the education grant had been applied to post-secondary studies. It was paid to Professional staff stationed outside their home country in order to provide partial assistance in meeting the additional, expatriation-related expenses for the education of their children. The education grant had been the subject of exhaustive reviews by various bodies. The findings were reflected in a paper prepared by FICSA. The conclusion had always been the same: the education grant (including its application to post-secondary studies) met the purpose for which it had been intended. The latest review would be undertaken in 1987 by ICSC, at the request of the General Assembly at its fortieth session.

The present grant was rather modest, given the cost of education in many countries. The grant covered 75 per cent of expenses actually incurred, with a limit of $4,500. Since it was paid only to expatriate staff and was one of the major expatriate benefits, its curtailment would lead to recruitment difficulties and would be an impediment to mobility.

The Group of 18 also recommended the establishment of a four-week annual-leave system for all staff members, who were at present entitled for six working weeks of annual leave, in other words, 30 days accrued at a rate of 2 1/2 days per month. The annual-leave entitlement had been established in 1946 and had been reviewed several times since. As early as 1949, a committee of experts had concluded that 30 days of annual leave was not unreasonable for an international civil service. In 1986, when considerable social progress had been made, it did not seem reasonable for the United Nations to consider curtailing the annual leave entitlement for its own staff.

If it was considered necessary, the review of the entitlement should be carried out by ICSC in the context of a total-compensation comparison. It should be noted, however, that at OECD and NATO, staff had 30 days of annual leave, that at IBRD/IMF, they had between 26 and 30 days depending on seniority, and that in the United States federal civil service, they had between 13 and 26 days depending on seniority, and 38 days in the case of expatriate staff with more than 15 years of service, with additional leave accruing at the rate of 1 day per month for expatriate service.

The Chairman of the Group of 18, in his statement to the press when the report had been released, had said that the Group had confined itself to the United Nations and its affiliated bodies. The curtailment of common-system entitlements mentioned in recommendation 61 did not appear to be consistent with such an approach. FICSA urged the Fifth Committee to consider the factual information available concerning recommendation 61 and to suggest that the General Assembly, in view of the ramifications in the common system, should remove the recommendation from the "package" and refer the matter to ICSC for study.

Many loyal and qualified staff members of the United Nations organizations remained dedicated to their work, even though the Assembly had frozen their salaries, reduced their pension entitlements and refused to improve their conditions of service. It was they who were responsible for providing development assistance and humanitarian relief or for providing the necessary administrative support for such activities. How would the punitive measures envisaged in recommendation 61 enhance the effectiveness of the United Nations and the specialized agencies? How would the negligible savings from a reduction in the annual-leave entitlement and in the education grant resolve the financial crisis of the Organization?

One might well ask whether it would be judicious for the General Assembly to approve those measures. Admittedly, the staff would be able to appeal to the Administrative Tribunals; but the damage would already have been done. Many staff members would be affected. Many might leave the organizations; others might lose some of their idealism. There might be protests at some duty stations. Indeed it would be a serious mistake to approve the recommendation as it stood."

Following the formal meetings, informal meetings were held between 24 October to 5 November in order to elaborate the Fifth Committee's report to the GA. That report was the work of a drafting group and the 'enlarged Bureau': delegations representing the regional groups, some other delegations the Chairman of the Fifth Committee had invited to attend and any other delegation that had chosen to take part. The report contained the conclusions of the Committee on the recommendations by the Group of 18. The Committee did not put forward conclusive proposals with regard to the most controversial issues, namely the programme budget process, budget outline, contingency fund and the intergovernmental machinery. They were shown in an indicative list of points to be resolved by the GA.

When introducing the draft report for approval by the Committee, Mr. Fontaine-Ortiz (Cuba), **Chairman of the Fifth Committee**[145], noted:

"The purpose of the Committee's findings was to assist the General Assembly in reaching a decision on item 38, which was one of the most essential on the agenda of the forty-first session. Paragraphs 64 and 68 (d) of the findings on section VI of the Group's report, planning and budget procedure, each contained a phrase in brackets to reflect the fact that their contents had not been accepted by consensus. There had, however, been agreement on some findings in regard to that section; paragraph 69 of the draft report contained a list of points that remained to be resolved. He hoped that the Committee would accept the approach, for reaching agreement on section VI was clearly not part of its mandate from the General Assembly."

The report (A/41/795)* was adopted by the Fifth Committee on the 5 November 1990. Before the adoption, following statements were made.

The representative of Czechoslovakia, speaking on behalf of **socialist countries**"[146]

"drew attention to the finding, in paragraph 57 of the draft report, to the effect that recommendations 55 and 57 by the Group of High-level Intergovernmental Experts had not enjoyed the necessary support within that Group. The Eastern European delegations and others had expressed fundamental reservations to those two recommendations both in the informal discussions and at the relevant plenary meetings of the General Assembly. Any decision by the General Assembly on the report of the Group should reflect the fact that there had not been agreement on those recommendations."

---

*See volume II, 2.4.
**Bulgaria, Byelorussian SSR, German Democratic Republic, Hungary, Poland, Romania, Ukrainian SSR, USSR.

The representative of **Algeria**[147]

"The conclusions in the draft report constituted an important basis for agreement between Member States on the planning and budgetary machinery and the implementation of all the recommendations of the Group of Experts.

He hoped that the Committee's findings on section VI would be strengthened by further compromises on the points of disagreement mentioned in paragraph 69. The list of points given there was not exhaustive. If it was expanded, the balance between the concerns of Member States reflected in the draft report should be respected."

The representative of the **United States of America**[148]

"indicated throughout the process that the Committee's appropriate role was to carry out a factual examination and to report its findings objectively. The Fifth Committee should not pre-empt action by the plenary Assembly by taking or recommending substantive decisions. As to the findings relating to sections II to V, his delegation believed that a great deal of useful information was being transmitted to the plenary Assembly which should assist that body in its deliberations. The Committee had rightly avoided making specific recommendations on courses of action. His delegation stressed, in that regard, that the Committee's findings concerning section VI were intended to describe only the points of agreement among the three options set out in section VI. It would be unfortunate and inaccurate if those points were construed as an agreed overall approach to the issue of the programme budget. In that respect, paragraph 69 contained an indicative list of points to be resolved during the plenary Assembly's consideration of the report of the Group of Experts. Those points were some of the central elements of the issue and would need to be discussed and negotiated in detail in the plenary Assembly."

2.2.4 Approval of the Resolution on the Review of the Efficiency of the Administrative and Financial Functioning of the United Nations (41/213)

The report of the Fifth Committee was presented to the Plenary Assembly on 6 November 1986. In order to reach agreement on the points on which there was still a divergence of view, the following procedure was approved. The President, assisted by the Vice-Presidents, contacted the different groups, sub-groups and individual delegations, with a view to identifying areas of agreement, as well as issues on which further consultations were needed. The results of the efforts of this contact group were placed before a consultative group comprising essentially representatives which had been selected from different regions during an early stage of the process. The consultative group, which deliberated over the matter from 12 to 18 November under the chairmanship of the permanent representative of Malaysia, Ambassador Yusof M. Hitam, in turn, attempted to narrow down the differences on the various issues. There was widespread despair of ever reaching agreement and a large number of ambassadors became involved in the final stages of negotiating the reform resolution. It was in the consultative group that the various positions were formulated, enabling the negotiating team to conclude its work successfully and submit the outcome of their efforts for consideration by the Committee of the Whole of the Plenary Assembly.

There had been substantial movements of positions during the session of the GA. The US Ambassador, General Vernon Walters, came to accept the first 'compromise' option rather than the third option on the programme budget procedure. He made it known that if option two was accepted, at least in broad outlines, the US government would seek to revise the Congress legislation on the withholding of the UN contribution. Another good-will offer was made in October by the US Secretary of State, George Shultz, when he announced that the USA would pay over $100 million for 1986 rather than the $60 million initially expected. Clearly, this represented a victory by the US State Department over the hardliners in the US Congress. Finally, the US delegation to the UN made it known that further payments would follow once option two of the budget process and cuts in the UN programme were accepted. In addition, the economy measures agreed so far were estimated to amount to $70 million rather than $100 million as previously expected from the Group of 18 report. This went a long way towards softening the attitude of the G77 in their insistence on option two, which involving only minimal changes. The African group, however, still insisted on option two with the aim of protecting the principle of sovereign equality. Although the supporters of option one developed from a minority to a majority group, it still took three weeks of intense and bitter negotiations during December 1986 before agreement could be reached. Among the final concessions to the African countries was the deferral of a decision on the contingency fund to the next GA session by which time the results of further studies by the Secretary-General would be available. In addition, the 25 per cent cut in high-level posts was now defined as target rather than a fixed number. The socialist countries appear not to have taken a strong stance in the final negotiations. They agreed with the US demands for budget reduction, but criticized the US position with regard to the withholdings and the demand for weighted voting. Finally, they indicated their agreement with option one. This was supported by an unprecedented move of the USSR, which advanced $25 million of its 1987 assessment in early December 1986. The fact that agreement could be reached was to a large extent also the result of the efforts by the Secretary-General, who made it known "that his acceptance of a new six-year term would depend on a significant progress on the Group of 18 proposals"[149].

Concluded during the last 36 hours of the 41st GA, the final agreement was closer to option one than to option two. The resolution which described the final agreement, defined the new role of CPC as the principal advisory and intergovernmental committee with regard to the programme budget. The Committee would consider the Secretary-General's budget outline one year prior to budget preparation ('off-budget year') and advise the Fifth Committee of the GA. The budget outline would include a total budget ceiling in US dollars not to be exceeded in the subsequent preparation of the proposed programme budget. In addition, as a new feature, CPC would agree on a contingency fund for financing any additional activities approved after the programme budget had been developed. The contingency fund would be defined as a percentage of the total programme budget. In the budget year, the Secretary-General would submit the detailed programme budget proposals to the CPC and ACABQ for consideration prior to their approval by the Fifth Committee. CPC would be entrusted with considering the medium-term plan and examining the relationship between the plan and the proposed programme budget. The Secretary-General was expected to consult with CPC on the broad concept he intended to reflect in the plan before actual preparation took place. This would allow for an early participation of member states in the planning process.

The resolution stipulated that all possible efforts should be made in the Fifth Committee to establish the broadest possible agreement. CPC, however, should "continue its existing practice of reaching decisions by consensus" (para 6). The practice of taking decisions by consensus was not considered very important at a time when CPC had only a modest role in the programme budget process. Now, however, the elevated role of CPC would make decision-taking by voting more likely, with the risk of larger contributors being outvoted. The explicit requirement for consensus would eliminate this risk and give the USA, as a member of this committee, greater leverage in shaping the programme budget. Once approved by CPC, the proposed budget could still be rejected by the Fifth Committee, where the current appeal for consensus still left room for voting. This would be difficult, however, since it would involve a breaking up of a carefully structured budget package at a rather late stage of the process. The agreement, therefore, tipped the balance of influence rather than institutionalised outright weighted voting procedures, as initially demanded by the USA. Nevertheless, the question was raised by those critical of the agreement as to whether insistence upon consensus in CPC was compatible with Article 18 of the UN Charter, which described the decision-making process. Previously consensus decision-making at CPC had only been an informal practice, and not a requirement. Prior to the approval of the resolution, the Legal Council of the UN had been asked for a legal opinion on this matter and had concluded that the agreement was not in conflict with Article 18 of the Charter.[150]

As noted, CPC was expected to play a more important role in the future programme budget process. The committee had 21 members, elected by the GA on the nomination by ECOSOC on the basis of geographical distribution. In order to increase their participation in CPC, developing countries demanded a larger say. Draft resolution A/41/L.48 submitted by Bolivia, included a proposal to increase membership in the CPC to 54 state from 1988 onwards with the following geographical distribution: 14 seats for African States, 11 seats for Asian States, 10 seats for Latin American and Caribbean States, 13 seats for Western European and other States and 6 seats for Eastern European States. The draft resolution was strongly opposed by the Western European States and the USA. The revised draft A/41/L.48/Rev.1 submitted by Bolivia, which included a smaller increase to 36 members and a geographical distribution of 10, 8, 7, 7, and 4, did also not meet with general approval. In order not to put into jeopardy the consensus reached on the recommendations of the Group of 18, the developing countries finally agreed to withdraw the draft resolution and it was decided to defer its consideration to the 42nd session of the GA.

The way was therefore clear for the Plenary Assembly to take decision on the recommendations of the Group of 18. Before doing so, the following statements were made.

The representative of Panama, on behalf of the **Group of Latin American and Caribbean States**[151]

"it is not acceptable that under the pretext of reviewing the efficiency ... or any other pretext, there should be an attempt to detract from the democratic nature of the decision-making process provided for in Article 18 of the Charter. Nor is it acceptable for the Organization's efficiency to continue to be affected by the intentional withholding by some Member States of their contribution to the regular budget, contributions they are obliged to make under Article 17 and 19 of the Charter. ...

The informal practice of arriving at resolutions and decisions by consensus, which should not be confused with unanimity, is useful and therefore tends to be employed in all the bodies of the General Assembly. However, as it is not a juridical norm, it is not obligatory and it does not interfere with the right of any Member States to seek recourse to a vote to achieve majority decisions when necessary. The practice of consensus is conceived of only within a process of decision-making governed by the fundamental rule of voting."

The representative of Cape Verde, speaking on behalf of the **Group of African States**[152]

"Firmly committed as we are to the purposes and principles of the United Nations, we were strongly against the consideration of any question which directly or indirectly threatened those principles or jeopardized the attainment of those purposes. We could in no way endorse positions that would subvert the democratic rights of all Member States, particularly in the General Assembly.

It is therefore with satisfaction that we acknowledge that those legitimate concerns and firm positions of the African States, which, after all, were shared by the overwhelming majority of Member States, if not by all, have been fully taken into account and are duly and clearly reflected in the text of the draft resolution and its annexes.

We come out of these difficult negotiations convinced that all Member States are aware of the utmost importance of the United Nations as an indispensable framework where nations of the world can debate and search for peaceful solutions to their conflicts and where all nations representing the human race as a whole can find agreed solutions to global problems.

The agreement reached on the reforms to be introduced into the Organization, with a view to improving its efficiency in the administrative and financial fields, gives us renewed hope that all countries will, in compliance with their Charter obligations, commit themselves to the dignifying task of preserving and strengthening the United Nations, in the interest of world peace and the well-being of all peoples."

Following these statements, and based on draft A/41/L.49/Rev.1˙, the GA approved by consensus the resolution entitled **Review of the Efficiency of the Administrative and Financial Functioning of the United Nations (41/213)˙˙** on 24 December 1986. The 'reform resolution' 41/213, as it became known, has two major parts. In part I on the recommendations of the Group of 18, the GA decided that the recommendations as agreed upon should be implemented in light of the findings of the Fifth Committee and subject to the following: the implementation of recommendation 5 should not prejudice the implementation of projects and programmes already approved by the GA; the percentage referred to in recommendation 15 should be regarded as targets in the formulation of the Secretary-General's plan to be submitted to the GA for the implementation of the recommendation; the Secretary-General should transmit to the ICSC those recommendations having direct impact on the UN common system (recommendations 53 and 61), with the request that it report to the GA at its 42nd session, so as to enable the Assembly to make a final decision. In part II on the planning, programming and budgeting process, the GA decided that the process shall be governed by: (a) strict adherence to the principles and provisions of the Charter, in particular articles 17 and 18 thereof; (b) full respect of the prerogatives of the principal organs of the UN with respect to the process, and of the Secretary-General as the chief administrative officer of the organization; and (c) recognition of the need for member states to participate in the budgetary preparation from its early stages and throughout the process. Annex I of the resolution provides a description of the new budget process. Annex II shows a communication dated 12 December 1986 addressed to the President of the GA by the Legal Counsel of the UN. By decision 41/468 the GA indicated its agreement with a legal opinion from the Legal Counsel on the implications of 3 paragraphs (5, 6 and 7) of the resolution *vis-à-vis* the provisions of article 18 of the UN Charter.

After the adoption of resolution 41/213, the **Secretary-General**[153] made following statement.

"The resolution just adopted by this Assembly on the report of the Group of High-level Intergovernmental Experts is of cardinal importance for the future of this Organization as an effective force for progress and for peace.

˙Submitted by Algeria, Bangladesh, Brazil, Cameroon, Cape Verde, China, France, Germany, Federal Republic of, Ghana, India, Iraq, Japan, Nigeria, Pakistan, Trinidad and Tobago, USSR, UK, USA, Yugoslavia. The initial draft resolution A/41/L.49 was identical with Rev.1 except for not including Annex II, Communication dated 12 December 1986 addressed to the President of the GA by the Legal Council of the UN.

˙˙See volume II, 1.2.

This notable achievement has been possible only because of the spirit of accommodation shown by all Member States. The measures endorsed for the improvement of the financial and administrative functioning of the Organization are without precedent in their scope and detail. I believe they provide a sound basis for changes that will bring new confidence in the effectiveness and efficiency of the Organization and facilitate the agreement among Member States on the programmes and budget that is necessary for financial and political viability. ...

There is now much to be done. Implementation of the measures decided upon by the Assembly will be a complex and demanding undertaking, to the success of which I am totally committed. I have already taken steps within my authority to improve resource utilization and I have made preparations within the Secretariat which should permit us to move ahead expeditiously and in orderly fashion to implement the broad measures foreseen in the report of the Group of 18.

In stating this I must add that a number of important strands will need to be woven into a coherent pattern during the coming year. Some of the measures decided upon by the Assembly require action by intergovernmental bodies. Others which can be implemented by the Secretary-General will need to be carried out with due regard for their relationship to such intergovernmental action. The year 1987 must also see extensive work accomplished on the programme budget for the next biennium, to include a contingency fund and the initiation of preparations for the 1990-1995 medium-term plan. The effect of the prospective reforms will have to be taken into account in the process.

The year 1987 will thus be a year of transition, a year in which we undertake purposefully the reforms that can be quickly begun and lay the groundwork for further rationalization of structures and operations through the reviews and studies that are to be made. Clearly, there will need to be flexibility in the modalities of implementation. In the progress report which I shall submit to the General Assembly this coming May I shall give a full account of what has been accomplished by then and define the approaches which I believe can best be taken in achieving the purpose of the measures agreed upon by the Assembly.

As a result of the far-sighted and painstaking work of the Group of 18 and of the constructive action taken by the Assembly today after thoughtful and constructive deliberation, we have in place the blueprint for a more efficient United Nations. The co-operation and understanding of Member States will be necessary as we build from this the stronger edifice that all desire. I must emphasize, as we end a year of severe financial crisis and enter another, that the major requirement in this respect, now and in the future, is full payment of assessed contributions in accordance with the Charter. The reform measures now to be undertaken must be accompanied by an end to the present financial uncertainties if the United Nations is to meet successfully the challenges and opportunities of the future."

Further statements were made after the adoption of resolution 41/213 as recalled below.

The representative of **Saudi Arabia**[154]

"I have accepted with a heavy heart the resolution just adopted without a vote. Despite its ambiguity, which initially we found difficult to accommodate, I consider your explanation, Mr. President, sufficient to eliminate any ambiguity that might have been created by the terms of the text itself, and believe that nothing in the text will really hamper the procedures adopted by the General Assembly in its normal deliberations."

The representative of **India**[155]

"With the adoption of the ... resolution 41/213, the General Assembly has taken a historic decision. It is historic not in the sense that it breaks any new ground or lays down new policies or principles: On the contrary, it reconfirms existing principles and provisions. It is historic in the sense that the Organization, which was facing one of the most acute crises in its 40-year life - some even say that it was the most acute crisis - has shown once again that, given political goodwill on all sides, it is possible to overcome seemingly insurmountable obstacles. There was a widespread perception that the very existence of the United Nations was in danger. Every Member, as it were, was on trial. Hence all of us might claim that we have passed the test with a least reasonably satisfactory grades."

The representative of **Bolivia**[156]

"my Government is concerned by the trend in international forums to seek consensus - or unanimity - even though it may sometimes result in a document of dubious value. A more accurate term might be "undemocratic", because the democracy which we try to preserve in our countries is based on the will of the majority, as expressed by the vote. Adoption by consensus, on the other hand, imposes criteria that mask delegations' positions. This is obviously inconsistent with the pluralism which should prevail in the international community.

... my delegation finds that the way in which the report was dealt with at this session - both in the plenary Assembly and in the Fifth Committee, under agenda item 38 - was partial and somewhat confusing: In the Fifth Committee factual, technical findings were discussed that did not make it possible for States Members duly to formulate their objections to the report as a whole or to its individual recommendations. Hence it might have been through that on the first five chapters of the report on which there was unanimity among the experts who prepared it there might also have been unanimity among the Member States. That is not the case. Indeed, in respect of the 67 recommendations contained in the first five chapters the Bolivian delegation stated that it did not agree with 18 of them and that it found seven of them unacceptable, specifically recommendations 6, 7, 24, 25 (3), 27, 37 (3) and 61. ...

I reiterate that the lack of efficiency resulting from the Organization's financial crisis is the responsibility of neither the Secretary-General nor the staff of the international civil service. My delegation does not agree that the international staff is overpaid or that it has too many privileges. On the contrary, the international civil service should be given every support and all the incentives needed so that it can accomplish its work.

My delegation stresses that if [the] resolution ... had been put to a recorded vote, we would have abstained on the draft resolution in general and voted against paragraph 6 for reasons of principle."

The representative of the German Democratic Republic, speaking on behalf of **socialist countries**[*][157]

"The countries I have the honour to represent have supported the resolution on the report of the Group of Experts although the document before us does not fully take into account all our ideas and interests."

The representative of the United Kingdom, speaking on behalf of the 12 member States of the **European Community**[158]

"We believe that the resolution we have just approved represents a careful, balanced approach to a complicated and intractable set of problems."

The representative of the **United States of America**[159]

"The United States believes that the adoption of this resolution is the beginning, not the end, of a process of reforming and improving the United Nations in the interest of all its Members. Central to this process, in our view, is the use of consensus in establishing the framework for the United Nations budget. Guidance given to the Secretary-General in this area will now reflect broad agreement among the membership. As has been suggested, it is unhealthy for an institution when Member States which contribute 75 per cent

---

[*]Bulgaria, Byelorussian SSR, Czechoslovakia, German Democratic Republic, Hungary, Mongolia, Poland, Romania, Ukrainian SSR, USSR.

of the funds of the United Nations still feel compelled to vote against or abstain on the United Nations budget in order to express their disagreement with the level or type of expenditure.

As a result of what we have achieved today, Member States, through good-faith negotiation, will now act by consensus on the important budget issues that previously proved so divisive. This is fundamental, indeed absolutely essential, for the long-term viability of the United Nations. Were this new process to break down, we would find ourselves back where we started, in a situation unacceptable to all of us."

The representative of **Sweden**[160]

"The Swedish delegation regards the resolution just adopted as a response to a generally recognized need for reforms in the financial and administrative areas. At the same time, it is obvious that the review of the Group of 18, as well as the Assembly's deliberations, has been undertaken during a period in which the United Nations faces a severe financial crisis.

With respect to the wider picture, the Swedish Government believes that a revision of the present method of assessing contributions is an essential reform which should be included in a comprehensive solution of the problem facing the United Nations. It remains the conviction of my Government that a more even apportionment of assessments would reflect, better than at present, the fact that the United Nations is the instrument of all nations. The Organization would be less dependent on contributions from any single Member State. This, in turn, would be likely to improve the balance and coherence in the functioning of the world body, thereby enhancing its efficiency and effectiveness."

The representative of **Zimbabwe**[161]

"My delegation believes that to most of us here the main purpose of the exercise we have gone through has been to improve the efficiency and effectiveness of the United Nations system. However, we are aware that there were other efforts that were not necessarily aimed at promoting the democratic character of this body. This was, is and will continue to be a cause of anxiety to most of us. It is for the reason that Zimbabwe wishes to place on record its understanding of the crucial paragraphs 6 and 7 on the budgeting process, which have a potential for subverting the democratic principles governing the Organization.

It is our understanding that the existing practice of the Committee for Programme and Co-ordination in reaching decisions is to do so without a vote. It is therefore our interpretation that the phrase "existing practice of reaching decisions by consensus" when applied to the Committee's present practice can mean only the practice of coming to decisions without a vote. Otherwise, it has no meaning at all. It is also my delegation's understanding that the Committee cannot be said to have a single practice of arriving at its decisions. Consequently, we take it that the word "practice" in the English text issued in the plural form, just as is the case in the unofficial language of the text, and therefore the Committee is not being restricted by paragraph 6 to following any one practice.

Zimbabwe recognizes that in the English language "consensus" has at least three meanings. First, it may be taken as being synonymous with general agreement - or unanimity, for short. Secondly, it may designate a judgement arrived at with the concurrence of most of those concerned. That is, it reflects the majority view. Finally, it may be equated with group solidarity, sentiment and belief.

Given this array of possible interpretations of "consensus", my delegation is of the view that the only interpretation that is in consonance with paragraph 5 is its second meaning: a judgement arrived at with the concurrence of most of those concerned - that is, it reflects the majority view.

Zimbabwe therefore rejects as invalid any interpretation that seeks by the purported codification of a delaying mechanism in the decision-making process of the Committee for Programme and Co-ordination to derogate from the operational provisions of the Charter and the General Assembly's rules of procedure.

With those few observations, we hope that those who have brought us here by withholding their assessed contributions will now accept their obligation to the Organization. For if that does not happen, this will have been an exercise in futility, significant only in that the sharks have had an opportunity to taste blood."

The representative of **Iraq**[162]

"If the euphoria sop clearly manifested this afternoon in this Hall is not be disappear into thin area ... at least some of the hopes I am about to express must be realized. First, nothing, in my humble opinion, would enhance the chances of translating the important resolution we have just adopted into reality so much as immediate action by those Members that are in arrears in their contributions to the regular budget - illegally in arrears - to end their delinquency without any further delay and promptly meet their obligations to the budget of the United Nations. ...

My second hope is that Member States - and their executive branches in particular - will do everything in their power to counter the constant "United Nations-bashing". ...

The third point I should like to emphasize once again is the enormous role of the Secretary-General in this very area of administrative and financial reforms. ...

The fourth point I want to make is by way of a reminder. I hate to sermonize, but administrative and financial reform and efficiency important and laudable though it be, should never in the context of the United Nations be seen as an end in itself. It can only make sense as a means to an end, because in the final analysis the success or failure of the Organization will never be measured by how much money it has spent, whether it is slightly less - as it is now - or slightly more than the cost of the nuclear submarine. Its success or failure will be measured by the ability or failure of the Organization to solve, and to remove from our agenda chronic political, economic and social items. ...

In conclusion, nothing would please my delegation more than to come back next year and see the adoption of this draft resolution without a vote have a material effect on the budget itself. Nothing would please us more than to see the major contributors, and others, who now pay 75 per cent of the budget, vote enthusiastically for the next budget."

The adoption of resolution 41/213 was generally perceived as having gone a long way to accommodate the critics of the UN. There was hope that the withholding would now be stopped. The US President Ronald Reagan telephoned the Secretary-General on the 22 December 1986 and described the resolution as a historical step as well as promising that he would ask the US Congress to restore most of the withholdings.[163]

A first main possibility to apply the decision on the reform would be in 1987 during the approval of the 1988-1989 programme budget. Preparation for this programme budget was already well under way and it was expected that not all the changes could be implemented in time. This period of transition would be followed by the first real test of the new programme budget procedure in 1988. During that year, the programme budget outline - the first of its kind - for the biennium 1990-1991 would be submitted and approved. This would be followed in 1989 by the consideration of the detailed programme budget for 1990-1991.

The reform of the UN was the subject of a conference during February 1987 sponsored by the Stanley Foundation. Participants included senior secretariat officials, UN diplomats and other outside experts who had been involved in shaping the decision on the reform. They met as individuals rather than as representative of their organizations or governments for several days of frank, informal discussion. The conference termed the adoption of resolution 41/213 a 'historic event'. "The historic proportion, however, does not stem from the sense that the content of the resolution is brilliant, uniformly farsighted, or likely to change the course of the world. Rather it gains its status from the fact that any agreement was found at all."[164] With regard to the agreement reached, it was noted in the report of the Conference that "it would be a denial of the complexity of the negotiations to suggest that the United States got everything it set out to achieve. ... the General Assembly resolution contain numerous compromises. In the word of one participant, the result is a 'judicious distribution of dissatisfaction'".[165] Nevertheless "though not set forth in any document, it is understood by all involved that the December 1986 agreement and all of the work which preceded it constitute a serious effort on the part of the United Nations to begin a reform process and thereby give cause for the United States to end the withholdings. Participants tacitly accept this connection but are anxious not to formalize it. To publicly acknowledge the connection effectively sanctions use of a tactic which most of the UN community interpret as illegal withholding in order to achieve a political goal. Beyond that there is a real cause of saying that the linkage is not as firm as it first appears. It is necessary for the entire international community to see that there is genuine value in reform. If the process is to succeed, it must be good for the United Nations and the world community and not just an exercise intended to appease the United States. ... So while it is clear on one level to say that the financial crisis drives the reform effort, it is important to note that only when a measure of ambiguity has been placed between the issues - that there is something less than a direct cause-effect relationship - has the context been created wherein agreement is possible. It is important because maintaining that measure of ambiguity is essential to preserving the atmosphere necessary for implementation of the reforms."[166]

Although improving the efficiency of the UN was seen as a good idea, participants of the conference "repeatedly called attention to the need to articulate a vision for the organization and some far-reaching programmatic goals. Without a political consensus on goals, the reforms will take place in a vacuum. In a positive sense, some participants believed that the current reform programme is forcing a more fundamental reexamination of the United Nations' role in the world. ... In an ideal world, it was argued, the goals would be set first and the organization would follow. However, the press for administrative reform is on, and the best that can be hoped for now is that the process of reform will facilitate broader rethinking. Some other more doubtful participants expressed concern that the reform effort might simply turn into a technical fix designed to avoid confronting broad political problems."[167]

"There was also concern raised about the possible rush to reduce the number of controversial issues with which the United Nations deals. One way to get the broadest financial support, it was argued, is to keep as many countries as possible happy. However, the United Nations was created to deal with controversy, and the institution must be able to rely on the support (including financial) of its members even when some of those members are unhappy with the outcome of a controversy."[168]

Finally, developing countries, in particular, suspected a hidden agenda of the major contributors in their push for reform. "They fear that the reform initiative is really an attempt to seize control of the organization's agenda and gain more political control of the organization thus thwarting the will of the majority. Several participants cautioned that they will be on guard to protect against what might be perceived as reshaping of the United Nations' programme to serve the needs of the developing countries at the expense of the developing. Some called for 'reform' of another kind - that is progress on the substantive concerns of many of the world's poorest nations."[169]

With regard to the new planning and budget process approved by resolution 41/213, the participants at the conference noted that "on the surface the changed process looks only modestly different from its predecessor, but ... the undocumented agreement which lies behind the new procedures is the key compromise. ... CPC will attempt to reach decision by consensus. That gives the major powers more say in the content and size of the budget than has been the case before. However, 41/213 provides that votes can be taken on the budget by any of the reviewing bodies. ... Here then is the undocumented but clearly held understanding: if the major powers are unreasonable in withholding support for certain programmes, the majority can resort to its voting power; conversely, if the majority is unreasonable and uses its voting power to pass a budget that is onerous to the major contributors, the new process will have collapsed and the major contributors are expected to resort to withholding. Obviously, the standard here is reasonableness. Can this be made to work?"[170]

Resolution 41/213 had called for a number of in-depth studies, in particular, to identify ways to simplify the intergovernmental structure and to strengthen the co-ordination activity in the economic and social fields. The aim was to reduce duplication and repetition of discussions and programmes. The likely success of this effort was judged cautiously by the participants of the conference, when stating "attempting to accomplish these various tasks will face numerous problems. Perhaps most fundamental is that there is no common view of the problem which the study seeks to address. Some see enormous overlap and duplication in the economic and social fields and would favour extensive reorganization to combine or eliminate some agencies. Others, with a more minimal view, call only for a slight fine tuning of the existing structure. ... the machinery in these areas is old and entrenched and is the result of certain member states' initiatives. Consequently, those nations may be unwilling to see them dismantled or subsumed into another organization."[171]

Little concern was expressed with regard to the changes envisaged for the secretariat, in particular the cut in posts and the reorganization. "These directives reflect the views held by many concerning the Secretariat. Its structure is seen as being top heavy and too complex. As a result, accountability, responsibility, and communication suffer. The fragmentation of the structure ... results in poor co-ordination and often duplication of work lowering the overall quality of output."[172]

Finally, on the implementation of the reform "concern was expressed that because of the time constraints - the reorganization and staff cuts are to be completed by January 1, 1990 - that decisions will be made in a hasty, ad hoc manner. ... Participants from the Secretariat urged member states to use restraint and give them an opportunity to get the reforms in place and operating before passing judgement on their value or instituting additional changes. As one participant noted, a gardener cannot keep pulling a plant up to check how the roots are doing, if the plant is to grow and prosper."[173]

Notes

1.   Arthur Kilgore, 'Cut Down in the Crossfire?', *International Relations*, XXXIII (November 1986), p. 600.
2.   *Ibid.*, pp. 601-602.
3.   A/C.5/41/24.
4.   *Official Records of the General Assembly, Fourty-first Session, Supplement No. 1* (A/41/1), p. 1.
5.   A/41/PV.1, pp. 17-22.
6.   A/41/PV.4, pp. 16-17.
7.   *Ibid.*, p. 62.
8.   A/41/PV.5, pp. 22-23.
9.   *Ibid.*, pp. 56-57.
10. *Ibid.*, pp. 67-72.
11. A/41/PV.6, pp. 62-63.
12. *Ibid.*, pp. 84-85.

13. A/41/PV.7, pp. 17-18.
14. *Ibid.*, p. 63.
15. *Ibid.*, p. 82.
16. A/41/PV.8, pp. 38-39.
17. *Ibid.*, p. 56.
18. *Ibid.*, p. 58.
19. A/41/PV.9, p. 11.
20. *Ibid.*, pp. 22-23.
21. *Ibid.*, pp. 47-49.
22. *Ibid.*, p. 108.
23. A/41/PV.10, p. 76.
24. *Ibid.*, p. 89-91.
25. A/41/PV.11, p. 37.
26. *Ibid.*, p. 41.
27. *Ibid.*, pp. 57-58.
28. *Ibid.*, p. 87.
29. A/41/PV.12, pp. 18-20.
30. *Ibid.*, p. 85.
31. A/41/PV.13, p. 22.
32. *Ibid.*, pp. 39-40.
33. *Ibid.*, pp. 66-67.
34. *Ibid.*, pp. 86-88.
35. A/41/PV.14, pp. 4-7.
36. *Ibid.*, p. 43.
37. *Ibid.*, pp. 46, 57.
38. *Ibid.*, p. 61.
39. A/41/PV.15, pp. 38-40.
40. *Ibid.*, pp. 68-70.
41. *Ibid.*, p. 84.
42. A/41/PV.16, pp. 78-80.
43. A/41/PV.17, pp. 6-7.
44. *Ibid.*, p. 107.
45. A/41/PV.19, p. 6.
46. *Ibid.*, p. 28.
47. *Ibid.*, pp. 41-43.
48. A/41/PV.20, p. 6.
49. A/41/PV.21, p. 12.
50. *Ibid.*, p. 22.
51. *Ibid.*, p. 47.
52. *Ibid.*, p. 61.
53. *Ibid.*, pp. 86-87.
54. A/41/PV.22, pp. 2-5.
55. *Ibid.*, pp. 37-38.
56. A/41/PV.24, p. 14.
57. *Ibid.*, pp. 52-53.
58. *Ibid.*, p. 42.
59. *Ibid.*, pp. 77-80.
60. A/41/PV.27, p. 33.
61. A/41/PV.28, pp. 17-18.
62. *Ibid.*, p. 58.
63. A/41/PV.29, p. 23.
64. A/41/PV.30, pp. 23-25.
65. A/41/PV.31, pp. 31-32.
66. A/41/PV.33, pp. 47-52.
67. *Ibid.*, pp. 57-61.
68. *Ibid.*, pp. 71-72.
69. A/41/PV.34, pp. 7-12.

70.   *Ibid.*, pp. 17-20.
71.   *Ibid.*, pp. 23-28.
72.   *Ibid.*, pp. 33-38.
73.   *Ibid.*, pp. 43-45.
74.   *Ibid.*, pp. 51-55.
75.   *Ibid.*, pp. 58-65.
76.   *Ibid.*, pp. 68-71.
77.   A/41/PV.35, pp. 4-6.
78.   *Ibid.*, pp. 9-10.
79.   *Ibid.*, pp. 12-20.
80.   *Ibid.*, pp. 21-30.
81.   *Ibid.*, pp. 33-36.
82.   *Ibid.*, pp. 41-46.
83.   *Ibid.*, pp. 48-55.
84.   *Ibid.*, pp. 64-65.
85.   A/41/PV.36, pp. 8-12.
86.   *Ibid.*, pp. 16-18.
87.   *Ibid.*, pp. 22-25.
88.   *Ibid.*, pp. 29-30.
89.   *Ibid.*, pp. 38-41.
90.   *Ibid.*, pp. 42-46.
91.   *Ibid.*, pp. 48-56.
92.   *Ibid.*, pp. 58-61.
93.   *Ibid.*, pp. 66-68.
94.   *Ibid.*, pp. 71-75.
95.   *Ibid.*, pp. 79-86.
96.   A/41/PV.37, pp. 4-7.
97.   *Ibid.*, pp. 9-12.
98.   *Ibid.*, pp. 16-27.
99.   *Ibid.*, pp. 31-35.
100. *Ibid.*, pp. 38-41.
101. *Ibid.*, pp. 43-47.
102. *Ibid.*, pp. 53-57.
103. *Ibid.*, pp. 61-70.
104. *Ibid.*, pp. 73-75.
105. *Ibid.*, pp. 79-82.
106. *Ibid.*, pp. 86-87.
107. *Ibid.*, pp. 92-95.
108. *Ibid.*, pp. 98-103.
109. *Ibid.*, pp. 107-108.
110. *Ibid.*, pp. 113-116.
111. *Ibid.*, pp. 117-121.
112. *Ibid.*, pp. 122-127.
113. A/41/PV.38, pp. 5-7.
114. *Ibid.*, pp. 11-14.
115. *Ibid.*, pp. 17-20.
116. *Ibid.*, pp. 24-27.
117. *Ibid.*, pp. 32-36.
118. *Ibid.*, pp. 38-42.
119. *Ibid.*, pp. 47-62.
120. *Ibid.*, pp. 72-73.
121. *Ibid.*, pp. 77-79.
122. A/41/PV.39, pp. 6-10.
123. *Ibid.*, pp. 17-18.
124. *Ibid.*, pp. 22-25.
125. *Ibid.*, p. 31.
126. *Ibid.*, pp. 36-40.

127. *Ibid.*, pp. 47-52.
128. *Ibid.*, pp. 57-60.
129. *Ibid.*, pp. 62-67.
130. *Ibid.*, p. 73.
131. *Ibid.*, pp. 82-100.
132. *Ibid.*, pp. 103-106.
133. *Ibid.*, pp. 116-120.
134. A/C.5/41/SR.27, pp. 2-3.
135. A/C.5/41/SR.13, pp. 2-7.
136. A/C.5/41/SR.14, pp. 3-4.
137. A/C.5/41/SR.15, pp. 2-14.
138. *Ibid.*, pp. 11-13.
139. *Ibid.*, pp. 14-15.
140. A/C.5/41/SR.16, pp. 2-11.
141. A/C.5/41/SR.17, pp. 2-6.
142. A/C.5/41/SR.18, pp. 2-4.
143. *Ibid.*, pp. 11-15.
144. *Ibid.*, pp. 15-17.
145. A/C.5/41/SR.21, p. 2.
146. *Ibid.*, pp. 2-3.
147. *Ibid.*, p. 5.
148. *Ibid.*, p. 8.
149. David R. Protheroe, *The United Nations and its Finances, A Test for Middle Powers* (Ottawa, Canada: The North-South Institute, 1988), p. 56.
150. A/41/PV.102, pp. 7-8.
151. *Ibid.*, pp. 11-12.
152. *Ibid.*, p. 14.
153. *Ibid.*, pp. 16-18.
154. *Ibid.*, p. 18.
155. *Ibid.*, pp. 21-22.
156. *Ibid.*, pp. 28-31.
157. *Ibid.*, p. 31.
158. *Ibid.*, p. 33.
159. *Ibid.*, p. 43.
160. *Ibid.*, p. 46.
161. *Ibid.*, pp. 48-49.
162. *Ibid.*, pp. 53-57.
163. Elaine Sciolino, 'President Will Ask Congress to Restore Millions for UN', *The New York Times*, 1 January 1987.
164. *Administrative and Budgetary Reform of the United Nations*, Report of the Eighteenth UN Issues Conference, Stanley Foundation, 20-22 February 1987, p. 9.
165. *Ibid.*, p. 11.
166. *Ibid.*, p. 11.
167. *Ibid.*, p. 13.
168. *Ibid.*, p. 16.
169. *Ibid.*, p. 15.
170. *Ibid.*, pp. 16-18.
171. *Ibid.*, p. 19.
172. *Ibid.*, p. 21.
173. *Ibid.*, p. 22.

CHAPTER 3
FIRST PROGRESS REPORT, 1987

3.1 Financial Situation

Actual payments by the USA under the regular budget amounted to $149 million in 1986 - substantially more than the $60 million initially expected - in accordance with the announcement by US Secretary of State, George Shultz, during the negotiation of the reform resolution 41/213. The US contribution, however, was still $61 million short of the total assessment of $210 million. This increased the total outstanding US contribution to $149 million and the total UN deficit to $258 million by the end of 1986.* The shortfall in payments to the regular budget had to be covered by the Working Capital Fund (WCF) of $100 million, the Special Fund which had been increased to $94 million, the suspension of the provisions of financial regulation amounting to $29.7 million and borrowing from special funds and accounts in the custody of the UN.[1]

The Secretary-General, Javier Pérez de Cuéllar, was reelected at the end of 1986 to a second five-year term for the period 1987 to 1991. At the beginning of 1987, it was widely reported that the US Administration would ask Congress to restore UN funding for 1987 to nearly its full annual assessment. It was not clear, however, if and to what extent the arrears would be addressed. Above all, the response of the US Congress remained a big unknown. Uncertainty over the forthcoming US contribution prompted the Secretary-General to continue the austerity measures initiated in 1986. These included cutbacks in meetings, a recruitment freeze and a reduction in travel and documentation. As one delegate noted, "it will be extremely difficult to reinstate support for the UN among members of the US Congress after the Reagan Administration spent five years convincing them of its weakness."[2] In fact, there was a feeling among developing countries that the US Administration had failed to deliver its part of the bargain implicit in the December 1986 agreement: payment of full contributions in return for consensus voting. There were, nevertheless, some bright spots in the financial picture. The cash-flow situation in early 1987 was substantially better than in the past. Major contributors other than the US, as well as several-middle income countries, had paid their assessments early, in effect delaying a possible cash crisis until the last quarter of 1987.

---

*For details on the financial situation see annex, table 3 and 4.

Additional support was announced during the meeting of the Fifth Committee by Japan, which intended to make a special contribution of $20 million.

Most importantly, the UN started to benefit from the beginning of the end of the cold war between the superpowers. The USSR had rediscovered the UN and produced a continuous flow of ideas on how to use the organization, which traditionally had always been put forward by western countries.[3] In a famous article, General-Secretary Gorbachev proposed a more active and independent role for the UN Secretary-General, more international verification and fact-finding missions which the USSR had previously opposed, the strengthening of peace-keeping activities and the resurrection of the Military Staff Committee, initially conceived as the teeth of the UN but inactive since 1946 due to disagreements among the five permanent members.[4] Of particular importance insofar as the financial crisis was concerned, was the announcement in September 1987 that the USSR would pay its debt of $197 million for peace-keeping operations.

This new support for multilateralism revived the activities of the UN in early 1987, when, at the suggestions of the Secretary-General, the permanent members of the Security Council decided to work for an end to the Iran-Iraq war.

3.2 First, Second and Third Sessions of the Special Commission of ECOSOC

In accordance with GA resolution 41/213, ECOSOC took the decision entitled **In-depth Study of the United Nations Intergovernmental Structure and Functions in the Economic and Social Fields (1987/112)*** during its organizational session in February 1987. By decision 1987/112, ECOSOC: (a) established a Special Commission open to the full participation of all member states; (b) requested the Special Commission to consider, in the context of the in-depth study, the relevant provisions of recommendation 2 of the Group of 18; and (c) appointed Ambassador Abdel Halim Badawi (Egypt) as Chairman of the Special Commission. The Special Commission was to start its work in March 1987 and submit a final report to the second regular session of ECOSOC in the summer of 1988. During the intervening period, ECOSOC would be kept informed of the progress achieved.

---

*See volume II, 1.3.

During its first session (2-6 March 1987), the Special Commission considered the organization of its work during, including the identification of the documentation required to conduct an in-depth study of the intergovernmental structure and its functions in the economic and social fields. The Commission also considered different methodological approaches for the study. The following opening statement was made by Mr. Badawi (Egypt), **Chairman of the Special Commission**[5]:

"there is widespread recognition today by members of the United Nations of the need for measures to improve the efficiency of the United Nations with a view to strengthening its effectiveness in dealing with the various issues on its agenda. It is also recognized that as a result of the evolution and development of the principles and scope of international economic co-operation, the interdependence of States, the interrelatedness of issues and the resulting need for an integrated approach, the United Nations as a universal forum for deliberations and negotiation had to cope with the changing circumstances and the new challenges as they emerged. Consequently, the agenda of the United Nations has grown continuously, with a concomitant growth in the intergovernmental machinery in the economic and social fields. A parallel growth in the United Nations Secretariat support structures to service the intergovernmental machinery resulted. The volume of documentation has also increased considerably, sometimes exceeding the average or even the super-human capacity for absorption, particularly for smaller delegations which have to cover the meetings of several committees or bodies with a limited staff. So, the general objective of this exercise is to increase the efficiency and enhance the effectiveness of the United Nations intergovernmental structure and functions in the economic and social fields with a view to achieving the ultimate objective of improving the quality of human life world wide. I have to plead with all members of the Commission to undertake the task entrusted to them in a positive spirit and with a common understanding that improvement of the delivery of the intergovernmental machinery and its secretariat support services should be the focus of the exercise, without any attempt to politicize issues. Without a clear consensus on this basic point, we may go astray and deviate from the genuine and objective target of reform."

It was agreed that the Commission should proceed with its substantive work on the basis of an integrated thematic and functional approach in order to address both the nature and structure of intergovernmental bodies, as well as their substantive activities. The Commission requested the secretariat to prepare a number of informal working papers providing additional information on the terms of reference of intergovernmental bodies in the economic and social sectors, the frequency and duration of meetings and the secretariat support structure. The secretariat was also requested to prepare a list of available UN studies on the functioning and restructuring of intergovernmental bodies in the economic and social sectors, as well as relevant legislative decisions. The secretariat was further requested to compile a list of resolutions and decisions adopted by the GA and ECOSOC relating to the functioning of intergovernmental machinery in the economic and social sectors since the adoption of GA resolution 32/197 of 20 December 1977.

At its second session (18-20 March 1987), the Special Commission reviewed informal working papers prepared by the secretariat, including some sample analyses of substantive areas in the economic and social sectors, with a view to providing further guidance to the secretariat on the format and content of future documentation to be prepared for the Commission. The Commission also continued its discussion of its future programme of work. An offer made by UNITAR was accepted to prepare an analytical study summarizing the conclusions and recommendations of relevant evaluations that had been made concerning the efficiency and effectiveness of UN activities in the economic and social sectors. Finally, the Chairman was requested to undertake consultations with delegations, with a view to agreeing on the format and content of further documentation to be prepared by the secretariat and the most appropriate manner to proceed with its substantive work beginning with its third session.

At the outset of the third session (27 April-1 May 1987), the Special Commission was informed that, as a result of informal consultations held by the Chairman, an understanding had been reached that the substantive work of the Commission should proceed "from the general to the specific" and that the Commission could begin its work with a preliminary exchange of views on the functioning of the GA and ECOSOC. For this purpose, the Commission agreed to establish an informal working group of the whole.

The informal working group met throughout the third session to undertake a preliminary review of the GA and ECOSOC. At the end of the session, the Chairman informed the Commission that the exchange of views had reaffirmed that the GA should function as the principal forum for policy-making and for the establishment of overall strategies, policies and priorities for the UN system as a whole in respect of international co-operation in the economic, social and related fields in accordance with the provisions of the UN Charter. There was equally a reaffirmation that ECOSOC should monitor and evaluate the implementation of overall strategies, policies and priorities established by the Assembly in the economic, social and related fields. Other major tasks of ECOSOC were to ensure the overall co-ordination of the activities of the UN system in the economic, social and related fields and to continue to assist in the preparation of the work of the GA in those fields. The Chairman also stated that it would be necessary, at a later stage of the Commission's work, to elaborate the necessary modalities to assist both the GA and ECOSOC in fulfilling their responsibilities under the UN Charter. With regard to its future programme of work, the Commission agreed to request ECOSOC to make the necessary arrangements for the Commission to meet for about 50 working days in 1988.

3.3 First Regular Session of ECOSOC

At the first regular session of ECOSOC in 1987, Mr. Badawi (Egypt), Vice-President of the Council and Chairman of the Special Commission, made an oral report on the progress of the first three sessions of the Special Commission as outlined above. Following his report, a number of statements were made as recalled below.

The representative of the **United States of America**[6]

"the Special Commission, to whose work his delegation attached great importance, had been entrusted with a huge and complex task. It was therefore justifiable - even advisable - to spend some time at the outset determining the best way to approach it. The Commission had devoted two full sessions to those procedural issues, and had reached broad agreement on the type of documentation required and the various methods for analyzing the information provided. In order to prove that the lengthy procedural debate had been time well spent, that rapid progress should be made to dealing with the substance at hand."

The representative of Denmark, speaking on behalf of the five **Nordic countries**[7]

"The Commission's two sessions spent on procedural questions had not resulted in agreement on a specific work programme and methodology. Although the so-called integrated approach was a useful guideline, its application needed further elaboration. Discussion of the role of the General Assembly and the Council had remained on a general and abstract level, and there had been a certain tendency to go over old, familiar ground. While conceding that a number of important questions had been raised, the Nordic countries felt that a process where the States members sounded out each others' intentions and objectives and reflected on their own objectives was probably needed. It would have been highly ambitious to expect the diverging views on the role and efficiency of the United Nations to be overcome speedily. On the other hand, divergent policy views and other overall political considerations concerning the state of affairs at the United Nations should not delay or dominate the work of the Special Committee.

There were evidently some institutional problems in the United Nations system in the economic and social fields, but that should not mean that interpretations of the Charter should be made the focus of the study. It might be useful to discuss how the General Assembly and the Council could best complement each other, and how the United Nations and its organs could improve their dialogue with the specialized agencies. The Nordic countries strongly recommended that a pragmatic approach be pursued in the future. ...

Practical proposals submitted at the Commission's third session included further enhancing biennialization, consolidating general debates and reports of a similar character, working on the basis of dynamic, rather than static, agendas, avoiding repetitive debates and resolutions, focusing more on co-ordination in the Council and developing criteria for the establishment and duration of subsidiary bodies. A number of interesting proposals, all of which merited further consideration, had also been submitted in the Secretary-General's report on co-ordination (A/42/232).

It must be recognized that the United Nations was currently unable to serve its Member States as well as it ought, partly because States often had different interests which were difficult to reconcile, but also because of the unplanned growth of the Organization. In a recent statement to the Committee for Programme and Co-ordination, the Secretary-General had suggested three criteria which should guide the Organization: the importance of an objective to Member States; the Organization's capacity to achieve that objective; and the effectiveness and usefulness of the results. While the United Nations had always taken the first criterion into account, the other two had been underemphasized. It should also be borne in mind that some areas of endeavour were more suited to United Nations involvement than others.

The continued expansion of United Nations programmes had been accompanied by a parallel growth in intergovernmental machinery, as demonstrated by the plethora of supervisory and co-ordinating bodies established in the economic and social fields. At the same time, attendance at many meetings was very low and the participation of experts in some expert bodies had decreased. The daily schedule of meetings shown in the *Journal* was often so heavy that it was impossible for many countries to be adequately represented at all the meetings on a given day, which led him to question whether all those meetings were indispensable. The overwhelming number of activities in specific areas, such as science and technology, gave rise to similar questions. The Nordic countries did not consider the study to be a budget-cutting exercise. However, they believed that an efficient use of resources was both a prerequisite for continued trust in the Organization as well as an objective pursued by all Member States."

The representative of **Jamaica**[8]

"The Special Commission should reaffirm the authority and clarify the respective responsibilities of the General Assembly and the Economic and Social Council. Obviously, there could be no derogation from the authority of the Assembly or from the rights of Member States to have any matter discussed there. The Special Commission should also consider practical ways to reinforce the functions of the Assembly and the Council, particularly with regard to policy-making and relations with other parts of the United Nations system.

The central role of the Council in formulating policy, monitoring and assessing the implementation of established priorities and co-ordinating activities in the economic and social fields should be strengthened. The detailed examination of all the subsidiary bodies which reported to the Council would need to be completed before practical proposals on the functioning of the Council could be made. ...

The Special Commission's adoption of a thematic and functional approach in its method of work would facilitate its examination of the subsidiary bodies of the General Assembly and the Council in the economic and social fields. In considering those bodies in relation to their functions as defined in their mandates, the Special Commission would be able to pinpoint aspects or procedures which could be improved and made more effective.

The Secretary-General was proceeding with a number of structural changes within the Secretariat. While Jamaica did not question the Secretary-General's authority and competence in that area, it hoped that the Special Commission would be able to review those changes in the light of its own recommendations."

The representative of Belgium, speaking on behalf of the 12 member states of the **European Community**[9]

"the Twelve were therefore concerned at the slow pace at which the work of the Special Commission was proceeding.

He welcomed the useful debate which had taken place during the most recent session of the Commission on the pivotal role of the Council as spelt out in the Charter. The proposals which had been put forward would enable both the General Assembly and the Council to play their own distinct roles more effectively. That discussion should be continued, in keeping with the agreement reached in the Special Commission on the need for an integrated approach. The Special Commission should also address the inseparability of the roles of the General Assembly and the Council from those of their principal subsidiary organs.

If the Commission's recent debate had been at all unproductive, it was largely because delegations were uncertain until the last minute as to the topic of discussion. In the future, the subject and structure of the debate should be agreed upon in advance. ...

During its most recent session, the Special Commission had met as an informal group of the whole, an arrangement which facilitated discussion. Yet, while proposals had been made by delegations and objections raised, there was no record of the debate to provide a basis for future work. He urged the Special Commission and its officers to consider that point, and suggested that it would be useful to have a small group from within the Secretariat assigned to the Commission as a support staff."

The representative of **China**[10]

"During the 1980s, the development process had suffered many setbacks, and the outlook for the future was not bright. Consequently, the deliberations of the Special Commission should lead to structural reforms that would help solve current economic and social problems and address future challenges. It was particularly important that the Organization's role as a forum for achieving consensus on international economic co-operation for development should be enhanced, as should its ability to implement its resolutions. Only then could the United Nations meet the expectations placed in it by its Member States, especially the developing countries.

The deliberations of the Special Commission should be practical and action-oriented. At its most recent session, the Commission had spent much time discussing provisions of the Charter and other texts. While such a review was necessary, it must be recalled that those provisions had not been fully or effectively implemented over the years. The Special Commission should therefore seek to ensure that such implementation occurred, with emphasis placed on enhancing the decision-making role of the General Assembly and the co-ordinating role of the Economic and Social Council. The Council's relationship with its subsidiary organs and the specialized agencies must also be addressed.

The Special Commission must deal adequately with the relationship between the restructuring of the Secretariat undertaken by the Secretary-General, upon instructions from the General Assembly, and the reforms that the Commission was mandated to explore. Exchanges of information and consultations must take place between the Secretary-General and the Special Commission to consider those areas where their responsibilities coincided, and a good working relationship between the two parties should be established."

The representative of the Union of Soviet Socialist Republics, speaking on behalf of **socialist countries**[11]

"In order to enhance the effectiveness of the General Assembly and of the Council in the social and economic fields, the work of those two bodies must be co-ordinated. The adoption of a biennial programme of work by the Second Committee and the Council helped to avoid duplication of work. However, the division of work was still largely a matter of a purely technical division of items. If all the economic bodies and specialized agencies of the United Nations system reported to the Council, its co-ordinating role would be enhanced, and the Second Committee, spared the task of a second consideration of reports, would be able to focus on major international economic problems and their solution.

At the third session of the Special Commission, the Chairman of the Group of 77 had stressed the importance of the Declaration on the Establishment of a New International Economic Order and the Charter of Economic Rights and Duties of States. The Soviet Union supported the position of the Group of 77 on the need to strengthen the role of the General Assembly as the principal forum within the United Nations for adopting political decisions on economic and social problems, and formulating comprehensive strategies, policies and priorities in the field of international co-operation."

---

[*]Bulgaria, Byelorussian SSR, Czechoslovakia, German Democratic Republic, Mongolia, Poland.

The representative of **Nigeria**[12]

"delegations should refrain from advancing proposals for reforms in subsidiary bodies which might conflict with or undermine the mandate of the Special Commission.   In that connection, his delegation welcomed the announcement by the representative of the United States of America at a recent meeting of the First (Economic) Committee that it would withdraw a draft resolution urging the biennialization of meetings of the Commission on Transnational Corporations, since the Special Commission would be seized of that matter at a later date.   It was to be hoped that significant gesture would be emulated by other delegations."

The representative of **Canada**[13]

"The Council had a twofold purpose: to provide a unique forum in which to discuss the current economic and social situation; and to ensure that the United Nations system made its full contribution to the resolution of major problems.   He suggested that Council members should assist the Special Commission by submitting guidelines and suggestions as to what the Council expected of the United Nations system and the subsidiary intergovernmental bodies, and what information it required in order to play its role effectively.

With regard to the substance of its work, the Council might consider questions according to subjects, sectors and geographical regions.   Its agenda might thus be organized along four main themes: (1) review and debate a limited number of socio-economic issues considered by the Member States to be the most crucial; (2) review the activities of the United Nations system on the basis of reports prepared by intergovernmental bodies given special responsibility for examining the activities in a particular sector or region; (3) identify the desirable adjustments to United Nations activities in the light of the review of the most crucial issues, the result of which would be either guidelines for the intergovernmental bodies or recommendations for the General Assembly; (4) recommend to the General Assembly the additional actions to be taken by the Member States, regional groups of Member States or non-United Nations multilateral institutions regarding the most crucial economic and social issues."

The observer for Guatemala, speaking on behalf of the **Group of 77**[14]

"The purpose of the exercise in which the Commission was engaged was not to eliminate bodies and reduce their functions but rather to increase the efficiency of the United Nations system in the economic and social fields with a view to achieving a new international economic order based on equity and justice."

The observer for **Uruguay**[15]

"The Commission's agreement to proceed from the general to the specific would enable it to avoid a study of each of the respective bodies in isolation. He supported the suggestion ... to complete the study on the General Assembly and the Economic and Social Council before reviewing the operation of the subsidiary bodies.

Greater co-ordination was necessary between the Secretary-General and the Special Commission regarding reforms made by the Secretariat in the support structures of the subsidiary bodies in the economic and social fields."

The representative of **Japan**[16]

"while not entirely satisfied with the deliberations of the Special Commission, was glad that the Commission had initiated its substantive discussions. ...

With regard to the substantive aspects, comparative study of the agendas of the Second and Third Committees of the General Assembly and that of the Council revealed that some topics were approached in the same manner and that debates were somewhat repetitive. There were no precise principles governing the manner in which tasks were distributed between the Assembly and the Council and their subsidiary bodies. An in-depth study should be conducted, in light of the terms of reference of the two bodies as set forth in the Charter, with a view to establishing rational principles for distributing and co-ordinating work between them. Deliberations should focus on recommendation 8, paragraphs 3 (a), 3 (c), 3 (e) and 3 (f) of the report of the Group of High-level Intergovernmental Experts (A/41/49). There was a clear need to improve co-ordination so that economic and social issues could be dealt with more comprehensively."

The observer for **Mexico**[17]

"It was clear that not all delegations meant the same when they said that United Nations activities in the economic and social area must become more responsive to Members' needs. The majority, including his own country, meant that the United Nations should resolve the major problems to economic and social development on a fair and equitable basis; others, however, meant that everything should continue as before, but that less should be done and at less cost. If the Special Commission was to make the best use of its time it was essential that all delegations should have the same interpretation. It was indeed necessary to make sure that resources were used effectively, but it was also necessary to simplify the institutional and administrative procedures."

Following these statements, the President submitted draft E/1987/L.30, which was approved as decision entitled **In-depth Study of the United**

Nations Intergovernmental Structure and Functions in the Economic and Social Fields (1987/64). By decision 1987/64, ECOSOC: (a) requested the Secretary-General to submit to the Special Commission a document incorporating the information received thus far from the subsidiary bodies of the GA in the economic and social sectors and the subsidiary bodies of ECOSOC, in accordance with Council decision 1987/112; (b) decided to convene the fourth session of the Special Commission from 1 to 4 September 1987; (c) recommended that conference services and facilities for at least 50 official meetings be made available to the Special Commission in 1988; and (d) requested the Secretary-General to take all appropriate measures to ensure the provision of adequate full-time secretariat support for the duration of the Special Commission's work.

The following statement was then made by Mr. McKintyre, **ASG, Office of the Director-General for Development and International Economic Co-operation**[18]

"the Director-General, after having reviewed the question of Secretariat support for the Special Commission's future work programme, had come to the same conclusions as were implicit in paragraph 5 of draft resolution ... namely, that a more formal Secretariat support system should be set up. Accordingly, the following arrangements had been made: an advisory group reporting to the Director-General had been set up, comprising senior representatives of Headquarters entities to provide overall guidance; he himself would supervise a working group with a limited number of full-time staff to ensure comprehensive Secretariat support."

3.4 Fourth Session of the Special Commission of ECOSOC

Prior to the fourth session, the **Secretary-General**[19] offered his own recommendations on how to re-organize ECOSOC:

"Today there is no representative intergovernmental body in the United Nations that is able to provide authoritative guidance to Member States and to the organizations of the United Nations system with regard to priorities of global programmes, the allocation of responsibilities, and the utilization of assistance resources. Most of the specialized agencies and some of the organizations of the United Nations itself have governing bodies that meet at the ministerial level. Yet, the Economic and Social Council, which is charged in the Charter with co-ordination and policy formulation for the economic and social activities of the system, is not constituted by representatives of such authoritative rank. I believe this should be corrected. For optimum effectiveness, the Council might become, in practice, a Council of Ministers for Economic and Social Affairs which would have the authority to review the medium-term plans or equivalent documents of all the organizations of the United Nations system, thus contributing to rational utilization of resources in the light of global priorities as defined by the Council and given greater strength and coherence to the system as a whole. The Council, with an enhanced participation of the specialized agencies, could keep world economic and social developments under review and suggest modifications of programmes to meet changing circumstances and new exigencies. The cabinet-rank Council members, who might vary, or be augmented, according to the economic or social issue under consideration, would be able to speak with much greater authority than is the case. Given the orientation of such a Council, the present deliberative function of the Economic and Social Council might, in part or in whole, be assumed by the Second and Third Committees of the General Assembly. This would require careful analysis.

This concept, if followed, would obviously lead to a radical change in the functioning of the Economic and Social Council, but I believe it might be more consonant with the original intent of the Charter than the way in which the Council has functioned until now. ...

I feel compelled to state that in recent years the effectiveness of the Council in providing intellectual leadership and the needed co-ordination of United Nations economic and cosmical activities has been inadequate. I would add also that the incremental reforms undertaken over the years to improve the functioning of the Economic and Social Council have not had the desired effect. We need to focus on what the Council should do rather than on how it can better perform what it has been doing."

At the fourth session[20] of the Special Commission (1-4 September 1987), the Chairman briefed the Commission on the informal consultations held with members states and executive heads of UN system organizations since the third session. The exchanges of views had focused mainly on the relationship between the UN and the other organizations of the system, including, in particular, the co-ordinating role of ECOSOC and modalities for harmonizing efforts for development and international co-operation in the economic, social and related fields. Consultations had also been held with the executive secretaries of the regional commissions. As a consequence, a special insight had been gained into the complex relationship between the UN and its specialized agencies, the latter's perception of the role of the Council, the functioning of the CPC/ACC joint meetings and the need for co-ordination at the national level.

Through its informal working group, the Commission extensively discussed the role and functions of ECOSOC, including the question of its relationship with the GA. The discussions were based on an informal paper put forward by the Group of 77.* In the course of the discussion, proposals were also made by the European Community, the Nordic countries, the German Democratic Republic on behalf of socialist countries", Australia, Canada, Japan and the USA.

In his closing statement, the Chairman stated that it had become obvious from the deliberations that the strengthening of ECOSOC would require the adoption of a number of interrelated measures in major areas affecting its work. Many of these areas had been identified by delegations and groups of delegations. A great degree of convergence had emerged on a number of issues; others would require further consideration by the Commission.

The Commission approved a tentative programme of work for 1988 and requested the Chairman, in consultation with member states and the secretariat, to prepare a more detailed work programme, indicating the order in which subsidiary bodies would be considered, and to make the programme available to delegations well in advance of the fifth session. Concerning the work undertaken by the Commission on the GA and ECOSOC, the Chairman expressed his hope that delegations would hold informal consultations among themselves in order to clarify some of the issues that had been identified in the course of the Special Commission's third and fourth sessions.

3.5 Second Resumed Regular Session of ECOSOC

The second resumed regular session of ECOSOC was concerned with three reform issues. Firstly, the progress report on the work of the Special Commission was discussed. Secondly, ECOSOC had to take up the issue of a new composition of CPC. This was in accordance with the understanding reached during the 41st session of the GA to defer this issue to the 42nd session. Thirdly, the introduction of a new agenda item to the second regular session in 1988 was considered. The new initiative focused on the functioning

---

*See volume II, 2.23, annex I.
"Bulgaria, Byelorussian SSR, Czechoslovakia, German Democratic Republic, Hungary, Mongolia, Poland, Ukrainian SSR, USSR.

of ECOSOC with the aim to improve the working methods of the Council, known as the revitalisation of ECOSOC.

With regard to the first issue, Mr. Badawi, **Chairman of the Special Commission**[21] reported on the progress achieved during the fourth session of the Commission as follows:

"The Commission had noted a great degree of convergence on a large number of issues; it was agreed that Member States should recognize the primacy of the Council in accordance with its responsibility under the Charter and that they should harmonize their policies regarding the Council and the governing bodies of the specialized agencies; that it was of crucial importance to strengthen the Council in the effective functioning of the United Nations system in the economic and social fields; that the strengthening of the effectiveness of the Council would serve to complement the functions of the General Assembly and its subsidiary organs, such as the United Nations Conference on Trade and Development; that the measures to strengthen the Council must include not only the enhancement of its authority and credibility buy also the improvement of its role in policy overview and co-ordination in order to improve harmonization of actions and promote an integrated approach in the social and economic fields and improvement of the interrelationships and modalities for dialogue among major intergovernmental bodies of the United Nations system in those areas. There was also agreement that a clearer distinction should be drawn between the respective roles of the apex bodies through more clearly defined programmes of work, consolidation of discussions and avoidance of duplication. It was also agreed that the Council should serve as an effective organ in the provision of policy recommendations to the General Assembly in the economic and social fields and should effectively monitor the work of the subsidiary machinery, thereby allowing the General Assembly to focus on carefully selected policy issues; for that purpose the reporting procedures of the subsidiary machinery should be rationalized.

There was general agreement that the work programmes of the Council and of the Second and Third Committee of the General Assembly should continue to be biennial and that the format and nature of the general debate in the Council should be improved. It had been agreed that there should be a more effective control and evaluation of the management and implementation of operational activities and that there was a need to implement the provisions of General Assembly resolution 32/197 regarding the role of the Council and that the Council should strengthen its review of the activities of the regional commissions and ensure that they provided effective inputs for deliberations of the global level. It had also been regarded as desirable that the schedule and duration of the meetings of the Council and its subsidiary bodies should be rationalized.

The Special Commission would consider issues relating to the membership of the Council, the work of the subsidiary bodies, Secretariat support for the Council and specific measures to enhance organization, co-ordination, evaluation and the supervisory functions of the Council. The programme of work of the Special Commission for 1988 was a vast endeavour, covering, as it did, such issues as the subsidiary organs of the General Assembly and Council (other than UNCTAD), including the Committee for Programme and Co-ordination, the regional commissions and their respective subsidiary organs; UNCTAD; operational activities; the regional commissions and their subsidiary organs; and, finally, the drafting and consideration of the Commission's own recommendations and report."

The Council took note with appreciation of the oral report by the Chairman of the Special Commission. In addition, the Council approved the Commission's work programme and the calendar of meetings for 1988 by the decision entitled **In-depth Study of the United Nations Intergovernmental Structure and Functions in the Economic and Social Fields (1987/190).**

As indicated during the 41st session of the GA, it was expected that the 42nd session would decide on a new composition of CPC. The representative of Bolivia introduced draft resolution E/1987/L.50/Rev.1 on behalf of the sponsors*, which called for membership of 36 states with following distribution of seats: eleven for African states, nine for Asian states, eight for Latin American and Caribbean states, five for Western European and other states and three for Eastern European states. In addition, the draft resolution recommended that members should be elected for 3-year terms and that the GA should elect the new members at the 42nd session. Furthermore, the GA should dispense with the requirement of nominations by the Council for the purpose of electing the new members."

During the introduction of the draft resolution, the following statements were made.

The representative of **Bolivia**[22]

"At the forty-first session of the General Assembly, Bolivia had expressed its concern about the unfair and obsolete composition of the Committee for

---

*Antigua and Barbuda, Algeria, Bangladesh, Bolivia, Colombia, Cuba, Mexico, Nicaragua, Panama, Peru, Philippines, Syria, Venezuela.

**The previous draft resolution E/1987/L.50 did not contain this provision.

Programme and Co-ordination (CPC) and had submitted a draft resolution (A/41/L.48/Rev.1) which sought to correct the anomaly of its limited and unrepresentative composition. However, at the request of a number of delegations, Bolivia had decided to postpone consideration of that draft resolution until 1987.

The future of the Organization was in jeopardy; consequently, the work to be carried out in the next decade was extremely important. The medium-term plan for 1990-1995 should reflect that concern and Member States should have an updated and democratic basis on which to participate in its implementation. The Committee was to consider the draft plan before it was adopted by the General Assembly, and it was therefore important that the representation of Member States in CPC should be appropriately adjusted as soon as possible. Moreover, Assembly resolution 41/213 assigned to CPC new activities which required it to be a body with broad and democratic representation.

His delegation shared the view of the great majority of States that CPC should be an efficient body and, in 1986, after many consultations, it had decided to reduce the number of members from 54 - as originally proposed in draft resolution A/41/L.48 - to 36. The latter number corresponded approximately to the number of delegations which attended as full members or observers."

The representative of **China**[23]

"at the forty-first session of the General Assembly and in one of the many informal groups which had met to discuss the proposals of the Group of 18, her delegation had proposed that representation in CPC should be broadened in order to ensure equitable geographical distribution. The current composition of CPC did not reflect the increased membership of the Organization and therefore required readjustment. In view of the importance of CPC as an intergovernmental body, its membership should not be too large. She hoped that the Council could reach a consensus on the regional formula proposed in draft resolution E/1987/L.50/Rev.1 so that election could be held at the current session."

The Vice-President of the Council was then authorized to begin informal consultations on the draft resolution. During the course of the consultations, the **Vice-President**[24] reported as follows:

"informal consultations ... had focused on two main themes, the first of which was the principle of increasing the number of members on the Committee for Programme and Co-ordination. While support for that principle had ranged from enthusiastic to reluctant, strong opposition to the principle continued to exist. Negotiations on the second theme - the number of seats by which the Committee should be increased and the apportionment of those seats among the regional groups - had been still more difficult. A number of delegations strongly believed that the principle of equitable geographical distribution must be strictly observed, while another view held that any enlargement of the Committee should reflect the existing balance among countries comprising the Committee."

Following informal consultations, the sponsors accepted a revision of the draft resolution to the effect that CPC should be composed of 34 member states rather than 36, with the following distribution of seats: nine for African states; seven for Asian states, seven for Latin American and Caribbean states, seven for Western European and other states and four for Eastern European states. Before the draft resolution was adopted, a statement was made by the representative of the **United States of America**[25]

"during the intensive consultations he had been opposed to a considerable increase in the number of States members of CPC, which would, in his view, adversely affect its operation. The United States would have been prepared to accept 10 additional seats, whereas the current proposal was for 13. Despite its continued interest in the work of CPC and its desire to help it carry out the additional responsibilities conferred upon it by General Assembly resolution 41/213, the United States could not join the consensus."

The representative of Mozambique, speaking on behalf of the **Group of African States**[26]

"in order to maintain the consensus, he was prepared to vote in favour of the draft resolution; he was not satisfied, however, with the number of seats allocated to the African countries, which, for historical reasons, were still underrepresented in nearly all United Nations organs. Thus, Africa should actually receive five additional seats instead of four. Although the African countries were being accommodating for the moment, that concession on their part, made in a spirit of co-operation, should neither constitute a precedent nor imply that they would always accept the situation, especially since other countries were overrepresented."

The representative of Bangladesh, speaking on behalf of the **Group of Asian States**[27]

"the proposal to change to 34 the number of members of CPC did not ensure equitable representation of all States in that body, since the Asian countries would receive the equivalent of 24.59 per cent of the seats, while they represented 25.48 per cent of States Members of the Organization. The Group of Asian States would, however, accept the will of the majority. ... Nevertheless, the decision should not be taken as a precedent."

The representative of Rumania, speaking on behalf of the **Group of Eastern European States**[28]

"the Group of Eastern European States had advocated an increase of fewer seats in CPC. ... The Group would, however, go along with the majority."

Following these statements, ECOSOC approved the resolution entitled **Broad Representation in the Committee for Programme and Co-ordination (1987/94)**, based on the draft E/1987/L.50/Rev.1, as orally amended. Approval was given by 45 votes to 1 with the USA voting against.

Following the adoption of the resolution, a statement was made by the representative of Malta, speaking on behalf of the **Group of Western European and Other States**[29]

"he had hesitated to join in the consensus on the proposal to create 13 additional seats in CPC, which he felt was excessive and might adversely affect the operation of the Committee. He regretted, however, that the revised draft resolution had to be put to the vote."

Finally, the slow progress achieved so far by the Special Commission, prompted the developing countries to initiate a new effort known as the revitalisation of ECOSOC. It was stimulated by the discussion in the Special Commission, but focused only on the work of the Council. This parallel effort reflected a certain impatience in creating the necessary conditions which would improve the functioning of the Council.[30] As a result, a request was submitted by Jamaica for the introduction of a new agenda item to the second regular session of ECOSOC in 1988 entitled "In-depth study of the United Nations intergovernmental structure and functions in the economic and social fields: the Economic and Social Council".

The delegation of **Jamaica**[31] argued that

"the Council, in decision 1987/112, ... requested all subsidiary bodies of the Economic and Social Council to submit to the Special Commission their views and proposals on achieving the objectives envisaged in recommendation 8 ... No provision has, however, been made for the Council, which is the only intergovernmental body established by the Charter of the United Nations responsible for economic and social issues, to carry out its own study of its structure and functioning in accordance with General Assembly resolution 41/212. The inclusion of the agenda item ... would enable the Council to fill this lacuna. A proper self-examination by the Council is clearly essential in

assessing its appropriate role and function in the economic and social area."
The inclusion of the agenda item was approved by decision 1987/189.

3.6 The 42nd Session of the General Assembly

As early as September 1986, a mechanism had been set up within the secretariat under the personal direction of the Secretary-General in anticipation of the outcome of the GA's deliberations for the co-ordination and planning of the reform effort. Margaret Anstee, Assistant-Secretary-General, was appointed special co-ordinator, supported by a small office, with staff redeployed from their regular functions. Activities were planned in close co-operation with the Director-General for DIEC and the USG for Administration and Management. The functions of the special co-ordinator were rather catalytic, aiming to provide a special impetus to the initial phase of the reform. Once the process was underway, the office was disbanded in 1987 and follow-up action was taken through the normal channels, with the key responsibility assigned to the USG for Administration and Management.

Immediately following adoption of resolution 41/213, the Secretary-General announced an energetic programme of activity for the implementation of the resolution as far as it affected the secretariat. The measures were divided into two broad categories. Firstly, the streamlining and rationalization of the organizational structure and secondly, measures concerned with personnel and administrative matters, including a reduction in the number of posts.

In response to recommendation 18 of the Group of 18, a new office was established in March 1987 to consolidate all activities related to the collection and dissemination of publicly available data. This Office for Research and Collection of Information (ORCI) was to assist the Secretary-General directly to identify threats to peace at an early stage. At the same time, in response to recommendation 32 of the Group of 18, the Office of Programme Planning and Co-ordination (in the DIEC) and the Budget Division (in the Department of Administration and Management, DAM) were merged to form the Office of Programme Planning, Budgeting, Monitoring and Evaluation (OPPBME) in DAM. This brought together the activities of the new planning and budgeting mechanisms approved by resolution 41/213. Many other changes took place to rationalize the organizational structures and procedures. For example, in the political sector, five offices were merged with other entities and the three executive offices within the Department for Administration and Management were consolidated into one office. Structural changes were implemented in

Geneva and Vienna. Activities in the social field were brought together in Vienna under the Director-General for UNOV. This extensive restructuring and rationalization allowed for a reduction of nine USGs and ASGs posts, or approximately 15 per cent, as a first step towards the 25 per cent reduction target. Furthermore, reviews were launched by the Secretary-General in many areas, such as public information.

With regard to personnel and related budgetary and administrative issues, recommendation 15 of the Group of 18 was of key importance. It mandated the reduction of posts by 15 per cent within a period of three years, i.e. by the end of 1989. The Department of Administration and Management, under the guidance of the Programme Planning and Budgeting Board (PPBB), set in train the process of implementing this recommendation. Consultations were held with programme managers and, in March 1987, PPBB issued recommendations calling for the establishment of a post review group to examine submissions by departments and relate them to overall needs. The group, comprising staff from all sectors of the organization, began work in June 1987. It was the intention not to reduce posts arbitrarily across the board in all departments and offices, but to take into account the current situation in each and the capacity to fulfil key mandated programmes.

The post retrenchment process had also to take into account the results of the recruitment freeze implemented since 1985. Previously, a vacancy rate of 5 per cent of posts at the professional level had been considered acceptable in the light of the time required for the filling of posts. The recruitment freeze had resulted in an increase in the vacancy rate to 10.8 per cent. This made the retrenchment process both easier and more difficult at the same time: easier in that it appeared possible to achieve a reduction in staff mostly through attrition; more difficult, since vacancies resulting from the recruitment freeze did not obviously correspond to the proposed post reductions arising from the reorganization of the secretariat. For example, the vacancy rate for professional staff at one regional commission had reached 25.5 per cent. Staffing tables had become unbalanced. Grave discrepancies had arisen between available skills and programme needs. In order to counteract this development, a new system of vacancy management and staff redeployment was introduced in December 1986. While this was essentially an emergency measure to alleviate the immediate impact of the recruitment freeze, the new procedures were designed in such a way as to allow for an orderly staff retrenchment process as required by the Group of 18.

The 42nd session of the GA was scheduled to approve the 1988-1989 programme budget. The requirement that the draft programme budget be submitted at the normal time to CPC and ACABQ did not permit consideration of the modified staffing table for the secretariat emanating from the recommendation of the Group of 18. Revised estimates for the 1988-1989 programme budget were therefore submitted towards the end of 1987, reflecting the various recommendations. The new staff structure would, therefore, be in place for, and reflected in, the 1990-1991 programme budget.

The actual reduction in staff would not be reflected in the 1988-1989 programme budget in a reduction of posts. Rather, the reduction would be presented as an increase in the vacancy rate of established posts. The financial implication of both options, i.e. the reduction of budget estimates, was the same. Increasing the vacancy rate, however, would provide more flexibility for the time being. Staff could slowly be reduced by attrition and a recruitment freeze, while planning for a streamlined and reduced post structure could continue in parallel. Once the final post structure was established, actual posts would be cut. This would not result in a reduction of financial resources - they would have already been reduced - but in a decrease of the vacancy rate. Accordingly, it was proposed that the 1988-1989 programme budget should reflect an increase of the vacancy rate from 5 to 12.5 per cent for the professional and higher categories and to 7.5 per cent for the general service and related categories. This would lead to a final post reduction of 15 per cent at the end of 1989 in accordance with GA resolution 41/212. In addition, the proposed programme budget reflected reductions of approximately $25.3 million in operating expenses for travel, consultants, *ad hoc* expert group meetings, printing and contractual services, furniture and equipment, supplies and materials, temporary assistance and other staff costs. The total proposed programme budget was estimated at $1,681,372,400. In addition to the decrease of resources as a result of the higher vacancy rates, the budget estimates reflected a real decrease (negative real growth) of 1.5 per cent. Following the review of the proposed programme budget by ACABQ, the Committee recommended to the GA the application of an even higher vacancy rate in accordance with actual development, resulting in a net reduction of $26.7 million. Although this would have no impact on the staffing situation, it would reduce the total assessment for 1988-1989 and thereby increase the cash flow problem. ACABQ also recommended further reductions under other line items totalling $8.8 million.

The GA was expected to agree on the establishment of a contingency fund to address the problem of add-ons to the programme budget, including those derived from inflation and currency fluctuations. A comprehensive solution in this area would further define the new programme budget process as approved by GA resolution 41/213. The Secretary-General submitted two reports to the GA on this subject in order to facilitate the deliberations. A report was also submitted by ICSC in response to a previous request by the GA to examine some recommendations of the Group of 18. With regard to recommendation 61, ICSC reiterated its earlier position and argued that the existing entitlement should not be changed. This related in particular to the education grant for post-secondary studies and the annual leave entitlement of 30 days per annum.

The 42nd session of the GA took up the reform issues in the following three forums: the Fifth Committee considered the reform of the UN in accordance with GA resolution 41/213 - see section 3.6.1; the Plenary Assembly considered the ECOSOC resolution 1987/94 on the increase in membership of CPC - see section 3.6.2; and the Second and Third Committee took up the reform in the economic and social fields in accordance with ECOSOC resolution 1987/64 - see section 3.4.3.

3.6.1   Approval of Resolutions on the Implementation of General Assembly Resolution 41/213 (42/211) and the Programme Budget for the Biennium 1988-1989 (42/226)

Under agenda item 41 (Review of the Efficiency of the Administrative and Financial Functioning of the United Nations: Report of the Secretary-General), the Fifth Committee considered the implementation of the UN reform in accordance with GA resolution 41/213[*]. The Committee had before it following documentation: (i) the Secretary-General's report on questions relating to inflation and currency fluctuation, and the level of the contingency fund (A/42/225 and Add.1), together with observations of ACABQ (A/42/7 and A/42/640) and CPC (A/42/16)[**]; (ii) the Secretary-General's progress report on the implementation of GA resolution 41/213 (A/42/234 and Corr. 1), together with the observations of ACABQ (A/42/7) and CPC (A/42/16)[***]; (iii) an update of the Secretary-General's progress report on the implementation of GA resolution 41/213 (A/C.5/42/2/Rev.1), together with the

---

[*]See volume II, 1.2.
[**]See volume II, 2.5, 2.11, 2.6, 2.12, 2.7, 2.13.
[***]See volume II, 2.8, 2.9, 2.10.

observations of ACABQ (A/42/7/Add.1-10)*; and (iv) the report of the ICSC on the recommendations of the Group of 18 (A/42/30)**. In addition, the report of ECOSOC (A/42/3), the Secretary-General's report on revised estimates for construction, alteration, improvement and major maintenance of premises (A/C.5/42/4), the Secretary-General's note on the timing of the submission of the outline of the programme budget (A/42/214) and the Secretary-General's note on supplementary rules and regulations necessary for the improvement in the planning, programming and budgeting process (A/42/532) were submitted. Agenda item 41 was considered concurrently with items 43 (Current Financial Crisis of the United Nations), 115 (Proposed Programme Budget for the Biennium 1988-1989), 116 (Programme Planning) and 117 (Financial Emergency of the United Nations).

Before recalling the Fifth Committee's debate under agenda item 41, the statements by the Secretary-General on the issues involved are presented.

In his report on the work of the organization, the **Secretary-General**[32] noted:

"The proposed programme budget for the forthcoming biennium that I have submitted to the General Assembly is 1.8 per cent less than the revised appropriation for the present biennium and reflects a number of the austerity measures that I have already taken. A rigorous programme-by-programme review has been launched in order to identify the specific functions where post reductions can best be accommodated. Secretariat structures in the political areas have been streamlined and more effectively organized, and a review of the economic and social sectors is under way. A restructuring of the Department of Administration and Management has been effected and substantial changes in the Department of Public Information are now being initiated. I am convinced that these measures will enhance the ability of the United Nations to discharge its responsibilities.

I must make clear that the necessary prolongation of austerity measures, including the freeze on staff recruitment and restrictions on meetings, has an adverse effect on programme implementation and on the Secretariat staff, although I have sought to minimize both. The mechanisms for staff-management consultations that have proven fruitful in the past have become especially important. In fact, the staff have been active partners in the search for the

----

*See volume II, 2.14, 2.15.
**See volume II, 2.16.

best means of implementing the reform measures mandated by the General Assembly. ...

In light of these developments and the reforms that are in progress, I look forward to the early restoration of the financial soundness of the Organization. I must emphasize, however, that this has not yet occurred. There is as yet no assurance that payment of assessed contributions will meet the minimum austerity operating expenses. Orderly administrative management is seriously handicapped when there is uncertainty as to receipt of a significant portion of the regular programme budget."

When addressing the Fifth Committee, the **Secretary-General**[33] made following statement during his introduction of the proposed programme budget for the biennium 1988-1989:

"the continuing financial crisis which confronted the United Nations jeopardized the very concept of programme planning and the orderly implementation of General Assembly resolution 41/213. It also undermined a soundly structured Secretariat and the morale of a dedicated and talented staff.

It was paradoxical that the crisis should persist when the role of the United Nations was becoming ever more vital. ...

His primary task as Secretary-General was to safeguard and increase the capability of the United Nations so that it can fulfil its historic duties. He was determined to carry through the essential changes now under way in order to ensure maximum operational efficiency and effectiveness. But continuing financial uncertainty rendered that task extremely difficult - even impossible - and in certain ways negated the efforts towards reform that were so vital for the future of the Organization. ...

The budgetary proposals he now submitted (A/42/6) had been formulated - not without difficulty - with the purpose of proceeding immediately with the mandates flowing from General Assembly decisions, including resolution 41/213. Certain structural changes had been made, aimed at streamlining functions, simplifying reporting channels, increasing efficiency and effectiveness and reducing staff and other costs. Thus the proposed programme budget amounted to $1.68 billion, $30 million below the current appropriation. The proposals would be subject to revision in 1988 - and perhaps in 1989 - while the Organization moved towards the programme budget for 1990-1991 and the future medium-term plan.

The proposals included significant budgetary innovations in the treatment of perennial activities and resources for conference services. In structural terms, it reflected measures he had taken in the political area, including research and the collection of information, and in those of programme planning, budgeting and finance, human rights and social development.

He urged members to fix the content, scope and level of the budget on the basis of the broadest possible agreement, for such agreement would be of fundamental importance to the viability of the United Nations, representing a clear commitment to provide timely political and financial support throughout the next biennium, for action to carry out the programme which Member States had mandated.

The financial prospects for the Organization in 1988 depended upon the full payment of assessed contributions early in the year. Otherwise he might later have to discuss with the Committee means of coping with grossly inadequate funds. The process of orderly change, now under way, must not be jeopardized by continuing financial uncertainty."

In a later address to the Fifth Committee, the **Secretary-General**[34] noted:

"Although he would be very happy if his forecasts proved inaccurate, the financial data and patterns of contributions over recent years indicated that the United Nations might become insolvent in the third quarter of 1988. ...

Paradoxically, the crisis had occurred just when there were indications of an increased awareness throughout the world of the need for a strong and effective United Nations. The means were available to Member States to ensure such effectiveness, and it was in their common interest to do so. It was essential, if irrevocable damage to programmes and structures was to be avoided, that Member States should meet their past and current financial obligations in 1988, promptly and in full. ... It was also necessary for the programme budget to enjoy the broad agreement and support of Member States.

The notable spirit of accommodation embodied in General Assembly resolution 41/213 constituted another important element in those endeavours. ...

Since the reforms approved by the General Assembly on the basis of the recommendations of the Group of High-level Intergovernmental Experts To Review the Efficiency of the Administrative and Financial Functioning of the United Nations would not be fully implemented until the end of the biennium, there was a need for flexibility during the period of transition."

In the following, the statements made under agenda item 41 are recalled. Before member states addressed the Committee, the Chairman of ACABQ and the Vice-Chairman of CPC introduce their reports, as outlined below.

Mr. Mselle, **Chairman of the ACABQ**[35]

"The Secretary-General's proposals showed, in monetary terms, the effects of initial action on some of the recommendations by the Group of 18: in particular, recommendations on reducing regular budget posts, including perennials in the initial estimates, and curtailing travel and consultancy costs...

The Committee ... endorsed the Secretary-General's view that the present budget proposals were essentially transitional, but held that the estimates, read in conjunction with the progress report, were an indispensable step in the transition to the 1990s. ...

The Committee recommended ... net reduction of $45,491,700. The bulk of the reductions related to the recommendations on turnover rates for calculating staff costs and on underutilized budget balances.

In view of the vacancy rates prevailing in the Secretariat in recent months, the Advisory Committee had concluded that higher average vacancy rates could be achieved over 1988-1989, to facilitate attainment of the objectives set in General Assembly resolution 41/213, than were proposed by the Secretariat. It had accordingly recommended an increase of 2.5 per cent in the turnover deduction proposed on the Secretariat for both Professional and General Service posts. The further adjustment did allow for the fact that the pattern of vacancies during 1988-1989 would vary, especially in view of the need to continue judicious recruitment of new personnel, but if necessary, the Committee would review the situation in the context of revised estimates during the biennium. ...

Other adjustments recommended by the Advisory Committee affected several objects of expenditure. While the Committee appreciated the way the reductions in spending on travel and consultants recommended by the Group of 18 had been applied by the Secretariat, it felt that the overall outcome did not fully reflect the reductions called for by the Group of 18. On such items as rentals and supplies, the Committee believed that the eventual number of staff in the Secretariat was bound to affect requirements. It also recommended adjustments in the requirements for printing and temporary assistance for meetings, and had given detailed explanations of the rationale for those recommendations. ...

Extensive discussions had been held on the question of a contingency fund; the detailed views of the Committee were given in its first report and an additional document (A/42/640). The proposal to establish a contingency fund for the 1988-1989 programme budget, while welcomed by some members, had surprised other members of the Committee. The Committee noted that the proposal for a contingency fund would be considered in the context of the programme budget outline submitted by the Secretary-General at the forty-third session. In the absence of a decision by the General Assembly on whether the 1988-1989 budget should have a contingency fund, it had been difficult to settle the issue in the Advisory Committee. A number of fundamental questions about the fund must be settled before the programme budget outline was approved by the General Assembly at its forty-third session. The Advisory Committee had attempted to identify technical issues, and made recommendations on several aspects of the fund. For example, the contingency fund should provide additional resources to finance activities with programme budget implications. Revised estimates should be divided into three categories: one to be considered in the context of the contingency fund, another to be reviewed by the General Assembly on an *ad hoc* basis, and a third to be dealt with in the context of the procedures for inflation and currency to be examined at the forty-third session. Recourse to the fund for activities covering a biennium would be made over a three-year period; the Committee recommended that, pending experience, no pre-determined proportion for a given year should be set. The Committee strongly believed that the procedures for operating the fund should be simple, not complicated or cumbersome, and its recommendations attempted to achieve that objective.

As indicated in paragraph 118 of its report, the Advisory Committee intended to look closely into the matter of additional expenditure resulting from fluctuations in currency or inflation and from revisions in standard rates for salaries and common staff costs, with a view to making specific recommendations to the General Assembly at its forty-third session. If no satisfactory solution was found to the problem of inflation and currency fluctuations, the overall level of the budget would be a source of disagreement among Member States for the foreseeable future. Such disagreement should be avoided, if only to spare the United Nations further damage to its financial health. The Advisory Committee, in its consideration of the subject, would be guided by the experience it had gained over the years and its continuing exchange of views with the specialized agencies. A number of the small specialized agencies had devised new mechanisms to deal with currency fluctuation problems, including split assessments, budgeting in a currency other than the United States dollar, and devising incentives to induce early payments. The Committee would examine the utility of those and other methods, and would appreciate any suggestions from Member States."

Mr. Cabric, **Vice-Chairman of the CPC**[36]

"the twenty-seventh session of CPC had assumed particular significance, as a result of the expanded role which had been given to CPC in budgetary matters under General Assembly resolution 41/213.

The session had been held during a transitional period, before the Committee's enhanced responsibilities in budgetary matters had because fully operational; moreover, the budget proposals for the biennium 1988-1989 had been termed "transitional" by the Secretary-General; the Committee had to take up certain fundamental issues of the budgetary process, namely, consideration of the nature of the proposed contingency fund and the overall level of the budget; finally, given the prevailing political atmosphere, a successful outcome of the session had assumed a great deal of symbolic value. Notwithstanding severe time constraints resulting from its increased responsibilities, CPC had been able to complete consideration of all the items on its agenda. ...

The Committee had considered the report of the Secretary-General on the implementation of his economy measures with particular attention to their programmatic implications but had decided to reserve judgement on the issue until the exact impact of those measures became known through the performance reports on the programme budget for 1986-1987. When programmatic adjustment appeared necessary, the Secretary-General should continue to seek the guidance of Member States through the appropriate intergovernmental bodies. ...

The priorities assigned by the Secretary-General to the issues of African economic recovery and the development and advancement of women had received general support. It had also been suggested that issues such as the external debt crisis, human rights, disarmament and development, and trade and development, should have received similar attention. The Committee had also expressed the view that the recruitment freeze should not be used as a policy instrument to achieve the target of 15 per cent reduction in staff, and a number of delegations had urged an early end to the freeze. ...

The Committee had noted the "sense of determination and vigour" on the part of the Secretary-General in implementing General Assembly resolution 41/213 and had noted his intention to pursue reforms in the Secretariat without waiting for the outcome of the in-depth study of the United Nations intergovernmental structure and functions in the economic and social fields which was being undertaken by the Special Commission of the Economic and Social Council. The final shape of the Secretariat's structure in those fields should, however, be determined only after the completion of the Special Commission's study. The Committee wished to emphasize that, while the Secretary-General should continue with his reform process in an effective and orderly manner, that process should not have adverse effects on programme delivery."

The representative of **Brazil**[37]

"With regard to the proposal of the Advisory Committee ... to increase the turnover deduction factor by 2.5 per cent, his delegation failed to understand the proposal, given the absence of any decision of the Secretary-General concerning how he planned to implement the 15 per cent cut in regular budget posts over the coming two years and whether or not he planned to suspend the recruitment freeze which had been in effect since 20 March 1986. It was unfortunate that the Secretariat had not been more forthcoming on those points, particularly since 75 to 80 per cent of the United Nations budget went to cover personnel costs. His delegation nevertheless would go along reluctantly with the Advisory Committee's recommendations. ...

In a departure from previous practice, the General Assembly would be dealing with the question of additional expenditures in the context of the contingency fund set up under resolution 41/213. ... The time of unlimited additional expenditures was over. Many countries, including Brazil, were experiencing hardships that necessitated stringent budgetary control. In Brazil, it was more and more difficult to assimilate additional expenditures after the Federal budget had been approved by the Congress. ...

There remained the question of the level of the contingency fund. Some members of the Group of 18 had been of the opinion that the contingency fund should not exceed 2 per cent of the budget (A/41/49), while the Secretary-General felt that 0.75 per cent of the budget would be a reasonable amount (A/42/225, para. 34). His delegation felt that the level of expenditures for new non-perennial activities, revised estimates and related conference costs in 1988-1989 should not exceed in nominal terms what had been allocated for additional expenditures in 1984-1985. The corresponding level of additional resources needed was roughly 3 per cent of the Secretary-General's initial proposal for gross expenditures in the coming biennium."

The representative of **Brazil**[38] continued

"CPC, which had formerly focused most of its attention on programmatic questions, would in future have to display still more openness and flexibility in order to meet the expectations of Member States and perform its responsibilities as a subsidiary body of the General Assembly for specific budgetary matters. The traditional practice of CPC of reaching decisions by consensus should be continued, in order to avoid stalemate and the consequent transmittal of questions to the General Assembly without the necessary conclusions and recommendations. Dissenting views should be presented to the General Assembly, a practice which had been recommended in General Assembly resolution 41/213 but which CPC had not observed at its last session."

The representative of **Japan**[39]

"The Secretary-General had proceeded to the speedy implementation of resolution 41/213, as was clear from the various measures taken to improve the administrative efficiency of the Secretariat, which were outlined in documents A/42/234 and A/C.5/42/2. Substantial progress had been made in post reductions and organizational restructuring, particularly in the political sector. Many measures were still under review and would not be implemented in the near future. Further efforts must therefore be made to accelerate implementation of all the reforms mandated by the General Assembly. Concerning the financial operations of the Organization, the new budgetary procedure approved by the General Assembly for the biennium 1990-1991 would benefit as a consequence of its partial implementation during the next biennium as the Secretary-General had proposed. On the same issue, it was disappointing that the members of CPC during its resumed session had been unable to agree on an overall level of resources for 1988-1989 or on the contingency fund. ...

The proposed programme budget for 1988-1989 must reflect the budgetary austerity and the retrenchment efforts on the agenda of most States. In view of the precarious financial situation of the Organization and the reforms under way, the proposed programme budget submitted by the Secretary-General was necessarily transitional. ... In the circumstances, the Secretary-General's budgetary proposals should be assessed in the light of two principles: first, the proposals should reflect the implementation of resolution 41/213, since the next biennium corresponded to the period when the mandated administrative reforms were to be completed; and, second, the overall level of the budget should be as realistic as possible, taking into account the actual level of expenditures during the current biennium. ...

The Advisory Committee had recommended increasing the staff turnover rate by a further 2.5 per cent to a total of 15 per cent so as to reflect more accurately the overall vacancy situation expected to prevail during the biennium. The 15 per cent goal for post reductions during the next biennium had already been met in part and, as the normal staff turnover rate was 5 per cent, the Advisory Committee's recommendation was more than justifiable. His delegation supported that recommendation although it favoured an even higher turnover rate. The recommendations for a 30 per cent reduction in the provisions for consultants and a 20 per cent reduction for official travel should be strictly complied with. On the basis of the pattern of expenditures during the previous complete biennium, the Advisory Committee had recommended a reduction of $10 million in the initial expenditure estimates for 1988-1989. His delegation would have supported a more substantial reduction, bearing in mind that the actual unspent balance of approved appropriations had been in excess of $20 million in each of the previous three bienniums. It supported the Advisory Committee's recommendations for reductions in expenditures relating to external printing and binding, temporary assistance, and rental and maintenance of premises. The Advisory Committee had also supported the policy of technological innovation. His delegation agreed with the efforts for enhancing the productivity of the Secretariat through office automation but considered that any proposal for the acquisition of new equipment should be based on a detailed examination of the needs of the services concerned and be accompanied by a statement of expected gains in efficiency and staff savings. ...

The General Assembly had ... decided to establish a contingency fund to deal with the problem of additional requirements. ... Bearing in mind the need to rationalize as quickly as possible the budgetary and programming procedure, his delegation agreed with the Secretary-General's view that the fund should be authorized at the current session at a level of 0.75 per cent of the budget. Finally, his delegation considered that the overall budgetary level for 1988-1989 should be kept down as much as possible in the light of the revised appropriations for the current biennium, subject of course to the revised estimates which would be submitted towards the end of the session. ...

In view of the persistence of the financial crisis, the prudence shown by the Secretary-General in his management and in his efforts to reduce expenditure was highly commendable. United Nations staff members had also risen to the situation notwithstanding the recruitment freeze, with regard to which his delegation had strong reservations. In the view of his delegation, financial uncertainty should not hamper implementation of administrative reform or the search for greater efficiency. While budgetary austerity was needed now more than ever, it was also essential that Member States should comply in full and promptly with their financial obligations. In that connection his delegation welcomed the decision of the Soviet Union to pay long outstanding arrears to the United Nations regular budget and peace-keeping forces. He announced that Japan would support the efforts of the Secretary-General by making a special contribution of $20 million."

The representative of Finland, speaking on behalf of the five **Nordic countries**[40]

"the proposed programme budget was the culmination of a state of affairs best described as uncertain, experimental, *ad hoc* and transitional. The Nordic delegations were concerned over the Secretary-General's recent statement that the continuing financial crisis could affect programme delivery. ...

The Nordic countries were mainly concerned with two questions: the level and content of the budget, and the implementation of resolution 41/213 with respect to the proposed budget. They recognized that the level of the proposed budget was chiefly a result of adjusting the vacancy rate for Professional and General Service posts, decreasing travel and consultants' costs and incorporating previously non-recurrent items into the resource base. At the same time, there were several pending matters. Some information had not yet been incorporated into the proposed budget figures and the impact of currency fluctuations and inflation had not been assessed. Another open question was the impact of any changes that might be recommended by the Special Commission of the Economic and Social Council which was reviewing the structure and functioning of the intergovernmental machinery in the economic and social fields, or of other reviews conducted by the Secretariat. ...

It seemed that some delegations viewed the new budgeting process as an exercise in reducing estimates. The Nordic delegations, however, believed that the more focused discussion of budget priorities was meant to elicit the greatest possible support from Member States. The budget process, an integral part of reform, would contribute to better, more efficient implementation of the General Assembly's political decisions. That, in turn, would make resource needs more predictable and allow far more orderly planning of activities. The new procedures would also constitute a more structured approach to budgetary planning, the defining of perennial activities, the contingency fund and the impact of inflation and currency fluctuations. ...

The new planning and budgetary procedures would give Member States a better basis for negotiating and, ultimately, agreeing on the content and level of resources. Resolution 41/213, however, did not emphasize reductions, but rather the full implementation of General Assembly resolutions. If it turned out that there was a need for agreement on a revised timetable for the implementation of resolutions or on the setting of priorities substantive decisions should be taken by relevant intergovernmental bodies, or even the Main Committees of the General Assembly.

While the proposed contingency fund would be geared primarily to programmatic contingencies, a much larger question was how to deal with additional expenditures related to cost increases. The Nordic countries welcomed the Advisory Committee's finding that recourse to the fund would extend over three years for activities covering a biennium. They hoped that a compromise could be reached on the basis of the Advisory Committee's observations. That compromise should aim to use experience acquired in 1988-1989 for the proper implementation of the fund in 1990-1991. A compromise should also reflect agreement on the scope, coverage and flexible use of the fund. In addition, procedures to be followed by the General Assembly for determining the use of the contingency fund must be clearly understood. In conclusion, while resolution 41/213 provided a basis for resolving the Organization's financial problems, it was no substitute for political agreement among Member States on the substantive issues."

The representative of **Australia**[41]

"Far from reducing programme output, reform would facilitate resource transfers from administrative to programme areas. In that regard, the proposed restructuring of the Department of Public Information was a useful paradigm. Australia looked to the Special Commission of the Economic and Social Council to make far-reaching recommendations on rationalizing the existing system. The Council's subsidiary bodies could be greatly reduced in number by abolishing some functions and combining others.

Australia had supported recommendations on a new budget process in the belief that they would yield three important results. The first would be that Member States would be able to determine resource allocations in accordance with more clearly defined priorities. The current system left too much responsibility to the Secretariat. Second, for the first time, Member States would have a precise indication of the upper limit of their financial obligations in any one biennium, because the overall level for the budget would include finite funds to cover additional expenditure. Third, the new procedure was expected to secure wider support for the budget since decisions would be taken by consensus. By failing to reach agreement on budgetary reforms at its recent session, the Committee for Programme and Co-ordination had missed an important opportunity to maintain the momentum of reform.

For the first time in several years, Australia was able to support the Secretary-General's initial budget estimates for 1988-1989. It agreed with the

Advisory Committee that whatever their shortcomings, preliminary estimates were an important transitional step in formulating future budgets. Australia welcomed budget innovations such as the incorporation of perennial activities and the structural changes introduced to increase efficiency and reduce costs. Like other delegations, it had hoped for a more detailed proposal from the Secretary-General on implementing recommendation 15 of the Group of 18.

Australia fully supported the Advisory Committee's recommendations on areas targeted for reductions. Along with Japan, it believed that in the light of the recent pattern of actual unspent balances, $20 million could have been cut from the estimates without loss of flexibility. ...

The withholding of regular budget contributions was placing an unfair burden on other major contributors who always paid promptly. What amounted to a *de facto* subsidy to a major contributor must not be perpetuated by reducing that country's assessment below its capacity to pay. Continued large-scale withholdings might well block the reform process and the major achievements of the forty-first General Assembly session. In Australia's view - which was not shared by everyone - the crisis and reform were two separate matters. The current financial crisis merely made the inevitable task of reform that much more pressing.

Australia was strongly committed to the United Nations, but was facing serious budget problems of its own and the difficulties of economic adjustment. That meant it did not have unlimited resources to finance the rising cost of multilateralism. The United Nations was already associated with too much rhetoric and not enough negotiation, a proliferation of subsidiary bodies and over-staffed secretariats. The Organization must address such image problems if its credibility was to be restored."

The representative of **Australia**[42] continued

"The proposed programme budget for the biennium 1988-1989 seemed to take into account the budget constraints facing the majority of Member States and was to be commended. It was unfortunate that not all Member States seemed willing to follow the path recommended by the Secretary-General. Some had suggested increasing the budget, apparently on the assumption that loyal contributors could be prevailed upon to pay more than their assessed level of contributions. Any device to extract more from the 66 members which paid in full would only discredit the Organization and further undermine confidence in it."

The representative of **China**[43]

"The arbitrary withholding of contributions, the subordination of the Charter to a State's national legislative action or the linking of payments to the institution of certain reforms all ran contrary to internationally accepted practice and could constitute a destructive precedent for the United Nations. Normal operations had already been jeopardized, and it was to be hoped that the Member State concerned would take immediate steps to repair the damage it had done to the Organization.

... the negative growth provided for in the initial estimates should be regarded as an exception necessitated by special circumstances and not be taken as a basis for future budget proposals. It was logical that, under normal conditions, United Nations activities should register a reasonable rate of positive growth, helping to ensure the implementation of programmes beneficial to Member States and to strengthen the Organization's role in international affairs. The fact that some programmes had already suffered adverse effects as a result of the financial crisis was a matter of grave concern. General Assembly resolution 41/213, among others, had emphasized that reform measures should not prejudice the implementation of programmes. The Secretariat should provide information indicating which programmes had been postponed or terminated, in order to ensure that there was no adverse impact on development-oriented programmes mandated by the General Assembly which were of vital importance to developing countries.

The continued recruitment freeze was disturbing in view of the problems it posed for application of the principle of equitable geographical distribution, as well as for countries whose nationals served mostly on fixed-term contracts. The freeze had been intended as a temporary measure in response to the financial crisis, and no endorsement had been given by the General Assembly for its use by the Secretariat as a mechanism to attain the 15 per cent staff reduction target. His delegation supported the view of the Committee for Programme and Co-ordination that the freeze should not be used as a policy tool in personnel matters and was particularly concerned by the impact of the freeze on language posts. ...

The establishment of a contingency fund to accommodate additional budgetary expenditures other than those arising from fluctuations in rates of exchange and inflation constituted an important reform which his delegation supported. However, the scope of application, method of allocation and operational procedure for such a fund must be decided after serious consideration and by consensus. The Secretary-General's outline of the programme budget for the following biennium in off-budget years should, as provided for in General Assembly resolution 41/213, contain an indication of the size of the contingency fund expressed as a percentage of the overall level of resources. ... Subject to a satisfactory solution of all pertinent questions, his delegation would be willing to accommodate the wishes of Member States if a majority should favour the earlier establishment of a contingency fund on an experimental basis.

While there was clearly a need to streamline the United Nations and to reduce unnecessary expenditure, the basic thrust of reforms must be positive."

The representative of **China**[44] continued

"All Member States supported the reforms outlined in General Assembly resolution 41/213. Any attempt by any country to impose reforms desired by it would only disrupt the activities of the Organization and prevent the reforms from being carried out in an orderly manner. Resolution 41/213 had been adopted by consensus and reflected a renewed commitment to multilateralism and to the strengthening of the role of the United Nations. Unless those objectives were achieved, the reforms would be meaningless."

The representative of **Yugoslavia**[45]

"Concern over the Organization's solvency was diverting attention from the most important international problems. Meanwhile, the use of political pressure in order to wrest certain concessions ran contrary to the basic democratic character of the Organization. His delegation refused to believe that political short-sightedness and national selfishness could prevail over reason and thus threaten the very survival of the United Nations. ...

Full implementation of the recommendations of the Group of 18 was more important than ever. However, the fulfilment of financial obligations could not be made contingent on the implementation of those recommendations. While the financial crisis might have provided impetus for the work of the Group of 18, the recommended measures remained independent of the crisis. It was essential that the measures should be based on thorough and comprehensive studies and not on concessions exacted by force.

Reorganization in the economic and social fields should be harmonized with measures to restructure the intergovernmental machinery. Hasty action might be seen as an attempt to pre-empt proposals by Member States and could even run counter to the basic intention of such reorganization. It should be possible to begin defining proposals for a reorganization of the intergovernmental structure - which was inefficient, and did not serve the interests of the developing countries - by early 1988. ... It was also essential that the recruitment freeze should be ended in order to redress the injustices suffered by those countries which were underrepresented in the Secretariat as well as to improve the overall quality of staff.

The transitional programme budget introduced by the Secretary-General reflected all the weaknesses and shortcomings that were inherent in the complex situation facing the Organization. Nevertheless, it had greatly surpassed his delegation's expectations: The reduction of 1.8 per cent over the gross revised appropriation for 1986-1987 was in line with the overall intention to reduce spending, in accordance with resolution 41/213. ... The Secretary-General should be encouraged to continue his efforts without, however, jeopardizing the implementation of programmes."

The representative of Hungary, speaking on behalf of **socialist countries**[*46]

"The socialist States ... were concerned over recent attempts to undermine the Organization and to replace the multilateral approach to international problems with the unilateral imposition by certain Member States of their wishes over those of others. Attempts to use financial blackmail against other Member States were doomed to failure.

Noting the urgent need for decisions by the Fifth Committee on the content, scope and level of the budget to be taken on the basis of the broadest possible agreement, the socialist States believed that the proposed programme budget for the biennium 1988-1989, together with the adjustments proposed by the Advisory Committee, provided an appropriate basis for the sound and economical operation of the Organization as it faced the challenges and opportunities of the years to come. They were aware of the concern of some Member States that the Secretary-General should be given a measure of flexibility in view of the current financial crisis but believed in view of the far-reaching extent of the reforms to be implemented during the next two years, that there should be further substantial reductions in estimated resource requirements. The overall level of expenditures in the next biennium should, therefore, not exceed the level of the current budget, and Member States should make concerted efforts to reduce expenditures even further."

The representative of **Trinidad and Tobago**[47]

"In striving for greater administrative and financial efficiency, Member States should not lose sight of the basic intention of General Assembly

---

[*]Bulgaria, Byelorussian SSR, Czechoslovakia, German Democratic Republic, Mongolia, Poland, the Ukrainian SSR, USSR.

resolution 41/213, namely that each Member State should renew its commitment to abide by the principles of multilateralism and to fulfil its obligations under the Charter.

The proposed programme budget was of a transitional nature and was thus not necessarily the standard on which any future budget should be based. His delegation was particularly concerned that the proposed reduction in expenditure was to be achieved by a decrease in programme activities. Although resolution 41/213 stressed that the implementation of projects and programmes already approved by the General Assembly should not be prejudiced, cuts were to be introduced in expenditures on official travel and on consultants. His delegation questioned the ability of the Organization to carry out its mandated tasks in such circumstances.

The criteria for the setting of priorities were not yet sufficiently clear to ensure that only the least important programme elements were affected, and his delegation did not fully understand the budgetary implications of the Secretary-General's selection of two particular issues for priority treatment. ... In the case of the Department of Public Information, for example, it appeared that a sweeping restructuring could take place before Member States had any chance, through the Committee on Information or the Committee for Programme and Co-ordination, to provide real inputs to the process. There was therefore a possibility that the restructuring might not address the real concerns of Member States with respect to the Department and, by extension, other units of the Secretariat.

In view of the important role played by the Committee for Programme and Co-ordination in ensuring that mandated activities were properly incorporated into the organizational structure, as well as its increased responsibilities under the provisions of resolution 41/213, the Committee should hold two sessions each year as a matter of course. Its membership should also be increased, though not excessively, in order to ensure broader representation of regional and subregional interests. Such an increase should take effect before initiation of the new budget process at the Committee's twenty-eighth session. ...

With regard to the vital issue of the contingency fund ... It was essential to spell out how the fund would operate and which body would have initial responsibility for the allocation of resources from it before the fund was established."

The representative of **Israel**[48]

"In urging that decisions on the proposed programme budget should be reached on the basis of the broadest possible agreement, the Secretary-General presumably had in mind the need, as stated in resolution 41/213, for Member States to participate in the budgetary preparation from its early stages and throughout the process. That process, as outlined in annex I to the resolution, provided for the submission in off-budget years, of an outline of the programme budget for the following biennium, to include an indication of the size of the contingency fund. The programme budget itself, including expenditures related to political activities of a "perennial" character, was to be submitted in the following budget year, in accordance with the existing procedures. The Secretariat, however, by including political activities of a perennial character before the outline was approved, was failing to comply with those existing procedures. His delegation was strongly opposed to the Secretariat's decision to deal with an individual aspect of its own choosing before resolving the issue of the contingency fund. It also found the Advisory Committee's failure to note that departure from existing procedures entirely unacceptable, particularly since the Committee for Programme and Co-ordination had clearly entertained reservations about the proposed programme budget for that reason. Since it was evident that Member States had not been able to participate in the preparation of the budget from the early stages, his delegation could not accept the proposed budget in its current form."

The representative of **Israel**[49] continued

"The call for a leaner, more efficient Secretariat made in resolution 41/213 was not reflected in the perspectives on the work of the United Nations as described by the Secretary-General, which showed a lack of the necessary self-criticism. ...

What changes should be made? To his delegation, it was clear that the basic ideas underlying the United Nations - the Organization's universality, and the sovereign equality of all Member States - must be recognized in all activities, and that the Organization's approach should be more balanced, drawing on a proper understanding of the positions of all countries concerned. It was inappropriate for plans for the future work of the United Nations to be discussed only in the Second or Fifth Committees: the United Nations was, first and foremost, a means to safeguard international peace and security, a subject dealt with by neither of those Committees. There should be less talk, fewer conferences and fewer documents, so that the United Nations could concentrate on the things that did reasonably well: operational activities for development, among other things. In short, when considering whether to support United Nations programmes, delegations should consider not only the resolutions adopted by the General Assembly but the attitude taken by each Member State to paying for them."

The representative of **Canada**[50]

"There had been steady progress in the implementation of resolution 41/213, but reform had raised a number of important practical issues which were complex and, to a certain degree, political. Furthermore, the continuation of the recruitment freeze into 1987 and the implementation of other economy measures in 1986 and 1987 had enabled the Organization to remain solvent for the current year, but at a considerable price. The delivery of certain programmes was threatened and the distortions in staffing patterns and staff remuneration were hardening and seemed to be taking on an air of permanence. ...

With proposed expenditures some $30 million below the $1.71 billion appropriated for the current biennium, it was the first time that at that stage in the consideration of the budget, the Fifth Committee was witnessing a decline in expenditures from one biennium to the next. ...

It was encouraging that the Secretary-General had been able to reflect the implementation of resolution 41/213 in his programme budget proposal, for example, by including for the first time, estimates of expenditures for certain political activities of a perennial character and conference-servicing costs.

His delegation concurred with the Advisory Committee's recommendations for reductions in consultant services and official travel, in the unobligated balance of appropriations and the balance of unliquidated obligations, and in certain other expenditures. It did, however, reserve its position on the recommendation to increase turnover rates by another 2.5 per cent for both Professional and General Service categories. It was, however, disturbing that the majority of economies had come from the recruitment freeze and other staff-related measures, measures which had introduced a number of distortions. Therefore, his delegation was prepared to endorse the Advisory Committee's proposal to save $31.7 million by increasing the rate of staff turnover only if the Secretary-General could give some assurance that measure would not affect programme delivery and would not prevent him from hiring and retaining top-quality personnel for the United Nations. ...

Canada was pleased with the restructuring already undertaken in the political sector, the important steps taken in the economic and social sectors and the proposed restructuring of the Department of Public Information. It was pleased at the appointment of three women Under-Secretaries-General and with the number of women appointed to management positions.

His delegation welcomed the analysis and contents of the reports of the Secretary-General and the Advisory Committee on the inclusion of a contingency fund in the programme budget for the biennium 1988-1989. The amount in the fund could represent 0.75 per cent of the regular budget, as the Secretary-General had proposed, or even 1 per cent. In any case, whatever decision would be taken for the biennium 1988-1989 on the scope and operation of the fund should not prejudice the final decision which would be taken for 1990 and beyond. ...

Lastly, his delegation fully shared the concern of the Secretary-General and several other delegations regarding the severity of the financial crisis. Actions which denied the Organization its assessed contributions were contrary to the Charter and penalized those Member States which paid their contributions on time. His delegation could not accept any linkage between the implementation of resolution 41/213 and the payment of assessed contributions, and it regarded the implications of such a linkage as damaging to the reform process."

The representative of **Canada**[51] continued

"the financial crisis of the United Nations was not only humiliating, but mortifying. Many of the excellent international public servants who managed the Organization, including the Secretary-General, spent their entire day on the exhausting, unproductive and debilitating quest for financial security. It was unconscionable that things had come to such a pass.

While everyone, including his own delegation, liked to target the United States as the chief culprit, it was important to emphasize two points. Firstly, a majority of countries did not pay their assessed contributions on time and an extraordinary number had not paid their arrears. The arguments about the United States would be a lot stronger if so many other countries were not themselves delinquent. Secondly, the exceptional efforts of the United States Mission to the United Nations and especially, the United States Permanent Representative, must be acknowledged. Canada had nothing but admiration for the attempts of the United States delegation to persuade the United States Congress to approve that country's full assessment.

Bearing those two points in mind, the unpleasant reality was that countries that did not pay their assessments were in violation of international law. Furthermore, any country which contracted to pay 25 per cent of the United Nations budget had a special obligation to pay in full and on time, since failure to do so clearly had disastrous consequences for the Organization. What made matters worse was that the current reform programme had in significant measure been worked out with the United States. When drastic reforms were implemented the promised contribution still did not materialize, that felt like bad faith bargaining to a number of countries."

The representative of **Bangladesh**[52]

"Since the budget for the biennium 1988-1989 was a transitional one, it should represent a judicious balance between the elements of continuity and those of change. With regard to continuity, he cited two aspects. First, it was heartening that the volume of outputs had not been scaled down in proportion to the resource reductions in each programme. It was important, however, that there should be no departure from full implementation of the programme of activities; any adverse effect on programmes brought about by the reform measures should be brought to the notice of Member States so that they could give the Secretary-General guidance. The second element concerned the rules and regulations regarding priority-setting, scrupulous adherence to which took on renewed significance in the context of resolution 41/213. In that connection, his delegation agreed with the Nordic delegations that the modification in the budgetary process envisaged in the resolution was aimed at a more focused discussion of priorities rather than an exercise in reducing estimates. ... CPC had recommended that efforts should be made to reduce the share of executive direction and management as well as support costs of the programme budget so that maximum resources would become available for substantive activities.

With regard to the elements of change in the proposed programme budget, he said that the budget proposed by the Secretary-General showed a negative real growth of 1.5 per cent as compared to the revised appropriations for the current biennium. That negative growth should be regarded as an exception deriving from the special circumstances brought about by resolution 41/213. Since the Organization was dynamic by nature its budget should reflect that dynamism in terms of positive growth and that trend should resume under normal conditions. Secondly, ... With regard to the 15 per cent post reduction called for in resolution 41/213, his delegation shared the concern expressed by CPC at the use of the recruitment freeze to achieve that target. Such a measure could have undesirable consequences for the distribution of expertise among programmes and for the efforts to recruit staff on as wide a geographical basis as possible. ...

The third element of change was the contingency fund to cover supplementary expenditures. In the light of the relevant reports of CPC and the Advisory Committee, his delegation felt that, for a comprehensive treatment of all aspects of the matter, further substantive deliberations were required. It would be flexible, however, with regard to the possibility of utilizing the contingency fund on an experimental basis during the biennium 1988-1989."

The representative of Denmark, speaking on behalf of the 12 member states of the **European Community**[53]

"resolution 41/213 marked an important step in the strengthening of the efficiency of the administrative and financial functioning of the United Nations, in that it called for a new budget procedure. Not all the elements in that procedure had been taken into account in the budget proposals now before the Committee, unfortunately, for they had been drawn up before the resolution was adopted. It was unfortunate also that CPC had been unable to agree on two central issues: the overall budget figure, and the manner in which the contingency fund would function. ...

Several innovations deserved mention. The proposed programme budget defined two principal priority areas: African economic recovery and development, and the advancement of women. Additionally, provision for temporary assistance at meetings in the three major United Nations conference centres had been included in the initial budget estimates, and add-ons were not envisaged provided there was no change in the pattern of conferences. For the first time, "perennial" activities were covered in the initial budget estimates, and the resources requested were less than had been appropriated in previous budget cycles. On the other hand, the list of programme outputs judged to be obsolete, of marginal usefulness or ineffective was very short. Member States should agree to drop activities of low priority, thus providing increased scope for urgent or new activities.

On the purely budgetary aspects of the issue, it was difficult to comment on the Secretary-General's proposals, for they were clearly only a starting point. The Advisory Committee had recommended sizeable reductions in them. Currency fluctuations and inflation could not be predicted, and allowance must also be made for revised estimates and the possible establishment of a contingency fund - something the Twelve would like to see. That said, the total estimates of expenditure for 1988-1989 were lower than the revised appropriations for 1986-1987, despite the inclusion of some "perennial" activities. It seemed that the familiar trend towards bigger budgets every biennium had been reversed. The Twelve hoped that the reforms would confirm the new trend; they regarded efforts to enhance efficiency as crucially important, being the only way that all mandated activities could be carried out at the least possible cost.

The cuts in spending were mainly due to the decline in the size of the Secretariat, but also derived from reductions in certain items of expenditure such as official travel and consultants, where the Advisory Committee recommended further cuts. The Advisory Committee also recommended a further increase in the standard turnover deduction, which the Twelve considered warranted by the current level of vacant posts.

The question of a contingency fund was an important aspect of the budget procedure. The Secretary-General considered it desirable to include a contingency fund of 0.75 per cent of the total budget in the proposals for 1988-1989. It was unfortunate that CPC had been unable to reach a decision on that proposal. The establishment of the fund obviously raised a number of questions and it was therefore important, as the Advisory Committee had emphasized, to lay down the precise rules and procedures that would govern its operation. The procedure suggested by the Secretary-General in document A/42/255 could serve as a good starting point. It had been suggested, during the CPC session, that a contingency fund should be established on an experimental basis for the biennium 1988-1989. The Twelve supported that proposal, believing that it would allow the fund to be tried out without in any way prejudging how it would eventually operate."

The representative of **Indonesia**[54]

"To try to link structural reform and settlement of the financial crisis would create an atmosphere of suspicion and could even make the exercise vulnerable to financial blackmail. ...

The progress report of the Secretary-General on the implementation of resolution 41/213 called for a number of comments. First of all, his delegation agreed with the general approach taken by CPC. ... it should be ensured that reforms would not have a negative impact on programmes. Secondly, it was necessary to wait for the findings of the in-depth study undertaken by the Special Commission of the Economic and Social Council before making adjustments to the Secretariat structure in the economic and social fields. ... Thirdly, the recruitment freeze sanctioned by decision 41/466 should not be an instrument for effecting the post reductions mandated by resolution 41/213. The freeze should be lifted as soon as the financial situation improved. His delegation had noted that the scheme to reduce posts had been designed in such a way as to lead logically into a longer-term retrenchment plan. Fourthly, the regrouping of social and economic activities into separate sectors should not adversely affect the integrated, or at least co-ordinated, approach followed so far by the Organization in dealing with economic and social development.

Given its features, the proposed programme budget was more a reflection of the past than a model for the future. The incorporation of activities of a perennial character and the systematic reduction of estimates for travel and consultant services were not particularly significant innovations. His delegation fully agreed with the Advisory Committee and the Secretary-General that it was necessary for the process of reform to proceed in an orderly, clear, coherent and timely manner but it wondered how a budget so heavily influenced by the financial crisis could contribute to that goal.

Turning to the question of the level of expenditures, he said that his delegation welcomed the prudence demonstrated by the Secretary-General and was confident that he would try to offset the cuts in resources by increases in efficiency so that the negative growth of the programme budget would not adversely affect programme delivery either quantitatively or qualitatively. He concurred with the view of CPC that efforts should be made to reduce the share of administrative and support services so that maximum resources would become available for substantive activities. It had no objection to the proposal to give priority to the issues of African economic recovery and development and the advancement of women but felt that follow-up activities to the major conferences which had taken place that year (UNCTAD VII, the International Conference on the Relationship between Disarmament and Development and the International Conference on Drug Abuse and Illicit Trafficking) also deserved priority treatment.

With regard to the contingency fund, given the interim nature of the proposed programme budget and the extraordinary circumstances in which it had been formulated, he was doubtful that it would be advisable to establish such a fund, even on an experimental basis. Having said that, his delegation was ready to co-operate with other delegations so that decisions on the content and level of the budget could be based on the broadest possible agreement."

The representative of **Jordan**[55] expressed

"his disappointment at the current atmosphere of uncertainty that was undermining the process of reform and the collective political will manifested in General Assembly resolution 41/213. ...

His delegation was concerned at the possible adverse effects the economic measures and certain reforms might have on staffing and on programmes requested by Member States. It shared the views expressed that the recruitment freeze was not a normal management tool and pointed out that it led to imbalances in staffing patterns with regard to age, sex and geographical distribution. It was deeply concerned at the exceptionally high vacancy rate (at least 25 per cent) noted in the Economic and Social Commission for Western Asia ...

With regard to CPC, there was no doubt that since the adoption of General Assembly resolution 41/213, it had assumed a more pivotal role in programme planning and budgeting. An enlargement of its membership should not become an obstacle to reaching the widest possible agreement on the budget. All regional and sub-regional groups should be represented and no single group should dominate. Decision-making in CPC should continue to be governed by the provisions of the Charter and the rules of procedure of the General Assembly."

The representative of **Ethiopia**[56]

"Taking advantage of the size of its financial contribution to the regular budget, the Member State in question had attempted to pressure the Organization not simply to undertake necessary reforms but also to follow its political thinking. Such an attitude was contrary to the Charter, in that it contravened the sovereign equality of Member States. It also undermined the reform process, management and programme planning and budgeting. ...

Although reforms must be implemented in an orderly, clear, coherent and timely manner, as recommended by the Advisory Committee, they must also faithfully respect the decisions of the General Assembly. That was far from the case for the construction projects in Addis Ababa and Bangkok. Efficiency and economy were not an end in themselves, but a means of attaining the purposes of the Charter. They should therefore not prevent the Organization from tackling issues requiring its urgent attention. His delegation was pleased that the Secretary-General gave priority to Africa's economic recovery and development but warned him against excessive rigidity in implementing the reform measures (reduction in staff, consultants and construction, for example) because that might defeat his stated intentions.

In view of the circumstances in which the budget proposals had been prepared, the reduction in expenditure should be seen as reflecting reform measures rather than a diminishing role for the Organization."

The representative of the **Union of Soviet Socialist Republics**[57]

"The Soviet Union strongly opposed any attempts to use the current financial difficulties to bring pressure to bear on the Organization or check its activities. It would co-operate actively with the efforts to overcome its difficulties and had already taken specific practical steps in that direction, as noted by several delegations. In particular, it had decided to pay its arrears and had already acted on that decision by paying over $28 million on 12

October 1987 in addition to its regular contribution for 1987. It was also ready to give favourable consideration to the question of its participation in eliminating the deficit in the budget of the United Nations peace-keeping forces.

The Soviet Union had played a very active role in the preparation of administrative and budgetary reforms. Those reforms focused primarily on three areas, namely, the reorganization of intergovernmental machinery, the restructuring of the Secretariat, and the introduction of a new budget process. Reform in the first area had been primarily entrusted to the Special Commission of the Economic and Social Council, whose report would not be submitted until 1988. As to the second area, it was still premature to draw conclusions on the results of the restructuring effort, but the Organization seemed to be headed in the right direction ... However, the process must take place in a spirit of openness and not entail *de facto* discrimination against any particular country or group of countries. Finally, the third area, which should be the focus of the current session, hinged on two major issues: the contingency fund and its operation, on the one hand, and a comprehensive solution to the problem of additional expenditures, including those deriving from inflation and currency fluctuations, on the other.

A decision on the contingency fund could be taken as early as the current session on the basis of the Advisory Committee's observations. The Soviet delegation fully concurred with the Committee that the operation of the fund should not be so intricate or so rigid as to complicate the work of the Assembly. Moreover, the fund should facilitate the redeployment of resources to priority programmes and the elimination of activities which were ineffective, outdated or of little value. There was a tendency to underestimate the resources which could be released through such redeployment and elimination, which, in fact, were consistent with the search for a more rational use of resources, stressed by the Secretary-General in his report (A/42/512). None the less, the slow pace of progress in that area was regrettable. ...

The in-depth study of the problem, which the Advisory Committee planned to conduct, must be accorded high priority and must cover the following points: first, it should summarize the views expressed by Member States at various General Assembly sessions, particularly in connection with the adoption of resolutions 36/230 and 37/130. It was in the context of those resolutions that the possibility had first been raised of absorbing the effects of inflation and currency fluctuations through contributions, including voluntary contributions, to be paid by developed countries which hosted United Nations offices and derived substantial benefits from doing so. Second, a study should be made of the specialized agencies' practice of budgeting additional expenses in the course of the biennium, and particularly the desirability of multi-currency financing. Third, a certain percentage of such expenses should be absorbed by savings, redeployment of resources or the rescheduling of low-priority activities. Fourth, in accordance with resolution 41/213, consideration should be given to constituting a reserve from gains on exchange, savings realized in the execution of the budget and returns on investments. Finally, it would be interesting to consider the possibility of introducing a system of material incentives that would induce Member States to pay their contributions on time. In putting forward those proposals, the Soviet Union stood ready to participate constructively in the search for a comprehensive solution acceptable to all parties.

The proposed programme budget for 1988-1989 was, as the Secretary-General had said, a "transitional" budget not subject to the planned reforms just getting under way. It would make more sense to consider each of its sections at the following session, by which time the Secretary-General would have submitted revised estimates reflecting the extent to which reform had progressed.

The Soviet delegation wished to make a number of comments on the proposed budget as a whole. Expenditures of $1,681,000,000 were too high and did not adequately reflect General Assembly decisions to reduce personnel by 15 per cent, and consultants' and travel expenditures by 30 and 20 per cent, respectively, all before 1989. For no valid reason, the initial estimates also incorporated several million dollars of unobligated balances and unliquidated obligations. Consequently, the Soviet delegation supported the Advisory Committee recommendations designed to correct such shortcomings, but felt that the proposed reductions could have been more substantial. It also supported the recommendations on printing costs, the recruitment of temporary personnel, rental and maintenance of premises.

The proposed budget for 1988-1989 was, in some respects, similar to previous budgets which had never been approved by the Soviet delegation. For example, it included a provision of $94 million for inflation and the Secretariat intended to add approximately $80 million before the end of the session as protection against fluctuations in exchange rates. Thus, it seemed that the Secretariat did not wish to adhere to resolution 41/213, which explicitly requested it to attempt, to the extent possible, to absorb such expenditures. It was also intolerable that in a crisis situation, resources from the regular budget were still being used to cover overhead expenses related to the execution of technical assistance projects carried out by other organizations, primarily UNDP. The UNDP Governing Council, UNITAR and other organizations should be fully responsible for the cost of conference services provided to them.

It should be borne in mind that the level of the budget proposed by the Secretariat was not final and that in the course of the session, Member States would be requested to approve a whole series of additional appropriations amounting to a rather significant sum. ...

The Soviet Union was inclined to agree with the conclusions of the Advisory Committee on the matter of establishing a contingency fund within the framework of the 1988-1989 budget. If the technical problems raised in connection with the establishment and operation of such a fund were resolved on time and if a majority of the Member States wished to establish it within the overall level of the 1988-1989 budget, the Soviet Union would be ready to play a part in solving the problem."

The representative of **Sri Lanka**[58]

"While it was true that an increase in United Nations activities must necessarily lead to an increase in the Organization's structure and size, it was necessary to guard against the proliferation of unproductive expenditures and to cut out the dead wood currently burdening the system. The resources currently available to the Organization should be devoted to programmes that were of use to the world community as a whole and to the developing countries in particular. Therefore, the cost-cutting exercise must not affect activities of special political and economic significance, such as the programmes relating to southern Africa, Namibia, Palestine, decolonization or environmental problems such as housing and water supply, public health and information. Issues such as the external debt, commodity prices, trade and protectionism should likewise be considered. While he welcomed the Secretary-General's reference to the recognition of women in the Organization's administrative hierarchy, their role in the development strategy should likewise be acknowledged in the United Nations programme activities.

The proposal to set up a contingency fund was in line with General Assembly resolution 41/213; however, there did not yet seem to be any agreement regarding the percentage of the budget that should be appropriated and what exactly the purpose of the fund should be. In his view, the fund should not be a means of remedying guesswork but an exercise in accountancy and auditing which took into account the planning, programming and budgeting processes.

His delegation agreed with the Chairman of the Advisory Committee that the "across the board reduction" in personnel under each budget section had been merely indicative. The 15 per cent reduction should not be applied uniformly to every unit; each unit should be examined individually in order to determine how Member States, particularly the developing countries, would be affected."

The representative of **Cameroon**[59]

"Resolution 41/213 clearly stated that the Secretary-General should make proposals on the subject of the contingency fund in the context of the outline of the budget which he was to present in 1988. It would therefore be better to stick to that timetable, which had been agreed to by consensus, and, in the mean time, to try to resolve the technical problems raised by the fund. His delegation believed that the fund should cover the budget period. With regard to the elements to be included therein - expenses arising from new activities mandated by the deliberative organs, budget extensions, inflation and currency fluctuations - ACABQ had estimated that the procedure adopted in regard to resolutions having financial implications should not be such as to hamper the work of the various committees and other deliberative organs. With regard to the revised estimates, the three categories indicated by ACABQ were relevant, on the understanding that revised estimates relating to unforeseen and extraordinary expenses would continue to be dealt with in accordance with the current practice. With regard to the last two elements, he supported the proposal by ACABQ to examine the question in greater detail in 1988. ...

Regarding the construction projects at Addis Ababa and Bangkok, it would be wise to confirm the consensus which had led to the adoption of resolution 41/213; there was no justification for reopening the debate on that matter, especially since no additional funds had been requested. If the consensus were challenged, it would introduce a note of discord and upset the delicate balance of interests reflected in resolution 41/213. Cameroon would be the first to extend such an imbalance to many other points in the resolution."

The representative of **Uganda**[60]

"The proposed programme budget for the biennium 1988-1989 had been referred to by the Secretary-General as a "transitional budget". The budgetary process should not be linked to the reform process. ...

The question of the contingency fund should not arise in the 1988-1989 programme budget, but rather in the context of the budget outline to be presented to the General Assembly at its forty-third session: the Assembly had not yet reached a decision on whether there should be a contingency fund and a number of important technical issues concerning its establishment, scope and operation would have to be resolved first. The Committee should spare no effort in seeking solutions to the question of inflation and currency fluctuation and in deciding on the content, scope and level of the budget outline.

Resolution 41/213 strengthened the role of CPC. Member States had agreed that the consultations on the programme and budget aspects should be as broad as possible. The present regional and subregional representation on CPC did not seem to meet that purpose. Fears had been expressed by some that an expanded CPC would be an added financial burden to the Organization. His delegation would agree to the present number of members remaining unchanged, if the membership were reorganized so as to respect and preserve the principle of equitable geographical representation. There was another consideration: CPC must remain financially viable. The Fifth Committee must be flexible in that respect in order to arrive at reasonable compromise agreements which reconciled the requirements of geographical representation and of the Organization's current financial situation.

The decision on the matter should be taken by the General Assembly before the start of consultations on the new budget process, i.e., before CPC started its consideration of the budget outline at its twenty-eighth session in 1988."

The representative of **Tunisia**[61]

"The transitional character of the budget, resulting from the partial implementation of the recommendations of the Group of 18, meant that it could only reflect the activity of the organization in an incomplete manner. ...

CPC had not been in a position to reach a decision on the overall level of the next budget nor on the creation of the reserve fund. It would be imprudent to accelerate the implementation of the new budgetary process, particularly during a period of transition, as the Advisory Committee itself had observed. ...

It would be wise to adopt the same procedure in connection with the creation of the reserve fund. The fund was calculated on the basis of a percentage of the budget; before setting it up, it would be advisable to wait until the budget incorporated all the reforms of resolution 41/213. The creation of the fund would be all the more premature as neither Member States, nor the Advisory Committee, nor CPC had yet reached agreement on the modalities for its operation or on its funding. There was therefore a need to hold consultations in greater depth in 1989 and at the same time to study the problem of additional costs resulting from currency fluctuations. For the moment, the General Assembly should continue to proceed as it had in previous budgets regarding the financial consequences of draft resolutions adopted after the proposed programme budget had been drawn up. Such a step should not cause any problems because of the integration of continuing activities in the budget.

His delegation welcomed the priority given in the proposed programme budget to two important questions, namely, the economic recovery and development of Africa on the one hand and, on the other hand, the advancement of women. There was however a risk that the systematic implementation of recommendation 15 of the Group of 18, regarding the substantial reduction of Secretariat staff, would seriously impede programme implementation and the normal operations of the Organization. Pursuant to the Advisory Committee's recommendation, efforts must be made to prevent the 15 per cent reduction from being applied uniformly to all departments."

The representative of **New Zealand**[62]

"Continuation and implementation of the reform process set in motion by General Assembly resolution 41/213 must not be made dependent on a solution to the problem posed by any State's withholding of contributions. The need for reform had emerged over a number of years and an interruption of the process would be counter-productive. In an era of rapid change, structural adjustment to ensure the most effective management of finite resources was as vital for the United Nations as it was for any individual Member State. Whatever reforms were eventually adopted should cater for the needs of the future without giving rise to another painful upheaval such as that which had been caused by years of runaway expansion. The Secretary-General's efforts to streamline structures and improve administrative efficiency enjoyed her delegation's full support, and it was to be hoped that the momentum of those efforts would be maintained in accordance with the General Assembly's instructions on programme activities and priorities. Given the great importance of programme review, it was to be hoped that the Special Commission of the Economic and Social Council would produce significant recommendations for the elimination of unproductive, outdated or overlapping activities.

The lack of a clear strategy for the achievement of a 15 per cent staff reduction within three years gave cause for concern. While appreciating the Secretary-General's concerns and believing that it was important not to introduce any fresh constraints on staffing distribution at the current stage, her delegation believed that reductions must be carefully planned and not brought about simply by attrition. Since much information on the subject was dispersed in different parts of the available budget documentation, it was difficult to visualize the shape of staff changes and restructuring currently in progress. ...

The proposed programme budget for the biennium 1988-1989 was transitional in that it had been necessary to make projections without yet knowing the full implications of the reform measures implemented so far. Nevertheless, the preparation of the proposed budget was, as noted by the Advisory Committee, an indispensable step in the transition to the 1990s. In conditions which were exceptional as well as transitional, the small reduction in real budget growth was both realistic and commendable, and it was to be hoped that the coming year's revised estimates would reflect similar restraint. The Advisory Committee's call for some further reductions should be explored. Her delegation also agreed that some of the new budgetary procedures should be incorporated in advance of the biennium for which their full implementation was scheduled.

It was disappointing that the Committee for Programme and Co-ordination (CPC) remained divided over both the overall level of the budget and the establishment of the contingency fund. The problem of additional expenditures derived from legislative mandates needed to be resolved. It was to be hoped that the Assembly would consider it worthwhile gaining technical and procedural experience through the establishment of an interim contingency fund for the biennium 1988-1989 at the experimental level suggested by the Secretary-General, in preparation for full implementation of the fund in the following biennium, and that the Assembly would reach provisional agreement on the fund's basic scope and coverage at its current session. Her delegation looked forward to working with others towards a constructive solution of that problem and hoped that progress would also be made on measures to deal with problems posed by inflation and currency fluctuations."

The representative of **India**[63]

"India agreed with CPC that the recruitment freeze should not become a reason for reducing posts. That would severely damage programmes and distort the geographical distribution of the Secretariat. It was to be hoped that the vacancy management and staff redeployment scheme would forestall such developments. India also hoped that the recruitment freeze would not entail undue cutbacks in the number of staff members from developing countries, particularly in the upper echelons, where they were already underrepresented. It supported the Secretary-General's observation that the 15 per cent staff reduction should not be arbitrarily applied across the board, but rather in the light of each department's particular situation. At a time when the responsibilities of CPC had been enhanced, the geographical distribution of seats in that Committee was still not equitable. As the last review of the membership of CPC had been in 1970 and the United Nations had grown since then, there was a need to increase the number of members to allow for a more balanced geographical distribution.

Past expenditure patterns indicated that the level of the contingency fund should be higher than the 0.75 per cent suggested. Member States should allow the Secretary-General flexibility in deciding the level of the fund, as it would be his only means for meeting unforeseen expenditures over a three-year period. India concurred with the Advisory Committee that the current adjustment system must remain in place, pending further examination by that Committee and CPC. ... India endorsed the suggestion to increase the number of CPC sessions from one to two each year, in line with the Committee's enhanced responsibilities. CPC could recommend an overall level of the budget at its second session, after the question had been examined by the Advisory Committee."

The representative of **Nigeria**[64]

"for the first time the budget was growing "down", and it would be counter-productive for Member States to carry on their discussions as if nothing had changed. Indeed, a lot had changed, and the changes were negatively affecting programmes of vital interest to developing countries. Despite further programme reductions, Nigeria would reluctantly support the Secretary-General's proposals in the interest of attaining broad agreement on the 1988-1989 budget. Such broad acceptance, it was to be hoped, would eliminate the need for withholding assessed contributions. ... Unfortunately, $140 million of the $189 million still in arrears was owed by one Member State. The remaining $49 million, owed mostly by developing countries, was not the sole cause of the United Nations financial problems. Late payment of contributions by those countries reflected economic problems and not a deliberate policy to ignore their legal obligations to the Organization. Therefore, the Member State chiefly responsible for the shortfall should settle its accounts in full. If the Organization was to become more efficient, the Secretary-General could not be denied the resources so vitally needed for reform.

While Nigeria was prepared to accept the Secretary-General's proposals, it was only on the condition that they would not become the basis for determining the levels of future budgets. A permanent commitment to zero or negative growth was not in order at a time when the Secretary-General himself had referred to the increasingly vital role of the United Nations in international affairs. The Organization would be called upon to do more, not less, in the years ahead and hence it would need more resources in the post-transitional period of the 1990s.

The economy measures put into effect in 1986-1987, which had been approved on an exceptional basis, should not influence the structure of the 1988-1989 budget. ...

Despite such praiseworthy innovations as the inclusion in the budget of resources for perennial activities and conference-servicing, the overall budget format remained complex, voluminous and comprehensible to only a few. The Secretary-General should therefore resume the suspended operation of improving the budget format.

The Advisory Committee's recommended adjustments in turnover rates, unobligated balances and unliquidated obligations were understandable. None the less, such adjustments would further reduce an already scaled-down budget and have a negative impact on programmes. The Secretary-General must have sufficient flexibility to implement mandated programmes, and the reductions recommended by the Advisory Committee should be reviewed in the light of any revisions submitted in 1988, and even in 1989. ...

The hasty introduction of the proposed contingency fund would be undesirable. A number of technical problems identified by CPC and the Advisory Committee needed to be addressed before any action was taken in that regard. ...

As matters stood, too much occurring in the name of reform was not brought to Member States' attention. It was the Secretary-General's prerogative to reorganize the Secretariat, but Member States had a right to know how that reorganization would affect the delivery of approved pro-grammes. His delegation was alarmed over developments in the Department of Public Information and believed that no action should create suspicion that the course of reform would be shaped only by those with the power to withhold their financial support."

The representative of the **United States of America**[65]

"the proposed budget for the biennium 1988-1989 which was currently before the Fifth Committee represented an important step forward. While each of the past two biennial budget submissions had called for increases of more than $100 million, the initial estimates of $1.68 billion for the biennium 1988-1989 were approximately $30 million lower than the revised appropriations for 1986-1987. In addition, higher vacancy rates had been used to reflect reductions in staffing and proposals had been made for cuts in spending on official travel and consultants.

Nevertheless, the amounts requested for the coming biennium were substantially higher than expected expenditures for the current biennium, which would amount to some $150 million less than the budgeted level. ...

He regretted that the Committee for Programme and Co-ordination had not been able to assume its new budgetary responsibilities during its September 1987 session, despite having agreed to do so previously. Although the Committee's deliberations had served to identify a number of technical issues which needed to be addressed, they had not produced any recommendation on either the level of the budget or the contingency fund.

Initially, the resources of the contingency fund were to be used to finance all the new programmes and activities approved by the General Assembly during the biennium but not included in the proposed budget. His delegation agreed with ACABQ that the establishment of that type of fund was only one step towards the comprehensive solution to the problem of budget add-ons. He looked forward to receiving the Secretary-General's proposals and ACABQ's recommendations on the issue at the forty-third session.

Concerning the operation of the contingency fund, the United States endorsed the procedures outlined in paragraphs 12 to 14 of ACABQ's report, which met many of the concerns expressed by delegations regarding the options presented by the Secretary-General. No provision had, however, been made for the implementation of paragraph 9 of annex I of resolution 41/213. His delegation also supported the Advisory Committee's recommendation that each statement of programme budget implications and each proposal for revised estimates should contain a specific plan to implement new activities through redeployment rather than additional expenditures. The Secretary-General was already required by paragraph 7 of resolution 38/227 to present such funding options to the General Assembly.

The issue of the level of the contingency fund would probably be the most difficult to resolve. The Secretary-General had recommended a level of approximately $12 million to finance additional programme expenditures during the coming bienniums. That proposal reflected the level of budget add-ons of previous biennium and took into account the revised methodology for determining the biennial budget estimates. The proposal therefore included resources for perennial political activities, additional conference-servicing requirements and construction which in the past had been provided through budget add-ons. Accordingly, the level of the fund proposed by the Secretary-General would provide the General Assembly with sufficient flexibility to finance new programmes during the coming biennium.

During the current session, agreement could be reached on an overall level of resources for the coming biennium exclusive of possible adjustments for changes in currency and inflation rates. His delegation could support an overall level - before recosting at exchange rates prevailing at the end of the session - at or slightly below the level recommended by ACABQ, that would include a contingency fund at the level of resources proposed by the Secretary-General. That level of funding would be sufficient to meet existing programmes and any which might be added later in the biennium. Such a decision would restore confidence in the United Nations by demonstrating the commitment of all Member States and the Secretariat to reform and economize. In adopting that position, account should be taken of the Secretary-General's intention to submit revised budget estimates to the General Assembly at its forty-third session.

In regard to the report of the Secretary-General on the implementation of the reforms (A/42/234), while there had been some progress much remained to be done and those reforms should result in additional savings during the biennium 1988-1989. In that connection, he supported the Advisory Committee's recommendation that the Secretary-General should complete the reviews and studies currently under way in time to submit revised estimates by 1 April 1988. He agreed with the approach taken by the Secretary-General to implement the approved reforms in accordance with paragraph 13 of the progress report. The proposals before the General Assembly should be examined in the light of the Secretary-General's guidance to programme managers.

Furthermore, it should be emphasized that there was a need for additional progress in some areas, particularly in the economic, social and public information sectors; revised estimates reflecting savings anticipated from streamlining those areas should be submitted for review by ACABQ and CPC. Additional proposals, which should take into account the recommendations of the Special Commission, could be submitted during the forty-third session.

He emphasized that resolution 41/213 would prove to be meaningless unless the Secretary-General and the Assembly implemented the kind of real reforms contemplated in that resolution. The United States continued to be vitally concerned with the reform efforts; it would be disastrous for the public perception of the United Nations if the momentum of reform were suddenly to collapse. Failure to proceed with the reforms would be extremely harmful. Conversely, successful implementation of the reforms would demonstrate that the spirit of revitalization existed among Member States."

The representative of the **United States of America**[66] continued

"As everyone knew, the current funding situation was one manifestation of the dissatisfaction felt by a large number of Member States concerning the growth and spending patterns of the United Nations budget. Another manifestation had been the establishment of the Group of 18, whose recommendations for improving the administrative and financial functioning of the Organization provided the means for correcting the situation which had fostered the crisis. The adoption of the Group's recommendations in General Assembly resolution 41/213 had been the turning-point which, in the view of the United States had represented the means for rebuilding the confidence in the Organization required to end what everyone agreed was an untenable situation.

Reflecting the adoption of General Assembly resolution 41/213, the United States budget for the current fiscal year had been amended to request sufficient funds to pay nearly the full regular-budget assessment for 1987. The United States legislative process was long and complex; even at the current stage, the Congress had not yet completed action on the funding request for 1987, and it might not do so until it reconvened in February. However, earlier in the week, conferees from both Houses of the legislature had agreed to authorize the full amount requested by the President for assessed contributions to international organizations, including $193 million for the United Nations. That was not the end of the process, because a separate set of committees had yet to agree on a final appropriation level, which was likely to be below the amount authorized. Full disbursement of authorized amounts would also require a Presidential certification regarding implementation of reforms. The action earlier in the week was a clear signal that the Congress was prepared to resume full funding of the United States share of the regular budget of the United Nations.

The United States was committed to paying its United Nations assessment. He had to state in all candour, however, that the willingness of the Congress to travel further down the path begun would only be affected positively by indications that Member States took seriously the implementation of the new budget process adopted by consensus in 1986. That was a critical point. Progress to date in that area had been less than all might have hoped for. The Committee for Programme and Co-ordination had been unable to come to grips seriously with its new mandate at both its regular and its resumed sessions of 1987, leaving the Fifth Committee with an even greater burden.

Time was short, but the Committee could still complete the tasks begun by CPC before the end of the session. His delegation believed strongly that the adoption of a restrained budget for the biennium 1988-1989, based on the Secretary-General's proposals as amended by the report of ACABQ and including an allowance that would, on an experimental basis, accommodate the additional expenses that would inevitably arise during the remainder of the biennium, would both advance the process begun in 1986 and demonstrate to the world that the United Nations was serious about reform. Such actions were the most practical means of ensuring future financial stability for the Organization.

The United States Administration had taken all possible steps to move towards full payment of its assessment, and had gone to great lengths in a time of extreme domestic fiscal constraint to provide sufficient funding to ensure that the United Nations continued to operate during the current period. The United States could not guarantee that it would resume full payment in the current year; however, it believed that the signs from Washington to which he had alluded, combined with a constructive result at the current session of the General Assembly that demonstrated seriousness of purpose, would lead to the end of the financial crisis. ...

The only way for the United Nations to continue to exist in the long run was to foster a level of confidence on the part of its Member States that would ensure timely payment of assessments on a regular basis. Different countries had different reasons for their inability to pay; at present, almost 60 per cent of Member States had such reasons. He had described his country's reasons and in so doing had indicated its strong interest in returning to a pattern of full payment in order to bring to a close the current difficult period in United Nations financial history. If all countries worked together on that effort in the short term, the Organization would be secure in the long term."

The representative of the **Philippines**[67]

"the General Assembly, in approving resolution 41/213, had sought to shape a more cost-efficient Organization which was nevertheless responsive to the needs of Member States, including the developing countries; it had also sought to meet the concerns of some Member States in order to induce them to reinstate contributions which had been withheld. Although the reform measures had been set in motion, the financial crisis continued unabated. ...

The budget was the essential tool in carrying out the reform process. The proposed programme budget for the biennium 1988-1989 had been formulated in circumstances which were hardly conducive to the preparation of a realistic budget.   Since it had been drawn up prior to the adoption of General Assembly resolution 41/213, the budget could not have reflected the mandated reforms and therefore did not lend itself to critical and in-depth financial analysis, particularly since most of those reforms would take three years to complete. ...

Concerning the overall level of the budget, his delegation welcomed the substantial decrease and the projected negative growth rate of 1.5 per cent. The development must however be viewed as tentative because the reforms were still in progress and vital issues, such as the treatment of inflation, exchange-rate fluctuations, "add-ons" and the contingency fund had not yet been fully resolved.   The contingency fund was an integral part of any well-thought-out budget because it minimized uncertainty in the budget preparation, and increased the overall predictability of financial requirements; its effectiveness, however, would depend on how well its mechanics were formulated so that specifications must be properly drawn from the outset. ...

The Secretary-General had drawn attention to the fact that the economy measures had affected programme implementation adversely.   That was disturbing, especially in the light of the injunction in General Assembly resolution 41/213 that the reform measures, at least those in recommendation 15, should not prejudice implementation of approved projects and programmes. Budget reductions should not be achieved at the expense of programme implementation. To use the level of the budget as the principal yardstick for measuring efficiency in the United Nations would be short-sighted and counter-productive; that approach should therefore be proscribed. It was, in fact, reasonable to expect that future budgets would show a reasonable percentage of increase reflecting implementation of the new activities natural to a dynamic organization.   Instead of simply pruning the budget it was necessary to try to achieve a greater cost-benefit ratio and to define needs and priorities clearly so as to be able to implement priority programmes effectively."

The representative of the **Ukrainian Soviet Socialist Republic**[68]

"despite the short time which had elapsed since the adoption of resolution 41/213, a number of fundamental reforms had already been introduced to improve the structure of the United Nations. ... His country ... supported the economy measures introduced by the Secretary-General to improve the administrative functioning of the Organization. The implementation of economy measures should not, however, jeopardize the fulfilment of the fundamental purposes of the Organization. ...

His delegation had carefully studied the Secretary-General's report on the implementation of resolution 41/213 (document A/42/234 and Corr.1) and supported the steps taken to rationalize the functioning and management of recruitment procedures and to improve personnel services. Any changes to be made in that respect should take into account the interests of Secretariat staff members holding fixed-term appointments and those seconded by their Governments. The adverse impact of the recruitment freeze was a cause of concern and should be mitigated through greater flexibility in dealing with personnel questions. A number of countries continued to be overrepresented, while the proportion of underrepresented countries had increased. It was vital to take practical steps to put an end to that unsatisfactory state of affairs and to comply with the principle of equitable geographical distribution provided for in the Charter of the United Nations."

The representative of **Venezuela**[69]

"he understood and accepted the reasons for proposing a transitional programme budget. However, the possible repercussion of reform on the Organization's programmes troubled him. Reform measures must not be confused with economy measures. The latter were temporary restrictions intended to meet the financial crisis and presupposed that part of the allocated resources would not be available at the time they were needed. Reform, on the other hand, presupposed only that a greater rationalization of activities was possible. That was the case for the staff reductions, an organizational measure that must be applied so as not to affect the quality and quantity of the work done and so as to maintain geographical representation. The recruitment freeze, on the other hand, was a step taken in response to the crisis and must not be prolonged indefinitely because it would have a serious negative impact...

It was commendable that the overall level of the proposed programme budget for the biennium 1988-1989 was lower than for the biennium that was drawing to a close. The reduction of the overall level, however, should not establish a precedent. Because of its magnitude, the reduction would have to be reviewed in greater detail in order to assess its repercussions on programmes and activities.

His delegation endorsed the priority given in the budget proposals to the economic recovery and development of Africa and to the advancement of women. It believed, however, that it was not entirely clear what effect the setting of such priorities would have in practice. It therefore thought that Member States should in the future have a greater hand in setting priorities both in the General Assembly and in CPC, whose membership should be extended to make it more representative of the diversity of interests within the United Nations.

With regard to the contingency fund, the procedures for its functioning should be more clearly specified before it was put into operation. The fund must, in particular, adhere strictly to its terms and, given its character as a fund for covering contingencies, the level of its resources should not be established as a fixed percentage of the budget and still less as a fixed sum. Moreover, its operation should be flexible enough to allow its adjustment to needs arising from General Assembly decisions and other factors. It would be useful to have a clearer idea of how the question of additional expenditures would be handled, such as those resulting from inflation and currency fluctuations."

The representative of **Chile**[70]

"It was clear that the crisis was creating uncertainty for the staff and was having an impact on the quality of the staff's work. Many officials, precisely those who were most highly qualified, were leaving the Organization. That was extremely serious and it was happening because the reforms were being implemented in an atmosphere of pressure and threats, which was adversely affecting the functioning of the Organization."

The representative of **Peru**[71]

"His delegation agreed with the views expressed by many delegations concerning the origin of the financial crisis and the inescapable responsibility in that regard of the major contributor. That unilateral action could not be linked in any way to the action of a large number of Member States which, because of the unfavourable international economic climate, were unable to meet their financial obligations towards the Organization as promptly as they should. The former was the result of political interests which were attacking the very essence of multilateralism and sovereign equality of States; the latter was a physical inability which was becoming increasingly difficult to overcome.

...

Another aspect of the reform concerned the planning, programming, and budgeting process. Given the importance of the new functions entrusted to CPC, the need to ensure the legitimacy of that organ by ensuring fair and full representation of all Member States and the need to ensure the efficiency of its work, it was to be hoped that the Assembly would be able to adopt a decision on the matter at the current session so that, when CPC took over its new functions fully the following year, it would reflect the essentially democratic nature of the Organization."

The representative of **Argentina**[72]

"If CPC was to discharge all its tasks as envisaged, it must continue to have the support of Member States as it had in the past. His delegation joined those delegations that had pointed to the need for the composition of the Committee to be more equitable geographically.

Despite the progress made by CPC and the Advisory Committee in determining the functioning of the contingency fund, various questions remained unresolved. The concept of the contingency fund had not yet been sufficiently developed, and it appeared that the time had not yet come to include it in a transitional proposed programme budget such as the one under consideration. To do so might distort the fund's experimental nature, and the results obtained with it might not be as useful as it was hoped they would be."

The representative of **Bulgaria**[73]

"The Advisory Committee's recommendations in document A/42/640 constituted a sound basis for resolving the intricate question of the contingency fund. In that connection, he shared the Advisory Committee's view that a set of procedures for the fund should be in place before it went into operation. The budget proposals should indicate how programmes of lowest priority could be modified, reduced or deferred, if necessary. That was the procedure followed for statements of programme budget implications and revised estimates. In the event of additional requirements exceeding the contingency fund, that procedure would make it possible to scale down or defer not only programmes and activities proposed by the Main Committees, but also programmes and activities of the lowest priority appearing in the initial budget proposals.

He shared the view of the Chairman of the Advisory Committee that there was an urgent need to solve the problem of additional expenditures arising from inflation and currency fluctuations. The Secretary-General's proposals for the establishment of a special reserve and budgeting in several currencies were worth considering. Any such reserve, however, once established, must not turn into another device for raising the assessments of Member States. The reserve must be kept level and in overall balance by offsetting increases in expenditures due to inflation and currency fluctuations in some years, against decreases in other years. If increases in expenditure over certain periods were much larger than decreases, economy measures should be introduced, and the reserve could be replenished with the savings realized. As the Soviet delegation had suggested, interest earned on United Nations assets and voluntary contributions by certain States could also be credited to the reserve. The establishment of a system which encouraged prompt payment of assessed contributions, thereby reducing losses due to inflation, would also help to maintain the reserve balance."

The representative of **Senegal**[74]

"In adopting resolution 41/213, Member States had given proof of their deep attachment to the United Nations as an irreplaceable tool of international co-operation. It was heartening to note that, in the proposed programme budget for the biennium 1988-1989, the Secretary-General had applied the principles of that resolution and proposed a reduction of 1.8 per cent, reflecting its policy of austerity and reform. His delegation supported the Secretary-General's budget proposals in so far as they corresponded to the new administrative and financial procedures decided upon by the Organization. Nevertheless, it considered that such austerity must not be allowed to impede efforts to achieve the Organization's noble objectives of development and peace. In order to end the Organization's permanent situation of financial instability, Member States must fulfil unconditionally their obligations under the Charter."

The representative of **Uruguay**[75]

"the review of the efficiency of the administrative and financial functioning of the United Nations and the Organization's current financial crisis had given rise to contradictions, since the crisis had made it necessary to take steps that were contrary to the very principles of efficiency and sound management on which the reform process outlined in General Assembly resolution 41/213 was based. Those transitional measures must not be allowed to set a precedent and should not be taken into account in future budget proposals and medium-term plans. ...

The expansion of the functions of the Committee for Programme and Co-ordination (CPC) provided for in Assembly resolution 41/213 would require an increase in the Committee's membership in accordance with the principle of equitable geographical distribution. The role of CPC in setting priorities would also need to be expanded, since it was in that body that the consultation process, subsequently completed with the participation of the Fifth Committee, was begun."

The representative of **Fiji**[76]

"Continuing to withhold payment of staff salaries and allowances would have deleterious repercussions on the operations of the Organization and an unregulated freeze on recruitment would seriously affect the delivery of programmes. Although his delegation had in the past criticized the high levels of remuneration, allowances and pensions in the Organization, and would do so again if circumstances so required, it currently took the view that in order to restore staff morale and ensure their efficient operation, they must be given their just and rightful reward, within the prescribed parameters. In the final analysis, it was the commitment of the staff to their duties that determined the success of the Organization's programme.

There were many other areas where economies could be effected, such as in the volume of documentation. The agenda of the General Assembly might also be seriously examined to see if the number of items could not be halved without any adverse effect.

His delegation considered that the Secretary-General had done a commendable job in reducing the proposed programme budget by 1.5 per cent in real terms compared with the revised budget for the current biennium. But it reiterated that greater economies could be achieved if rationalization measures were adopted in the areas mentioned previously. In addition, the Secretary-General's task would be much easier if he received more co-operation from Member States, *inter alia*, through a reduction in the number of resolutions adopted by the General Assembly.

... his delegation took the view that the proposed programme budget could have provided more guidance about its future direction. For example, there seemed to be no clear linkage between the budget and the reform process. His delegation hoped that the Administration would be able to provide a better and clearer picture in the near future."

The representative of the **German Democratic Republic**[77]

"The levels of savings proposed for individual budget sections differed enormously, and his delegation therefore supported the recommendation of the Committee for Programme and Co-ordination (CPC) that all programme elements should be subject to a survey of priorities. It fully endorsed the priority treatment of economic recovery and development in Africa and was also pleased to note an improvement in the position of women in the Secretariat. However, the latter question should not divert attention from such vital questions as the preservation of world peace, comprehensive international security and peaceful co-operation in the political, economic, ecological, social and humanitarian fields.

The various sections of the proposed budget appeared to imply that United Nations travel costs had been reduced only by about 15 per cent. A further reduction was required, as well as an effort to ensure the relevance of all programme activities. Costs for consultants should be reduced yet further, particularly through the recruitment of highly qualified staff on fixed-term contracts. The proposals submitted by the Secretary-General provided a good basis for further discussion of that subject.

It was regrettable that most of the savings so far had been achieved through the continuation of the recruitment freeze. If the freeze were to be lifted and vacancies filled with staff employed on fixed-term contracts, equitable geographical distribution would be enhanced and the work of the Organization would be enriched by new blood."

The representative of **Austria**[78]

"the process of reform should not promote short-term over long-term interests. Temporary assistance, for example, was not necessarily less expensive than the provision of a minimum level of permanent staff. The recruitment freeze should not impede the orderly management and implementation of programmes, particularly in the case of certain regional commissions affected by extremely high vacancy rates. ...

It was unfortunate that CPC had been unable to make recommendations concerning the establishment of a contingency fund. A simple set of procedures should be in place when the fund came into operation, and her delegation welcomed the Advisory Committee's intention to address the problem of additional expenditures. Disagreement on such problems would be detrimental to the Organization, and it might be useful for the Advisory Committee to draw on the relevant experience of some specialized agencies in its search for alternative solutions. Her delegation was willing to discuss the establishment of a contingency fund for the biennium 1988-1989 on an experimental basis, without prejudice to the future, and to negotiate matters such as the scope, period covered and procedures for the fund, since it was convinced that a consensus on those issues remained essential."

The representative of **Mexico**[79]

"Experience had shown that hasty action was unlikely to yield the desired result, and some of the ambiguities in General Assembly resolution 41/213 might have been eliminated if more time had been provided for negotiations. With respect to the establishment of a contingency fund, resolution 41/213 clearly stated that the outline of the programme budget submitted in off-budget years should contain an indication of the size of the fund. No mandate existed for the establishment of an experimental fund, nor did it appear appropriate to introduce such a fund during a transitional budget period. Problems relating to the fund should be solved on the basis of the Advisory Committee's suggestions before it was actually established, rather than allowing the Organization's reform process to degenerate into a constant pattern of "trial and error".

His delegation agreed with the view ... that the budget process approved in resolution 41/213 was designed to produce a more focused discussion of programme budget priorities, rather than to be an exercise in reductions, and that intergovernmental bodies should participate in the new process to an even greater extent. ...

For the time being, it wished to express its support for the Advisory Committee's view that it was impossible at the present stage to set an overall figure for the revised estimates for the 1988-1989 proposed programme budget, its agreement with the view of certain delegations that the proposed budget could not set the pattern for future budgets, and its concern that the implementation of certain recommendations of the Group of High-level Intergovernmental Experts were having an adverse effect on programmes, particularly with respect to the activities of regional commissions. ...

While it was important to achieve the broadest possible agreement among Member States on the outline programme budget, the current geographical distribution of seats in CPC needed to be modified if such agreement were to be reached. In view of the need for Member States to participate in the budgetary preparation from its early stages and throughout the process, the Committee's membership should also be expanded prior to its twenty-eighth session, and its timetable of activities revised."

The representative of **Poland**[80]

"the decrease in the overall level of resources requested for the forthcoming biennium might well be a turning-point. For many years, Poland had advocated a lower, stabilized rate of growth in the budget, which would not necessarily have decreased efficiency and programme delivery. ... If the Secretariat became more efficient and productive, the cuts would not adversely affect programmes. ...

His delegation agreed with the Advisory Committee that a contingency fund would be only one step towards a comprehensive solution to the problem of add-ons. At the forty-third session of the General Assembly, the Secretary-

General should submit proposals for incorporating such additional costs - including those resulting from inflation and currency fluctuations - into the overall level of resources for the biennium. His delegation had noted with interest that the Advisory Committee intended to undertake an in-depth study of the question."

The representative of **Algeria**[81]

"Negative growth in the budget was being proposed at a time when the Organization was being called upon to play a wider role in resolving conflicts and dealing with an ailing world economy. Since the proposed programme budget had been drafted at a time of crisis, and, hence, of transition, it should not serve as a precedent for the 1990-1991 outline.

His delegation agreed with the Advisory Committee that pending a comprehensive examination of the technical issues relating to the operation of the proposed contingency fund, it was premature to include any provision for such a fund in the 1988-1989 programme budget. It was regrettable that CPC had been unable to deal with those technical issues. ...

His delegation questioned the reconsideration of estimates for construction projects at the Economic Commission for Africa (ECA) and the Economic and Social Commission for Asia and the Pacific (ESCAP). The General Assembly had approved those projects three years earlier, and at a time when reform and renewal were the order of the day, it was not particularly appropriate for it to reverse its decision on two projects which exemplified the trend towards universality and decentralization. The ECA and ESCAP construction projects had been delayed for too long. As a result, the Organization would incur even greater expenditures and lose credibility. For those reasons, the projects must be completed as early as possible."

The representative of **Pakistan**[82]

"He emphasized ... that the negative growth in the proposed programme budget should be considered an exception, made in response to particular conditions, and should not form the basis of future budget proposals. Once the reforms had been carried out, positive growth in the budget would demonstrate the Organization's vitality and enhanced role in international affairs.

An important reform in the budgetary process was the establishment of a contingency fund, as called for in resolution 41/213. ... On the question of expenditure over and above appropriations, his delegation agreed with the Advisory Committee that the current procedure for authorization should continue, to apply pending further examination of the question by the Advisory Committee and CPC.

Resolution 41/213 emphasized that the reform measures should not have an adverse effect on programmes. His delegation was concerned that had not been the case. Levels of programming must be maintained unless the General Assembly decided otherwise. In the mean time, his delegation would like to receive information on the programmes affected by the economy measures and how the reforms, as they progressed, led to reductions in the budget.

He was concerned at the continued recruitment freeze which, he hoped, would not be used as means of bringing about the mandated reduction in Secretariat posts. Such a move would not only damage programmes but distort the geographical distribution of posts in the Secretariat. Measures such as the vacancy management scheme and the staff redeployment scheme should serve to minimize the effect of the freeze.

The Secretary-General had begun changes in important Secretariat departments without awaiting the results of the in-depth study of the United Nations intergovernmental structure and functions in the economic and social fields. His delegation maintained, nevertheless, that the final shape of the Secretariat in the economic and social fields should be determined only after the Economic and Social Council's Special Commission had completed its study."

The representative of **Saudi Arabia**[83]

"The proposed programme budget for the biennium 1988-1989 showed a reduction of $30 million from the appropriations for the current biennium, or a decrease of 1.5 per cent in real terms. Unfortunately, that had been achieved through a decrease in programme activities. His delegation urged that reform should be carried out in such a way as to avoid further adverse effects on important programmes with special political and economic significance, such as Palestine, southern Africa, Namibia and decolonization. ...

In carrying out the 15 per cent reduction in posts, account must be taken of the relative importance and requirements of each organizational unit. It might be necessary for some units to be reduced by more than that figure, and others by less. Some, such as interpretation services, should be exempted from the reduction, for evident reasons. The current financial crisis had forced the Secretary-General to impose a recruitment freeze. His delegation agreed with the Committee for Programme and Co-ordination (CPC) that the freeze should not be an instrument solely for reducing posts. The effects of the freeze should be closely monitored with a view to rectifying the unfair distribution of posts.

The contingency fund, the establishment of which had been approved by the General Assembly at the preceding session, should provide a greater degree of stability in the Secretary-General's initial budget estimates by accommodating add-ons and revised estimates without raising the overall level of resources required. There was merit in the proposal to establish a prototype of such a fund for the biennium 1988-1989, with full operation starting during the biennium 1990-1991. It would be helpful to have an assessment of the operation of the provisional fund before taking a final decision on the size of the contingency fund."

The representative of **Cuba**[84]

"While ... one part of the political agreement represented by resolution 41/213, the reform process, was already under way, the other part, the abandonment of withholdings on political grounds, had not yet been put into practice. His delegation believed that the reform process could proceed against the background of implicit blackmail created by the financial crisis. Those who asserted that the reform process ought not to be influenced by the financial crisis were utterly mistaken, and would make a more positive contribution if they used their good offices to convince the principal contributor to end the current state of financial uncertainty.

The tendency to apply some recommendations of the Group of 18 selectively, partially or subject to unilateral interpretations was disturbing. His delegation called on intergovernmental bodies and the Secretariat to ensure that the recommendations were carried out in a complete and balanced manner.

He agreed with the Advisory Committee's recommendation that the contingency fund should not yet go into operation. The size of the fund must be suggested by the Secretary-General in the outline he submitted in 1988 of the proposed programme budget for the biennium 1990-1991."

The representative of **Kenya**[85]

"His delegation hoped that one result of the full application of the measures contained in resolution 41/213 would be increased efficiency and cost-effectiveness, but could not accept the increasingly widespread notion that efficiency and cost-effectiveness were synonymous with cuts in United Nations activities or with arbitrary limits on the resources made available to the Secretary-General for carrying out approved programmes. Nor could the refusal by one Member State to pay its assessed contribution, or the failure of many others to pay their contributions in time, be used as a pretext for wholesale unwarranted condemnation of the United Nations. ...

One of the units which had reached an advanced stage of reorganization pursuant to resolution 41/213 was the Department of Public Information which was to be restructured so as to reduce its staff and make it more efficient. Before his delegation could endorse the new structure of the Department, it would like to be assured that mandated programmes, such as the anti-*apartheid* radio programme, would be continued without jeopardizing their unique and intrinsic character. It also sought assurances that the Section to which the former Division of Economic and Social Information was to be reduced would be able to do a better job than the former Division: if so, how?"

The representative of **Norway**[86]

"His delegation expressed appreciation of the efforts made by the Secretary-General and his staff to carry out the reform process. However, much remained to be done. It was particularly important to establish, as soon as possible, a clear, coherent and transparent personnel policy. He also urged the administration to complete the post-by-post review within the next month in order to ensure the rational use of personnel resources.

With respect to the responsibilities of Member States as established in resolution 41/213, his delegation regretted that at its latest session CPC had been unable to reach agreement on some important matters concerning the new budget procedure, and sincerely hoped that the problems would be solved in the near future."

The representative of **Finland**[87]

"The General Assembly must urgently address long-term solutions to the Organization's financial problems, solutions which promised a more predictable flow of resources and a more stable foundation for the United Nations. General Assembly resolution 41/213 must continue to be implemented, for it was an important element of any long-term solution. However, assessments must also be addressed as part of a long-term solution to the Organization's difficulties. The time had come to agree on a revised scale which would leave the United Nations less vulnerable to the failure of a few to pay their full assessed contributions."

The representative of the **Libyan Arab Jamahiriya**[88]

"Despite the generally held belief that all parties had accepted the package deal embodied in General Assembly resolution 41/213, an attempt was now being made to apply the recommendations of the Group of 18 in a partial and selective manner. However, if certain States chose, for political reasons, not to meet the financial obligations imposed on them by the Charter, the reform process would inevitably be affected. That process was intended to strengthen the Organization, and the withholding of contributions could only cause further instability and place the very existence of the United Nations in jeopardy. The current financial crisis was primarily political in nature since it resulted from a deliberate attempt to impose certain policies on the United Nations."

The representative of **Malaysia**[89]

"The reforms set forth in General Assembly resolution 41/213 could only enhance the effectiveness of the United Nations. However, their implementation must continue to be based on the principle of sovereign equality among States. No single country could seek to impose changes without the agreement of other Member States or through the unilateral enactment of laws. Such actions could only be detrimental to the Organization."

Before the resolutions on the implementation of the reform process (i.e. the implementation of resolution 41/213) and the 1988-1989 programme budget could be adopted, the controversy over the funding of the construction projects (paragraph 10 (a) of the draft resolution) needed to be resolved. The **Controller**[90] gave the following interpretation:

"paragraph 10 (a) would take it to mean that the Secretary-General was instructed to proceed with the necessary work within the funds available in the construction-in-progress account so as to be in a position to return to the Advisory Committee and the General Assembly in due course with the technical and financial information required to substantiate further resource allocations for both projects already approved by the Assembly".

A legal opinion on paragraph 10 (a), obtained from the **Office of Legal Affairs**[91], reads as follows:

"Sub-paragraph 10 (a) provides guidelines to the Secretary-General with a view to implementing plans for the construction of the United Nations facilities. It states that the General Assembly had before it recommendation 5 of the Group of 18 and that it also considered the report of the Secretary-General (A/C.5/42/4) containing his views on the question.

After considering this document, the Assembly invited the Secretary-General to undertake, as requested, the implementation of two drafts approved in paragraph 1 (a) of section I of resolution 41/213, it being understood that no additional credit would be requested in this connection for the biennium 1988-1989. In other words, the expression 'take note' in paragraph 10 (a) has the usual meaning in this context, bearing in mind its goals and objectives, as is true of any term or expression used in a legislative instrument. The interpretation turns initially on the formulation used; then, if here remain uncertainties, the circumstances in which the text was drafted; and, in the final analysis, of course, on the intentions of the organ adopting an instrument. In the present case, 'take note' means that the General Assembly has read the report of the Secretary-General and has studied it without either approving or disapproving it.

In short, the interpretation is the following. The Secretary-General has received instructions to undertake necessary work within the limits of funds available in the construction account in order, in timely-fashion, to give the Advisory Committee on Administrative and Budgetary Questions and the General Assembly the technical and financial information needed to justify a new allocation of resources under the two drafts already approved by the General Assembly."

After having obtained the legal opinion, the **Chairman of the Fifth Committee**[92] noted that

"he was in a position to state that paragraph 10 (a) provided guidelines for the Secretary-General for proceeding with the construction of United Nations conference facilities. Those guidelines stated that the General Assembly had before it recommendation 5 of the Group of High-level Intergovernmental Experts and had also had before it and read the Secretary-General's report A/C.5/42/4 giving his views on the matter. The Assembly, after reading those documents, was inviting the Secretary-General to proceed as requested on the two projects it had approved in resolution 41/213, section I, paragraph 1 (a), with the added provision that no additional appropriation would be required in that regard for the biennium 1988-1989.

The meaning of the words "takes note" in paragraph 10 (a) of the draft resolution was to be determined in the light of their ordinary meaning in such a context, and their object and purpose. As was the case with all legal instruments, the interpretation of any term depended initially on the wording and, if any uncertainty persisted, on the circumstances of the drafting of the text and ultimately, of course, on the intention of the body adopting the instrument. In the case of the draft resolution in question, the words "takes note" meant that the General Assembly had read the Secretary-General's report and taken cognizance of it, without expressing either approval or disapproval. The interpretation of the paragraph, in short, would be the one just formulated by the Controller."

Following these statements, the Chairman of the Fifth Committee submitted a draft resolution drawn up on the basis of informal consultations. The draft A/C.5/42/L.23 was approved by consensus in the Fifth Committee and subsequently in the Plenary Assembly as resolution entitled **Implementation of General Assembly Resolution 41/213 (42/211)**[*]. By resolution 42/211, the GA stressed that, in order to carry out successfully the process of reform and restructuring, it was essential that the present financial uncertainties were dispelled; it reiterated that implementation of resolution 41/213 must not have an adverse effect on mandated activities and programmes; stressed the importance of the timely and successful completion of the in-depth study of the intergovernmental structure and functions in the economic and social fields being undertaken by ECOSOC; stressed the importance of the revised estimates for the biennium 1988-1989 that the Secretary-General would submit to the GA at its 43rd session; noted that the Secretary-General's implementation of certain recommendations of the Group of 18 adopted by the GA in its resolution 41/213 was not in accordance with the decisions of the Assembly; approved the guidelines for the contingency fund as annexed to the present resolution; decided to consider at the 43rd session the question of a comprehensive solution to the problem of all additional expenditures, including those deriving from inflation and currency fluctuations, on the basis of the reports to be submitted by the CPC and ACABQ; and also decided that the date for the submission of the outline of the programme budget should be 15 August of the off-budget year.

Following the approval of the draft resolution by the Fifth Committee, the representative of Denmark, speaking on behalf of the 12 member states of the **European Community**[93] in explanation of their position noted that:

"they welcomed the fact that it had been possible to reach a consensus, since the implementation of General Assembly resolution 41/213 was always likely to be as controversial as the initial agreement on the resolution itself had been. However, while opinions in the Committee might differ on the quality of such implementation so far, the Twelve would have welcomed some recognition in the draft resolution of the efforts by the Secretary-General and his staff to proceed with the reform process, particularly in the current difficult financial circumstances. They wished formally to express their own recognition of those efforts and to encourage their continuance."

The Fifth Committee then proceeded to approve the draft resolution on the programme budget for 1988-1989. The net expenditure for the biennium 1988-1989 was estimated at $1,703,276,000. This amount reflected the budget as proposed by the Secretary-General, reductions as recommended by ACABQ,

---

[*]See volume II, 1.5.

a small number of add-ons resulting from newly mandated activities and a recosting taking into account the most up-to-date exchange rate and inflation figures. The following statements were made before the vote was taken.

The representative of **Italy**[94]

"while some attempt had been made to implement the reforms outlined in resolution 41/213, much remained to be done to restore confidence in the United Nations by enhancing the effectiveness of its machinery, reducing its complexity and rationalizing its methods of work. The proposed programme budget had been formulated before the adoption of resolution 41/213.

... his delegation had seen no convincing evidence of reform of the Organization's machinery, as intended by the Group of High-level Intergovernmental Experts to Review the Efficiency of the Administrative and Financial Functioning of the United Nations and as called for in General Assembly resolution 41/213.

He trusted that it might yet prove possible to adopt the proposed programme budget by consensus. If a vote proved necessary on the budget appropriations for the biennium 1988-1989, however, Italy had reservations concerning the need for further efforts to absorb expenditures and the need for further cost-cutting and rationalization of budgetary procedures in accordance with resolution 41/213. He hoped that the revised budget presented by the Secretary-General in April 1988 would show evidence of progress in those areas. Now that the Committee had taken a decision on the contingency fund, his delegation would be able to vote in favour of the appropriations. In the rationalization of the number of regular budget posts, account should be taken of the fact that Italy was grossly underrepresented in the Secretariat.

There was no doubt that the Organization faced a structural crisis which could not be remedied by occasional contributions or changes in the scale of assessments. Delegations must face up to the necessary changes in management and budgetary structures at the United Nations and in the specialized agencies so as to promote the revitalization of the United Nations system."

The representative of **France**[95]

"the Committee was being asked to take a decision on what was a transitional budget, it being the first budget to follow the adoption of resolution 41/213. Since approval of the appropriations would provide impetus to the Organization, his delegation would vote in favour of them.

The fact that the proposed programme budget showed a decrease in real terms over the previous biennium was evidence of the efforts to promote rationalization, as was the constructive decision just taken by the Committee on the contingency fund. It was his hope that, at the forty-third session the Committee would be able to take a decision on the contingency fund that allowed for full implementation of the new budgetary procedures. ...

The $139,491.3 million difference in the estimates attributable to changes in rates of exchange and inflation could not have been foreseen by the Secretariat, but any further cost increases should be absorbed in accordance with resolution 41/213."

The representative of **Japan**[96]

"his delegation was anxious to keep in check the overall level of appropriations for the biennium and to ensure that the budget reflected the aims set forth in resolution 41/213. Regrettably, CPC had failed to establish clear guidelines for the overall level of resources or for the contingency fund. The decision to consider the question of the contingency fund in the context of the second year of the biennium was unfortunate and agreement on that question must be reached in the early part of the forty-third session. His delegation also regretted the decision to make 15 August of the off-budget year the deadline for submitting the outline of the programme budget. Setting a date so close to the beginning of the session of the General Assembly would not facilitate the attainment of consensus within CPC.

His delegation was perturbed at the revised estimates submitted on the basis of changes in rates of exchange and inflation. It was clear from General Assembly resolution 41/213, annex I, paragraph 11, that the Secretary-General should make efforts to absorb the additional costs resulting from currency fluctuations and inflation. Accordingly, his delegation would have to reserve its position on the proposed programme budget until it had an opportunity to assess the revised estimates to be submitted in 1988."

The representative of **Cameroon**[97]

"Member States should, in the interests of the Organization, support the initiatives taken by the Secretary-General to promote reform. In particular, caution should be exercised in what was a transitional phase in so far as the budget was concerned. His delegation, like those of other third world countries, supported the proposed appropriations."

Following these statements, the Fifth Committee approved and the Plenary Assembly adopted the resolution entitled **Programme Budget for the Biennium 1988-1989 (42/226)**. By resolution 42/226, the GA approved net expenditure of $1,703,276,000 for the biennium 1988-1989. The draft resolution had been put to a vote and adopted with 3 abstentions (Australia, Japan, USA) and one vote against (Israel). Although not approved by consensus, this result was a big improvement compared to the many votes against previous budgets, in particular by the major donors. It was also seen as an indication that the overwhelming majority of the GA were in favour of the reform process.

3.6.2 Endorsement of ECOSOC Resolution 1987/94 on Broad Representation in CPC (42/450)

Under agenda item 12 (Report of ECOSOC), the Plenary Assembly considered the ECOSOC recommendation to increase in the membership of CPC from 21 to 34 states (1987/94)*. Before the GA voted on the recommendation, the following statements were made.

The representative of the **United States of America**[98]

"My delegation objects to the proposal to expand the membership of the Committee for Programme and Co-ordination, and we have four major reasons for voting against it.

As a supporter of independence for Non-Self-Governing Territories since before the drafting of the Charter, the United States has welcomed the near universality of the United Nations and the consequent need for widespread geographical representation in its committees and commissions, but while history allows no doubt on this point my delegation also supports the well-established practice of considering additional factors in determining the composition of some subsidiary United Nations bodies.

Due regard to equitable geographical distribution has not meant disregard for the size of Member States's economies in determining the scale of assessments, nor has it meant disregard for the size of their populations in allocating Secretariat posts. Similarly, the composition of several administrative and budgetary bodies throughout the United Nations system reflects the contributions factor as well as geographical equity. This time-honoured practice of giving due regard to such other factors has been a key concept producing widespread agreement on administrative and budgetary matters.

Although my delegation made it clear in the consultations that it would have accepted some expansion and adjustment in the membership of the Committee for Programme and Co-ordination to reflect changing circumstances, we believe that the proposal before us represents too radical a deviation from well-established practice.

---

*See section 3.5 above.

Secondly, the United States delegation views this change in the Committee's membership as an unwarranted departure from the consensus underlying General Assembly resolution 41/213. That resolution gave the Committee the task of determining the amount of the overall level of the budget. One of the reasons for lodging that responsibility in the Committee was its small but representative size and composition, which were expected to facilitate the give and take needed to work through the complicated issues involved. This proposal changes an important factor of that agreement. My delegation accepts the idea that experience will show where we need to build on the provisions of resolution 41/213, but we believe that the spirit of that resolution will best be maintained if such departures are arrived at by consensus. Otherwise, the Assembly runs the risk of invoking that resolution as a delicately balanced package not to be tampered with and then turning around and running roughshod over that consensus.

Thirdly, the central problem with the Committee has been its inability to take up its now mandate and complete its work on time. In 1987 the Committee not only had to hold a resumed session, but repeatedly found it necessary to extend that session. This proposal will not improve that situation. We do not believe that the problem has been an unrepresentative membership, as there is no group or point of view that has not been represented at sessions of the Committee for Programme and Co-ordination - sessions, it should be noted, where consensus is the rule. Nor is there any way to conclude that expanded membership will speed up the Committee's work.

My delegation certainly agrees that the Committee needs to be strengthened, but, as a matter of strongly held principle, we reject the view that strengthening a body means expanding its membership.

Finally, my delegation joins with those who question the additional costs for the Committee entailed in the proposal. We do not believe that the Committee is entitled to an exception to pay for travel and subsistence. If, however, this practice is continued in 1988-1989, we believe that the additional costs can be absorbed within existing resources. Many statements at this session have referred to the ongoing review of the intergovernmental economic and social machinery, as part of which the Fifth Committee will be making recommendations regarding the Committee's role.

De facto, then, this decision to expand the Committee is an element of the economic and social restructuring plan to be completed next year. The review should result in substantial savings to the organization, even though its primary aim is streamlining intergovernmental machinery. Since the 1988-89 proposed programme budget does not reflect those anticipated savings, we believe that there is sufficient flexibility in the budget to absorb the additional costs resulting from the recommendation of the Economic and Social Council.

In summary, the United States delegation has called for a recorded vote and intends to oppose the proposal, since it represents a departure from the well-established practice and from the consensus spirit of resolution 41/213. It will not facilitate consensus-based budgeting in the Committee for Programme and Co-ordination and it entails questionable costs that should be absorbed."

The representative of Mozambique, speaking on behalf of the **Group of African States**[99]

"I wish to make it clear that our acceptance of the four additional seats out of the new 13 in no way signifies that the African group accepts being underrepresented, as it is in the whole United Nations family. We are not happy at remaining on the threshold of this family house. We have accepted the four seats as a gesture of goodwill, and hope that others will not only understand us in this light but extend the hand of co-operation when the need arises in the future. We shall continue to fight for our fair share of regional representation in the whole United Nations system. Therefore, we do not consider that our acceptance of four additional seats on the Committee for Programme and Co-ordination constitutes a precedent for the Committee itself, or any other organ or body of the United Nations."

The representative of **Bolivia**[100]

"The delegation ... wishes it to be clearly understood that the whole exercise that began last year with the changes in various mechanisms, including the Committee for Programme and Co-ordination, presupposed the need to have a balanced Committee. All the efforts made were aimed at not merely its enlargement, but an enlargement permitting a redistribution taking into account the importance of the regions of the third world, which since independence in the 1960s have not been adequately represented in the United Nations system.

Consequently, the sponsors demonstrated the maximum flexibility to try to achieve harmony and agreement in a spirit of consensus. Unfortunately, although we could count on the consensus of all the regional groups, that was not possible in the Council, because one country called for a recorded vote. Nevertheless, it is clear to all Member States that although the formula accepted is still not in accordance with strict geographical representation, it is part of a process that should prompt consideration within the United Nations on how the nations of Africa, Asia and Latin America, through their regional groups, may participate with their correct proportional representation within the system, while allowing the correct representation of the countries of Western and Eastern Europe."

Following these statements, and based on the recommendations of ECOSOC, the Plenary Assembly approved the resolution entitled **Broad Representation in the Committee for Programme and Co-ordination (42/450)**. The resolution had been put to a vote and supported by 152 votes to one, with the USA voting against. By resolution 42/450, the GA approved the increase in the membership of CPC from 21 to 34 states.

3.6.3 Consideration of ECOSOC Resolution 1987/64 on the In-depth Study of the UN Inter-governmental Structure and Functions in the Economic and Social Fields (42/431)

Under agenda item 12 (Report of ECOSOC), the Second and Third Committees considered the reform in the economic and social fields in accordance with ECOSOC resolution 1987/64*.

On behalf of the Group of 77 the representative of Guatemala submitted to the Second Committee the following draft resolution entitled **Implementation of General Assembly Resolution 41/213 in the Economic and Social Fields (A/C.2/42/L.39)**:

"*The General Assembly,*

Recalling its resolution 32/197 of 20 December 1977 on the restructuring of the economic and social sectors of the United Nations system and 41/213 of 19 December 1986 on the review of the efficiency of the administrative and financial functioning of the United Nations, both of which are elements of a common process,

Recalling also Economic and Social Council decision 1987/180 of 8 July 1987 on enhancing the co-ordination of activities of the organizations of the United Nations system,

1.   *Affirms* that resolution 41/213 should be implemented at the intergovernmental and secretariat levels in a timely, orderly, integrated and well-co-ordinated manner, taking strictly into account the interests of the developing countries and the need to ensure that the development-oriented programmes and activities of the United Nations are not jeopardized;

---

*See section 3.3 above.

2. *Considers* that resolution 41/213 should be implemented in the economic and social fields, taking into account the fact that the in-depth study of the United Nations intergovernmental structure and functions in the economic and social fields, as called for in section I, paragraph 1 (e), of that resolution is under way;

3. *Affirms* that provisional measures taken in the course of the implementation of 41/213 in the economic and social fields, should be reviewed or adjusted in accordance with the decisions taken on the matter by the General Assembly."

Following informal consultations on draft resolution A/C.2/42/L.39, the Vice-Chairman of the Second Committee submitted draft resolution A/C.2/42/L.89. The draft was approved by consensus in the Second Committee and subsequently in Plenary Assembly as resolution entitled **Implementation of General Assembly Resolution 41/213 in the Economic and Social Fields (42/170)**[*]. By resolution 42/170, the GA considered that the implementation of resolution 41/213 should take into account the fact that the work of the Special Commission was under way and recognized that adjustments in the structure of the secretariat would be required as a result of ongoing reviews and of the work of the Special Commission. In addition, the Second and Third Committees approved and the Plenary Assembly adopted by consensus the decision entitled **In-depth Study of the United Nations Intergovernmental Structure and Functions in the Economic and Social Fields (42/431)**. By decision 42/431, the GA requested the intergovernmental bodies in the economic and social fields that had not yet done so to submit their views and proposals to the Special Commission in accordance with ECOSOC decision 1987/112.

---

[*]See volume II, 1.4.

Notes

1. ST/ADM/SER.B/288; A/C.5/42/31.
2. Peter S. Ross, 'UN - Back on its Feet?', *International Perspectives*, XVII (January/February 1988), p. 16.
3. Brian Urquart, 'The United Nations System and the Future', *International Affairs*, LXVIII (1989), p. 226.
4. *Pravda*, 17 September 1987.
5. E/1988/75, annex VII, pp. 132-133.
6. E/1987/SR.12, pp. 7-8.
7. *Ibid.*, pp. 8-10.
8. *Ibid.*, p. 11.
9. *Ibid.*, pp. 11-12.
10. *Ibid.*, p. 13.
11. *Ibid.*, p. 14.
12. *Ibid.*, p. 15.
13. E/1987/SR.13, p. 2.
14. *Ibid.*, p. 3.
15. *Ibid.*, pp. 3-4.
16. *Ibid.*, p. 4.
17. *Ibid.*, pp. 4-5.
18. E/1987/SR.19. p. 4.
19. *Official Records of the General-Assembly, Forty-second Session, Supplement No. 1* (A/42/1), p.7.
20. E/1988/75, pp. 10-11.
21. E/1987/SR.38, pp. 4-6.
22. E/1987/SR.39, p. 2.
23. *Ibid.*, p. 3.
24. E/1987/SR.40, p. 2.
25. E/1987/SR.41, p. 3.
26. *Ibid.*, p. 4.
27. *Ibid.*
28. *Ibid.*
29. *Ibid.*
30. Traian Chebeleu, 'The Administrative and Financial Reform of the United Nations. Some Reflections', *Revue Roumaine d'Études Internationales*, XXII (1988), p. 544.
31. E/1987/131, p. 2.
32. *Official Records of the General Assembly, Forty-second Session, Supplement No. 1* (A/42/1), pp. 7-8.
33. A/C.5/42/SR.12, pp. 9-11.
34. A/C.5/42/SR.56, p. 3.
35. A/C.5/42/SR.12, pp. 13-15.
36. *Ibid.*, pp. 16-18.
37. A/C.5/42/SR.14, pp. 3-5.
38. A/C.5/42/SR.23, p. 15.
39. A/C.5/42/SR.24, pp. 6-8.
40. A/C.5/42/SR.15, pp. 12-14.
41. *Ibid.*, pp. 14-15.
42. A/C.5/42/SR.59, p. 9.
43. A/C.5/42/SR.15, pp. 15-17.
44. A/C.5/42/SR.59, p. 7.
45. A/C.5/42/SR.15, pp. 17-18.
46. A/C.5/42/SR.16, p. 2.
47. *Ibid.*, pp. 3-4.
48. *Ibid.*, p. 4.

49. A/C.5/42/SR.24, pp. 10-11.
50. A/C.5/42/SR.17, pp. 6-9.
51. A/C.5/42/SR.60, p. 8.
52. A/C.5/42/SR.17, pp. 9-10.
53. A/C.5/42/SR.18, pp. 2-3.
54. *Ibid.*, pp. 5-6.
55. *Ibid.*, pp. 6-7.
56. *Ibid.*, p. 8.
57. *Ibid.*, pp. 8-11.
58. *Ibid.*, pp. 11-12.
59. *Ibid.*, p. 13.
60. *Ibid.*, pp. 14-15.
61. *Ibid.*, pp. 16-17.
62. A/C.5/42/SR.19, pp. 2-3.
63. *Ibid.*, pp. 3-4.
64. *Ibid.*, pp. 4-6.
65. A/C.5/42/SR. 20, pp. 6-9.
66. A/C.5/42/SR.61, pp. 3-4.
67. A/C.5/42/SR.20, pp. 9-10.
68. A/C.5/42/SR.21, p. 3.
69. *Ibid.*, pp. 3-4.
70. *Ibid.*, p. 6.
71. *Ibid.*, p. 7.
72. *Ibid.*, pp. 9-10.
73. A/C.5/42/SR.23, p. 12.
74. *Ibid.*, pp. 13-14.
75. *Ibid.*, p. 14.
76. *Ibid.*, pp. 17-18.
77. A/C.5/42/SR.24, pp. 2-3.
78. *Ibid.*, pp. 3-4.
79. *Ibid.*, pp. 4-5.
80. *Ibid.*, pp. 5-6.
81. *Ibid.*, pp. 7-8.
82. *Ibid.*, pp. 9-10.
83. A/C.5/42/SR.25, pp. 2-3.
84. *Ibid.*, pp. 4-5.
85. *Ibid.*, pp. 5-7.
86. A/C.5/42/SR.59, pp. 8-9.
87. A/C.5/42/SR.60, p. 11.
88. *Ibid.*, p. 12.
89. *Ibid.*, p. 13.
90. A/C.5/42/SR.67, p. 11.
91. A/42/PV.99, p. 4.
92. A/C.5/SR.67, pp. 11-12.
93. *Ibid.*, p. 12.
94. *Ibid.*, pp. 16-17.
95. *Ibid.*, pp. 17-18.
96. *Ibid.*, pp. 18-19.
97. *Ibid.*, p. 19.
98. A/42/PV.98, pp. 12-16.
99. *Ibid.*, pp. 16-17.
100. *Ibid.*, p. 17.

CHAPTER 4
SECOND PROGRESS REPORT, 1988

4.1 Financial Situation

There was a marked change in 1988. The end of the cold war and a new pragmatism in the relations between North and South had led to a remarkable renaissance of the UN. The UN had won newfound prestige by successfully facilitating a cease-fire in the Iran-Iraq war and the withdrawal from Afghanistan of Soviet troops. The Secretary-General's proposal for a settlement of the problem of Western Sahara had been accepted by all parties concerned. Under the good offices of the Secretary-General, the leaders of Cyprus had come back to the negotiating table. The independence process for Namibia would commence shortly under the supervision of the UN. Finally, there were promising negotiations on the problems of Cambodia and its neighbouring states. This was quite a different UN from the one which had been under siege in 1986.

Despite these successes, the financial situation remained serious.[*] Total outstanding contributions to the regular budget amounted to $353 million at the end of 1987. Out of this, the USA owed $253 million. Its payment for 1987 amounted to $107 million against an assessment of $212 million. The total deficit in 1987 resulted in a cash shortage for the day-to-day needs. In order to meet its obligations, the UN had used the $100 million Working Capital Fund (WCF) as well as the funds available in the Special Account ($99 million). Furthermore, amounts realized from the suspension of the financial regulations relating to the return to member states of unused appropriations as credit against their future assessed contributions amounted to $52 million. The total amount of $251 million had to be supplemented by borrowing, temporarily, from peace-keeping funds.[1]

In the face of a possible funding shortfall in 1988, including cash depletion in August 1988, the Secretary-General had requested from the GA in 1987 the following measures: (i) an increase of the WCF by $100 million to a level of $200 million, effective 1 January 1988; (ii) authority to resort to commercial borrowing in the open market of up to $50 million; and (iii) authority to issue interest-free certificates of indebtedness for subscription by members states

---

[*]For details on the financial situation see annex, table 3 and 4.

and international entities. The GA, however, would not approve any increase in the WCF or authorize the Secretary-General to borrow money commercially. It only approved the issuance of certificates of indebtedness, without payment of interest, to international institutions and member states. No government, however, agreed to purchase the certificates.

The economy measures implemented during the 1986-1987 biennium had been expected to reduce expenditures by some $113.6 million or about 7.8 per cent. This excluded a balance of $18 million which, although not disbursed in 1986/87, was transferred to the construction-in-progress account in December 1987. The savings, together with the absorption of the effects of inflation and currency exchange fluctuations in 1987, met the original reduction target of $146 million. The biggest part of these reductions had been effected in salaries and staff-related expenditures, achieved through the application of a recruitment freeze and the deferral of cost-of-living adjustments, as well as by reductions in overtime, staff travel and the use of consultants. Savings had also been achieved by curtailing contractual services by more than 22 per cent, general operating expenses by almost 10 per cent, and supplies, furniture and equipment by more than 36 per cent. Finally, major construction projects and alterations amounting to $25 million had not been carried out or had been deferred. The recruitment freeze and the increase in the vacancy rate had resulted in a worsening shortage of skilled staff in the different areas, for example in the language services, and affected the quality of outputs. In fact, it was clear that the economy measures had taken a toll on the overall level of programme delivery.[2] The 1988-1989 programme budget already incorporated many of the reductions in resources foreseen in GA resolution 41/213. It was therefore considered impossible to implement another set of economy measures in 1988 of sufficient magnitude to avoid cash depletion without grave damage to the mandated programmes and structure of the UN.

For the fiscal year 1988, the US Congress had allocated $144 million for the UN, compared to the total US assessment of $215 million. Of the allocation, $100 million was to be paid immediately. The release of the remaining $44 million would depend on the satisfactory implementation of UN reforms. This would be the case, once three criteria, devised by Senator Nancy Kassebaum, had been met. Firstly, the UN programme budget had to be adopted by consensus. No consensus had been reached in 1987 on the 1988-1989 programme budget. Although the USA had only abstained and not voted against the programme budget as in previous years, it disagreed strongly with the African countries on the construction of conference facilities in Ethiopia and the overall level of the budget. The first real test, however, would be the events leading to the approval of the 1990-1991 programme budget, in particular the review and approval of the programme budget outline by CPC and the GA. Secondly, UN staff needed to be cut by 15 per cent. Staff reductions proceeded through a hiring freeze and attrition. By mid-1988, approximately 11 per cent of UN posts were unfilled. Thirdly, 50 per cent of UN staff from any country had to be awarded permanent contracts. At that time, approximately 90 per cent of the staff from the USSR, China and Eastern European countries were seconded by their governments. Some changes in this direction seemed to be possible. The USSR had announced that it would support the issuance of more permanent contracts to its citizens.[3]

A number of important issues had to be solved in 1988. Firstly, the Special Commission of ECOSOC was to conclude its work. After submission of the ECOSOC report to the GA, the second major part of the reform emanating from resolution 41/213 - the reform of the intergovernmental structure and functions in the economic and social fields - was expected to be approved. Secondly, the GA would review the progress made in implementing reforms as well as a programme budget outline and the modalities of a contingency fund.

4.2 Special Commission of ECOSOC[4]

The fifth session of the Special Commission (19-29 January 1988) approved a detailed programme of work for 1988 and agreed to proceed with a review of the functioning of the subsidiary bodies in an informal working group. The secretariat was requested to assist in such meetings by responding to questions that delegations might have on the functioning of the bodies. The secretariat was also requested to prepare informal summaries of comments and proposals made by delegations during the discussions.

The Commission carried out an in-depth review of the functioning of individual bodies within the UN intergovernmental machinery in the economic and social fields during the fifth, the sixth (8-19 February 1988) and seventh (7-18 March 1988) sessions.[*]

---

[*]Commission on Transnational Corporations, Intergovernmental Working Group of Experts on International Standards of Accounting and Reporting, *Ad Hoc* Intergovernmental Working Group on the Problem of Corrupt Practices, Statistical Commission, United Nations Group of Experts on Geographical Names, Committee for Development Planning, Meeting of Experts on the United Nations Programme in Public Administration and Finance, *Ad Hoc* Group of Experts on International Co-operation in Tax Matters, Committee of Experts on the Transport of Dangerous Goods, Committee for Programme and Co-ordination, Committee on Non-

At the eighth session (18-29 April 1988), the Special Commission had before it the informal papers submitted at the end of the seventh session by Australia, Canada, China, the Federal Republic of Germany (on behalf of the 12 member states of the European Community), Japan, Norway, Tunisia (on behalf of the Group of 77), the USSR (on behalf of Bulgaria, the Byelorussian SSR, Czechoslovakia, the German Democratic Republic, Hungary, Mongolia, Poland, the Ukrainian SSR and the USSR) and the USA.* These papers were introduced and discussed in informal meetings prior to the eighth session.

At its 31st meeting, on 18 April 1988, the Commission requested the Chairman to prepare an informal consolidated discussion paper on the proposals and suggestions made so far on the functioning of the UN intergovernmental machinery in the economic and social fields, including secretariat support. The Chairman was further requested to indicate, to the extent possible, areas of convergence and divergence in the paper, which was issued on 21 April 1988". Informal consultations on the paper were subsequently held by the Chairman with interested delegations. In introducing the informal consolidated discussion paper, the Chairman stated that it did not cover all the issues addressed during the Commission's discussion. He said that a supplement covering the remaining issues would be circulated in due course. This supplement was presented by the Chairman on 23 May 1988 and was not the subject of informal consultations in the Special Commission""".

At its 32nd meeting, on 29 April 1988, the Commission requested the Chairman to prepare a text on its conclusions and recommendations. In response to that request, the Chairman stated that the Commission had thus far

---

Governmental Organizations, Committee on Negotiations with Intergovernmental Agencies, Trade and Development Board, Executive Board of the United Nations Children's Fund, Committee on Food Aid Policies and Programmes, Executive Committee of the Programme of the United Nations High Commissioner for Refugees, Governing Council of the United Nations Development Programme, High-level Committee on the Review of Technical Co-operation among Developing Countries, Governing Council of the United Nations Environment Programme, Commission on Human Settlements, Population Commission, Intergovernmental Committee on Science and Technology for Development, Advisory Committee on Science and Technology for Development, Committee on the Development and Utilization of New and Renewable Sources of Energy, Committee on Natural Resources, World Food Council, Economic Commission for Europe, Economic and Social Commission for Asia and the Pacific, Economic Commission for Latin America and the Caribbean, Economic Commission for Africa, Economic and Social Commission for Western Asia, Commission for Social Development, Commission on the Status of Women, Commission on Narcotic Drugs, Committee on Crime Prevention and Control, Commission on Human Rights, Committee on Economic, Social and Cultural Rights.

*See volume II, 2.23, annex II.
"See volume II, 2.23, annex III, A.
"""See volume II, 2.23, annex III, B.

managed to conduct the in-depth study entrusted to it and had diagnosed the problems.   Despite the convergence of views on many issues, there still remained much ground to be covered on the means and modalities needed for effective and practical reform.   In view of the absence of sufficient common ground on some issues, the Chairman made it clear that, while he was willing to prepare a text as requested, he would have to exercise his judgement in putting together a balanced package of elements that were reasonable and that could be implemented, based on the views and preliminary ideas contained in the informal papers circulated by a number of delegations and groups to serve as a basis for negotiations.

The Special Commission concluded its work during its ninth session (2-6, 11 and 23 May 1988).   All in all, it had undertaken in-depth studies of 37 intergovernmental bodies.   All these bodies had submitted to the Special Commission their proposals for achieving the objectives of the reform process. Only a few, however, had prepared their proposal as seriously as ECE.   ECE convened a special session in November 1987 and approved the following reform measures: a cutting of programme activities; a reduction of principle subsidiary bodies from 16 to 15 and of other subsidiary bodies from 91 to 32; to cut by 15 per cent the number of days of meetings serviced by the secretariat and documentation by 20 per cent; and new procedures for policy formulation and programme implementation.[5]

Two main issues were at the centre of the discussion. Firstly, the definition of the roles and responsibilities of the GA and ECOSOC.   Secondly, the rationalization of the subsidiary bodies of the GA and ECOSOC in the economic and social fields.   Proposals included:[6]
-   universal membership of ECOSOC; an extension of the duration of ECOSOC meetings; improving the secretariat support structure; recognising the authority of ECOSOC over other bodies in the UN system; and improving the organization of work and reporting procedures: G77;
-   reducing the duplication of debates in the GA and ECOSOC: Australia;
-   shortening of the debates in the Second and Third Committees; substantive annual sessions of ECOSOC to run concurrently with the GA but prior to the meetings of the Second and Third Committees: Canada, Norway, USA;
-   one regular annual session of ECOSOC to consider reports by subsidiary organs, to decide on recommendations to be submitted to the GA, to carry out policy planning and co-ordination; *ad hoc*, subject-oriented, high-level meetings when necessary: G77, China;

- suppress general debate in ECOSOC and focus on co-ordination of system-wide programme activities: European Community;
- one annual session; substantially reduce the agenda of ECOSOC: Japan;
- all UN bodies in the economic and social fields to report to ECOSOC, which would submit a consolidated annual report to the GA; the GA should concentrate on the annual report and major economic and social problems of a global dimension: some socialist countries;
- Committee on Natural Resources and the Committee on the Development and Utilization of New and Renewable Sources of Energy: abolish (Australia, European Community, Japan, Norway, USA);
- World Food Council: biennialize (European Community), abolish (USA);
- Commission on Transnational Corporations: biennialize (Japan), abolish (USA);
- Intergovernmental Committee on Science and Technology for Development: suppress (European Community, Japan, Norway, USA);
- High-level Committee on Technical Co-operation among Developing Countries: suppress (European Community, Norway);
- *Ad hoc* Group of Experts on International Co-operation on Tax Matters: meetings should be *ad hoc* rather than biennial (Japan);
- Committee for Social Development: abolish (Australia, European Community, Japan, USA);
- UN Group of Experts on Geographical Names: triennialize (Japan).

The universalization of ECOSOC was vigorously supported by the Group of 77 and opposed by Western countries. The latter countries attached great significance to the proposals to abolish or merge subsidiary bodies and reduce duplication in the Second and Third Committees of the GA, ECOSOC and UNCTAD. This, again, was resisted by the Group of 77.

At its 34th meeting, on 4 May 1988, the Special Commission had before it the Chairman's draft on the conclusions and recommendations of the Commission[*]. In introducing the text, Mr. Badawi, **Chairman of the Special Commission**[7] made following explanatory remarks:

"At its 32nd meeting, on 29 April 1988, the Special Commission requested the Chairman to prepare a Chairman's text to facilitate the process of negotiation in the Special Commission.

I explained then that, despite the absence of a sufficient common ground which would help me produce a compromise text, I was willing to bend to the

---

[*]See volume II, 2.23, annex IV.

desire of the Commission. I made it clear that much would have to be left to the judgement of the Chairman of what he believed could be the elements of a package which is reasonable and implementable. ...

Section 1 of the text diagnoses the ailment and reflects the agreement thereon. It also states that the Commission has undertaken the in-depth study entrusted to it. More important still, it makes clear the fact that reform is a continuing process. What we have done in the Special Commission is one link in a chain. I therefore suggest that a process of periodic review and evaluation of the United Nations intergovernmental structure be established.

On the body of the text itself, I wish to make the following explanatory remarks.

The General Assembly

Paragraph 6 reiterates functions and responsibilities of the General Assembly, as contained in the Charter and in relevant General Assembly resolutions. It only spells out measures aimed at enhancing the effectiveness of the General Assembly. So, the intention is not to introduce new functions, nor is it intended to cite an exhaustive list of the responsibilities of the General Assembly.

I hope paragraph 6 will be looked at in the context of this explanation.

Paragraph 7 deals with the method of work, organization and agenda of the General Assembly, aimed at enabling it to perform its responsibilities in a rationalized and more effective manner.

The agenda and duration of the Second and Third Committees are still controversial issues. In a compromise text, I had to exercise my personal judgement in what could be reasonable agenda and duration.

The Economic and Social Council

Since the bulk of the restructuring process centres on the Council and its subsidiary bodies, this section is the most detailed. Paragraph 9 elaborates the responsibilities of the Council, not the present Council, but an enhanced and a more effective Council with universal membership.

Again, those functions are drawn from the Charter, from relevant General Assembly and Council resolutions and from the new responsibilities to be entrusted to the Council as expressed by various groups and delegations. Paragraph 9 deals with the programme of work of the new Economic and Social Council. Here again, there are wide-ranging and sometimes divergent views on the agenda and the duration of the new Council. I have tried to list a number of organizational issues and some ideas about the organization of work of the new Council in a manner that would ensure a reasonable duration and pragmatic agenda.

I also tried to present some practical ideas on the form and content of the kind of report which the Council may submit to the General Assembly, with concrete suggestions on the possible allocation of its chapters to the plenary and the relevant main Committees of the General Assembly.

Paragraphs 10, 11 and 12 are devoted to the reporting procedure and the reports to and from the Council.

Paragraph 13 deals with the idea of subject-oriented sessions and their agenda.

Paragraph 14 is the subject of various views and proposals as it concerns the role of the Bureau of the new Council. Several useful ideas have been advanced, but I have preferred to leave the decision on the composition and role of the Bureau to the Council itself.

Paragraph 15 contains an invitation to the executive heads of the specialized agencies to participate more actively in the work of the Council. It is my hope that the new Council will be able to attract them to regain their confidence in it and to contribute positively to its deliberations. Paragraph 16 is also related to the specialized agencies and it reiterates article 64 of the Charter, according to which the Council can request regular reports from the agencies reflecting the measures taken by them to translate General Assembly and Economic and Social Council recommendations into concrete action.

Paragraph 17 is a natural consequence of the radical reforms suggested earlier in the text. A new Economic and Social Council, which will perform a filtering role of the social and economic issues and which will assume the responsibility of some of its subsidiary bodies should, in a democratic organization, encompass all actors in the international arena. Hence the universal membership of the Council.

Paragraph 18 deals with documentation: how to rationalize it and how to render it more useful and more intelligible in order to facilitate the work of the Council.

Paragraphs 19 to 24 are devoted to the subsidiary bodies. The list suggested may be incomplete, but I had to rely on many of the views already expressed. However, in the absence of specific suggestions from some groups on this issue, I had to exercise some personal judgement. Still, I believe this issue may need further consultations between various groups and delegations.

Section 5 of the text (paras. 25 to 29) attempts to incorporate most of the views expressed on operational activities for development and their governing bodies.

Section 6 (paras. 30 to 33) cites some general recommendations related to regional commissions. Since this is one of the issues on which there is not much controversy, the Commission may wish to expand it. There are naturally certain recommendations that may apply to specific regional commissions, and I will advise interested delegations to contact the Secretariat and pronounce themselves on such points.

Section 7 deals with the Secretariat support and lists some guidelines that the Secretary-General could take into account when preparing proposals for the restructuring of the Secretariat in the economic and social fields, to be submitted to the General Assembly at its forty-third regular session.

Section 8 refers to the views and proposals agreed upon by members of the Trade and Development Board on the rationalization of its work.

Paragraph 36 suggests a swap in the agenda of the two parts of the regular session of the Trade and Development Board to enable it to conduct its debate on the interrelated issues in spring with a view to ensuring better co-ordination and complementarity between the Trade and Development Board, the Economic and Social Council and the General Assembly.

Section 9 deals with the modalities for the implementation of the proposed recommendations. As the proposed recommendations as a package would entail an amendment to article 61 of the Charter related to the composition of the Council, ratification in accordance with the provisions of article 108 will have to take place before the elements of the package are implemented. However, good faith and determination to strengthen the efficiency of our organization may create an atmosphere conducive to constructive dialogue on the modalities for the implementation of the recommendations, including the possibility of envisaging transitional arrangements. That is why the Special Commission may find it appropriate to recommend to the Council to request the Secretary-General to submit a report to the General Assembly at its forty-third session on such modalities, including suggestions on draft pro- grammes of work of the Second and Third Committees of the General Assembly and of the Council, the draft calendar of meetings of subsidiary bodies of the Council, draft organization of work, etc.

Whatever recommendations we may approve in the Special Commission, they will need to be translated into applicable arrangements. The General Assembly, on the basis of data to be submitted to it, could elaborate on the modalities and the calendar for implementation of the Commission's recommendations.

With less than three days left before the Commission to complete its work, the need for the spirit of compromise and the sincere determination to conclude our mission successfully is more dire than ever."

At its 35th meeting, on 11 May 1988, the Chairman informed the Special Commission of the outcome of the informal consultations held on the Chairman's text with the spokesmen of the various groups and delegations. He said that, after three lengthy sittings, it appeared that the divergent views on major outstanding issues could not be reconciled. He stated that, while such a development was disappointing and that, as Chairman, it was his duty to co-ordinate the work of the Special Commission with a view to assisting members to reach agreement, he could not impose an agreement on them. The following statements were made at the 35th meeting.

The representative of Tunisia, on behalf of the **Group of 77**[8]

"The task the Economic and Social Council entrusted to you when it elected you Chairman of the Commission in February 1987 is surely one of the most complex and sensitive ever undertaken in the United Nations. In 1977, the General Assembly adopted a non-exhaustive, global package of reforms in its resolution 32/197. At that time, however, the United Nations, particularly in the economic and social sectors, was characterized by an unprecedented dynamism which had its basis in a consensus objective, the establishment of the new international economic order.

Despite such favourable circumstances, it must be acknowledged that the implementation of the measures recommended has been somewhat lacking. While this has undoubtedly pointed up the need for a further reform, it has also constituted one of the obstacles to the formulation of measures that can actually be implemented. It taking stock of these 15 months of intense labour, which have allowed us to conduct a true in-depth study and draw certain conclusions from it, we are compelled to recall how the Special Commission came into being. ...

A great many of our developed-country partners found it quite difficult to depart from their original agenda, which involved a few superficial, small-scale reforms aimed essentially at reducing the Organization's operating costs. Obviously, such an approach was intended to do no more than make substantial cuts in the regular budget of the Organization, thereby justifying the withholding by certain Member States of a portion of their contributions. Actually, this took us farther from the agreed objective of strengthening the structure of the

United Nations machinery in the economic and social fields and improving its functioning. In any event, many delegations from industrialized countries stated at that time that the goal of any reform should not be a reduction of operating costs.

At last, the Special Commission's deliberations, at the urging of the Group of 77, were directed towards the concept of genuine reform. All intergovernmental bodies, from the organs established under the Charter to the subsidiary bodies, were studied in detail by the Group of 77 as well as by other delegations in September 1987 and, subsequently, in January, February and March 1988. The conclusions reached by the various participants in these deliberations were marked by a high degree of homogeneity and revealed the existence of a common point of view in certain areas. ...

Any genuine reform that is to be more than a mere patch job or an *ad hoc* reduction of bodies must necessarily include:

(a) A strengthening of the weak link in the United Nations machinery, namely the Economic and Social Council and its secretariat, and the improvement of its functioning so that it may fully play the role ascribed to it by the Charter;

(b) Expansion of the Economic and Social Council so that it becomes truly representative, thereby ensuring its credibility and effectiveness. This strengthening measure might lead the General Assembly, whose prerogatives and role as chief decision-making body and co-ordinator of international efforts in the economic and social fields cannot undergo any modification whatsoever, to consider making adjustments in the agenda and duration of sessions of its Second and Third Committees. This measure might also lead to consideration of the question of subsidiary bodies, some of whose statutes might be revised, albeit in the light of clearly identified and agreed criteria. ...

For the delegations of many industrialized countries, however, the studies and conclusions formulated during the Special Commission's debates have been distorted so that they focus on objectives that are incompatible with the collective desire for reform and with the letter and philosophy of the United Nations Charter, implying a fundamental modification of the Charter and at the same time criticizing one of the proposals of the Group of 77, the expansion of the Economic and Social Council.

These objectives are the following:

(a) To prevent the General Assembly from discharging its role and functions by limiting the duration of sessions of the Second and Third

Committees to the holding of a general debate. The negotiating and deliberating functions of the Assembly would thus be suppressed;

(b) To limit the length of deliberations of an Economic and Social Council that would be revamped but rendered incapable of dealing with the questions submitted to it in an exhaustive and decisive manner, including its role as central co-ordinator of the United Nations system in the economic and social fields;

(c) To eliminate all activities of the Organization dealing with questions of vital interest to the international community, particularly the developing countries, by abolishing the subsidiary bodies responsible for science and technology, natural resources (including energy), new and renewable sources of energy, food and agriculture, social development and technical co-operation among developing countries.

What then would a reform undertaken on the basis of such proposals have accomplished? The atrophy of the United Nations, the marginalization of international economic co-operation and a worsening of the impediments to the economic and social development of the developing countries. Where, under these conditions, would the standing commitment of all countries to work relentlessly for peace and world security fit in? We need look no further to understand why the Special Commission was unable to draft joint recommendations.

Here we wish to commend the initiative you took in providing the Special Commission's informal working group with a Chairman's text, dated 4 May 1988. Despite the considerable problems it is raising, the Group of 77, it will be recalled, was the only group to declare itself fully prepared to accept that text as a basis for negotiation. Yet this acceptance, far from unanimous, is apparently not enough to have this document considered as anything more than an informal proposal from the Chairman, to be tucked away in our delegation's files. ...

The Special Commission has concluded its work by stating unanimously that the Economic and Social Council continues to be the Organization's central problem in the economic and social and related sectors. We are thus confident that together with our partners, the industrialized countries, we shall in the near future overcome this problem and make it possible for the Council to work as effectively as we desire, particularly as it plays its central role of co-ordinating the activities of the United Nations system in the economic, social and related fields. We should also resolve to improve its performance in the review of and follow-up to the operational activities for development of the United Nations system."

The representative of the Federal Republic of Germany, on behalf of the 12 member states of the **European Community**[9]

"Speaking on behalf of the States Members of the European Community, let me first of all say that we share your sense of regret that, after months of serious work done by all of us in the Special Commission, you have come to the conclusion that at this moment the time does not seem to be ripe for an agreement on a far-reaching reform of the United Nations in the economic and social fields. ...

As far as further procedures are concerned, we share your view that it is up to the Council and the forty-third session of the General Assembly to take the necessary action. The States Members of the European Community remain committed to a meaningful reform which on the basis of General Assembly resolution 41/213 should be in the interest of all Member States. We continue to be committed to strengthening the United Nations in accordance with the Charter as an indispensable instrument for international co-operation in the economic and social fields. We are ready at any time to continue discussions and to do our share to bring the reform efforts to a successful conclusion."

The representative of **China**[10]

"We are now in a situation where the "clock has come to a stop". And for this we feel extremely regretful. ...

We do hope that a basis for a possible consensus leading to a meaningful reform package could be found. However, we are certainly not in favour of the concept of the so-called "back to back" formula, i.e. the simultaneous or concurrent holding of the regular session of the Economic and Social Council and that of the General Assembly. We are also strongly sceptical about the feasibility for the Council to subsume a number of very important subsidiary bodies, such as the Intergovernmental Committee on Science and Technology for Development."

The representative of the **United States of America**[11]

"We are saddened that the Commission could not accomplish more after so great an investment of time, commitment and work. In this regard we urge that what was achieved will not be lost. Valuable common positions and practical proposals were developed. There was meaningful progress and it should be preserved and implemented.

We further suggest that mechanisms be found to keep up the momentum towards improving the United Nations system. We can and should build upon this just completed exercise, taking further steps to heighten efficiency and credibility. This benefits everyone. One approach might be to assign small task forces to concentrate on specific areas of activity. Examples could be consolidation of publications, streamlining of subsidiary bodies, more effective structuring of meetings."

The representative of the Union of Soviet Socialist Republics, on behalf of **socialist countries**[12]

"In our opinion, the Special Commission could undertake an in-depth, comprehensive analysis of the work of the United Nations in the economic and social fields, expose the many problems and difficulties existing therein and enhance the common understanding of ways to improve that work.

Unfortunately, at the present stage the members of the Special Commission have been unable to find a unified approach to all the problems and to overcome the residual divergence of views. We feel, however, that on the whole useful work has been accomplished, and a worthwhile fund of ideas has been accumulated which should be kept for future use."

The representative of **Canada**[13]

"My delegation joins others in supporting your introductory statement and its recommendations. The in-depth study which the Special Commission has been engaged in, going on 16 months, has been of major value to all participants. Many of us started out with only a hazy understanding of the Economic and Social Council and its subsidiary machinery. Now most of us, including the secretariat, I dare say, have learned a great deal about United Nations intergovernmental bodies in the social and economic field, including the specialized agencies and regional commissions. ...

Indeed we have gone further. We have identified certain key elements of possible convergence as well as major differences still separating us. If we have fallen short of agreement, it is due to such facts as the essential conditions of timing, the complexity of the process itself and that sufficient understanding and mutual confidence were not yet adequately advanced. In the meantime, Canada's informal reform proposal of 18 April remains on the table.

My delegation agrees with your approach, Mr. Chairman, both in terms of procedure and substance. It provides the Economic and Social Council with an opportunity to review the results achieved thus far to decide on a future course of action."

---

*Bulgaria, Byelorussian SSR, Czechoslovakia, German Democratic Republic, Hungary, Mongolia, Poland, Ukrainian SSR, USSR.

The representative of **Norway**[14]

"The Special Commission has had a twofold mandate:

(a) To undertake an in-depth study of the intergovernmental structure and its secretariat support services in the economic and social fields of the United Nations;

(b) To present recommendations aimed at enhancing the effectiveness and the efficiency of the United Nations in these fields.

It is the view of my delegation that the Commission has succeeded in fulfilling the first part of this mandate. It cannot be claimed, however, that the Commission has fulfilled the second part of its mandate, despite more than 15 months of hard work. My delegation deeply regrets that beyond the general agreement on the need for, and even the framework for a possible comprehensive reform, no consensus could be reached with regard to specific measures. We have a feeling that a somewhat higher degree of flexibility on the part of the delegations would have facilitated a more concrete end result.

It is our intention, Mr. Chairman, to assess more in detail the work of the Special Commission when this issue is being dealt with at the second regular session of the Economic and Social Council in July. We will on that occasion also revert to another important issue, which is the future follow-up of our efforts in the Special Commission through the last months. But let me on this occasion congratulate you, Mr. Ambassador, on the manner in which you have discharged your extremely difficult task. You certainly contributed to the work of the Commission in a consensus-seeking spirit which is highly appreciated."

The representative of **Japan**[15]

"We knew that our task was a difficult one, perhaps one of the most important attempts in the history of the United Nations, particularly in view of the fact that most of the past attempts to reform the intergovernmental structure in the economic and social fields were unable to achieve their envisaged objectives.

Frankly speaking, my delegation is disappointed that our efforts and endeavours did not lead the Commission to a successful conclusion within the scheduled time. However, we note that we could learn many things about the United Nations system through our analytical work on the intergovernmental bodies and their subsidiary organs, and that we could enhance our mutual understanding on a variety of issues. ...

As my delegation has repeatedly said in our exercise of restructuring, Japan, in principle, is against the universalization of the Economic and Social Council, because we are not convinced of the wisdom of introducing universalization into the Council. We have serious doubts about the possible consequences which would be brought about by the universalization of the Council. If the Council is universalized without clear division of labour between the General Assembly and the Council, it would unavoidably lead to duplication of work between the Assembly and the Council and would make the United Nations system more complicated and unworkable. We firmly believe that most of the measures for strengthening the efficiency and effectiveness of the function of the intergovernmental structure can be realized without the universalization of the Council.

With regard to the question of how we should proceed from now, I should like to point out, first, that we should not lose sight of our fundamental objective of our work entrusted to us by General Assembly resolution 41/213 based on the Group of 18 report. We should not continue our exercise just for the sake of reform, neither should we accept unsatisfactory reforms based upon inadequate compromise, which would certainly turn out to be unrealistic and unworkable solutions.

After a long, assiduous work in the Commission, this is the time for us to reflect upon our past endeavours and achievements so far made from a wider perspective. We could resume our work in a more efficient and effective manner during the summer session of the Council. My delegation would like to express its readiness and willingness to participate actively in the continuing exercise."

The representative of **Australia**[16]

"Unfortunately, despite your efforts and those of delegations, agreement on major issues has eluded us. Delegations have lacked an overriding sense of urgency and concern for the efficiency of the whole multilateral system. We would note, however, that delegations are now better informed and we would hope that they are perhaps better able to be flexible in the future in consequence. ...

We will be working hard to use the knowledge we have gained to secure tangible gains from the process later this year at the second regular session of the Council in Geneva and at all other opportunities which present themselves."

The representative of **Austria**[17]

"The exercise in itself was a useful one - we have educated ourselves, studied previous reform attempts, familiarized ourselves with the highly complex subsidiary machinery which we have created over the years, we have identified many lacunae, we have come to realize that the overly complex structure of the intergovernmental machinery at the United Nations suffers from a lack of cohesion which renders co-ordination difficult.

We now realize that the cumbersome organizational and structural set-up in the economic and social fields needs to be reflected upon with a view to render the intergovernmental machinery and the respective Secretariat structure more responsive to the needs of Member States in the outgoing twentieth century. We also seem to have agreed that we need to make the system simpler in order to make it more responsive, that the respective roles and interrelationships of the General Assembly, the Economic and Social Council, but also the Trade and Development Board, the main bodies of deliberation and negotiation in the economic and social fields, need to be clearly defined and their working arrangements so organized as to allow Member States to come to a clearer understanding of global world problems with a view to finding adequate solutions. We also have identified some areas in which organizational streamlining is needed.

I believe that I can say that we all agree that reform of the United Nations in the economic and social fields is necessary, that it is a continuous process and that this reform process ought to be continued. The fact that we have not been able to produce a report or set of recommendations that command the consensus among all participants indicates that we, the Member States, are not quite clear about the role the United Nations ought to play in the economic and social fields within the system of international relations. In this context, I want to draw the attention of this Committee to the fact that my delegation has invariably stressed the importance to increase and strengthen the role of the United Nations in the social sector."

The representative of **Sweden**[18]

"The Swedish delegation of course regrets that the Special Commission has not been able to reach a common understanding on reforms that should be undertaken. We believe, however, that the Special Commission - after a hesitant start - has carried out a useful analytical work and has identified areas where reforms should be considered. Constructive ideas and proposals have been put forward from many quarters and could be used for further considerations.

We must now look at what can be done in the future on the basis of the work of the Special Commission. At the Economic and Social Council meeting in July we must consider how the work of the Special Commission can be continued in one way or another."

A concluding statement was made by Mr. Badawi, **Chairman of the Special Commission**[19] in which he assessed the work of the Special Commission as follows:

"I wish now to make my closing statement which contains my personal assessment of the work of the Special Commission as well as my assessment of the outcome.

At the beginning of the exercise, the residual fear, suspicion, mistrust and lingering resentment spilling over from the forty-first regular session of the General Assembly and the spectre of the financial crisis tarnished the atmosphere in the Special Commission. Then a period of genuine interest in the in-depth study evolved and delegations and Member States got involved in an intellectual and challenging process of scrutinizing a much proliferated and intricate intergovernmental structure. It was certainly a useful, informative and educating process for everyone. ...

The final stage, that of formulating the recommendations of the Special Commission on the basis of the findings of the in-depth study, ran into serious difficulties for several reasons, among which I may cite the following:

(a) Political considerations;

(b) A sense of frustration, triggered by a series of setbacks, foremost among which is the financial uncertainty besetting the United Nations. Such setbacks and uncertainties cannot be overlooked and they have certainly had a negative impact on the prospects of, let alone the interest in, genuine reform;

(c) Difficulties within several groupings and delegations to agree on a solid position regarding the substantive recommendations and the modalities for their implementation. It was not the failure to identify the divergences and the issues to be addressed which obstructed such an undertaking. Rather, it was the fear that some elements of a package could compromise vested interests;

(d) Vested interests have not been limited to the political dimensions. They have transgressed those bounds into the realm of preferences. This was demonstrated when negotiations started on the subsidiary bodies of the Economic and Social Council and the attempt to rationalize them through their absorption by the new Council, their elimination or their conversion into expert groups;

(e) One of the main stumbling-blocks which impeded an agreement on a set of recommendations was the inability to make a clear-cut, logical and implementable division of labour between the General Assembly and a universalized Economic and Social Council.

Within this spectrum, trends ranged from converting the Council into an economic and social general assembly, even if such an arrangement detracted from the powers and responsibilities of the General Assembly as enshrined in the Charter, to having a strengthened and hopefully more effective Council with universal membership, without being specific on the impact that such an arrangement should have on the method and organization of work of the General Assembly. A third trend opted for introducing minor changes by trimming down a few intergovernmental bodies while adhering to the saying that "Whatever is, is right". Had a genuine willingness to reach a compromise existed, it would have enabled the Special Commission to bridge the gap between the various positions. There was a necessary prerequisite that everyone should rise above narrow interests and engage in dialogue on the merit of each element of a package of measures. ...

On the positive side, I could cite some of the areas on which there is a convergence of views among the members of the Commission:

(a) Review of the functioning of the United Nations should be seen as a continuing process aimed at bringing about appropriate reforms to enhance the capacity of the Organization to meet the changing needs of its members. Resolution 32/197 was thus the beginning of a process. However, we have to take into account the developments that have taken place since then and the prospects for the future so that any restructuring could respond to those changing needs. Many delegations duly recognized the fact that the work of the Special Commission was part of a political compromise reflected in General Assembly resolution 41/213 and that recommendations 2 and 8 were two out of 72 recommendations adopted by the Group of High-level Intergovernmental Experts to Review the Efficiency of the Administrative and Financial Functioning of the United Nations;

(b) The common interests of all countries in the effective and efficient functioning of the United Nations in the economic and social fields;

(c) There is a reaffirmation of the principle that the General Assembly should function as the principal forum for policy-making and for the establishment of overall strategies, policies and priorities of the system as a whole in respect of international co-operation in the economic, social and related fields, in accordance with the provisions of the Charter;

(d) There is a reaffirmation that the Council should monitor and evaluate the implementation of overall strategies, policies and priorities established by the General Assembly in the economic, social and related fields. Another major task of the Council, which has to be strengthened, is to ensure the overall co-ordination of the activities of the United Nations system in the economic, social and related fields;

(e) In order to enable the Council of fully and effectively carrying out its Charter responsibilities, particularly in the field of co-ordination, Governments should harmonize their positions in the various governing bodies of the organs, organizations and bodies of the United Nations system;

(f) The strengthening of the Council and its functioning is of crucial importance to the effective functioning of the United Nations system in the economic and social fields. It was the common feeling that the Council is the weakest link in the chain and that the enhancement of its effectiveness is a major objective;

(g) A strengthened and effective Economic and Social Council should be seen as complementing and strengthening the respective roles of the General Assembly and its subsidiary bodies;

(h) Measures to strengthen the Council must include specific steps which would enhance its authority and credibility, improve its role in policy overview and co-ordination in order, *inter alia*, to improve harmonization of actions and promote an integrated approach in the social and economic fields and improve the interrelationships and the modalities for dialogue among major intergovernmental bodies of the United Nations system in the economic and social areas, particularly in the context of operational activities;

(i) The Council should recommend to the General Assembly overall priorities and policy guidance on operational activities for development of the United Nations system;

(j) Continued effort should be made to biennialize the agendas and work programmes of the Council and of the Second and the Third Committees of the Assembly with a view to ensuring the necessary complementarity between the General Assembly and the Council;

(k) The recognition of the need to rationalize the subsidiary bodies of the General Assembly and the Council on the basis of agreed criteria;

(l) Executive heads of the organizations of the United Nations system or their senior representatives should participate more actively in the deliberations and informal discussion of the Economic and Social Council and should provide all assistance to the Council;

(m) In accordance with Article 64 of the Charter, the Council should obtain regular reports from the specialized agencies on the steps taken by them to give effect to relevant recommendations of the General Assembly and the Council in the economic and social fields;

(n) In accordance with the global development strategy and policies adopted by the General Assembly, the Economic and Social Council should put greater emphasis on the consideration of the reports of the regional commissions with a view to effectively integrating the regional inputs into the global discussion of substantive issues. The Council should also review and co-ordinate, on a global basis, interregional co-operation among the regional commissions. Regional commissions should draw the attention of the Council to questions with global implications or which are of relevance to other regions;

(o) Relevant provisions of General Assembly resolution 32/197 should be fully implemented in order to allow the regional commissions to exercise fully and effectively their role, under the authority of the Economic and Social Council, as the main economic and social development centres within the United Nations system for their respective regions;

(p) The Office of the Director-General for Development and International Economic Co-operation should be strengthened and adequately staffed in order to enable the Director-General to effectively carry out his responsibilities, particularly in the areas of co-ordination and operational activities for development;

(q) Secretariat departments and divisions in the economic and social fields should be strengthened and/or modified in such a way as to provide adequate substantive and technical support commensurate with the functions of the respective organs, organizations and bodies of the United Nations in the economic and social fields."

At its 36th meeting, on 23 May, the Special Commission adopted its report (E/1988/75)* for submission to the second regular 1988 session of ECOSOC. The lack of agreement prevented the Special Commission from putting forward a set of reform proposals. In fact, little had been achieved during the lengthy negotiations. Further clarifications on the report were made by the Chairman who noted that Annex III, A (Informal Consolidated Discussion Paper Presented by the Chairman)** did not encompass all the views expressed during the informal discussions and that its contents were thus not binding. In addition, several delegations explained that they had reservations about specific paragraphs of Annex III, B (Supplement to the Informal Consolidated Discussion Paper Presented by the Chairman)***. In fact, the representative

---

*See volume II, 2.23.
**See volume II, 2.23, annex III, A.
***See volume II, 2.23, annex III, B.

of Mexico expressed reservations on the inclusion of Annex III, A and B and Annex IV (Chairman's Text on the Draft Conclusions and Recommendations of the Special Commission)*. The representative of **Mexico**[20] noted at the meeting:

"I have express instructions from my Government to reiterate its opposition to the inclusion in the report of the Special Commission (document E/SCN.1/L.1) of annexes III and IV consisting of texts by the Chairman of the Commission, dated 21 April and 23 May (annex III) and 4 May (annex IV). While it is clear that these texts have not been adopted, they contain views whose articulation alone calls into question the very existence of our Organization and the authority of the General Assembly and, in our judgement, they threaten the vital interests of the developing countries and do not help to strengthen multilateralism in the economic and social fields.

We believe that the above-mentioned texts will severely hamper consultations on the report in the Economic and Social Council."

4.3 Second Regular Session of ECOSOC: Consideration of the Report of the Special Commission and Approval of the Resolution on the Revitalization of ECOSOC (1988/77)

The second regular session was concerned with two reform issues. Under agenda item 3 (a)**, ECOSOC considered the report of the Special Commission (E/1988/75)***. Under agenda item 3 (b)****, the Council considered the revitalization of ECOSOC in accordance with decision 1987/189 as approved during the resumed second regular session in 1987. The two agenda items were covered together.

The debate started with the introduction of the report of the Special Commission by Mr. Badawi, **Chairman of the Special Commission**[21], who noted that

"the Commission had begun its work in March 1987 and had devoted its early meetings to consideration of the procedures and methods by which it

---

*See volume II, 2.23, annex IV.

**In-depth Study of the United Nations Intergovernmental Structure and Functions in the Economic and Social Fields: Report of the Special Commission of the Economic and Social Council on the In-depth Study of the United Nations Intergovernmental Structure and Functions in the Economic and Social Fields.

***See volume II, 2.23.

****In-depth Study of the United Nations Intergovernmental Structure and Functions in the Economic and Social Fields: the Economic and Social Council.

could best carry out the task entrusted to it by the Council in the context of the implementation of recommendation 8 of the report of the Group of 18. It had taken the Commission some time to determine first of all the nature of the documentation required for an integrated study of the Organization's structure and functions in the economic and social fields. A combination of functional and thematic approaches had enabled it to carry out a consistent and in-depth review of both the intergovernmental machinery and the Secretariat.

The Commission had begun its review of the intergovernmental machinery during its fourth session, and the exchange of views throughout its work had proved extremely useful. The documentation prepared by the Secretariat and contributions submitted by the subsidiary bodies in response to Council decision 1987/112 had also facilitated its task.

Consultations following completion of the study had revealed that, while delegations recognized the need for overall reforms, they could not agree on a set of practical measures for recommendation to the Council. He nevertheless wished to put forward some ideas concerning the ways in which the Council could carry out the task entrusted to it by the General Assembly and to identify areas in which it might be possible to reach an agreement so as to facilitate the work of the Assembly at its forty-third session.

A number of delegations had suggested that the Council should consider renewing the mandate of the Commission so as to enable it to draw up a set of agreed recommendations. He did not share that view: the Commission had clearly concluded its work, since it had completed the study requested and had set out the findings of that study in its report. The considerations detailed in that report had prevented it from reaching agreement on specific recommendations and it was now for the Council to decide what would be the best means of completing the task.

Another idea was to establish a small group to pursue the Commission's reforms. He personally doubted the usefulness of such a course of action and felt that what was needed now was a process of negotiation and a political decision by all parties on a set of agreed recommendations concerning operational measures for reform based on the vast array of information and analyses available.

Furthermore, it seemed to be the unanimous view of delegations that the work already done by the Commission must not be ignored. Every effort should be made by the Council or the Assembly to utilize the available information for an overall package of reforms. Consultations with delegations showed that many would have preferred the Commission's report to be transmitted, together with appropriate recommendations or comments, directly to the Assembly for consideration and action.

He wished to underscore the fact that agreement already existed on a number of proposals to enhance the efficiency and effectiveness of subsidiary bodies and that those proposals should be pursued as their implementation would contribute to the ultimate objectives of reform. Under agenda item 3 (b), the Council now had an opportunity to review its own functioning and therefore help to achieve an agreement. Its report, along with that of the Commission, would no doubt be extremely useful for the Assembly in its consideration of reforms aimed at enhancing the efficiency and effectiveness of the United Nations intergovernmental structure in the economic and social fields and its Secretariat support.

In conclusion, he wished to reiterate his conviction that the Commission's hard work had not been in vain and hoped that more propitious circumstances would soon bring about the results which it had not been possible to attain as a result of the Commission's work."

The statements made following this introduction are recalled below.

The representative of Norway, speaking on behalf of the five **Nordic countries**[22], pointed out that

"the Special Commission had been given a twofold mandate, both to undertake an in-depth study of the United Nations intergovernmental structure in the economic and social fields and of its Secretariat support services, and also to present recommendations aimed at enhancing the efficiency and effectiveness of the United Nations in those fields. The Nordic countries felt that the Commission had succeeded to a reasonable extent in fulfilling the first part of its mandate. The review of intergovernmental machinery had shown that the performance of most subsidiary bodies of the Council and the General Assembly - albeit with some exceptions - was satisfactory, a fact which came as an agreeable surprise in view of the relatively numerous criticisms which had been levelled at the United Nations system in recent years. The weakest link in the system had been clearly identified as the relationship between the superior organs, notably the Assembly, the Council, and the Trade and Development Board. All delegations appeared to recognize that the division of labour between those organs was blurred and that the Council was not fulfilling its mandate as envisaged in the Charter. They had also broadly accepted the need for reforms, although common conceptions on the direction of such reforms had not yet materialized.

Regarding the review of Secretariat support structures, the work of the Commission had been less fruitful because of lack of time, resources and information. In that respect, the Nordic countries welcomed the Secretary-General's efforts to implement recommendation 25 of the Group of 18. However, as there was a link between the intergovernmental machinery and the Secretariat support structures, those efforts had been hampered by the lack of conclusions from the Commission.

It was even more regrettable that the Commission had been unable to fulfil the second part of its mandate and had reached no consensus on recommending specific reform measures to the Council. A higher degree of political will could no doubt have facilitated a more concrete end-result. The Nordic countries had participated actively in the work of the Commission in the conviction that the economic and social sectors of the United Nations system could be made more effective and that there was scope for major improvements. Against that background, they had been pleased that a considerable number of package proposals for reform had been introduced in the Commission, but they would have welcomed a more open and frank discussion of some of them.

Regarding the question of the universalization of the Council's membership, such a reform would clearly not in itself make the intergovernmental machinery more efficient or effective and, in that regard, all delegations had agreed in principle that the prerequisites for such a transformation were as important as universalization itself. Consideration of those prerequisites, however, had turned out to be very difficult and delegations had been unable to agree on the institutional arrangements that would ensure a clear distinction between the role of the Council and that of the Assembly. Moreover, the question of the relationship between those bodies and UNCTAD had hardly been raised.

The Nordic countries very much regretted that the Commission had failed to present a reform package which could have improved the efficiency and usefulness of United Nations activities in the economic and social fields and enhanced the credibility and prestige of the system as a whole. Surely it was in the collective interest to streamline the Organization in order to provide for greater responsiveness to emerging needs, and in particular the pressing problems of developing countries. Nevertheless, at the current session the Council should give further consideration to the Commission's findings - despite their shortcomings - in order to facilitate the deliberations of the Assembly on that subject. In more general terms, the Nordic countries would like the question of restructuring to remain on the agenda of the Council and the Assembly. They would also be in favour of a more thematic approach in the work of the Council, as advocated in proposals to which the Commission had given its support. In addition, there seemed to be a consensus on the need to strengthen the management role of the Bureau of the Council: the Bureau could be mandated to deal with the organizational issues which, in the current circumstances, were taking up an unreasonable amount of the Council's time at the organizational session. Lastly, he wished to emphasize that the Nordic countries remained committed to the reform process and had an open mind about procedures and modalities for future discussions. The existing momentum should not be lost and it was important to build upon the work that had already been done."

The observer for Tunisia, speaking on behalf of the **Group of 77**[23]

"Agreement had been reached on the diagnosis, in particular with regard to the weak link in the chain, the Economic and Social Council. However, it must also be recognized that the work of the Commission had not resulted in recommendations acceptable to all. Undoubtedly, the shadow of the financial crisis and its underlying political causes had largely contributed to that failure. ...

In conclusion, he said that the Group of 77 had noted with interest the suggestions made by Mr. Badawi, in his personal capacity, regarding future action on the question of restructuring the United Nations system in the economic and social fields."

The representative of **China**[24]

"it was regrettable to have to note that, despite the joint efforts of the parties concerned, the Special Commission had failed to reach a consensus on a package of recommendations for the restructuring of the United Nations system in the economic and social fields. ...

His delegation was not at all in favour of the idea of merging the Second and Third Committees with the Economic and Social Council. Efforts to enhance the Council's work should in no way weaken the role of the Second or Third Committee, or *vice versa*. The utmost care must be taken with regard to the merging of subsuming of a number of intergovernmental or subsidiary bodies. The Intergovernmental Committee on Science and Technology for Development should be retained and revitalized in view of the important role it could play in promoting the economic development of developing countries. Lastly, a set of criteria would have to be established before any action could be taken to subsume intergovernmental bodies.

His delegation endorsed the pragmatic suggestion to seek practical and feasible ways to strengthen the Council. It suggested that measures should be taken in such areas as the continued biannualization of the programme of work, improvement of the reporting system, expeditious preparation and distribution of documents, effective co-ordination of programmes of work within the United Nations system, enhanced co-ordination of operational activities for development, a shortened list of agenda items, the prompt convening of meetings, etc."

The representative of the **United States of America**[25]

"The study of the Council by the Commission had dealt in large part with the issue of its membership. On the one hand, delegations had found it difficult to assign specific functions to the Council while the issue of its membership remained unresolved; on the other hand, the issue of membership could not be resolved until the Council's role was clarified. Nevertheless, there were many ways to improve the functioning of the Council irrespective of its membership. Some of those were acceptable to all sides: for example, the gradual introduction of changes focusing on specific points and the reduction of documentation and meeting times, as well as the number of committees and commissions.

The Council should adopt a more thematic approach to its work. The general debate was already guided by one priority issue each year, a practice which should be expanded to cover the entire agenda. While concentrating on major issues, the Council would still fulfil its role as co-ordinator of the activities of subsidiary bodies. Improved documentation would assist the Council in its task. Summaries which clearly listed the recommendations made by each reporting body would enable the Council to carry out its task in a more efficient manner. Strengthening the Council's role in reviewing the recommendations of its subsidiary bodies would relieve the General Assembly of that task and allow it to focus only on the key issues.

Lastly, the Council's meeting calendar and the role of its organizational session should be re-evaluated. His delegation supported the idea of holding a shorter session and giving a larger role to the Bureau in organizing the annual work calendar. Those proposals were not politically sensitive; they were practical, specific and designed to improve the functioning of the Council. It was necessary to be realistic and to remain committed to pursuing the reform process."

The observer for **Austria**[26]

"He wished to take the opportunity to re-emphasize the need for a stronger United Nations role in the social sector. Of the 44 intergovernmental bodies reviewed by the Commission, only four were active in the social field. In spite of that lack of proportion, and to the great surprise of his delegation, some members had proposed the elimination of one of those social bodies. In fact, the discussions in the Commission had proved once again that, in the social sector, no subsidiary body could be eliminated or reduced and that the existing bodies must, on the contrary, be strengthened. In the future, greater attention should be paid to the social implications of economic adjustment measures, and the United Nations could play an important role in efforts to mitigate the negative effects of adjustment measures on the populations concerned, in particular the most vulnerable groups. It must not be forgotten that restructuring was not an end in itself and that its purpose was to improve the quality of life throughout the world."

The representative of the Union of Soviet Socialist Republics, speaking on behalf of **socialist countries**[*27]

"The study enabled delegations to appreciate that the machinery for regional and global co-operation was performing well and flexibly enough to respond quickly and effectively to developments in the world economic and social situation. Moreover, the study had highlighted sectors in which changes were needed and in which professional competence should be enhanced. The socialist countries were convinced that the proposed reforms must be undertaken without delay, in a carefully considered and balanced manner, taking into account the responsibilities of each individual body, its mandate and field of competence, as well as the interests of all Member States, on the basis of the principle of consensus and through compromise. They were opposed to the attempts which had been made in the Commission by some countries to use the Commission as a means of promoting their interests or limiting in some way or other the activities of subsidiary bodies which were not to their liking. At the same time, the ideas which had been put forward regarding changes in the preparation of documents, the submission of reports and the meeting calendars of some bodies should be acted on.

At the meetings which were to be held in order to secure a rapprochement of the various delegations and achieve consensus, it would undoubtedly be essential to underscore the role of the General Assembly and of the Economic and Social Council as the principal organs responsible for adopting recommendations on ways to resolve the most serious global economic and social

---

[*]Bulgaria, Byelorussian SSR, Czechoslovakia, German Democratic Republic, Hungary, Mongolia, Poland, Ukrainian SSR, USSR.

problems. The Council must also effectively carry out the co-ordination functions entrusted to it under the Charter in respect of all economic and social activities in the United Nations system. That, of course, meant not only technical co-ordination of plans and programmes, but above all political co-operation between all Member States in devising global strategies and identifying priorities in the field of international co-operation for the entire system, so as to achieve the objectives of international social and economic co-operation, as defined by the Assembly. The socialist countries believed that the Council should be entrusted with final consideration of reports by United Nations economic and social bodies, as that would facilitate the formulation of well-balanced and carefully considered recommendations on the most serious international economic problems. The Council must undertake the functions of political co-ordination for all operational activities carried out within the framework of the United Nations. A rational division of labour between the Council and the competent committees of the Assembly and the other economic and social bodies in the United Nations would enable the intergovernmental machinery to function more effectively in the economic and social fields. It would also enable the Assembly to focus on consideration of the key issues of the world economy and international economic relations, and to adopt political decisions on them.

The activities of the Secretariat's economic and social departments should be aimed in particular at identifying the new problems created by the world economic and social situation and facilitating in-depth analysis of those problems in relation to one another and in the light of long-term trends in economic and social development, as well as drawing up recommendations on ways to resolve them before they were submitted to the competent intergovernmental bodies. Furthermore, the structure of the Secretariat departments should be modified in line with that of the intergovernmental bodies. It would therefore be inadvisable to modify the structure of the Secretariat before agreement was reached on the reform of the Organization itself.

The socialist countries believed that the search for ways to improve the economic and social activities of the United Nations was inseparable from the obligation of all Member States to find mutually acceptable political solutions and to fulfil their obligations under the Charter, in particular their financial obligations. However, the restructuring of the economic and social activities of the United Nations must not become an end in itself, nor should it be a permanent process. The most important point was to resolve the problems of the world economy and international economic relations through the political will of all States and not to resort continually to new forms of bodies to discuss them when the provisions of Assembly resolution 32/97 remained unfulfilled. Nevertheless, in the light of the work of the Commission, it should be possible for the Council to reach an consensus with a view to improving the technical and organizational aspects of its working methods and those of the other economic and social bodies within the United Nations. That consensus should also extend to matters such as the periodicity and agenda of sessions and documentation, on which the Council could already take action to facilitate the adoption of practical measures concerning the efficiency and effectiveness of the intergovernmental machinery."

The representative of **Japan**[28]

"The members of the Commission had not agreed on the final report for two reasons: first, several delegations and groups of countries had failed to agree on substantive recommendations and procedures for their implementation; and secondly, the negotiation process had been conducted among members in meetings open to all Member States. However, recommendation 8 of the report of the Group of 18, in response to which the Commission had been established, had envisaged that the body responsible for carrying out the in-depth study should be made up of a limited number of eminent persons chosen on the basis of the principle of equitable geographical distribution. In order to pursue the exercise, therefore, his delegation believed that agreement should be reached, at the current session - or at the Assembly's forty-third session - on a forum and methods of work similar to those which had been advocated by the Group of 18.

Turning to substantive points, he said that his country opposed the universalization of the Council, because that would unavoidably lead to duplication of work between the Council and the Assembly and would make the functioning of the United Nations system even more complicated. It firmly believed that most of the measures for strengthening the efficiency and effectiveness of the intergovernmental machinery could be implemented without universalization of the Council. There was a clear need for better co-ordination and division of labour between the Council and the Assembly. ...

The reform of the United Nations should be a continuing process. The results so far achieved by the Commission were only a first step in restructuring the intergovernmental machinery to make it more responsive to the ever-changing needs of the international community. Fundamental reforms should be envisaged in a longer-term perspective."

The observer for **Mexico**[29]

"the spirit of reform had encountered two serious obstacles: the widespread crisis in the world economy and the internal financial crisis in the United Nations. While confronting the economic crisis, the Member States had at the same time endeavoured to undertake a reform of the structure established by the United Nations for the consideration of economic and social issues. The financial crisis in the United Nations was itself due in large measure to the failure of certain countries to honour their financial obligations. As the Secretary-General had stated, the United Nations would soon become insolvent unless special efforts were made and the very existence of the Organization was at stake. That uncertainty concerning the future of the United Nations had influenced the work of the Commission."

The representative of **Australia**[30]

"his Government regretted that the Special Commission, despite its lengthy labours, had failed to arrive at agreement on a package of wide-ranging structural reforms as envisaged in recommendation 8 of the report of the Group of 18.

His Government believed that one of the most important conclusions to be drawn from the Commission's work, as the Chairman of the Commission had emphasized, was the agreement of Member States that the review of the functioning of the United Nations should be seen as a continuing process aimed at bringing about appropriate reforms to enhance the capacity of the Organization to meet the changing needs of its Members.

That task must be undertaken without delay, building on the work of the Commission, in order to reach rapid decisions on specific reforms. To that end, in his delegation's view, it was necessary first to keep the reform objective high on the agenda, secondly, to find a way to overcome the difficulties posed by certain political obstacles and to study the question on a more technical level, and thirdly, to define clearly the terms of reference so as to give structure and logic to future work. He hoped that the Council would at its current session consider appropriate means to carry forward the task of reform. He would have no objection to the proposal made in informal discussions for the establishment of a small group of high-level experts chosen on the basis of the principle of equitable geographical distribution."

The representative of **Egypt**[31]

"The view that the Council was incapable of living up to its responsibilities was extreme. The substantial expansion of programmes and intergovernmental machinery in the economic and social fields had made the Council's co-ordinating role more complex and at the same time the increasing interdependence of nations and issues and the need for an integrated approach to social and economic development had made its task more difficult. The main reason for the Council's failure was that reform had bypassed some of its major functions, while the Council itself had either waived some of its Charter powers or had not made full use of them. The objectives of international economic and social co-operation set out in Chapter IX of the Charter had taken second place to logistical matters, such as the organization and programme of work, documentation and the like. It was necessary instead to consider the Council's functions and powers under the Charter.

With regard to policy formulation, the general discussion in plenary, the Council's only substantive discussion of international economic and social policy and development, more often than not did not culminate in policy recommendations addressed to the Assembly, the specialized agencies and Member States. Even attempts to arrive at agreed conclusions had been frustrated. If the Council let slip that fundamental function, its very existence might be called in question.

With regard to the Council's second major function, it had to be recognized that co-ordination would not work if Member States failed to co-ordinate their national positions in the various organizations of the United Nations system.

While both the Assembly and Council were given a central co-ordinating role by the Charter, some organ had to co-ordinate co-ordination, and the Council was the only one with a constitutional basis for that task in the economic and social fields. It was the central intergovernmental body for the co-ordination of the system. If the Council failed in its co-ordinating role, the output of the system would be scattered and meaningless, a waste of time, effort and resources, which was more or less the present situation. One reason was the proliferation of programmes, activities and subsidiary bodies. Another was the absence of political determination on the part of Member States to make full use of the Council. A third reason was a negative attitude to the concept of co-ordination on the part of Member States and of entities within the system. The situation had not been helped by the lack of a clear distinction between the roles of the Assembly and the Council, which had led to overloading of the Council's agenda, and the fragmentary approach.

The Council was also failing in its third function of monitoring the implementation of its own decisions and those of the General Assembly on economic and social issues. It was not using its Charter powers or the provisions of relationship agreements to obtain reports from the specialized agencies on the effect given to Assembly and Council recommendations. Substantive co-ordination had been neglected.

Turning to specific proposals, his delegation proposed that as part of the general discussion all members of the Council should strive to reach agreement on a set of recommendations or, failing that, as a transitional measure, a set of agreed conclusions, to assist the Assembly in focusing on a limited number of major issues. The Council should identify issues requiring its priority consideration in time to enable other organizations of the system to participate actively in their discussion. It should organize its work in such a way as to enable it to concentrate on a limited number of carefully selected major policy issues for in-depth study with a view to formulating concrete, action-oriented recommendations. It should monitor the implementation of the overall strategies, policies and priorities established by the Assembly in the economic, social and related fields, and consider means of carrying out the Assembly's recommendations in those fields. In that context, the Secretary-General should be requested to prepare a consolidated report on relevant Assembly decisions, highlighting matters requiring action by organizations of the system, and indicating the priorities laid down by the Assembly. The reports should be circulated to all organizations of the system and made available to the Council at its organizational sessions. The specialized agencies should be requested to include information on steps taken to give effect to the Assembly and Council recommendations in their analytical summaries. The Council should make recommendations to the Assembly for the preparation of the medium-term plan, and the outline of the draft programme budget, particularly with regard to priorities. The Council should recommend to the Assembly overall priorities and policy guidance for operational activities throughout the system and should continue to carry out comprehensive policy reviews of system-wide operational activities. It should concentrate on the policy review and co-ordination of regional co-operation activities, particularly with regard to issues of interregional interests. Where issues for its consideration were similar or related, the Council should consolidate them under a single agenda item so that they could be considered and acted on in an integrated manner, and it should endeavour to bring the economic and social activities of the system closer together. The Secretary-General should be requested to ensure that meetings of subsidiary bodies of the Council ended at least eight weeks before the Council session at which their reports were to be considered. The Council should continue to consider the biennialization of the meetings of its subsidiary bodies with a view of achieving greater synchronization between General Assembly and Council activities. Consolidated reports on social, economic and related fields should be prepared by the Secretariat for the Council on the basis of the reports submitted by relevant bodies within the system. To ensure proper consideration of the interrelationship between economic and social issues, the Council might, on a biennial or triennial basis, review both the economic and social dimensions of the world situation.

System-wide co-ordination should be an integral part of the Council's work, and reports by subsidiary bodies should highlight the substantive and co-ordination issues in the respective fields of activities. Co-ordination instruments such as COPAS, CORS, ACC/CPC meetings, and reports from the ACC and its subsidiary bodies should be strengthened to enable the Director-General to carry out his responsibilities more effectively, particularly in the areas of co-ordination and operational activities for development. The relevant provisions of General Assembly resolutions 32/197 and 33/202 should be fully implemented.

In order to ensure that the measures his delegation proposed were duly implemented, he proposed that the revitalization of the Council should be included in the Council's agenda for its second regular session in 1989 and discussed in plenary with ample time for full consideration. His delegation favoured holding a consolidated session at Headquarters and suggested that the Secretary-General should be asked to prepare a report on the feasibility of doing so.

Many of these proposals were not new and had indeed been adopted by consensus by the Assembly and the Council. What he was advocating was that they should be consolidated in the form of agreed and coherent recommendations without prejudice to any future decisions the Assembly might wish to take."

The representative of **Jamaica**[32]

"The Council had specific responsibility for the follow-up of those issues in the economic and social fields, and over the years, it had established a structure of subsidiary bodies to assist it in carrying out its mandate of responsibilities. There was, however, general agreement that the Council had not performed effectively, and recent discussions had focused on ways and means of restoring its authority and efficacy. Many of its subsidiary bodies had taken on an independent life of their own and were reluctant to accept the Council's authority.

He hoped the Council would be able to agree on an approach to restructuring itself and its subsidiary bodies, a step that would require vision and boldness to go beyond the constraints of the current financial crisis.

As a first step, it was crucial for Member States to agree on identifying the areas - such as money, finance, debt, trade and development; food and agriculture; technical co-operation and assistance; human resources and development - which the United Nations should continue to address, bearing in mind growing world interdependence and the need for multilateral action on various fronts. Other issues could be identified, but consideration should focus on those for which the Council had direct responsibility. The bodies involved in those issues should then be grouped under the headings of policy formulation, operations and support. It would be found that most policy-making was carried out elsewhere than in the Council; the aim should be to restore to the latter many of those policy-making functions, with a view to resuming high-level debate in the Council itself and fostering an integrated, co-ordinated approach to the relevant issues. The Council's various operational and support mechanisms such as commissions, committees and *ad hoc* expert groups should have their mandates, periodicity and output carefully monitored. Duplication and overlapping could not be entirely avoided, of course, given the nature and complexity of many issues, such as that of population - in which the Council itself would be found not to play a substantive part in policy formulation. If the Council was to enhance its role it needed to decide which policy functions it should deal with direct and which ones were better handled elsewhere.

If that general approach was acceptable, the Council could then begin to examine existing bodies with a view to restructuring them and improving procedures, reorganizing the Secretariat where appropriate. The Council's calendar, including agendas and reporting procedures could then be arranged more easily, and it could be seen which of the recommendations made by the Group of High-level Intergovernmental Experts, and the proposals emerging from document E/1988/75, were applicable."

The representative of **Peru**[33]

"The Council was not alone in having its authority diminished or disregarded. The Security Council's decisions, especially those aimed at establishing peace and justice for the South African and Palestinian peoples, had been flouted on many occasions. But the gravity of the Council's situation lay in the fact that its function as the highest forum for economic and social affairs and its responsibility for subordinate bodies such as IMF, the World Bank and others, were being eroded. As a result, none of those bodies was succeeding in its tasks. IMF had failed to achieve world financial stability and the Bank's efforts had led to some reconstruction but had not achieved development. GATT had not succeeded in bringing about a truly multilateral trade system and UNCTAD's efficiency was declining.

Not only had the Council lost prestige and authority, but the world's structural economic problems were as far from solution as ever and seemed to be worsening. Piecemeal efforts were of no use. As the Secretary-General had said, global problems required global solutions arrived at through global consultations. The Council was the right forum for that purpose; its authority must be reasserted. It was the place to achieve the expression of genuine political consensus without which mere technical reforms would achieve little.

A first step could be a meeting at ministerial level with officials from the major agencies, in order that all could participate with a view to policy decision in which all views were fairly represented. It was time to recognize, for one thin, that the huge imbalance in economic growth rates between North and South would go on giving rise to instability and crises unless rectified."

The representative of **Yugoslavia**[34]

"Consideration of the structure and functioning of the Council was of great importance, not only for its own work but for any further efforts to restructure the economic and social sectors of the United Nations. The Council's role could not be separated from that of the Assembly, under whose authority it functioned. The current crisis in multilateral co-operation meant that the United Nations' role in international economic decision-making was being questioned. The Council constituted one of the Organization's weakest links, although its original purpose had been to interlink and co-ordinate the overall United Nations system. ...

There was no lack of ideas or proposals, but the many recommendations that had been adopted had not been put into practice. The question was what must be done to make sure that they were implemented. The greatest number related to the Council and its functioning and their basic objectives was to enable it to fulfil its mandate under the Charter. The Council, under the guidance of the Assembly, was the central intergovernmental body for co-ordinating the activities of the United Nations system. It had never been successful in doing so and steps must therefore be taken to enable it to fulfil its major task. The Council's role in monitoring the implementation of the overall strategies, policies and priorities established by the Assembly for carrying out its decisions should be strengthened. Only through the implementation of the decisions of the various forums in the United Nations system could confidence in the Organization be built. One of the crucial issues was the relationship between the Council and the specialized agencies, which was characterized by formalism and an almost complete absence of United Nations influence on their work. If that weakness could be redressed, the Council could regain its role as one of the major organs of the United Nations system in the economic and social fields. Steps should be taken to ensure that, in accordance with Article 64 of the Charter, the specialized agencies reported to the Council on the steps taken to give effect to the recommendations of the Assembly and the Council in the economic, social and related fields.

To enhance the Council's own efficiency and effectiveness, the items of its agenda should be strictly biennialized, the volume of documentation should be reduced, and the general debate should be better structured and action-oriented. A single consolidated session of the Council should be considered, together with the related question of its venue. The Council should produce a consolidated report covering economic and social matters and United Nations operational activities for development, which would facilitate the proceedings in the General Assembly and enhance overall efficiency."

The representative of the **German Democratic Republic**[35]

"Twice since its inception, in General Assembly 32/197 and 41/213, the United Nations had set itself the task of revitalizing its work in the economic and social fields and making it more action-oriented. The aim was to make the United Nations and its agencies a more efficient forum for dialogue and co-ordinated co-operation in tackling economic and social issues of the present and the future. A number of proposals in that connection had been put forward during the meetings of the Special Commission. Efforts were already being made to reshape work programmes, new structures were emerging, the calender of conferences were being streamlined and documentation rationalized. Steps were being taken to make the secretariats more efficient and open, through strict adherence to the principles of professional competence and equitable geographical distribution.

The fact that the Special Commission had been unable to reach a consensus on recommendations for the General Assembly was no indication of efficiency on the part of the Council, however. The General Assembly, and those United Nations organs which had already adopted concrete measures for restructuring, expected the Council to complete its task as a prerequisite for continued successful activities by the United Nations.

A number of decisions for the revitalization of the Council had been taken and pursued by the Council and the General Assembly since 1982, including the

1983 decision of the General Assembly on the biennialization of the work of the Second committee and of the Council. Those decisions provided sufficient guidance and their clear provisions should now be put into practice. The need was not for further theoretical discussions but for political will and a readiness on the part of all concerned to take concrete action. ...

Some established practices of the Council which had proved useful should be continued. It should, for example, continue its general discussion of international economic and social policy, including regional and sectoral developments. The identification of priority issues would make the discussion increasingly significant for the full range of United Nations economic activities. The World Economic Survey should continue to be produced and CDP and CPC should continue to present timely reports to serve as a basis for a high level general discussion. The strengthening of the Office of the Director-General, proposed by the socialist countries in their position paper, was part of that approach. That applied particularly to its functions in regard to the review and monitoring of operational activities and its co-ordination function in regard to the specialized agencies. Co-ordination with the specialized agencies was extremely important and his delegation supported the Group of 77's proposal in that connection."

Following the debate, a number of draft resolutions were submitted.

Under agenda item 3 (b), the delegation of Tunisia submitted on behalf of the Group of 77, the draft resolution E/1988/L.45 on the revitalization of ECOSOC. As an observer noted, the draft resolution was "proposed in too great a hurry and without a thorough debate in the Council on the various points of view and tendencies regarding the role of ECOSOC."[36] It reflected a sense of frustration among the developing countries at the lack of results achieved by the Special Commission. At the very least, it was now hoped that the reform effort in the social and economic fields could lead to improvements in the functioning of ECOSOC through rather modest changes, such as modifications of reporting procedures, the structure of debates and documentation. The draft resolution entitled **Revitalization of the Economic and Social Council (E/1988/L.45)** reads as follows:

"The Economic and Social Council,

Recalling, General Assembly resolution 41/213 of 19 December 1986, 42/170 of 11 December 1987 and 42/211 of 21 December 1987, concerning the review of the efficiency of the administrative and financial functioning of the United Nations,

Recalling also General Assembly resolution 32/197 of 20 December 1977 on the restructuring of the economic and social sectors of the United Nations system,

Recalling further section IV of General Assembly resolution 33/202 of 29 January 1979 concerning the role of the Director General for Development and International Economic Co-operation,

Recalling Economic and Social Council resolutions 1458 (XLVII) of 8 August 1969 and 1982/50 of 28 July 1982,

Reaffirming the primary responsibility of the General Assembly as the supreme organ of the United Nations system in the economic and social fields,

Aware that the work of the Economic and Social Council can be streamlined in order to make the United Nations system more responsive to the challenges of development in the coming years,

Fully aware of the urgent need to revitalize the Council in order to enable it, under the authority of the General Assembly, to exercise effectively its functions and powers as set out in the Charter of the United Nations and in relevant resolutions of the General Assembly and the Council,

Having heard statements by Member States on this item,

1.   *Affirms* that the Economic and Social Council can make an important contribution to the major issues and concerns facing the international community and, in particular, the economic and social development of developing countries,

2.   *Decides* to adopt, without prejudice to future decisions that the General Assembly or the Council may wish to take, the following measures aimed at revitalizing the Council, improving its functioning and enabling it to exercise effectively its functions and powers as set out in chapters IX and X of the Charter of the United Nations:

(a) The Economic and Social Council shall undertake annually an in-depth discussion of major policy issues, especially those relating to acute international economic and social problems, with a view to elaborating concrete action-oriented recommendations for their resolution; to this effect, the Secretariat shall, upon conclusion of the General Assembly, prepare the basic documentation in the form of an analytical report with appropriate conclusions or recommendations;

(b) The Council shall make recommendations with respect to international economic, social and related matters as part of its annual general discussion. In this connection:

(i)   The executive heads of all the specialized agencies or their senior representatives should participate actively in the general discussion;

(ii)   The Secretariat should prepare documentation of high quality to facilitate the process of discussion and dialogue;

(iii)   The specialized agencies should be invited to resume submission of analytical summaries of their reports and to submit other relevant documentation that could enrich the discussions of the Council;

(c) The Council shall monitor the implementation of the overall strategies, policies and priorities established by the General Assembly in the economic, social and related fields as contained in relevant resolutions of the Assembly and the Council. It shall also consider all appropriate modalities for carrying out the recommendations of the Assembly on matters falling within the Council's competence. In this regard:

(i)   The Secretary-General shall prepare each year a consolidated note on the decisions adopted by the General Assembly in the economic, social and related fields, highlighting matters that require action by the relevant organs, organizations and bodies of the United Nations system. This note should also indicate, in an integrated manner, the priorities laid down by the Assembly and the Council. It shall also consider all appropriate modalities for carrying out the recommendations of the Assembly on matters falling within the Council's competence. In this regard:

(ii)   The Secretary-General shall prepare each year a consolidated note on the decisions adopted by the General Assembly in the economic, social and related fields, highlighting matters that require action by the relevant organs, organizations and bodies of the United Nations system. This n economic, social and related matters that fall within their respective mandates and areas of competence. Such information is to be included in the analytical summaries referred to in paragraph 2, subparagraph (b)(iii), above;

(d) The Council shall make recommendations to the General Assembly for the preparation of the medium-term plan and its introduction, and on the outline of the programme budget, particularly in regard to the priorities to be established therein.

(e) The Council shall recommend to the General Assembly overall priorities and policy guidelines for operational activities for development undertaken by the United Nations system.

(f)   The Council shall carry out its function of co-ordinating the activities
of the United Nations system as an integral part of its work. To this effect:

(i)   The consideration of co-ordination questions should, to the extent
possible, be integrated in the discussion of relevant substantive items
of the Council's agenda;

(ii)   Co-ordination instruments, such as cross organizational reports, the
Joint Meetings of the Committee for Programme and Co-ordination
and the Administrative Committee on Co-ordination and reports of
the Administrative Committee on Co-ordination and its subsidiary
bodies should be adapted in order to enable the Council to carry out
its co-ordination functions in an effective manner, based on the
measures contained in the present resolution; the Committee for
Programme and Co-ordination should assist the Council in this
regard and submit specific proposals thereon to the Council at its
second regular session of 1989;

(iii)   The Administrative Committee on Co-ordination, through its
Consultative Committee on Substantive Questions (Operational
Activities), and the Joint Consultative Group on Policy should
prepare suggestions to assist the Council in fulfilling its central co-
ordinating role in the field of operational activities for development
for submission to the Council at its second regular session of 1989;

(iv)   The Council shall review the United Nations programmes in the
economic, social and related fields as well as their programme budget
implications, and shall recommend to the General Assembly relative
priorities for the activities of the United Nations system in those
fields; to that end, beginning at its second regular session of 1992,
the Council shall, in the framework of a six-year programme, review
selected major issues in the medium-term plans of the organizations
of the United Nations system; for that purpose, the cross-organizational programme analyses shall be discontinued in their present
form and be replaced by mini-analyses on the major issues contained
in the medium-term plan, to be considered directly by the Council;
the Secretary-General should submit to the Council, immediately
after the adoption by the General Assembly of the medium-term plan
for 1992-1997, draft proposals on a multi-year programme for such
a review;

(v)   In considering the question of regional co-operation, the Council
shall concentrate on the policy review and co-ordination of activities,

particularly with respect to issues of common interest to all regions and matters relating to interregional co-operation;

(g) In formulating its biennial programme of work, the Council shall consolidate similar or related issues under a single agenda item in order to consider and take action on them in an integrated manner; the Council shall pay particular attention to bringing closer together the economic and social activities of the United Nations system. To this effect:

(i) The Secretary-General shall, in proposing future calendars of conferences, ensure that meetings of the subsidiary bodies of the Council will end at least eight weeks before the session of the Council at which their reports are to be considered; the Committee on Conferences should be requested to act accordingly;

(ii) The Council shall continue to consider the biennialization of the meetings of its subsidiary bodies and of its own agenda items and programme of work, taking into account the need for a balance between economic and social issues;

(iii) The Council shall receive consolidated reports on the various economic, social and related issues considered by it, to be prepared by the Secretariat on the basis of the reports submitted by relevant bodies and organizations of the United Nations system;

(iv) The Council shall report to the General Assembly on the outcome of its work in a manner that would enable the Assembly, in its Main Committees, to consider the recommendations made by the Council in an integrated manner;

(v) The Council shall review all the documentation prepared for the consideration of questions in the economic, social and related fields;

(h) The Secretary-General, in the context of the implementation of General Assembly resolution 41/213, should submit to the Council, at its second regular session of 1989, proposals on the structure and composition of a separate and identifiable secretariat support structure for the Council to undertake the substantive functions and technical servicing that will be required as a result of the implementation of the measures recommended in the present resolution;

(i) In order to achieve better and more effective co-ordination of the economic, social and related activities of the United Nations system, as well as the system-wide co-ordination of operational activities for development, the Office of the Director General for Development and International Economic Co-operation should be strengthened and adequately staffed; in this context, the relevant provisions of General Assembly resolutions 32/197 and 33/202 should be fully implemented;

(j) In the recruitment of staff for the United Nations Secretariat in the economic and social fields, consideration should be given to the principle of equitable geographical representation;

(k) The Third (Programme and Co-ordination) Committee of the Council shall henceforth deal solely with:

(i)   Co-ordination of the activities of the United Nations and the United Nations system;

(ii)   Programme questions;

(iii) Operational activities for development of the United Nations system and system-wide co-ordination of those activities;

3. *Requests* the Secretary-General to submit a report to the Economic and Social Council at its second regular session of 1989 on the feasibility and comparative costs of holding one consolidated regular session or two regular sessions of the Council at United Nations Headquarters;

4. *Decides* to include an item entitled "Revitalization of the Economic and Social Council" in the provisional agenda for its second regular session of 1989 and to consider under that item a report of the Secretary-General on progress in the implementation of the present resolution;

5. *Requests* the Secretary-General to report to the Economic and Social Council at its organizational session for 1989 on the progress made in the implementation of the present resolution and to incorporate in the draft biennial programme of work of the Council steps to implement the measures contained in the present resolution, as well as measures to implement the recommendations related to the secretariat structure;

6. *Also requests* the Secretary-General, in order to continue discussions on how the work of the Council can be enhanced so as to make it more responsive to the challenge of development in the coming years to submit to the General Assembly at its forty-third session a note containing:

(a) A classification of the functions of the Council and its subsidiary bodies according to the relevant chapters of the medium-term plan and the following categories: (i) policy formulation, co-ordination and monitoring; (ii) operations and implementation; (iii) technical support;

(b) A listing of the mandates of the bodies established to assist the Council in carrying out its functions, grouped into the categories set out in subparagraph (a) above."

Belgium, France, the Federal Republic of Germany, Greece, Ireland, the Netherlands, Portugal, Spain, the UK and the USA submitted a draft resolution under agenda items 3 (a) and 3 (b) which went beyond the issue of the revitalization of ECOSOC and also focused on reforming the structure of the subsidiary bodies. The draft resolution was entitled **Reform of the intergovernmental structure and functions in the economic and social fields, including the functioning of the Economic and Social Council (E/1988/L.49)** and reads as follows:

"*The Economic and Social Council,*

Recalling General Assembly resolution 41/213 of 19 December 1986 and 42/211 of 21 December 1987 on the review of the efficiency of the administrative and financial functioning of the United Nations,

Recalling also General Assembly resolution 32/197 of 20 December 1977 on the restructuring of the economic and social sectors of the United Nations system,

Reaffirming the primary responsibility of the General Assembly as the supreme organ of the United Nations system in the economic and social fields,

Aware that the working methods of the Economic and Social Council should be improved in order to make the United Nations system more responsive to current and future challenges,

Fully aware of the urgent need to exercise more effectively its functions under the authority of the General Assembly,

Noting the report of the Special Commission of the Economic and Social Council on the In-depth Study of the United Nations Intergovernmental Structure and Functions in the Economic and Social Fields,[37]

I. *In-depth study of the United Nations intergovernmental structure and functions in the economic and social fields*

1. *Recommends* to the General Assembly that it take immediate steps to formulate recommendations on structural reform of the United Nations intergovernmental machinery in the economic and social fields, taking due account of the suggestions made by Governments at the second regular session of 1988 of the Economic and Social Council;

2. *Further recommends* to the General Assembly that it conduct negotiations with a view to establishing common ground on the positions developed by the Special Commission of the Economic and Social Council on the In-depth Study of the United Nations Intergovernmental Structure and Functions in the Economic and Social Fields;

3.   *Requests* the Secretary-General to assist the General Assembly in this task;

II.   *Working methods of the Economic and Social Council*

  1.   *Decides:*

  (a) To adopt a thematic approach in the consideration of its agenda, which should be drawn up in accordance with a multi-year work programme; to adopt this work programme in accordance, *inter alia*, with the priorities established in the medium-term plan of the United Nations and the work programmes of other relevant United Nations bodies; to address at each of its sessions a limited number of themes, including co-ordination issues that may fall under them; every three years one of the themes should be a general review of operational activities for development to coincide with the triennial policy review of the operational activities for development of the United Nations system;

  (b) To elect its Bureau early in the calendar year and prior to the organizational session of the Council;

  (c) To discontinue the practice of holding a general discussion of international economic and social policy in plenary meeting;

  (d) To consider reports, including those of its subsidiary bodies, in accordance with the thematic agenda established in the multi-year work programme; there should be no general debate on reports submitted to the Council when these are not being considered under one of the major themes of the Council's agenda as established in the multi-year work programme; in such cases, the Council should limit itself to the consideration of recommendations requiring action, unless it decides otherwise;

  2.   *Further decides:*

  (a) That all reports submitted to the Council should be prefaced by an executive summary that highlights the main issues addressed and the recommendations made thereon; reports should not exceed 32 pages in length;

  (b) To adhere strictly to the six-week rule for the circulation of substantive reports of the Secretariat and the eight-day rule for the annotated agenda of the Council; reports of intergovernmental bodies should be made available at least eight days in advance of their consideration by the Council; reports not available within these time-limits should not be considered;

  (c) To receive one consolidated report on each of the main themes to be considered in accordance with the multi-year work programme; such reports should synthesize the work of the subsidiary bodies of the Council having a mandate related to the themes in question; the Secretariat, after consultation with the Bureau, should prepare such reports;

(d) To report to the General Assembly in a manner that will focus the attention of the Assembly on a limited number of major items and recommendations on which action or policy guidance by the Assembly is required;

(e) That the Bureau of the Council, assisted by the Secretariat, should formulate proposals relating to the draft programme of work and the allocation of agenda items; the Bureau should ensure that the greater part of the work of the Council is devoted to the thematic agenda items; the Bureau's recommendations should be summarized in a document prepared for the organizational session; items should be included in the provisional agenda only if a decision of the Council is likely to be required, unless the Council decides otherwise; the duration of the organizational session should be limited to three days;

(f) To include the question of the working methods of the Council on the provisional agenda for the session of the Economic and Social Council in 1989;

3. *Requests* the Secretary-General to make recommendations to the Council at its organizational session for 1989, in order to facilitate the implementation of the decisions taken in section II of the present resolution."

After intensive consultations, a compromise was finally reached in the form of two resolutions (1988/77 and 1988/182).

Under agenda item 3 (b), ECOSOC approved by consensus a revised version of draft E/1988/L.45 (E/1988/L.45/Rev.1) submitted by Tunisia on behalf of the Group of 77 as resolution entitled **Revitalization of the Economic and Social Council (1988/77)**[*] By resolution 1988/77, ECOSOC decided to adopt measures to revitalize the Council, improving its functioning and enabling it to exercise effectively its powers with respect to policy formulation, monitoring, operational activities, co-ordination, working methods and organization of work. Furthermore, the Secretary-General was requested to submit to the second regular session of ECOSOC in 1989 a report on the feasibility and comparative costs of holding one consolidated or two regular sessions of the Council. The resolution did not mandate major changes in the working system of the Council, which continued to hold one organizational and two substantive regular sessions each year. In order to strengthen the Council's policy formulation functions, it was agreed to reserve the first five working days of the summer session for an annual general debate on international economic and social policy, including regional and sectoral develop-

---

[*]See volume II, 1.6.

ments. The debate was expected to attract the participation of member states at a high political level. It was further decided that ECOSOC should hold annual in-depth discussions of previously identified major policy themes. Other changes were of a more technical nature and were not expected to lead to major improvements.

Following the adoption of resolution 1988/77, a number of statements were made.

The representative of **Norway**[38]

"did not interpret operative paragraph 2 (a) (i) as a reconfirmation of the need to hold an annual general discussion in the Council, since that duplicated similar discussions in the Trade and Development Board and the General Assembly. Where paragraph 2 (g) was concerned, his delegation interpreted it as a proposal for rearrangements within the Secretariat through the consolidation of existing units and, if necessary, the redeployment of staff. Further, it was convinced that paragraph 2 (h) could only be implemented through such redeployment."

The representative of **China**[39]

"the Chinese delegation had pleasure in joining the consensus on the draft resolution on the revitalization of the Council, which represented a welcome step forward towards the goal of strengthening the United Nations system in the economic and social fields.

His delegation supported the reform of the documentation and reporting system of the Council and hoped that reform would lead to a reduction of documents, an improvement of their quality and their timely distribution. It supported the strengthening of overall policy guidance by the Council for operational activities for development in the hope that it would help the governing bodies of subsidiary organs to exercise their mandated functions more effectively. It supported the strengthening of the co-ordinating role of the Council in activities and programmes within the United Nations system as a whole, which it hoped would facilitate the full functioning of the system's existing machinery of co-operation."

The representative of the **United States of America**[40]

"the language used in paragraph 2, section III (d) (i) of the draft resolution just adopted should not be interpreted in such a way as to interfere with the full exercise of their programme responsibilities by the governing bodies of the specialised agencies.

With reference to section V (g) on working methods, his delegation firmly opposed any action with would counteract decisions already taken by the

Secretary-General concerning the restructuring of the Secretariat. The Secretary-General had not asked for a separate and identifiable secretariat for the Council, and the United States delegation believed that would be reflected in any proposals he submitted."

The representative of **Japan**[41]

"For the purpose of revitalizing the Council, more clear-cut language might possibly have been required. The new amendments were somewhat confusing as, for example, in the question of the thematic or sectoral approach. His delegation had questioned the idea of "a separate and identifiable secretariat support structure for the Council" and wondered how large such a secretariat might be. In the interest of co-ordinating the activities of the United Nations system, a strong Office of the Director-General for Development and International Economic Co-operation was indeed required. In the current circumstances of financial stringency maximum use should be made of existing resources to implement the requests made in paragraph 2 (g) and (h)."

The representative of **Egypt**[42]

"His delegation had accepted the idea of having themes considered by the Council with a view to rationalizing its agenda, but had simultaneously encountered opposition to the consolidation of related items under a single agenda item. That seemed to be a double standard."

The representative of **Belgium**[43]

"his delegation had been somewhat reluctant to join the consensus on the draft resolution, for three reasons. Firstly, that document concerned only the functioning of the Council in isolation whereas the Council was only one part of a vast and complex intergovernmental mechanism in the economic and social field. The resolution did not take sufficient account of the problem of the relationship between the Council and the General Assembly and between the Council and its principal subsidiary organs, thus leaving the way open for some duplication.

Secondly, the resolution, while containing many provisions of which his delegation approved, did not take sufficient account of proposals made by his delegation with a view to improving and simplifying the Council's working methods; the resolution modified those methods but did not simplify them sufficiently.

Thirdly, the resolution had been drafted, negotiated and amended at the current session of the Council, in other words the economic session. The procedures of the social session were different, and insufficient account had been taken of that fact. The implementation of some provisions of the resolution at the social session of the Council was likely to cause difficulties."

The representative of the **Federal Republic of Germany**[44]

"his delegation had serious doubts as to whether the draft resolution would have the desired effect of making the Economic and Social Council more efficient. It shared the concern of the delegation of Belgium, particularly regarding the work of the Council in the social field. It considered that the resolution addressed only some aspects of the reform envisaged by the Group of 18 in recommendation 8 of its report and General Assembly resolution 41/213."

The observer for Tunisia, speaking on behalf of the **Group of 77**[45]

"There was a contradiction between the stated desire of many delegations to reform the economic and social sectors of the United Nations and their declared aim of reducing the United Nations programme budget.

Referring to paragraph 2, section I on policy formulation, he said that the Group of 77 was satisfied with subparagraph (a) (i) dealing with the annual general discussion, which it considered to be of great importance for the developing countries. Although it had accepted the use of the expression "major policy themes" in subparagraph (a) (ii), it found that term unclear and hoped that the Council and the General Assembly would at some stage define it.

Section II on monitoring functions was important, since it allowed the Council to fulfil the mandate set out in the Charter of the United Nations.

Section III on operational activities provided adequate assurance in subparagraph (d) (i) that the governing bodies of the organizations responsible for operational activities in the United Nations system would not exceed their mandates.

Section IV (e) ensured clarity in inter-agency relations and the introduction of a spirit of constructive competition in the activities of the agencies in their respective sectors.

Section V on working methods and organization of work sought to enable the Council to balance its economic and social activities. The reports referred to in subparagraph (f) (iii) did not duplicate those of subsidiary bodies and would enable the Organization to make considerable savings, and reduce the quantity and improve the quality of documentation. Subparagraph (g) had been based on recommendation of the Group of 18; the Group of 77 wished thereby to give the Council the means of carrying out its functions without placing any further burden on the United Nations budget. Subparagraph (i) was important for the Group of 77, which was concerned about recruitment trends and redeployment in the Secretariat, which did not take adequate account of equitable geographical representation. Regarding subparagraph (k) and (l), the Group of 77 was convinced that the Bureau and the President of the Council could play a role that would help to enhance the efficiency of the Council."

The representative of **Denmark**[46]

"While his delegation had no reservations to the text just adopted it considered that an opportunity had been missed for a genuine reform of the Council which would enable it to regain the political credibility it needed in international economic discussions. Rather than simplifying the work of the Council, the tendency was in the opposite direction. Most of the provisions of the resolution were a repetition of principles already adopted in earlier Council and General Assembly resolutions. The problem - which continued to exist even after the adoption of the resolution - was how to translate those principles into specific measures to serve the objective shared by all delegations. His delegation would have liked to see more specific proposals put forward for consideration and regretted that its amendments had not been taken into account."

Following these statements, the ECOSOC turned to agenda item 3 (a). Based on draft E/1988/L.46 submitted by Tunisia on behalf of the Group of 77, ECOSOC approved by consensus the decision entitled **Report of the Special Commission of the Economic and Social Council on the In-depth Study of the United Nations Intergovernmental Structure and Functions in the Economic and Social Fields (1988/182)**. By decision 1988/182, ECOSOC took note of the report of the Special Commission and transmitted the report to the 43rd session of the GA for consideration and appropriate action.

Once the decision had been adopted, the representative of **Australia**[47] noted

"His delegation's greatest regret was that the Council had been unable to provide the General Assembly at its forty-third session with suggestions concerning possible practical steps to follow up the work of the Special Commission to implement fully General Assembly resolution 41/212. One such step was the establishment of a high-level body based on the principle of equitable geographical distribution and preferably with a limited membership. Unfortunately, no other practical suggestion had been made at the current session of the Council for a mechanism to carry forward the reform process, and he urged that matter should be given full and careful consideration at the forthcoming session of the General Assembly."

In his annual report, the **Secretary-General**[48] commented on the two ECOSOC decisions (1988/77, 1988/182) concerning the revitalization of ECOSOC and the report of the Special Commission, noting:

"The Special Commission, established by the Council, has carried out a thorough and useful review of the intergovernmental machinery of the United Nations in the economic and social sectors. It was unfortunate that the Commission could not agree on a set of recommendations about the many activities in the economic and social fields which it discussed. Nevertheless, its discussions reveal substantial areas of agreement on important general principles, which could provide a basis for future action.

I welcome the Council's resolution on revitalization which, when implemented, can greatly enhance its ability to give policy guidelines as well as to monitor and co-ordinate the economic and social activities of the United Nations system. The Council's resolution and the report of the Special Commission will be extremely helpful for further deliberations in the context of the ongoing reform process. I should like to touch upon two elements relevant to this process.

First, the Council's effectiveness depends upon its ability to provide authoritative guidance towards a clear definition of priorities. I continue to believe that this ability will be strengthened if the Council meets at a sufficiently high political level, preferably ministerial, to consider issues of major importance for the international community. Such meetings would enhance the Council's status, credibility and effectiveness.

Second, and closely related to the above, Member States need to consider practical steps to identify those issues which are relatively more important and timely for intergovernmental consideration. In doing so, full consideration needs to be given to the fact that financial, monetary, trade and development issues are interrelated and have profound political and social implications. The concept of sustainable development in its broadest sense has relevance in this context."

4.4 The 43rd session of the General Assembly

Unlike the disappointing outcome of the Special Commission, other reform efforts proceeded successfully. First of all, CPC recommended to the GA by consensus the approval of the programme budget outline for the biennium

1990-1991. The estimates amounted to $1,763,700 which represented a reduction of 9.6 per cent in real terms. This was the first outline proposed by the Secretary-General in accordance with the new budget procedure. It was also the first major test of how the new budget process agreed in December 1986 would work. The Secretary-General estimated that a contingency fund amounting to 0.75 per cent of the budget was reasonable to accommodate additional expenditures, excluding those arising from extraordinary expenses and the fluctuations in exchange rates and inflation. The proposal for the use and operation of a contingency fund had been reviewed by CPC and ACABQ. Extensive restructuring had been completed in the political and administrative areas and was well under way in the Department of Public Information. In addition, the implementation of the post reductions had reached a crucial stage. This GA would decide on the new staffing tables and set an upper limit for the number of posts.

The elaboration of the new post structure proposal by the secretariat had been a rather difficult exercise. In February 1988, after seven months of intensive study, the post review group had submitted its report to the Secretary-General and Programme Planning and Budgeting Board (PPBB). The Board decided to circulate the report to all programme managers for comments. In the light of additional information and comments from programme managers, the PPBB met in February and March 1988 for a final review of the report. The Chairman of the post review group had attended the meetings of the Board, which had also been addressed by the Chairperson of the staff union. The PPBB had based its final review on information on programme implementation for the period from 1984 to the first semester of 1987 and, in some cases, on information about work-loads. Estimating the work-load for 1990-1991 had been a somewhat theoretical exercise, inasmuch as the programme had not yet been finalized, but the experience of programme managers had helped to temper that problem.

The detailed recommendations on the reductions in personnel were issued in July 1987 as document A/C.5/43/1/Rev.1. The proposal included a reduction of 1,465 posts from 11,422 to 9,957, detailed down to the budget section level. Out of the 11,422 posts, 167 could not be included in the posts reduction exercise since they were funded jointly with other UN agencies. The adjusted base was therefore 11,255 posts and the proposed reduction of 1,465 posts accounted for 13.02 per cent, which fell short of the target of 15 per cent. With regard to the senior level, the proposal included a cut of 14 of USG and ASG posts. This corresponded to approximately 23 per cent of the total and fell short of the target of 25 per cent. The lower reductions were essentially justified by the lack of progress achieved in the Special Commission of ECOSOC. Only when the organizational and structural changes were in place in the economic and social fields, could further staff reductions be implemented. The current proposal included a reduction in the Department of Conference Services by 14.1 per cent. This proposal was based on the assumption that the GA would approve a streamlined calender of conferences and meetings during 1990 and 1991. If this could not be achieved, some of the cuts in this area would need to be restored. Following a review of the post reduction proposals, the ACABQ recommended that 100 posts should be restored to the Department of Conference Services, to be partly offset by a reduction of 50 posts in other areas, a noted in the report A/43/651. The total number of posts reduced would, therefore, be 1,415 or 12.57 per cent, resulting in a final figure of 10,007 posts. The ACABQ recommended that the Secretary-General should submit a report to the GA before 1 November reflecting this recommendation.

Prior to the commencement of the 43rd session of the GA, a representative of the Secretary-General informed the Advisory Committee that no further proposals on post reductions could be submitted until the results of the various intergovernmental and secretariat reviews under way were known, since any further cuts would have an adverse affect on programmes. The Secretary-General's representative was not been in a position, however, to inform the ACABQ of the precise effect on programmes of the reductions in question. In a further report (A/43/651/Add.1), the ACABQ therefore recommended a total of 10,007 posts, including the increase of 100 posts in the Department of Conference Services. Further reductions in other budget sections should be proposed by the secretariat in 1989 in the context of the proposed programme budget for 1990-1991. There were, of course, two other options. Firstly, to approve a staffing table of 9,957 posts as proposed by the Secretary-General on the assumption that conference servicing demands would be considerably reduced. Secondly, the GA could approve 10,007 posts without further reductions in the following biennium. A representative of the secretariat had indicated that for the biennium 1988-1989, the restoration of the 100 posts could probably be financed from savings within the existing appropriation. There would, however, certainly be an increase in the real value of the budgetary requirements in the next programme budget proposals.

The 43rd session of the GA took up the reform issues in the following three forums: the Fifth Committee considered the reform of the UN in accordance with GA resolution entitled Implementation of General Assembly Resolution 41/213 (42/211) - see section 4.3.1; the Plenary Assembly considered the report of the Special Commission of ECOSOC in accordance with ECOSOC decision 1988/182 - see section 4.3.2; and the Second Committee considered ECOSOC resolution entitled Revitalization of the Economic and Social Council (1988/77) - see section 4.3.3.

4.4.1 Approval of the Progress Report and Revised Estimates (43/213) and the Programme Budget Outline and Contingency Fund (43/214)

Under agenda item 49 (Review of the Efficiency of the Administrative and Financial Functioning of the United Nations), the Fifth Committee considered the implementation of the UN reform in accordance with GA resolution entitled Implementation of General Assembly Resolution 41/213 (42/211)[*]. The Committee had before it following documentation: (i) the Secretary-General's second progress report on the implementation of GA resolution 41/213 (A/43/286), together with observations of ACABQ (A/43/651) and CPC (A/43/16)[**], (ii) the Secretary-General's note on the use and operation of the contingency fund (A/43/324), together with observations of ACABQ (A/43/929) and CPC (A/43/16)[***], (iii) the Secretary-General's report on revised estimates for the implementation of recommendation 15 on the reduction of personnel (A/C.5/43/1/Rev.1), together with observations of ACABQ (A/43/651 and A/43/651/Add.1) and CPC (A/43/16)[****], (iv) the Secretary-General's report on the proposed programme budget outline for the biennium 1990-1991 (A/43/524), together with observations of ACABQ (A/43/929) and CPC (A/43/16)[*****]. Agenda item 49 was considered in conjunction with revised estimates for the biennium 1988-1989 under item 114 (Programme Budget for the Biennium 1988-1989).

Comments on the reform effort made by **Secretary-General**[49] in his annual report are given below, followed by statements made during the debate under agenda item 49.

---

[*]See volume II, 1.5.
[**]See volume II, 2.17, 2.18, 2.19.
[***]See volume II, 2.20, 2.21, 2.22.
[****]See volume II, 2.24, 2.25, 2.26, 2.27.
[*****]See volume II, 2.28, 2.29, 2.30.

"Reform and renewal in the United Nations has been one of my main preoccupations. As Secretary-General, I have shared the feeling that the accretions of four decades and a certain inflation of activity had encouraged a bureaucratic resistance to self-review and that we needed a leaner and more effective apparatus. ... I might summarize some of the main points here:

Reform is the joint responsibility of both Member Sates and the Secretariat. As far as the Secretariat is concerned, a good part of the process pertaining to administrative and finance has been completed ahead of the three-year schedule. The appropriations for the programme budget of the current biennium assume an overall vacancy rate of 15 per cent in the Professional and 10 per cent in other categories of staff.

Extensive restructuring has been undertaken in the political and administrative areas of the Secretariat and is under way in the area of public information.

A number of steps have been taken to improve co-ordination among the organizations of the United Nations system and a close look has been taken at field offices so as to avoid duplication and share resources, wherever possible.

A thorough assessment of our management information systems, in the light of current technology, has been initiated with a view to their eventual integration and the better provision of information required by Member States and the Secretariat. ...

There are limits to the economies that can be effected in the Secretariat. An example is the provision of conference and documentation services essential to the conduct of discussions on issues on the international agenda. Without a decrease in meetings included in future calendars of conferences, post reductions of the size that were recommended in this area would gravely disrupt these services. But a decrease in meetings would mean some curtailing of the activities of the intergovernmental machinery and this would require a decision not by the Secretariat, but by Members States.

This brings us face to face with the fact that the Secretariat has grown not through a self-propelled process, but in response to the demands of the more extended intergovernmental machinery it must service. A rationalization of the structures of the Organization at the intergovernmental level would require decisions by Governments based on a re-examination of priorities among programmes and decisions, if acceptable to the generality of membership, would lend further substance to the process of reform."

In the following, the statements made under agenda item 49 are recalled. Before members states addressed the Committee, the USG for Administration and Management presented the issues involved and the Chairman of ACABQ and the Chairman and Vice-Chairman of CPC introduced their reports, followed by the Controller, as outlined below.

Mr. Ahtisaari, USG for Administration and Management[50]

"In the political sector, many reforms had now been completed. The Committee for Programme and Co-ordination had requested some clarifications - on, for instance, the new structure of the Office of the United Nations Commissioner for Namibia. The matter had been reviewed by the Council for Namibia; the Secretariat hoped that the arrangements were now satisfactory.

Reform in the economic and social sector had not proceeded so fast since, under paragraph 6 of resolution 42/211, the Secretary-General was required to take into account the reviews, studies and decisions entrusted to intergovernmental bodies. Discussions were now taking place on possible reforms, taking into account Economic and Social Council decision 1988/77 on the revitalization of the Council.

Many recommendations of the Group of 18 in the administrative area had been put into effect; others, particularly those relating to personnel management, depended upon the completion of other recommendations. That was especially true of recommendation 15, on post reductions. Priorities had to be established among the many tasks proposed by the Group of 18 and approved by the General Assembly; a work programme had been drawn up with a view to putting as many as possible into effect before December 1989. It should also be noted that many recommendations in the administrative area required implementation on a continuous basis extending well beyond 1989. One of the most important related to the integration of Secretariat management systems. ...

The Secretary-General's plans for post reductions had been drawn up after complex and serious analyses and consultations. The dominant objective had been to increase the efficiency and effectiveness of the Secretariat while limiting as far as possible the adverse effects of a staff cut on the Organization and its future. ...

One possible effect of the reduction in personnel which the Secretary-General had tried to avoid was an adverse impact on programmes. There was not an automatic link between a smaller Secretariat and a reduced role for the United Nations; efficiency and productivity could be improved in various parts of the Organization through technological innovations, improved management procedures, and the consolidation of programmes and units. Further progress towards effectiveness and efficiency was needed and could be made if reform and renewal were pursued with the full and active support of Member States, including compliance with their financial obligations. The design and delivery of some programmes might need to be improved, and a number of administrative and legislative processes needed to be rationalized. Once the retrenchment was over, however, all parties would be freer to pursue the changes that would demonstrate that the United Nations could effectively play its enhanced role."

Mr. Mselle, **Chairman of the ACABQ**[51]

"Of the recommendations by the Group of 18, recommendation 15 had been one of the most thoroughly negotiated and debated, and the General Assembly had laid down a series of guidelines to be followed by the Secretary-General in implementing it. Although they attempted to address the concerns of various States and groups of States, the guidelines were unfortunately not definitive statements of what should and should not be done, or how. The General Assembly had assumed that the cuts called for had been arrived at in a pragmatic manner instead of being, as they were, arbitrary. The Group of 18 had never carried out a work-load analysis of the various departments and offices in the Secretariat: the Secretary-General had been asked to do so. The requirement that the Secretary-General should implement recommendation 15 with flexibility, in order to avoid negative impact on programmes and on the structure and composition of the Secretariat, left a good deal to be arrived at by the Secretary-General on the basis of his own judgement. Thus the Secretary-General's proposals for implementing the recommendation were bound to be interpreted differently by different Member States or groups of Member States.

The Secretary-General proposed a target 13.02 per cent reduction in an adjusted base of 11,255 regular-budget posts; if the calendar of conferences for 1990-1991 was not modified, however, he would recommend a target reduction of 12.1 per cent overall, reflecting a reduction under section 29 of 10 per cent instead of 14.1 per cent. After extensive examination and discussion of the Secretary-General's proposals, the Advisory Committee had concluded that, if the calendar of conferences from 1990 onwards was not modified, 100 of the 357 posts under section 29 originally proposed for elimination should be restored, bringing the target for reduction under that section to approximately 10.1 per cent. The Advisory Committee held that the 100 posts, apportioned between grades as indicated in paragraph 15 of its report, should be allocated to translation, interpretation of meetings, publishing, editorial control and official records, due regard being paid to the need for the proportionate treatment of language services.

In present circumstances, the Advisory Committee had been unable to recommend additional appropriations to cover the restoration of 100 posts under section 29. It had been informed that the biennial cost of those posts would be $12,893,900, net of staff assessment. In paragraphs 15 to 19 of its report, it proposed a series of measures to accommodate the estimated gross cost of almost $15 million, among them a compensatory adjustment of 50 posts from other parts of the Secretariat. He did not believe that adjustment and the other measures outlined in paragraph 19 of the Advisory Committee's report ought to affect the regional commissions (other than the Economic Commission for Europe), in view of their special circumstances."

Mr. Mselle, **Chairman of the ACABQ**[52] continued

"For the moment, the Secretary-General had neither rejected nor embraced the Advisory Committee's recommendation. He had simply said that a number of studies were still being carried out (inter-agency-funded machinery, liaison functions, etc.) and that it was therefore impossible at the present stage to indicate where the 50 additional posts could be eliminated. If the Advisory Committee's recommendation was accepted, the Secretary-General would make the consequential changes in proposed budget for the biennium 1990-1991, taking due account of the result of the studies, the views of CPC as to which administrative units had suffered most in the initial proposals, and the views of the Fifth Committee."

Mr. Mselle, **Chairman of the ACABQ**[53] continued

"The organizational changes outlined in chapter III of the revised estimates (A/C.5/43/1/Rev.1) were difficult to evaluate in the absence of complete information on functional allocation and programmes. The Advisory Committee felt that the proposed programme budget for 1990-1991 should incorporate all the changes described in the various progress reports and revised estimates.

The Advisory Committee had accepted the proposal for an Evaluation and Management Advisory Services Division under section 8, as indicated in paragraphs 31 and 32 of its report. It had reserved its position on joint and common services at Nairobi pending a precise indication of how the findings of a review of such services would be implemented (para. 33).

In examining the revised estimates for the Department of Public Information (A/C.5/43/1/Rev.1, chap. IV), the Advisory Committee had refrained from duplicating the debate on public information activities which had been carried out in CPC and the Committee on Information. Having heard from the representatives of the Secretary-General, it would not object to the restoration of five D-1 posts in the manner indicated in paragraph 45 of its report. With regard to the new main organizational units in DPI, it questioned the rationale for the existence of the Bureau of Programme Operations and felt that there was some potential for duplication between the activities of the Division for Committee Liaison and Administrative Services and some other substantive units.

During its consideration of the revised estimates for DPI, the Advisory Committee had been given the results of a survey of public information activities conducted by other Secretariat departments. The survey had concluded that, for a number of reasons, it would not be feasible to consolidate those activities within DPI at present. Some of those activities were carried out in accordance with long-standing mandates; besides, DPI was being reorganized and could not assume more responsibilities before its new structure became fully operational. The Advisory Committee had accepted the findings of the survey, and welcomed the offer by the Secretariat to conduct another survey not later than 1992. It believed that DPI and other departments should co-operate to use public information resources to optimum effect, and it also called for more emphasis on training."

Mr. Mselle, **Chairman of the ACABQ**[54] continued

"The Advisory Committee had noted some improvements following the steps taken by the Secretary-General to reduce the high vacancy rates in the regional economic commissions and certain Secretariat units, in particular through internal redeployment and exceptions to the recruitment freeze. ...

In chapter VI of the revised estimates, the Secretary-General proposed that temporary posts authorized on a recurrent basis should be converted to established posts. ... The Advisory Committee found it difficult to take a position on the proposal in the absence of specific information on the functions related to the posts in question and believed that the proposal should be reformulated and submitted, with justification, in the context of the proposed programme budget for biennium 1990-1991. ... The Advisory Committee, for its part, believed that the proposals should be dealt with in the context of the consideration of the programme budget for 1988-1989 and maintained that the matter was one which fell within its own sphere of competence."

Mr Mselle, **Chairman of the ACABQ**[55] continued

"With respect to activities relating to Namibia ... there had been a proposal to merge the posts of Director of the Office of the Commissioner for Namibia and the Secretary of the United Nations Council for Namibia (para. 6). ... As was indicated in document A/C.5/43/1/Rev.1/Add.1, the United Nations

Council for Namibia had considered the question at its 516th meeting on 23 June 1988. As was apparent from paragraphs 3 and 4 of that addendum, the proposal to consolidate the functions of Director of the Office of the Commissioner and Secretary of the Council for Namibia had not been endorsed by the Council. It therefore seemed that those two functions would continue to be separate.

The addendum also contained a proposal which had not been before ACABQ at its spring session, namely, the reclassification of the post of Secretary of the Council from the D-1 to the D-2 level and the establishment of a D-2 post for that purpose. ACABQ had, however, considered a similar proposal in the context of the programme budget for the biennium 1986-1987, and its observations at that time were summarized in paragraph 5 of the addendum. Unfortunately, no detailed substantiation of the reclassification proposal had been provided to ACABQ in response to its request. In the circumstances, ACABQ was unable to endorse the proposed reclassification. It would, moreover, point out to the Fifth Committee that proposals designed to reduce the number of posts at the levels of Under-Secretary-General, Assistant Secretary-General and D-2 were under study. If the two functions mentioned earlier had been consolidated, they could indeed have been entrusted to a D-2 official; but, since the Council had rejected the proposed consolidation, the reclassification sought appeared to be unjustified in the present circumstances. ACABQ had no objection to the other changes proposed by the Secretary-General in section A of chapter IV.

Section B, which related to the implementation of recommendation 29 concerning the functions of the Office of Secretariat Services for Economic and Social Matters, was contained in paragraphs 19 to 30 of chapter IV. ACABQ dealt briefly with it in paragraphs 38 and 39 of its report (A/43/651), and the recommendation of CPC was in paragraph 40 of its report (A/43/16). The issue had been discussed at length at the forty-second session. As was apparent from the revised estimates, the Secretary-General maintained the position which he had formulated at that time, namely, that the functions of the Office relating to the technical secretariat servicing of intergovernmental meetings should be assigned to the Office of the Under-Secretary-General for Political and General Assembly Affairs and Secretariat Services.

Section C of chapter IV dealt with the implementation of recommendation 37 concerning public information activities. That issue had been discussed in depth by CPC and ACABQ, and the latter's comments were contained in paragraphs 40 to 60 of its report (A/43/651). Following the deliberations of

CPC, additional information had been provided by the Secretariat, and it was reproduced in section D of chapter IV. ACABQ had taken that information into account in formulating its recommendations, especially in relation to the restoration of five D-1 posts (A/43/651, paras. 42-45). In the light of the observations of ACABQ, the Secretariat had issued document A/43/16 (Part II) Add.1, which ACABQ had not yet discussed in detail. He nevertheless advised the Fifth Committee not to await the outcome of that discussion for the purposes of its own deliberations on chapter IV, since the substance of that addendum was in no way inconsistent with the recommendations which ACABQ had formulated in paragraphs 42 to 45 of its report. The Secretary-General stated in the addendum that the restoration of five D-1 posts would entail the elimination of the following posts: one P-4, three P-2 and one P-3. The units in which the posts were to be abolished were given in paragraph 6."

Mr. Mselle, **Chairman of the ACABQ**[56] continued

"paragraphs 2 to 16 of the Advisory Committee's report (A/43/929) explained how the preliminary estimate of the proposed programme budget outline for the biennium 1990-1991 had been calculated. The Secretary-General had estimated total programme resources for the biennium 1990-1991 at $1,763.7 million at 1988 rates, compared with the initial appropriations of $1,769.6 million for the biennium 1988-1989. After detailed examination of the Secretary-General's proposals, ACABQ had recommended that a 5 per cent vacancy rate rather than the proposed rate of 3 per cent be used to calculate staff costs for the outline, leading to a reduction of $16,155,000 (at 1988 rates) from the preliminary estimate. On the other hand, it had recommended an addition of $14,264,800, representing the cost (at 1988 rates) of programme decisions proposed so far for adoption at the forty-third session of the General Assembly and approved by the Advisory Committee, together with an addition of $5,308,000 (at 1988 rates), being the cost of a net addition of 50 posts over and above the 9,957 posts proposed for the biennium 1990-1991 in document A/C.5/43/1/Rev.1.

The total preliminary estimate recommended by the Advisory Committee at 1988 rates was therefore $1,767,060,000, without taking into account charges for unforeseen and extraordinary expenditures. A problem with regard to the outline submission date was addressed in paragraph 3 of the report of the Advisory Committee, which had recommended that the Secretary-General should exercise the best possible discretion to anticipate changes in programme activities to be introduced during the year in which the outline was considered. Although it would seem to be impossible for the Secretary-General to anticipate all programme changes arising from intergovernmental decisions, the delay experienced in 1988 in estimating requirements within the Secretary-General's jurisdiction, and particularly for such a substantial project as the Integrated Management Information System, should not be repeated. Recosting at 1990-1991 rates would bring the total preliminary estimate recommended by the Advisory Committee for the biennium 1990-1991 to $1,982,523,700.

Paragraphs 17 to 31 of the Advisory Committee's report addressed the difficult problem of how to deal with future changes in currency and inflation rates. The General Assembly, in resolution 41/213, had expressed the desire that additional expenditures to cover such fluctuations should be accommodated within the overall level of the budget. The Advisory Committee had once again held extensive consultations with representatives of the specialized agencies and the United Nations and noted the various new procedures adopted by certain of those agencies. Those included the expression of budgets in the local currency of the host country, the collection of "split assessments" and the forward purchasing of currency. Further details of all those systems could be provided if necessary. The Advisory Committee had, however, concluded that no method so far tried was fully satisfactory. It had therefore proposed two options for consideration by the General Assembly. Either the current system of annual adjustments could continue, or a reserve might be established, as briefly explained in paragraphs 27 to 30 of document A/43/929. ...

ACABQ had recommended that the contingency fund be set at $15 million at 1990-1991 rates and had provided, in paragraphs 35 and 36 of its report, technical guidelines with respect to the determination of its size. The amount of the fund was in addition to the preliminary estimate of resources at 1990-1991 rates. As indicated in paragraph 34, no advance appropriation should yet be made in respect of the contingency fund but amounts, within its limit, should be appropriated as needed."

Mr. Murray, Chairman of the CPC[57]

"Among its conclusions and recommendations in connection with document A/43/286, the Committee had endorsed the view of the Secretary-General that, for the process of reform to reach fruition, Member States must provide their full support, politically and financially, to the Organization and had noted that action relating to reform in the economic and social fields would need to take into full account the results of the in-depth study of the intergovernmental structure and functions in those fields. It had also emphasized that the restructuring exercise should avoid negative impact on programmes, particularly in relation to the implementation of recommendation 15 of the Group of High-level Intergovernmental Experts, while bearing in mind the necessity of securing the highest standards of efficiency, competence and integrity of the staff, with due regard to equitable geographical distribution.

Following consideration of the options proposed by the Secretary-General for reductions in conference-servicing posts at New York and Geneva, the Committee had recommended acceptance of a 10 per cent reduction in such posts, with further reductions to be made, when possible, in the process of implementation of General Assembly resolution 41/213 as a whole. It had also expressed its concern with respect to the situation in smaller offices and regional commissions and recalled that a decision on the consolidation and strengthening of support activities relating to Namibia should take full account of the opinion of the United Nations Council for Namibia.

Conclusions and recommendations relating to the Department of Public Information were contained in both parts (I and II) of the Committee's report and should be considered together. The Committee continued to harbour many reservations about the reorganization of the Department and recommended that its performance should be closely monitored and evaluated. Indeed, the entire restructuring exercise required further monitoring in order to ensure that the overall result was a more efficient and more effective Organization."

Mr. Chabala, **Vice-Chairman of the CPC**[58]

"CPC considered that the report of the Secretary-General (A/43/524) constituted the basis for a decision by the General Assembly. The eight points reflected in paragraph 30 of the CPC report included such important reminders as the need for a strict observance of the financing of the programme budget once it had been approved and appropriated; the need to have a budget outline that would preclude a negative impact on mandated programmes; the need to treat the outline as an evolving exercise to be approached with flexibility, while respecting the provisions of General Assembly resolutions 41/213 and 42/211; and the recognition that the level of the contingency fund, expressed as a percentage of the overall level of resources, was to be in addition to the proposed preliminary estimates of the Secretary-General as adjusted by appropriate estimates of inflation and currency fluctuations.

With regard to the level of the contingency fund, the views of CPC were reflected in paragraph 18 and 19 of its report. Some delegations had supported the 0.75 per cent initially recommended by the Secretary-General, others considered the percentage to be too low, while still others felt that it could be subject to review during the biennium.

A third issue concerned the treatment of priorities. CPC felt that the paragraphs on priorities in the Secretary-General's report (A/43/524, paras. 8 and 9) did not satisfactorily address the request made in General Assembly resolution 41/213 for the submission of "priorities, reflecting general trends of a broad sectoral nature". In paragraph 31 of its conclusions and recommendations, CPC pointed out that the distribution of staff resources among the various parts of the budget did not represent the establishment of priorities among the various activities of the Organization. CPC emphasized the need for the Secretary-General, in developing his detailed programme budget for the biennium 1990-1991, to reflect the priorities deriving from the current medium-term plan as revised. ...

Lastly, in paragraph 35, CPC noted that the proposed programme budget outline was reflected in the revised estimates of the Secretary-General, and reiterated that the level of resources for the biennium 1990-1991, while reflecting the negative real growth of 9.6 per cent proposed by the Secretary-General, should be adequate for the fulfilment of the objectives of the Organization."

Controller[59]

"The Secretary-General agreed with the Chairman of ACABQ that the 15 per cent reduction rate proposed by the Group of 18 was not a scientifically arrived-at figure, but a target to be achieved over a certain period while abiding by certain parameters (no adverse impact on programmes, the maintenance of geographical balance within the Secretariat, etc.). His proposed target was that given in paragraph 15 of document A/C.5/43/1/Rev.1: an overall cut of 13.02 per cent from a base of 11,255 posts. To arrive at that figure, he had to take account of the effect of the planned reductions on a programme budget whose size and content would not be defined till much later. His position was that a reduction of that order would inevitably have repercussions and, as mandated by the relevant regulations, Member States would have to define their priorities clearly so that the Secretariat could amend programmes intended for execution in 1990-1991 to prevent any adverse impact."

The **Controller**[60] continued

"CPC and the Advisory Committee, which found the reduction excessive, were both proposing the restoration of 100 posts for conference services in New York and Geneva, and the Advisory Committee was further proposing that the restoration should be partially offset by a reduction of 50 additional posts in other sectors. The Secretary-General maintained that, since the

Member States had not completed their study of the intergovernmental structure in the economic and social fields ... and the various studies requested by the Advisory Committee were still under way, he was in no position to determine where the 50 additional posts should be eliminated. It had taken 18 months of hard work to establish, in consultation with the departmental managers and bearing in mind the many directives and caveats formulated by Member States, the retrenchment plan currently proposed. It was simply not possible for the Secretariat to redo all that work in one week. He could, however, state which would be the additional reductions in the context of the proposed programme budget for the biennium 1990-1991, provided that the Member States specifically asked him to do so. Given that the Member States themselves had not completed their work on the rationalization of the calendar of conferences and meetings, it was imperative that the Secretary-General should have sufficient time to determine which other posts could be eliminated, and on the basis of what criteria, so that those proposals, carefully pondered, could be the subject of a consensus."

The representative of **Yugoslavia**[61]

"expressed appreciation for the results achieved by the Secretary-General in the reforms requested by the General Assembly in resolutions 41/213 and 42/211. ...

In the economic and social fields, the review of the intergovernmental structure had not yet been completed and the General Assembly still had to make recommendations. It was, therefore, important that the discussions that were now, according to the Under-Secretary-General for Administration and Management, taking place in the Secretariat should not prejudge the solutions to be reached at the intergovernmental level. Still, the Secretariat should not be discouraged from trying to eliminate overlapping, streamline its activities and enhance co-operation between its various individual units, particularly in the fields of research and analysis.

It was not surprising that the questions of personnel management and post reductions had attracted particular attention. Recommendation 15 by the Group of High-level Intergovernmental Experts to Review the Efficiency of the Administrative and Financial Functioning of the United Nations ("Group of 18") must be put into effect; his delegation agreed, however, with the Committee for Programme and Co-ordination (CPC) on the need to proceed with flexibility in order to avoid an adverse effect on programmes and the structure and composition of the Secretariat. The Secretary-General's proposed target of a 13.2 per cent reduction in posts by the end of 1989, with adjustments in conference-servicing staffing in New York and Geneva, was a reasonable one.

Minimizing the adverse effects of a reduction in posts on programme execution was a major task, which should be carried out jointly by the Secretariat and Member States. The Secretariat should explore every opportunity to increase its productivity and make better use of its resources. Member States must make additional efforts to define their priorities and express them in a more concrete form. Clearer agreement on priorities would help the Secretariat to implement programmes successfully while continuing the reform process - probably the only way to ensure an orderly, limited and balanced reduction in the total volume of United Nations activities, the seemingly unavoidable consequence of a smaller budget and a smaller Secretariat. That was not to imply a reduced role for the Organization: the United Nations could only benefit if its numerous activities were less dispersed, more action-oriented and more focused on crucial issues of common interest.

Equitable geographical distribution among the staff of the Secretariat remained an important concern for his delegation. Beside the need to take due account of that point in implementing recommendation 15 by the Group of 18, it was important to arrive at an adequate balance at senior levels of the Secretariat, as called for in recommendation 49."

The representative of **New Zealand**[62]

"supported the recommendation of the Committee for Programme and Co-ordination (CPC) that the amount for the contingency fund for the 1990-1991 biennium should be additional to the preliminary estimates, and was of the opinion that the fund should represent 0.75 per cent of total resources. ...

His delegation would confine its remarks to the reform of the Department of Information, referring to the relevant paragraphs of the report of the Advisory Committee (A/43/651). First, the possible restoration of certain posts in the Department seemed acceptable, on the understanding, as the Advisory Committee emphasized (para. 45), that there would be no additional appropriations under section 27 for the biennium 1988-1989, which meant that commensurate savings must be made elsewhere. The Advisory Committee questioned the rationale for the existence of the Bureau of Programme Operations, at least in its current form, and recommended that the Secretary-General should re-examine the question (para. 49), and his delegation fully supported that opinion. It also agreed that staff training for information officers was essential, not only within the Department but also in other areas of the Organization involved in public information activities (para. 51).

The Group of 18 had called for consolidating information activities in the Department of Public Information to the greatest possible extent. The Advisory Committee had underscored the Department's crucial role in making the work of the Organization better known and better understood and thus contributing to the support and financial backing that were so essential to it. His delegation was surprised to see that public information work conducted outside the Department amounted to 36 work-years annually (para. 55). That figure seemed much too high and the matter should be reviewed not in 1992 at the earliest, as the Secretary-General had suggested, but well before."

The representative of **Canada**[63]

"In his delegation's view, the reforms undertaken by the Secretary-General were consistent with both the spirit and the letter of resolutions 41/213 and 42/211 and the rate of progress was generally satisfactory.

As the Committee for Programme and Co-ordination had recommended, the Secretary-General should strive towards the full implementation of recommendation 15 of the Group of 18 for a 15 per cent reduction in the number of posts. That target, which was an important aspect of the drive for improved efficiency, must not, however, be attained at the expense of programme implementation. His delegation would support the Secretary-General's general proposals for post reductions as adjusted by a 10 per cent reduction in the staffing of Conference Services in New York and Geneva, making a total of 1,365 posts (12.1 per cent of the total establishment). The Advisory Committee proposed a further reduction of 50 posts in areas of the Secretariat other than Conference Services and his delegation was prepared to support that proposal, provided the Secretary-General indicated in his report that there would be no adverse programmatic impact.

However, it was not convinced that unit-by-unit post cuts did not impair the delivery of programmes, especially when the cuts were severe. Post reductions must therefore be functional and take into account the order of priorities established by Member States. The case of administrative units which already had only a small staff was particularly worrying. For example, the Centre for Human Rights in Geneva must not be reduced to paralysis. If the Organization fragmented the mechanisms for protection of human rights, it might lose part of the stock of public sympathy which it had acquired, particularly in Canada. It was also necessary to ensure that the Vienna-based units which administered the high-priority programme to combat drug abuse and illicit trafficking continued to have sufficient resources to fulfil their mandate. The Department for Disarmament Affairs, which had increasing responsibilities in an area of universal interest, must also have sufficient staff. Furthermore, as Africa was one of two priority areas for the United Nations, it was essential that the Economic Commission for Africa (ECA), which was already under-staffed, should not suffer any cutback in its ability to deliver programmes. His delegation commended in that connection the special measures taken to reduce the vacancy rates in the regional commissions.

It also noted with pleasure that since the beginning of 1987 three women had been appointed to posts at the level of Under-Secretary-General and four others promoted to the Director level; women had been appointed to some 30 per cent of the posts subject to geographical distribution. In contrast, it was disappointing to learn that the preparation of a complete personnel administrative handbook would take 18 months, that the training programmes envisaged under recommendation 58 appeared insufficient to meet the demand, and that no clear action had yet been taken to eliminate delays in the appeals process.

His delegation favoured an approach which, rather than focusing on further reductions, would emphasize the improvement of recruitment and placement, in order to ensure that units servicing high-priority programmes and field activities received priority treatment. In the future there must be greater flexibility in the movement of staff. With regard to the problem of renewable temporary posts, his delegation agreed with the Advisory Committee that a "blanket" conversion of such posts into permanent posts was not desirable in 1988. Proposals for conversion should be considered case by case within the context of the proposed programme budget for 1990-1991, in accordance with established procedure.

In paragraph 9 of document A/43/16 (Part I)/Add.1, the Secretary-General stated that the overall post reduction of 12.1 per cent, instead of the 13.02 per cent originally envisaged, would not entail a change in the overall level of appropriations for 1988-1989. The Advisory Committee had recommended in its report (A/43/651) a series of compensating measures which should eliminate the requirement for an additional appropriation in the second performance report on the programme budget for the biennium 1988-1989. The overall budget would thus remain unchanged, and the revised budget estimates would confirm the decline of budgetary growth rates - something which his delegation could only welcome.

It also noted with satisfaction that the structural changes in the political sector were near completion, at an opportune time to furnish the Organization with the means to take even more effective action in that area. However, the reforms undertaken in the economic and social sectors were marking time, and the Special Commission had been unable to reach agreement on a final document. His delegation thought nevertheless that it ought to be possible to reach an early agreement on the basis of the work done by the Special Commission and Economic and Social Council resolution E/1988/77.

The Canadian delegation looked forward to the completion of the restructuring of the Department of Public Information on the basis of the CPC recommendations. It also supported the Secretary-General's initiatives in the area of improved management information systems, for such measures could only increase the Organization's efficiency and productivity."

The representative of **Uganda**[64]

"Resolution 41/213 could not bear fruit unless all Member States showed flexibility and expedited decisions on the studies relating to economic and social activities. Those decisions should be reflected in the revised budget estimates for the biennium 1988-1989.

In paragraphs 15 to 21 of his report (A/C.5/43/1/Rev.1), the Secretary-General had proposed targets for post reductions to be attained by 31 December 1989, but without indicating the basis on which those targets had been established or which posts were to be abolished. It was clear that the way in which recommendation 15 of the Group of 18 was implemented at present had a direct impact on the geographical distribution of posts in the Secretariat. The majority of Member States attached particular importance to the adequate representation of developing countries, particularly at the higher levels, and was concerned that some posts seemed to be the exclusive preserve of certain Member States. It was therefore important for the Secretary-General to strive to correct that situation.

Drastic cuts could not be made in the conference service budget without impairing the Organization's performance. His delegation found it difficult to support proposals along those lines but it had nevertheless accepted, as a compromise, the reduction of 10 per cent in the staffing of conference services in New York and Geneva recommended by CPC (A/43/16, para. 36). ...

The situation in the regional commissions remained a matter of concern, especially the situation in ECA where the high vacancy rate had become a chronic problem, for which the Secretariat had not really given a satisfactory explanation. His delegation welcomed the action taken by the Secretary-General in that connection but called for urgent measures to correct the problem. It would be particularly useful for the Secretary-General to make known the timetable for filling the vacancies. It was also important to ensure the full and timely implementation of paragraph 1 (a) of resolution 41/213 concerning the implementation of all the projects and programmes already approved by the General Assembly, in particular the development of conference facilities in ECA and the Economic and Social Commission for Asia and the Pacific.

His delegation fully subscribed to the recommendation made by CPC in paragraph 45 of its report (A/43/16) that the final decision on the consolidation and strengthening of support activities relating to Namibia should be made by the General Assembly at the present session, taking full account of the opinion of the United Nations Council for Namibia. The fact that South Africa was giving the appearance of accepting Namibia's early access to independence should not be used as an excuse for downgrading the functions of the Council for Namibia.

His delegation was keenly interested in the reorganization of the Department of Public Information, and believed that full account should be taken of the views of Member States, summarized in paragraphs 47, 50, 52 and 53 of the report of CPC (A/43/16), paragraphs 10 (f) and 11 of resolution 41/211 and elsewhere, as recommendation 29 of the Group of 18 was put into effect. While appreciative of the efforts by the Secretariat to meet some of the concerns it had expressed at the twenty-eighth session of CPC, his delegation considered that the new structure should take effect only after the approval of the General Assembly, as stipulated in resolution 42/211. It was regrettable that the proposed plan was already being put into effect, contrary to the assurances given to the Fifth Committee at the previous session. There were still fundamental problems with the structure of the Department, its programmes, and the level and distribution of resources for priority topics such as Palestine, Namibia and *apartheid*. Some programme activities covered by the medium-term plan for the period 1984-1992 had been abolished, despite the increasing problems posed by the *apartheid* régime and the Israeli occupation. He hoped that the Fifth Committee would take full account of those concerns during its consideration and final adoption of the revised estimates under section 27 of the programme budget.

The Committee must remember that reforms introduced pursuant to resolution 41/213 should be designed to strengthen the Organization, not weaken it."

The representative of **Japan**[65]

"Urgent action had long been necessary to eliminate duplication of the agenda items of intergovernmental bodies and to co-ordinate their work, as well as to reduce the number of such bodies and the meetings and documentation they generated. It was thus regrettable that the work of the Special Commission of the Economic and Social Council on the In-depth Study of the United Nations Intergovernmental Structure and Functions in the Economic and Social Fields had ended so inconclusively. Many rationalization measures had been agreed upon in individual forums during the course of the In-depth Study, in view of which his delegation saw no reason why implementation of those measures should be further delayed. The Secretariat should provide a thorough analysis of the measures in question to determine what economies could be achieved, so as to encourage further reform.

The Group of 18 had described the structure of the Secretariat as being too complex, fragmented and top-heavy. According to the second progress report on the implementation of General Assembly resolution 41/213 (A/43/286), there was now a clear delineation of responsibilities in the political sector, while many recommendations had also been implemented in other sectors. Nevertheless, his delegation was under the impression that real reform had been initiated in only a limited number of areas, albeit significant ones. In other instances it appeared that the Secretary-General was still reviewing the issues involved and had simply announced a future programme of action. For example, despite the stated intention to reduce regular budget posts at the Assistant and Under-Secretary-General levels by 25 per cent - some 14 posts - and the expectation that provision would be made for further reductions in the budget outline for the biennium 1990-1991, by April 1988 only 11 such posts had been frozen, and no provision for further reductions had in fact been made. Indeed, three such posts had been created and filled during 1988 in respect of peace and security activities relating to Afghanistan and to Iran and Iraq. His delegation was concerned over the tendency to perpetuate a top-heavy and overly complex structure, thus risking erosion of recommendations 14 and 15(2) of the Group of 18. Appropriate rules applicable to senior appointments should be developed.

In response to the recommendations of the Group of 18, the Secretary-General had issued a series of guidelines for post reductions at various levels, with the exception of the P-2/P-1 levels. Yet none of those guidelines had been observed, and there had been virtually no change in the proportions of posts at various levels. His delegation trusted that the Secretary-General would continue to alleviate the top-heaviness of the staffing structure in the context of the restructuring of intergovernmental machinery and the Secretariat called for in recommendation 15(4).

Attrition, retrenchment, the regrouping of Secretariat components and post reclassification should be carried out within the coherent framework of the personnel policy recommended by the Group of 18. ...

The Secretary-General was to be congratulated on having sought the co-operation of all the offices which acted as substantive secretariats to intergovernmental bodies in encouraging restraint in the use of meeting and documentation services. Co-operation between the Department of Conference Services and the substantive secretariats should go further, so as to eliminate all duplication of work, from typing and proofreading to the provision of secretaries and the drafting of reports. ...

The Secretary-General's proposed target of 1,465 regular-budget posts for possible abolition (13.02 per cent of an adjusted base of 11,255 posts) represented a firm offer based on a thorough, internal, post-by-post review designed to facilitate the implementation of recommendation 15. Although the target agreed upon by the General Assembly had been 15 per cent, his delegation would accept the Secretary-General's proposals, adjusted to reflect a 10 per cent reduction in the staffing of Conference Services in New York and Geneva as recommended by CPC. It endorsed the view of CPC that further reductions should be made where possible during the implementation of resolution 41/213.

The Group of 18 had specified that the Secretary-General should be guided by an analysis of work-loads, with reference to the principle of equitable geographical distribution, in identifying posts for abolition. There was little evidence that those two points had been taken into consideration in the preparation of the Secretary-General's plans. No work-load standard appeared to have been used or developed; the plans took no account of the need to rectify a distorted staffing structure which ran counter to the interests of underrepresented States. Furthermore, the process agreed upon for restructuring the intergovernmental machinery had not yet been put into effect. A far-reaching consolidation and integration of the intergovernmental machinery would require the Secretariat to streamline its own structure further. If it wished to serve its Member States better and meet the changing needs of the international community, the United Nations must not be complacent about its achievements. No change in the staffing structure should be regarded as final or permanent.

His delegation concurred in the reinstatement of 100 posts under section 29, subject to the results of the in-depth study of the United Nations intergovernmental structure and functions in the economic and social fields. The arrangement should be reflected in the revised estimates for the following biennium, it being understood that the results of further restructuring in intergovernmental machinery and the Secretariat were basic to determining the actual level of resources for the biennium 1990-1991.

His delegation supported the Advisory Committee's recommendation that the Secretary-General should indicate, by budget section and grade level, 50 posts which could be cut to offset in part the restoration of the 100 posts under section 29. Any upward adjustment in staffing levels should be absorbed through vacancy management. Given the built-in and actual vacancy rates in the Secretariat, the full biennial costs of the posts reinstated under section 29 should be met from within existing appropriations. Even if the Secretariat could not offset half the increase under section 29 by trimming 50 posts in other areas, no additional appropriation should be made.

His delegation supported the thrust of the Secretary-General's plans for the restructuring of the Department of Public Information, and strongly supported the conclusions and recommendations of CPC in paragraphs 82, 83, 84 and 86 of its report (A/43/16 (Part II)). It could go along with the recommendation to reallocate D-1 posts to United Nations information centres and services, but believed that the availability of resources must be taken into account. As regards the proposed Bureau of Programme Operations, headed by a D-2, his delegation understood the concerns of the Advisory Committee but was convinced that a practical solution to the problem could be found, taking the real needs of the Department into account."

The representative of **Japan**[66] continued

"the proposed programme budget outline was a creditable basis for formulating the budget estimates for the next biennium. His delegation concurred with the CPC recommendations on the outline, and supported the Advisory Committee's recommendation for a staff turnover rate of 5 per cent. It agreed that the General Assembly should approve $1,767,060,000 at 1988 rates as the overall level of the preliminary estimate of resources in order to provide for activities during the 1990-1991 period, subject to recosting to reflect the latest forecast of inflation and exchange rates when the budget was adopted. In preparing the draft budget outline, the Secretary-General should also take into account the latest developments and trends in the legislative bodies. Prior to final approval of the outline, consideration should be given to changes in programme activities approved in 1988 for implementation in the biennium 1990-1991. ... In preparing future outlines, subsequent changes in programme activities should be anticipated, taking into account intergovernmental discussions of any proposals likely to modify existing mandates. ...

His delegation concurred with the procedures for the use and operation of the contingency fund (document A/43/324), and to the proposed rate of 0.75 per cent for the biennium 1990-1991. It endorsed the Advisory Committee's recommendation that no appropriation should be approved for the fund as yet. It also shared the Advisory Committee's view that the contingency fund should remain at the level set in the budget outline, on the understanding that the amount approved was a ceiling.

Clearly, the current system for dealing with inflation and currency fluctuation had proved to be ineffective. The General Assembly must decide in principle at the current session to establish a mechanism which would bring about a comprehensive solution to the problem of all additional expenditures (General Assembly resolution 41/213, annex I, para. 10). In that connection, his delegation noted with appreciation the Advisory Committee's recommendations in paragraphs 27 to 30 of document A/43/524. It concurred with CPC's conclusion that the budget outline was predicated on full implementation of resolution 41/213 and strict compliance with the decisions on the financing of approved programmes under the 1990-1991 budget. A real solution to the problem of additional expenditures could not be found until the financial crisis was over. However, the United Nations recent experience had pointed up the necessity of establishing an effective mechanism to deal with increased costs deriving from inflation and currency fluctuations. The General Assembly should therefore request the Secretary-General to formulate and submit a complete set of procedures for the operation of the contingency fund, including any changes it might bring about in the financial rules and regulations, for approval at the forty-fourth session. It would be essential to strengthen the Organization's financial and accounting procedures. A more sophisticated approach would be needed to consider inflation-related cost increases on the basis of data broken down by object of expenditure rather than on the basis of an overall rate. The same would apply to increased costs of imported goods and services resulting from currency fluctuations. The integrated management information system (IMIS) should facilitate the preparation of the budget outline and the establishment of an accounting system which could identify variations between estimates and actual expenditures based on sophisticated inflation and exchange rate forecasts."

The representative of **Pakistan**[67]

"The implementation of recommendations 25 to 27 of the Group of 18 must await the final outcome of the in-depth study of the United Nations intergovernmental structure and functions in the economic and social fields. The results of any departmental reviews in that area must, therefore, await the report of the Special Commission of the Economic and Social Council. The reorganization of the Department of Public Information was a source of continuing concern, and deserved the Committee's close attention. Recommendation 47, on due representation of developing countries at senior levels of the Secretariat, must be fully respected in the reform process. ...

Her delegation was concerned by the proposed reductions in posts in the small offices, especially in the areas of international peace and security, disarmament affairs, economic development and social programmes, including narcotics control, and the regional commissions. Disproportionately large cuts seemed to have been proposed for small departments, and more posts were proposed for abolition in the second and third largest regional commissions than in the largest. Such imbalances needed to be redressed, and her delegation would like further information on how the Secretary-General's targets had been arrived at.

Her delegation fully supported the recommendation by CPC that conference services posts in New York and Geneva should be reduced by 10 per cent; it wanted more details, however, on how the Advisory Committee's recommendation to offset the restoration of 100 posts to section 29 by cutting 50 posts elsewhere would be effected."

The representative of **Bangladesh**[68]

"The recommendations of the Group of 18 had been more difficult to apply in the economic and social fields because of the complexity of the secretariat structure and the task of reviewing the intergovernmental bodies. Despite one year of effort, the Special Commission of the Economic and Social Council entrusted with the responsibility of making an in-depth study of the structure and functioning of the economic and social bodies had not been able to complete its work successfully. During the summer session, the Economic and Social Council had finally adopted a resolution on its own revitalization (resolution 1988/77). He hoped that the General Assembly would deal with that problem during the session and make recommendations on the study in progress. Therefore, no step should be taken at the present stage that would prejudge the outcome of those efforts.

Since they covered a wide range of issues, the recommendations of the Group of 18 concerning personnel must be studied carefully. Despite the details given by the Secretary-General in paragraphs 15 to 21 of his report in document A/C.5/43/1/Rev.1, it was unclear how he had determined the number of posts that could be eliminated by 31 December 1989 and what posts were involved. If recommendation 15 was to be pursued at all levels, flexibility was required in order to avoid any negative impact on programmes. The 15 per cent target in the recommendation was therefore hard to reconcile with the latter requirement. On the other hand, the overall target of 13.2 per cent proposed by the Secretary-General and the adjustments for conference services in New York and Geneva seemed reasonable.

It was of the greatest importance for the developing countries to be adequately represented at the higher levels of the Secretariat; the implementation of recommendation 15 could be an opportunity to correct the existing imbalance. ...

As for the uncertainty that recommendation 15 created among the staff, his delegation stressed that its implementation alone would not make the United Nations more effective. Ensuring the future of staff was another way to help do that. The high vacancy rate of certain administrative units, particularly the regional economic commissions, was very disturbing. ...

His delegation had taken particular interest in the restructuring of the Department of Public Information. The Secretary-General and the Under-Secretary-General of the Department of Public Information had tried to meet certain concerns expressed by Member States during the twenty-eighth session of the Committee for Programme and Co-ordination (CPC), but the fundamental problems persisted in terms of structure, programmes and the level and distribution of resources allocated to priority items, especially *apartheid*, Namibia and Palestine.

Despite the reforms there would be no notable improvement without proper system-wide co-ordination. That was a complicated issue, particularly because of the proliferation of institutional arrangements and programmes of work of the United Nations and the specialized agencies. In that connection he stressed the importance of joint meetings of CPC and the Administrative Committee on Co-ordination (ACC), which enabled the organization of the United Nations system to exchange views and formulate specific recommendations amenable to follow-up by the Secretariat and the governing bodies. Those meetings and other instruments of co-ordination (interorganizational analysis of programmes,

ACC reports, etc.) should enable Member States to carry out co-ordination in an effective manner."

The representative of **Zimbabwe**[69]

"His delegation had studied attentively the Secretary-General's plans for the reduction of personnel as called for in recommendation 15 of the Group of 18 and endorsed the factors the Secretary-General had taken into account in formulating those plans (A/C.5/43/1/Rev.1, para. 14). It felt, however, that the principle of equitable geographical distribution of posts must be fully respected. It attached great importance to that principle, which should guarantee in particular the representation of the developing countries in the Secretariat. He wished to voice in that connection the concern caused by the reorganization of the Department of Public Information. His delegation was not alone in thinking that geographical representation must be more equitable in the upper echelons of that Department, not only in New York, but also in the United Nations information centres in the field. The restructuring in progress offered a unique opportunity to redress existing imbalances.

His delegation associated itself with the many delegations which had stressed the need to ensure that the restructuring did not have a negative impact on the implementation of programmes, a result which would be contrary to the aim of enhancing the effectiveness of the Organization. In that context, it agreed with the Advisory Committee that "the target for reductions in conference service posts under budget section 29 should be adjusted downward, with the "restoration" of 100 posts of the total of 357 posts originally proposed for elimination under section 29" (A/43/651, para. 15). However, it could not support the recommendation in paragraph 17 that the restoration of the 100 posts should be partially offset by a reduction of 50 posts in other areas of the Secretariat. Such a procedure would have an adverse effect on the productivity of the units from which those posts would be taken.

Regarding the Department of Public Information, he noted with particular satisfaction that the Secretary-General intended to highlight, in the structure of the Department, the prominence accorded to questions relating to *apartheid*, Namibia and Palestine. However, to ensure that such prominence was also reflected in substantive activities, the units responsible for the programmes should have the appropriate complement of staff. His delegation could not but express some concern on that issue. Originally, the anti-*apartheid* unit had 15 Professional staff, but his delegation now understood that it was proposed to reduce that number to 7, representing a 53 per cent cut. Such a drastic reduction could only have a deleterious effect on the anti-

apartheid radio programmes. His delegation felt that, on the contrary, consideration should be given to appointing persons who were knowledgeable about the situation in South Africa, competent in the languages involved and sensitive to the plight of the victims of *apartheid*. Furthermore, his delegation feared that the programmes would lose their focus if one section were to be entrusted with questions relating to the struggle against *apartheid* as well as questions relating to Palestine. The situation of South Africa under the *apartheid* régime and the situation of occupied Palestine were now regarded as among the most critical issues facing the international community, and deserved special and concentrated attention.

A reduction in personnel was always a difficult and unsettling process, but it should not be forgotten that the staff were called upon to play a critical role in the process of reform. Member States could do much to allay their fears and improve their morale. They had the duty to show their readiness to make sacrifices themselves and to commit resources in the interest of revitalizing the Organization."

The representative of **Kenya**[70]

"He noted that, since the adoption of resolutions 41/213 and 42/211, some delegations had taken contradictory approaches with regard to the measures needed to enhance the effectiveness of the Organization. Although there had been unambiguous agreement on the two resolutions, certain Member States had relentlessly attacked the fundamental principle on which the Organization was based, namely the principle of sovereign equality of all Member States, which was reflected specifically in the fact that each State had one vote. It was surprising that those delegations which put themselves forward as champions of democracy were to be found leading a crusade with the aim of suppressing democracy within the United Nations. Those same Member States, which already enjoyed the right of veto as permanent members of the Security Council, were now seeking to exercise that right in other organs of the United Nations, and particularly the Committee for Programme and Co-ordination, by using consensus as another form of veto.

The effect was to modify the Organization's agenda, starting with a reduction in programmes. A vicious circle was thus established: on the one hand, contributions due to the Organization were being withheld, and on the other hand, the Organization was being ordered to carry out reforms. It was clear that the United Nations could not carry out reforms without the financial resources which were due to it and which it needed in order to function. His country was convinced that the Organization was useful and viable, and that it was capable of doing much more, given the necessary political will and financial resources, to put into practice the general agreement reflected in resolutions 41/213 and 42/211.

The Organization was, in particular, an indispensable instrument for the preservation of peace and the safeguarding of justice in the world. For that reason, its effectiveness and dynamism must be maintained. His delegation doubted, however, that measures such as reductions in personnel and programmes would of themselves achieve the objective of efficiency. In its view, Member States must demonstrate in practical fashion that they had the political will to achieve that end by making optimum use of available financial and human resources. Kenya considered that the international community must do much more in the economic and social fields, and that human rights would remain meaningless unless all peoples of the world enjoyed their basic and fundamental rights to food, shelter, education and health, to mention only a few.

While the Organization had recently been playing a particularly commend-able role in the field of peace-keeping, peace was not an end in itself for the vast majority of the developing countries, but rather an indispensable requirement if those countries were to enjoy all their rights, including the right to sustainable development in all areas. For them, the reform process must be reflected in an increase rather than a reduction in operational programmes, and such programmes should be implemented with maximum cost-effectiveness.

In adopting resolution 41/213, the General Assembly had stipulated that the reform process should be carried out in such a manner as to avoid a negative impact on programmes, and that in cases where it was necessary to make changes to such programmes, the Secretary-General should seek prior approval from the General Assembly. His delegation wished to congratulate the Secretary-General on the way in which he had conducted the reform process as a whole. However, the reorganization of the Department of Public Information did not seem to have achieved the desired results. In his delegation's view, the rapid reorganization of the Department had not fully taken into account the letter and spirit of resolution 41/213, and was likely to have an adverse effect on programmes, particularly the anti-*apartheid* radio programmes. ...

With regard to recommendation 15, on the reduction in the number of posts, his delegation hoped, first of all, that the reduction in posts subject to geographical distribution would pay due regard to recommendation 47, which provided that the Secretary-General should ensure that the nationals of developing countries were duly represented at senior levels, in accordance with the relevant resolutions of the General Assembly.

Secondly, his delegation hoped that the reduction in posts would not have a disproportionate effect on some units of the Secretariat. It noted in particular, with deep concern, that a disproportionate reduction rate was envisaged for the two United Nations organs based at Nairobi, the United Nations Environment Programme (UNEP) and the United Nations Centre for Human Settlements (Habitat). In its view, it was unacceptable that two organs whose programmes were so important to all, and in particular to the developing countries, should be so adversely affected that they might be incapable of carrying out their mandates efficiently. His delegation supported the recommendation of the Advisory Committee concerning the reinstatement of 100 conference service posts and the consequent reduction of 50 posts in other areas of the Secretariat. In addition, it wished to congratulate the Secretary-General on his efforts to reduce the vacancy rates in the regional commissions, in particular the Economic Commission for Africa."

The representative of Greece, speaking on behalf of the 12 member states of the **European Community**[71]

"The Twelve ... were disappointed by the findings of the Special Commission of the Economic and Social Council responsible for reviewing the intergovernmental structure and functions in the economic and social fields. The intergovernmental bodies still had much to do to improve their operation and to rationalize their working methods and the calendar of their meetings. It was clear that reform of the intergovernmental apparatus would affect the structure of the Secretariat, but the Twelve felt that it was not necessary for the Secretary-General to wait for the results to take the measures he thought appropriate. ...

They were prepared to accept the recommendation of CPC for a reduction of 10 per cent in conference service staff and noted that, according to the Secretariat, it would not be necessary for that purpose to request additional appropriations in the current budget. ...

In connection with the restructuring of the Department of Public Information, the Twelve were concerned by the changes made in the initial project and by the delay in its implementation. They considered that the recommendations of ACABQ on that matter, including the proposal for a new and more detailed study before 1992, deserved the Committee's attention, and they believed that the benefit to users of the Department's products should be one of the principal criteria for evaluation."

The representative of Greece, speaking on behalf of the 12 member states of the **European Community**[72] continued

"the new budget procedure mandated by General Assembly resolution 41/213, of which the outline mechanism was a basic element, represented an important step towards strengthening the efficiency of the administrative and financial functioning of the United Nations. Budgetary reform, meanwhile, was based on a recognition of the need for involvement by Member States in the preparation of the budget from its early stages and throughout the process.

It was disappointing that the Secretary-General had so far been unable to propose priorities for consideration by CPC, and the Twelve therefore looked forward to the consideration in 1989 of the Secretary-General's report on the setting of priorities of a broad sectoral nature, as well as his concrete proposals in the programme budget for the biennium 1990-1991. It was also regrettable that there should be a discrepancy between the views of the Secretary-General and those of the Advisory Committee with respect to the putative reduction in real growth of resources over the current biennium. The Twelve had expected, on the basis of their understanding of the budgetary process as set out in General Assembly resolution 41/213, that the level of resources indicated in the Secretary-General's proposal would be all-inclusive. While recognizing that an exceptional procedure was necessitated by the lack of any precedent for the new process, they believed that in the future the Secretary-General's proposal should be of an all-inclusive nature.

The Twelve agreed with the Advisory Committee's recommendations to retain the standard 5 per cent vacancy rate for Professional and higher categories and to allow a net addition of 50 posts. The recommendation that the total preliminary estimate for the coming biennium, at 1990-1991 rates, should amount to $1,982,523,700 was also acceptable. With regard to the contingency fund, the Twelve could accept the Secretary-General's recommendation that the level of the fund be set at 0.75 per cent of the preliminary estimate at 1990-1991 rates. They agreed with the Advisory Committee that the fund should remain at the level set in the outline, on the understanding that level was a ceiling, and wished to stress that the size of the fund for any biennium must not be subject to change once it had been adopted by the General Assembly. It was important that the General Assembly should, in accordance with General Assembly resolution 41/213, adopt at the current session an overall level of resources which should not be subject to any subsequent modification.

Since the Twelve were not in favour of maintaining the current system for dealing with additional expenditures caused by inflation and currency fluctuations, they believed that the Advisory Committee's proposal to establish a new reserve fund deserved serious consideration."

The representative of **Tunisia**[73]

"In the two years since that reform had been initiated, most of the recommendations of the Group of 18, reaffirmed by the General Assembly in its resolution 41/213, had been or were being implemented and had produced a distinct improvement, both quantitatively and qualitatively, in the activities and output of the Organization. The progress reports submitted on the subject by the Secretary-General showed the scale of the changes already made, but they also made it clear that there was a threshold beyond which the reform process could have adverse effects. ...

The difficulties encountered by the Special Commission of the Economic and Social Council resulted specifically from disagreement between the developing countries and certain industrialized countries as to the reductions to be made in the subsidiary bodies of the Council which dealt with economic and social issues. The developing countries would be unable to accept any reform of the Organization which was at the expense of their common interests. His country therefore invited the Secretary-General to take due account of the viewpoint of the developing countries and to refrain from imposing drastic cuts in staff in the economic and social sector of the Secretariat in the name of administrative and financial efficiency.

In some cases, the reforms had led to a modification of the priorities established by the Member States and of the geographical distribution of posts within the Secretariat. Accordingly, the systematic application of recommendation 15 of the Group of 18 was not unrelated to the difficulties experienced by the Department of Public Information. The new structure of that Department, despite the adjustments made by the Committee for Programme and Co-ordination, continued to give rise to serious problems for many Member States and to a certain malaise among staff in the Department. His delegation fully appreciated the efforts made by the Under-Secretary-General for Public Information to remedy that situation, but it considered that decisions must be taken to preserve the geographical balance in the upper echelons of the Secretariat.

His delegation welcomed the fact that ACABQ, aware that the Department of Conference Services was working at full capacity, had recommended the restoration of 100 posts in that Department. It regretted, however, that

ACABQ had, at the same time, recommended the elimination of 50 posts in other departments, which would inevitably have far-reaching implications as far as programmes were concerned and deprive the Secretary-General of every iota of the latitude which was required to run an organization as complex as the United Nations. ACABQ had shown flexibility in proposing that the elimination of those 50 posts could be postponed, if necessary, until the next financial year. In any case, the Tunisian delegation could not, at the present juncture, support a measure with such significant implications. The United Nations would be unable to achieve the objectives laid down in resolution 41/213 if it continued to suffer such substantial staff cuts."

The representative of **Tunisia**[74] continued

"the Fifth Committee would not be able to decide on the Advisory Committee's recommendations until it knew which departments and programmes were targeted by the proposed additional reductions. He mentioned the case of the Department of Public Information, where the current retrenchment plan would reduce from 14 to 7 persons the number of staff in an administrative unit concerned with information relating to such high-priority questions as Palestine, Namibia and *apartheid*."

The representative of the **Union of Soviet Socialist Republics**[75]

"For the moment, the reform process seemed to be proceeding satisfactorily, particularly as far as the political organs of the Secretariat and those responsible for administration and management were concerned. His delegation was nevertheless disappointed at the lack of progress by the Special Commission of the Economic and Social Council. It hoped that efforts in that direction would continue and bear fruit, thus allowing the problems raised by the pattern of conferences to be dealt with. ...

His delegation had noted the Secretary-General's intention to trim the staff of the Secretariat by 13 per cent by the end of the current budgetary period. At the same time, it endorsed the recommendation of CPC calling upon the Secretary-General to make every effort to implement recommendation 15 of the Group of 18 in full. That was a vital aspect of the reform, and his delegation counted on the Secretary-General to take steps to that end when the budget proposals for 1990-1991 were drawn up.

As to the staffing of the Department of Conference Services, his delegation supported the Advisory Committee's recommendation that the costs of restoring 100 posts within the Department should be met from existing appropriations by, among other things, making further cuts in the staff of other units."

The representative of the **Union of Soviet Socialist Republics**[76] continued

"given the upward adjustment of the Secretary-General's preliminary estimate - due to recosting at 1990-1991 rates - by some $215 million, it could hardly be said that predictability had been achieved with respect to United Nations expenditures. Nor had a major objective of the current reforms, namely, the achievement of the broadest possible consensus on the Organization's budget. In the opinion of his delegation, without a solution to the problem of additional expenditures caused by inflation and exchange rate fluctuations, the adoption of other elements of the budgetary reform process, such as the budget outline and the contingency fund, would be of limited practical value. The Advisory Committee, however, had proposed a simple, effective, and economical mechanism by which to address the problem. ...

Despite certain reservations with respect to the methodology used to prepare the outline, his delegation was prepared to support the conclusion of CPC that the Secretary-General's report should constitute the basis for a decision by the General Assembly. It was its understanding in doing so that the level of resources envisaged in the outline would provide for the full implementation of all measures listed in General Assembly resolution 41/213, including recommendation 15 of the Group of High-level Intergovernmental Experts to Review the Efficiency of the Administrative and Financial Functioning of the United Nations (Group of 18). If that principle were respected, it calculated that the Secretary-General's estimate could be reduced by $25.8 million."

The representative of **Bulgaria**[77]

"his delegation was generally satisfied with the progress of the reforms undertaken by the Secretary-General. It was, however, concerned that the Special Commission of the Economic and Social Council had not completed its study of the structure and functioning of the economic and social bodies.

The reduction in staff proposed by the Secretary-General, 13.02 per cent, was fairly close to the 15 per cent called for in recommendation 15. None the less, his delegation expected the recommendation to be implemented in full in the next budgetary biennium. On the subject of conference services, his delegation supported the Advisory Committee's recommendation to restore 100 posts in New York and Geneva, partly offsetting the cost by cutting a further 50 posts in other departments.

The information on organizational changes provided in the third chapter of the revised estimates (A/C.5/43/1/Rev.1) was insufficient to permit any final judgement to be made, apparently owing to the transitional nature of the budget. ... As regards the final chapter of the Secretary-General's report, his delegation reiterated its concern at the practice of converting temporary posts into permanent ones, and endorsed the Advisory Committee's intention of reviewing each proposal for conversion in future."

The representative of **China**[78]

"Her delegation supported the principle of a 10-per-cent cut in posts for conference services in New York and Geneva, believing that the 15-per-cent reduction recommended by the Group of 18 had not been based on a rigorous analysis of needs and need not be followed to the letter. It should be recalled that the Secretary-General had been requested to implement recommendation 15 with flexibility so that programmes did not suffer. It was clear in that light that the 14.1-per-cent cut originally planned for the Department of Conference Services was not acceptable.

Concerning the proposed reduction of 50 posts to offset the restoration of 100 posts in Conference Services, her delegation believed the reduction plan proposed by the Secretary-General for sections other than section 29 was the result of extensive consultations with the heads of department concerned and took account of the requirements of programme implementation. It was doubtful, therefore, whether the further cuts proposed could be made without affecting activities under other sections of the budget. The Secretariat had told the Advisory Committee that any further reduction in resources would adversely affect programmes. As for absorbing the costs of the 100 posts within existing appropriations, her delegation agreed that every effort should be made to restrict budgetary growth and avoid additional expenditure, but considered that carrying out the programmes approved by the General Assembly must continue to be the primary objective."

The representative of **China**[79] continued

"the reorganization of the Department of Public Information should be carried out in conformity with General Assembly resolutions and in consultation with as many Member States as possible. It should not produce a negative impact on already approved programmes; should fully reflect the priorities established by legislative bodies; and should respect the equitable geographical distribution of posts.

With regard to *apartheid*, Namibia and Palestine, which were considered priority issues by the General Assembly, the organizational adjustments made by the Secretary-General should be accompanied by practical actions on programme planning, staff arrangements and project implementation. His delegation supported the CPC recommendation that separate sections should be clearly identified in the Communications and Project Management Service to handle issues of economic development and of human rights and social development. With regard to the new organizational structure of the Department, his delegation had questions, as did ACABQ, about the Secretary-General's recommendation that the Bureau of Programme Operations should oversee and co-ordinate the work of the Communications and Project Management Service, the Information Products Division and the Dissemination Division. ...

The reorganization of the Department of Public Information had not been carried out in the same way as it had in other departments in the Secretariat, causing concern in various quarters. His delegation, for its part, hoped that the Department would pay particular attention to the impact of reorganization on the morale of staff members and on the geographical distribution of posts."

The representative of **China**[80] continued

"Given that the preparation of the programme budget outline was a new exercise, which would take some time to perfect, a measure of flexibility should be demonstrated both in the methodology employed and in the components of the outline. ...

The rate of 0.75 per cent proposed for the contingency fund was acceptable. Nevertheless, that figure should not be taken as unchangeable or as constituting a precedent, and should be reviewed carefully at the end of the first year, at which time the Advisory Committee should report on whether it considered the rate to be appropriate. A suitable level for the fund was closely related to the overall level of resources, so that his delegation's final position depended on the decision taken on the latter issue.

The methodology for dealing with inflation and currency fluctuations was an important part of the budgetary process. A conservative approach should be taken so as to minimize the Organization's potential losses as a result of those two factors. ...

As requested by the General Assembly in its resolution 41/213, the Secretary-General had indicated priorities reflecting general trends of a sectoral nature by actual increases in resources under various sections of the budget. His delegation did not believe that such an approach could fully indicate programme priorities; neither could it see how the method adopted by the Secretary-General was linked to the priorities established in the medium-term plan."

The representative of **Ghana**[81]

"pointed out that recommendation 15 had been drawn up by the Group of 18 on the basis of a survey which had revealed duplication and fragmentation of responsibilities and too many senior-level staff in many sectors. The reductions proposed sought to remedy those shortcomings and made the Organization more efficient. As the Secretary-General stated in paragraph 23 of document A/C.5/43/1/Rev.1, the reductions planned would certainly have an effect on programmes and the volume of activities. His delegation would like the Secretariat, the Advisory Committee and CPC to prove that the steps they advocated would really enable the problems of wastage he had mentioned to be dealt with."

The representative of **Sweden**[82]

"The objective of the reform process was to make the United Nations more efficient, and that was the purpose of resolution 41/213; cutting expenditures was not, in itself, a means of doing so. As it considered the revised estimates, therefore, the Fifth Committee should be mindful of the need to prevent cuts in staff from adversely affecting programmes, particularly in areas of vital importance to the success of multilateral efforts in disarmament and peace-keeping, the promotion of human rights, the fight against drug abuse and trafficking, the advancement of women and the protection of the environment. Her delegation was also troubled by the possibly harmful effects of the cuts on Secretariat services with small numbers of staff, thinking in particular of the Department of Disarmament Affairs, whose terms of reference were likely to be expanded in the years to come. Within the framework of the reform process, the United Nations must be provided with enough resources to play the central role which rightfully belonged to it. Her delegation believed that the Secretary-General had satisfactorily carried out the reform mandate given to him by the General Assembly."

The representative of **Australia**[83]

"the Advisory Committee had made laudable attempts to impose some discipline on the Secretariat in applying recommendation 15 of the Group of 18. His delegation was therefore concerned that the Secretariat had not fully implemented the recommendation, and viewed the manner in which post reductions had been effected as unacceptable. The reductions had not been determined on the basis of clearly defined priorities or accepted professional standards, but had been the subject of internal conflict and "horse trading". It was clear that the Under-Secretary-General for Conference Services and Special Assignments had been quicker than his colleagues, which was little consolation to other parts of the Secretariat or to Member States. The fact that the Department of Conference Services was requesting exemption from the full staff reductions identified in the post-by-post review created serious difficulties for his delegation, which recognized the direct link between the number of conferences and the volume of services required, but had not been presented with any detailed evidence to convince it of the validity of the Department's claim. In the absence of such evidence, his delegation would continue to believe that recommendation 15 should be fully implemented. It seemed unfair that other areas of the Secretariat should be penalized in order to subsidize one very large department, with over 2,500 staff and an appropriation in excess of $330 million.

While being prepared to accept the Advisory Committee's recommendation as a short-term measure, his delegation thought that the Fifth Committee should also envisage a long-term solution. To that end it needed much more detailed information on work-loads and productivity levels before it could accept the Secretariat's unsubstantiated claim that any further reduction in resources would have an adverse impact on programmes.

His delegation noted that the Advisory Committee had been informed that it was not possible to quantify precisely the effect on programmes of the offsetting post reductions. If the Secretary-General could not produce convincing evidence to support his claim, the Fifth Committee should not be so naive as to allow itself to be manipulated into putting Secretariat interests above those of Member States."

The representative of **Australia**[84] continued

"His delegation had explained in the course of discussions in CPC the reasons why it found the Secretary-General's initial outline unacceptable but was pleased to say that most of its major concerns had been addressed by the Advisory Committee, with the result that it could fully support all that Committee's recommendations. An overall budget outline of $1.98 billion for the next biennium, at 1990-1991 rates, would be acceptable provided that figure was regarded as firm. The amount should, if properly allocated, allow for full implementation of all mandated programmes. While fully recognizing the difficulties inherent in any attempt to solve the problem of additional and unforeseen expenditures, his delegation could not support continuation of the present system. In the belief that a reserve fund, to cover not only currency and inflation costs but also statutory cost increases for staff, would remove the element of unpredictability and facilitate a wider level of support for future United Nations budgets."

The representative of the **United Kingdom**[85]

"Like CPC, his delegation considered conference services to be one of the principal areas where further reductions should be made in the process of implementing General Assembly resolution 41/213 as a whole. It would certainly not be realistic to expect full implementation of the resolution by the end of 1989, but it was important to continue to make vigorous efforts to that end during the coming year and into the next budgetary biennium, efforts which should apply at least as much to the Department of Conference Services as to any other unit of the Secretariat. His delegation would welcome further detailed scrutiny of the Department's activities and work-load, but accepted the Secretary-General's judgement as to the posts which could not properly be cut at the current stage, as well as his judgement on the posts which could be cut. ...

As for the inter-agency joint services referred to in paragraph 16 of the report on the revised estimates, his delegation noted that consultations would be conducted through ACC on the subject of the Secretariat posts servicing ICSC and the Joint Inspection Unit and that any reduction would be reported in the context of the proposed programme budget for the biennium 1990-1991. That undertaking appeared to be consistent with the request by ACABQ that the additional 50 regular budget posts recommended for abolition need not necessarily be identified immediately but should be identified in the proposed programme budget for the next biennium."

The representative of the **United Kingdom**[86] continued

"He was still perturbed, however, by the Secretariat's request for an additional appropriation for the Office for Research and the Collection of Information to cover overtime and staff travel. That proposal was contrary to recommendation 38 of the Group of 18. Furthermore, he was not wholly convinced that the additional amount would enable the Office to carry out its work better. ...

In the case of the Board of Auditors, he supported the ACABQ's recommendations and shared the view that an analysis of the distribution of external costs between the regular budget and extrabudgetary sources should be undertaken. Care must be taken to see that external audit costs were not themselves too high.

He also supported the ACABQ recommendation concerning the conversion of temporary to established posts. It emerged from the CPC's conclusion on the subject that the conversion would have neither negative nor positive programmatic implications. It would appear, therefore, that the proposal should be considered from a purely technical point of view, which came within the ACABQ's terms of reference."

The representative of the **United Kingdom**[87] continued

"although he had no objection to the proposed staffing table for the United Nations Council for Namibia, he did object to the reclassification of the post of Secretary of the Council from the D-1 to the D-2 level. He noted that the Advisory Committee had not expressed support for that proposal.

With regard to recommendation 37, concerning public information activities, the Secretariat's initial proposals had been revised on the basis of the recommendations of the Committee for Programme and Co-ordination (CPC). However, his delegation had accepted those recommendations only in order to maintain consensus. Noting the position expressed in paragraph 48 of the CPC report (A/43/16 (Part I)), his delegation underlined the importance of evaluation in the case of the Department of Information. Before the reorganization, the Department had a tendency to evaluate its accomplishments on the basis of the number of its products, whereas the essential criterion was their impact on the final user. Some progress had been made, but a great deal remained to be done. It should be noted in that regard that there was no measurable relationship between the degree of priority attached to an activity and the staff needed to carry it out."

The representative of **Austria**[88]

"Her delegation fully concurred with the view of CPC to the effect that recommendation 15 of the Group of 18 should be implemented with flexibility in order to avoid negative impact on programmes and on the structure and composition of the Secretariat. Account should be taken of the priorities set by Member States and of the specific requirements of smaller offices. That consideration applied in particular to the United Nations Office at Vienna, which had always suffered from a low staffing level and now had to take on new responsibilities in the area of social affairs. The proposed post reductions would affect the functioning of the Office, as her delegation had emphasized during the course of discussions in CPC. It was of the utmost importance that the Office should be provided with all the resources it needed in order to perform its important task and that the recommendation made by CPC in paragraph 37 of its report should be applied in full."

The representative of **Algeria**[89]

"noting that discussions had focused on recommendation 15, recalled that the other recommendations of the Group of 18 were just as important, whether they called, for example, for measures to ensure that nationals of developing countries were duly represented at senior levels or urged that the services of Under-Secretaries-General and Assistant Secretaries-General should not be extended beyond 10 years. The Secretary-General's first two progress reports did not address those other recommendations. ...

The information on implementation of recommendation 15 was not complete. The Secretariat did not state what its intentions were with respect to posts at the Under-Secretary-General and Assistant Secretary-General levels, which were supposed to be subject to a 25 per cent reduction, It might also be asked exactly what plans had been drawn up by the Secretary-General for the implementation of recommendation 15. Two years had already passed since the beginning of the reforms; the Secretariat had therefore had ample time to determine its staffing requirements. However, it had not produced any study on the subject and went no further than to provide figures. For lack of information, CPC had not been able to judge what impact the reductions might have on programmes. That, indeed, was a very important aspect of recommendation 15, which called for a 15 per cent reduction in the number of staff while avoiding any negative effects on the implementation of programmes. ...

Similarly, with regard to reductions of conference-servicing staff, CPC had been obliged to choose between two sets of figures without knowing how they had been arrived at. One of the reasons invoked to justify a rate of no more than 10 per cent was the need to respect the principle of equal treatment for all the Organization's official languages, in accordance with General Assembly resolution 42/207 C. That argument was not very convincing. The figures provided should in fact be supported by an internal study showing the staffing requirements of the Department of Conference Services."

The representative of **Algeria**[90] continued

"As far as the economic and social areas were concerned, it must be emphasized that recommendations 8 and 25 of the Group of 18 were aimed not so much at a reduction of personnel as at a rationalization of activities. For that reason, and because of the need to preserve the balance between the economic and social sector and the political sector, it would be helpful to know the planned reduction percentages in each of those two sectors and also the reductions to which the restructuring of the political sector had already given rise."

The representative of **Algeria**[91] continued

"The level of resources approved for the biennium 1988-1989 was no longer an appropriate basis for the outline, since the budget for that biennium had been transitional and, as implicitly recognized in General Assembly resolution

41/213, the outline was to reflect the major programmes of the medium-term plan rather than programmes under way during the transitional period. The estimate of resources in the outline was not intended to be final. Therefore, the provisional figures recommended by the Advisory Committee for the biennium 1990-1991 should be interpreted with flexibility.

Taking into account the impact which recommendation 15 of the Group of 18 would have and the high vacancy rates at the regional commissions, his delegation favoured the 3 per cent turnover rate proposed by the Secretary-General. The implementation of recommendation 15 had created uncertainties over the overall level of resources included in the outline. In his submission to CPC, the Secretary-General had not taken into account the revised estimates, while the Advisory Committee had, in calculating the total level of expenditures for the biennium 1990-1991, taken into account its own recommendations on revised estimates. The Secretary-General's proposal of an overall staff reduction of 12.1 per cent (10 per cent in the Department of Conference Services) was likely to win the support of almost all Member States. The estimate of resources should therefore be based on that figure. The Secretariat had indicated that normal operations might be disrupted even with a reduction of that magnitude. Unless the General Assembly was prepared to reduce the duration and number of the meetings of its subsidiary bodies and those of the Economic and Social Council, there was little justification for pressing for a 15 per cent reduction in Secretariat posts.

His delegation shared the Advisory Committee's view that the contingency fund should be added to the preliminary estimate and must be included in the total amount of resources. At the twenty-seventh session of CPC and the forty-second session of the General Assembly, his delegation had expressed serious doubts about the Organization's ability to meet additional expenditures arising over a three-year period with a contingency fund set at 0.75 per cent. Moreover, that percentage had not been accepted by the General Assembly or CPC as yet. ... In the interest of reaching a compromise at the earliest possible date, the 0.75 per cent rate might be adopted initially and reviewed in 1990-1991 in order to take account of new developments.

The negative rate of real growth of 9.6 per cent proposed in the outline would be acceptable only to the extent that it reflected the rate of post reductions alone.

It was regrettable that neither the Secretary-General nor CPC was in a position to make concrete proposals on priorities reflecting general trends of a broad sectoral nature. Presumably, the question would be taken up in future discussions of the budget for the biennium 1990-1991. At that time, priorities should be established on the basis of the General Assembly mandates. Such priorities should include development and the economic situation in Africa in the economic sector; the anti-*apartheid* activities, Namibia and the self-determination of the Palestinian people, in the political sector; and human rights and the rights of peoples in the social sector. Some of the Advisory Committee's recommendations on the budget outline were acceptable to his delegation. They included the recommendation that prior to final approval of the outline, the Assembly should take into account any changes approved in 1988 to programme activities scheduled for implementation in 1990-1991."

The representative of **United States of America**[92]

"referring to the implementation of recommendation 15 of the Group of High-level Intergovernmental Experts (Group of 18), said that the number of posts to be abolished was an absolute, whereas the distribution of the actual cuts might vary as the effects of the reorganization became apparent. The Secretary-General therefore had a reasonable degree of flexibility, which he should use to ensure that small units were not subjected to disproportionate reductions.

The Committee for Programme and Co-ordination (CPC) had recommended acceptance of the Secretary-General's revised estimates for the Department of Conference Services (DCS), but without prejudice to the full implementation of recommendation 15. Member States expected that after the initial phase the Secretary-General would draw up a list of additional posts to be eliminated so that the 15 per cent target figure could be met. His delegation strongly supported the ACABQ proposal that the 100 posts restored to DCS should be offset by the elimination of 50 posts from other services. The Secretariat claimed that it could not eliminate 50 posts - i.e., less than 0.5 per cent of its staff - without "programme disruption". However, since it had given no specific indication of what "programme disruption" would entail, there was reason to doubt that it would actually occur. As at 31 August 1988, the vacancy rate in DCS was 11.3 per cent for Professional staff and 12.5 per cent for General Service staff without any obvious disruption in servicing. Staffing levels should not, in any case, be established on the basis of work-loads at "peak" periods. Moreover, another look should be taken at work-load standards, particularly in the support services, because United Nations standards might well have sunk to below average. Finally, technological advances were another means of realizing savings.

The implementation of recommendation 15 had thus far been affected by the political pressures of a bureaucracy and those of an international organization which had to deal with the wishes of its Member States. The Member States acknowledged that the Secretary-General's task had not been easy, but that did not mean that they did not expect recommendation 15 to be fully implemented."

The representative of the **United States of America**[93] continued

"recalled that submission of a budget outline was the first stage in the new budget process approved by the General Assembly in resolution 41/213 and said that document A/43/524 represented a creditable first effort to produce such an outline. ...

The Secretary-General's proposal reflected a small decline in real terms from the level of the current budget, although the decline was less than the negative growth rate stated in the outline. The use of existing methodology to determine the 1988-1989 budget base had resulted in a measurement of growth as it might have been if General Assembly resolution 41/213 had not been adopted. Negative growth was imperative. The small decline did not imply the degree of programme disruption suggested in the Secretary-General's proposed budget outline.

Had the staffing calculations been based on a 15 per cent reduction - rather than the level initially proposed by the Secretary-General in the 1988-1989 revised estimates - the negative growth reflected in the outline would have been still less in real terms. If the CPC recommendation to restore 100 posts was accepted, the number of posts eliminated by the start of the 1990-1991 biennium would represent only 12.5 per cent of the previous total. Her delegation took very seriously CPC's statement that acceptance of the revised estimates was without prejudice to the implementation of recommendation 15 of the Group of High-level Intergovernmental Experts to Review the Efficiency of the Administrative and Financial Functioning of the United nations (Group of 18). Every effort must be made during the biennium 1990-1991 to meet the target for staff reductions approved in resolution 41/213. In CPC, her delegation had questioned the use of a 3 per cent Professional vacancy rate in calculating the level of the 1990-1991 budget outline. It welcomed the Advisory Committee's recommendation that the outline should be costed on the basis of a 5 per cent rate.

Since the budget outline would make provision for so-called add-ons and resources to finance activities approved at the forty-third session, there was no justification for approving more than the 0.75 per cent level proposed for the contingency fund. Her delegation agreed with the Advisory Committee's recommendation in paragraph 36 of its report that the levels for the contingency fund should be a ceiling which did not necessarily have to be reached. That was consistent with the conclusion reached by CPC.

Although it was regrettable that the Advisory Committee should have been unable to recommend a comprehensive solution to the problem of additional expenditures, as called for in General Assembly resolution 41/213, the reserve mechanism referred to in paragraphs 27 to 29 of the Advisory Committee's report deserved support. Her delegation therefore recommended that the General Assembly endorse, in principle, the approach suggested by ACABQ and request that final recommendations be presented to its forty-fourth session, with a view to implementing the mechanism during the biennium 1990-1991. Following the establishment of a good basis for future progress on specific programme priorities during discussions in CPC, her delegation also wished to emphasize its commitment to efforts to ensure that future budget outlines contained priority designations. Notwithstanding certain reservations, it supported the recommendations of CPC on the Secretary-General's draft outline, as updated and clarified by the Advisory Committee's report, and hoped that other delegations would do so too."

The representative of **Cameroon**[94]

"One thing was certain: the Secretary-General categorically affirmed that the elimination of 50 additional posts would have an adverse impact on programmes, without being able to say exactly how. The Secretary-General added that he would take account in his future decisions of those sectors in which the initial reductions had been considered excessive. He also proposed to take account of the views of Member States. However, each time the Secretariat made use of that formulation it placed itself in a difficult situation, particularly when the views of Member States were contradictory."

The representative of **Cameroon**[95] continued

"It had been rightly emphasized that the new budgetary process was in a developmental period and should be applied with flexibility and that the outline of the proposed programme budget was a part of the process of improving the efficiency and effectiveness of the Organization in serving the international community. A negative impact on the programmes to be included in the proposed programme budget for the biennium 1990-1991 should be avoided. It was gratifying to note the unanimity of views - on the part of the Secretary-General, the Advisory Committee and CPC - to the effect that financing of the

budget would be strictly observed once it had been approved and appropriated.
...

His delegation supported the total preliminary estimate of $1,982,523,700, as recommended by ACABQ, and also believed that the adjustment procedure suggested by the Secretary-General and endorsed by ACABQ in paragraphs 3 and 13 of document A/43/929 was appropriate. That support should be seen in the context of its initial observations and of the pertinent conclusions and recommendations of CPC and ACABQ. It must, however, be emphasized that the recommended level of resources and the contingency fund should not cover extraordinary and unforeseen expenditures, expenditures relating to peace-keeping operations, expenditures arising from statutory cost increases for staff or those arising from inflation and exchange rate fluctuations. Those categories should continue to be treated in the usual manner. In his delega-tion's view, the option mentioned in paragraph 26 of the Advisory Committee's report represented the least inconvenient way of dealing with changes caused by inflation and exchange rate fluctuations. It did not consider the alternative suggested in paragraphs 27 to 31 of the Advisory Committee's report to be appropriate, but believed that it would be consistent with paragraph 10 of the annex to General Assembly resolution 41/213 if the Committee were to accept as a lesser evil a solution which would amount to reimbursing Member States for any surplus resources arising from inflation or exchange rate fluctuations only at the end of each biennium, even if a decision must be taken on the percentage of resources to be left in the special fund.

With regard to the contingency fund, his delegation again believed in the need for flexibility in view of the importance of not jeopardizing the United Nations growing responsibilities in the quest for universal peace, security and well-being. It therefore believed that the amount and procedures for use and operation of the contingency fund must be reviewed, notwithstanding paragraph 15 of General Assembly resolution 42/211, even earlier than the Assembly's forty-seventh session."

The representative of **Cuba**[96]

"the basic problem posed by the implementation of recommendation 15 was political and admitted of only two solutions: either the Committee accepted the proposed recommendations knowing in advance that they would have an adverse impact on programmes, or it refused to. That being the case, many delegations, including his own, declined to opt for the first solution without knowing which sectors of activity would be affected."

The representative of **Mexico**[97]

"It was ... regrettable that the Secretariat had been unable to indicate clearly the impact which the planned reductions would have on the programmes. Without that information, the Fifth Committee and the General Assembly would have to rely on guesswork."

The representative of Denmark, speaking on behalf of the five **Nordic countries**[98]

"the budget outline was an innovation, allowance must be made for trial and error. ...

The Nordic countries concurred with the Advisory Committee that the traditional vacancy rate of 5 per cent for Professional and higher level posts should be retained. They supported the proposal that the level of the contingency fund should be 0.75 per cent for the biennium 1990-1991, on the understanding that it would be subject to review by the Assembly. With regard to additional expenditures, he said that the United Nations budget should be shielded as far as possible against inflation and currency fluctuations. There seemed to be no immediate alternative to the current system. However, the Advisory Committee should continue to study the problem.

In view of the difficulty of setting priorities of a broad sectoral nature, the detailed programme budget for 1990-1991 should reflect the priorities deriving from the current medium-term plan as revised."

The representative of Bulgaria speaking on behalf of **Group of Eastern European States**[99]

"The Secretary-General, in his report (A/43/524), had made a fair attempt to produce a concise and transparent programme budget outline for the biennium 1990-1991, although it would have been preferable for the report to have contained an indication of programme priorities, a matter on which agreement should be reached at the next session of the Committee for Programme and Co-ordination (CPC).

The budget outline suggested a modest decline in real terms from the current budget, although the Eastern European countries were concerned that, for the first time, the overall level would be close to $2 billion. The Eastern European countries concurred with the Secretary-General's proposal that, with respect to the contingency fund, a rate of 0.75 per cent should be adopted for the biennium 1990-1991, and with the Advisory Committee that the contingency fund should remain at the level set in the budget outline, with the understanding that the amount so approved was a ceiling, which need not be reached but could not be exceeded.

The treatment of currency fluctuations and inflation still presented difficulties. Although the problem was complex, there was no need for further postponement of a decision on the matter. The Eastern European States supported the Advisory Committee's proposal for the establishment of a reserve to cover currency fluctuation, non-staff costs inflation, and statutory cost increases for staff, as well as the means proposed for its operation. The Secretary-General should submit proposals thereon at the forty-fourth session."

Following these statements, the Vice-Chairman of the Fifth Committee submitted a draft resolution on the basis of informal consultations. The draft A/C.5/43/L.19 was approved by the Committee and subsequently adopted by the Plenary Assembly by consensus as resolution entitled **Implementation of General Assembly Resolution 42/213: Progress Report and Revised Estimates for the Biennium 1988-1989 (43/213).** By resolution 43/213, the GA requested the Secretary-General to take into account the following guidelines when implementing recommendation 15 of report A/41/49: (a) the recommendation should be implemented in a flexible manner, taking due account of work-load analyses, where applicable; (b) there should be no negative impact on programmes; (c) there should be no adverse effect on the structure and composition of the secretariat, bearing in mind the necessity of securing the highest standards of efficiency, competence and integrity of staff with due regard to equitable geographical distribution; (d) it should be implemented in a balanced manner, taking into account recommendations 41, 46, 47 and 54.

Prior to approving of the draft resolution, the Fifth Committee reached an understanding that the outline for 1990-1991 would include the funding of 50 of the 100 posts referred to in paragraph 9 of the resolution. Once the draft resolution had been approved, the following statements were made at the Fifth Committee.

The representative of **Algeria**[100]

"his delegation trusted that resolution 41/213 would be implemented in a balanced way and with flexibility, as recommended in paragraph 8 of the draft resolution just adopted. With regard to paragraph 9, it was his understanding that the overall post reduction in the Secretariat would be 12.1 per cent and that reduction would not have a negative impact on United Nations activities. He understood further that paragraph 13 referred to the modalities and

---

*See volume II, 1.8.

guidelines to be applied in attaining the percentage reduction referred to in paragraph 9."

The representative of the **United Kingdom**[101]

"his delegation had joined the consensus reluctantly. The item dealt with the implementation of resolution 41/213 as a whole, whereas draft resolution A/C.5/43/L.19 related only to specific aspects of that resolution. The Secretary-General should continue to pursue the objective of achieving staff reductions established under resolution 41/213, and it was to be hoped that the restructuring exercise would be continued in the interest of the Organization as a whole. His delegation interpreted paragraph 15 solely in terms of the prerogatives of the Secretary-General as the chief administrative officer of the Organization."

The representative of **Kenya**[102]

"paragraphs 5 and 8 stressed the need to avoid any negative impact on programmes and, to that end, to implement resolution 41/213 in a balanced way and with flexibility. The substance of paragraphs 11 and 12 was gratifying, since it was essential to the sound administrative and financial functioning of the United Nations for various units not to be adversely affected. With regard to the report requested in paragraphs 18 and 19, his delegation trusted it would clarify whether the implementation of resolution 41/213 would continue to improve the efficiency of financial administration in general and of that of small units, such as Nairobi, in particular."

Following the approval of the resolution on the progress report and revised estimates for the biennium 1988-1989 (43/213), the Chairman of the Fifth Committee introduced draft resolution A/C.5/43/L.20, drawn up on the basis of informal consultations. The draft was approved by the Committee and subsequently adopted by the Plenary Assembly by consensus as resolution entitled **Proposed Programme Budget Outline for the Biennium 1990-1991 and Use and Operation of the Contingency Fund (43/214).** By resolution 43/214, the GA decided that the Secretary-General should prepare his proposed programme budget for the biennium 1990-1991 on the basis of the total preliminary estimates of $1,767,060 at 1988 rates (equivalent to $1,982,523,700 at 1990-1991 rates) as shown in paragraph 16 of the ACABQ report; decided that the contingency fund of the programme budget for the biennium 1990-1991 should be established at a level of 0.75 per cent of the preliminary estimate at 1990-1991 rates, i.e. $15 million, which would be

---

*See volume II, 1.9.

appropriated as needed and used according to the purpose and procedures set out in the annexes to resolutions 41/213 and 42/211; reaffirmed the need for a comprehensive and satisfactory solution to the problems of controlling the effects of inflation and currency fluctuations on the budget of the UN.

The approval by consensus of the budget outline for the biennium 1990-1991 constituted a major successful test of the new programme budget procedure. Clearly, the reform resolution 41/213 appeared to provide a foundation for establishing broad based agreement in budgetary matters.

4.4.2 Approval of the Resolution on the Review of the Efficiency of the Administrative and Financial Functioning of the United Nations in the Economic and Social Fields (43/174)

Under agenda item 49 (Review of the Efficiency of the Administrative and Financial Functioning of the United Nations), the Plenary Assembly considered the report of the Special Commission of ECOSOC in accordance with ECOSOC decision 1988/182. The Plenary had before it document A/43/785, a note by the Secretary-General referring the GA to the report of the Special Commission of ECOSOC (E/1988/75)*. The following statements were made during the debate.

The representative of **Australia**[103]

"The Australian Government regrets that the Special Commission, despite its long labours, could not arrive at agreement on a package of wide-ranging structural reforms in the economic and social fields as originally envisaged in recommendation 8 of the report of the Group of 18 high-level intergovernmental experts. Several factors contributed to this, but lengthy post-mortems would not be constructive. We should rather turn our attention to the positive outcomes to date and seek to build on these. ...

In our view, it would be wrong to believe that this activity is about simple cost-cutting. Throughout the life of the Special Commission, our objective has been to make the United Nations more responsive to the contemporary needs of all Member States, for example by seeking to reallocate scarce human and financial resources to new and emerging priority areas.

At the second regular session of the Economic and Social Council this year, a resolution entitled "Revitalization of the Economic and Social Council" was adopted. My delegation joined the consensus in the adoption of this text, and

---

*See volume II, 2.23 and section 4.3 above.

we earnestly hope that concrete reforms will flow from that decision. However, we do not believe that the Economic and Social Council resolution represents the end of the reform process envisaged by Member States in 1986. In my Government's view, the urgent task before us is to carry forward this reform task in a way that - building on the foundations laid by the Special Commission - will lead to decisions being taken at the earliest possible time on concrete reforms.

We have considered carefully ways to carry forward the reform effort. In doing so, we have taken several principles into account, including the need, first, to keep the reform objective high on the United Nations agenda; secondly, to find a way to overcome the difficulties posed by certain political obstacles and to place the exercise on a more technical level; and thirdly, and finally, to define clearly the terms of reference to give structure and logic to future work.

Furthermore, the context for our consideration of these informal ideas is the undoubted merits of the role of the Special Commission in collecting and sorting the basic data about the present intergovernmental machinery, including the subsidiary bodies. It also provided a valuable forum in which the views of Member States were usefully elaborated.

In our view, a mechanism or framework needs to be established through which reform work can continue. Without such a programmatic approach, reform will falter or become piecemeal. Our belief is that the most efficient way to proceed is to request that further work be done, in conjunction with a group of eminent persons who have in-depth experience of the United Nations system, so that by the next session of the General Assembly we are in a position to take action.

My delegation has therefore commenced discussions with a number of other interested delegations in order to produce a draft resolution on furthering the work of reform, based on the principles I outlined earlier. My delegation believes that work on this item would benefit if those discussions continued for several more days. Hence, we would suggest that you consider, Mr. President, whether the debate on this item might not usefully be postponed for the time being, to see if these consultations can bear fruit in the form of a widely supported text."

The representative of Greece, speaking on behalf of the 12 member states of the **European Community**[104]

"The work of the Special Commission was inspired by the report of the Group of 18 and was envisaged as a comprehensive and necessary process aiming at the simplification of the intergovernmental structure and functions in the economic and social sectors of the United Nations. Unfortunately, the Special Committee has not been able to fulfil the task set forth in recommendation VIII of the Group of 18. The outcome of its work has fallen short of our expectations.

The Twelve remain committed to reform. We played an important part in the arduous task of the Special Commission, and we want to draw upon the many areas of agreement revealed in the Commission's report that can form the basis for further work by the General Assembly.

It is our understanding that informal proposals are being discussed among a number of delegations with regard to ways of bringing this process of reform forward. The streamlining of the intergovernmental machinery remains a major concern and should be addressed, and we are ready to work with others in creating a basis for further fruitful deliberations."

The representative of Tunisia on behalf of the **Group of 77**[105]

"The Special Commission established by the Council in its resolution E/1986/112 produced a report after a great deal of work. It was, however, unable to reach any conclusions or recommendations, despite the availability of a package of proposals by the Group of 77, contained in the annex to the Commission's report - which indeed is purely factual.

What conclusions can one draw from this situation?

First, the carrying out of a thorough and genuine reform depends, of course, on the support of all parties to the commitments entered into in this respect, in accordance with their obligations under the United Nations Charter. Moreover, it is conceivable only if there is respect for the statutes and mandates of the various organs of the United Nations.

The reform of the economic and social structures in fact began on the initiative not of the developed countries but, rather, of the developing countries. Thanks to their resolve, their constructive spirit and the flexibility they have constantly demonstrated, a consensus emerged, following their many initiatives, that made possible the adoption of resolution E/1988/77, on the revitalization of the Economic and Social Council. Any subsequent reform must therefore, in our view, be based on that important, unique decision by Member States to improve and strengthen the Economic and Social Council - this United Nations organ - as well as its support structures in the Secretariat.

...

We could legitimately ask ourselves how we should proceed in future and further the reformatory process in the economic and social fields. Clearly, the new objectives and priorities of the Organization for the 1990s have yet to be defined. The Secretary-General is engaged in preparing the next United Nations medium-term plan, and is currently consulting with Member States on that subject. ...

In the mean time we are of the view that any functional or structural reforms must proceed from the decisions to be taken on the basis of the reports that the Secretary-General was requested to submit under Economic and Social Council resolution E/1988/77 in 1989. At present, the General Assembly, although aware of its responsibilities, is not called upon to take any decision and must not in any way prejudge the implementation of that resolution or the report to be submitted by the Secretary-General to the forty-fourth session pursuant to General Assembly resolutions 41/213 and 42/211.

Accordingly, in the view of the Group of 77, the General Assembly at this session can only take note of the report of the Economic and Social Council on the matter, along with the report of its Special Commission, whose mandate has now been fulfilled. Member States will undoubtedly envisage some future action, particularly in light of the reports of the Secretary-General called for in Economic and Social Council resolution E/1988/77."

The representative of **Mexico**[106]

"it has not been possible to reach conclusions in the Special Commission's work and studies that could lead to a profound reform of intergovernmental structure and functions in the economic and social fields. Nor, as the report notes, was the Special Commission able to achieve any convergence, owing to the unilateral approach adopted, which was objected to by the Group of 77 and other countries, particularly since the report dealt with reforms in the structure and functions of subsidiary bodies with a view to achieving greater universality within the Economic and Social Council.

My country would therefore like to stress the fact that the Special Committee's report should not serve as a basis for further reform, although it contains valuable elements that should be taken into account. Mexico would also like to reiterate its reservations with regard to the report, which are set forth on the final page of document E/1988/77.

In conclusion, our country is firmly committed to a genuine, authentic process of reform of the United Nations, but we believe that in order to embark upon such reform and to succeed it must at least have the following features: first, it must be carried out without any kind of pressure, such as the threat of withholding a country's legally assessed contributions to the

Organization; and secondly, it must be carried out without any overt or covert attempt to give greater specific weight to a few countries over and above the majority, without any desire to dismantle bodies, without prejudice to the fact that the United Nations should indeed curb its expenditures, which is a goal in itself, and without undermining the instruments needed for the Organization's economic and social work or the legitimate rights of its staff. In short, reform must be carried out with a view to strengthening the United Nations, not to weaken it."

The representative of **New Zealand**[107]

"As a small State ourselves we believe that it is particularly in the interests of small countries that the existence and effectiveness of the Organization is not threatened. We want to see it strengthened, not weakened. We small States - more so than the large or even the middle-sized - have the most to lose if the difficulties of the United Nations are not resolved.

It is fundamental that all Members fulfil their financial obligations under the Charter. We cannot lose sight of that basic point. But, beyond that, we are not so blinkered as to believe that the United Nations is without blemish. The Organization has become unwieldy and wasteful of both funds and the skills of its staff. We have expressed concern previously over duplication of activities, out-dated programmes and the like. In addition, for small States it has simply become too difficult to follow responsibly even a modest range of activities of interest. We often feel we are drowning in a sea of paper.

It is fair to say, however, that since the Assembly adopted resolution 41/213 we have undeniably made progress. But it is equally fair to say that progress has been patchy and that in some areas it has been limited or far from adequate. This is not altogether surprising since the issues are often very complex, but the fact of complexity requires additional will to find means of resolution, we suggest. The Special Commission established by the Economic and Social Council to conduct an in-depth study of the United Nations intergovernmental structure and functions in the economic and social fields achieved a great deal during its existence. While we regret that it proved impossible to adopt a final report containing specific recommendations for subsequent action, its work to date should not be under-valued. It is our firm view that the time is right to carry forward the process of reform.

What we are saying quite simply is that we do not like the way in which the present financial situation has developed, and we look to see it remedied. The situation, carefully handled, provides an incentive for us to look at underpinning the recent welcome resurgence in the Organization's authority by maintaining steady and coherent progress in reform, including in the economic and social fields. Our objective should be a streamlined, well-managed and above all responsive structure."

The representative of Sweden, speaking on behalf of the five **Nordic Countries**[108]

"Many speakers in the general debate observed that the role of the United Nations in the political field had been enhanced by recent events, but that progress towards the solution of many economic problems was lagging behind.

We for our part consider that the United Nations can count a number of considerable achievements in the economic field also. The United Nations system has many times proved its strength both by contributing to greater awareness of global problems and offering solutions to them. We share the view, however, that further progress is called for. We must make the United Nations a more efficient tool for solving the problems that face mankind and require a multilateral solution.

Of course, increased political will to tackle together the economic and social problems is a prerequisite. The Nordic countries believe, however, that internal reforms aimed at making the United Nations more responsive and more efficient have an impact on how Member States view the activities of the United Nations and on their willingness to participate actively and constructively in the work of the United Nations.

The activities of the United Nations in the economic and social fields are very broad. As new tasks have emerged, generally without old ones being phased out, the agenda of the United Nations has shown sustained and considerable growth. This expansion has been accompanied by a parallel growth in the intergovernmental machinery, which in some cases has resulted in duplication of agendas and duplication of work. We should also bear in mind that the present structure is not the result of a comprehensive analysis of the needs of the system or of its member States but to a great extent the product of *ad hoc* decisions. The present structure must therefore not be taken as the ultimate response to our needs.

There are a great number of committees, commissions and sub-committees dealing with economic and social issues. A number of co-ordination mechanisms exist but there is still a lack of co-ordination. Overlapping and duplication are recurrent phenomena. Even though there is a feverish meeting schedule, the productive value of all these activities and meetings could at times be questioned.

The Nordic countries for their part find it of paramount importance to replace unnecessary bureaucracy by efficiency; paralysis by effectiveness; duplication by concentration; repetition by action; and vagueness by priorities. In short, there is a need for a more focused and efficient Organization responsive to the needs of its Member States, in particular the developing countries.

The open societies of the Nordic countries are closely linked to the world at large. We therefore have an obvious interest in an effective multilateral Organization. It would be difficult to build new multilateral forums. The United Nations already exists, it is needed, and it must be improved. This applies to all the various roles of the United Nations: as a forum for negotiations, as a peace-maker, as a norm-giver, and as a channel for development assistance. We are convinced that all United Nations Members have the same genuine interest in a strong and effective world Organization.

...

We can now take stock of the work carried out by the Special Commission entrusted with this in-depth study. Our evaluations are somewhat mixed. On the one hand a reasonably substantial review of the intergovernmental machinery did take place. It showed that the performance of subsidiary organs of the Economic and Social Council and the General Assembly, although with some important exceptions, is satisfactory.

The weakest links in the system were clearly identified as the relationship between the superior bodies and organs - notably the General Assembly, the Economic and Social Council and the Trade and Development Board. All delegations seemed to agree that the distribution of tasks and functions is blurred and that the Economic and Social Council is not fulfilling its mandate as envisaged in the United Nations Charter. On the positive side it must also be noted that a considerable number of proposals for comprehensive reforms were introduced in the Special Commission. There seemed to be a willingness to consider wide-ranging changes and not merely minor adjustments of a cosmetic nature. In addition, there seems to be a growing awareness that solutions to the pertinent problems of today are sought on multiple levels and in several international forums, some of them only loosely linked to the political process of the United Nations.

The Nordic countries regret, therefore, that the Special Commission was unable to fulfil the essential part of its mandate, namely to present recommendations aimed at enhancing the effectiveness and efficiency of the United Nations in the economic and social fields. It is disappointing that, beyond the general agreement on the need for comprehensive reform, no consensus could be reached with regard to specific reform measures.

The need for reform is still with us. I will not dwell here on all possible reforms but only point to a few areas in which the Nordic countries believe that further efforts could and should be made.

First, we are still of the opinion that the aims and usefulness of the general debates in the Economic and Social Council and the Second Committee should be re-examined. They should either be consolidated or emphasize different themes in order to avoid duplication. We believe that reform in this direction would increase the value of the deliberations in the Economic and Social Council and contribute to increased political attention being given to the Council so that it could fulfil its central role as envisaged in the Charter.

Secondly, a new attempt should be made to rationalize and streamline the structures of the subsidiary bodies. In that way the discussions of the topics that these bodies deal with could be made more relevant and tangible.

Thirdly, another look should be taken at the roles of the Economic and Social Council and the General Assembly. Reports to the Council for subsidiary bodies must be referred to the General Assembly only if it is explicitly decided that this be done. The Council's role as a filter for reports, resolutions and topics should be strengthened. This would make it possible for the General Assembly to concentrate its attention on major policy issues confronting the international community. In this context I should like to reiterate that the Nordic countries attach great importance to the biennial work programmes and meetings.

The reform process should be a continuing one, and appropriate measures to enhance the efficiency of the United Nations must be considered and implemented on a regular basis. We must therefore consider how, within the framework of a continuing reform process, the valuable analytical work carried out by the Special Commission and the proposals for reform put forward in the Special Commission can be used to promote further necessary reforms. The question on our minds must be how we can build on the work that has already been achieved, and move forward.

The momentum of reform must not be lost. The Nordic countries are committed to the reform process and would like to see substantial reform measures adopted at this session of the General Assembly. We must at least come to common conclusions concerning modalities and procedures for further discussion. One possibility could be to entrust the Economic and Social Council with further consideration of some issues. Another possibility would

be to make use of outside experts in preparing reports for further consideration. A third possibility could be to ask the Secretary-General to put forward
reform proposals after appropriate consultations with Member States. We are
quite open-minded and flexible in this respect, but we believe that it is of
fundamental importance that the reform process remain on the agenda of the
Economic and Social Council and of the General Assembly. In this context we
would also like to encourage the Secretary-General to proceed with reforms of
the structures of the Secretariat, in conformity with resolution 41/213."

The representative of the Union of Soviet Socialist Republics, speaking on
behalf of **socialist countries**[*][109]

"Although the Commission was not able to arrive at agreed decisions on the
restructuring of the economic and social structures of the United Nations - a
fact recognized by all - it did useful work in a very thorough study of the
situation. The main thing is that, under the Special Commission, a dialogue
was established to allow for better understanding of the functions of the United
Nations, taking into account contemporary requirements and needs.

On the practical level, the work of the Special Commission made possible
at the summer session of the Economic and Social Council this year an
important decision designed to strengthen and, in practical terms, implement
the work and functions of the United Nations and the Council under the
Charter, particularly at the level of organizing solutions to problems in the
economic and social fields. We trust that the experience acquired by the
Special Commission will enhance a continued and fruitful search for mutually
agreed approaches to improving the economic and social mechanisms of the
United Nations, duly taking into account the balance of interests of the various
groups of countries.

Our delegation still adheres to the goal of enhancing the effectiveness of the
economic and social activities of the United Nations in the interests of all
countries, and we are willing constructively to continue work in that direction
in any forums acceptable to all other countries and regional groups."

The representative of **Egypt**[110]

"The work of the Special Commission, despite the absence of agreed
recommendations, has proved very useful and has presented a reservoir of
knowledge that should not be ignored or forgotten.

---

[*]Bulgaria, Byelorussian SSR, Czechoslovakia, German Democratic Republic, Hungary,
Mongolia, Poland, Ukrainian SSR, USSR.

However, the reform of the United Nations inter-governmental structure in the economic and social fields should be considered as part and parcel of the overall reform of the administrative and financial functioning of the United Nations.

We therefore believe that the final consideration of the report of the Special Commission should take place together with the final report of the Secretary-General on the implementation of resolution 41/213 and his reports to be prepared in implementation of Economic and Social Council resolution 1988/77 on the revitalization of the Economic and Social Council, as we believe reform is indivisible. We fully recognize that reform aimed at enhancing the efficiency and effectiveness of the United Nations is and should be a continuing process."

Following these statements, two draft resolutions were introduced. The first draft was submitted by Australia, Finland, Italy, Japan, the Netherlands, New Zealand, Norway, Sweden, the UK and the USA entitled **Review of the Efficiency of the Economic and Social Machinery of the United Nations (A/43/L.29)**, which reads as follows:

"The General Assembly,

Recalling its resolutions 41/213 of 19 December 1986 on the review of the efficiency of the administrative and financial functioning of the United Nations, 42/170 of 11 December 1987, on the implementation of General Assembly resolution 41/213 in the economic and social fields, and 42/211 of 21 December 1987 on the implementation of General Assembly resolution 41/213,

Recalling also Economic and Social Council resolution 1988/77 of 29 July 1988 on the revitalization of the Economic and Social Council,

Conscious of the fact that reform is an ongoing process and that resolution 41/213 should be fully implemented,

Recognizing that the review called for in recommendation 8 of the report of the Group of High-level Intergovernmental Experts to Review the Efficiency of the Administrative and Financial Functioning of the United Nations,[111] as adopted by General Assembly in resolution 41/213, requires continued attention,

Emphasizing that the work of the subsidiary bodies in the economic and social fields of the United Nations should be enhanced and streamlined in order to make the United Nations more effective and responsive to the needs of Member States,

Fully aware of the urgent need to examine and take appropriate action on subsidiary bodies in the economic and social fields of the United Nations in order to enable them to meet effectively their evolving priorities as set out in relevant resolutions of the General Assembly and the Economic and Social Council and to be responsive to the needs of the Member States,

Taking note with appreciation of the work of the Special Commission of the Economic and Social Council on the In-depth Study of the United Nations Intergovernmental Structure and Functions in the Economic and Social Fields,[112] which was forwarded to the Assembly by the Economic and Social Council in its decision 1988/182.

1. *Affirms* that the subsidiary bodies in the economic and social fields of the United Nations should make an important contribution to addressing the major issues and evolving priorities facing the international community, in particular, the economic and social development of developing countries;

2. *Invites* the Secretary-General to implement without delay those recommendations in General Assembly resolution 41/213 pertaining to the economic and social fields of the United Nations within his purview and to report thereon through the Committee for Programme and Co-ordination and the Economic and Social Council to the General Assembly at its forty-fourth session;

3. *Requests* the Secretary-General, taking into account the work done by the Special Commission and the views expressed by Governments, and following consultations with Member States, eminent persons who have in-depth experience of the United Nations system in the areas of its economic and social activity, and the organizations concerned, to prepare and submit, through the Economic and Social Council, to the General Assembly at its forty-fourth session, a report containing options for an appropriate intergovernmental structure in the economic and social fields of the United Nations for consideration and decision thereon by Member States, and including consideration of:

(a) The possible abolition, merging or expertization of some subsidiary bodies and subsuming of bodies by the General Assembly of the Economic and Social Council;

(b) The possible transfer of the responsibilities of the work or part thereof of some of the subsidiary bodies to the General Assembly, the Economic and Social Council, the regional commissions or other relevant parts of the United Nations system;

4. *Decides* to consider at its forty-fourth session the report of the Special Commission together with the report of the Secretary-General called for in paragraph 3 above and the report of the Secretary-General on the implementation of resolution 41/213;

5.   *Decides* to include in the provisional agenda of the forty-fourth session a sub-item entitled "Review of the efficiency of the economic and social machinery of the United Nations", under the item entitled "Review of the efficiency of the administrative and financial functioning of the United Nations".

The second draft resolution **(A/43/L.40)** was submitted by Tunisia on behalf of the Group of 77 and reads as follows:

"*The General Assembly,*

Recalling General Assembly resolution 32/197 of 20 December 1977 on the restructuring of the economic and social sectors of the United Nations system,

Recalling also General Assembly resolutions 41/213 of 19 December 1986, 42/170 of 11 December 1987 and 42/211 of 21 December 1987 on the review of the efficiency of the administrative and financial functioning of the United Nations,

Recalling further Economic and Social Council resolution 1988/77 of 29 July 1988 on the revitalization of the Economic and Social Council,

Emphasizing that the financial stability of the Organization will facilitate the orderly, balanced and well co-ordinated implementation of resolution 41/213 in all its parts,

Recognizing that the reform of the economic and social sectors of the United Nations is a continuing process aimed at strengthening the effectiveness of the United Nations in dealing with those issues,

Noting the report of the Special Commission of the Economic and Social Council on the In-depth Study of the United Nations Intergovernmental Structure and Functions in the Economic and Social Fields[113] and its secretariat support structures and recognizing that, although the Special Commission had conducted the in-depth study entrusted to it, it was unable to reach agreed recommendations,

1.   *Stresses* the common interest of all countries in the effective functioning of the United Nations in the economic and social fields, which are of particular importance to the developing countries;

2.   *Requests* the Secretary-General to consult with all Member States and to seek their views on ways and means of achieving a balanced and effective implementation of recommendations 2 and 8 of the Group of High-level Intergovernmental Experts to Review the Efficiency of the Administrative and Financial Functioning of the United Nations,[114] taking into consideration all relevant reports, including the report of the Special Commission of the Economic and Social Council on the In-depth Study of the United Nations

Intergovernmental Structure and Functions in the Economic and Social Fields and the outcome of the discussions on the revitalization of the Economic and Social Council, to be held during the second regular session of the Council for 1989, and to report thereon, through the Economic and Social Council, to the General Assembly at its forty-fourth session, under the item entitled "Review of the efficiency of the administrative and financial functioning of the United Nations".

After informal consultations, the two draft resolutions A/43/L.29 and A/43/L.40 were withdrawn by the sponsors. The new draft A/43/L.48 was submitted by Malta and approved by the Plenary Assembly by consensus as resolution entitled **Review of the Efficiency of the Administrative and Financial Functioning of the United Nations in the Economic and Social Fields (43/174).** By resolution 43/174, the GA requested the Secretary-General to consult with all member states and seek their views on ways and means of achieving balanced and effective implementation of recommendations 2 and 8 of the Group of 18, taking into consideration all relevant reports, including the report of the Special Commission of ECOSOC, as well as the outcome of the 1989 discussions on the revitalization of ECOSOC, and to submit to the 44th session of the GA a detailed report in order to enable member states to consider and take appropriate action with a view to enhancing the effectiveness of the intergovernmental structure and its secretariat support structures as well as programme delivery in the economic and social fields.

Prior to the approval of the draft resolution, the representative of Tunisia made a statement on behalf of the **Group of 77**[115]

"The Group of 77 wishes to reiterate its belief that the United Nations can and should deal more effectively with international economic co-operation to fulfil its responsibilities and objectives in those fields as set out in its Charter and in relevant resolutions. We equally believe that reform of the economic and social sectors of the United Nations is a continuing process, aimed at strengthening the effectiveness of the United Nations in dealing with those issues.

Reform will, however, be devoid of any substance or content if it is not coupled with the requisite political will on the part of all Member States and the necessary determination to match words with deeds, to honour commit-

---

See volume II, 1.7.

ments and to work in good faith to give effect to the decisions adopted in a democratic way by this universal forum.

Attempts at eroding or questioning the role of the United Nations in dealing with the economic and social issues and problems besetting the world are tantamount to questioning multilateralism and the very existence of the United Nations itself, and the *raison d'être* of international economic co-operation for development.

We have embarked on the process of reform in good faith. The Group of 77 has been forthcoming in coming up with initiatives to this end. We therefore expect all Member States to be as forthcoming and to demonstrate their commitment to the principles of the Charter and to work constructively towards utilizing the full potential of the United Nations in resolving the economic and social problems of our contemporary world, particularly those related to the development of developing countries."

After the Plenary Assembly had adopted the resolution, the representative of **Denmark**[116] made following statement:

"While my delegation has joined in the consensus on draft resolution A/43/L.48 ... it has done so without enthusiasm as it considers this resolution to be a disappointing and meagre outcome of the extensive deliberations and negotiations on the functioning of the United Nations in the economic and social fields that have taken place over the past two years. Regrettably, these considerations have not, up to now, led to any results. In the view of my Government, improved efficiency and functioning of the United Nations is a *sine qua non* for an enhancement of the role of the United Nations in these fields.

The adoption of draft resolution A/43/L.48 postpones further consideration of this question to the forty-fourth session of the General Assembly. It is the sincere hope of my Government that appropriate decisions to streamline and enhance the effectiveness of the intergovernmental structure in the economic and social fields will be taken at the forty-fourth session. We strongly encourage the Secretary-General to include in his report to the General Assembly at its forty-fourth session - the report requested in paragraph 2 of the resolution - specific proposals on ways and means of achieving this objective in order to enable Governments to take the necessary decisions."

4.4.3   Endorsement of ECOSOC Resolution 1988/77 on the Revitalization of ECOSOC (43/432)

Under agenda item 12 (Report of the ECOSOC), the Second Committee considered ECOSOC resolution on the revitalization of ECOSOC (1988/77)*. The following statements were made during the debate.

The representative of Tunisia, speaking on behalf of the **Group of 77**[117]

"the second regular session of the Economic and Social Council had taken place in a spirit of constructive co-operation.

Resolution 1988/77 on the revitalization of the Economic and Social Council had been adopted following nearly two years of effort by the Group of 77 to reach agreement on the restructuring of the economic and social sectors. It constituted a sound basis upon which to pursue the objective of increasing the United Nations impact in those areas."

The representative of **China**[118]

"Another important achievement was the adoption by consensus of resolution 1988/77 concerning revitalization of the Economic and Social Council, which provided not only a point of departure for reform of the Council itself, but was also a first step towards the reform of the United Nations system as a whole in the economic and social fields. In that connection, he praised the work of the Special Commission on the In-depth Study of the United Nations Intergovernmental Structure and Functions in the Economic and Social Fields."

The representative of the **Union of Soviet Socialist Republics**[119]

"Economic and Social Council resolution 1988/77 contained good suggestions for enhancing the efficiency and role of the Council, and the General Assembly should give it serious attention. The key role of the Council as co-ordinator of all the social and economic activities of the United Nations system could be enhanced by a political streamlining of the efforts of all bodies and agencies of the United Nations system in the implementation of comprehensive international co-operation strategies and policies. It was important to return to the practice whereby all the specialized agencies submitted regular reports to the Council. That would help bridge the existing gap between the political recommendations worked out by the international community and the practical activities for their implementation, and would help harmonize the activities of the entire United Nations system."

---

*See volume II, 1.6 and section 4.3 above.

The representative of **Egypt**[120]

"described the Economic and Social Council as the weakest link in the United Nations chain and said that its revitalization was a prerequisite for a more efficient and more effective system. Accordingly, the adoption by consensus of resolution 1988/77 was a major achievement and the Group of 77 should be commended for producing a substantive and comprehensive draft, which affirmed that the Council had an important contribution to make with regard to major international issues, in particular, the economic and social development of developing countries.

The resolution clearly set out the Council's threefold functions and powers, namely, policy formulation, monitoring and co-ordination, providing a set of principles and guidelines for its working methods, guaranteeing a maximum of co-ordination between the Council and the subsidiary bodies and rationalization of its output and capacity. It also contained specific measures which would call for joint efforts on the part of Member States and the Secretariat.

With regard to the reports to be prepared by the Secretary-General in that connection, he said that without co-ordinated effort and well-prepared reports, endeavours to improve the functioning of the Council and to maximize its contribution would be doomed to failure. There should, therefore, be consultations between the Secretariat and Member States prior to preparation of reports. Furthermore, consolidating reports was not just a matter of juxtaposing, compressing or listing material submitted by various bodies. It meant giving various inputs concise and intelligible form.

With regard to achieving more effective co-ordination of activities, including operational activities for development, within the United Nations system, the resolution not only emphasized the need to reinforce the Office of the Director-General for Development and International Economic Co-operation, but it also provided for action on the part of the Secretary-General and the specialized agencies. All such measures required careful co-ordination.

The final restructuring of the Secretariat in the economic and social sectors would probably have to take account of the provisions of resolution 1988/77 and of the final decisions ensuing from discussion of the report of the Special Commission on the In-depth Study of the United Nations Intergovernmental Structure and Functions in the Economic and Social Fields. The Committee should hold informal exchanges of views between members and the Secretariat on ways and means of implementing the resolution. In that connection, he drew attention to the issues raised in paragraphs 2(b)(i), 2(f)(iii), 2(f)(vi), 2(g), (h), and (k) and 6. The main purpose of such an exchange of views would be to ensure that Member States and the Secretariat assumed their responsibilities and honoured their commitment to reform. It would also help to expedite the reform process."

The representative of **Canada**[121]

"there had been a significant loss of momentum and energy at the Council's second regular session of 1988. Attendance had been poor, and meetings had often been cancelled owing to a lack of speakers. If the Council was to heed the call of many delegations for expanded membership, participants should be genuinely committed to making the Council work.

His delegation was concerned that the Special Commission had failed to come up with agreed recommendations on improving the intergovernmental structure and functions of the United Nations in the economic and social fields. Although Council resolution 1988/77 had contributed a little to keeping alive the momentum towards greater efficiency and better use of resources, it had not gone far enough. Greater commitment was needed to eliminate - or at least limit - the general debate, cut back the production of reports, avoid overlapping and duplication and clarify the organization of the debates."

The representative of **Mexico**[122]

"Council resolution 1988/77 provided the Council with the necessary institutional bases for increasing its efficiency and its ability to deal with the economic problems of the developing world. The re-introduction of the practice whereby the specialized agencies submitted reports on measures which they had taken to implement General Assembly and Council resolutions was of great importance and, in conjunction with the Council's new role in operational activities for development, would enable the entire system to set common goals and priorities and would ensure coherence and complementarity in the work of the various specialized agencies.

The efficiency and effectiveness of the United Nations should be measured by the quality and promptness of its response to the challenges and problems of development. The seriousness of the economic situation in the developing countries required lasting and just solutions and the General Assembly should, as a matter of urgency, hold a special session on the reactivation of economic growth and development of developing countries."

The representative of **Philippines**[123]

"Perhaps too much had been expected from the work of the Special Commission on the In-depth Study of the United Nations Intergovernmental Structures and Functions in the Economic and Social Fields. None the less, the wealth of information gathered could be used in future, for the United Nations system must continually undergo reforms in order to keep up with the needs of the time, particularly those concerning greater integration of the developing countries into the mainstream.

For the time being, the Philippines continued to attach great importance to the preponderant role the General Assembly must play in economic and social matters within the United Nations system, particularly through the Economic and Social Council. The Council must be the primary focus of any reform of the overall operation of the system. In that connection, the important provisions of resolution 1988/77 must be scrupulously implemented, particularly those concerning the monitoring of the implementation of the overall strategies, policies and priorities established by the General Assembly in the economic and social fields, and the co-ordination of the activities of the United Nations system. The monitoring of activities required urgent attention. An extensive and complex bureaucracy such as the United Nations too often gave rise to confusion, lack of transparency, and a shortage of information and integrated data. Brilliant and well-meaning initiatives could readily come to naught for that reason. An improved monitoring system would, at the same time, enhance the co-ordinating function performed by the Economic and Social Council. The consideration of co-ordination issues should therefore be integrated in the discussion of relevant substantive items so that the Council could recommend to the General Assembly guidelines and priorities that were both integrated and comprehensive. It was equally important for the Administrative Committee on Co-ordination (ACC) and the Joint Consultative Group on Policy to provide support to the Council, as set forth in resolution 1988/77."

The representative of the **German Democratic Republic**[124]

"His delegation attached great importance to strengthening the role of the Economic and Social Council as the principal organ for international economic and social co-operation under the Charter of the United Nations. In that connection, the revitalization of the Council and the adoption of resolution 1988/77 were particularly welcome. Resolution 1988/77 might be helpful in efforts to streamline the work of the Council. In particular, his delegation reaffirmed the importance accorded by all States to the continuation of the Council's work. What mattered now was to translate its provisions into reality. His delegation would continue to work to that end."

The representative of **Yugoslavia**[125]

"The adoption of resolution 1988/77, which should facilitate the revitalization of the Economic and Social Council and thus improve its functioning, was a major success. However, the agreements reached would be of value only if they were implemented.

Measures to strengthen the co-ordinating role of the Council and to rationalize its activities were of particular significance. In that connection, her delegation looked forward to the report of the Secretary-General on the feasibility and comparative costs of holding, with the present in-sessional arrangements, one consolidated or two regular sessions of the Council. In her view the number of participants at the second regular session had been insufficient. It would be useful if the report could deal with the organizational issues which influenced participation at Council sessions.

In a more general context, the reorganization of the Economic and Social Council should enable the United Nations to play a more active role in dealing with world economic problems and in responding to the expectations of the international community. The current favourable political climate should facilitate such an endeavour."

The representative of the **United States of America**[126]

"Much had been said about the reform of the Economic and Social Council, and sustained efforts had been made in that direction. Between January and May 1988, the Special Commission of the Council responsible for that question had laboured hard and the reform had progressed; it was real and should not be belittled. Improvements could only be made step by step. Sudden, sweeping changes were difficult to bring about. The second regular session of the Economic and Social Council had been constructive, resulting in the adoption by consensus of resolution 1988/77. The United States Government had, however, expressed reservations, which it maintained, on two parts of that resolution. Finally, it was vital to keep up the momentum of reform. Pending the response which would be provided in July 1989 to several recommendations, specific action could be taken on specific subjects, such as the streamlining of several subsidiary bodies of the Council."

The representative of **Peru**[127]

"the adoption of resolution 1988/77 had been a decisive step towards strengthening the Council's role as a co-ordinating body on economic and social matters. In that connection, the decision to revert to the practice of asking the specialized agencies for reports on measures they had taken to give effect to the recommendations of the General Assembly and the Council was gratifying. However, that was not enough. If the Council was to play effectively its role as the main United Nations body responsible for considering truly important economic and social questions and making recommendations thereon, it would be necessary to deal with substantive questions, such as the composition of the Council and of its subsidiary bodies, and the agenda and organization of Council sessions."

The representative of **Bulgaria**[128]

"1988 had been an important year for the Economic and Social Council. Although it had not been possible to reach agreement on the adoption of a common document, one positive result of the Council's summer session had been the adoption by consensus of resolution 1988/77. That resolution was an important step forward in enhancing the efficiency and role of the Council, and Bulgaria hoped that the General Assembly would adopt a positive decision on it."

The representative of **Czechoslovakia**[129]

"fully supported the efforts made to increase the effectiveness of the Economic and Social Council. It was regrettable, therefore, that the Special Commission on the In-depth Study of the United Nations Intergovernmental Structure and Functions in the Economic and Social Fields had been unable to reduce the differences in approach of individual countries and groups of countries on many key issues. The adoption of resolution 1988/77 was significant in that it would make the Council better able to provide political guidelines, and to monitor and co-ordinate the economic and social activities of the United Nations system. The resolution also provided a point of departure for further efforts to strengthen the Council's role as one of the main United Nations bodies. He hoped that, in his report on the possible merging of the two sessions into one, the Secretary-General would take account of the relevant resolutions on the geographical distribution of sessions and on conference rules, and of the views of the Committee on Conferences. He welcomed the comments of the Director-General for Development and International Economic Co-operation with regard to restructuring."

The representative of Greece, speaking on behalf of the 12 member states of the **European Community**[130]

"resolution 1988/77 on the revitalization of the Economic and Social Council was part of a wider reform exercise to which the Community attached great importance. The resolution, which was a further step towards remedying problems which had beset the Council for a number of years, represented a modest but none the less satisfactory approach to some critical areas where improvement was needed. The Community attached particular importance to the provision calling for in-depth discussions of previously identified major policy themes, and fully agreed with the emphasis placed on the Council's role in operational activities. The Council's contribution was important for the implementation of General Assembly resolution 42/196 on operational activities for development.

Some of the principles set out in resolution 1988/77 needed to be translated into practical arrangements in the form of a coherent package aimed at improving the Council's work. Past experience had shown that some resolutions had not produced the expected results largely because of difficulties associated with implementation. The Community expected that the proposed new working methods and organization of work would contribute substantially to the more effective operation of the Council. Reform was not an end in itself but a means of improving international economic and social co-operation for development, and efforts towards that end were taking place in an improved political climate. The member States of the Community attached particular importance to the success of the Council's omission and were ready to contribute actively and effectively in that regard."

The representative of the **Byelorussian Soviet Socialist Republic**[131]

"Further joint efforts were required to enhance the Council's activity, and resolution 1988/77 envisaged specific measures in that regard. The resolution corresponded to the provisions of Chapters IX and X of the Charter and was based on resolutions already adopted by the General Assembly and the Council. It was therefore essential to achieve the complete implementation of the provisions of resolution 1988/77 and to agree upon a more effective division of labour between the Council and the General Assembly. In that connection, it might be possible to discuss certain ideas which had already been put forward such as making the membership of the Council universal, abolishing some of its subsidiary bodies while ensuring that ways and means of supporting United Nations activities in the relevant spheres of co-operation were secured, holding special sessions of the Council on specific important problems and also sessions at ministerial level, and other proposals which had emerged during the work of the Special Commission.

Improvements in the intergovernmental structure and functions in the economic and social fields must be accompanied by enhanced effectiveness of the Secretariat. The Council should make greater efforts to implement the relevant provisions of General Assembly resolutions 42/93 ("Comprehensive system of international peace and security") and 41/59 D. In addition, questions concerning the protection of the environment must be given special attention. ...

There were still many unresolved problems with respect to the effective co-ordination of the activity of the United Nations system in the economic and social spheres, and while resolution 1988/77 was a step in the right direction it was also necessary to enhance the effectiveness of the Administrative Committee on Co-ordination. Enhancing the effectiveness of the Council and the Second Committee was an integral part of the general task of enhancing the role of the United Nations in solving all global problems, and as such required new political thinking. To ensure that the United Nations functioned properly as the universal forum for the collective settlement of global problems it was essential that all States members should strictly observe their financial obligations towards the Organization. Financial pressure on the United Nations was inadmissible."

The representative of **Indonesia**[132]

"his delegation firmly believed that there was an urgent need to reactivate world economic growth and to put multilateral co-operation for development back on the global agenda. Although the Economic and Social Council, as the main co-ordinating body for social and economic activity in the United Nations system, had an important role to play in that regard, it had no major impact on the formulation of world economic and development policies. The adoption of resolution 1988/77 was, therefore, extremely gratifying. Full implementation of its provisions would ensure that the Council and its subsidiary bodies properly fulfilled their mandate, and that the structures involved could be adapted to the new priorities, objectives and needs of the Member States. Although the Special Commission had been unable to reach consensus, its deliberations would provide basis for future activities within the framework of resolution 41/213."

The representative of the **Ukrainian Soviet Socialist Republic**[133]

"The Ukrainian SSR wholeheartedly supported the strengthening of the role of the Economic and Social Council. Although the Special Commission on the In-depth Study of the United Nations Intergovernmental Structure and Functions in the Economic and Social Fields had not reached consensus, its work had been fruitful and there was reason to hope that the reform process currently under way would be completed. Council resolution 1988/77, on the revitalization of the Council, was an important step in that direction, because it set out precise guidelines for improving the Council's working methods. His delegation would actively support its implementation."

The representative of **India**[134]

"With respect to the issue of the reform of the United Nations intergovernmental structure and functions in the economic and social fields, he recalled that the positions adopted by the Group of 77 during the discussions and negotiations of the Special Commission constituted an integrated package whose diverse elements could not be dealt with in isolation. It was regrettable that the Special Commission had not been able to agree on an agreed set of conclusions on the restructuring; however, a certain convergence of views had emerged during the negotiations, and it should facilitate future work. It would, however, be prudent, before considering the question of subsidiary bodies and Secretariat support structure, to see how Council resolution 1988/77 was being implemented and what was happening to the various proposals made by the Group of 77 in the Special Commission."

The representative of **Colombia**[135]

"welcomed the many results obtained by the Council during the past year and the adoption by consensus of resolution 1988/77 on the revitalization of the Council. The latter should constitute, together with the in-depth study of the United Nations intergovernmental structure and functions in the economic and social fields, a point of departure for an overall reform of the activities of the United Nations system in those areas."

The representative of the **Libyan Arab Jamahiriya**[136]

"Member States should undertake to ensure implementation of resolution 1988/77 on the revitalization of the Council, which was intended to enable the Council to carry out better the mandate entrusted to it under Chapters IX and X of the Charter and subsequent resolutions of the General Assembly, particularly with respect to policy formulation, monitoring of the implementation of overall strategies, policies and priorities established by the General Assembly in the economic and social and related fields, operational activities and co-ordination of activities of the United Nations system in the economic and social fields. He drew attention to the need for Member States to undertake effective consultations with the Secretariat in order to implement the part of resolution 1988/77 entitled "Working methods and organization of work", to strengthen the Office of the Director-General for Development and International Economic Co-operation and to give due consideration to the principle of equitable geographical distribution in the recruitment of staff of the United Nations Secretariat in the economic and social fields."

The representative of **Mongolia**[137]

"the work of the Economic and Social Council in 1988 had been fruitful.
The spirit of co-operation and dialogue which delegations had generally
displayed had enabled a greater number of resolutions to be adopted by
consensus. Resolution 1988/77, which dealt with the revitalization of the
Council, was particularly important since it specified the Council's functions
and its relations with other bodies which had parallel responsibilities. Its
implementation would certainly contribute to improving the operation of the
Council and strengthening its role within the United Nations system.

Consideration had continued to be given to the manner in which the Council
could help in solving the urgent international problems which came within its
competence. It was in that light that one had to evaluate the work of the
Special Commission of the Economic and Social Council on the In-depth Study
of the United Nations Intergovernmental Structure and Functions in the
Economic and Social Fields. It had not been possible to reach a consensus but
on the whole the discussion had been fruitful. Many useful ideas and proposals
had been put forward. For example, the delegation of Mongolia found the
proposal of the Group of 77 on broadening the composition of the Council to
embrace all Member States very interesting. It supported the proposal
periodically to organize sessions at ministerial level. Such an initiative would
give the Council increased authority and enable it to play a more important
role in analyzing and solving international problems."

Following these statements, the representative of Tunisia submitted the
draft resolution A/C.2/43/L.21 on behalf of the Group of 77. The draft was
approved by consensus in the Second Committee and subsequently in the
Plenary Assembly as resolution entitled **Revitalization of the Economic and
Social Council (43/432).** By resolution 43/432, the GA endorsed the
ECOSOC resolution on the revitalization of the Council (1988/77). Following
approval of the draft resolution by the Second Committee, the representative
of Tunisia, speaking on behalf of the **Group of 77**[138], noted that the Group

"welcomed the adoption by consensus of the draft decision. As far as the
Group of 77 was concerned, implementation of the recommendations contained
in the draft, and of the decisions to be taken by the Economic and Social
Council at its 1989 summer session, would make it possible to lay the
foundations for an effective process of reform in the economic and social
sectors."

Notes

1.   ST/ADM/SER.B/295; A/C.5/43/29.
2.   A/42/841, p. 3.
3.   Ruth Pearson, 'U.N. Cries "Uncle"', *Bulletin of the Atomic Scientists*, XLIV (October 1988), pp. 37-38.
4.   E/1988/75, pp. 11-15.
5.   E/ECE/1150/Rev.1.
6.   Traian Chebeleu, 'The Administrative and Financial Reform of the United Nations. Some Reflections', *Revue Roumaine d'Études Internationales*, XXII (1988), pp. 542, 547-548.
7.   E/1988/75, annex V, pp. 107-110.
8.   *Ibid.*, annex VI, pp. 111-114.
9.   *Ibid.*, p. 116.
10. *Ibid.*, p. 117.
11. *Ibid.*, p. 118.
12. *Ibid.*, pp. 119-120.
13. *Ibid.*, p. 121.
14. *Ibid.*, p. 122.
15. *Ibid.*, p. 123.
16. *Ibid.*, p. 125.
17. *Ibid.*, p. 126.
18. *Ibid.*, p. 128.
19. *Ibid.*, annex VII, pp. 129-132.
20. *Ibid.*, annex X, p. 142.
21. E/1988/SR.29, pp. 8-10.
22. *Ibid.*, pp. 10-12.
23. *Ibid.*, pp. 12-13.
24. *Ibid.*, pp. 13-14.
25. *Ibid.*, pp. 14-15.
26. *Ibid.*, pp. 15-16.
27. *Ibid.*, pp. 17-18.
28. *Ibid.*, p. 20.
29. *Ibid.*, p. 21.
30. *Ibid.*, p. 22.
31. E/1988/SR.30, pp. 2-5.
32. *Ibid.*, pp. 6-7.
33. *Ibid.*, pp. 8-9.
34. *Ibid.*, pp. 9-10.
35. *Ibid.*, pp. 12-13.
36. Chebeleu, *op.cit.*, p. 544.
37. E/1988/75.
38. E/1988/SR.41, p. 10.
39. *Ibid.*, pp. 10-11.
40. *Ibid.*, p. 11.
41. *Ibid.*, pp. 11-12.
42. *Ibid.*, p. 14.
43. *Ibid.*
44. *Ibid.*, p. 15.
45. *Ibid.*, pp. 15-16.
46. *Ibid.*, p. 16.
47. *Ibid.*, p. 17.
48. *Official Records of the General Assembly, Forty-third Session, Supplement No. 1* (A/43/1), p. 8.
49. *Ibid.*, pp. 9-10.

50. A/C.5.43.SR.7, pp. 2-3.
51. *Ibid.*, p. 4.
52. A/C.5/43/SR.21, p. 9.
53. A/C.5/43/SR.7, pp. 4-5.
54. A/C.5/43/SR.23, pp. 2-3.
55. *Ibid.*, pp. 5-7.
56. A/C.5/43/SR.46, pp. 3-5.
57. A/C.5/43/SR.7, pp. 6-7.
58. A/C.5/43/SR.46, pp. 5-6.
59. A/C.5/43/SR.21, p. 7.
60. *Ibid.*, p. 13.
61. A/C.5/43/SR.10, pp. 2-3.
62. A/C.5/43/SR.11, pp. 2-3.
63. *Ibid.*, pp. 3-5.
64. *Ibid.*, pp. 5-7.
65. A/C.5/43/SR.12, pp. 3-6.
66. A/C.5/43/SR.48, pp. 8-9.
67. A/C.5/43/SR.12, p. 6.
68. A/C.5/43/SR.14, 4-5.
69. *Ibid.*, pp. 6-7.
70. *Ibid.*, pp. 7-9.
71. A/C.5/43/SR.16, pp. 2-3.
72. A/C.5/43/SR.48, pp. 5-6
73. A/C.5/43/SR.16, pp. 3-4.
74. A/C.5/43/SR.21, p. 12.
75. A/C.5/43/SR.18, p. 10.
76. A/C.5/43/SR.48, p. 7.
77. A/C.5/43/SR.18, pp. 10-11.
78. *Ibid.*, pp. 12-13.
79. A/C.5/43/SR.24, p. 3.
80. A/C.5/43/SR.48, pp. 4-5.
81. A/C.5/43/SR.18, p. 13.
82. A/C.5/43/SR.19, p. 7.
83. *Ibid.*, p. 8.
84. A/C.5/43/SR.48, pp. 6-7.
85. A/C.5/43/SR.19, pp. 9-10.
86. A/C.5/43/SR.23, p. 3.
87. A/C.5/43/SR.24, p. 2.
88. A/C.5/43/SR.19, p. 11.
89. A/C.5/43/SR.19, p. 12.
90. A/C.5/43/SR.21, p. 14.
91. A/C.5/43/SR.48, pp. 10-11.
92. A/C.5/43/SR.21, pp. 5-6.
93. A/C.5/43/SR.47, pp. 4-5.
94. A/C.5/43/SR.21, p. 9.
95. A/C.5/43/SR.48, pp. 7-8.
96. A/C.5/43/SR.21, p. 11.
97. *Ibid.*, pp. 11-12.
98. A/C.5/43/SR.47, pp. 3-4.
99. A/C.5/43/SR.48, p. 3.
100. A/C.5/43/SR.50, p. 14.
101. *Ibid.*
102. *Ibid.*
103. A/43/PV.46, pp. 68-71.
104. *Ibid.*, p. 72.
105. *Ibid.*, pp. 72-77.
106. *Ibid.*, pp. 77-80.

107. *Ibid.*, pp. 81-82.
108. *Ibid.*, pp. 82-90.
109. *Ibid.*, p. 91.
110. *Ibid.*, p. 92.
111. *Official Records of the General Assembly, Forty-first Session, Supplement No. 49* (A/41/49).
112. E/1988/75.
113. *Ibid.*
114. *Official Records of the General Assembly, Forty-first Session, Supplement No. 49* (A/41/49).
115. A/43/PV.76, pp. 62-66.
116. A/43/PV.76, p. 71.
117. A/C.2/43/SR.11, p. 2.
118. *Ibid.*, p. 3.
119. *Ibid.*, p. 4.
120. *Ibid.*, pp. 5-6.
121. *Ibid.*, p. 6.
122. *Ibid.*, p. 7.
123. A/C.2/43/SR.12, p. 2.
124. *Ibid.*, p. 4.
125. *Ibid.*, p. 5.
126. *Ibid.*, p. 6.
127. *Ibid.*, pp. 6-7.
128. A/C.2/43/SR.13, p. 3.
129. *Ibid.*, p. 4.
130. *Ibid.*, p. 6.
131. *Ibid.*, p. 7-8.
132. *Ibid.*, p. 8-9.
133. A/C.2/43/SR.14, p. 3.
134. *Ibid.*, p. 4.
135. *Ibid.*, p. 6.
136. *Ibid.*, p. 7.
137. *Ibid.*, p. 8.
138. A/C.2/43/SR.44, p. 6.

CHAPTER 5
FINAL PROGRESS REPORT, 1989

5.1 Financial Situation

Following its involvement in stopping the Iran-Iraq war and in facilitating the withdrawal of the Soviet army from Afghanistan, the UN success story continued. It provided the peace-keeping force necessary for the supervision of the free elections in Namibia and for South Africa's withdrawal from the area. The UN was also expected to assist in solving the Cambodian question, supervise elections in the Western Sahara and help to restore peace in Central America. The financial situation, however, remained bleak.[*] At the end of 1988, total outstanding contributions amounted to $395 million, out of which the USA owed $308 million. Contributions for 1988 amounted to $160 million. This was considerably more than expected and more than had been contributed in 1987, but still less than the 1988 assessment of $215 million.[1] In September 1988, President Reagan announced that the US Administration now intended to pay its full contribution.[2] This still left open, however, the question of the US accumulated debt, which would probably be dealt with by the newly elected administration in 1989. Nevertheless, Reagan's announcement was seen as the end of US reluctance to announce its satisfaction with the outcome of the reform process.

5.2 Revitalization of ECOSOC and Review of the United Nations in the Economic and Social Fields: Subsequent Events

GA resolution 43/174[**] on reform in the economic and social fields, approved during the previous session, had set in motion two main activities which were to follow up the reform effort. Firstly, the resolution mandated the revitalization of ECOSOC. Secondly, recognizing that the Special Commission of ECOSOC had been unable to agree on recommendations, the GA called upon the Secretary-General to consult with members states on ways and means of reforming the intergovernmental structure and functions in the economic and social fields.

---

[*]For details on the financial situation see annex, table 3 and 4.
[**]See volume II, 1.7.

With regard to the effort to revitalize ECOSOC, the Council considered further reports by the Secretary-General (E/1990/14 and E/1990/75) and adopted a series of resolutions and decisions (1989/114, 1990/69 and 1990/205). This process resulted in a number of improvements, such as a sharper focus in ECOSOC's work through a reorganization of its working methods, better presentation of documentation, more analytical reports and a reduction in the overall volume of documentation. The focus on the revitalization of ECOSOC also revealed the limitations. The Council was itself part of the machinery of intergovernmental meetings. Appropriate changes and improvements would need to be introduced in the overall intergovernmental framework before the Council and the UN could realize their full potential in the economic and social sectors.

The reform of the intergovernmental structure and functions in the economic and social fields was the subject of two further reports by the Secretary-General (A/44/747 and A/45/714) and two GA resolutions (44/103 and 45/177). With the adoption of resolution 45/177, the GA launched a new reform attempt, reconvening the 45th session in May 1991 for one week to discuss reform of the UN in the economic and social fields. The reconvened session concluded with the approval of the resolution entitled **Restructuring and Revitalization of the United Nations in the Economic, Social and Related Fields (45/264)**. By resolution 45/264, the GA decided that, starting with 1992, ECOSOC would hold an annual organizational session of no more than four days in early February and an annual substantive session of four to five weeks between May and July. The substantive session, which would alternate between New York and Geneva, would include four days of high-level discussions with ministerial participation, open to all member states. The remaining part of the session would be limited to members of ECOSOC and include meetings devoted to co-ordination, operational activities and committee matters. The latter were to include specific economic, social and related issues. The resolution also listed issues to be addressed in the future, such as the complementarity between the work of ECOSOC and GA, the composition of the Council, subsidiary machinery in the economic, social and related fields and the restructuring of the secretariat. This new reform effort - a follow-on to the Group of 18 initiative - will be described in detail in a forthcoming publication.˙

˙Joachim Müller, *The Reform of the United Nations in the Economic and Social Fields* (Dobbs Ferry, New York: OCEANA, forthcoming).

5.3 The 44th Session of the General Assembly: Approval of Resolutions on the Implementation of Resolution 41/213 (44/200) and on the Programme Budget for 1990-1991 (44/202)

By the end of 1989, the reforms had mainly been completed. There was a clear distribution of responsibilities in a number of organizational entities, in the political, social and common service areas. Several departments had undergone a detailed review of their structure in order to enhance their efficiency and implement recommendation 15 on post reductions. New activities launched during the year under review related to the establishment of an integrated information system in the administrative area. The system was not expected to yield immediate results, but to improve the functioning of the organization in the long run. In addition, information was made available through the Secretary-General's final progress report on recommendations which had been referred to ICSC, JIU and the Board of Auditors for consideration.

In addition to reviewing the implementation of the reforms, the GA was expected to approve the programme budget for 1990-1991, and in so doing would complete the first cycle of the new programme budget procedure which had started with the adoption of a budget outline. It was thus a major test of the viability of the new procedure. The secretariats' proposed programme budget for 1990-1991 amounted to $1,983,863,700 and reflected a negative growth of 0.4 per cent in real terms as compared to 1988-1989. The proposal was for a slightly higher amount - $1,300,000 more - than the estimates of resources in the outline adopted by GA one year previously by resolution 43/214. Moreover, in the end only 10 out of the 14 ASG and USG posts indicated during the 1988-1989 programme budget exercise had been cut.

The Fifth Committee reviewed the implementation of the reform in accordance with the GA resolutions 43/174, 43/213 and 43/214*, under agenda item 38 (Review of the Efficiency of the Administrative and Financial Functioning of the United Nations). The Committee had before it following documentation: (i) the Secretary-General's report on all aspects of priority-setting in future outlines of the proposed programme budget (A/44/272), together with the observations by ACABQ (A/44/7) and CPC (A/44/16)**; and (ii) the Secretary-General's report on the establishment and operation of

---

*See volume II, 1.7, 1.8, 1.9.
**See volume II, 2.34, 2.35, 2.36.

a reserve fund (A/44/665), together with observations of ACABQ (A/44/729)˙. The Fifth Committee considered agenda item 38 in conjunction with item 123 (Proposed Programme Budget for the Biennium 1990-1991) and item 124 (Programme Planning).

Before recalling the Fifth Committee's debate under agenda item 38, the statements by the Secretary-General on the issues involved are presented.

In his annual report on the work of the Organization, the **Secretary-General**[3] noted:

"The administrative and financial situation of the Organization differs significantly from previous years. This is because of the impact of administrative reform, the addition of major new peace-keeping responsibilities and the continuing financial crisis.

The programme of administrative reforms initiated in 1986, based on the recommendations of the Group of High-level Intergovernmental Experts to Review the Efficiency of the Administrative and Financial Functioning of the United Nations, has been largely implemented. However, administrative reform is essentially a continuing process. The reforms have unquestionably produced a leaner and, in many ways, a more efficient Secretariat. Staff reductions undertaken since 1986 are now nearing the recommended target of 15 per cent. Unfortunately, in several areas, the capacity of Secretariat to fulfil its tasks is already under considerable strain. In view of additional responsibilities placed on the Secretariat, it may well be necessary to limit the cuts to the level already attained. Several offices have been restructured in order to provide a more effective response to new demands while also adjusting to continuing constraints on available resources. Management information systems and the introduction of new technologies have yielded benefits in substantive, conference and administrative services.

Despite these changes, other factors have detracted from their potential net benefit. Although the Group of High-level Intergovernmental Experts envisaged less demand for conference and documentation services owing to the reductions and reforms, such a decrease has not occurred. Few bodies have decided to schedule biennial rather than annual meetings, or to reduce the duration of their sessions. As a result, the calendar of meetings is not significantly different this year from 1986, before the reform process began."

˙See volume II, 2.37, 2.38.

When introducing the proposed programme budget for the biennium 1990-1991, the **Secretary-General** stated:

"The proposals before the Committee were the first to have been prepared in accordance with the new budgetary procedures established under resolution 41/213 and were based on the outline for the proposed budget for 1990-1991 adopted in resolution 43/214. They should also be seen within the context of the implementation of a number of measures called for in resolution 43/213.

In considering those proposals, the Committee should bear in mind that his programme budget submission, derived from the outline, did not cover factors such as adjustments for inflation and currency fluctuations. Those adjustments would have to be made towards the end of the session and, barring the adoption by the General Assembly of an alternative method, they would continue to be undertaken in the traditional manner.

Furthermore, as stated in his reports to the Committee in previous years and reiterated by the Secretariat staff in introducing or elaborating on those reports, the commitment authority granted to him, as well as to the Advisory Committee on Administrative and Budgetary Questions (ACABQ), subject to certain limitations, under the label of unforeseen and extraordinary expenditures, was outside the outline and therefore outside the scope of his budget proposals. He could not stress strongly enough how essential that commitment authority was to the performance of the duties entrusted to him under the Charter in relation to the maintenance of international peace and security. ...

The proposed programme budget for the biennium 1990-1991 amounted to $1,983,863,400. That represented a negative rate of real growth of 0.4 per cent of the revised final appropriations for the biennium 1988-1989. It included a post reduction of 12 per cent and either no change or a decrease in most objects of expenditure including travel of staff, consultants, expert groups and external printing. The only increases in expenditure related to strictly mandated activities, notably construction of new premises and technological innovations. The proposals also reflected a number of organizational changes, particularly in the departments and offices dealing with political and administrative matters. He was pleased to note that ACABQ, in its first report on the proposed programme budget, stated that the whole budget process was still in its formative stage (A/44/7, para. 9). Similarly, the Committee for Programme and Co-ordination (CPC) in its report, cited the complexity and evolving nature of many of the issues embodied in the programme budget and emphasized the need for flexibility (A/44/16, para. 55 (a)). The latter quality would indeed be needed in the collective efforts to deal with a number of issues which were both technical and political.

He trusted that the current year's discussion would be productive in terms of clarifying further some of those basic technical and political issues. For his part, he would welcome further elucidation of points such as the methodology for budget preparation, including the treatment of real growth. He believed that, on the basis of the contribution of ACABQ, dialogue should continue on the relationship between the outline and the programme budget. That relationship should be explored not only in terms of the outline being a target in developing his budget submission, but also in terms of its significance during the process of consideration of his submission and at the time of its approval. He had already mentioned the treatment of the issue of inflation and currency fluctuation in the budget. He would also like to mention the operation of the contingency fund, where refinements might be required in light of the experience to be gained during the current session. ...

It was clear therefore that, while the reform process had covered a significant number of areas and programmes in the organization, some were yet to be effected. The results of the process, so far, were contained in his budget programme proposals; further reforms that might be decided upon at the current session of the General Assembly. ...

Reform was a continuing process, not an end unto itself. It implied a constant review of the organization to ensure that it remained capable of attaining the objectives for which it had been established. To perceive reform primarily as a post-reduction exercise was to lose sight of its purpose, in the present case the enhanced effectiveness of the United Nations for the fulfilment of the objectives of the Charter. He was sure that all would concur at that level of analysis, but there might be different perceptions concerning the details of the implementation of the reform process."

Before member states addressed the Committee on agenda item 38, the Chairmen of ACABQ and CPC introduce their reports, as outlined below.

Mr. Mselle, **Chairman of the ACABQ**[5]

"proposed expenditure, at $1,983.8 million, was $195.1 million more than the 1988-1989 revised appropriation. Projected inflation in 1990-1991 accounted for $128.9 million of the increase; the rate of real growth was put at minus 0.4 per cent. The proposed establishment comprised 10,054 posts, 50 of them temporary. ...

In addition to the budget proper, ... the estimates ... included a contingency fund of $15 million to be used in accordance with resolution 42/211.

The budget outline for the biennium 1990-1991 (see resolution 43/214, para. 5) showed a total $1.3 million lower than the Secretary-General's estimates. Some members of the Advisory Committee and CPC argued, as a matter of principle, that the outline total should not be exceeded; others, that the excess was too small to worry about. It must be remembered that the preliminary resources cited in the outline and the estimates of the proposed programme budget used different variables, costed at different starting points, and the various stages of preparation of the outline and the budget estimates thus could not be completely harmonized, but that did not fully explain the $1.3 million increase. The General Assembly had recognized, however, that the outline resources were preliminary and the procedure was evolving. The experience of preparing the estimates and the debate on them should give the Secretariat guidance on the preparation of the next outline and related estimates.

One objective of resolution 41/213 was to create a mechanism for predicting the overall level of resources for the next biennium. Two elements of such a mechanism had been agreed on: the preliminary resources of the outline, and the contingency fund. The third element, additional funds to finance the effects of currency and inflation after the budget had been appropriated, would be considered during the current session in accordance with resolution 43/214. Pending a final decision, the effects of currency fluctuations and inflation would be handled in accordance with present practice.

The reorganization and other reforms in progress had prevented the Secretariat from reporting, in the context of the proposed estimates, on a number of improvements recommended by the Advisory Committee. By the time the proposals for the 1992-1993 biennium were considered, in 1991, he hoped that work on improving the budget document and refining work-load standards and statistics wherever feasible would have been completed. Progress would be enhanced by success in the current efforts to improve the content of the medium-term plan.

The Advisory Committee recommended an initial expenditure estimate of $1,976.9 million, compared with the Secretary-General's estimate of $1,983.8 million. The proposed estimates and related recommendations of the Advisory Committee would be affected mainly by additional amounts relating to the contingency provision, to the recommendations of ICSC as accepted by the General Assembly, and to the effects of inflation and currency changes. ...

The 1990-1991 manning table proposed by the Secretary-General was smaller by eight posts than the revised establishment approved by the General Assembly for 1988-1989. The net effect of the recommendations of the

Advisory Committee would be a reduction by six posts instead of the eight proposed by the Secretary-General. The General Assembly had not yet decided where posts at the Assistant Secretary-General and Under-Secretary-General levels should be trimmed. The number to be trimmed had been reduced to 10 from the 14 indicated in the 1988-1989 revised estimates. As one of those 10 had been reclassified to D-2, the actual proposed reduction was 9 posts - or 10, if a post abolished earlier was included.

Experience and time would show whether one of the objectives sought under the new budgetary process, namely that Member States should be involved in decisions on the programme budget from the very beginning, had been achieved, and at what cost. The budget outline, as one avenue to such involvement, was partly to blame for recent difficulties with the timely submission of documentation, as were some of the reform measures and the new peace-keeping operations. He hoped that the observations of the Advisory Committee, including those on the outline, would assist the Secretariat in that regard. Effective involvement of Member States in reviewing the programme of work for 1990-1991 required more focused attention by legislative bodies on the activities under their jurisdiction. Too often, their debates on the programme of work did not lead to any definitive conclusion which could guide the Secretariat in its task. In any event, an increased role for the specialized bodies in reviewing the programme of work should in no way infringe on the procedures for decision-making on the programme budget as set out in resolution 41/213.

The contingency provision was a challenge to the Secretariat to provide the information and the intellectual guidance necessary for intergovernmental bodies to indicate alternative courses of action in the use of the contingency fund. The procedures for use and the adequacy of the fund would be reviewed by the General Assembly no later than 1992. In the mean time, to avoid serious disagreement, the Secretariat and intergovernmental bodies must come to understand the procedures and co-operate fully in efforts to implement them. Statements of programme budget implications would have to be made more useful. It should be borne in mind, however, that not all legislative decisions could be analyzed in detail for programmatic content, and attempts to do so might create excessive and unnecessary work in the Secretariat units concerned. ...

The extraordinary international movement away from confrontation towards peaceful co-existence, together with renewed enthusiasm for a more assertive Organization, afforded the United Nations a unique opportunity. To play an effective role, the Organization must have, and must be seen to have, effective administration and sound financial management. He hoped that the current session would consolidate the progress made towards achieving the most realistic possible budget and help to provide the United Nations with the tools to carry out the tasks entrusted to it by the international community."

Mr. Mselle, **Chairman of the ACABQ**[6] continued

"on the establishment and operation of a reserve fund (A/44/729), said that the Advisory Committee had some doubts about the solution proposed by the Secretary-General. Firstly, if the reserve was funded even before the actual needs had been determined, the result would be an additional, and needless, charge on Member States. Secondly, the failure to establish in advance the procedure to be followed if the reserve proved insufficient might cause confusion. Thirdly, Member States had indicated that they would like to have a precise idea, well in advance, of the total amount of resources that they might be called upon to provide. The solution proposed by the Secretary-General did not satisfy those criteria. Accordingly, the Advisory Committee believed that the question of the reserve fund warranted further consideration, especially as the new budgetary procedure was not yet run in. It recommended that the General Assembly should defer consideration of the item to its forty-sixth session, inviting the Secretary-General to submit a new report which would take into account the experience gained and present a new analysis of the ideas put forward by the Advisory Committee in paragraphs 17-41 of its 1988 report (A/43/929). Meanwhile, it was necessary to continue with the current arrangements for dealing with currency and inflation in accordance with paragraph 11 of annex I of General Assembly resolution 41/213."

Mr. Monthe, **Chairman of the CPC**[7]

"The Committee's conclusions and recommendations on the proposed programme budget for the biennium 1990-1991 (paras. 47 to 69) concerned such matters as the interpretation of the new budgetary process, the clear identification of changes in programmatic content from the previous budget, documentation, programme implementation, the implementation in the various sections of the budget of the relevant provisions of General Assembly resolution 41/213, the growth of programmes and overall resource requirements. In that connection, the Committee, while stressing the necessity for the Secretary-General to adhere to the consensus reached by Member States as expressed in resolution 43/214, nevertheless recognized the equally important need for flexibility, taking into account the factors listed in paragraph 55 of the report. ...

The Committee had noted with interest the Secretary-General's very useful report on the various aspects of priority-setting in future outlines of the proposed programme budget (A/44/272). In transmitting that report to the Economic and Social Council and the General Assembly for further consideration, the Committee had noted that it shed only partial light on the problem, given its complexity and that such important issues as mandates and sources of funding warranted further analysis with a view to weighing their effects and defining more closely the parameters of priority-setting. The Committee's conclusions and recommendations on that very important topic appeared in paragraphs 271 to 275 of the report. In the resolution adopted at its summer session, the Economic and Social Council had requested CPC to redouble its efforts in that area, and he was sure that the Committee would do so at its future sessions, with the assistance of any additional analysis provided by the Fifth Committee. ...

During its consideration of co-ordination questions, the Committee had before it a very full and useful background note by the Secretariat on the rationalization of co-ordination instruments (E/AC.51/1989/CRP.1). It noted in its conclusions (paragraph 330) that, in its resolution 1988/77, the Economic and Social Council had put an end to cross-organizational programme analyses in their current form and that the Council would need to define the scope and character of the future thematic analyses called for in the resolution. At its summer session in Geneva, the Council, after lengthy and difficult consultations, had adopted a resolution providing guidelines in that connection and requesting CPC to continue to assist it in formulating appropriate recommendations on matters of programme and co-ordination. ...

On the important question of the implementation of General Assembly resolution 41/213, the Committee welcomed the progress so far achieved through the efforts of Member States, the Secretary-General and the staff as a whole, although it noted that results differed in different sectors. In the economic and social sector in particular, the Special Commission established by the Economic and Social Council was still only starting its work, and a fresh impetus was required for the implementation of certain important recommendations of the Group of High-level Intergovernmental Experts. The Committee suggested an overall methodological framework for the Secretary-General's next report on the implementation of the reform process."

The representative of the **United States of America**[8]

"the proposed programme budget for 1990-1991 was the first one to be prepared in accord with the new process approved by consensus in General

Assembly resolution 41/213. It exceeded the level agreed upon by the General Assembly in resolution 43/214 by $1.3 million. While that amount was relatively small, such a departure endangered the credibility of the whole budget process. In its report, the Committee for Programme and Co-ordination (CPC) had recommended that the Secretary-General should adhere to the provisions of resolution 43/214. His delegation supported that recommendation and expected that the Assembly's decision on the budget estimates would provide further evidence that the new process was being respected.

The rate of growth in the proposed budget for 1990-1991 was 0.4 per cent less in real terms than in the approved 1988-1989 budget. That reduction had been accomplished without a negative impact on the Organization's activities, thus proving that the United Nations could deliver mandated programmes while applying strict budgetary discipline. The Advisory Committee on Administrative and Budgetary Questions (ACABQ) had recommended reductions of $6.9 million in the Secretary-General's estimates. The proposed reductions were less in dollar terms than in previous years, reflecting efforts made by the Secretariat to eliminate waste and marginal activities. His delegation would address many of the Advisory Committee's proposals during the detailed review of the budget; it did, indeed, support all of the recommended reductions.

In resolution 41/213 and subsequent resolutions, the General Assembly had mandated a 15-per-cent staff reduction, with a view to rationalizing operations and eliminating duplication. A major reason for the inability to reach the target to date, in the Secretary-General's view, had been the failure of Member States to agree on rationalizing the calendar of conferences and restructuring the economic and social sectors. None the less, considerable flexibility had been given to the Secretariat, and decisions on where to cut back had been left to programme managers. The proposed budget did not represent significant further progress beyond the 12-per-cent reduction approved for 1988-1989. His delegation was aware that progress had been made but was concerned about the failure of the Secretary-General to absorb the costs associated with 50 conference servicing posts restored by the General Assembly at its forty-third session. ... In order to meet the goal of a 25-per-cent reduction in posts at the level of Under-Secretary-General and Assistant Secretary-General, 14 such posts should have been abolished, instead of the 10 posts envisaged in the proposed programme budget. His delegation was prepared to work with the Secretariat and other delegations in order to meet that modest target.

None the less, the proposed programme budget did reflect progress in other areas, particularly with regard to recommendation 44 of the Group of 18, which called for an increase in appointments at the junior professional level. His delegation hoped that trend would continue. The budget also included savings in a number of non-staff objects of expenditure. However, his delegation had expected much larger savings in the area of rental and maintenance of premises. ...

The 1990-1991 budget would be the first to provide for a contingency fund, for which the General Assembly, by resolution 43/214 had approved a level of $15 million. That amount was sufficient to cover any new programmes authorized at the forty-fourth and forty-fifth sessions. The Secretariat should ensure scrupulous implementation of those procedures in all Main Committees; should the level of budget add-ons for new activities exceed the resources of the fund, existing programmes should be terminated or implementation of the new programmes deferred until the following biennium. In view of the Secretary-General's statement, in his introduction, that some 20 per cent of the outputs in the budget were discretionary, rather than strictly mandated, his delegation saw no reason why the reprogramming proposals were not feasible. It could be that the Secretariat might not propose in all cases the termination of lower priority programmes. ...

His delegation agreed with the Secretary-General that implementation of resolution 41/213 was not a finite process but rather an ongoing one aimed at contributing to a more effective and efficient Secretariat. Indeed, rigorous reviews such as those called for in the resolution should be a normal part of the Organization's operation.

The report of the Secretary-General contained in document A/44/222 indicated that substantial progress had been made in implementing many of the recommendations of the Group of 18, and the benefits thereof were already evident. However, more needed to be done. Member States had not moved quickly enough in implementing those recommendations with which they had been entrusted, particularly with regard to the calendar of conferences, restructuring the economic and social sectors and improving the intergovernmental decision-making process. The process of restructuring the economic and social sectors was a complex undertaking which would probably require several years of negotiation. It was essential to begin it immediately; the Secretariat should be requested to provide Member States with recommendations on how best to proceed.

The Secretary-General said that no further staff reductions could be made in the Department of Conference Services until the calendar of conferences and meetings was simplified. That was only partly true, for it seemed that some more posts could be deleted without waiting for the intergovernmental machinery to be restructured. As the Advisory Committee recommended, work-load and productivity statistics also urgently needed review: that should be an absolute priority at the current session. Member States, for their part, should make a special effort to streamline the calendar of conferences. The number of meetings and volume of documents had hardly been reduced at all. The negotiating process had become too complicated. His delegation was convinced that meetings would be more useful if there were fewer of them, conducted to more focused agenda.

As the three-year period set for implementing of the recommendations of the Group of 18 reached its end, many reforms had been only partly applied and no action at all had been taken on some. Considerable progress had been made, thanks to the actions of the Secretary-General and Member States, but the reform process was not over. The world expected much of the United Nations in many important areas - the environment, drug control, human rights, peace-keeping and so forth. The needs were great, but resources were limited. It was thus most important to apportion resources optimally."

The representative of the **United States of America**[9] continued

"the reserve fund was an essential element of the new budget process approved in resolution 41/213 and that the General Assembly had agreed in principle at its forty-third session to establish a fund. The Secretary-General's report was an important first step towards solution of the problem of determining the overall level of budgetary resources, but his delegation had a number of difficulties with the Secretary-General's proposals. Many of those difficulties were addressed in the Advisory Committee's report, notably in paragraph 9. While the United States remained committed to the concept of a reserve fund, it believed that the course of action recommended by the Advisory Committee in paragraph 10 of its report should be approved."

The representative of France, speaking on behalf of the 12 member states of the **European Community**[10]

"welcomed the consensus on the reform process but pointed out that although the three-year period set for implementing the recommendations of the Group of 18 was coming to an end, not all its targets had yet been met. The job must go on, and the Secretary-General should continue to report to

Member States on the follow-up to the guidelines adopted by the General Assembly. ...

The Secretary-General had to execute an unprecedented programme of reform against a background of acute financial crisis, whilst Member States had not always been able to move forward with the restructuring of the intergovernmental machinery. Some structural reforms had been carried out in the administrative and political sectors of the Secretariat; others were encountering internal resistance. The Twelve believed that where the organization and structure of the Secretariat were concerned everyone should respect the authority of the Secretary-General, and the measures adopted must be applied.

Recommendation 15 of the Group of 18 was difficult to implement but efforts must continue, with due regard for the recommendations made by CPC in paragraph 66 of its report (A/44/16). The restructuring of the intergovernmental machinery in the economic and social sectors should result in a reorganization of support services and, among other benefits, allow better use to be made of available resources. The Twelve also noted that, despite laudable efforts, the reduction in senior posts had not yet reached the 25 per cent recommended by the Group of 18; further cuts would be necessary.

The Twelve were pleased that, as called for under the new budgetary procedure, the budget proposals had already been the subject of extensive consultations. The extension of the consultative process to cover more subsidiary bodies should allow the programmatic content of the budget to be improved and priorities to be set more easily among the various budget elements. The emergence of broad agreement on the outline was proof that the new procedure was viable and effective and had gone beyond the experimental stage. It would take on its final form when the Assembly decided how to deal with inflation and exchange-rate fluctuations and when certain shortcomings had been put right. In that connection, he drew the attention of the Secretariat to the need to remain within the total value of the outline adopted by the Assembly. The projected excess stretched the rules set by resolution 41/213 and repeatedly confirmed by the Committee. The Twelve were not convinced by the Secretariat argument that the cost of the 50 posts restored by the General Assembly under resolution 43/213 sufficed to explain the excess. It would have been easy, for example, to propose cuts in expenditure on equipment. The Twelve hoped that the steps recommended by the Advisory Committee would bring the total budget back down to an acceptable level."

The representative of Finland, speaking on behalf of the five **Nordic countries**[11]

"remarked that the new budget process adopted by the General Assembly in resolution 41/213 and first applied in full in the proposed programme budget for 1990-1991 was not designed to limit the resources of the Organization, but to allow the United Nations to plan its activities on a more orderly basis in order to carry out effectively the political decisions of the General Assembly. ...

The proposed budgetary package represented an increase of $1.3 million over the figure indicated in the outline. The Nordic delegations did not consider the difference to be too alarming; they stressed the preliminary nature of the forecasts in the outline which, moreover, reflected budget paring made necessary by the financial crisis. The new budget process clearly needed to be broken in; with experience, its various elements would become easier to master and the way in which the outline related to the proposed budget would become easier to grasp. As things now stood, the proposed budget as presented was in keeping with the spirit of resolution 43/214.

The budget proposal did not include many examples of the redeployment of resources. Yet it might have been possible, using the work-load analyses of the various departments, to indicate the sectors where redeployment was a possibility. The evaluation of the Department of Conference Services referred to in document A/44/222 ought to provide more explicit information on the Department's work-load and therefore on the resources which it actually needed. ...

The Nordic delegations had repeatedly emphasized the need to involve the intergovernmental bodies more closely in the planning and programming process. Such involvement was now all the more essential in view of the need to identify alternative solutions, especially in connection with the use of the contingency fund. The table which appeared in paragraph 70 of the Advisory Committee's report showed that the degree of involvement of specialized bodies in programme planning had been uneven to say the least.

With regard to the financing of activities as such, it must be stressed that between 1980-1981 and 1990-1991 extrabudgetary resources had increased by 116 per cent, as against 74 per cent for regular-budget resources. It might be asked whether the administrative and budgetary reform had not contributed to that increase. It was moreover probable, as the Advisory Committee pointed out, that the creation of 261 additional posts financed from extrabudgetary funds - in fact, on the basis of the initial estimates for 1988-1989, the increase was 637 posts - would partly offset the reduction in the number of regular-budget posts.

The increasing practice of using extrabudgetary resources, in particular in areas of activity normally financed from the regular budget, raised many questions. In view of the growing importance of that mode of funding, it would be useful to have more detailed information about the number and the amount of trust funds and "sectoral" funds, the volume of extrabudgetary resources in the various areas of activity, their growth rate compared with the increase in regular-budget resources, and the role played by intergovernmental organs in determining their use. It was extremely important to know the extent to which voluntary contributions, and especially the trust funds, affected the setting of priorities and the implementation of the Organization's programmes - an issue which the CPC also touched on in its report. The Advisory Committee had also indicated the practical problems of the management of such funds owing to the lack of approval, control and forecasting mechanisms. ... It was essential to make a thorough study of the whole question, so that Member States could assess in particular the extent of the sliding-away from the principle of collective responsibility in the financing of United Nations activities. ...

For the Nordic delegations the draft programme budget demonstrated that the reform process had produced tangible results and they were therefore ready to approve it."

The representative of Norway, speaking on behalf of the five **Nordic countries**[12] continued

"At the present stage ... the Nordic delegations were relatively satisfied with the follow-up of resolution 41/213, in particular with respect to the new planning and budgetary procedures, the restructuring of the policy and administrative sectors, the reductions in the costs of travel and the use of consultants and the staff cut-back of approximately 12 per cent.

On the other hand, the results of the restructuring of the economic and social sector were very disappointing, with respect to the intergovernmental machinery as well as the Secretariat. It was regrettable that the work done by the Special Commission had not led to the adoption of any recommendations. The question must be taken up again and the Secretariat should contribute to the resumption of the process by making concrete proposals. Furthermore, although Member States had not reached an agreement on the intergovernmental machinery, it did seem that a start could now be made on the restructuring of the economic and social sectors of the Secretariat.

Follow-up was also required with respect to the inter-institutional co-ordination machinery; and little had been achieved with respect to reduction of the duration of meetings and conferences and limitation of documentation. Member States had not done everything they could to make best use of the available time and conference services. It was disappointing that the Committee on Conferences, despite the strengthening of its mandate and the enlargement of its membership, had not been able to discharge its responsibilities as envisaged in the report of the Group of 18. On the other hand, it was satisfying to see that the trend for the demand for conference services to increase had not been maintained and that many bodies had adopted a biennial work programme. ...

The measures to be used in the reform process had initially been conceived as a whole. Owing to the financial crisis the emphasis had been mainly on reductions of expenditure and staff, and there had been some neglect of the recommendations concerning personnel management, recruitment policy, training, job rotation, etc. The "human dimension" of the reform, which was the subject of recommendations 41 to 61 of the Group of 18, had not received sufficient attention. It was regrettable in particular that the staff reductions had not been carried out more rationally, on the basis of a work-load analysis of the departments, as suggested in recommendation 15.

The Nordic delegations were satisfied that the recommendations concerning monitoring, evaluation and inspection were being followed up, and they wished to recall the importance which they attached to the work of the Joint Inspection Unit; it was essential for the bodies which had been reported on by the Inspectors to ensure proper follow-up of the Inspector's recommendations.

The Nordic delegations believed that the implementation of resolution 41/213 had already led to more prudent management of the Organization's resources, a result which, of itself alone, showed that the reform had not been in vain. It had also led to a search for broader agreement on budgetary and administrative questions; at its last session, for example, most of the important decisions of the Fifth Committee had been taken by consensus."

The representative of Sweden, speaking on behalf of the five **Nordic countries**[13] continued

"Priority-setting was a complicated process, but without it financial management lost much of its meaning. The proposed new system, which would mean setting priorities at the subprogramme level, would make the process less complicated inasmuch as it would be simpler to define objectives and means at that level than at higher levels. Furthermore, priority-setting at the subprogramme level was logical, since the subprogramme was the principal link between the medium-term plan and the programme budget. Accordingly, the Nordic countries had little difficulty in endorsing the introduction, on a trial-and-error basis, of the modified system proposed by the Secretariat and its evaluation at the end of the 1992-1993 budget period."

The representative of **China**[14]

"observed that the Secretary-General attributed the difference of $1.3 million between the amount in the proposed programme budget and the amount estimated in the budget outline to the restoration of a number of posts in the Department of Conference Services, at the request of the General Assembly. ACABQ saw the discrepancy as the result of a number of factors. So long as the budget outline and the proposed programme budget were based on different data (the initial estimates for the preceding biennium and the revised estimates, respectively), the two series of figures would never be exactly the same, especially as there were other variables. It would therefore not be realistic to regard the outline as the ceiling of the programme budget. Since the new budgetary procedure was still in a developmental phase, and since, therefore, flexibility was required, his delegation endorsed the conclusions and recommendations formulated by CPC at the end of its twenty-ninth session and recalled that, as it had proposed, CPC had suggested a future review of budgetary procedures in the light of the experience gained. ...

His delegation had noted the reductions which ACABQ had recommended for technical reasons. A number of matters which would have a direct impact on the overall level of the proposed programme budget had yet to be settled (reduction of posts at the Under-Secretary-General and Assistant Secretary-General levels, budgetary implications of the 1992 United Nations conference on environment and possible additional appropriations arising from proposals made by ICSC and the Joint Staff Pension Board)."

The representative of **China**[15] continued

"the joint efforts by Member States, the Secretary-General and the entire staff of the Secretariat had enabled the Organization to make considerable achievements in the reform process, particularly in the area of structural adjustment, the budgetary process and staffing matters. Nevertheless, the reforms were parts of a continuing process whose objectives had still to be reached. In the economic and social field, the two resolutions on the revitalization of the Economic and Social Council had yet to be fully implemented. ...

As it had been presented before the end of the three-year period assigned for the reform process, the Secretary-General's report, while useful and objective, could not satisfactorily reflect the successes, the setbacks and the effects of the reform and could not therefore serve as the basis for an overall evaluation of the process. His delegation concurred with the recommendation of CPC that the Secretary-General should present, at the forty-fifth session of the General Assembly, an analytical and critical report on the reform process covering the full three-year period, in the light of the objectives set in resolution 41/213, and focusing on issues of common concern.

Throughout the reform process the Member States had insisted on the importance of a number of principles. First, the objective of reform was to improve the efficiency of the Organization's administrative and financial functioning, and not only to streamline its institutions and curtail expenditure. Secondly, the programmes already approved by the General Assembly should not be adversely affected by the reform measures, something which could not be guaranteed unless there were objective criteria to determine the impact of reform measures on the implementation of programmes. Finally, personnel questions should be governed by the principle of equitable geographical distribution, a principle whose application was also affected by the recruitment freeze and staff retrenchment. His delegation hoped that the report to be presented by the Secretary-General at the forty-fifth session of the General Assembly would give a fuller account of the situation in that respect."

The representative of **China**[16] continued

"the point made by the Secretary-General in his report on the establishment and operation of a reserve fund (A/44/665) that such a fund must be properly financed, for otherwise requests for additional appropriations in connection with currency fluctuation, inflation in non-staff costs and statutory cost increases for staff would have to be dealt with in accordance with the existing arrangements. Although the Secretary-General believed that the soundest way to determine an adequate level of financing was to analyze past experience, it was impossible to predict future developments.

Both of the alternatives for the establishment of a reserve fund suggested by the Secretary-General would entail an additional burden on Member States. Furthermore, the Secretary-General emphasized the consequences of an inadequate reserve but disregarded the impact of a surplus on Member States. The programme budget was not the final account, and revised estimates were sometimes inevitable. The additional requirements resulting from inflation and other factors could not be limited by the amount of a predetermined reserve fund; instead they should be determined by means of revised estimates. The procedure was different in the case of a contingency fund, when additional financing might be obtained by absorption in the budget or by changing or postponing programmes. His delegation therefore shared the view given by the Advisory Committee in its report on the question (A/44/729) that the concept of a reserve fund needed further study, that the General Assembly should postpone taking a decision, and that the current system should continue to be used in the meantime."

The representative of **Mexico**[17]

"the debate on the efficiency of the administrative and financial functioning of the United Nations provided an opportunity for reflection on the results and limitations of the process of reform initiated three years earlier. From the outset, the reform had given rise to lively controversy. While there seemed to be general agreement concerning the need for greater efficiency in the Organization's functioning, opinions differed as to the measures that should be employed to that end. The administrative reform had been launched at a point in time when the Organization had been at the mercy of the principal contributors and strong pressures had been exerted in order to subordinate multilateral negotiations to the interests of certain countries. In his delegation's view, the efforts made would ultimately enhance the Organization's capacity for action in the face of economic, political and social problems to promote the fuller realization of the purposes and principles of the Charter. That goal would be difficult to achieve by concentrating exclusively on budget savings and simplified administrative procedures.

There were other important factors, including a sincere desire to co-operate on the part of all Member States; the fulfilment of financial obligations; the full and prompt payment of assessments; and the need to set priorities while giving due consideration to the problems facing the international community. Above all, there must be respect for the democratic nature of the Organization.

He was confident that the administrative and financial functioning of the United Nations could be further improved, and he supported the efforts made in that regard. However, such efforts should not be confined to the elimination of certain programmes and a reduction in the number of international conferences.

Despite the guidelines formulated by the General Assembly with regard to the implementation of resolution 41/213, the recommendations of the Group of High-level Intergovernmental Experts still had not been implemented in a balanced way. That was true, for instance, with regard to the recommendations on the structure of the Secretariat and personnel management. In recent years, a significant effort had been made to curtail the number of staff, which obviously had been in the interests of certain countries. As the Secretary-General had pointed out, those measures had entailed significant constraints on the performance of the work of the Secretariat. At the same time, there had been no evidence of a similar eagerness to ensure an equitable representation of developing countries in the higher-level posts. The report of the Secretary-General revealed the maintenance of a *status quo* which was not commensurate with the role played by those countries within the international community.

Moreover, the report of the Secretary-General did not contain satisfactory details on the implementation of recommendations 54 and 55 of the Group of High-level Intergovernmental Experts. With regard to the recommendation to limit appointments at the Assistant Secretary-General and Under-Secretary-General levels to 10 years, no corresponding measure had been mentioned. Nor was there any indication of what had been done to ensure that posts did not become the exclusive preserve of any country or regional group. In both cases, practices contrary to the spirit of General Assembly resolution 41/213 had been maintained.

The administrative reform in progress would necessarily have an important impact on the Organization's structure, functioning and future political prospects. For the time being, no one knew with any certainty what effect the measures taken had, or whether they had already led to any improvement in the functioning of the United Nations. On the other hand, the costs of the reform were clearly visible in several sectors. Strong pressures were being exerted for the elimination of certain organs and the limitation of conferences on issues of concern to the developing countries. The procedures governing budget preparation and implementation had become more rigid, limiting the Organization's possibilities for action in carrying out new mandates. The reductions in the Secretariat staff now threatened to hamper the delivery of existing programmes and had led to delays in the preparation of documentation.

In such a context, the question of priority-setting in the proposed programme budget took on critical importance. His delegation believed that the new method proposed by the Secretary-General represented a step forward to the extent that it made it possible to set more specific and more objective priorities. It believed that priority-setting in the medium-term plan should take place mainly at the sub-programme level and not between programmes.

Similarly, it was preferable to use greater flexibility in determining the number of outputs to which a maximum or minimum priority was to be assigned within each programme, rather than to continue to apply the rigid 10 per cent rule. However, since the proposal submitted by the Secretariat did not resolve all of the conceptual and methodological problems identified in the report, the study of the criteria relating to priority-setting should be continued.

The decisions taken in the context of the administrative reform would shape the Organization for several decades to come. He did not see how it was possible, therefore, merely to reduce expenditures and simplify procedures. The search for enhanced effectiveness should go hand in hand with an ongoing effort to adapt the Organization to the changing realities of the contemporary world and to prepare it for the new challenges awaiting it."

The representative of **Nepal**[18]

"A number of recommendations had already been implemented by the Secretariat, which deserved praise for its efforts. The decision to maintain the Committee on Conferences as a permanent subsidiary organ should help to check parallel growth in the intergovernmental machinery and ensure the optimum utilization of conference-servicing resources. The detailed report requested in General Assembly resolution 43/174 would pave the way for further actions to enhance the effectiveness of the intergovernmental structure and its Secretariat support structures, as well as programme delivery in the economic and social fields. He could cite other examples: the additional measures being considered by the Administrative Committee on Co-ordination, the informal consultations scheduled to take place among the executive heads on major policy questions, the reaffirmation of the central co-ordinating role of the United Nations Development Programme, the review of the functions of the resident co-ordinators, the sharing of premises and services in the United Nations system and a study of budgeting techniques to be conducted by the Joint Inspection Unit. All those measures would undoubtedly lead to enhanced effectiveness.

On the other hand, he was disappointed by the rather meagre results achieved with regard to priority-setting, although considerable time had been devoted to that question. He fully endorsed the modified system proposed in document A/44/272. In view of the conceptual and methodological problems encountered, he recommended a prudent approach, in other words the Secretary-General should be allowed to implement the modified system during a reasonable trial period so as to enable him to devise a set of priorities acceptable to all Member States.

He noted with satisfaction that the restructuring in the political sector of the Secretariat had been completed as recommended by the Group of High-level Intergovernmental Experts. The simplification of the organizational structure and the reorganization in the political, administrative and information areas had already yielded the desired results. With regard to the post reductions, although some progress had been achieved, much remained to be done to implement General Assembly resolution 41/213. As the Secretary-General had been requested to exercise extreme caution in order to avoid negative impact on mandated programmes and activities and at the same time to secure the highest standards of efficiency, competence and integrity of the staff, it was natural that detailed studies should be undertaken prior to certain post reductions. In view of those considerations, he was confident that vital recommendation of the Group of High-level Intergovernmental Experts would also be implemented as endorsed by the General Assembly."

The representative of **Hungary**[19]

"the first proposed programme budget prepared in accordance with the new budgetary procedures established by General Assembly resolution 41/213 seemed to be a step in the right direction, since the difference between the total in the budget outline and the total in the proposed programme budget was less than 0.1 per cent, and the total reduction recommended by the Advisory Committee on Administrative and Budgetary Questions (ACABQ) in its first report was less than $6.9 million. None the less, an effective priority-setting mechanism and a consistent medium-term plan would further improve the budgetary and planning procedure.

His delegation noted with satisfaction that significant efforts had been made, and results achieved, with regard to the post reductions, even if, in percentage terms, the reductions did not yet comply with the provisions of General Assembly resolution 41/213. In most instances, the staff reductions had been carried out in a humanitarian manner, without any obvious decline in programme delivery. However, the reductions at the level of Under-Secretary-General and Assistant Secretary-General seemed inadequate since only 10 posts were to be abolished instead of 14 initially foreseen, especially as in one case a post had been reclassified to the D-2 level, and in another case a temporary recurrent post had been abolished. Although he appreciated the efforts of the Secretary-General to preserve the necessary work-force at the higher levels, further steps should be taken to comply with the resolution, and those Member States directly concerned by the reductions should show self-restraint. ...

As for the medium-term plan consultative progress, his delegation noted with regret that 17 out of the 41 programmes of work for 1990-1991 of the organizations of the United Nations system had not been reviewed by any intergovernmental body. That made the planning and programming process more difficult and a well-defined medium-term plan, and hence a sound programme budget, unrealistic."

The representative of **Japan**[20]

"after the establishment of the Group of 18 and the adoption of General Assembly resolution 41/213, the United Nations had undertaken a series of short-term and long-term reforms that had given it more dynamism despite the chronic financial crisis. The Organization had for some time also been assuming greater responsibilities, particularly with regard to the settlement of regional conflicts, and was expected to perform a greater role in multilateral efforts addressing such global issues as the environment, disaster prevention, disarmament, narcotic drug control and human rights. It was appropriate, nevertheless, to ask whether all the reform measures within the competence of the Secretary-General had been implemented and whether the Member States were providing the Secretariat with the necessary tools for the effective implementation of the tasks they had entrusted to it. ...

As CPC had said in connection with the final report of the Secretary-General on the implementation of General Assembly resolution 41/213, the purpose of the reforms was to enhance the effectiveness of the United Nations and not merely to effect savings or staff reductions. The United Nations should, of course, pursue more seriously the efforts undertaken to improve control of its operations, but so far that had not been done in the sense of proper management of human resources: lack of rational work-load standards, uneven impact on the work of various departments, implementation of personnel policies (recruitment freeze and staff attrition or retrenchment) which, together with the vacancy management system, had more to do with solving the financial crisis than carrying out reforms, had prevented the United Nations from attracting new and competent personnel and had perpetuated top-heaviness in the staffing structure instead of injecting new blood into the Organization, as the Secretary-General would like.

The qualitative aspects of personnel policy also seemed to have been somewhat neglected. In the absence of objective methods and clear criteria for recruitment, performance evaluation and promotion, the Organization could lose its most able staff members as well as its competitive edge *vis-à-vis* other international institutions. His delegation therefore urged the Secretary-

General to review the effects of the staff reduction plan on the implementation of programmes and on the structure and composition of the Secretariat. In addition to rejuvenating the staff structure, maintaining staff quality and achieving equitable geographical distribution, the Secretariat must try, as CPC had requested, to achieve greater transparency and coherence in personnel management. That also required refinement of work-load standards and statistics to facilitate a better distribution of resources among various departments.

Over the past three years there had been considerable delay in implementation of the approved recommendations in the area of human resources management, the restructuring of intergovernmental machinery in the economic and social sectors and servicing conferences and meetings, as well as in the implementation of the modernization plans for administration and management. His delegation also hoped that further progress would be made in the area of public information.

... he recalled that at the twenty-ninth session of CPC his delegation had expressed concern at the disparities in approach and presentation between the introduction of the proposed programme budget and the outline of the budget approved by the General Assembly at its forty-third session with respect to the basis for their formulation, adjustment for inflation and programmatic content, differences which were all the more important because it was the first proposed programme budget prepared under the new budget process. The excess of $1.3 million over the budget outline had been attributed to the impossibility of fully absorbing the costs of the 50 posts that had been restored pursuant to General Assembly resolution 43/213, but a full explanation had not yet been provided on that point, not even by ACABQ. His delegation wished to point out that according to the table in paragraph 7 of ACABQ's first report, the difference between the two total amounts of resources was $3 million at 1989 rates. In addition, the proposed programme budget contained no estimate that was directly comparable to the Secretary-General's proposals for $1,767.1 million at 1988 rates, an amount that had been officially adopted by the General Assembly in resolution 43/214. If the outline was to serve as a basis for predicting the overall level of the programme budget, there must be a credible basis for comparison between the two documents. The Secretariat must define for the next outline a more precise method making possible a direct comparison of the two sets of estimates.

Japan regarded the outline of the budget not simply as a means of enabling the Secretariat to predict more accurately what resources would be available to it, but also as a means of letting Member States know the total amount of resources required. His delegation therefore urged the Secretariat to give the Committee more realistic estimates for the biennium 1990-1991, based on the latest assumptions for exchange rates and inflation rates. The outline should not be a guarantee of the total amount of resources available to the United Nations. It should rather serve as a basis for dialogue between the Secretariat and Member States for the preparation of the proposed programme budget and therefore describe the content of programmes and set priorities, not only within a sector but also among sectors.

The lack of clear priority-setting among departments was particularly worrying with regard to staff reductions, which had been more strongly felt in sectors whose importance could only grow (peace-keeping, disarmament, environment, etc.) than in the Department of Administration and Management or the conference and library services. Paradoxically, it was those sectors whose efficiency had been enhanced by technological innovations and improved management procedures which maintained more or less stable staffing levels. The Secretary-General was, of course, right to emphasize the responsibility of Member States for determining priorities, but he should re-examine the formulation of the programme budget to bring it more clearly into line with the policy priorities that he considered important. ...

With regard to the proposed programme budget itself, the Japanese delegation welcomed the Secretary-General's statement that any further reforms and new programmes decided upon by the Economic and Social Council or the General Assembly, on the basis of recommendations from ICSC in particular, should be financed within the limits of the budget proposals, including the Contingency Fund. It was the view of his delegation that the additional requirements to be accommodated by the Contingency Fund in the first year of the biennium should not exceed half the amount of that Fund.

With regard, finally, to programme planning, his delegation considered it useful for certain specialized bodies to participate in a thorough examination of the respective chapters of the draft medium-term plan which the General Assembly was to adopt in 1990. The Secretariat of the United Nations should demonstrate leadership and at the same time sufficient flexibility to absorb such specialized external inputs. On the question of monitoring, evaluation and management of programme planning, his delegation noted with satisfaction that the Secretariat had come to realize that the findings of monitoring and evaluation reports should serve as a basis for formulating the medium-term plan and programme budget. The same was true of priority-setting in future outlines of the proposed programme budget. His delegation therefore supported the conclusions and recommendations contained in the Secretary-General's reports on those two subjects (A/44/233 and A/44/272), on the understanding that they would be implemented on a trial basis and that CPC would review the results within the next several years."

The representative of **Tunisia**[21]

"his delegation concurred with the observation by CPC concerning the Secretary-General's report on the implementation of resolution 41/213. That document (A/44/222) which only related to a period of 26 months, did not reflect in a global and integral way the process of implementation of the reforms. In certain cases it went no further than to mention studies which had already been examined, for example by the Economic and Social Council, without noting the reactions of the Member States. Furthermore, it contained a number of repetitions and inappropriate passages which detracted from its quality. ... His delegation also supported the observations by CPC regarding the layout of the analytical and critical review which was to be submitted to the General Assembly during its forty-fifth session.

Significant progress had been achieved in the application of resolution 41/213, particularly in view of the fact that the reforms had been effected at the very height of the financial crisis. While taking note of the staffing measures, his delegation wished to recall that the reform process was aimed at improving the efficiency of the Organization's functioning and not simply at making economies or retrenching staff. ...

While there was now a clearer distribution of responsibilities in a number of organizational entities, as indicated by the Secretary-General in paragraph 11 of document A/44/222, the same did not hold true for the economic and social sectors. Certain contradictions pertaining to that matter were noted in the report of the Secretary-General. For example, in paragraph 50 of that document, the Secretary-General indicated that it would be advisable to extend the reform period for the economic and social sectors, while in paragraph 76 he stated that he would make every effort to enhance the efficiency and effectiveness of the present structure of those sectors of the Secretariat."

The representative of **Bangladesh**[22]

"the proposed programme budget largely maintained the elements of continuity, whether of programmes or of allocation of resources. In most of the sectors of activity, estimates had declined relative to the 1988-1989 revised appropriations. The proposed programme budget for 1990-1991 amounted to $1,983,863,400, or an increase of $1.3 million over the amount established in the budget outline and approved in resolution 43/214. His delegation was of the view that increase was sufficiently small to be able to state that the spirit of resolution 43/214 had been observed. The new budgetary process was still in the formative stage, and it was to be hoped that once the methodology had been refined, especially with regard to the operation of the reserve fund and all the additional requirements, the Secretary-General would be in a position to predict with greater accuracy in the budget outline the level of resources necessary for the implementation during the following biennium of the programmed activities mandated by the legislative bodies. It was also important to associate the Member States and the intergovernmental bodies more closely with the preparation of the proposed programme budget, so as to ensure its adoption on the basis of the widest possible agreement. ...

The reform, his delegation wished to reaffirm, was not an end in itself; it was not synonymous with staff reductions and it would not adversely affect the mandated programmes. Staff reductions should be carried out flexibly, so as not to undermine the Organization's effectiveness or demoralize the staff."

The representative of **Bangladesh**[23] continued

"noted with satisfaction that despite the unfavourable circumstances, the Secretariat had applied a substantial number of the recommendations made by the Group of 18, particularly those relating to the distribution of responsibilities among the different administrative units. Recalling the different stages in the reform process, he noted that, while considerable progress had been made in the political sector, the task had proved more difficult in the economic and social fields. The work of the Special Commission of the Economic and Social Council had not resulted in recommendations in those two fields. ...

With regard to recommendation 15 of the Group of 18, his delegation would like to reiterate the statement made by CPC at its twenty-ninth session that the recommendation should be implemented with flexibility to avoid negative impact on programmes. The overall target of 13.2 per cent in post reduction to be achieved by the end of 1989 as proposed by the Secretary-General together with the adjustments in the staffing of conference services, appeared to be a reasonable one. Implementation of that recommendation could also serve to improve the representation of developing countries in higher-level posts, in observance of General Assembly resolution 35/210. Full implementation alone, however, would not make the United Nations more effective; it was also important to ensure a secured future for the staff. Recalling the concern expressed at the high vacancy rate in the regional economic commissions, he called upon the Secretariat to provide a timetable to fill those vacancies. He noted with satisfaction the measures that had already been taken to implement recommendation 37 of the Group of 18 concerning the Department of Public Information. ... He stressed the importance of addressing the fundamental problems (structure, programmes and the level and distribution of resources allocated to priority items, especially *apartheid*, Namibia and Palestine).

Although it was very interesting, document A/44/272 had such serious shortcomings that it limited the scope for decisions on implementation of the modified system proposed in section IV, even on a trial basis. Although at the twenty-ninth session of CPC, the Bangladesh delegation had asked the Secretariat to take into account Economic and Social Council resolution 1988/77, there was no mention of it in the document under consideration. So far, CPC had been the prime actor in priority-setting and the Economic and Social Council had been endorsing the recommendations of CPC without engaging in any in-depth study. Resolution 1988/77 appeared to have changed that procedure by making the Economic and Social Council responsible for submitting some recommendations on priority-setting to the General Assembly. However, that was the case only for the economic and social fields; in other spheres, priority-setting would still be the responsibility of CPC. Resolution 1988/77 also implied changes in regulation 3.2 of the Regulations Governing Programme Planning, the Programme Aspects of the Budget, the Monitoring of Implementation and the Methods of Evaluation. Indeed, all the implications of resolution 1988/77 should be studied in depth before the Committee considered adopting the modified system proposed by the Secretary-General. The Secretariat should not have assumed that resolution 1988/77 would not change anything in connection with priority-setting. It should be mindful of developments in the intergovernmental machinery which affected mandates of CPC and of the points raised by various delegations.

The significance of co-ordination in the United Nations system could hardly be over-emphasized. The aim of co-ordination exercises should be to identify shortcomings, to make the activity of the organizations of the United Nations system more responsive to the needs of Member States, to eliminate duplication and to improve cost-effectiveness. The joint meetings of CPC and ACC could play a crucial role by offering a regular forum for exchanges of views between the organizations of the system and the Member States, which would help in coming up with action-oriented recommendations amenable to follow-up by the Secretariat and the governing bodies. All the co-ordination instruments should be so conceived as to enable Member States to carry out co-ordination in an effective manner.

Stressing that reform measures were an ongoing process, he expressed the hope that the analytical report to be submitted by the Secretary-General in 1990 would review the entire gamut of measures taken, bearing in mind the views expressed by delegations."

The representative of **Morocco**[24]

"The proposed budget showed a slight total increase of $1,339,700 relative to the amount of the total preliminary estimate included in resolution 43/214. The reason for the increase given by the Secretary-General was the impossibility of fully absorbing the cost of the posts restored by resolution 43/213. In his delegation's view, that reason alone did not suffice to justify the increase. There were other causes: the budget outline and the proposed budget had each been established on a different basis and the amount set by the budget outline was simply a preliminary estimate which could not be considered either a ceiling or a floor. In any event, the increase should not give rise to any substantial difficulties in view of its small size.

One of the major indicators in the proposed programme budget was real growth, whose rate remained negative. His delegation hoped that the negative growth would not have an adverse effect on programme implementation and asked the Secretariat to give its assurances to that effect. It was stated in the introduction to the proposed programme budget that all mandated outputs were included in the budget but that there had been some regroupings and deletions. It would be desirable for the Committee to be informed of the cases of regroupings and deletions so that it could consider them in full knowledge of the facts.

As CPC had stated in its report, in many sections of the proposed budget there was a trend towards an increase in administrative costs and costs associated with the use of experts and consultants travel, external printing and equipment. His delegation supported the CPC recommendation to the effect that the efforts should be continued with a view to reducing all such costs for the benefit of programmes. Moreover the reduction of staff should not have an adverse effect on programme implementation or on small entities, such as the regional commissions. ...

According to paragraph 21 of the report on priority-setting, the current system was encountering three categories of difficulties: definitional, conceptual and methodological. The criteria governing priority-setting gave rise to important conceptual problems: (a) the importance of the objective to Member States; (b) the Organization's capacity to achieve the objective; and (c) the real effectiveness and usefulness of the results. His delegation considered that it might be more appropriate to take all the criteria into consideration in priority-setting, since those criteria complemented and balanced each other."

The representative of **India**[25]

"for the second consecutive biennium the proposed programme budget presented by the Secretary-General showed a negative rate of growth. Since the United Nations had to play an increasing role in many areas, particularly in providing assistance to the developing countries, its budget should not continually decline in real terms but should instead show a modest rate of increase.

The total amount requested in the proposed programme budget was somewhat higher than the preliminary estimates approved in General Assembly resolution 43/214. His delegation emphasized the preliminary nature of the estimates included in the outline. The Advisory Committee had pointed out that the outline and the proposed programme budget had different points of origin. It had, moreover, recommended reductions totalling approximately $6.9 million, which would bring the budget below the level provided for in the outline.

The level of extrabudgetary resources for the biennium 1990-1991 showed an increase of 17.72 per cent in nominal terms compared to the previous biennium, while the increase in expenditure under the regular budget was only 10.91 per cent. It was therefore clear that when certain Member States asked for zero growth in the regular budget, it was not because they were short of resources.

Provision was made for the reduction of eight posts compared with the revised staffing table approved for 1988-1989. His delegation believed that any further post reductions should await the conclusion of the work on the restructuring of the intergovernmental machinery in the economic and social fields. ...

With regard to the establishment of a reserve fund which would cover additional expenditures due to currency fluctuation, non-staff costs inflation and statutory cost increases for staff, he hoped that, if the concept of such a reserve was accepted, care would be taken to ensure that expenditures over and above the amount of the reserve would not be offset against the budget appropriations to the detriment of mandated programmes and activities. ...

Several measures had been taken to streamline many departments in the political sector, but the restructuring of the intergovernmental machinery in the economic and social sectors had not yet been completed. Final judgment on the reform process would therefore have to wait until the Secretary-General submitted the analytical report requested by CPC. However, at the present stage, it could be said that, while positive results had been achieved in a number of areas, the restructuring of certain Secretariat departments and post reductions had a negative impact on various activities. Further efforts must be made with regard to the geographical distribution of high-level posts within the Secretariat and the specialized agencies and the membership of various United Nations organs, the duration of conferences and meetings, and the timely issuance of documentation."

The representative of **Australia**[26]

"As far as the level of expenditure was concerned, it was imperative to adhere to the outline established by the General Assembly in resolution 43/214, since that was an essential element of the new budget strategy. While his delegation commended the efforts made by the Secretary-General to achieve negative real growth, it supported the proposals of the Advisory Committee concerning ways to narrow the gap between the level set in the outline and that proposed by the Secretary-General.

With regard to supplementary expenditures, the new budgetary procedure should put an end to the practice of opening credits at the last minute to offset the effects of inflation, currency fluctuations and statutory increases in personnel expenditure. The principle of a reserve to cover those categories of expenditure would precisely eliminate the need to resort to that type of practice. ...

With regard to structural reform, particularly in the economic and social sectors, some progress had been made but there was still much to be done. The precise objectives to be attained in those sectors and the strategies to be followed should be defined at the highest level. On those bases, action might be taken on the restructuring of the intergovernmental machinery of the Secretariat."

The representative of **New Zealand**[27]

"the proposed amount was higher than the amount fixed by the Assembly in resolution 43/214; that disparity, moreover, had not been satisfactorily justified. That raised a number of questions regarding the methods of the outline. It was therefore necessary to formulate precise guidelines to enable the Secretariat to improve the method of establishing the next budget, particularly with regard to the calculation of real growth, the processing of non-renewable expenditures, the presentation of the budget and the establish-

ment of priorities. The comparison with the outline would thus be facilitated.
...

Her delegation awaited with interest the analytical report on the effectiveness of the reforms instituted during the past three years that the Secretary-
General was to submit at the forty-fifth session. It hoped that the progress
made in the political and administrative sectors would soon be complemented
by a revitalization of the economic and social sectors."

The representative of the **Union of Soviet Socialist Republics**[28]

"when drawing up the draft budget, the Secretary-General should not, in any
event, have exceeded the platform indicated in the outline. There must be an
analysis of the reasons that had led the Secretariat to misinterpret the
provisions concerning the new budgetary process, and the necessary measures
must be taken to ensure that did not occur again in the future.

It was regrettable that the draft budget did not envisage new provisions for
the integral implementation of recommendation 15 of the Group of 18
concerning the reduction of staff by 15 per cent. Nor had the Secretariat
indicated how it intended to absorb the expenditures relating to the temporary
re-establishment of 100 posts in the Department of Conference Services. When
the budget estimates were considered, concrete decisions must be adopted with
a view to obtaining the 15 per cent target during the biennium 1990-1991. As
indicated in paragraph 4 of recommendation 15, a more substantial reduction
might even be envisaged following the restructuring of the intergovernmental
machinery and the Secretariat.

With regard to the senior posts, it seemed that the Secretariat had not made
all possible efforts to achieve the objective approved by the General Assembly,
namely, a 25 per cent reduction. As was known, at the time of the approval of
the revised estimates for the biennium 1988-1989, the Assembly had decided
to abolish 14 posts. However, the Secretariat was submitting proposals that
tended to reintroduce several posts, and it was not impossible that certain
Member States would do likewise. Those initiatives were clearly contrary to
resolution 41/213 and other resolutions relating to administrative and
budgetary reforms. His delegation was fully aware that a delicate political
question was involved. It was necessary to find an adequate solution which,
without encroaching on the prerogatives of the Secretary-General, would make
it possible to ensure a more equitable representation of States at the higher
levels. ...

The total amount of the proposed budget could and should be reduced
considerably. The reductions suggested by ACABQ seemed modest. The

necessity of making further reductions became all the more imperative because the Fifth Committee had yet to consider a whole series of recommendations submitted by ICSC and the Joint Staff Pension Board."

The representative of the **Union of Soviet Socialist Republics**[29] continued

"his delegation was on the whole satisfied with the results achieved in the area of administrative reform, in particular with regard to the reorganization of the United Nations executive apparatus. On the other hand, the restructuring of the intergovernmental structure in the economic and social fields had not progressed. In that regard, the Soviet Union shared the concerns expressed by most Member States and hoped that the Secretary-General would propose effective corrective measures in the report that he would submit in implementation of resolution 43/174. ...

With regard to the recommendations of the Group of 18, there were a number of gaps to note. Although implementation of the recommendations concerning the Committee on Conferences and the organization of conference services was practically complete, the situation in that area had scarcely improved. The Committee was not justifying the hopes placed in it and was refusing to settle certain extremely important questions pertaining to its new mandate. With regard to conference services, the considerations on which the Group of 18 had based itself should be re-examined. In the current period of revitalization, it was no longer justified to place an artificial limit on growth in one of the United Nations main areas of activity. It might become necessary to review the rules governing the holding of conferences and meetings, in particular the one which stipulated that bodies must meet at their headquarters. In certain cases, that rule was perhaps not justified; on the other hand, the dispensations from that rule granted to other bodies, such as the International Law Commission and the United Nations Commission on International Trade Law, should be reconsidered.

Recommendations 9 and 10, dealing with inter-agency co-ordination, were of particular importance in the current circumstances. Member States were conscious that United Nations bodies had to combine their efforts if solutions were desired to major world problems, such as disarmament, protection of the environment, and elimination of underdevelopment. That was why the Soviet delegation supported the recommendations of CPC, which advocated making the annual report of the Administrative Committee on Co-ordination (ACC) an effective instrument of co-ordination and strengthening the role of ACC and of its Chairman and secretariat. On the other hand, his delegation considered that the secretariat of ACC should be attached, not to the Office of the Director-General for Development and International Economic Co-operation, but to the Executive Office of the Secretary-General.

Recommendation 13 on harmonizing the format of the programme budgets of United Nations bodies was being implemented too slowly. ...

With regard to the changes made to the structure of the Secretariat, much work had been done, especially in the area of administration. Nevertheless, it might perhaps be necessary to take additional steps in the light of the recommendations of CPC and the conclusions reached by joint meetings of CPC and ACC on questions of inter-agency co-ordination. The Soviet delegation was in favour of carrying out a study of the productivity and efficiency of the Department of Conference Services and noted that the Committee on Conferences intended to take part in it. Although, in general, the Soviet delegation had no objections to make concerning the reorganization of the Secretariat's political services, it thought that the Secretary-General was drawing a rather premature conclusion when he affirmed in paragraph 50 of his report that the restructuring was complete. The changes that had taken place in international relations and the new prospects opening up for multilateral diplomacy in the areas cited by the Secretary-General in his report on the activities of the United Nations could require the adoption of additional measures at a later date. Restructuring was also far from complete in the economic and social sectors. Results there would depend to a great extent on the changes made in the intergovernmental structure.

His delegation had already stated its position on recommendation 15 concerning the reduction in Secretariat staff: it trusted that the Secretary-General would continue to take the necessary steps to ensure the recommendation's complete implementation.

The process of reform implied its continuation into the long-term future; its content had to be changed if circumstances so required. The immediate priority was to co-ordinate the efforts and resources of all United Nations bodies so that they could solve the major problems faced by mankind in their respective spheres of competence. At the current stage, it was far more important to decide the main directions in which to pursue reform than to engage in interim stocktaking."

The representative of the **Union of Soviet Socialist Republics**[30] continued

"a comprehensive solution to the problem of controlling additional requirements due, *inter alia*, to inflation and currency fluctuation was essential in order to ensure the broadest possible agreement on the budget of the United Nations. The General Assembly had, in paragraph 10 of its resolution 43/214, agreed to a means of dealing with that problem, namely, the concept of a reserve. However, an analysis of the Secretary-General's report (A/44/665) showed that the Secretariat had responded to the request contained in that paragraph in a very peculiar manner, which was a source of great disappointment.

His delegation agreed with some of the specific comments of the Advisory Committee on the Secretary-General's report. In particular, it had serious doubts about the idea of financing the fund from the outset through assessment, even before the need for recourse to it had been identified. The absence of a predetermined procedure for dealing with an insufficiency in the reserve would lead to confusion, and the calculation of amounts for each component of the reserve should not present insurmountable difficulties. However, his delegation could not endorse the Advisory Committee's recommendation to defer consideration of the question of a reserve until the forty-sixth session. Its participation in an agreement on the proposed programme budget would depend to a great extent on the adoption of a decision on the reserve."

The representative of the **Philippines**[31]

"Under the new budget process, the requirements included in the programme budget were calculated on the basis of the ceiling given in the budget outline. As emphasized by ACABQ and CPC, the new procedures must be applied with flexibility, the relationship between the outline and the programme budget having yet to be established with precision. ...

The reforms based on the recommendations of the Group of 18 had not yet been fully implemented, despite the efforts made by the Secretary-General. The reductions advocated must not in any way impair the improved administrative and financial functioning of the Organization. It was gratifying that the Department of Conference Services, in spite of staff reductions, was making more efficient use of its available resources."

The representative of **Indonesia**[32]

"involving Member States as early as possible in the budget process had caused delays in the submission of budget documents. ...

As far as his delegation was concerned, the difference between the global amount in the budget outline and the total level of the budget set by the Secretary-General was not truly important, since the amount expressed in the outline was of a preliminary nature and thus could never be considered a fixed ceiling. It should have been understood from the outset that a reasonable margin of flexibility would be allowed. The controversies surrounding the question were undermining the search for the widest possible agreement on the programme budget. Accordingly, Member States should endeavour to achieve a common perception, and improvements in the methodology for preparing the budget outline should continue to be made so as to avoid any discrepancies between it and the programme budget.

The proposed negative real growth rate of 0.4 per cent for 1990-1991 was sensible provided that there was an assurance that the Organization would truly be able to perform the mandated programmes and activities. A thin dividing line existed between a reduced budget in the name of efficiency and a reduced budget which would impair the functioning of the Organization. An increase in the share of the budget devoted to substantive programmes, in relation to support services, would be the best proof of enhanced efficiency. Yet, according to the information in paragraph 46 of the ACABQ report, the reverse was apparently the case. ...

His delegation shared the Advisory Committee's concern with regard to the management of extrabudgetary funds. The idea of establishing a mechanism to ensure that adequate control was exercised had merit. It was true that the utilization of extrabudgetary funds should not influence unduly the setting of priorities. Some were jumping to the hasty conclusion that the increase of those resources necessarily implied a shift away from the Charter principle of collective responsibility of Member States. It would be extremely difficult to determine whether it was the increase of extrabudgetary funds or the reduction of the regular budget which threatened to jeopardize that principle. It should be recalled that the growth of the various extrabudgetary funds was generally the wish of the legislative bodies concerned and was supported by the recipient countries and the donor community. It was thus his delegation's belief that the increase should be considered a positive sign and an indication of the revival of multilateralism."

The representative of **Canada**[33]

"for the second successive biennium, the rate of real growth of the proposed budget was negative. Nevertheless, the overall level of expenditure proposed for 1990-1991 was some $1.3 million greater than the level agreed in the programme budget outline. Her delegation regretted that it had not been possible to remain within that ceiling or to offer a satisfactory explanation for the increase over the ceiling. ...

Certain aspects of the new budgetary procedures needed to be defined with greater precision and rigour. As ACABQ had pointed out, the preliminary estimates in the outline and the estimates of the programme budget had not been prepared on the basis of the same variables and were therefore not entirely comparable. It was desirable, for that reason, that the comments made at the current session should be used to refine the methodology for preparing the programme budget outline so that the required level of resources could be more precisely estimated.

The budget proposal was the first ever to incorporate the contingency fund, the level of which had been established at $15 million on the basis of past trends in add-ons and taking into account the incorporation of perennial activities into the budget itself. Experience would show whether the amount was sufficient and whether the procedures for the operation of the contingency fund were adequate. On the other hand, she doubted whether another reserve fund would be needed in order to accommodate inflation and currency fluctuations.

The issue of priorities required further examination at all levels in the context of the consideration of the medium-term plan. It was satisfactory to note that the Secretary-General had established international narcotics control and the implementation of the Programme of Action for African Economic Recovery and Development as major objectives for the coming biennium. On the other hand, the list of programme elements and outputs terminated as being obsolete or of marginal usefulness was rather modest. Greater efforts were required in that area. ...

The level of post reductions as currently proposed was acceptable, but Member States also had to fulfil certain obligations, particularly in the area of rationalizing the calendar of conferences, if the original target of 15 per cent was to be reached. The Secretariat had not done all it could to achieve a 25 per cent reduction at senior levels. The vacancy management system should be improved so as to take the "human dimension" more fully into account. No real work-load analysis of the various units had been carried out to facilitate redeployment. Despite the requests made in the General Assembly and in CPC, it was precisely the small units that bore the brunt of post reductions, a situation which was difficult to accept.

The reduction or stabilization of certain expenditures (travel, consultants, expert groups and external printing) had enabled the Secretary-General to increase expenditures on technological innovations, a key area for increasing the Organization's efficiency.

As the Secretary-General had pointed out, reform was a continuing process. Results had undeniably been achieved in certain areas, while others were yet to be affected by the reform process. Thus, more action should be taken to improve the Secretariat's structure in the economic and social areas. The analytical report on the implementation of resolution 41/213, which would be submitted to the forty-fifth session and would facilitate a full evaluation, should serve as a point of departure for further reforms, particularly in the area of personnel policy."

The representative of **Cuba**[34]

"the reasons given by the Secretary-General in explanation of the $1.3 million discrepancy between the total amount of the proposed programme budget and that of the programme budget outline. ... To treat the programme budget outline as sacrosanct would be harmful to the Organization's efficiency. Her delegation, for its part, would always be ready to give favourable consideration to any justified budgetary proposal. ...

Some progress had been made, but much remained to be done; as the Secretary-General had remarked, reform was by its nature a continuous process. Her delegation hoped that the functioning of the Committee on Conferences, whose responsibilities and composition had been modified, would continue to improve so that its recommendations might be reflected in greater efficiency in the conference field. It also hoped that the co-ordination activities entrusted to ACC would develop further in such a way that the dialogue with Member States begun in the framework of joint CPC/ACC meetings could be intensified. Recalling that under the terms of General Assembly resolutions the implementation of recommendation 15 should have no negative impact on programmes or on the structure and composition of the Secretariat, it noted with concern the statement in paragraph 55 of the report of the Secretary-General that the number of new appointments to posts subject to geographical distribution had been severely curtailed. On the other hand, it welcomed the steps taken to recruit Professional staff members at the P-1 and P-2 levels from among nationals of non-represented or under-represented countries.

With regard to recommendation 47, her delegation noted that the figures mentioned by the Secretary-General related in part to the period preceding the commencement of reforms. It would appreciate further information on that point, and also on the implementation of recommendation 54. It noted with concern the abolition of a post of Assistant Secretary-General of UNCTAD, whose holder was a national of a developing country, and hoped that important post could be re-established.

Two points on which the operation of the Organization still left much to be desired were documentation and conference services. Delegations were receiving their documents very late, sometimes even after the work had begun. Moreover, sometimes only the English version was available, and interpretation services likewise were not always available in the other official languages. He therefore wondered whether, after all, the cutbacks in staff might not have impaired the Organization's ability to perform its work."

The representative of **Argentina**[35]

"The outline should not be viewed as a rigid framework. On the contrary, it should allow for the necessary manoeuvring room, as recommended by CPC in paragraph 55 of its report. His delegation was aware, as was ACABQ, that the budgetary procedure was still in a trial stage. Hence, it was concerned to see that the real growth rate envisaged in the proposed programme budget was a negative one (-0.4 per cent). ...

Referring to the recommendations of the Group of 18, he noted that they had not been applied evenly in every sector, although they should be considered as a whole. With regard to recommendation 15, the Organization should develop a consistent personnel policy that took into account the mandates set forth in the Charter. Since the purpose of reform was not merely to reduce the budget, but to enhance the effectiveness of the Organization, it was also important to be flexible so that the staff cutbacks would not have a negative impact on programmes.

His delegation noted with satisfaction the great contribution made by the Special Committee of the Economic and Social Council to reforming the economic and social sectors of the Organization. In that regard, Economic and Social Council resolution 1988/77 was especially important.

Given the diversity of the tasks entrusted to the United Nations, it was difficult to develop a strict system for establishing priorities. A method must be found, however, which would make it possible to reconcile the three criteria to be applied, namely, the importance to Member States of the objectives envisaged (the political aspect), the capacity of the Organization to attain them (the technical aspect) and the usefulness of the results obtained (the practical aspect). It was also important to address the question of whether the amount of funds allocated to a given activity should always be increased as the priority assigned to it was raised. The proposals contained in document A/44/272 could provide a starting-point for negotiations aimed at setting up an objective and clear-cut system for establishing priorities at the level of programmes, subprogrammes and output."

The representative of **Bahamas**[36]

"Under the new budgetary procedure, Member States had participated more actively throughout the process and had approved by consensus an outline for the budget. Unfortunately, it had not been possible to remain within the limits of that outline. In future, therefore, the outline should be based on a detailed programme profile ensuring maximum predictability by avoiding the need for the agreed level of resources to be exceeded.

One of the purposes of the reform process was to remedy the problem of fragmentation of efforts and activities. However, careful study of the budget proposals revealed that programmes in the area of development activities and political and security matters were considered by an increasing number of bodies, leading to duplication and a resultant squandering of resources. Priority must therefore be given to implementing recommendations 16 to 24 of the Group of 18, by defining clearly the scope of programmes and centralizing related activities. Such implementation would facilitate the 25 per cent cut in high-level posts."

The representative of **Yugoslavia**[37]

"his delegation considered the proposed programme budget for 1990-1991 to be acceptable, although the total amount of resources proposed was $1.3 million above the outline figure approved. In that regard, it should be recalled that the outline resources were preliminary and the procedure was evolving. ...

It should be borne in mind that implementation of the new budget process was still in the experimental stage and that a number of more or less complex questions, such as the treatment of real growth, and the issues of inflation and currency fluctuation would have to be dealt with patiently. ...

It was obvious that the scope of the implementation of reforms varied greatly in different sectors. Thus, while the reforms in the political sector were almost completed, which was commendable in view of the role played by the Organization in peace-keeping, the situation was different in the economic and social sectors, where the Secretariat structure was more complex. Likewise, the review of the intergovernmental structure had not yet produced concrete results.

Implementation of recommendation 15 of the Group of 18 was certainly one of the most sensitive issues. Nevertheless, it had to be pursued with due flexibility, so as to avoid a negative impact on programmes as well as on the composition of the Secretariat. Due regard should also be given to equitable geographic distribution of senior-level posts. The elimination of overlapping and excessive dispersion - which was the focal point of that recommendation - would improve the effectiveness of the Organization."

The representative of **Egypt**[38]

"Document A/44/222 illustrated numerous aspects of the progress made so far. However, reform was an ongoing process, implying not only financial savings and staff reductions but, essentially, an improvement in programme performance. In that connection, he looked forward to the analytical report to be submitted by the Secretary-General to the General Assembly at its forty-fifth session. At a time when hopes were high for an expansion of the role of the United Nations role in many spheres yet financial resources remained limited, the need for a continuation of the reform process was particularly evident.

It was to be hoped that the proposed programme budget would, after minor amendments, serve as a basis for broad agreement among Member States. The slight decline, in real terms, in the level of the programme budget was to be welcomed, provided that programme activities were not negatively affected. The extremely small difference between the levels of the budget outline and of the proposed programme budget was acceptable, given the preliminary character of the outline and the fact that the new budget process was at an experimental stage of its development. Indeed, the improvement in the budget procedure was indicated by the low incidence of conflict between the budget proposals and the recommendations of the Advisory Committee. However, it was the hope of his delegation that future budget proposals would indicate to what extent the proposals for specific programmes diverged from the level of funding for those programmes in the current budget.

Given the political nature of priority-setting, it was unreasonable to expect the Secretariat to take difficult decisions in that area on behalf of intergovernmental bodies. ...

The atmosphere of financial crisis which had prevailed in recent years should not blind Member States to the fact that it was in the interests of all to ensure the continued health of the Organization. General Assembly resolution 41/213, and the related resolutions which had succeeded it, constituted a sound basis upon which the United Nations might be enabled to fulfil its responsibilities more effectively. It was essential to ensure that reforms were not put at risk by continued anxiety over the Organization's financial future."

The representative of **Romania**[39]

"His delegation had noted with satisfaction that there had been a negative rate of growth of 0.4 per cent, in real terms, in the proposed budget for

1990-1991, compared with the revised estimates for 1988-1989. The fact that the reduction had been accomplished without a negative impact on the Organization's activities proved the validity of the reform measures adopted and the need for their full implementation. It was, however, disturbed at the discrepancy of $1.3 million between the level of the outline approved by the General Assembly in resolution 43/214 and the final estimates for the next biennium. He hoped that such a discrepancy did not signal a slackening of the Organization's efforts to curtail expenditure.

His delegation strongly supported the recommendation in paragraph 54 of the report of CPC (A/44/16), that the Secretary-General should adhere to the provisions of General Assembly resolution 43/214 regarding the total amount of resources requested for the biennium 1990-1991. It also urged the Secretary-General to implement the recommendation in paragraph 60 calling for the continuation of the effort to reduce administrative costs and the costs associated with the use of experts and consultants, travel, external printing and equipment, for the benefit of substantive programmes.

His delegation supported the reductions proposed by the Advisory Committee in its report and it welcomed the Secretary-General's statement that the financial implications of further reforms and new programmatic initiatives that might be agreed upon at the current session by the General Assembly would have to be accommodated within the boundaries of the budget proposals, including the contingency fund.

The Secretary-General's report on the implementation of resolution 41/213 (A/44/222) clearly indicated the significant progress achieved in implementing many of the recommendations of the Group of High-level Intergovernmental Experts. His delegation was, however, disappointed that little progress had been achieved in reducing the number and duration of meetings, as well as the volume of documentation, and in setting in motion the reform process in the economic and social areas. It hoped that the current session would advance the process of reform in the economic and social sectors in line with the agreement already reached in the two resolutions on the revitalization of the Economic and Social Council.

His delegation was satisfied with the reforms made in the political and administrative sectors and the measures being implemented in the budget process and the management of human resources. Further serious efforts were, however, needed to prevent any unnecessary expansion of the Organization's activities and budget in coming years and to achieve the staff reductions mandated by resolution 41/213. His delegation shared the concern of other delegations that the staff retrenchment measures implemented so far had not yielded the best possible results. The lack of work-related standards, the preferential and uneven distribution of staff cuts, and the failure to give due consideration to the principle of equitable geographical distribution were only some of the issues that needed to be given serious consideration by the Secretariat. It therefore urged the Secretary-General, in implementing the mandated programmes, to give due consideration to the need to rejuvenate the staff structure, improve staff performance and ensure equitable geographical distribution at both senior and junior levels.

On the issue of programme planning, his delegation hoped that the various intergovernmental bodies would become more closely involved in the entire planning and programming process so that Member States could have a greater say in translating legislative mandates into planned activities and in establishing programme priorities and alternative courses of action. ...

In the area of priority-setting, his delegation supported the view expressed by the Secretary-General in his report (A/44/272, para. 42 (b)) that the primary focus of priority-setting should be the medium-term plan, which would then form the basis for defining priorities both in the outline and in the draft programme budget. Otherwise the issue of priority-setting threatened to create increasing tension between Member States and the Organization. In regard to the appropriate level and modalities of priority-setting, his delegation agreed that the Secretary-General's recommendations should be implemented on a trial basis, subject to final review and approval by CPC."

The representative of **United Republic of Tanzania**[40]

"commended the Secretary-General on having presented a proposed programme budget which exceeded the budget outline by no more than $1.3 million, thus reflecting the realities of the circumstances and his flexibility in carrying out the demands of the General Assembly. His delegation noted that the methodology used needed further refinement and that the disparity between the outline and the programmatic content of the budget might narrow as the reforms progressed. Furthermore, the appropriateness and adequacy of the contingency fund would have to be reviewed.

His delegation noted that, while some activities in the regular budget were being curtailed, others were being replenished from extrabudgetary resources. It expressed its appreciation to those countries which continued to provide such funds, but wished to make it clear that extrabudgetary resources should in no way distort the priority decisions for regular budget activities. It was greatly concerned at the criteria being used to earmark extrabudgetary resources for different activities and wished to emphasize that Member States should become more involved in deciding the placement and utilization of those funds. ...

In connection with the implementation of recommendation 15 of the Group of High-level Intergovernmental Experts regarding staff reductions, his delegation sympathized with the Secretary-General who, on the one hand, was required to implement the recommendation and, on the other hand, must ensure that, in so doing, no negative programmatic impact would arise. In balancing those seemingly conflicting directives, the Secretary-General must take into consideration the views of Member States on the reforms and their implementation."

The representative of **Algeria**[41]

"The United Nations was increasingly being called on to deal with conflicts that threatened world peace and security; development efforts were facing serious obstacles, such as the external debt problem; the economic situation of the entire continent of Africa was more critical than ever; and yet, for the second time running, the proposed budget showed a negative real rate of growth. It was regrettable that the Committee for Programme and Co-ordination had been unable to verify the impact of negative growth on programmes and activities. Every care must be taken to avoid adverse repercussions on mandated activities.

The Secretary-General was to be congratulated on keeping his formal budget proposals so close to the amounts forecast in the budget outline. Maintaining, as some delegations did, that the preliminary forecasts should not be exceeded was tantamount to saying that, by adopting the new budget procedure, the General Assembly had put a cap on the expenses of the Organization. His delegation was emphatically not of that view, believing that programmes must not be forced to conform to any arbitrary limit on resource growth. Before rendering a final opinion on the Secretary-General's estimates, the Fifth Committee should bear in mind that the budget was more up to date and comprehensive than the outline; that resolution 41/213 called for preliminary estimates not definitive appropriations; and that the insignificant extra amount was more than covered by the reductions recommended by the Advisory Committee.

By recommending only eight further posts for deletion, as against the 50 called for by the General Assembly in resolution 43/213, the Secretary-General had reminded Member States that he could not cut more than 12 per cent of the posts in the budget without seriously endangering some of the basic activities of the Organization. The Advisory Committee's recommendation to restore two posts to the Joint Inspection Unit should be proof enough that a 15 per cent cut simply was not possible. On the other hand, his delegation shared the Advisory Committee's views on the Secretariat's failure to explain its reasons for trimming only 10 instead of 14 posts at the Under-Secretary-General and Assistant Secretary-General levels. It would favour a solution to that question which upheld the prerogatives of the Secretary-General as far as possible.

His delegation was deeply disappointed at the lack of haste to comply with recommendation 15 of the Group of 18 shown by bodies financed by extra-budgetary contributions. If applied, that recommendation would have enabled them to redeploy resources from the administrative sector to operational and development activities.

At the forty-third session his delegation had voiced doubts as to whether the United Nations could meet any additional expenditure approved over a possible three-year period out of a reserve fund amounting to 0.75 per cent of total resources. Its doubts had been increased by the prospect of special meetings and session of the Assembly during the biennium 1990-1991. ... It must be borne in mind that the purpose of the contingency fund was to strengthen budgetary discipline, not artificially restrict the growth of United Nations activities. Pending the feasibility study on a reserve, additional outlays occasioned by currency fluctuations, inflation in non-salary costs and statutory increases in personnel costs should be covered in accordance with current practice and procedures, as the Advisory Committee recommended. ...

What was missing from the outline and proposed programme budget was any attempt to set priorities. Some features of the budget proposals, however, showed the importance of priority-setting. Paradoxically, the proposed budget for UNCTAD continued to decline although the interlinked problems of trade, debt, currencies and finance was highly topical and the situation of the least developed countries were more precarious than ever. As official development assistance and voluntary support for United Nations operational programmes stagnated and shrank, the tiny increase in the budgets for the regional commissions, notably the Economic Commission for Africa, hardly seemed to promise the requisite stimulus for development or to reflect the priority attached by the United Nations to the economic situation in Africa. Priority-setting among programme elements and subprogrammes must remain the prerogative of intergovernmental bodies. Some of the guidelines and criteria set forth in resolution 36/228 A should be reviewed in the light of the Organization's discouraging experience. Priorities must be set with due regard for the interests and concerns of all parties. His own country's priorities were still development, the right of peoples, in particular the Palestinian people, to self-determination and independence, and the abolition of the system of *apartheid*.

His delegation continued to feel that the recommendations of the Group of 18 had not been given balanced implementation. A number of recommendations designed to produce greater transparency in personnel management had still not been put into effect. His delegation firmly supported the CPC recommendation for increased staffing for the activities of United Nations Information Centres, and emphasized the importance it attached to Department of Public Information activities relating to Palestine, Namibia and the campaign against *apartheid*."

The representative of **Peru**[42]

"Although the Special Commission of the Economic and Social Council had not yet agreed on the restructuring of the economic and social sectors of the Organization, his delegation did not believe it would be appropriate for reforms in those areas to be discussed elsewhere. The recommended 15 per cent cut in staff had not been achieved, but the Secretariat had made great efforts, and much of the burden of the reforms had been borne by the staff. The progress made on travel and the use of consultants must be acknowledged; on the other hand, he wondered what progress had been made in ensuring that no post was regarded as the preserve of any one country or regional group. ...

The procedures for budget formulation and execution were tending to become more rigid, limiting the ability of the Organization to respond to new mandates. The trend could be corrected by setting flexible standards for the operation of the contingency fund and the fund designed to cover the costs of inflation and currency fluctuations. On the other hand, his delegation agreed on the desirability of an integrated programming system which would allow both the growth of the programme and the financial implications of that growth to be clearly seen. ...

His delegation had never regarded the budget outline as a limit, but merely as a preliminary frame of reference. When the international community was expecting so much of the United Nations, it was regrettable that the proposed budget should show negative real growth of nearly 1 per cent. The trend must be reversed, otherwise it would be very difficult for the Organization to accomplish the purposes set forth in the Charter. In the long run, his delegation believed, there was a direct relationship between the size of the Secretariat and the growing role of the Organization.

On the subject of priority-setting, his delegation felt that the method proposed by the Secretariat was a step forward, and it agreed that priority-setting in the context of the medium-term plan should focus on the sub-programme level."

The representative of **Venezuela**[43]

"the difference of 0.06 per cent between the proposed programme budget and the budget outline was acceptable, given that the latter was intended to be only a preliminary estimate of resources. ...

In his delegation's view, technological innovations were necessary in a reform process aimed at improving the efficiency of the administrative and financial functioning of the United Nations. At the same time, it hoped that those innovations would be conceived as part of a well-considered plan that would result, once the level of staff was stabilized, in improved productivity and savings in costs. The introduction of new technologies was not in itself a panacea. It implied additional costs, which would have to be amortized, and the availability of additional skills if full effects were to be enjoyed. ...

His delegation was also concerned about the possible negative impact of post reductions on programmes. General Assembly resolutions 43/213, 42/211 and 41/213 had all established that such measures should have no negative impact on programmes, and CPC made the same point in paragraph 66 of its report (A/44/16)."

The representative of the **German Democratic Republic**[44]

"His delegation noted with satisfaction that considerable progress had been made in such areas as the restructuring of the political sector, clearer statements of goals, more rational approaches, and staff reductions. His delegation also welcomed the positive changes in the budget process, including the introduction of the programme budget outline and the contingency fund, as well as progress in improving co-operation among units of the Secretariat and United Nations organs dealing with planning and budgeting matters. The process was, however, still at the introductory stage and new decisions might need to be taken as a result of experience. Moreover, some important tasks remained to be tackled, for example, the reorganization of the economic and social sector of the United Nations. ...

The continuous updating of all programme activities was essential, and greater efforts must be made to identify and terminate outmoded programmes more quickly. ...

Despite the efforts that had been made to fulfil the mandates relating to the budget, and to implement resolution 41/213, the proposed programme budget for 1990/1991 revealed a number of deficiencies. The proposed programme budget exceeded the budget outline for 1990-1991 agreed upon in resolution 43/214 by $US 1.3 million. That outline, which had been adopted after lengthy and thorough negotiations based on a balance of interests, should be taken very seriously and should be exceeded only if special circumstances arose. According to paragraph 11 of the introduction to the proposed programme budget (A/44/6/Rev.1), perhaps 20 per cent of outputs were not strictly mandated. In future, Member States should consider carefully such outputs were required or justified.

His delegation felt that the Office of Programme Planning, Budget and Finance should exert a more consistent influence to ensure a unified format for the programme budget and the soundness of arguments with regard to expenditures. In the circumstances, his delegation was in favour of the changes recommended by ACABQ. It was essential, given the existing difficulties, that priorities should be set, but the proposed programme budget for 1990-1991 did not offer a fundamental solution to the problem of priority-setting. It was hard to understand how a thorough review of possible financing for new activities could be made in a short space of time in the event that the contingency fund was exhausted, if even during the protracted process of drawing up the proposed programme budget, the value of individual programmes was not assessed."

The representative of **Ghana**[45]

"his delegation attached great importance to the cluster of agenda items under discussion. The various instruments involved in the effort to lay the foundation for an efficient administrative and financial structure of the United Nations - the medium-term plan, the programme budget outlined the programme budget, priority-setting, and the review envisaged in General Assembly resolution 41/213 - were all designed to enhance predictability and offer increased opportunities for evaluation.

The excess of only 0.06 per cent in the proposed programme budget over the budget outline was a significant achievement. Such a small increase over a 12-month period should normally be welcome. It should be pointed out, however, that the methodology currently employed was likely to continue to produce a programme budget that exceeded the resources predicted in the outline and until a methodology was found that enhanced predictability, the outline should not, and could not, be regarded as a ceiling. Such a position would adversely affect the Secretariat's ability to implement mandated programmes.

The contingency fund was another instrument that required consideration. According to the guidelines annexed to General Assembly resolution 42/311, any programme activity based on a decision taken in the year preceding the biennium, in other words in 1989, and during the biennium, 1990-1991, would be chargeable to the contingency fund, for which a sum of $US 15 million had been appropriated. In his delegation's view, the fund's operations would have to be carefully monitored to ensure that mandated programmes were not financially starved into premature termination or deferment. In that connection, it would be advisable for the Committee to pay particular attention to any statements of programme budget implications that might be submitted. His delegation would find it difficult to accept the usual practice of according approval with the proviso that the activity should be funded from available resources, but would require a clear indication of the source of funding, whether at the programme, subprogramme or programme element level. It would revert to the issue of the proposed reserve fund to cover charges for unforeseen and extraordinary expenditures outside the scope of the proposed budget and on the contingency fund at a later stage, but wished to state at the present stage that if the reserve fund was to be a credible alternative to the existing arrangement its liquidity must be guaranteed.

The role of priority-setting in programme planning could not be overstated. His delegation had examined the Secretary-General's report (A/44/272) with care and endorsed his diagnosis of the ailment of the existing legislative framework and its application. It did not, however, believe that his prescription would have the desired effect. The additional criterion proposed would merely add to the current confusion. The concept of "multilateral action" lacked clarity and was unhelpful as a guide. Priority-setting need not be related to the importance of multilateral action. Priority should be rooted in the effect of an activity on the realization of the Organization's objectives as spelled out in the Charter.

First and foremost, priority needed to be properly defined. The current definition whereby it was expressed in terms of claims on resources, with 10 per cent of resources being allocated in the programme budget to programmes of "high priority" and 10 per cent also to programmes of low priority, was contradictory. Priority-setting should be the result of political dialogue rather than any mathematical equation or set of rules. In any event, CPC should be requested to consider the Secretary-General's proposal and submit recommendations on it to the General Assembly at its forty-fifth session.

Referring to the report of the Secretary-General on the implementation of resolution 41/213 (A/44/222), he said his delegation had noted the recurrent concern about possible adverse effects on mandated programmes, particularly if the projections in the medium-term plan went wrong. ...

Until the Assembly had reviewed the effect of the reforms on the efficiency of the administrative and financial functioning of the United Nations, caution was advisable in respect of further staff reductions. While the reform process could be expected to continue, it was proper that the review mandated under resolution 41/213 should be formally brought to an end."

The representative of **Botswana**[46]

"The proposed programme budget exceeded the outline by some $US 1.3 million. While he understood the concern expressed by some delegations on that score, it should be remembered that the procedures were new and that, as they were refined and as experience was gained, excesses might not recur. It was, moreover, his delegation's understanding that the outline was a guide and should therefore provide room for flexibility. ... In his delegation's view, the Secretary-General was to be congratulated on having prepared a budget proposal which was as close to the outline as possible.

While his delegation appreciated the need for reform, it believed that it should not be seen merely as a cost-saving measure or as an end in itself. It hoped that the 12 per cent cut in posts would not seriously hamper the work of the regional commissions or such important departments as the Department of Public Information."

The representative of the **Ukrainian Soviet Socialist Republic**[47]

"Considering that the total approved by the General Assembly for the budget outline appeared to be adequate, the $1.3 million increase envisaged in the proposed budget did not seem to be fully justified. As the Chairman of ACABQ had noted, the controversy regarding that discrepancy could have been settled more easily if the Secretariat had offered some detailed explanations in the budget proposals.

The Ukrainian Soviet Socialist Republic shared the concern expressed by CPC with regard to the increase in administrative costs and in the costs associated with the use of experts and consultants, travel, external printing and equipment (A/44/16, para. 60). Further efforts must be made to reduce those costs. Moreover, decisions concerning the reduction in the number of permanent posts taken by the General Assembly at its forty-third session had not been fully implemented."

The representative of the **Islamic Republic of Iran**[48]

"welcomed the fact that the Secretary-General's proposed programme budget represented a reduction of 0.4 per cent in real terms, but only in so far as that did not have a negative effect on the programmes mandated by the legislative bodies, especially programmes of assistance to developing countries. Likewise, the total estimate in the budget outline should not be regarded as a limit that it was forbidden to exceed in the proposed programme budget. It was necessary to show flexibility and give the Secretariat more time to gain experience with the new budget process. His delegation hoped that, with the advantage of experience, the Secretariat would be able to ensure that all the resources necessary to attain the objectives of the Organization were available in the budget outline. It also hoped that the Member States and intergovernmental bodies would be more closely involved in the preparation of the programme budget. It noted with satisfaction that international control of narcotic drugs and the United Nations Programme of Action for African Economic Recovery and Development were among the major objectives of the proposed programme budget for the biennium 1990-1991. ...

Implementation of the General Assembly resolutions calling for a 15 per cent staff reduction had made substantial progress, since a reduction of 12 per cent had already been achieved. There too, however, it was necessary to show flexibility so that programme implementation would not be negatively affected. With regard to the target of 25 per cent set for the reduction in the posts of Under-Secretary-General and Assistant Secretary-General, his delegation wished to point out that the principle of equitable geographical distribution should be maintained and measures should be taken to guarantee the adequate representation of developing countries in such posts."

The representative of **Pakistan**[49]

"that since the proposed programme budget submitted by the Secretary-General was the first prepared in accordance with the new budget procedures, it was appropriate to treat the product with flexibility, as the General Assembly had affirmed in its resolution 43/214. Certain features would have to be refined, in particular the question of the relationship between the budget outline and the subsequent proposed programme budget. He had no problem with the fact that the latter slightly exceeded the former. The outline was simply intended to provide a greater level of predictability of the necessary funds and it was only a preliminary figure. ...

He noted that the real rate of growth was negative and emphasized that the reform process should not have any adverse effect on programme delivery.

Some delegations had stressed the need to implement certain recommendations of the Group of 18 to the letter, especially those on the reduction of posts. His delegation firmly believed that to be a most sensitive matter which required further study. The elimination of so many posts in the highest echelons of the United Nations should be seen in its broad political context, as CPC had emphasized at its twenty-ninth session. His delegation therefore wholly endorsed the recommendation made by CPC in paragraph 67 of its report. ...

With regard to the implementation of resolution 41/213, he agreed with the Secretary-General that reform was a continuing process which must not become an end in itself. Some Member States had expressed concern that specific recommendations of the Group of 18 had not been implemented in full. But among its other objectives, the resolution had addressed the vital necessity of restoring the financial viability of the Organization. It was therefore inconsistent that Member States continued not to pay their dues on time as required by the Charter, which could not be regarded as being less important than a resolution. Given the progress already achieved and the increased responsibilities entrusted to the Organization, it was imperative for Member States to honour their financial obligations."

The representative of **Uganda**[50]

"the outline approved by the General Assembly should not be considered as fixing the overall level of budgetary resources definitively. It was obviously not a budget that had been considered on a section-by-section basis.

It was clearly inconsistent that the rate of growth was negative at a time when the Organization was playing an ever-increasing role in the international sphere. ...

The process of reform initiated by the implementation of resolution 41/213 should remain integrated and balanced. ... While supporting the proposed 12 per cent reduction in posts, his delegation found it difficult to understand the way in which the reduction was being carried out and hoped that the matter would be clarified during future negotiations.

The restructuring of the Department of Public Information was a cause of concern for many delegations, in particular because of the imbalances noted both in the geographical distribution of staff in senior level posts and in the allocation of resources within units. His delegation wished to have information about the distribution of posts in the Anti-*Apartheid*, Namibia and Palestine Programmes Section. ...

The process of reform must not serve to reorient the Organization towards certain areas to the detriment of others. It was with that consideration in mind that his delegation would continue to monitor the work of the Committee on Conferences closely. His delegation recalled that the Fifth Committee had informed the General Assembly that it had expressed its opinion on the status of the Committee on Conferences on the understanding that nothing in it could be construed as giving that Committee any role in the budgetary process or any power to disregard decisions duly taken by United Nations bodies concerning programmes, meetings and conferences. His delegation was therefore surprised that some people were trying to call in question that interpretation of the mandate given to the Committee on Conferences."

The representative of **Byelorussian Soviet Socialist Republic**[51]

"the preparation of the programme budget outline, despite some shortcomings and the oversimplified method used to calculate the preliminary estimates, had played a positive role in the establishment of the programme budget. In particular, although a number of reservations had to be entered on the score, it was to be noted that the proposed expenditure increase was also a positive development, facilitating a better utilization of resources and more effective avoidance of duplication and overlapping. The most important point, however, was that the intergovernmental organs and the Secretariat of the United Nations were now giving very close attention to the problems and shortcomings of programme and resource planning and, in a constructive manner, seeking means of correcting them.

It should not be concluded, however, that his delegation was unconcerned by the problems arising from the lack of acceptable methods and procedures for the preparation and consideration of the outline, the delays in formulating procedures to govern the utilization and operation of the contingency fund, or the conservatism of the Secretariat, whose efforts to contain the proposed programme budget strictly within the limits of the preliminary estimates had been less than persistent.

What worried his delegation were not so much the $1,300,000 requested over and above the preliminary estimates as the fact that a unanimously adopted decision of principle was being ignored. Corrective action should be taken when approving the proposed programme budget; the preliminary resource estimate and the amount set aside for the contingency fund were ceiling figures which should on no account be exceeded. The reasons for strictly applying that rule were twofold: first, if precedents - even isolated ones - were tolerated, the new budgetary process became meaningless, not to mention the fact that requests for funds to cover additional expenses had never been a sign of efficiency; and, second, it was well known that unused possibilities whose correction or utilization, if only in part, would release sufficient resources to meet unforeseen requirements.

His delegation ... approved the recommendations of ACABQ on the proposed programme budget while regretting their lack of vigour in certain cases; for example, the figure of $6,898,800 proposed by way of reduction in the expenditure estimates was altogether inadequate."

In response to the issues raised by member states, the **Controller**[52] noted:

"The target set by the Group of 18 of a 15 per cent reduction in posts was not based on any scientific criterion. The recommendation therefore needed to be implemented with the utmost flexibility. Several delegations had deplored the fact that the reductions proposed by the Secretary-General had not been based on an analysis of the work-loads of the various departments. But, in view of the extremely short period of time (about four months) available in which to decide what posts should be abolished, it had not been possible to make such a thorough analysis. In any case, the 13.5 per cent reduction proposed by the Secretary-General at the forty-third session had been decided on the basis of the most thorough and objective examination possible in the light of the constraints, *inter alia* financial, with which the United Nations had been faced.

In the proposed programme budget for the biennium 1990-1991, the Secretary-General was proposing a net additional reduction of eight posts. As indicated in the introduction to the programme budget, given the need not to jeopardize programme execution, the absence of concrete results in the economic and social sector, the impossibility of limiting the number of meetings and, furthermore, given the additional responsibilities entrusted to the United Nations in recent months, he was not in a position to propose further cuts. Regarding high-level posts, the position of the Secretary-General remained as stated in paragraph 19 of the Introduction to the programme budget, namely, that he was most definitely not in a position to propose further reductions in that area."

Following the debate, the draft decision A/44/L.54 was introduced by Malaysia, which reads as follows:[53]

"*The General Assembly*,

(a) *Takes note* of the note of the Secretary-General on the review of the efficiency of the administrative and financial functioning of the United Nations;[54]

(b) *Decides* to review the efficiency of the administrative and financial functioning of the United Nations in the economic and social fields, including the secretariat support structure, in the light of the outcome of the major intergovernmental deliberations scheduled to take place in the beginning of the 1990s, including, in particular, the special session of the General Assembly on international co-operation against illicit production, supply, demand, trafficking and distribution of narcotic drugs, the special session of the Assembly devoted to international economic co-operation, in particular to the revitalization of economic growth and development of developing countries, the Second United Nations Conference on the Least Developed Countries, the elaborations of the international development strategy for the fourth United Nations development decade, the eighth session of the United Nations Conference on environment and development;

(c) *Stresses* the need for the full implementation of Economic and Social resolutions 1988/77 of 29 July 1988 and 1989/114 of 28 July 1989, including the provisions related to the secretariat support structure of the Council."

After further informal consultations, the Vice-Chairman of the Fifth Committee submitted draft resolution A/C.5/44/L.24. The draft was approved by consensus in the Fifth Committee and subsequently in the Plenary Assembly as resolution entitled **Implementation of General Assembly Resolution 41/213 (44/200).** The resolution was in three parts. Part A dealt with implementation of GA resolution 41/213. The GA decided to recognize the progress achieved to date in the overall post reduction exercise mandated by resolution 43/213; acknowledged that the Secretary-General was not in a position to propose further post reductions at present; decided to consider, in the light of the analytical report to be submitted to the GA at its 45th session, any proposals put forward by the Secretary-General for further implementation of recommendation 15 of resolution 41/213; stressed the need to strengthen the role of the Secretary-General with respect to co-ordination within the UN system, as well as the role of member states, through the relevant intergovern-mental bodies; requested the Secretary-General to provide to the 45th session of the GA a compendium of the mandates of the Assembly's subsidiary administrative and budgetary bodies, together with information on relevant reviews carried out over the past 5 years; requested the Secretary-General to submit to the 45th session of the GA an analytical report assessing the effect of the implementation of resolution 41/213 on the organization and its activities. Part B dealt with the budget process. The GA requested the Secretary-General to provide statements of programme budget implications to

---

*See volume II, 1.12.

all subsidiary bodies of the GA and ECOSOC, in order to facilitate decision-making, and to keep under review the format and content of statements of programme budget implications in the context of the new budgetary process; requested the Secretary-General to submit to the 46th session of the GA a single report on the review of the procedures for the provision of statements of programme budget implications and for the use and operation of the contingency fund; decided to keep under review the question of a comprehensive solution to the problem of all additional expenditures, including those deriving from inflation and currency fluctuation, and to consider it again at its 46th session; requested the Secretary-General to take fully into account the conclusions, recommendations and observations of the CPC and ACABQ on the treatment of extrabudgetary resources when preparing and presenting the outline and the proposed programme budget for the biennium 1992-1993. Part C dealt with technical innovations. The GA requested the Secretary-General to prepare a report on the status of the introduction of electronic data-processing and new technologies into the UN for submission to the 45th session of the GA.

A number of statements were made following approval of the resolution by the Fifth Committee.

The representative of **Cuba**[55]

"her delegation was in general agreement with the provisions of the draft resolutions just adopted and would be especially interested in the information requested in draft resolution A, paragraph 14, since it believed that the administrative and budgetary area was one in which the recommendations of the Group of High-level Intergovernmental Experts had not been fully applied. While meaningful reforms had been carried out, the report that was to be submitted pursuant to paragraphs 15 and 16 should allow the General Assembly to assess the overall results of the reform process."

The representative of **Algeria**[56]

"underscored the importance his Government attached to certain provisions of the draft resolutions, particularly paragraph 15 of draft resolution A calling for an analytical report, and paragraph 6 regarding a balanced and flexible implementation of the recommendations of the Group of High-level Intergovernmental Experts, some of which - such as recommendations 42 and 47 - needed to be implemented immediately. Also, Algeria understood paragraph 14 as in no way restricting the sovereign right of Members to bring up the question of the composition of administrative and budgetary bodies, especially in relation to the geographical distribution of posts."

The representative of the **United Kingdom**[57]

"it was of critical importance to pursue reform and renewal so that the administrative and budgetary arrangements of the United Nations could command confidence. The matter had been dealt with as early as in the very first session of the General Assembly and it was noteworthy that the current session was the first since then at which such broad agreement had been reached on administrative and budgetary questions. His delegation believed that paragraph 14 of the draft resolution must be considered as a whole and construed in its plain meaning."

The representative of **Uganda**[58]

"stressing the importance of paragraphs 6 and 15 of draft resolution A, said that the analytical report requested in the latter paragraph should make clear the impact of reform - negative and positive - and the manner in which recommendations 41, 46, 47 and 54 of the Group of High-level Intergovernmental Experts had been implemented. Also, it was his understanding that in paragraph 14 the Secretary-General was being asked to give information, and the paragraph was not to be construed as a request for a review of administrative and budgetary bodies."

The representative of the **Libyan Arab Jamahiriya**[59]

"referring to the questions regarding Professional staff dealt with in draft resolution A, observed that recommendations 15, 54 and 55 of the Group of High-level Intergovernmental Experts were aimed at political renewal, especially in the stipulations that Under-Secretary-General and Assistant Secretaries-General should not serve for more than 10 years, and that, in accordance with the principle of equitable geographical distribution, no post should be considered the exclusive preserve of any State or group of States."

Following the conclusion of the item on the implementation of the reform by resolution 44/200, the GA turned to the consideration of the programme budget. The Assembly adopted by consensus the resolution entitled **Programme Budget for the Biennium 1990-1991 (44/202)**, approving a net expenditure of $1,974,634,000 for 1990-1991.

The adoption of the programme budget by consensus was considered a major success and very much in contrast to the negative votes cast on previous occasions. All member states appeared to support the reforms, which particularly fulfilled the expectations of the major contributors.

Once the programme budget was adopted, the representative of the **United States of America**[60] made following statement:

"The forty-fourth session of the General Assembly has been one of the most constructive sessions in the history of the United Nations. Member States and the Secretary-General deserve credit for the important contributions made towards addressing key international political, economic and social problems. The United States delegation is gratified not only by the concrete accomplishments of the forty-fourth session but also by the positive signals they send about the role of the Organization. The capacity of the United Nations to contribute to the solution of the many critical problems on the international scene has been strengthened by important steps taken at this session of the General Assembly towards further implementation of administrative and budgetary reforms.

Among the most significant accomplishments of the forty-fourth session has been the consensus adoption of the 1990-1991 programme budget. That decision represents the successful completion of the new budgetary process approved by the Assembly at its forty-first session. We can take satisfaction in that positive result and in the important contributions made by the Secretary-General and delegations to rebuilding confidence in the work of the United Nations.

My delegation would like to highlight those elements of the budget resolution which are of major significance to the United States.

The 1990-1991 United Nations budget of $1.975 billion is below the level agreed upon at the last General Assembly session in the context of approval of the budget outline. It therefore reflects the continued restraint shown by the Secretary-General and Member States. Also, the Organization is continuing to make progress towards achieving the reductions called for in resolution 41/213 regarding overall staffing levels, in high-level posts in particular. While some delegations expressed reservations about the approved reductions in senior posts, they worked with others to permit a consensus on the budget. We look forward to receiving proposals next year for the elimination of the four remaining high-level positions that is required to meet the target set in resolution 41/213.

Another major accomplishment has been the successful operation of the new contingency fund. Budget add-ons charged to that fund total less than $2 million, well below the level approved for the biennium as a whole. ...

Let me stress the importance of the resolution adopted by the Assembly on the implementation of the reforms. That resolution continues the effort begun in 1986 to improve the efficiency and effectiveness of the Organization. While significant progress had been made towards achieving the previously agreed target of 15 per cent for staff reductions, we are not there yet. More needs to be done, and we are encouraged that the General Assembly will address this issue next year. The reform resolution also requires further action by Member States to restructure the intergovernmental decision-making process in the economic and social areas. Through co-operative efforts on the part of the Secretary-General and Member States, full implementation of all the reforms approved by the General Assembly at its forty-fourth session can be achieved."

In a concluding statement, the **Secretary-General**[61] acknowledged the adoption of programme budget as follows:

"We have just witnessed the adoption without a vote of all the reports of the Fifth Committee, including the programme budget for the biennium 1990 to 1991. I could not let this historic occasion pass without expressing my gratification of the spirit of co-operation which has led to the adoption by consensus of the budget necessary to fulfil the goals and objectives of the Organization over the next two years. I regard the Assembly's approval of this budget, the first to be prepared in accordance with the new budgetary procedures approved by the General Assembly in resolution 41/213, as a further indication of the renewal of confidence in multilateralism and its agents which I noted in my annual report on the work of the Organization. I trust that Member States will demonstrate their commitment tangibly through timely and prompt payment of assessed contributions, as well as of arrears."

Notes

1. ST/ADM/SER.B/309; A/C.5/44/27.
2. David R. Protheroe, *The United Nations and its Finances, A Test for Middle Powers* (Ottawa, Canada: The North-South Institute, 1988), p. 61.
3. A/44/1, p.12.
4. A/C.5/44/SR.11, pp. 2-4.
5. *Ibid.*, pp. 7-10.
6. A/C.5/44/SR.46, p. 7.
7. A/C.5/44/SR.11, pp. 11-13.
8. A/C.5/44/SR.12, pp. 2-4.
9. A/C.5/44/SR.49, p. 14.
10. A/C.5/44/SR.12, pp. 4-5.
11. *Ibid.*, pp. 6-7.
12. *Ibid.*, pp. 8-9.
13. *Ibid.*, p. 10.
14. *Ibid.*
15. A/C.5/44/SR.13, pp. 11-12.
16. A/C.5/44/SR.49, p. 13.

17.   A/C.5/44/SR.13, pp. 4-6.
18.   *Ibid.*, pp. 6-7.
19.   *Ibid.*, pp. 7-8.
20.   *Ibid.*, pp. 8-11.
21.   *Ibid.*, p. 12.
22.   *Ibid.*, p. 13.
23.   A/C.5/44/SR.16, pp. 3-4.
24.   A/C.5/44/SR.13, pp. 14-15.
25.   A/C.5/44/SR.14, pp. 2-3.
26.   *Ibid.*, p. 4.
27.   *Ibid.*, pp. 4-5.
28.   *Ibid.*, pp. 5-6.
29.   A/C.5/44/SR.16, pp. 5-7.
30.   A/C.5/44/SR.49, pp. 13-14.
31.   A/C.5/44/SR.14, p. 7.
32.   *Ibid.*, pp. 8-9.
33.   *Ibid.*, pp. 9-10.
34.   *Ibid.*, pp. 10-12.
35.   *Ibid.*, pp. 12-13.
36.   *Ibid.*, p. 14.
37.   *Ibid.*, pp. 14-15.
38.   A/C.5/44/SR.15, pp. 6-7.
39.   *Ibid.*, pp. 7-9.
40.   *Ibid.*, p. 9.
41.   *Ibid.*, pp. 10-12.
42.   *Ibid.*, pp. 12-13.
43.   *Ibid.*, pp. 13-14.
44.   *Ibid.*, pp. 14-15.
45.   *Ibid.*, pp. 16-17.
46.   *Ibid.*, p. 17.
47.   A/C.5/44/SR.16, p. 2.
48.   *Ibid.*, pp. 4-5.
49.   *Ibid.*, pp. 7-8.
50.   *Ibid.*, pp. 8-9.
51.   A/C.5/44/SR.17, p. 2.
52.   A/C.5/44/SR.18, p. 13.
53.   A/44/L.54.
54.   A/44/747.
55.   A/C.5/44/SR.49, p. 8.
56.   *Ibid.*
57.   *Ibid.*
58.   *Ibid.*, p. 9.
59.   *Ibid.*
60.   A/44/PV.84, pp. 17-21.
61.   *Ibid.*, p. 23.

6.1 Financial Situation

The financial situation had become worse during 1989.[*] Total outstanding contributions to the regular budget at the end of 1989 amounted to $461 million out of which $365 million was owed by the USA. The US contribution for 1989 had amounted to $159 million against an assessment of $216 million. Short term cash relief amounted to $438, available from the Working Capital Fund ($100 million), the Special Account ($123 million) and suspension of the provisions of financial regulations ($215 million). It continued to be necessary on occasions to resort to temporary borrowing from peace-keeping and other funds to meet some of the cash requirements for the regular budget. With respect to peace-keeping operations financed from assessed contributions, total unpaid debts amounted to some $444 million at the end of 1989. This was even $182 million higher than in 1985. The member states which contributed troops continued to bear the full burden of the effect of the shortfall in payment of assessed contributions for peace-keeping operations.[1]

During 1990, the financial situation remained extremely fragile for the regular budget. For the first time since 1986, the UN had to borrow from peace-keeping funds to meet regular budget obligations as all cash reserves had been fully depleted. There were serious doubts on a number of occasions as to whether the UN would be able to meet its payroll obligations. Despite the precariousness of the financial situation, the GA again declined to agree to the Secretary-General's request that the Working Capital Fund be increased from $100 to $200 million. There was, however, a major improvement towards the end of 1990. The USA not only resumed payment of its full assessed contribution but also paid part of its previous withholdings. Total contributions for 1990 amounted to $303 million against assessments of $234 million. As a result, at the end of 1990 the total of outstanding contributions was reduced to $403 million, $296 of which was owed by the USA. Of this $403 million only $61 million had been withheld on the basis of principle compared to $93 million in 1985 and late payments accounted for $342 million compared to $149 million in 1985. Of the $61 million which had been withheld, $41

---

[*]For details on the financial situation see annex, table 3 and 4.

million was owed by South Africa. Apart from the USA, the main countries in arrears under the regular budget were Brazil ($13 million), Argentina ($9 million), Iran ($6 million) and Yugoslavia ($5 million). The deficit under the peace-keeping budgets had also declined by the end of 1990 to $346 million, with the USA owing $156 million and the USSR $74 million. The UN had now lived for a number of years with a serious cash crisis and there appeared to be growing complacency on the part of many member states about the financial situation. One sign of this was that the pattern of payments of assessed contribution was worse in 1990 than it had been in 1989. However, a major improvement in the financial situation appears possible for the coming years. In early 1991, at the request of President Bush, the US House of Representatives authorized payment of all outstanding arrears to international organizations. This initial step could clear the way for the payment of all US arrears both to the regular and the peace-keeping budgets. If approved by the US Senate, payments will be made over a four-year period.[2]

The return of the USA to full payment came at a time when the UN had established a new relevance in international affairs. The successes of the period from 1987 to 1989 have already been highlighted. With the easing of East-West tensions, the sessions of the GA had been viewed more positively by the major powers. The representative of the USA, appointed by the Bush Administration, described the 44th session held in 1989 as 'one of the most constructive and realistic within memory' and the UN as 'a useful place'. His counterpart from the USSR also noted that the UN had moved into 'the non-confrontational world'.[3] The new international climate continued to be reflected in the working of the UN in 1990. Its was successful supervision of elections in Nicaragua brought about an end to the fighting in that country. The Gulf crisis and the concerted action by the permanent members of the Security Council, however, brought about the most dramatic involvement of the UN in international affairs.

As for the outstanding decisions with regard to the programme and the budget, the 45th session of the GA adopted by consensus the medium-term plan for 1992-1997, the revised budget appropriation for 1990-1991 and the programme budget outline for 1992-1993. The revised appropriation amounted to $2,100 million, approximately $160 million more than the initial appropriation. This increase was essentially due to currency fluctuation and inflations. The policy was still one of maximum restraint, which was a euphemism for zero growth. The same applied to the approval of the outline, estimated at a preliminary figure of $2,400 million at 1992-1993 prices. Again the apparent increase compared to the biennium 1990-1991 was essentially due to the decline of the dollar, notably *vis-à-vis* the Swiss franc, and to projections of higher inflation rates.   Apart from non-recurrent items, such as the construction projects in Addis Ababa and Bangkok, the preliminary estimates left a very small margin for increases in the programmes. The contingency fund for the 1992-1993 biennium was again established at 0.75 per cent of the preliminary estimate, or \$19 million as compared to \$15 million for the biennium 1990-1991.

The GA also set out to review the analytical report of the Secretary-General on the reform process approved by resolution 41/213. The session constituted the concluding point of the reform process and gave a final assessment of the progress achieved.

6.2   The 45th Session of the General Assembly: Approval of the Resolution on the Review of the Efficiency of the Administrative and Financial Functioning of the United Nations (45/254)

The Fifth Committee considered agenda item 117 (Review of the Efficiency of the Administrative and Financial Functioning of the United Nations) the implementation of the reform in accordance with GA resolution 44/200'. The Committee had before it the following documentation: (i) the Secretary-General' analytical report on the implementation of reform in accordance with GA resolution 41/213 (A/45/226), together with the observations of ACABQ (A/45/617) and CPC (A/45/16, Part I)''; (ii) the Secretary-General's report on the proposed programme budget outline for the biennium 1992-1993 (A/45/369), together with the observations of ACABQ (A/45/878) and CPC (A/45/16, part II); (iii) the Secretary-General's report on the compendium of mandates of the subsidiary administrative and budgetary bodies of the GA (A/45/370); and (iv) the Secretary-General's report on the status of technological innovations in the UN (A/45/478). Agenda item 117 was considered in conjunction with agenda item 119 (Programme Planning).

Before recalling the Fifth Committee's debate under agenda item 117, the statement made by the **Secretary-General'** in his report on the work of the organization is noted below:

'See volume II, 1.10.
''See volume II, 2.39, 2.40, 2.41.

"Following the reform programme instituted by General Assembly resolution 41/213, the Secretariat has undergone a major internal restructuring and considerable reduction in staff. At the same time, new procedures have enhanced mutual confidence between Member States and the Secretariat in administrative and financial matters. By adopting all relevant resolutions without a vote, the last session of the General Assembly showed greater convergence of views on questions related to administration, budget and management. Equally encouraging were the consensus votes on revised estimates and the programme budget for 1990-1991.

The reforms in the budgetary process have thus concluded the first cycle, and I believe, have largely achieved their purpose. They have brought about a better awareness among Member States - and within the Secretariat - of the way in which the United Nations utilizes its resources, and encouraged their more judicious use. They have also largely allayed the concerns of the major contributors. This is the result of fruitful co-operation between all, Member States and the Secretariat."

In the following, the statements made under agenda item 117 are recalled. Before member states addressed the Committee, the Chairman of CPC introduced his report and the USG for Administration and Management providing some introductory comments, as outlined below.

Mr. Abraszewski, **Chairman of CPC**[5]

"While noting areas in which progress had been limited or not possible, *inter alia*, in the economic and social sectors, the Committee concurred with the Secretary-General that the Organization had, in a number of areas, fulfilled the mandate for reform to the best of its abilities. The Committee also agreed that the improvement of the efficiency and effectiveness of the administrative and financial functioning of the Organization was a continuing process and that the Organization should enter a stage of consolidation in order to strengthen its capacity to meet the challenges of the 1990s. It emphasized the need for continuing action in the political sector, personnel questions and posts, conference services, economic and social sectors, construction, and co-ordination, and recommended that the Secretary-General be requested systematically to highlight progress achieved in those areas. It noted, however, that, despite the many difficulties encountered, the role of the Organization had been enhanced and agreed that the Governments of Member States were increasingly seeking the assistance of the United Nations.

The Committee had noted a number of shortcomings in the analytical report. With respect to methodology and structure, it noted that the report did not adhere strictly to the provisions of paragraph 28 of the Committee's report on its twenty-ninth session, as reflected in paragraph 16 (a) of General Assembly resolution 44/200 A. It did, however, follow the structure of the report of the Group of High-level Intergovernmental Experts to Review the Efficiency of the Administrative and Financial Functioning of the United Nations, thus providing updated information on the status of implementation of the specific recommendations of that Group. In general, it provided a useful account of action taken to implement General Assembly resolution 41/213 and of the areas in which further action was required. The report did not facilitate a precise assessment of the real impact of the implementation of recommendation 15 on programmes, and the relationship between posts and programmes funded from the regular budget and those funded from extrabudgetary resources required further analysis and consideration. However, the Committee recalled that the new budgetary process was still in a developmental stage and that several methodological issues were still pending. Financial viability was required if the objectives of Member States were to be achieved, and paragraph 23 of document A/45/16 (Part I) indicated certain necessary measures to ensure such viability.

In conclusion, the Committee recognized that the credit for progress on the reforms called for in resolution 41/213 was due to the joint efforts of Member States, the Secretary-General and the Organization's staff."

Mr. Ahtisaari, **USG for Administration and Management**[6]

"With the adoption by consensus of resolution 41/213 and a number of other resolutions, of revised estimates for the 1988-1989 biennium and of the programme budget for the current biennium, one of the fundamental objectives of the reform, namely to facilitate agreement among Member States on the content and level of the Organization's budget, had been achieved. Credit was due to the Committee for its role in that process. As could be seen from the analytical report, the Secretariat, for its part, had, in essence, implemented the very diverse recommendations of the Group of 18 endorsed by the General Assembly in resolution 41/213. The programme of administrative reform initiated in 1986 had thus largely been accomplished, despite continuing financial uncertainty and other serious difficulties and the addition of new major responsibilities. The remaining problems which the Secretariat had yet to address or solve in continuing co-operation with Member States included that of the revitalization of the economic and social sector.

Two apparently paradoxical ideas - that the Organization must consolidate itself and move forward, and that reform was not a finite process but implied a constant review of the functioning of the United Nations in relation to its objectives - merited some clarification. Consolidation was needed because no organization could sustain a prolonged period of upheaval, and the renewed confidence in the Organization's capacity to act efficiently and respond to new challenges had to be translated into concrete improvements. Consolidation of the results of the reform could be achieved only through the restoration of the financial viability of the Organization. Consolidation did not, however, mean ossification, and further structural reforms would be required, but the overriding consideration must be to increase the Organization's capacity to fulfil its role. It remained important to keep under review the relationship between the level of staff resources and the volume of programmes and activities, and he hoped that member Governments would maintain a realistic approach to that question, since it was not possible to continue to increase programme contents without reference to resources. Even the new planning and budget procedure would need to be progressively adjusted to new circumstances. Technological innovations, such as the creation of an integrated management information system, would contribute to greater flexibility and effectiveness."

The representative of Italy, speaking on behalf of the 12 states members of the **European Community**[7]

"the Twelve wanted to emphasize that the report of the Group of High-level Intergovernmental Experts (Group of 18) remained the basic document which must guide the current reform process. Like the Secretary-General, they thought that the experience of the past five years had been on balance positive. There was no doubt that significant results had been achieved in a number of areas: several Secretariat services had been restructured and the post-reduction exercise had been continued. For the first time in over 40 years the budget appropriations had been adopted by consensus at the forty-fourth session of the General Assembly. By supporting the reforms undertaken Member States had demonstrated their commitment to the work of the Organization and had thereby helped to strengthen it.

However, more needed to be done in order to consolidate those achievements. An improvement in the financial situation of the United Nations was now overdue. Fulfilment by Member States of their financial obligations would be the most tangible evidence of their political commitment. In some areas the comments of the Group of 18 remained valid: for example, the overly complex structure of the intergovernmental machinery or the proliferation of conferences and meetings of intergovernmental bodies. The Twelve strongly supported the appeals of the President of the General Assembly for a reduction in the number of resolutions and of reports requested from the Secretary-General, as well as in night and week-end meetings. It was for the Fifth Committee to give a lead. With regard to the restructuring of the Secretariat in the economic and social sectors, the Twelve were convinced that the Secretary-General would be able to act with the authority which he had demonstrated in other areas. They again urged all concerned to respect the Secretary-General's prerogatives as chief administrative officer of the Organization.

Even in cases where the results obtained had been relatively satisfactory there must be no relaxation of effort. One of the main benefits of the reform exercise was that it obliged the Secretariat to engage in permanent self-evaluation. The Twelve thought that increasing account should be taken of changing requirements and work-loads in future reviews of staffing tables. Any proposed retrenchment, redeployment or reinforcement of staff must take those factors into consideration. As the Secretary-General had said, redeployment was a constant necessity in the functioning of a dynamic organization.

There was, of course, a close link between the distribution of human resources and the distribution of financial resources. Resolution 41/213 had established for the first time a framework to enable Member States to agree on the overall level of the programme budget. As experience had shown in 1989, that had facilitated agreement on the content of the programme budget and a broader measure of support for the funding of activities. The subsidiary bodies of the Fifth Committee had played an important role in that respect, and the Twelve wanted them to continue to function effectively in accordance with their mandates.

The Secretary-General had recently referred to confidence-building. But the Twelve thought that it was too early to say that the reform process had achieved its purposes. If the results were to prove of lasting value, Member States and the Secretariat, as the Secretary-General implied in paragraph 3 of his analytical report on the implementation of General Assembly resolution 41/213 (A/45/226), must sustain the effort in a spirit of compromise and in the common interest."

The representative of **Yugoslavia**[8]

"Significant progress had been achieved in many areas and it could be said that the Secretary-General had accomplished the essentials of what had been requested from him. Nevertheless, in some areas little or no progress had been made. That was particularly true with respect to recommendations 2 and 8. Despite the action taken by the United Nations Conference on Trade and

Development and some regional commissions, the implementation of the two recommendations depended almost entirely on the conclusion of an agreement on the structure of the intergovernmental machinery in the economic and social fields. Until that problem was solved it would be difficult to decide whether the Economic and Social Council should have only one session per year.

The question must also be addressed in the context of the work which the international community would have to undertake in the years to come: the programme was a very heavy one in the economic and social fields. That did not reduce in any way the urgent need for concerted action to rationalize and co-ordinate better the work of intergovernmental bodies and administrative services throughout the United Nations system. The choice of the type of intergovernmental machinery to be introduced would depend largely on the spirit of co-operation demonstrated by Member States, a spirit which currently prevailed in the work in the political sphere. In any event, in the interim the two annual sessions of the Economic and Social Council should be maintained.

His delegation noted with satisfaction that the Secretary-General has succeeded in reducing by 11.95 per cent the number of posts funded from the regular budget without detriment to the programmes or the functioning of the Secretariat; however, that reduction had been largely offset by the increase in the number of posts funded from extrabudgetary resources. Parallel with the internal restructuring of the Secretariat a new approach to administrative and financial matters had been introduced. The adoption of resolutions by consensus was an encouraging development which should become the regular pattern.

The reform of the United Nations was a continuing process which must embrace not only the activities of the Secretariat but also the work programmes of intergovernmental bodies, which should be more resolute in eliminating or phasing out outdated programmes in favour of new programmes which responded better to the new needs of the international community.

The Yugoslav delegation thought, that the proposed medium-term plan for the period 1992-1997 might be more easily discussed after it had been considered by CPC and the Advisory Committee. The number of programmes and subprogrammes contained in the plan was impressive. Given the new trends in international political and economic relations, it would certainly be necessary to revise some programmes. The Secretary-General's introduction of the medium-term plan was particularly important in that respect, because it reflected the changes taking place in the world and the opening-up of new perspectives for international co-operation."

The representative of **Nepal**[9]

"the Economic and Social Council had not yet taken a decision on the question of holding a single session each year, and that the number of subsidiary bodies of the Council which had decided to biennialize their sessions had scarcely increased. Furthermore, the Conference-Servicing utilization factor, which had reached the level of 70 per cent, remained well below the standard which had been set. His delegation hoped that the Department of Conference Services would propose practical ways of improving the effectiveness and cost-efficiency of those services, and that the Committee on Conferences would come up with a refined methodology, to take account of information on the holding of informal meetings, and of time lost, in calculating the utilization factor. On the other hand, his delegation was encouraged by the results obtained with regard to implementation of the recommendations that United Nations bodies should meet at their respective headquarters, that construction work should be undertaken only when sufficient resources were available to complete them, and that the number of claims for delegation travel should be reduced. Also encouraging were the measures adopted by a number of bodies, such as UNCTAD, ECE and ECLAC, to streamline their structures; other bodies should follow their example.

With regard to co-ordination, ACC should substantially modify the format and content of its annual overview report, in accordance with the recommendations of CPC, in order to rationalize the meetings of its subsidiary bodies and substantially reduce their cost. Co-ordination of operational activities for development, both within the United Nations system and at the national level, could not fail to be strengthened by the reaffirmation of the central funding and co-ordinating role of UNDP. His delegation noted with satisfaction that a number of organizations with country and subregional offices had endorsed the principle of common premises and shared facilities, subject to the practical constraints referred to by the Director-General for Development and International Economic Co-operation. Greater efforts should also be made to harmonize budgeting practices among the bodies of the United Nations system.

In view of the delay in restructuring the economic and social sectors, it was important that decisions should be taken rapidly at the intergovernmental level so as to enable the Secretary-General fully to implement recommendation 14 of the Group of 18. As for staff reductions (recommendation 15), the Secretariat had managed to reduce the number of posts without any resultant negative impact on programmes. In that regard, his delegation agreed with the Secretary-General that a proper balance must be maintained between the number of staff funded from the regular budget and the number funded from other contributions and that any further structural reforms should be aimed at increasing the capacity of the Organization to accomplish its role, not at reducing its staff. Given the importance of peace-keeping operations, special care must be taken to provide the Field Operations Division with the means to carry on normal activities. Member States must support the measures aimed at ensuring the availability of a cadre of core personnel for its operations and at establishing a reserve stock of commonly used equipment and stores items.

His delegation noted with satisfaction that significant changes had occurred, both in terms of organizational structure and in procedures and methods of work, which had resulted in clearer lines of responsibility and better co-ordination. It also welcomed the reduction in staff travel expenses affected by reducing the number of staff sent on mission and by strictly controlling first class travel. The independence of the internal audit function, reaffirmed by a self-evaluation exercise performed by the Division, presupposed that the Division should have the staffing and resources necessary to carry out the auditing work required, particularly in connection with activities away from Headquarters.

With regard to the planning and budget procedure, the Organization would benefit greatly from fuller involvement of intergovernmental bodies in the preparation of both the medium-term plan and the programme budget, despite the difficulty, for Member States and the Secretariat, of developing a common language on matters of programming and budgeting. Problems relating to priority setting should also be resolved as early as possible. His delegation hoped that, as in the case of the contingency fund, guidelines for the use and operation of which had been approved, a solution would be found to the comprehensive problem of additional expenditures, including those deriving from inflation and currency fluctuations, and that the solution would be submitted to the General Assembly at its 1991 session. In any case, improvement of the format and methodology of the programme budget and of the outline budget must be viewed as an ongoing and flexible exercise, in order to consolidate the reforms achieved thus far and to be in a position to meet the challenges of the 1990s.

The results of the process of enhancing the administrative and financial functioning of the United Nations, while not entirely in line with the objectives set forth in resolution 41/213, were none the less very encouraging. Furthermore, one could not but welcome the renewed confidence shown in the United Nations by Member States and the close co-operation and mutual support between Member States and the Secretary-General, which had enabled the Fifth Committee to adopt all its resolutions unanimously at the forty-fourth session. The public perception of the United Nations had also improved noticeably. The Secretariat had done its part, and programmes had suffered few adverse effects in consequence; it was now up to Member States to do theirs, by fulfilling their financial obligations in full and on time, to enable the Secretary-General to complete the implementation of Assembly resolution 41/213."

The representative of the **United States of America**[10]

"the reduction in international tensions had created a political climate favourable to the revitalization of the United Nations, but that the reform effort also had made a significant contribution to restoring its prominence and credibility in peace-keeping. Member States must ensure that the limited resources available were directed to priority programmes in respect of which the United Nations had a special ability to act. The areas highlighted by the Secretary-General in his analytical report on the reform process (A/45/226) and by the Committee for Programme and Co-ordination at its thirtieth session were a framework within which the General Assembly should take measures at its current session to strengthen further the Organization's ability to deal constructively with such critical global problems as drug trafficking and pollution.

In the economic and social sectors, insufficient reform had taken place, at both the intergovernmental and the Secretariat levels. The comprehensive approach adopted by the Special Commission in 1988 had failed to produce the expected results. The rationalization of the agendas and working methods of the many economic and social bodies of the United Nations must be addressed with a view to developing a decision-making process more oriented towards practical solutions. The structures and methods established over the past forty-five years must be swept away. The restructuring of the Secretariat in the economic and social sectors should not depend on progress made at the intergovernmental level. His delegation hoped that, in the report to be submitted to the General Assembly on that topic, the Secretary-General would propose the significant changes required, because the existing Secretariat offices and departments, and many of the programmes they were implementing, were clearly ill-suited to the future tasks of the Organization.

The resolutions of the General Assembly and the actions taken by the Secretary-General in implementation of the recommendations of the Group of 18 concerning co-ordination, while significant, were only the initial steps of a multi-year effort towards the goal of achieving system-wide co-operation in planning, budgeting and implementation. His delegation was ready to work with other delegations in order to build on the accomplishments of the forty-fourth session and to develop the practical measures needed to strengthen co-ordination functions. Regarding evaluation, the existing mechanisms were ineffective because the necessary follow-up measures were seldom taken. Shortcomings in that area, which had to do with the maintenance of programmes of marginal interest and the lack of concerted action to simplify administrative procedures, had been amply documented by the auditors, the Joint Inspection Unit, internal evaluation units and ACABQ. It was now up to the Secretariat to exercise leadership and act on the recommendations of those bodies.

The Organization must adapt its structures and working methods to the changing needs of the world community, and the General Assembly must continue to give priority to reform efforts. In the area of staff retrenchment and reduction of high-level posts, in particular, the mandated reductions should be implemented fully. While care must, of course, be taken to avoid negative impact on programmes, a further effort must be made to achieve the objectives in recommendation 15 of the Group of 18, as recommended by CPC at its thirtieth session. His delegation had accepted two extensions of the deadline beyond 1989 in meeting the agreed staff reduction goals, and understood the arguments put forward by the Secretary-General in requesting a further extension, but regretted that no further proposals had been made at the current session. It therefore urged the Secretary-General to renew his commitment to identify and abolish unneeded posts, particularly high-level posts. Elimination of one Assistant Secretary-General post had been proposed; that left three more posts to be eliminated in order to meet the agreed goal, which in his delegation's opinion, was not impossible to achieve. At its forty-fifth session the General Assembly should approve the elimination of those additional high-level posts while providing the Secretary-General with the necessary flexibility regarding the modalities for implementing the decision.

The reform process begun in 1986 must be consolidated and preserved. His delegation therefore proposed that the Secretary-General should submit an annual report, in the context of the programme budget, providing an in-depth analysis of the measures taken by the Secretariat to improve staff efficiency, achieve economies and reorient programmes to meet the needs of Member States. Such a report would provide a clear and concise picture of the steps taken by the Secretary-General to implement the recommendations of the auditors, the Joint Inspection Unit and ACABQ, as well as a detailed description of proposals to complete the implementation of the recommendations of the Group of 18. That report would also include a section directed to Member States proposing the legislative action required for the further rationalization of programmes and operations.

Despite serious financial difficulties, the United Nations had been able to improve its image and capabilities greatly, but heightened public interest brought with it more intense scrutiny of the way in which it conducted its business. Like its Member States, the United Nations was faced with difficult choices, since its resources were limited while needs were growing. It must, however, be able to respond effectively to the many expectations of the international community. Continuing the reform process was one of the best ways to achieve that goal."

The representative of **Bulgaria**[11]

"The Secretariat had made commendable efforts to implement most of the recommendations of the Group of 18. The achievements of the Special Commission of the Economic and Social Council were also considerable, making possible a significant improvement in the work of the Organization in those fields. As it had been issued in April, the analytical report of the Secretary-General (A/45/226) did not reflect all that had been done in that regard. In the opinion of his delegation, reforms did not consist only in reducing unnecessary expenditure, but were also a means of strengthening the role of the United Nations. Tasks must be better distributed among the various bodies of the system, and priorities must be more clearly defined. The role of CPC should be enhanced so that it could guide and monitor the improvement of efficiency in all spheres of the work of the Organization. His delegation attached particular importance to joint meetings of CPC and ACC and believed that full implementation of recommendations 9 to 13 of the Group of 18 and of General Assembly resolution 44/194 would guarantee greater efficiency in the activities of the United Nations and its specialized agencies and would help to avoid duplication.

Care should be taken to ensure that financial restrictions had no negative impact on programmes already approved. The prevailing climate of mutual understanding should facilitate the elimination of many practices which resulted in waste (multitudes of nearly identical resolutions, numerous and lengthy communications from Governments issued as official United Nations documents, lengthy conferences and sessions of various bodies, specialized agencies and committees, meetings held at night and at the weekend, etc.).

His delegation placed great importance on the full implementation of recommendation 15 of the Group of 18. It welcomed the commendable efforts of the Secretariat, which had resulted in an 11.95 per cent reduction of staff. It believed, however, that the principle of equitable geographical distribution should be even more firmly applied in the appointment of staff, provided that, the Organization was not prevented from recruiting the highly qualified specialists it needed."

The representative of the **Bahamas**[12]

"concerted action was needed to accelerate change in those sectors in which progress had been inadequate, particularly the economic and social sector, which was of considerable importance since it accounted for over 80 per cent of the resources of the Organization. In the view of her delegation, the difficulties encountered in restructuring the United Nations could be attributed to the failure fully to implement resolution 32/197. She also recommended for consideration and appropriate action the recommendations of CPC on the report of the Joint Inspection Unit on the subject, particularly in order to ensure the full implementation of paragraph 2 of that resolution. What was required was the full utilization of existing machinery. Nevertheless, it was also necessary to re-examine any firmly entrenched positions which might be impeding necessary reforms.

Reform was an ongoing process which should be based on results already achieved. Those results should be consolidated. However, the major reduction in the staff of the Secretariat should not have a negative impact on programme delivery.

The new procedures instituted in the administrative and financial sectors appeared to be working well, since during the forty-fourth session the Fifth Committee had adopted all its resolutions without a vote. Similar progress should occur in the payment of contributions, so that the Organization's programme delivery would not be jeopardized by a weak financial position. In view of the tensions triggered by recent events and the *de facto* solidarity uniting all States, they, as well as the Secretariat, had the obligation to provide the United Nations with the means to function effectively."

The representative of **China**[13]

"Pointing out that the financial crisis and the increasing demands on the United Nations had made the reform process extremely difficult, he stressed that a sound financial base was a prerequisite for the normal functioning of the United Nations and for the success of the reforms.

His delegation agreed that, to the best of its ability, the Organization had fulfilled the mandate assigned to it. His delegation also agreed with the Secretary-General's assessment of the progress achieved with respect to restructuring in the political field, the reduction in posts and the improvement in budgetary procedures. In the current phase, it was vital to consolidate the achievements in those fields so that the United Nations could meet the challenges of the 1990s.

Progress, however, had been uneven and much remained to be done in certain fields. First of all, the United Nations should play a more important role in the economic and social sectors. Any reforms in that regard must aim at strengthening the role of the Economic and Social Council and be in strict conformity with the mandate of that organ. Moreover, the revitalization of the Economic and Social Council must proceed gradually and reflect the common desire of Member States.

With regard to the budgetary process, the outline of the programme budget did enable Member States to participate at an earlier stage in the process, but could hardly make a reliable projection of the overall level of resources required for the next biennium since the final level had to be approved by the Assembly at the same time as the budget. The problem required an immediate solution. The rate fixed for the contingency fund must also be subject to timely revision to take account of needs.

Despite the importance attached to priority-setting, no feasible methodology had yet been devised. The question, raised both by the Advisory Committee and by CPC, of the impact of extrabudgetary resources on programmes, especially priority programmes, also remained to be settled as a matter of urgency.

Although it was too soon to assess the effect of the measures concerning personnel, the Secretary-General had shown commendable realism in deciding not to reduce regular budget posts by 15 per cent, as had been called for in recommendation 15. It was regrettable, however, that he had failed to mention in his report the effect of post reduction on geographical distribution and that he had not drawn the appropriate conclusions from the figures given in paragraph 185 of his report with regard to the percentage of posts at the D-1 level and above held by nationals of developing countries, which showed a slight decline. It was to be hoped that he would take effective measures to redress that situation without delay.

Finally, the Secretary-General stated in paragraph 258 of his report that the reform had been carried out without serious negative effects on programmes.

He did not give any further details on that point, but, elsewhere, mentioned postponing outputs that could not be produced because the number of vacant posts had been higher than anticipated. In addition, the figures showed a declining trend in overall programme delivery rates since the 1984-1985 biennium. The matter warranted serious attention by the Secretariat and Member States.

The considerable resurgence of interest shown in the Organization by Member States was not so much the result of the reform undertaken as a sign of the international community's conviction that the United Nations could play a positive role in world affairs. The Organization could maintain its vitality only by continually improving the efficiency and effectiveness of its work. His delegation was prepared to join with other delegations in contributing to such an improvement."

The representative of **Morocco**[14]

"It noted that considerable progress had been made despite the financial crisis. The restructuring of the Secretariat had been successfully completed in respect of political affairs, administration and information, and it was to be hoped that the improvement in the international climate would help to revitalize the system in the economic and social sectors.

With regard to post reductions, his delegation considered that any further reduction might have a negative impact on programme implementation and the structure of the Secretariat. Noting the contradiction between the Secretary-General's comment that the programmes had, on the whole, been implemented and the fact that the rate of programme implementation had dropped from 82 per cent to 74 per cent since the 1984-1985 biennium, his delegation agreed with CPC that the indices contained in the report of the Secretary-General did not lend themselves easily to an overall assessment of the real impact of recommendation 15 on programmes. It hoped that the activities provided for in the programme budget for the current biennium would not be affected by the implementation of that recommendation.

His delegation further stressed the need to display the utmost flexibility in implementing the new budgetary process, given the numerous methodological problems which remained to be solved and, while agreeing on the importance of consensus, pointed out that the decision-making process was still governed by the relevant provisions of the Charter and the rules of procedure of the General Assembly.

If the administrative and financial reform was to have a lasting effect, the United Nations must continually adjust to developments in the international situation and put an end to the financial uncertainties affecting the functioning of the Organization. In order to enable it to discharge its growing responsibilities with regard to peace-keeping and development effectively, all Member States must pay their contributions punctually and in full."

The representative of **Kenya**[15]

"despite universal and repeated reaffirmations of the crucial role of the Organization, some of the Member States which had been most insistent in their calls for reform had yet to meet their financial obligations. The result was that, at a time when the Organization was called upon to perform many new tasks, it was still threatened by bankruptcy. Moreover, at the same time as the United Nations was being urged to expand its activities in certain fields, demands were still being made for further across-the-board reductions in its resources, without any regard for the difficulties already encountered in some services.

Her delegation agreed that the Organization had fulfilled its mandate to the best of its abilities, but it believed that it should now proceed with caution and endeavour to consolidate the results achieved. It could be seen that the implementation of recommendation 15 had resulted in a reduction in the rate of programme implementation. The Organization's capacity had been stretched to its maximum limits, it did not have the means to carry out the new tasks entrusted to it and, in order to avoid jeopardizing certain programmes, had to resort to posts funded from extrabudgetary resources. Her delegation was therefore opposed to any further post reductions and fully endorsed the CPC recommendation that the relationship between posts and programmes funded from the regular budget and those funded from extrabudgetary resources required further analysis.

Her delegation was disappointed by the poor results achieved regarding the representation of nationals from developing countries in the higher levels, and urged the Secretary-General to intensify his efforts in that regard. In that connection, it regretted that he had not provided more information on the implementation of recommendation 55.

With regard to the new budgetary process, while welcoming the willingness of all delegations to reach a consensus, she did not believe that consensus was an absolute necessity and reaffirmed that the decision-making process was governed by the provisions of the Charter and the rules of procedure of the General Assembly. No State, when it deemed an issue to be important to itself or to its region, could be prevented from seeking majority decisions. Resolution 41/213 had indeed been adopted on that understanding."

The representative of **Romania**[16]

"it emerged from the analytical report of the Secretary-General that the programme of administrative reform initiated in 1986 had been largely implemented. That augured well for the Organization's ability to evolve in an ever-changing world.

During the past four years, remarkable progress had been made in improving co-ordination, particularly in the area of operational activities. Resolution 44/211 laid down a number of basic principles in that regard. Much remained to be done, however, to improve co-ordination in other sectors, and his delegation was therefore satisfied with the conclusions and recommendations adopted at the recent joint meetings of CPC and ACC on that issue.

The simplification of the organizational structure of the Secretariat had mainly affected the political, administrative and information sectors. The restructuring of the economic and social sectors was still pending. As the chief administrative officer of the Organization, the Secretary-General was undeniably entitled to take certain decisions in that regard without awaiting the restructuring of the intergovernmental machinery; if necessary, he could anticipate such restructuring. The proposed medium-term plan, particularly the approved priorities, could serve as a guide to him in carrying out that task. It went without saying that any decision should be taken in consultation with Member States.

As regards the implementation of recommendation 15, he noted that considerable efforts had been made to achieve a 12 per cent reduction in the number of regular budget posts. While agreeing with the Secretary-General that, on the whole, the reductions had not made a negative impact on mandated programmes, his delegation failed to see the connection between the implemented reduction and the Organization's capacity to produce new outputs (para. 79 of document A/45/226). The number of outputs added during the biennium might be an indicator of the Organization's adaptability, but a lower rate of newly added outputs would prove a better level of planning. His delegation did agree that, as stated in paragraph 80 (c), the reduction had stretched the capacity of "some parts" of the Secretariat, a formulation which suggested that there were other parts of the Secretariat whose capacities could be stretched too. That was not, however, a call for further staff reductions; on that point, the Rumanian delegation shared the Secretary-General's cautious approach. The staff reductions was not an end in itself, but only one possible option in the general effort to increase the Organization's efficiency. When contemplating any option, it was important to inquire whether it was commensurate with the volume of outputs which the Organization was required to produce."

The representative of **Chile**[17]

"any reform should be so designed as to strengthen its efficiency and enable it to perform a greater number of activities with the limited resources at its disposal. With that end in view, it was essential to keep a close watch on the operation of newly established bodies and to make sure that existing ones were still of use. That had been the objective of the work of the Group of 18, and due vigilance was called for in all the areas to which the Group's report drew attention. However, the purpose of the exercise would not be served by instilling a sense of permanent instability in the Organization's officials.

So far as the implementation of the Group's recommendations was concerned, considerable progress had been achieved with regard to recommendations 1 to 4. The reduction in the number of plenaries held by the General Assembly despite the increased number of agenda items suggested that conference services had been better utilized. On the other hand, the reasons for the drop in the rate of delivery of programmed outputs needed to be closely looked into. It was to be hoped that the decline was not an indirect consequence of the reform process.

With regard to recommendation 5 relating to the construction and maintenance of conference facilities, his delegation agreed with the Secretary-General that necessary work should be carried out in good time so as to prevent facilities falling into disrepair. Seen from that angle, a sound maintenance programme was not a superfluous item of expenditure because it led to savings in the long run.

With regard to staff reductions, the analytical report of the Secretary-General did not make it clear whether or not a net reduction had been achieved; while the number of regular budget posts had diminished, that of posts funded by extrabudgetary resources had risen. The figures supplied might give rise to confusion, and the Secretariat should furnish more precise information on developments with regard to all posts, including those funded by extrabudgetary resources, since the beginning of the reform.

Three years after the reforms had begun to be introduced, the Organization was no longer the same. It had achieved greater flexibility and had proved capable of adapting to developments in the world situation while causing the attitudes of Member States towards it to change. That its efficiency had been strengthened was indisputable. What was needed today was to consolidate those gains so that the United Nations might continue to play a leading role on the international scene."

The representative of the **Philippines**[18]

"In its recommendation 15, the Group of 18 had called for a reduction by 15 per cent of regular budget posts; a reduction of 12 per cent having now been achieved, his delegation would be interested to know the timetable for achieving the 3 per cent reduction still outstanding. It was essential to maintain the efficient delivery service of the Department of Conference Services, and his delegation hoped that any further post reduction would not prejudice that Department's very satisfactory performance. Continuity of staff levels and programme continuity were essential to the efficient functioning of the Organization. The fact that, despite difficulties, there had been no negative impact on mandated programmes proved that the creation of posts was not the only means of meeting the growing volume of the Organization's tasks.

The administrative efficiency of peace-keeping activities called for priority attention. Special training should be given to staff participating in those operations. In view of recruitment difficulties, the Secretariat might envisage offering some incentives within existing sources. Assistance to disaster-affected countries was another activity in which efficient delivery service depended on the quality and training of staff. It was to be regretted in that connection that the United Nations devoted only 0.46 per cent of its budget to training - a small percentage indeed compared with other agencies. In view of the steadily increasing volume and urgency of the world-wide refugee problem, attention should also be given to the efficiency of the activities of UNHCR.

The improved world political climate meant that in the reform process the Secretary-General could now focus his attention on economic and social activities. The Economic and Social Council, the intergovernmental body most prominent in those activities, should assert its role by recommending appropriate measures that took into account the requirements of Member States. So far as Secretariat units were concerned, the departments concerned, and in particular the Department of Technical Co-operation for Development, should be in the forefront of responsibility. The regional economic commissions should also play a greater role in the economic advancement of countries within their respective regions.

With regard to public information, his delegation took the view that all United Nations activities in that field should be placed under the aegis of the Department of Public Information. Such a step was not only desirable for reasons of economy but would also avoid duplication of activities in separate United Nations information offices.

As the integration of the medium-term plan, the programme budget and the monitoring and evaluation system recommended by the Group of 18 had not yet been achieved, information on progress achieved in that field might be included in a report to be considered, say, at the same time as the draft programme budget for the biennium 1992-1993. In that connection it was to be noted that the trend towards consensus adoption of decisions on budgetary matters should hasten agreement concerning the programme budget's level and contents.

With regard to financial and budgetary procedures, the bodies in charge of budgetary control - the Joint Inspection Unit, the Advisory Committee and the Board of Auditors - had submitted comments and recommendations which would help to strengthen the Organization's efficiency in those fields. It was to be hoped that the Secretariat would study those suggestions with care. His delegation also considered that the application of uniform accounting procedures throughout the system would facilitate the consideration of the financial reports of different agencies, while the use of standardized budgeting techniques would be helpful to decisions on budgetary matters. The financial rules and regulations should be more adaptive to the development of the budgetary process.

A new era had dawned for the United Nations, but the Organization could not be expected to rise to greater heights if its coffers were bare. In order to fulfil its political mandate and extend its humanitarian and economic assistance throughout the world, it had to enjoy financial stability."

The representative of **Canada**, speaking also on behalf of **Australia** and **New Zealand**[19]

"Like any Member State, the Organization was expected to undertake an ambitious programme of work and at the same time keep costs within reasonable limits. To that end, the reform of the Organization should do more than just implement the recommendations of the Group of High-level Intergovernmental Experts (Group of 18) aimed at improving the information systems in the Secretariat, using the medium-term plan to improve system resource allocation, and integrating programme budgets fully into the medium-term plan.

Considerable progress had been made in implementing many of the recommendations of the Group of 18, but the process that had been set in motion was not yet complete. In that connection and in connection with the development of the medium-term plan, the Secretariat had stated that it lacked the information necessary to implement the recommendations.   Such an admission was a clear indication that high priority should be given to developing appropriate management systems, a point on which the Board of Auditors and the Joint Inspection Unit (JIU) had already made some interesting suggestions.   It would be useful to the Fifth Committee if the Secretariat could keep it up to date on the implementation of the recommendations of those two bodies.   More vigorous evaluation would also help to improve programme delivery and would make it much easier to establish realistic priorities.   Much remained to be done in the area of co-ordination, both within the Secretariat and among the agencies.   The development of common terminology and common reporting systems, as recommended by the JIU and the Board of Auditors, would help the Secretary-General to administer mandated programmes more effectively.   With respect to personnel, the Secretariat did not currently appear to be in a position to make the best use of available resources.   To rectify that situation, the administrative structure of the Organization should be simplified, and responsibilities should be more clearly defined.

According to the Secretary-General, numerous difficulties had been encountered in programming and co-ordination in the economic and social fields.   Those difficulties, which might be due in large measure to an unwillingness among Member States to come to grips with some of the issues, should not prevent the Secretariat from trying to improve co-ordination among the divisions of the Secretariat operating programmes in those fields. Improved management practices and administrative structures could be put in place immediately and would enable the Secretariat to be prepared for the day when Member States could agree on the revitalization of the Economic and Social Council. He did not want what he hoped would be viewed as constructive criticism to detract from the great accomplishment of the Secretary-General in implementing most of the recommendations of the Group of 18 under adverse and uncertain financial conditions. It would be an error to stop the process now."

The representative of **Togo**[20]

"he was pleased to note that, in the space of three years, the administrative and budgetary reform process had produced significant results: the restructuring of services of the General Assembly, the Economic and Social Council and the Secretariat; the introduction of technological innovations to modernize the Organization's administrative and financial management; the adoption by subsidiary organs of biennial cycles in order to improve efficiency and cut expenditures; the measures taken by the Committee on Conferences to improve the utilization of conference services, for which the utilization factor now exceeded 70 per cent; the reduction in the number of meetings involving additional costs; the application of the principle that bodies should meet at their respective headquarters; the decrease in travel expense reimbursements to Member States; the exercise of restraint by Member States in their requests for the circulation of communications as official documents; and so on. Those results were, however, insufficient and should be expanded.

With respect to the implementation of recommendation 15 of the Group of 18, the programme budget for the biennium 1990-1991 showed a reduction of 1,365 regular budget-funded posts in comparison with the previous biennium, or a reduction of 11.95 per cent over three years. With regard to that recommendation, however, it should be remembered that the General Assembly had requested the Secretary-General to avoid any negative impact on programmes and on the structure and composition of the Secretariat. It was also necessary to take into account the consequences of the Organization's increased membership, the end of the cold war and the emergence of a new climate of understanding and co-operation, as well as the adjustments that would have to be made in the economic, social, peace-keeping and disarmament programmes as a result of those upheavals.

While the Special Commission of the Economic and Social Council on the In-depth Study of the United Nations Intergovernmental Structure and Functions in the Economic and Social Fields established to carry out a study of the intergovernmental machinery in those fields had not been able to submit a report that could be adopted by consensus, its work did have the merit of demonstrating that all the Member States wanted to see the efficiency of the United Nations improved in those fields; that the revitalization of the Economic and Social Council should take into account the legitimate and vital interests of all States and groups of States, while scrupulously respecting the purposes and principles of the Charter; and that revitalization should be aimed at creating ways of stimulating international economic co-operation, thereby ensuring economic and social progress in the developing countries. ...

In view of the absolute necessity of putting scientific and technological progress to work to modernize the management of the Organization, special attention should be given to its data collection, processing and transmitting and global network capacities; the periodic evaluation of the results of technological innovations; the training or retraining of the staff concerned in the use of modern management techniques; and the development of a global strategy for the introduction and use of technological innovations in the future. With respect to the United Nations system as a whole, efforts to harmonize budgeting practices among the different organizations, in accordance with recommendation 13 of the Group of 18, should continue, as JIU and ACABQ had recommended."

The representative of **Mexico**[21]

"regretted that, in his report, the Secretary-General had concentrated more on describing the measures taken to give effect to the recommendations of the Group of 18 than on analyzing their impact on the effectiveness of the Organization. Given their heterogeneous character, it was to be expected that the recommendations would not all be dealt with in the same detail, but the information on the implementation of some of the most important was too brief for one to be able to determine the impact of the reforms. It would appear that some of the recommendations had not received the desired attention, in particular recommendations 47, 54 and 55 relating to personnel. It would be noted, for example, that the number of high-level posts occupied by nationals of developing countries had decreased since 1986. It was to be hoped that steps would be taken to remedy that situation.

It was appropriate that, at a time when the results of the reform process were being evaluated, the Secretary-General should recall that the enhancement of the administrative and financial functioning of the United Nations was not an end in itself but a means of enabling the Organization to attain its objectives. In paragraph 258 of his report, the Secretary-General stated that the process had largely achieved its purpose, in that the Organization's overall effectiveness had been enhanced. There was no doubt that several mechanisms and procedures had been improved. The reforms had allowed Member States and the Secretariat to be more aware of the way in which the United Nations spent its resources. In the Fifth Committee, the changed climate was reflected in the fact that all resolutions had been adopted by consensus. In that connection, his delegation wished to emphasize that development, although welcome, could not be interpreted as a renunciation of the inalienable right of Member States to vote on draft decisions.

Given the absence of sufficiently detailed information, it was difficult to reach any decision on the cost-benefit ratio of the measures taken. The Secretary-General had indeed said that their implementation had not had a negative impact on programme delivery, but the figures provided showed that the delivery rate had declined since 1986. Given those contradictory indications, it was essential that the impact of the reforms on programme delivery should be followed closely so that the necessary corrective measures could be taken in time.

As the Secretary-General had pointed out, the reform process implied a constant review of the functioning of the Organization. The administrative reorganization measures should now be followed by measures to strengthen the economic and social sector, so that the Organization could be as active in that field as it was in the maintenance of peace and security. To that end, all Member States must demonstrate a greater will to co-operate. It was essential that they should respect the democratic principles of the Organization and, in particular, discharge their financial obligations in full and on time."

The representative of **Trinidad and Tobago**[22]

"it was difficult to determine whether the tasks set by the Group of 18 had been successfully completed because its recommendations included general proposals as well as detailed administrative instructions and, in many cases, had not been predicated on research or scientific findings. The Secretary-General was right to consider that much had been done since 1986 and that what was now required was to consolidate what had been accomplished and move forward. However, the reforms initiated so far must be given time to work, particularly in the planning and budgetary area.

The Group of 18 had set the Secretary-General the target of reducing regular budget and high-level posts by 15 and 25 per cent respectively. Those targets had not been achieved, but it was important to recall that the Secretary-General had also been requested to avoid any negative impact on programmes or on the composition of the Secretariat. There was a functional relationship between the necessary level of staff resources and the volume of programmes and activities to be implemented; care must therefore be taken to see that the capability of the Organization was not impaired at a time when it was continually being requested to undertake new tasks. The Secretary-General stated that a negative impact on programmes and activities had on the whole been avoided, but that statement, although it might be true, was not conclusively proved in his analytical report, which indicated, for example, that a number of outputs had been eliminated. It also emerged from the report on the programme performance of the United Nations that programme delivery rates had declined from 82 per cent in 1984-1985 to 74 per cent in 1988-1989, although that was only a quantitative analysis and did not attempt to assess the quality and relevance of the outputs. Lastly, the increased use of extra-budgetary resources during the period under review had masked the negative effects of post reductions. He was not opposed to the use of extrabudgetary resources, but they should not be programmed in the same manner as regular budget resources, or their use might seriously disrupt the planning and budgetary process.

The Special Commission established to study the reform of the economic and social sectors had been unable to arrive at agreed conclusions and recommendations. It was essential that Member States and the Secretariat should bring that work to a conclusion. That would require a less piecemeal approach and a courageous re-examination of positions on the matter. A major achievement of the reform process was the light it had thrown on the willingness of Member States to work together with the Secretary-General; in-depth consultations should continue, thus giving concrete manifestation to the sovereign equality of all Member States.

Some progress had been made with regard to co-ordination. The joint meetings of the Administrative Committee on Co-ordination (ACC) and CPC were evolving into an extremely useful mechanism for fostering co-ordination within the system. The annual report of ACC would help to promote greater understanding of the potential of the United Nations. Effective co-ordination, however, required a "culture of co-ordination" and a locus of authority within the system responsible for that activity. The Secretary-General, as Chairman of ACC, and the Director-General for Development and International Economic Co-operation should undertake that task. Evaluation was still not accepted as a management tool and was not utilized in accordance with the Regulations and Rules Governing Programme Planning. Self-evaluation and in-depth evaluation should therefore be more extensively used, and the intergovernmental bodies should devote sufficient time to the substantive consideration of reports on such evaluations.

The United Nations must be allowed to consolidate its position in order to move confidently into the 1990s and beyond. Member States must allow the reforms already instituted to take root. Above all, the Organization must be supported with adequate financial resources for it to play the enhanced role requested by Member States."

The representative of **Ghana**[23]

"referring to recommendations 1 to 13 of the Group of 18, said he had noted with some concern that, instead of decreasing, the number of items on the Organizations's agenda and the number of resolutions adopted had increased, and that efforts to implement recommendation 8 on the intergovernmental structure in the economic and social fields had proved inconclusive. While it was true that the implementation of those recommendations rested primarily with Member States, the Secretariat had a not inconsiderable part to play, for example by advising Member States on the possibility of eliminating duplication in agenda items. With regard to recommendation 5, he pointed out that delays in implementing approved projects, specifically construction projects, was as much a reflection on efficiency as the excessive utilization of resources for a programme. With regard to recommendation 6, the Secretary-General's report indicated that the number of claims for delegation travel had decreased. Given the large number of empty seats at Committee meetings, there were grounds for wondering what were the real effects of the measures taken.

The failure of the initiatives taken to reform the intergovernmental machinery in the economic and social fields could be attributed primarily to the diverging views of Member States. Recent developments in the international political climate gave grounds for hope that they would finally agree on the need to secure peace through development.

It was the will of the General Assembly, as expressed in resolution 41/213, that the implementation of the Group's recommendations 14 to 40 concerning the structure of the Secretariat should not have a negative impact on programme implementation. In paragraph 80 of his report, the Secretary-General stated that programmes had not, on the whole, been negatively affected by the reorganization of the Secretariat. Nevertheless, according to paragraph 79, the rate of implementation had declined during the biennium 1988-1989 as compared with the two previous bienniums, whereas the rate of termination of programmed outputs had risen to 15 per cent. According to the Secretary-General, the latter figure suggested that more attention had been given to redressing the deficiencies of the programming process. The fact remained that the level of activities had decreased even though the number of staff had remained about the same.

It emerged from paragraph 77 that, on the basis of a 15 per cent staff turnover rate, the 12 per cent reduction in the number of authorized posts - and not in the number of posts filled - had not had any significant impact on the number of staff of the Organization. It might therefore legitimately be asked whether recommendation 15 had really been implemented, particularly since the reduction in regular budget posts had been largely offset by a significant increase (+33 per cent) in the number of posts funded by extra-budgetary resources. His delegation welcomed the measures taken to restructure the units dealing with political affairs, but encouraged the Secretary-General to take additional steps to eliminate duplication, improve co-ordination, and thereby enhance the productivity of the departments concerned.

A more comprehensive approach should have been taken to the implementation of the recommendations on personnel, and particular care should have been taken not to jeopardize career development. It was regrettable that the Secretary-General had failed to indicate the impact of the implementation of recommendations 43 and 44 on the geographical composition of the Secretariat, since equitable geographical representation was one of the cardinal principles of the Organization's personnel policy. For the same reason, the implementation of recommendation 47 must be pursued with greater vigour, since the number of high-level posts occupied by nationals of developing countries remained insufficient.

His delegation regretted that the General Assembly had not yet been able to find a comprehensive solution to the problem of additional expenditures, including those deriving from inflation and currency fluctuation, and requested the Advisory Committee to redouble its efforts to devise the most appropriate mechanism. In conclusion, it recalled that payment by Member States of their contributions to the Organization's budget in full and on time was decisive in determining the level of efficiency of the Organization."

The representative of **Bangladesh**[24]

"was pleased to note that the process initiated in 1986 had attained its objectives in many areas. If the reform, which was essentially a continuing process, was to be pursued, Member States must provide the Organization with the necessary political and financial support. The remarkable improvement in the global political climate and the additional responsibilities entrusted to the United Nations should encourage all Member States to play their part in putting an end to the Organization's financial crisis.

With regard to the recommendations of the Group of 18 on personnel, his delegation noted with satisfaction that the proportion of women had increased, particularly at the higher levels. Further efforts must be made, however, to recruit more women from developing countries and, in general, to increase the number of nationals of those countries in senior-level posts. He was pleased to note that the Secretary-General stated that he had implemented recommendation 15 in a pragmatic manner, with flexibility, in order to avoid any negative impact on programmes, and that the programmes that were part of the programme budget for the current biennium would not be negatively affected by the post reduction (12 per cent) carried out between 1987 and 1989. Clarification from the Secretariat would be useful on that point, however, given the fact that the rate of implementation of programmes had decreased during the preceding biennium, as compared with the two previous bienniums, and that the Secretariat itself stated that "the capacity of the Organization to expand its programmes and produce new outputs, while retained, was, nevertheless, reduced" (para. 79). Any further initiative should aim to increase the capacity of the Organization to play a greater role in a changing world.

In the economic and social fields, the implementation of the recommendations of the Group of 18 had not been so easy on account of the divergent views of Member States. Despite some progress, much remained to be done. For instance, programming and co-ordination of activities must be improved, a proper balance must be maintained between operational activities funded by extrabudgetary resources and mandated programmes, and the interrelationship between research and policy analysis and operational activities must be further studied. Reform in a sector that was so important for developing countries could not be dealt with in a piecemeal manner.

A welcome development was the confidence-building between the Member States and the Secretariat in the administrative and financial areas. The adoption without a vote of resolutions concerning those questions at the forty-fourth session of the General Assembly had been encouraging. It was also to be hoped that the reform of the budgetary process would result in a better utilization of available resources."

The representative of **Argentina**[25]

"not all the recommendations of the Group of 18 had been dealt with in the same manner and regretted that the report of the Secretary-General did not furnish a reply to the many questions that might be asked about the reasons why individual recommendations had not been implemented, or not fully implemented, about the difficulties encountered, the solutions envisaged, and so on.

Despite the reforms carried out and the efforts made by most Member States, the financial situation of the Organization remained precarious. His delegation recalled that every Member State was required by the Charter to participate in the financing of the approved budget and could not shirk that obligation under any pretext, especially not for political reasons. Despite a particularly difficult economic situation, Argentina, for its part, was sparing no effort to meet its commitments.

The work of the Special Commission of the Economic and Social Council and the Council's resolution 1988/77 were two important contributions to the process of reform of the intergovernmental machinery in the economic and social sector. Progress had been made on such matters as the adoption of a biennial cycle by the subsidiary organs, the streamlining of the calendar of meetings and the elimination of duplication, but the work in that area was far from finished and efforts must be continued.

With regard to the recommendations of the Group of 18 on personnel, the Organization must adopt a clear and coherent personnel policy and display the necessary flexibility so as not to jeopardize programme implementation. It must recruit staff with the highest standards of efficiency, competence and integrity, with due regard to equitable geographical distribution.

The new budget process established pursuant to General Assembly resolution 41/213 enabled Member States to participate more actively in the formulation of the medium-term plan, the budget outline and the programme budget, and to reach a consensus, respecting the principle of the sovereign equality of all States in accordance with the Charter. In that connection, his delegation stressed that, while it favoured the adoption of resolutions by consensus, the practice did not represent any kind of obligation and Member States were always entitled to request that a decision should be put to a vote.

As the Secretary-General had remarked, the achievements of the reform begun in 1986 must now be consolidated. He hoped that the recent successes in the political domain would have an impact in the economic and social sphere. The great merit of the Group of 18 would have been to instil an awareness, not only in Member States, but also in the Secretariat, of the need to make effective use of resources. That said, it should not be forgotten that the quest for efficiency did not necessarily mean the elimination of programmes, reductions in staffing tables or budgetary restrictions. Being efficient meant attaining established objectives, namely, in the case of the Organization, implementing approved programmes and outputs."

The representative of Norway, speaking on behalf of the five **Nordic countries**[26]

"the analytical report of the Secretary-General (A/45/226) marked an important milestone in work on the reform process. Now that streamlining of procedures and efficiency had become underlying concerns in all the Organization's deliberations, the perception of its efficiency had been enhanced. The Nordic countries were, in general, satisfied with the results of the reform process so far and agreed that the time had come to consolidate them. However, the process itself must continue in order for its achievements to be maintained. A consolidation of budgetary reforms did not mean that the regular budget had reached an appropriate permanent level. A zero real growth rate could not be an end itself. If new challenges appeared, the Organization must not be prevented from carrying out its tasks. Indeed, following the completion of the first full budgetary cycle since reforms were introduced, it was clear that the process remained in an experimental phase.

While the number of regular budget-funded posts had decreased by 1,365 as a result of recommendation 15 of the Group of High-level Intergovernmental Experts to Review the Efficiency of the Administrative and Financial Functioning of the United Nations (Group of 18), posts funded from extra-budgetary resources had increased by 637 since the beginning of the biennium 1988-1989. Such an increase could only partially be explained by the new demands placed on the Organization and illustrated the need for continued monitoring of extrabudgetary resources. In the context of post reductions, the Nordic countries were appreciative of the efforts made by the Secretariat during the often painful process of reform and streamlining. They hoped that the co-operative spirit marking relations between the Secretariat and Member States would continue. It was also worth recalling that, while much of the responsibility for better co-ordination, improved efficiency and the avoidance of duplication rested with the Secretariat, Member States, too, must take their share of the burden in implementing reforms.

A greater willingness to pursue reforms in the economic and social sectors, particularly with respect to the intergovernmental machinery, had been noted during recent informal discussions. The Nordic delegations looked forward to the relevant report of the Secretary-General, which they hoped would contain substantial proposals. They believed that conditions were now propitious for a debate on enhancing United Nations efficiency in the economic and social fields and hoped that such a debate would be pursued and broadened during the current session of the General Assembly.

The entire reform process remained heavily dependent on a rapid solution of the Organization's difficult financial situation. The Nordic States once again urged all Members of the Organization to pay their assessed contributions promptly and in full."

The representative of **Algeria**[27]

"although the Secretary-General's analytical report (A/45/226) was an improvement over previous reports on the subject, it did not analyze sufficiently how far the reform process had improved the functioning of the Organization and strengthened its capacities and means of action at a time of growing challenges. However, the report, and the conclusions and recommendations of the Committee for Programme and Co-ordination (CPC), would help the

Committee to assess the results achieved and determine those fields in which more effort needed to be made.

Thanks to the joint efforts and determination of Member States and the Secretariat, the reform of the Organization had, in general, been successfully completed. However, the recommendations of the Group of 18 had been implemented in a very unbalanced manner, and he wondered whether that was attributable to practical difficulties, or to a particular order of priority, or to the absence of real political will.

The most decisive achievements of the reform process had been a profound restructuring of Secretariat services, substantial post reductions, and the establishment of a new budget procedure. The Secretary-General had succeeded in reducing the number of regular budget posts by 12 per cent and the General Assembly had agreed that it would be difficult, if not impossible, to go beyond that without jeopardizing the Organization's capacity to carry out its increased tasks. It would have been desirable to include an analysis of the effects of those reductions on the acquired rights and career prospects of staff, on respect for the principle of equitable geographical distribution and on the implementation of the programmes and activities of the United Nations. In that connection, his delegation took note of the Secretary-General's assurance, in paragraph 81 of his report, that programmes that were part of the programme budget for the current biennium would not be negatively affected by the staff reductions.

The corner-stone of the reform process - the establishment of a new planning, programming and budgeting procedure - had been laid at the forty-fourth session of the General Assembly; the joint efforts of Member States and the Secretariat had resulted in an unprecedented consensus on all the questions before the Fifth Committee, including the adoption of the programme budget for the biennium 1990-1991. However, the uncertainties, questions and methodological problems that had emerged showed that the procedure was not perfect. The preliminary estimates and the level of growth of the programme budget had given rise to varying interpretations and approaches. The contingency fund for financing additional activities was still at an experimental stage. Moreover, although the search for consensus was desirable, it remained understood that only the relevant provisions of the Charter and the rules of procedure of the General Assembly could govern decision-making.

There had been a number of improvements in regard to co-ordination. The joint meetings of CPC and the Administrative Committee on Co-ordination

(ACC), and the annual report of ACC, were improving steadily. The efforts of Member States and the Secretariat should be directed towards making the best possible use of the existing mechanisms at the intergovernmental and inter-secretariat levels, as CPC recommended in paragraph 392 of its report (A/45/16 (Part I)).

Despite the acute developmental problems confronting many developing countries, the recommendations on the restructuring and revitalization of the intergovernmental system in the economic and social sectors had not been fully implemented. It was to be hoped that the improved political climate would help to build a consensus among Member States which would make it possible to provide the Organization with the structures and resources it needed for the effective discharge of its growing responsibilities in the priority area of economic and social development.

Personnel was another sensitive area in which resolution 41/213 had not been sufficiently implemented. Instead of increasing, the number of nationals of developing countries in senior posts had declined considerably as compared with 1986. Moreover, the recommendations calling for the strengthening of the capacity of the Office of Human Resources Management (OHRM), greater transparency with regard to promotion and appointment, a career development plan for all staff, and the periodic renewal of the leadership of departments and offices had still not been put into effect.

The restructuring of the Department of Public Information (DPI) had been carried out without taking certain mandates into account. The representation of developing countries in DPI, particularly at the senior levels, had not improved and the resources of the United Nations Information Centres remained as restricted as ever. With regard to the project to build conference facilities for the Economic Commission for Africa, the Secretary-General should take steps to ensure that the delay in starting the work did not affect the timetable agreed on by the General Assembly at its forty-third session.

As to whether the reform process, despite its inadequacies, had helped to make the United Nations function more effectively, he said that, while the confidence of States in the Organization and the political will to make better use of its potential seemed to have been renewed, the objective of strengthening its capacities and means of action had not yet been achieved. The United Nations was still undergoing a serious financial crisis because of the refusal of some Member States to pay their assessed contributions on time and in full. Its resources should be used to achieve common priority objectives. However, the selective financing of activities through the withholding of statutory contributions and the use of special trust funds, as well as the indirect effects of extrabudgetary funds, hampered and distorted the establishment of priorities. Moreover, the attempts to impose zero budget growth would not help the United Nations to carry out the mandates entrusted to it.

The implementation of resolution 41/213 was a continuing process that demanded flexibility. Greater efforts should be made to repair the shortcomings that had been noted and to complete the implementation of those recommendations which had not yet been fully implemented. Since they were linked to external factors, the Organization's recent successes in the field of international peace and security alone did not prove that its functioning had been improved. In the end, the United Nations would be judged on its capacity to assume effectively its many responsibilities with regard to the economic and social development of the developing countries."

The representative of the **Union of Soviet Socialist Republics**[28]

"a continuous and forward-looking process of administrative and budgetary reform was one means by which the United Nations could adapt to rapidly changing circumstances. The analytical report of the Secretary-General provided a detailed picture of progress made in that area. Overall, the results of efforts to implement the recommendations of the Group of 18 had been positive but modest, and reform should not be limited only to the areas covered by those recommendations.

The area in which least had been achieved was the rationalization of intergovernmental machinery, particularly in the social and economic fields. Neither had much headway been made in the restructuring of the Secretariat departments dealing with social and economic matters. His delegation urged the Secretary-General to follow up the initial accomplishments mentioned in his analytical report. It also urged him to ensure that the staff reductions envisaged under recommendation 15 of the Group of 18 were fully implemented, making use, *inter alia*, of the redeployment of staff among programmes. There was a need to develop a lean and efficient executive machinery adequate to the tasks facing the Organization; that implied the termination of obsolete programmes and the avoidance of duplication and parallelism.

Although some reforms had been achieved in the political area, the unprecedented growth of United Nations involvement in peace-making and peace-keeping operations and use of the good offices of the Secretary-General made it necessary to take a critical look at the existing structures of the departments concerned and to carry out a substantial and possibly radical overhaul.

The two initial objectives of the new budget procedure had been to create an effective mechanism by which to limit the Organization's expenses and, at the same time, to ensure that Member States played a decisive role in determining an acceptable level of spending at the earliest stage of the budgeting process. Following the completion of the first experimental budget cycle, his delegation was disappointed to observe that those objectives had not been achieved. The resumed session of CPC had apparently failed to give a clear answer to the crucial question as to whether the outline of the new budget provided for any real growth by comparison with the current one. The record so far inspired little optimism as to any substantial limitation of the Organization's expenditure. The question therefore merited serious consideration in the course of the Fifth Committee's deliberations.

It could not be denied, however, that there was a new atmosphere of trust and consensus in the Committee. The lessons learned from implementation of the new budget procedure should now be applied throughout the United Nations system. In that context, there was a need further to improve co-ordination in the United Nations system in order to avoid the overlapping of programmes. The frank discussion of that issue in the joint meetings held by CPC and ACC had indicated that there was a growing awareness of the need for such co-ordination in order to draw the maximum benefits from the system's existing material and intellectual resources. The discussion had seen a reaffirmation of the need to strengthen the role of the Secretary-General as Chairman of ACC, to enhance the central co-ordinating role of the General Assembly and to upgrade the importance of the annual overview reports of ACC, which, in the view of his delegation, should become a key instrument of co-ordination in the United Nations system. There was a need for specific measures in that regard, which could yield prompt and tangible results. A particular area which might be addressed immediately was that of the administrative and budgetary aspects of co-ordination, which should concentrate in particular on the activities of the Advisory Committee on Administrative and Budgetary Questions (ACABQ), with a view to ensuring full implementation of the provisions of Article 17, paragraph 3, of the Charter.

The drastic changes in the international situation called for fresh and unorthodox approaches. Consideration might perhaps be given to some of the recent unconventional suggestions on ways of improving the Organization's effectiveness. What was needed was not just an ability to deal with present realities but a capacity to cope with situations which might arise in the future. The long and continuous process of reform was really only just beginning."

The representative of **Uganda**[29]

"the Secretary-General's analytical report (A/45/226) had been intended to provide a comprehensive and objective assessment of the way in which the reform process had enhanced the financial and administrative efficiency of the Organization. It had been hoped that it would show clearly which reforms had been fully implemented, which had been partially implemented and which had not been implemented at all, and in the latter two cases the reasons why. In his delegation's view, the report failed to bring out the full impact, negative or positive, and provided no clear reasons for the partial implementation of certain recommendations or the failure to implement others. Detailed explanations from programme managers would have helped the Fifth Committee to hold an informed discussion that would have paved the way for appropriate remedial action.

With regard to the impact of the implementation of the recommendations on conference-servicing, he reaffirmed the views put forward by his delegation during the consideration of the item on pattern of conferences. The current session of the General Assembly and other intergovernmental meetings continued to be hampered by the delays in the issuance of documents. He doubted whether the Department of Conference Services (DCS) was any more efficient than when resolution 41/213 had been adopted. He sympathized with the Department's predicament and recognized that many of the factors that had brought about that unfortunate situation were beyond its control. Member States and the Secretariat shared the responsibility, but that did not mean that the Committee should shy away from assessing the impact of resolution 41/213 on DCS.

His delegation welcomed the enhanced role assigned to the Committee on Conferences under resolution 43/222 B. The Committee had carried out its mandate successfully, but it should be careful not to stray into budgetary matters. However, that positive development had been frustrated, in particular, by the late issuance of documents, which had impaired the ability of various deliberative bodies to conduct meetings efficiently. A number of intergovernmental bodies were no longer provided with summary records; that made it increasingly difficult for them to refer to previous discussions and to ascertain what had led to the conclusions reached. The biennialization of meetings or agenda items had become a common feature and, while it might be necessary because of the financial crisis, his delegation could not accept the notion that the curtailment of documentation and the discontinuance of summary records made the conduct of business more efficient. The Committee on Conferences should keep those matters under continuous review in the light of the financial situation and should, as appropriate, formally recommend measures to repair that unfortunate situation.

His delegation recognized the delicate nature of the issue of the restructuring of the intergovernmental machinery and its intricate links with the restructuring of the economic and social sectors. It endorsed the conclusions and recommendations in paragraph 19 (d) of the CPC report (A/45/16 (Part I)) and in General Assembly resolutions 42/211, paragraph 7, and 43/213, paragraph 3. Those measures proposed by the Secretary-General that had administrative and budgetary or programme implications should, of course, first be reviewed by CPC and ACABQ, in accordance with their mandates.

With regard to co-ordination, his delegation welcomed the new spirit of dialogue among Member States and between Member States and the various secretariats of the United Nations system. It had been generally encouraged by the discussions on co-ordination at the most recent session of CPC and at the joint meetings between CPC and ACC. The dialogue should continue, with a view to identifying further obstacles to enhanced co-ordination and proposing measures to overcome them within the framework of the approved legislative mandates of various intergovernmental bodies. It was, however, important that the joint meetings should not be used to address issues and press for new mandates that should normally be the province of intergovernmental bodies. They should be a forum for a frank exchange of views in which organizations and agencies should be encouraged to participate freely. That would not be possible if the meetings were perceived solely as an occasion for criticism.

The implementation of the recommendation on post reductions remained a major issue. He noted that, although the Secretary-General stated, in paragraph 80 of his analytical report, that a negative impact on mandated programmes had, on the whole, been avoided, he also stated that the full effect would be felt in future. It was reasonable to conclude that neither Member States nor the Secretariat could assess precisely the full impact of the reform process. It was already very clear, however, that it had adversely affected the representation of developing countries. As paragraph 185 of the report clearly showed, the representation of developing countries at senior levels of the Secretariat had been reduced, and he noted that, in each senior category, the representation of developed countries had increased by a corresponding percentage. In resolution 44/200 A, the General Assembly had accepted the Secretary-General's view that it was not possible to propose further post reductions without an adverse impact on mandated programmes, a view that was reiterated in paragraph 82 of his analytical report. However, the Secretary-General seemed to be receiving conflicting signals regarding further post reductions and the creation of new high-level posts. The situation was further complicated by the fact that the mixed signals came from the quarters pressing hardest for post reductions. The only conclusion was that those countries wished the reductions to be carried out at the expense of the developing countries.

His delegation remained firm on the need to improve the structure and geographical composition of the Secretariat, a view shared by a large majority of delegations. He welcomed the reference by the representative of Australia, during the debate on agenda item 126 (a), to the undesirability of regarding high-level posts as the exclusive preserve of particular countries. When his own delegation had raised the matter in CPC, the picture that had emerged, of vacated posts being filled by persons from the same country as before, had not been encouraging.

He reaffirmed his delegation's commitment to the planning, programming and budgeting process adopted by the General Assembly in resolution 41/213 and welcomed the Secretary-General's efforts to involve Member States in the formulation of the medium-term plan and the programme budget through the process of consultation. It also agreed with the Secretary-General's view, in paragraph 235 of his report, that the obstacles to be overcome were extremely severe. Even at the level of the Main Committees of the General Assembly, there was little or no substantive discussion in order to evolve a common response to various chapters of the medium-term plan, or even to understand the import of statements of programme budget implications to be sent to the Fifth Committee for decision. As far as the medium-term plan was concerned, delegations were simply requested to submit written comments to the Committee Chairman and, without any further discussion, a compendium of views was prepared and submitted to the Fifth Committee with no clear recommendation from the Committee concerned. The Fifth Committee should make its requests to the other Committees more explicit, and the Secretariat should review the format and content of statements of programme budget implications in order to facilitate their consideration. His delegation concurred in the views expressed by ACABQ in that connection.

Commenting on the decision-making process, he said that, when the reforms had first been discussed, some Member States had been apprehensive about the voting procedure in budgetary matters and had even suggested that a weighted voting system should be introduced. The General Assembly had moved expeditiously to adopt resolution 41/213, which reaffirmed the provisions of the Charter, but the impression seemed to linger that resolution had amended the rules of procedure by introducing consensus as a way of making decisions on budgetary matters. That misrepresented both its letter and its spirit. His delegation was prepared to discuss the possible amendment of the General Assembly's rules of procedure and even of the Charter, but only as part of a broader package that would entail, among other things, a review of the privileges enjoyed by some Member States in the Security Council. Consensus was desirable but, rather than being an objective, it constituted a means of achieving the widest possible agreement during negotiations. His delegation had always worked to achieve consensus and had welcomed the adoption of the programme budget for 1990/1991 by consensus. Nevertheless, that decision did not derogate from the decision-making procedure outlined in the Charter and reaffirmed in resolution 41/213.

The United Nations had been preoccupied by reform and restructuring ever since 1986. As his delegation had stated at the thirtieth session of CPC, changes might be necessary. However, the Organization must spend more time focusing on the priority problems that faced the international community. The United Nations could not be efficient if it spent most of its time discussing itself and how it could improve, rather than the programmes it was supposed to implement."

The representative of **Pakistan**[30]

"his delegation concurred in the Secretary-General's assessment in his analytical report (A/45/226) that the United Nations had, to the best of its abilities, carried out the reforms mandated by the General Assembly. The purpose of the reform process should be to strengthen the Organization's ability to discharge its responsibilities under the Charter and the challenges currently facing the world. The United Nations must remain a dynamic organization. Reform was not a finite process, nor an end in itself but implied a constant review of the functioning of the United Nations in relation to its objectives. As to the Organization's capacity to attain those objectives, his delegation agreed with the Secretary-General that no organization could sustain a prolonged period of upheaval.

The difficulties of carrying out the reforms had been aggravated by continuing financial uncertainty. It should be borne in mind that an implicit objective of resolution 41/213 had been to restore the Organization's financial viability. Until that was achieved, the reforms could not be said to have been successful. Unfortunately, some of those delegations which continued to press for the full implementation of particular recommendations had yet to meet their financial obligations in full. At a time when so much was expected of the United Nations, his delegation earnestly hoped that situation would soon be corrected.

His delegation had other misgivings about the manner in which resolution 41/213 had been implemented. A reform process aimed at enhancing the Organization's performance had instead become a budget-cutting exercise which had undermined staff morale and adversely affected programme delivery. In the case of recommendation 3, for example, both the number of agenda items and of resolutions adopted had increased since the forty-first session of the General Assembly. As far as the rational distribution of agenda items among Main Committees was concerned, another Main Committee was also considering an issue relating to personnel. As to restraint in requesting reports, a proposal for a new report had actually been made during the consideration of the current item.

The wisdom of some of the recommendations of the Group of High-level Intergovernmental Experts had been called into question by ACC (recommendation 13) and ICSC (recommendations 53 and 61). Recommendation 24 had been that UNDP should consider the feasibility of taking over the functions of UNDRO, yet, by its resolution 41/201, the General Assembly had reaffirmed UNDRO's mandate. Recommendations 25, 26 and 33 had also not been found practicable. It was not clear how placing the functions of planning, programming, budgeting and monitoring in a single organizational unit, in response to recommendation 32, had benefited activities in the economic and social sectors. In that context, he recalled that many Member States had repeatedly stressed the importance of keeping substantive considerations in view when carrying out any restructuring exercise. The benefits if any, of the changes introduced, should be demonstrated by the Secretariat through a comparative analysis of the new and former procedures.

The General Assembly had made clear its position that the reform should not result in any negative impact on programmes. The Secretary-General had indicated that a negative impact on mandated programmes had been avoided, primarily because post reductions had fallen short of the mandated 15 per cent level at 11.95 per cent. The Secretary-General stated, in paragraph 81 of his analytical report, that programmes included in the current budget would not be negatively affected at that level of post reductions.

While 1,365 posts had been eliminated from the programme budget for the current biennium provision had been made for 2,549 posts to be funded from extrabudgetary resources. He wondered whether that figure should be interpreted as reflecting a 22 per cent increase in the number of posts actually required by the Organization to carry out its mandated activities. Reflecting its concern over that trend, CPC had called for further analysis of the relationship between posts and programmes funded from the regular budget and those funded from extrabudgetary resources. In paragraph 258 of his report the Secretary-General stated that the reforms had been carried out without serious negative effects on programmes. However, the suggestion that there had, in fact, been a negative impact was borne out by the programme performance report for 1988-1989, showing a decline in overall delivery rates from 82 per cent in 1984-1985 to 76 per cent in 1986-1987 and 74 per cent in 1988-1989. The fact that the post reductions had been effected arbitrarily, without regard to work-load analyses, might have contributed to that decline.

There was no analysis in the report of the effect of post reductions on equitable geographical distribution. Despite recommendation 47, the representation at senior levels of nationals from developing countries had declined during the biennium 1988-1989. The Secretary-General should be urged to redouble his efforts to correct that situation. Information on any changes that might have resulted from the implementation of recommendation 55 would be helpful.

Regarding reforms in the economic and social sectors, his delegation had taken note of the efforts to revitalize the Economic and Social Council, as reflected in its resolutions 1988/77 and 1989/114. The work of the United Nations in the economic and social fields was of special importance and his delegation looked forward to the Assembly's consideration of the Secretary-General's report on restructuring in those sectors, to be considered in the plenary Assembly under agenda item 121. Although that report would address the restructuring of the intergovernmental machinery and the Secretariat in the economic and social sectors, there were other areas of direct concern to the Fifth Committee, in particular the implementation of recommendation 32.

While the introduction of a budget outline had enabled Member States to participate in the formulation of the budget at an earlier stage, it had not proved a reliable indicator of the level of resources required for the next biennium. Whether the Contingency Fund could operate effectively, given the demand for new programmes, remained to be seen. The new budgetary procedure was still in the process of evolving and must be kept under review. His delegation recognized that the new procedures had in 1989 enabled the General Assembly for the first time, to adopt the programme budget by consensus. Nevertheless, he emphasized that those procedures did not preclude any Member from calling for a vote, in accordance with the understanding on which resolution 41/213 had been adopted.

The question of extrabudgetary resources remained a grey area. His delegation fully concurred in the view of ACABQ that those resources could have an impact not only on the work programme but on the ordering of priorities and that it was essential to define the role of extrabudgetary financing in the Organization's overall financial structure.

The restoration of the Organization's financial viability was increasingly important. Since 1986, the United Nations had assumed vast responsibilities for solving new problems of global significance. The Organization needed staff of the highest calibre and in sufficient numbers to carry out its new activities and the necessary financing had to be provided on a sound and assured basis. It was, therefore, unrealistic to insist that budgetary levels should remain unchanged."

The representative of **Japan**[31]

"the relaxation of tensions among major Powers had resulted in a more effective use of the United Nations, thus helping to revive the confidence of Member States in the Organization's ability to resolve international conflicts and global problems. In response to rising expectations, however, the United Nations now had to shoulder greater responsibilities. In the field of peace-keeping and peace-making, in particular, its activities had grown dramatically to a total of 11 missions in the field at the end of 1989, compared with 5 at the beginning of 1988.

The Organization had managed its increased work-load well, thereby enhancing its image. That improved performance, however, had been accompanied by an increase in its financial requirements which Member States had to meet. He noted that missions in the field had been provided with extensive human and financial resources and had recorded sizeable unencumbered budgetary balances at the end of their mandate. While his delegation recognized the difficulties of organizing peace-keeping operations, which were in large part "unprogrammable", it attached importance to the cost-effectiveness and efficiency of every programme and activity carried out by the Organization. It therefore attached great importance to the Secretary-General's commitment to maintaining administrative and financial effectiveness and efficiency. While cost-effectiveness and increased efficiency were not ends in themselves, they were essential means of strengthening the United Nations.

The Group of High-level Intergovernmental Experts had noted that over the years the increase in the number of posts had not been matched by an increase in the management capacity of the United Nations to maintain overall administrative efficiency, productivity and cost-effectiveness. That had been the fundamental problem to be resolved through the administrative reform envisaged in General Assembly resolution 41/213. Better management and redeployment were expected to create conditions whereby any increase in resources would result in greater output. The process had obviously heightened the consciousness of Member States and the Secretariat about the way in which the United Nations used its resources.

One of the major achievements of the reform was the new planning, programming and budgeting process. That process would help to ensure that priority-setting and the establishment of resource requirements in the medium-term plan and programme budget would result in the elimination of obsolete, marginally useful or ineffective activities. Implementation of the programme budget within the overall level of resources agreed upon would encourage the effective utilization and, eventually, the redeployment of available resources in accordance with priorities. Not only must there be a continued effort to adopt decisions on budgetary matters by genuine consensus, but much also remained to be done to consolidate the new budgetary process. A comprehensive solution must be found to the problem of additional expenditures, including those deriving from inflation, currency fluctuations and other add-ons not chargeable to the Contingency Fund. It was necessary to examine, in the light of past budget performance, the extent to which resources could be redeployed from low- to high-priority areas before the adequacy of the Contingency Fund was reviewed in 1991. The surplus indicated in the performance report for the biennium 1988-1989 was much larger than the $15 million Contingency Fund, which amounted to 0.75 per cent of total budget appropriation. For the biennium, there had been an uncommitted balance of $23.6 million, or 1.3 per cent of the total amount appropriated, and unliquidated obligations of $63.9 million, representing 3.7 per cent of actual expenditures for the biennium 1988-1989. When resources of that order were available, there was no basis for the fear that the new budgetary process might jeopardize the Organization's ability to fulfil its changing role and mandate.

The staff reductions effected so far had no negative impact on mandated programmes. The United Nations should continue to work to control any unnecessary expansion of its functions and budget, taking into account the staff reductions mandated by resolution 41/213. A positive indication of such restraint had been the reduction by nearly 50 per cent of the number of programme outputs added through legislative decision or at the initiative of the Secretariat over the past four years. The Secretary-General should also continue his efforts to reduce the number of high-level posts, in accordance with General Assembly resolution 44/201.

The Group of High-level Intergovernmental Experts had recommended that there should be further post reductions following the restructuring of the intergovernmental machinery and the Secretariat after the completion of the initial three-year period. In that connection, his delegation had three suggestions: first, a rational work-load standard should be established to prevent the impact of reductions from varying from department to department; second, the number of junior Professional staff should be increased and there should be recruitment from outside to ensure that not just the numbers of staff but also the staffing structure would be changed; third, there should be more transparency and coherence in personnel management, which should be based on objective methods and clear criteria for recruitment, evaluation and promotion. Serious attention should be paid to improving the quality of the staff, which was the Organization's most important asset.

Delays in restructuring the intergovernmental machinery and the Secretariat in the economic and social sectors had endangered major achievements in other areas, and reform in that area was long overdue. Functions must be revitalized so that it would be possible to respond better to the requirements of developing countries. His delegation welcomed the level of agreement reached in such organs as UNCTAD and the Economic Commission for Europe with regard to streamlining structures, reducing documentation and the number of meetings, and improving the organization of work by shortening agendas and streamlining calendars. It was also gratifying that four important United Nations bodies had decided on biennialization. Vigorous efforts to those ends should be made by all intergovernmental bodies of the United Nations. The Secretary-General should take the initiative in rationalizing the intergovernmental machinery necessary for each of the forthcoming major international conferences and meetings on such priority issues as the environment, the least developed countries, international debt and drugs, rather than awaiting the results of deliberations in those forums. The role of the Committee on Conferences should also be strengthened to help it to contribute to a better utilization of conference facilities and resources, not only of the United Nations but of the entire United Nations system. The Committee should also enforce strict observance of the established rules on the control and distribution of documentation and improve conference servicing by making use of recent technological innovations.

He emphasized the importance of strengthening the Administrative Committee on Co-ordination (ACC). The United Nations system was expected to play a major role in multilateral co-operation aimed at solving problems that were increasingly multidisciplinary and global in scope. It was essential, therefore, for the United Nations and the specialized agencies to develop a truly integrated approach to those problems. With enhanced co-ordination within the system, it would be possible to make better use of scarce resources and avoid waste and duplication. For that reason, his delegation believed that the time had come for CPC to consolidate and evaluate its own performance and establish a work programme designed to enhance and strengthen co-ordination within the United Nations system on the basis of input from ACC, particularly the prospective annual overview report. Under the direction of the General Assembly, the Committee for Programme and Co-ordination (CPC) was responsible for the process of reforming the United Nations and for system-wide co-ordination. If it took the steps suggested, it would contribute substantially to promoting the reform and increasing the efficiency and effectiveness both of the United Nations and the system as a whole."

The representative of **Cameroon**[32]

"supported the Secretary-General's adjustments to the structures of the Secretariat in the political and administrative areas and believed that conditions were now propitious for similar action in the economic and social sectors. Care should, however, be taken to avoid the hasty elimination of any organ and to promote the process of decentralization, in accordance with General Assembly resolution 32/197, in particular by strengthening the regional commissions. In that connection, his delegation was following closely the Secretary-General's endeavours to make the Economic Commission for Africa more effective, looked forward to the Fifth Committee's consideration of measures recommended by the Secretary-General to strengthen that Commission's administrative structure and was also awaiting the Secretary-General's report on the strengthening of the Commission's language services. The timetable drawn up by the General Assembly for construction work at the headquarters of the regional commissions in Addis Ababa and Bangkok should be scrupulously observed.

While reserving the right to revert to personnel questions at a later stage, his delegation wished to emphasize, in connection with recommendation 15 of the Group of High-level Intergovernmental Experts to Review the Efficiency of the Administrative and Financial Functioning of the United Nations (Group of 18), that staff reductions should be applied with flexibility in order to avoid any negative impact on programmes. Serious attention should also be devoted to the question of high-level posts, the representation of developing countries in such posts and the mandate of the Office for Human Resources Management (OHRM).

Member States must ensure that the Organization had sufficient resources to meet both its traditional and its new responsibilities. Although the new budget process was being applied in a generally satisfactory manner, his delegation fully agreed with CPC that the decision-making process must be governed by the provisions of the Charter and the rules of procedure of the General Assembly. The level of the contingency fund must also be adjusted to changing circumstances: given the new challenges faced by the Organization, that issue must receive fresh consideration at the forty-sixth session of the General Assembly. Meanwhile, extraordinary expenses, including those relating to fluctuations in rates of exchange and inflation, should continue to be treated in accordance with established procedures. There was a need to redefine what was constituted by unforeseen and extraordinary expenses.

The Secretary-General's generally positive assessment of the impact of General Assembly resolution 41/213 was to a large extent warranted. It was more or less possible to state that confidence had been restored in the Organization. Endeavours to restore the Organization's financial viability were as yet incomplete, further consideration being required of matters such as extrabudgetary resources, an equitable scale of assessments, the prompt and regular payment of contributions and management procedures. There had been considerable improvement in the system of programme planning, implementation and monitoring, although much remained to be done in the economic and social sectors. Reform, it must be remembered, was a continuous process: there was a need to consolidate progress already made, to find lasting solutions to existing deficiencies and to devise new instruments to enable the Organization to fulfil its vital tasks."

The representative of **Hungary**[33]

"every organization, particularly those with huge bureaucratic staffs, tended to favour the conservation of old structures rather than the introduction of new ones. In the case of the United Nations, everything possible must be done to create a flexible administrative structure which could respond rapidly to changes. The process of reform provided for under General Assembly resolution 41/213 must be kept in motion. Accordingly, the limited resources available to the United Nations must be focused on priority activities; outdated programmes should be abolished; and the corresponding administrative structures should be eliminated. In that connection, he proposed that the Secretary-General should, in the introduction to his budget proposals, give a brief description of reform measures taken or planned, together with suggestions for necessary legislative action."

The representative of **Colombia**[34]

"efficiency was a relative concept connected with the result obtained from the use of a given quantity of resources. A reduction of resources, for example a staff cut or a freeze on budget growth, was not in itself a sign of efficiency unless it could be demonstrated that an equal or greater product had been obtained. Several delegations had pointed out that the defective evaluation machinery still impeded an accurate determination as to whether the products obtained by the United Nations system were tending to increase or decline. In view of the new challenges facing the Organization, an absolute increase in resources would seem reasonable, but there were no reliable indicators of efficiency.

Another matter of crucial importance was a suitable policy for the selection of the Organization's managerial staff. Without prejudice to the usefulness and urgency of the structural reorganization, in the short term it was essential to carry out the recommendations approved by the General Assembly in its resolution 41/213 that objective technical criteria should be applied to personnel selection and that both the monopoly of posts by certain countries and the indefinite occupation of high-level posts should be avoided. Experience showed that the administrative efficiency of any team of workers depended largely on the abilities of its managers. In order to achieve excellence in that respect it was necessary to avoid placing the selected staff members under the pressure of the possibility of reappointment. The intellectual freedom which a prohibition on their reappointment would give to the most senior managerial staff, including staff in the specialized agencies, would substantially enhance their performance. That could mean modification of their terms of office and their mandatory separation from the system for a reasonable period once they had served their terms. Similar criteria could be applied to top-level officials, such as those at the Assistant Secretary-General and higher levels, whose appointment should be for a fixed term and non-renewable, in order to ensure a healthy renewal of the Organization's personnel.

The recent joint meeting of CPC and ACC had shown that a technical body was needed to evaluate the large number of proposals arising from resolution 41/213. Only thus would it be possible to submit to the General Assembly the proposals which were most viable and most consistent with the established goals. In order to carry out that task CPC might establish a group of experts, including as far as possible experts from non-governmental organizations and having specific terms of reference."

The representative of **Tunisia**[35]

"the analytical report of the Secretary-General on the implementation of General Assembly resolution 41/213 (A/45/226) contained very little analysis and no critical examination. It was therefore inconsistent with the recommendation made by the Committee for Programme and Co-ordination (CPC) in paragraph 28 of its report (A/44/16). Nevertheless, the information provided was interesting and topical and gave an impression of the resolution's impact on the functioning of the United Nations. The results were not those which had been expected. The figures provided in the report did not facilitate a precise and comprehensive evaluation of the real impact on programmes of recommendation 15 of the Group of 18, and it was questionable whether the reform process had improved the administrative and financial functioning of the Organization or strengthened its capacity.

Little progress had been made in the economic and social fields, which were areas of unquestionable priority. The time had come for Member States to show that the Organization really was the forum in which to solve all problems by means of dialogue and collective action and that it had outgrown the era of systematic refusals to carry out certain activities, particularly those relating to the mandate of the Economic and Social Council, as well as the era of the cold war and the sterile confrontation of different systems. The reform's success would be measured by the extent to which it was possible to develop and establish a fully comprehensible system of collective security, which must be achieved through economic and social development and the establishment of environmental priorities. Following the Organization's recent successes in peace-making activities and those relating to the independence of Namibia, the United Nations was in a better position than ever effectively to address development issues. Its objectives and activities must not be restricted as a result of deliberate limitations on resources. Zero-growth budgeting, which for some had become an end in itself, would not allow the Organization to meet its ever growing requirements, and his country opposed such an approach. The reduction of international tension should serve to convince the unwilling that the Organization must be given the financial security required to fulfil its mandates, meaning that Member States must pay their contributions on time.

The reform plan had not been entirely successful in the areas of personnel and programmes. Developing countries' representation had been declining constantly since 1986, particularly in high-level posts. Paragraph 83 of the Secretary-General's report clearly indicated the adverse effects on equitable geographical distribution of a reform process which must not be allowed to lead to a systematic elimination of posts, thus depriving the Organization of its staff. Much, moreover, remained to be done to make the reform of conference services effective. Post reductions and rationalization by means of a reform process with obvious limits would not make it possible to re-establish the effectiveness and capacity of those services. The budget process introduced under resolution 41/213 did not alter the provisions of Article 18 of the Charter; while it was convenient to reach a consensus, great care must be taken not to jeopardize the sovereign equality of States, which was one of the fundamental principles of the Organization."

The representative of **Cuba**[36]

"under recommendation 71 of the Group of 18, the report on the implementation of reform measures submitted in 1989 by the Secretary-General in document A/44/222 should have been his final report. That, however, had not been possible because the report was compiled before the end of the envisaged three-year period. Meanwhile, the analytical report now before the Committee (A/45/226) did not conform with the guidelines set out in paragraph 16 of General Assembly resolution 44/200. It was to be hoped that the Secretariat would, during the current session, provide the Committee with the information required to draw final conclusions on application of the recommendations.

The reform process was continuous in the sense that it required a whole series of measures to make the Organization more efficient. That did not mean it was necessary to continue applying the recommendations of the Group of 18, which had already run their course and whose implementation was being analyzed. It was now a matter of consolidating the progress achieved.

The strengthening of the Committee on Conferences was related to the new responsibilities which that body had assumed under recommendation 1 of the Group of 18. The current composition of the Committee more accurately reflected the geographical composition of the United Nations. Improving the composition of organs was a factor which should always be borne in mind, just as had been done in the report of the Secretary-General on the compendium of mandates of subsidiary administrative and budgetary bodies of the General

Assembly (A/45/370). It should, however, be noted, as was clear from the discussions on shortcomings in the area of publications, that full efficiency had not been achieved in conference services.

Nor had the objective set forth in recommendation 3 (d) of the Group of 18, concerning the distribution of General Assembly agenda items, been fully attained, because some committees were still considering items for which they were not directly responsible or because different committees were considering very similar items. In that context, the report on the intergovernmental structure of the United Nations and its functions in the economic and social fields to be submitted by the Secretary-General in accordance with resolution 44/103, which was to be considered in plenary meetings, should also be provided to the Fifth Committee as a reference document relating to the item under consideration. The reform process should be global and intersectoral, and it was difficult to understand why an attempt should be made to deal with a process of change in the economic and social sectors outside the framework of the Fifth Committee when that Committee was the body responsible for addressing administrative and budgetary problems and, therefore, for the analysis of those sectors' efficiency. She hoped that the Secretariat would give appropriate guidance to Member States with a view to avoiding the overlapping of functions and duplication of work.

Member States had always been concerned that the post reductions provided for under recommendation 15 of the Group of 18 should not have negative effects on programmes. In paragraph 258 of the analytical report, the Secretary-General indicated that such effects had been avoided, but not without pain. It was nevertheless a cause of concern that, as indicated in paragraph 6 of the report on programme performance (A/45/218), the overall rate of implementation for the biennium 1988-1989 had amounted to only 74 per cent. The Secretariat should inform the Committee how the reduction of permanent posts had affected the level of performance, bearing in mind the contents of paragraph 11 of that report. The Secretariat should also draw up a document comparing the level of programme performance in the three-year period 1987-1989 with performance during the period 1984-1986.

Although the number of regular budget posts had been reduced, those funded from extrabudgetary resources had increased, evoking doubts as to the real effects of recommendation 15 and highlighting the need for stricter control by the Assembly over extrabudgetary funds.

With regard to the emphasis on reduction of high-level posts called for in recommendation 15, at the forty-fourth session of the General Assembly there had been serious discussion about the reduction of posts of special importance to the developing countries, such as the Assistant Secretary-General post in the United Nations Conference on Trade and Development (UNCTAD) which was occupied by an official from the region of Latin America and the Caribbean. Lastly, paragraph 3 of section I of General Assembly resolution 44/201 B requested the Secretary-General to identify four additional high-level posts for reduction. It was therefore disheartening to read in the list of staff members contained in document ST/ADM/R.44 that, contrary to the General Assembly's instructions, there was a new Under-Secretary-General post at the United Nations Office at Geneva. The Secretariat ought to explain the situation.

With regard to the process for adoption of administrative and budgetary decisions, his delegation reaffirmed its comments made at the previous session concerning the fragility of consensus, which applied equally to the consideration of the proposed medium-term plan, i.e., that certain concepts, programmes or programme elements which were unacceptable or not included in the General Assembly's mandates should be rejected."

The representative of **Mongolia**[37]

"The analytical report of the Secretary-General indicated that considerable progress had been made in the political sector, in which many measures had been taken to strengthen the capacity of the Organization to deal with its primary responsibilities. Furthermore, a number of organs of the system had made laudable efforts to streamline their structures, check the proliferation of documentation, biennialize their sessions, rationalize their work programmes and improve the planning and organization of their meetings. Notable progress had also been made in reducing the staff of the Secretariat. It was worth noting that those many encouraging changes had been introduced despite the continuing financial crisis of the Organization. In that connection, a change was also necessary in the attitudes of the Member States, which must scrupulously honour their financial obligations to the world body.

The process of reform and restructuring should be extended to encompass other areas, in particular economic and social issues. His delegation agreed with other delegations that high priority should be accorded to the reform of the economic and social activities of the Organization. It was regrettable that, after two years of negotiations, the Special Commission established by the Economic and Social Council had failed to reach agreement. He was looking forward to the proposals which the Secretary-General would be submitting to the General Assembly at its current session, following several important meetings and deliberations that had taken place in that field in 1990.

With respect to personnel questions, geographical distribution remained unbalanced, and special attention should be given to the recruitment of nationals of unrepresented or severely underrepresented Member States. In that connection, his delegation shared the disappointment of the Ghanaian delegation regarding the inadequate representation of developing countries at senior levels in the Secretariat."

Following the debate, draft A/C.5/45/L.45 was approved by consensus in the Fifth Committee and subsequently in the Plenary Assembly as resolution entitled **Review of the Efficiency of the Administrative and Financial Functioning of the United Nations (45/254).** By resolution 45/254, the GA recognized the importance of the new budget process for enhancing the effectiveness of the organization; invited the Secretary-General to consolidate and build upon the achievements of the reform process; encouraged the Secretary-General to continue to implement the provisions of resolution 41/213 on questions of personnel and posts; invited the Secretary-General to ensure greater transparency in the management of extrabudgetary resources to permit a more precise assessment of their impact on the activities, programmes and priorities of the organization and requested the Secretary-General to present to the 46th session of the GA a report on all aspects of the use of extra-budgetary resources; requested the Secretary-General to present a further report to the 46th session on the review of the procedures for the provision of statements of programme budget implications and for the use and operation of the contingency fund; requested an updated version of the report on the status of technological innovation in the UN in the context of the proposed pro-gramme budget for 1992-1993; and decided to consider an annual report by the Secretary-General on the administrative, structural and other aspects of the improvement of the efficiency of the organization.

6.3 Concluding Comments

Resolution 45/254 essentially marked the end of the reform process set in motion in 1986 with the work of the Group of 18 and the approval of resolution 41/213. This was acknowledged by **Mr. Ahtisaari**[38], USG for Administration and Management in the following statement to senior UN officials:

"As you may recall, the Assembly had before it the analytical report of the Secretary-General on the implementation of the reforms in those areas that fell within his competence. The Assembly expressed its appreciation to the Secretary-General for this last report on the Review of the efficiency of the administrative and financial functioning of the United Nations, and in a sense one might say that the process initiated in 1986 thus ended. At the same time the Assembly endorsed the view that reform as such should be a continuing process. Hence, it encouraged the Secretary-General and Member States as well to pursue the objectives of resolution 41/213 particularly those that have yet to be met and invited the Secretary-General to consolidate and build upon the results achieved through the reform process."

As noted, the Group of 18 had put forward 71 recommendation relating to the intergovernmental machinery, the structure of the secretariat, personnel, monitoring, evaluation and inspection as well as the planning and budget procedures. Many of the recommendations called for further studies, particularly on the structure of the intergovernmental machinery in the economic and social areas and on the organizational structure of a number of departments and the regional economic commissions. With regard to the most controversial issue, namely the reform of the budget procedures, the group could not agree on a single proposal but recommended three alternatives for further discussion. The recommendations of the Group of 18 were considered by the GA in an atmosphere of suspicion and confrontation. The Assembly finally succeeded, however, in approving reform resolution 41/213 by consensus. This was seen as a major achievement and set the stage for the search for common ground between the member states' diverging views and objectives. Resolution 41/213 was further elaborated upon in subsequent sessions of the GA through other resolutions.

The acceptance of the new procedures in the programme planning and budgeting areas was evidence of the success of the reform effort. The approval of the 1990-1991 programme budget by consensus was possibly the clearest indication that the new procedure would work. It has contributed to a greater convergence of views, preempted the criticism of the major contributors and safeguarded the national sovereignty of members states as upheld by the UN Charter. In addition, the new procedures have resulted in the closer involvement of member states in the programming and budgeting exercise and increased consciousness in the secretariat about the way resources are spent.

Reforms of the organization of the secretariat in the political and administrative fields were approved and swiftly implemented and changes in the administrative field have contributed to a more efficient operation. Although the 45th session of the GA reviewed all the reform measures introduced, the process of improving the administrative and financial functioning is still ongoing and, at the GA's request, the secretariat will submit annual reports summarising the administrative measures undertaken to enhance the efficiency of the organization.

The staff retrenchment exercise was both painful and disruptive: painful for the individuals affected and disruptive of programme implementation. Initially intended to increase efficiency, the staff cuts seriously limited the capacity of the secretariat to undertake new tasks the organization was called upon to perform. The negative effect of staff cuts under the regular budget was somewhat eased by an increase in extrabudgetary resources. While calling for restraint under the regular budget, the major contributors were prepared to increase their contribution towards voluntary activities. The overall implication of this development has still to be examined. A proper balance has to be found between activities funded from extrabudgetary resources and the programme mandated under the regular budget. New planning and control procedures have to be established to integrate activities funded from voluntary contributions more effectively into the programme budget process.

Reform efforts were less successful in the area which had been considered of particular importance. As a result of their complexity and magnitude, the economic and social fields were seen to be prime candidates for change. The thrust for reform was expected to come from the Special Commission established by ECOSOC to deal with the rationalization of the intergovernmental machinery. The Special Commission, however, was unable to make any recommendations. Whereas consensus could, as noted, be reached on the structure of the secretariat in the political and administrative areas, member states found it more difficult to streamline intergovernmental bodies. Indeed this failure demonstrated that each of the intergovernmental bodies had an influential constituency and was supported by political priorities. The divergence of opinion concerning those priorities as well as on the functioning of various UN organs and their relations to other forums within the UN system, prohibited an agreement.

Following this setback, a new attempt was launched to restructure UN operations in the economic and social fields, starting with a reform of the intergovernmental structure to be followed by a reorganization of the secretariat. It is still to early to assess the outcome of this effort. First decisions were taken in April 1991 during the reconvened session of the 45th GA, which concluded with resolution 45/264 outlined in section 6.2. The reform effort in these fields, however, has yet to find the same spirit of co-operation that has evolved in the political and administrative areas. In addition to the efforts in the economic and social areas, a new reform initiative was launched by the President of the 45th GA, Mr. Guido de Marco, aimed at improving the work of the GA. Proposals were discussed in 1991 in an open-ended working group, made up of the chairs of the GA committees and the regional groups. The changes considered ranged from a reduction of the number of items on the GA agenda, a reduction of the number of main committees, the extension of the GA session, and the improvement of information processing and computer support to the development of follow-up procedures for the implementation of GA resolutions. The working group receives support from the secretariat in the form of assistance with background material.

Interest in the process of UN reform has remained strong both inside and outside the organization. New initiatives have been launched, this time not in response to a crisis as in the past, but to seize new opportunities and face the challenge created by the dramatic improvement in the political climate. Sponsored by the Ford and Dag Hammarskjöld Foundations, reform proposals were put forward by Brian Urquhart and Erskine Childers* in 1990, supported by a steering group and a large number of international experts.[39] The issues covered included an international agenda for the 1990s, the restriction of the term of office of the Secretary-General to seven years and improvements in the process for appointing the Secretary-General and the executive heads of specialized agencies, funds and programmes. The focus of the recommendations was to ensure the best possible leadership in order that the UN system might realize its full potential. In 1991, the Stockholm Initiative on Global Security and Governance was able to draw together a group of distinguished personalities who put forward a number of proposals for reforming the UN.** These included a review of the composition of the Security Council and the use of the veto; the strengthening of the role of the Secretary-General; a review of the methods of appointing of senior staff; the strengthening of interagency co-ordination and co-operation; a review of the finance system to encourage prompt payment of assessed contributions; and the rationalization of UN activities in the economic and social fields.[40] The Stockholm Initiative

---

*Brian Urquhart was a former UN Under Secretary-General for Special Political Affairs, and Erskine Childers, a former senior advisor to the UN Director-General for Development and International Economic Co-operation.

**Participants included Presidents Aylwin Azócar (Chile) and Vaclav Havel (CSFR), Prime Ministers Gro Harlem Brundtland (Norway), Ingvar Carlsson (Sweden) and Michael Manley (Jamaica), former Presidents Jimmy Carter (USA) and Julius Nyerere (Tanzania), former Chancellor Willy Brandt (Federal Republic of Germany) and former Prime Ministers Benazir Bhutto (Pakistan), Edward Heath (United Kingdom), Salim Salim (Tanzania) and Kalevi Sorsa (Finland).

concluded with a call for a World Summit on Global Governance, similar to the meetings in San Francisco and at Bretton Woods in the 1940s, to set in motion preparations for strengthening international institutions.

In conclusion, one might argue that the UN reform process which ended in 1990 can be regarded as successful. It certainly contributed to overcoming the crisis of the mid-1980s and helped to save the organization at a time when its existence was in jeopardy. Although financial viability has not yet been restored, the main contributor has recently resumed payment of its full assessment under the regular budget. In addition, the confrontational atmosphere of the initial stages of the reform process has given way to a greater convergence of views on questions related to the budget, administration and management. As such, the reform process may be seen as a contributing factor in renewing confidence and changing attitudes towards the UN. The reform of the UN did not, however, give rise to a new vision which would enable the organization to meet the new opportunities and challenges ahead. This is not surprising. The reform effort was born out of a crisis - political and financial - rather than a new consensus as to how the organization should work and what it should do. For this a political environment quite different from the one existing the first half of the 1980s would have been required. At that time, the divisions between North and South as well as East and West only allowed a minimum degree of consensus, reached through a painful process. The lessening of ideological competition, the end of the Cold War and the emergence of a new, constructive dialogue between North and South during the second half of the 1980s opened up a wealth of new possibilities for reforming the UN. Now is the time to rebuild the organization by setting new priorities and implementing the required institutional and procedural changes. Courageous decisions are needed to implement genuine reforms and to use the window of political opportunity opened up by changes in the global, political environment.*

---

*The new reform efforts will be the subject of a future publication: Joachim Müller, *The Reform of the United Nations in the Economic and Social Fields* (Dobbs Ferry, New York: OCEANA, forthcoming).

Notes

1. ST/ADM/SER.B/325; ST/ADM/SER.B/345; A/C.5/45/17.
2. 'US Congress Okays UN Payment', *Secretariat News*, May 1991, p. 9.
3. 'Seriouser', *The Economist*, 27 January 1990, p. 60.
4. A/45/1, p. 32.
5. A/C.5/45/SR.12, pp. 8-9.
6. *Ibid.*, p. 9.
7. A/C.5/45/SR.14, pp. 2-3.
8. *Ibid.*, pp. 3-4.
9. *Ibid.*, pp. 7-9.
10. *Ibid.*, pp. 9-10.
11. *Ibid.*, p. 11.
12. *Ibid.*, pp. 11-12.
13. A/C.5/45/SR.17, pp. 6-7.
14. *Ibid.*, p. 8.
15. *Ibid.*, pp. 8-9.
16. *Ibid.*, pp. 9-10.
17. *Ibid.*, pp. 10-11.
18. *Ibid.*, pp. 11-12.
19. A/C.5/45/SR.18, pp. 2-3.
20. *Ibid.*, pp. 3-4.
21. *Ibid.*, pp. 4-5.
22. *Ibid.*, pp. 5-6.
23. *Ibid.*, pp. 7-8.
24. *Ibid.*, pp. 8-9.
25. *Ibid.*, pp. 9-10.
26. A/C.5/45/SR.19, pp. 8-9.
27. *Ibid.*, pp. 9-11.
28. *Ibid.*, pp. 11-12.
29. *Ibid.*, pp. 13-15.
30. A/C.5/45/SR.20, pp. 2-4.
31. *Ibid.*, pp. 4-6.
32. A/C.5/45/SR.21, pp. 2-3.
33. A/C.5/45/SR.23, p. 3.
34. *Ibid.*, pp. 4-5.
35. A/C.5/45/SR.26, pp. 2-3.
36. *Ibid.*, pp. 3-4.
37. A/C.5/45/SR.35, pp. 10-11.
38. Statement to Senior Officials by Mr. Ahtisaari, 25 January 1991.
39. Brian Urquhart, Ershine Childers, *A World in Need of Leadership: Tomorrow's United Nations* (Uppsala, Sweden: Dag Hammarskjöld Foundation, 1990).
40. *Common Responsibility in the 1990s* (Stockholm, Sweden: The Prime Minister's Office, the Stockholm Initiative on Global Security and Governance, 22 April 1991).

ANNEX

Table 1[*]
1991 Scale of Assessments

Member State	per cent		
		Côte d'Ivoire	0.02
		Cuba	0.09
		Cyprus	0.02
Afghanistan	0.01	Czechoslovakia	0.66
Albania	0.01	Denmark	0.69
Algeria	0.15	Djibouti	0.01
Angola	0.01	Dominica	0.01
Antigua and Barbuda	0.01	Dominican Republic	0.03
Argentina	0.66	Ecuador	0.03
Australia	1.57	Egypt	0.07
Austria	0.74	El Salvador	0.01
Bahamas	0.02	Equatorial Guinea	0.01
Bahrain	0.02	Ethiopia	0.01
Bangladesh	0.01	Fiji	0.01
Barbados	0.01	Finland	0.51
Belgium	1.17	France	6.25
Belize	0.01	Gabon	0.03
Benin	0.01	Gambia	0.01
Bhutan	0.01	Germany	9.36
Bolivia	0.01	Ghana	0.01
Botswana	0.01	Greece	0.40
Brazil	1.45	Grenada	0.01
Brunei Darussalam	0.04	Guatemala	0.02
Bulgaria	0.15	Guinea	0.01
Burkina Faso	0.01	Guinea-Bissau	0.01
Burundi	0.01	Guyana	0.01
Beylorussian Soviet		Haiti	0.01
Socialist Republic	0.33	Honduras	0.01
Cambodia	0.01	Hungary	0.21
Cameroon	0.01	Iceland	0.03
Canada	3.09	India	0.37
Cape Verde	0.01	Indonesia	0.15
Central African Republic	0.01	Iran (Islamic Republic of)	0.69
Chad	0.01	Iraq	0.12
Chile	0.08	Ireland	0.18
China	0.79	Israel	0.21
Colombia	0.14	Italy	3.99
Comoros	0.01	Jamaica	0.01
Congo	0.01	Japan	11.38
Costa Rica	0.02	Jordan	0.01

---

[*]ST/ADM/SER.B/354.

Member State	per cent
Kenya	0.01
Kuwait	0.29
Lao People's Democratic Republic	0.01
Lebanon	0.01
Lesotho	0.01
Liberia	0.01
Libyan Arab Jamahiriya	0.28
Liechtenstein	0.01
Luxembourg	0.06
Madagascar	0.01
Malawi	0.01
Malaysia	0.11
Maldives	0.01
Mali	0.01
Malta	0.01
Mauritania	0.01
Mauritius	0.01
Mexico	0.94
Mongolia	0.01
Morocco	0.04
Mozambique	0.01
Myanmar	0.01
Namibia	0.01
Nepal	0.01
Netherlands	1.65
New Zealand	0.24
Nicaragua	0.01
Niger	0.01
Nigeria	0.20
Norway	0.55
Oman	0.02
Pakistan	0.06
Panama	0.02
Papua New Guinea	0.01
Paraguay	0.03
Peru	0.06
Philippines	0.09
Poland	0.56
Portugal	0.18
Qatar	0.05
Romania	0.19
Rwanda	0.01
Saint Kitts and Nevis	0.01
Saint Lucia	0.01

Saint Vincent and the Grenadines	0.01
Samoa	0.01
Sao Tome and Principe	0.01
Saudi Arabia	1.02
Senegal	0.01
Seychelles	0.01
Sierra Leone	0.01
Singapore	0.11
Solomon Islands	0.01
Somalia	0.01
South Africa	0.45
Spain	1.95
Sri Lanka	0.01
Sudan	0.01
Suriname	0.01
Swaziland	0.01
Sweden	1.21
Syrian Arab Republic	0.04
Thailand	0.10
Togo	0.01
Trinidad and Tobago	0.05
Tunisia	0.03
Turkey	0.32
Uganda	0.01
Ukrainian Soviet Socialist Republic	1.25
Union of Soviet Socialist Republic	9.99
United Arab Emirates	0.19
United Kingdom of Great Britain and Northern Ireland	4.86
United Republic of Tanzania	0.01
United States of America	25.00
Uruguay	0.04
Vanuatu	0.01
Venezuela	0.57
Viet Nam	0.01
Yemen	0.01
Yugoslavia	0.46
Zaire	0.01
Zambia	0.01
Zimbabwe	0.02
Total	100.01

Table 2[*]
Programme Budget 1990-1991

Section	US$

Part I: Overall Policy-making Direction and Co-ordination

1. Overall policy-making, direction and co-ordination	59,705,000
Total, part I	**59,705,000**

Part II: Political and Security Council Affairs: peacekeeping activities

2a. Political and Security Council affairs, peacekeeping activities	88,089,300
2b. Disarmament affairs activities	11,184,500
2c. Office for Ocean Affairs and the Law of the Sea	8,196,900
Total, part II	**107,470,700**

Part   III: Political   Affairs,   trusteeship   and decolonisation

3. Political affairs, trusteeship and decolonisation	35,988,200
Total, part III	**35,988,200**

Part IV: Economic, social and humanitarian activities

4. Policy-making organs (economic and social activities)	2,163,100
5a. Office of the Director-General for Development and International Economic Co-operation	4,670,800
5b. Regional Commissions New York Office	855,300
6. Department of International Economic and Social Affairs	46,814,800
7. Department of Technical Co-operation for Development	23,853,200
8. Activities of global social development issues	9,985,700
9. Transnational corporations	10,919,200
10. Economic Commission for Europe	33,089,300
11. Economic and Social Commission for Asia and the Pacific	39,791,400
12. Economic Commission for Latin America and Caribbean	49,010,700
13. Economic Commission for Africa	57,725,700
14. Economic and Social Commission for Western Asia	38,395,400
15. UN Conference on Trade and Development	73,107,600
16. International Trade Centre	15,400,800

[*]*United Nations Handbook 1990* (Wellington, New Zealand: Ministry of External Relations and Trade, 1990).

Section	US$
17. Centre for Science and Technology for Development	4,298,800
18. UN Environment Programme	11,195,600
19. UN Centre for Human Settlements (Habitat)	9,937,800
20. International Drug Control	8,333,600
21. Office of the UN High Commissioner for Refugees	34,180,100
22. Office of the UN Disaster Relief Co-ordinator	6,481,200
23. Human rights	16,105,700
24. Regular programme of technical co-operation	36,163,200
Total, part IV	**532,679,000**
Part V: International Justice and Law	
25. International Court of Justice	13,333,000
26. Legal activities	18,766,500
Total, part V	**32,099,500**
Part VI: Public Information	
27. Public Information	87,225,400
Total, part VI	**87,225,400**
Part VII: Common Support Services	
28. Administration and management	397,759,500
29. Conference and library services	352,777,600
Total, part VII	**750,537,100**
Part VIII: Special Expenses	
30. United Nations bond issue	-
Total, part VIII	-
Part IX: Staff Assessment	
31. Staff assessment	298,390,400
Total, part IX	**298,390,400**
Part X: Capital Expenditure	
32. Construction, alteration, improvement and major maintenance of premises	70,538,700
Total, part X	**70,538,700**
GRAND TOTAL	**1,974,634,000**

Table 3*
Status of Contributions to the United Nations Regular Budget
(in thousands of United States dollars)

Year	Total annual assessment	Total accumul. arrears at the end of the year	USA				USSR			
			annual assessment	annual contribution paid	accumul. arrears at the end of the year	accumul. arrears as per cent of annual assessment	annual assessment	annual contribution paid	accumul. arrears at the end of the year	accumul. arrears as per cent of annual assessment
1990	826,818	402,952	233,654	302,616	296,170	126.8	79,008	79,008	2,640	3.3
1989	776,605	461,238	216,287	158,840	365,131	168.8	74,633	79,209	2,640	3.5
1988	758,027	394,914	214,910	160,062	307,685	143.2	73,861	77,189	7,217	9.8
1987	756,294	353,431	212,876	107,041	252,838	118.8	73,903	80,001	10,545	14.3
1986	735,609	257,846	210,277	148,789	147,004	69.9	71,444	95,584	16,643	23.3
1985	691,869	242,431	197,897	123,886	85,515	43.2	69,368	71,119	40,783	58.8
1984	677,803	166,220	190,521	206,451	11,504	6.0	68,477	67,114	42,534	62.1
1983	612,605	170,516	171,329	147,298	27,434	16.0	62,012	61,230	41,172	66.4
1982	633,994	147,949	180,339	201,144	3,402	1.9	67,098	65,543	40,389	60.2
1981	595,884	145,616	167,347	143,331	24,208	14.5	63,412	60,939	38,834	61.2
1980	531,926	115,928	149,736	149,544	192	0.1	56,638	55,205	36,331	64.1
1979	500,358	95,816	143,025	143,025	0	0.0	55,232	55,269	34,927	63.2

*ST/ADM/SER.B/245, 252, 265, 271, 276, 283, 288, 295, 303, 325, 345.

Table 4*
Status of Contributions to the United Nations Peace-keeping Budgets
(in thousands of United States dollars)

Year	Total annual assessment	Total accumul. arrears at the end of the year	USA annual assessment	USA annual contribution paid	USA accumul. arrears at the end of the year	USA accumul. arrears as per cent of annual assessment	USSR annual assessment	USSR annual contribution paid	USSR accumul. arrears at the end of the year	USSR accumul. arrears as per cent of annual assessment
1990**	268,925	346,213	83,725	80,461	156,005	186.3	32,787	69,424	74,018	225.8
1989***	720,741	444,197	224,612	166,000	152,742	68.0	88,086	128,799	110,656	125.6
1988****	180,952	355,217	56,006	29,400	94,130	168.1	22,526	42,321	151,368	672.0
1987*****	194,880	362,949	60,399	29,400	67,523	111.8	24,246	24,213	175,540	724.0
1986*****	201,572	312,286	62,412	31,249	31,194	50.0	25,173	16,260	173,369	688.7
1985*****	87,412	262,129	26,834	53,638	32	0.1	11,156	8,321	164,455	1474.1
1984*****	174,524	323,506	53,558	53,441	26,835	50.1	22,277	3,678	161,621	725.5
1983*****	256,113	291,578	78,461	51,737	26,723	34.1	32,759	3,233	143,023	436.6
1982*****	211,475	208,412	64,110	64,110	0	0.0	28,195	3,597	113,497	402.5
1981*****	87,427	216,966	26,496	52,991	0	0.0	11,647	2,689	65,853	565.4
1980*****	164,146	263,835	49,722	55,947	21,993	44.2	21,871	4,935	56,184	256.9
1979*****	104,057	134,617	30,572	66,101	0	0.0	14,063	14,014	27,203	193.4

*ST/ADM/SER.B/245, 252, 265, 271, 276, 283, 288, 295, 303, 325, 345.
**ONUCA, UNAVEM, UNDOF, UNEF, UNIFIL, UNIMOG, UNTAG.
***UNAVEM (3 June 1989 to 2 Feb. 1990), UNDOF, UNEF, UNIFIL, UNIMOG, UNTAG (1 April 1989 to 31 March 1990).
****UNDOF, UNEF, UNIFIL, UNIMOG.
*****UNDOF, UNEF, UNIFIL.

BIBLIOGRAPHY

UNITED NATIONS DOCUMENTS

The UN documents are not listed individually. Rather, a description of the various document classifications is given below. The description in bold indicates the number or text of the individual document.

A/**document number:**
documents of the General Assembly

A/**session number/document number:**
documents of the General Assembly.

A/**session number/PV. meeting number:**
verbatim records of the General Assembly plenary.

A/C.2/**session number/SR. meeting number:**
summary records of the Second Committee of the General Assembly.

A/C.5/**session number/document number:**
document submitted to the Fifth Committee of the General Assembly.

A/C.5/**session number/SR. meeting number:**
summary records of the Fifth Committee of the General Assembly.

E/**year/document number:**
documents of the Economic and Social Council

E/**year/SR. meeting number:**
summary records of the Economic and Social Council.

Official Records of the General Assembly, **session number spelled out** *Session, Supplement No.* **supplement number (A/session number/document number):**
documents of the General Assembly, previously issued as document under number indicated in brackets.

Official Records of the Economic and Social Council, **year,** *Supplement No.* **supplement number (E/year/document number):**
documents of the Economic and Social Council, previously issued as document under the number indicated in brackets.

ST/ADM/SER.B/**document number:**
document of the secretariat on administration.

PUBLICATIONS

Administrative and Budgetary Reform of the United Nations, Report of the Eighteenth UN Issues Conference, The Stanley Foundation, February 1987.

Aga Kahn, Sadruddin, Prince; Strong, Maurice F., 'United Nations: Reform Might Help its Work', *International Herald Tribune*, 9 October 1985.

Aga Kahn, Sadruddin, Prince; Strong, Maurice F., 'Proposals to Reform the UN, 'Limping' in its 40th Year', *The New York Times*, 8 October 1985.

Basic Facts About the United Nations (New York: United Nations, Department of Public Information, 1990).

Beigbeder, Yves, *Management Problems in United Nations Organizations. Reform or Decline?* (London: Frances Pinter, 1987).

Berlin, Michael J., 'Lowering the Boom', *The Interdependent*, March-April 1986.

Bertrand, Maurice, *Some Reflections on Reform of the United Nations*, JIU/REP/85/9, Joint Inspection Unit, United Nations, Geneva, 1985.

Bertrand, Maurice, *The Third Generation World Organization* (New York: UNITAR, and Dordrecht, the Netherlands: Martinus Nijhoff Publishers, 1989).

Chebeleu, Traian, 'The Administrative and Financial Reform of the United Nations. Some Reflections', *Revue Roumaine d'Études Internationales*, XXII (1989), No. 6, pp. 533-553.

Collins, P. 'Administrative Reforms in International Development Organizations', *Public Administration and Development*, VII (1987), Special Issue, pp. 125-142.

Common Responsibility in the 1990s (Stockholm, Sweden: The Prime Minister's Office, the Stockholm Initiative on Global Security and Governance, 22 April 1991).

Congressional Record, S7793, 7 June 1985.

deCooker, Chris (ed.), *International Administration: Law and Management Practices in International Organizations* (Dordrecht, Netherlands: Martinus Nijhoff Publishers, 1990).

deGara, John, *Administrative and Financial Reform of the United Nations: A Documentary Essay* (Academic Council on the United Nations System, 1989).

Frank, Thomas M., *Nation Against Nation* (Oxford: Oxford University Press, 1985).

Fromuth, Peter J. (ed.), *A Successor Vision - The United Nations of Tomorrow* (Lanham: United Nations Association of the United States of America and University Press of America, 1988).

Jonah, James, 'The United Nations has its Problems', *International Affairs/ Mezhdunarodnaya Zhizn*, XXXIV (November 1988), p. 102

Kilgore, Arthur, 'Cut Down in the Crossfire?', *International Relations*, XXXIII (November 1986), pp. 592-610.

Lyons, Gene M., 'Reforming the United Nations', *International Social Science Journal*, XLI (May 1989), pp. 249-271.

Mathiason, John R., 'Who Controls the Machine? The Programme Planning Process in the Reform Effort', *Public Administration and Development*, VII (1987), pp. 165-180.

Mathiason, John, R.; Smith, D.C., 'The Diagnostics of Reform: the Evolving Tasks and Functions of the United Nations', *Public Administration and Development*, VII (1987), pp. 143-163.

Narasimhan, C.V., *The United Nations. An Inside View* (New York: UNITAR, and New Delhi: Vikas, 1988).

Nicol, David; Renninger, John, 'The Restructuring of the United Nations Economic and Social System: Background and Analysis', *Third World Quarterly*, IV (1982), No. 1, pp. 74-92.

Pearson, Ruth, 'U.N. Cries "Uncle"', *Bulletin of the Atomic Scientists*, XLIV (October 1988), pp. 36-39.

Pitt, David; Weiss, Thomas G. (eds.), *The Nature of United Nations Bureaucracies* (London: Croom Helm, 1986).

Protheroe, David R., *The United Nations and Its Finances, A Test of Middle Powers* (Ottawa, Canada: The North-South Institute, October 1988).

Ramcharan, B.G., *Keeping Faith with the United Nations* (New York: UNITAR, and Dordrecht, Netherlands: Martinus Nijhoff Publishers, 1987)

Renninger, John P. (ed.), *The Future Role of the United Nations in an Interdependent World* (New York: UNITAR, and Dordrecht, Netherlands: Martinus Nijhoff Publishers, 1989).

Ross, Peter S., 'UN - Back on its Feet?', *International Perspectives*, XVII (January/February 1988), p. 16.

Renninger, John P., 'The International Civil Service Commission and the Development of a Common Personnel Policy in the United Nations System', *Public Administration and Development*, VII (1987), pp. 181-194.

Sciolino, Elaine, 'UN Chief Suggests U.S. Contribution to be Cut', *The New York Times*, 29 April 1986.

Sciolino, Elaine, 'President Will Ask Congress to Restore Millions for UN', *The New York Times*, 1 January 1987.

'Seriouser', *The Economist*, 27 January 1990, p. 60.

'The Knife Next Time', *The Economist*, 17-23 May 1986, p. 41.

Tomuschat, Christian, 'Die Krise der Vereinten Nationen', *Europa-Archiv*, XLII (1987), No. 4, pp. 100-101.

Taylor, Paul, 'Reforming the UN System: Value for Money', *The World Today*, XLIV (July 1988), pp. 123-126.

UN Press Release WS/1304.

United Nations Handbook 1990 (Wellington, New Zealand: Ministry of External Relations and Trade, 1990).

Urquhart, Brian, 'The United Nations System and the Future', *International Affairs*, LXVIII (1989), pp. 225-231.

Urquhart, Brian; Childers, Ershine, *A World in Need of Leadership: Tomorrow's United Nations* (Uppsala, Sweden: Dag Hammarskjöld Foundation, 1990)

'US Congress Okays UN Payment', *Secretariat News*, May 1991, p. 9.

Williams, Douglas, *The Specialized Agencies and the United Nations - The System in Crisis* (New York: St. Martin's Press, 1987).

Wiznitzer, Louis, 'Sweden's Combative Prime Minister Stands Firm on Austerity', *The Christian Science Monitor*, January-February 1983.

INDICES

1. Subject and Name Index

2. Index of Draft Decisions and Resolutions

3. Index of Adopted Decisions and Resolutions*

---

*II stands for Volume II.

4. Document Index[*]

---

[*]II stands for Volume II.